SECURITY STUDIES

Security Studies
Critical Perspectives

EDITED BY
XAVIER GUILLAUME
AND
KYLE GRAYSON

Great Clarendon Street, Oxford, OX2 6DP,
United Kingdom

Oxford University Press is a department of the University of Oxford.
It furthers the University's objective of excellence in research, scholarship,
and education by publishing worldwide. Oxford is a registered trade mark of
Oxford University Press in the UK and in certain other countries

© Oxford University Press 2023

The moral rights of the authors have been asserted

All rights reserved. No part of this publication may be reproduced, stored in
a retrieval system, or transmitted, in any form or by any means, without the
prior permission in writing of Oxford University Press, or as expressly permitted
by law, by licence or under terms agreed with the appropriate reprographics
rights organization. Enquiries concerning reproduction outside the scope of the
above should be sent to the Rights Department, Oxford University Press, at the
address above

You must not circulate this work in any other form
and you must impose this same condition on any acquirer

Published in the United States of America by Oxford University Press
198 Madison Avenue, New York, NY 10016, United States of America

British Library Cataloguing in Publication Data

Data available

Library of Congress Control Number: 2022923811

ISBN 978–0–19–886748–7

Printed in the UK by
Bell & Bain Ltd., Glasgow

Links to third party websites are provided by Oxford in good faith and
for information only. Oxford disclaims any responsibility for the materials
contained in any third party website referenced in this work.

Praise for *Security Studies: Critical Perspectives*

'I have been waiting for a long time for an introduction to security studies that provides a clear set of tools for critically analysing security as a political practice with consequences for living in common. Xavier Guillaume and Kyle Grayson have delivered just that. *Security Studies: Critical Perspectives* is a fantastic teaching resource that will help students and scholars to methodically interrogate the bewildering multiplicity of security registers and issues today.'

Dr Jef Huysmans, Professor of International Politics, University of London

'This is a sophisticated new textbook that approaches students as fellow thinkers. The content is designed to help the students develop their critical thinking skills and be able to offer their own independent analysis of developing events. Highly recommended as an introduction to the politics of security in its multiple facets.'

Dr Pinar Bilgin, Professor, International Relations, Bilken University, Turkey

'Essential reading for anyone looking for a guide that helps them choose their own routes to navigate a sea of insecurity. Routes that lead us to new questions and, contrary to those of colonial navigation, that challenge the inevitability of violence and inequalities which are routinely authorized in the name of security for the few.'

Dr Marta Fernández, Associate Professor, The Institute of International Relations, The Pontifical Catholic University of Rio de Janeiro, Brazil

'*Security Studies: Critical Perspectives* unpacks the politics of security with finesse. It debunks the conventional understanding of security, unsettles the predominant narratives, enables the readers to raise profound questions, and offers a holistic treatise anchored in critical insights. Lucidly written, elegantly articulated and effectively communicated, the book is a must-read for all those who are grappling with the critical interpretations of security.'

Dr Madhan Mohan Jaganath, Professor, School of International Studies, Jawaharal Nehru University, India

'This is an innovative and comprehensive introduction to the field, asking important critical questions about security.'
Dr Elisabetta Brighi, Lecturer in International Relations, University of Westminster, UK

'An excellent introductory resource for students who are fresh to the field of critical security studies, focusing on a wide range of cases and topics that together encourage a more nuanced understanding of security in today's complex global environment.'

Dr Kiran Phull, Lecturer in International Relations, King's College London, UK

Acknowledgements

This book would not have been possible without the inspiration and feedback of many students, colleagues, and friends over a period that goes beyond its actual conception and writing. We would like to thank all the participants in this project who continued to collaborate with us even in the face of the hardships of the COVID-19 pandemic. We would like to especially thank the students in our different courses that have challenged us constantly to become (hopefully) better students of security ourselves. They have done so by decentring us from our own preconceptions and by reminding us that to teach is to learn.

Xavier would especially like to thank his PSIA students who have been a source of joy, inspiration, and self-reflection, as well as one of the key influences for this book. In Groningen, we would like to particularly thank Andreea Dascalu, Lisa Dudek, Dianne Kok, Johanna Krebs, Esther Ploeger, Jan Sedlacek, Nina Valentini, and Lisa Varwijk, who took the time to read and discuss many chapters of this book and help us to make them much better. Kyle would like to thank students at Newcastle on POL 1032: Key Concepts in International Relations, POL 2078: Critical International Politics, and POL 8044: Critical Geopolitics whose questions, interests, enthusiasm, and frustrations influenced the approach taken here. We would also like to thank and express our gratitude to Luise Fischer and Moana Verbeek van der Sande who provided us with invaluable research support to develop the pedagogical apparatus of this book. We would like to thank Axel Keber for his work on the index. At Oxford University Press, we would like to thank Sarah Iles, Katie Staal, and Makalah Moore for their support in challenging circumstances, as well as the anonymous reviewers who provided very useful feedback that has made this book better.

Foreword

Security surrounds us. Its impacts are widespread. Its consequences are significant. Yet we should not confuse security's ubiquity with its legitimacy. Security is a **political claim and a mobilization** that defines threats and what is under threat. As a political claim, security can, and should, be questioned. As a form of mobilization, security provides access to scarce resources. Moreover, security demands attention in ways that other forms of public policy do not. In doing so, security can eclipse important concerns such as human rights, the environment, and social justice.

Security Studies: Critical Perspectives reflects upon how security shapes our daily lives. The mobilization of security can result in positive outcomes. It may cultivate the conditions for peace and to live free from fear and want. However, security can also lead to unevenly distributed negative outcomes within societies and around the world, reinforcing inequalities and injustices. To capture its variable outcomes, we believe that as students of security and global citizens, we must view security as **a political choice that has consequences for our life in common**. By doing so, we can make sense of the different, and often violent, ways that security shapes our lives, the lives of others, and the worlds we live in. Furthermore, we can see that there are political alternatives that the mobilization and legitimation of security hides. Within the worlds we inhabit, security is *always a political choice*.

Our reference to **worlds** in the plural is not to deny that we all live in **a** world connected directly or indirectly to one another. Rather, it is a recognition that we nonetheless also inhabit specific worlds that are defined by where we live, who we understand ourselves to be, and how others identify us (e.g., via factors such as class, gender, sexuality, race, ethnicity, culture, religion, nationality, ideological beliefs, and/or disability). These worlds are subjective and intimate but they also have objective qualities. Our worlds are always at work within 'the world'. They shape how we navigate the economic, political, and social spaces that we traverse daily.

We are constantly reminded of the opportunities and obstacles within our worlds, including how these change in light of events, where we are, and our interactions with others. Events, spaces, and interactions can accommodate our different worlds by enabling us to live in common and engage in respectful co-existence with one another, however complex and potentially conflictual co-habitation may be at times. When our different worlds co-habit and co-exist, it becomes possible to rethink the parameters of our own worlds and contemplate how parochial they may be. Unfortunately, for too many of us, these events, spaces, and interactions restrict our opportunities to participate in the worlds of others as respected equals. Thus, in seeking to separate different ways of being, we lose the chance to live lives in common enriched from learning with, and from, one another.

> In the foundation **Chapters 1** to **5**, bold text is used to highlight key terms or points

> See **Section 1.4** for key elements of security

Over the past three decades, security has increasingly defined our own worlds and those of others. We use passcodes and passwords to conduct daily tasks. We consent to the monitoring and analysis of our online activity in exchange for 'free' services. We are subject to searches of varying degrees of intrusion to gain entrance to buildings, sporting events, and forms of transport. Many governments around the world do not recognize basic individual and collective rights. Some of us live in countries where government policy explicitly seeks to create a hostile environment for migrants in the name of fostering physical and cultural 'security'. In other places, LGBTQ+ communities are targeted for violence with spurious reference to securing public health and morality. Femicide is a global crisis.

For some of us, the politics of security plays out in our schools. For some of us, the politics of security is in our workplaces. For some of us, it is in the streets. And for some of us, it may be in our homes. For these reasons, we believe that we are living in times in which **security provides a window into our world(s)**. Security shapes how we live and what we do to get by. Moreover, security is how our worlds, and those of others, are constructed, contested, and/or controlled. It is thus vital to take account of the contingent character and transformative potential of security.

To critically investigate security requires a set of analytical skills. These skills are not just for academic settings. They also enable us to be global citizens who can ask important questions about how security is mobilized within societies around the world. To 'problematize' security—that is, to ask questions that do not take security as a given—is central to any analysis of security. We firmly believe that the strength of any problematization of security comes from the quality, relevance, and rigour with which key questions have been posed. Questions are therefore important.

Security Studies: Critical Perspectives does not engage with specific approaches, theories, or disciplinary debates within security studies, as important as these may be to the academic field—you can see our online resources (http://www.oup.com/he/Grayson-Guillaumele) for short introductions to key security theories if you are curious. Rather, this volume enables you to develop your own critical perspective that will empower you to ask probing questions about security, and beyond. Critical perspectives make sense of our worlds by acknowledging their complexity and interconnectedness. Developing your own critical perspective will reveal what security does and empower you to make informed judgements about security's consequences.

For us, the primary ambition for any introduction to security should be to develop the reader's critical capabilities so that they can better understand it. Thus, *Security Studies: Critical Perspectives* provides a **methodology** that enables you to develop your own critical perspective. By methodology, we are referring to a general guide that will help you to ask probing questions about security, justify why these questions are important, and start answering them. This methodology can be summed up as follows (see Figure 0.1): **to ask critical questions about security is to identify the hierarchies and forms of power that affect our worlds via identities, ideas, interests, institutions, and infrastructures that co-produce political violence.**

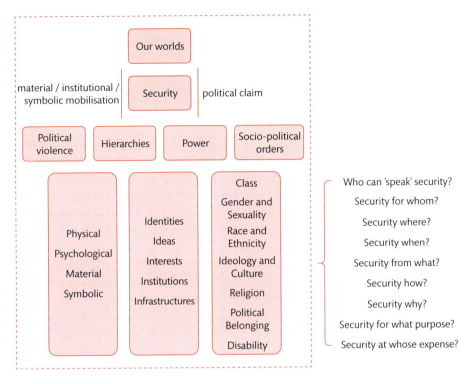

Figure 0.1 *Security Studies: Critical Perspectives*' methodology.

To do so, we can ask nine questions to analyse what security does in a given context: **who (can) speak** security, security **for whom**, security **where**, security **when**, security from **what**, security **how**, security **why**, security **for what purpose**, and security **at whose expense**?

Security tends to present itself in contemporary discussions as a necessary and prudent response to a problem. Chapters 1 to 5 of *Security Studies: Critical Perspectives* present a case for why we should not take this characterization for granted. In Chapter 1, we introduce the notion of **critique** as a perspective that pays attention to multiple historical, sociological, economic, and political contexts when analysing security. By adopting a critical perspective, we can understand security's roots and consequences such that we can consider how we might foster social, political, and environmental justice in our worlds via transformations in socio-political orders. As we will see in Chapter 2, **security** is always a claim that is both political and contingent. Thus, it should be subject to scrutiny. All security claims are shaped by a history and sets of social relations that require careful analysis. As we will see in Chapter 3, these factors potentially reinforce **forms of power** that produce hierarchies. These **hierarchies** are present in our worlds in terms of **class**, **gender** and **sexuality**, **race** and **ethnicity**, **ideology** and **culture**, **religion**, **political belonging**, and **disability**, as well as at their **intersections**. These hierarchies—as **expressions of forms of domination and oppression**—are enabled and articulated through **identities, ideas, interests, institutions**, and **infrastructures**.

Inevitably, asking critical questions about security will mean that you need to make some choices about what to prioritize in your analysis. For example, which hierarchies should be highlighted? How do they express themselves in identities, ideas, interests, institutions, or infrastructures that shape our daily lives? Choices about what to emphasize may be based on what you experience or discover through research; however, decisions may also reflect how hierarchies are challenged in ways that are often not obvious to most observers. As students of security, we must remember that facts do not speak for themselves. They are always embedded in arguments that require careful examination. We have a responsibility, as students of security and as global citizens, to examine security's truth claims because they often give rise to myriad forms of political violence that are committed in its name.

In Chapter 4, we therefore show how security is connected to **political violence**. Security often generates **physical, psychological, material**, and **symbolic forms of violence**, even when security is a response to mitigate the threat of violence. What is political about violence is not always self-evident. Therefore, we need to demonstrate how violence functions politically and be prepared to justify our claims. There are two important political questions that we can ask about violence that can help us connect it to security: what makes an act of violence legitimate and who has the authority to make these determinations? By establishing the potential links connecting security to violence, the precise stakes of security are brought into sharper focus. Finally, in Chapter 5, we will discuss how the nine core questions of our **methodology** can identify security as a political claim, how it is mobilized, and its consequences for people and our worlds in general.

After the introductory conceptual and methodological material of Chapters 1 to 5, the remainder of *Security Studies: Critical Perspectives* presents key themes in contemporary security. Their purpose is to show you what we can learn by approaching these themes through critique (see Contents). Written by leading security analysts, these chapters will provide you with the means to pursue important questions in relation to these contemporary security themes. Each chapter engages with its thematic focus with the aim of encouraging you to ask follow-on questions about the issues that are raised. As such, they explicitly avoid providing ready-made answers or telling you what to think.

We have divided these chapters into five sections that relate to how security affects different aspects of our worlds. The first is **socio-political orders** (Chapters 6, 7, and 8). Socio-political orders capture the different ways that authority is instituted, organized, and practised via security at local, national, and global levels, as well as across them. The second is **identity** (Chapters 9, 10, and 11). Identity refers to how we are classified, based on specific characteristics, by others, and ourselves, in connection with security. The third section is **political economy** (Chapters 12, 13, and 14). Political economy captures the economic dimensions of security with the political calculations that shape them. The fourth section is **technology** (Chapters 15, 16, and 17).

Here, the thematic chapters explore how security is materialized, mobilized, and challenged through infrastructure, practical objects, and processes. The last section is **security as space** (Chapters 18, 19, and 20). By space, we are referencing the physical environments that shape, and are shaped by, the possibilities and opportunities for security mobilizations, as well as the forms that these mobilizations take. In the online resources, you will find a series of illustrative cases written by leading experts that explore these themes further. Each case highlights specific questions to ask and provides a preliminary analysis of what security is doing. We hope these case studies will inspire you to investigate the issues they raise in more detail, or across different cases.

In writing, editing, and curating this collection, our underlying ambition has been to provide you with an understanding of how security becomes manifest in our worlds and how we can identify its effects, and to establish its connections to political violence. Security can be a condition of impossibility for some. It limits what people can do and who they are able to be. This includes determining who is entitled to the protections offered by laws and universal rights. But security may also be a condition of possibility. Here, security opens up new opportunities, freedoms, and spaces for action. To determine whether security enhances or limits conditions of possibility, for whom it does so, and where it does so requires that we examine security critically. In these challenging times, we need to know how security transforms lives as well as how security, our worlds, and the world we share can be transformed via security. By developing your ability to ask critical questions, you will become both a skilful security analyst and an informed global citizen. Critical thinking is not just about asking pertinent questions, using rigorous evidence gathering procedures, or undertaking robust forms of analysis. It should also instil the confidence to ask difficult questions, including of ourselves, and to accept that the complex challenges of the twenty-first century will go unaddressed if we are unprepared to tackle their messiness.

By harnessing the power of fear, security thinking and security practices too often seek to drive our worlds apart rather than bringing them together. We realize that some will not see this as a problem and may even dismiss our approach to security as overtly political. We do not deny this; at the heart of our thinking about security is a hope that violence and inequalities are not inevitable. But we are not alone in 'politicizing' security. We would note that claims that security, and its outcomes, are natural and inevitable are also political. So too are positions that advocate for security practices that accentuate forms of political, social, economic and/or environmental injustice, or that otherwise excuse it as a price worth paying for security outcomes enjoyed by some at the expense of others. Likewise, attempts to treat security as a technical issue hide the political stakes at the heart of security and the politics of its outcomes, thereby reproducing inequalities and injustice.

Political violence is a harm that results from political structures—whether patriarchy, structural racism, socio-economic inequalities, or crude ends/means analysis—that are often ignored. Yet these are political structures that shape hierarchies which generate suffering. A concern with how violence permeates societies is what lies at the core of perspectives that analyse security critically. Thus, by examining security critically, we gain insight into how our worlds, and the world, are structured around forms of socio-political, economic, and environmental injustice. Moreover, we can understand how we might initiate positive transformations. We hope that *Security Studies: Critical Perspectives* will help you build up your confidence and skills to question and challenge how the politics of security shapes our worlds.

Groningen and Newcastle, March 2023
Xavier and Kyle

Foreword to instructors

Our aim differs from most introductory books: we want to help students *become* security analysts and global citizens. Instead of introducing readers/students to specific theories they need to understand, compare, and contrast to meet course learning outcomes, we wish to empower them to scrutinize security mobilizations by using questions that deepen their understanding of the role of security in our worlds. After more than four decades of combined teaching experience, we no longer believe a theory-first approach is an inclusive or pragmatic starting point to achieve our aim. Moreover, we believe that subjecting security to a critical analysis is an endeavour that extends beyond a single field of study—for example, (critical) security studies—or discipline—for example, international relations.

To be inclusive and pragmatic means starting from the events and dynamics that will have attracted students to a security course in the first place. The point is to help them to see the range of questions they can ask and how they can start to do so. We often tend to teach them about how predominant positions in an abstract academic discipline theorize security and then assess how well they perform in reproducing these positions. Most of our students, however, do not go on to graduate study, nor do they become academics. Thus, we should be preparing them to engage in security discussions in ways that are most appropriate for the contexts in which these discussions will take place for them. Finally, theoretical expertise is much easier to develop with a strong conceptual background in what is being theorized, alongside a good understanding of the kinds of questions that one can ask. *Security Studies: Critical Perspectives* aims to establish a strong conceptual background by introducing students to key notions and questions, and how these help us to think about what security does to our worlds. For those who wish to include theories in their course design, we have included a short coverage of key security theories in the online resources to align with the broader approach taken here. In this case, we suggest that it would be appropriate to cover security theories after Chapter 5.

About the editors

Xavier Guillaume is Associate Professor in International Relations at the University of Groningen, the Netherlands and has also taught at the Université de Genève, the University of Edinburgh and Sciences Po Paris. A citizen from Geneva and Switzerland, Xavier was born and raised in Geneva's suburbs by a working poor, divorced mother. Xavier specialises in security and international issues connected to the mundane ways by which people constitute their identities in relation to others, the state, or to other international actors.

Kyle Grayson is Head of the School of Geography, Politics, and Sociology at Newcastle University, UK and Professor of Security, Politics, and Culture. A Canadian-British dual-national, he was born and raised on the traditional territory of many nations including the Mississaugas of the Credit, the Anishnabeg, the Chippewa, the Haudenosaunee, and the Wendat peoples. He is the third successive generation in his family to have migrated for economic reasons. Currently, he is Co-Editor-in-Chief of the journal *International Political Sociology* and Chair of the British International Studies Association.

About the authors

Victoria M. Basham is Professor of International Relations in the School of Law and Politics at Cardiff University, UK. Victoria's research focuses on how war, and war preparedness, shape people's daily lives; and how daily life in turn influences and facilitates war and other forms of violence. Victoria is particularly interested in how gender, race, ethnicity, sexuality, and social class shape the prioritization, use, and perpetuation of military force, especially in liberal democratic societies, and in how scandals can expose the role of societies in the reproduction of violence and harm. Victoria's work has been published in a range of journals including *Review of International Studies*, *Security Dialogue*, *International Political Sociology*, *Critical Studies on Security*, *Critical Studies on Terrorism*, and *International Feminist Journal of Politics*. Victoria is also Editor-in-Chief of *Critical Military Studies* and co-edits the Edinburgh University Press book series, Advances in Critical Military Studies.

Rocco Bellanova is Research Professor at the Vrije Universiteit Brussel (in the research group Law, Science, Technology, & Society) and the Principal Investigator of the DATAUNION project (ERC Starting Grant—2022–2027). Rocco's work sits at the intersection of politics, law, and science and technology studies (STS), and focuses on digital data as pivotal elements in the governing of societies. Using qualitative and interpretative methods, his research mainly focuses on European data-driven security practices and the role played by data protection and infrastructures in their governance. He has notably carried out research on security technologies and their infrastructural politics, as well as on the European governance of machine learning algorithms and data exchanges in the domain of justice and home affairs.

Mike Bourne is Reader in International Security Studies in the School of History, Anthropology, Philosophy, and Politics at Queen's University Belfast, UK. His research explores the entanglements of security politics and technology. Drawing on critical security studies, science and technology studies, and posthumanist/new materialist thought and process philosophy, he has conducted research on arms control and weapons politics, border control technologies and practices, and illicit trafficking. Recent journal articles have been published in *Security Dialogue*, *Social Studies of Science*, *Critical Studies on Security*, *International Politics*, and *Criminology and Criminal Justice*.

Sara E. Davies is Professor of International Relations at the School of Government and International Relations, Griffith University, Australia. Her most recent book, *Containing Contagion: The Politics of Disease Outbreaks in Southeast Asia* (Johns Hopkins University Press, 2019), charts Southeast Asian states' political cooperation in response to a wave of emerging and endemic infectious disease outbreaks between 1998 and 2015. Sara has researched global health governance for over a decade and published *Politics of Global Health* (Polity Press, 2010) and *Disease Diplomacy* (Johns Hopkins University Press, 2015, with Adam Kamradt-Scott and Simon Rushton).

Madeleine Fagan is Associate Professor in the Department of Politics and International Studies at the University of Warwick, UK. Her work focuses on the politics of ethical claims in relation to themes of political community and security, drawing on post-foundational and critical social and political theory. Her current research explores the politics and ethics of knowledge production practices around the Anthropocene as they mediate relationships between temporality, subjectivity, spatial imaginations, political community, and security. Outputs from this research appear in *Political Geography*, *European Journal of International Relations*, and *British Journal of Politics and International Relations*.

Melody Fonseca Santos has a doctoral degree in international relations from the Autonomous University of Madrid, Spain. Currently, she is a term assistant professor in the Department of Political Science and researcher at the Institute of Caribbean Studies of the University of Puerto Rico, Río Piedras Campus. Dr Fonseca Santos co-coordinates the Working Group Feminisms, Gender, and Memories in Latin America and the Caribbean of the Latin American Council of Social Sciences and is Editor-in-Chief of the journal *Caribbean Studies*. Her topics of interest are critical theory of international relations, critical feminist studies, post-colonial and decolonial studies, race and racism, Latin American and Caribbean politics, and US imperialism. She is also a member of Colectiva Feminista en Construcción, a black and decolonial feminist political organization based in Puerto Rico.

Philippe M. Frowd is Associate Professor in the School of Political Studies at the University of Ottawa, Canada. His research draws on critical security studies and focuses on emerging transnational forms of governance of security in the Sahel region of West Africa. His research has primarily focused on irregular migration and border control in the region and has been the focus of his latest book, *Security at the Borders: Transnational Practices and Technologies in West Africa* (Cambridge University Press, 2018). Philippe also works on the politics of non-state security provision and dynamics of militarization and intervention in the Sahel more broadly. His work has most recently appeared in *Third World Quarterly*, *Geopolitics*, and *African Affairs*. He is Associate Editor of *Security Dialogue*.

Jennifer Hobbs is Lecturer in International Relations at the University of Leicester, UK. Her research brings together feminist and queer approaches to security with the politics of global health. In particular, her work explores how the politics of race, sex, and gender are challenged and re-articulated through biomedicine.

Jessica Kirk is Research Fellow in the Centre for Governance and Public Policy at Griffith University, Australia. Her work draws upon debates within critical security studies, global health, and science and technology studies (STS) to examine the politics of disease outbreaks and pandemics. She has particularly focused on state-level emergency response and the increasingly contested role of expertise within this, with her recent work exploring the US response to the 2013–16 Ebola outbreak in West Africa and the response to COVID-19.

Mark Lacy is Senior Lecturer in the Department of Politics, Philosophy, and Religion at Lancaster University, UK. His work focuses on the changing technologies, tactics, and terrains of war and international conflict in the twenty-first century and the different techniques used by governments and militaries to prepare for 'future operating environments'. He is Lead Editor of the series Routledge Studies in Conflict, Security and Technology and author of *Theorising the Future of Conflict: War and International Politics Out to 2049* (Routledge, forthcoming).

Laura McLeod is Senior Lecturer in International Politics at the University of Manchester, UK. Her research focuses on gender, feminism, security, and peacebuilding in post-conflict contexts, particularly the Former Yugoslavia. Her current research examines how indicators matter in the implementation and achievement of feminist and gendered goals in international peacebuilding. Her work has been published in *International Studies Quarterly*, *Journal of International Relations and Development*, *Security Dialogue*, *Journal of Intervention and Statebuilding*, *Peacebuilding*, and *International Feminist Journal of Politics*. Her first book, *Gender Politics and Security Discourse: Personal-Political Imaginations and Feminism in 'Post-Conflict' Serbia*, was published by Routledge (2016).

Cédric Moreau de Bellaing is Associate Professor in Sociology at the École Normale Supérieure, Paris, France and a researcher at LIER-FYT (EHESS/CNRS). His research focuses on police practices and, more specifically, on the historical evolution of policing protest in France, as well as on the transformations of violence and its modes of regulation. He is the author of *Force publique. Une sociologie de l'institution policière* (Economica, 2016) and, with Danny Trom, of 'Sociologie politique de Norbert Elias', *Raisons Pratiques* 30, Presses de l'EHESS, 2022. He has also worked with Dominique Linhardt on enemy criminal law doctrine and recently published 'The "Enemization" of Criminal Law? An Inquiry into the Sociology of a Legal Doctrine and of Its Political and Moral Underpinnings', *International Political Sociology* 13(4), 2019, 447–463.

Benjamin J. Muller is Associate Professor at King's University College at Western University in London, Ontario, Canada. His research examines a range of issues including borders, mobility, security, identity, technology, sovereign power, exceptionalism, and post-colonialism. Critically engaging the application and implication of surveillance and identification technologies on borders and the bodies that cross them, his published work has appeared in journals such as *Citizenship Studies*, *Security Dialogue*, *Geopolitics*, and *International Political Sociology*, as well as in monographs and book chapters.

Christian Olsson is Professor in Political Science and International Relations at Université libre de Bruxelles (ULB), Belgium, director of its research unit in international relations (REPI), and affiliated to its Observatory of the Arab and Muslim Worlds (OMAM). His research deals with security practices in the context of military interventions (counter-insurgency, privatization of security), especially in Afghanistan and Iraq. At the theoretical level, he engages in his approach to international relations with global historical sociology, international political sociology, and critical war studies. He currently is working on a research project on the internationalization and transnationalization of armed conflicts in the 'wider' Middle East, focusing on non-state armed groups and the role of long-distance solidarities. He has recently published in *Millenium*, *Critical Military Studies*, *Canadian Journal of Political Science*, and *PArtecipazione e COnflitto*.

Caitlin Ryan is Assistant Professor in International Security at the University of Groningen, the Netherlands. Her work draws on debates in post-colonial and feminist security studies and on methods from anthropology to engage with the political and economic dynamics in post-war contexts. She has particularly focused on the global-local political economies of natural resources, the expansion of the Women, Peace and Security agenda, and women's post-war economic empowerment. She currently works on large-scale land deals and land reform in Sierra Leone and Liberia through considering the relations of power bound up in land. She has published recent articles in *Environment and Planning A*, *European Journal of International Relations*, and *Third World Quarterly*.

Anna Schliehe is Research Associate in Cultural Geography at the University of Bonn, Germany and holds an MSCA fellowship at the University of Oldenburg, Germany. Her work is located at the interface of carceral geographies and criminology and she has worked on several interdisciplinary research projects in and around prisons in different countries in Europe. She has particularly focused on the experiences of confinement for young women. She has published in *British Journal of Criminology* and *European Journal of Criminology* and has recently published a monograph with Emerald titled *Young Women's Carceral Geographies: Abandonment, Trouble and Mobility*.

Maria Stern is Professor in Peace and Development Studies at the School of Global Studies, University of Gothenburg, Sweden. Maria's work focuses on the question of violence in relation to security, warring, militarism, development, peace, identity and belonging, coloniality, and sex. She explores these subjects through a feminist lens that seeks to recognize intersecting relations of power and that is attuned to the politics of methodology. She has published in a variety of journals and publishing houses, enjoys the collaborative process of co-authorship, and has served as Editor/Associate Editor at *Security Dialogue* for many years.

Guide to using this book

Security Studies: Critical Perspectives provides a rich learning experience in which theories and contemporary security themes and concepts are brought to life and set in a real-world context. Outlined here are the key features and online resources included in the book to ensure that you understand each topic and, importantly, that you can critique this knowledge and form your own views.

 Access the online resources at: http://www.oup.com/he/Grayson-Guillaume1e

Apply theory to current events

Illustrative case studies available on the online resources provide detailed analysis of real-life issues from around the world which to help demonstrate security studies approaches in action.

Master the essentials

Short introduction to key theoretical approaches available on the online resources take your learning further by introducing you to different approaches to the study of security, written by the expert editors. Furthermore, extensive **marginal cross-references** encourage you to see the connections between topics and the issues explored.

Take your learning further

Boxes complement the text with thoughtful insights and additional information, expanding on key topics, and **Zoom-in boxes** provide brief snapshots of essential concepts.

Reflect on your knowledge

Questions for further reflection at the end of each chapter prompt you to further consider the concepts in each chapter, form your own views and perspectives, and consider the real-world implications of security studies.

Resources for lecturers

 http://www.oup.com/he/Grayson-Guillaume1e

Adopting lecturers can access the following online resources:

- An instructor guide to help incorporate the book into your teaching, supporting an issue-centred, critical approach to security studies.

Outline contents

1 What is critique?   1

2 Security   18

3 Orders, power, and hierarchies   36

4 Political violence   53

5 Critical questions   71

6 Policing   87
Cédric Moreau de Bellaing

7 War and socio-political orders   104
Victoria M. Basham

8 Terrorism and asymmetric conflicts   121
Christian Olsson

9 Identity and othering   139
Melody Fonseca Santos

10 Gender and sexuality   155
Jennifer Hobbs and Laura McLeod

11 Nationalism, racism, and xenophobia   171
Philippe M. Frowd

12 Securing development; developing security?   188
Maria Stern

13 Health   205
Sara E. Davies and Jessica Kirk

14 Property, extraction, and accumulation   223
Caitlin Ryan

15 Digital, (in)security, and violence   239
Rocco Bellanova

16 Security and design   256
Mark Lacy

17 Weapons-systems   273
Mike Bourne

18 Environment   291
Madeleine Fagan

19 **Borders and mobility** 309
    Benjamin J. Muller

20 **Prisons and camps** 325
    Anna Schliehe

Index 343

Detailed contents

1 What is critique? — 1
- 1.1 Introduction — 1
- 1.2 What is critique? — 4
  - 1.2.1 Contingency — 4
  - 1.2.2 Historicity — 5
  - 1.2.3 Sociology — 5
  - 1.2.4 Transformation — 6
- 1.3 Why do we need to approach security critically? — 8
- 1.4 Key factors for security, our worlds, and ourselves — 11
- 1.5 Conclusion — 14

2 Security — 18
- 2.1 Introduction — 18
- 2.2 Security: the history of an ambiguous term — 20
- 2.3 Security as a threshold/security as a process — 24
  - 2.3.1 Security as a threshold — 25
  - 2.3.2 Security as a process — 28
- 2.4 Security as a political mobilization — 29
- 2.5 Conclusion — 33

3 Orders, power, and hierarchies — 36
- 3.1 Introduction — 36
- 3.2 Socio-political orders and relations of power — 37
- 3.3 Hierarchies: identities, ideas, interests, institutions, and infrastructures — 42
- 3.4 Challenging and resisting security — 47
- 3.5 Conclusion — 49

4 Political violence — 53
- 4.1 Introduction — 53
- 4.2 Political violence as an analytical concept — 55
  - 4.2.1 Four forms of violence — 57
  - 4.2.2 Identifying and demonstrating the relations between security and violence — 59
- 4.3 The political question of legitimacy — 61
- 4.4 The political question of authority — 64
- 4.5 Conclusion — 67

5 Critical questions — 71
- 5.1 Introduction — 71
- 5.2 The global drug war — 72
- 5.3 Nine security questions — 73
  - 5.3.1 Contextualizing security — 75
  - 5.3.2 Understanding security — 81
- 5.4 Conclusion — 84

6 Policing — 87
Cédric Moreau de Bellaing
- 6.1 Introduction — 87
- 6.2 Policing, violence, and the state — 89
  - 6.2.1 Policing: a euphemism for political violence in social relations? — 91
- 6.3 The professional organization of policing — 92
- 6.4 Police and society — 95
  - 6.4.1 Reforming police institutions and denouncing illegitimate police practices — 96
- 6.5 The police in the face of changes in crime and war — 97
  - 6.5.1 Policing and transnational crime — 98
  - 6.5.2 The militarization of the police? — 98
- 6.6 Conclusion — 100

7 War and socio-political orders — 104
Victoria M. Basham
- 7.1 Introduction — 104
- 7.2 Where is war? — 105
  - 7.2.1 Locating war and what counts as war — 107
  - 7.2.2 Sites of perpetual war? — 107
  - 7.2.3 Securing civilization through war — 108
- 7.3 How is war possible? — 109
  - 7.3.1 Gender, racialization, and war — 110
  - 7.3.2 Agents and agency in war — 111
- 7.4 Who or what does war secure? — 112
  - 7.4.1 Why do we think war makes us secure? — 112
  - 7.4.2 Societal benefits and costs of war — 113
- 7.5 Conclusion: should we continue to wage and prepare for war? — 115

8 Terrorism and asymmetric conflicts — 121
Christian Olsson
- 8.1 Introduction — 121
- 8.2 What is asymmetric conflict? What is terrorism? — 122
- 8.3 Security, violence, and the struggle for political order — 125
- 8.4 The relation between clandestine political violence and counterterrorism — 127
  - 8.4.1 Counterterrorism as war — 128
- 8.5 Terrorism and counterterrorism: locating the political — 129

8.6	Civilians caught between rival political orders	132
8.7	Conclusion	134

9 Identity and othering
Melody Fonseca Santos

139

9.1	Introduction	139
9.2	Conceptualizing identity	142
	9.2.1 Identity/difference	142
9.3	Predatory identities	143
9.4	Alternative identity practices: relationality between/within differences	149
9.5	Conclusion	151

10 Gender and sexuality
Jennifer Hobbs and Laura McLeod

155

10.1	Introduction	155
10.2	Gender, sexuality, and security	158
10.3	Intersectionalities	160
10.4	The everyday	162
10.5	Transformative politics	164
10.6	Conclusion	166

11 Nationalism, racism, and xenophobia
Philippe M. Frowd

171

11.1	Introduction	171
11.2	Nationalism, racism, and xenophobia	172
	11.2.1 Nationalism	173
	11.2.2 Racism	174
	11.2.3 Xenophobia	176
11.3	Global security dynamics and the politics of belonging	177
	11.3.1 What are the transnational facets of nationalism?	178
	11.3.2 How do race and racism structure global politics?	179
	11.3.3 How do we decide who belongs and who doesn't?	181
11.4	Conclusion	183

12 Securing development; developing security?
Maria Stern

188

12.1	Introduction	188
12.2	Securing development; developing security?	190
	12.2.1 Development? The dominant storyline	190
	12.2.2 Security development?	193
12.3	Asking critical security questions	194
	12.3.1 Security for whom and from what?	194
	12.3.2 Security when/where?	198
12.4	Conclusion: the question of political violence	201

13 Health — 205
Sara E. Davies and Jessica Kirk

- 13.1 Introduction: health in the context of security — 205
- 13.2 Health security: origin story — 207
- 13.3 Health as security: who, what, how, and for what purpose? — 208
  - 13.3.1 National security — 209
  - 13.3.2 Human security — 211
  - 13.3.3 Why (health) security? For what purpose? — 213
- 13.4 Global health as security: non-Western experiences — 216
- 13.5 Conclusion — 218

14 Property, extraction, and accumulation — 223
Caitlin Ryan

- 14.1 Introduction — 223
- 14.2 Classifying land as 'open' for extraction — 226
- 14.3 Accumulating territory through accumulating property — 228
- 14.4 Securing processes of extraction in order to secure accumulation — 233
- 14.5 Conclusion — 235

15 Digital, (in)security, and violence — 239
Rocco Bellanova

- 15.1 Introduction — 239
- 15.2 Imagining the digital, imagining violence — 241
- 15.3 Critically questioning security and surveillance — 246
- 15.4 How local–global tensions matter — 249
- 15.5 Conclusion — 251

16 Security and design — 256
Mark Lacy

- 16.1 Introduction — 256
- 16.2 The visibility of security — 258
- 16.3 Design and invisible wars — 261
- 16.4 Design, security, and war: critical perspectives — 263
  - 16.4.1 Security through critical design — 263
  - 16.4.2 The future of war and the military designers — 266
- 16.5 Conclusion — 268

17 Weapons-systems — 273
Mike Bourne

- 17.1 Introduction — 273
- 17.2 What are weapons and what do they do? — 275

17.3	Does the manner of violence matter?	279
17.4	How are weapons controlled?	282
17.5	How is weapons-politics entangled with other forms of violence and security?	284
17.6	Conclusion	286

18 Environment
Madeleine Fagan — 291

18.1	Introduction	291
18.2	How should we think about the environment and security?	294
18.3	Three approaches to environment and security	296
	18.3.1 Environment, conflict, and security	296
	18.3.2 Human security	298
	18.3.3 Ecological security	300
18.4	Conclusion: environmental insecurities	303

19 Borders and mobility
Benjamin J. Muller — 309

19.1	Introduction	309
19.2	Identity: whose security?	313
19.3	Surveillance, ID technology, and the virtual border: where is security?	316
19.4	Deadly deterrence: when enhanced security leads to insecurity	318
19.5	Conclusion	320

20 Prisons and camps
Anna Schliehe — 325

20.1	Introduction	325
20.2	Building secure states through incarceration and encampment?	328
	20.2.1 Mass incarceration and the prison industrial complex	328
	20.2.2 Looking beyond the European camp complex	329
	20.2.3 Camps, prisons, and the production of security	331
20.3	Designing security—institutional creation of order and control	331
	20.3.1 Planned prisons	332
	20.3.2 Camps as constructions (of power)	332
20.4	Living in securityscapes—enforced intimacy and the microworlds of prisons and border camps	334
20.5	Conclusion	337

Index — 343

1

What is critique?

1.1	Introduction	1
1.2	What is critique?	4
1.3	Why do we need to approach security critically?	8
1.4	Key factors for security, our worlds, and ourselves	11
1.5	Conclusion	14

READER'S GUIDE

In this chapter we introduce the notion of critique. We outline its main elements: contingency, historicity, sociology, and a concern with transformation. We present the benefits of adopting a perspective that is critical of security. To understand the impacts of security within worlds and across them, we show that it is important to look at security in relation to class, gender and sexuality, race and ethnicity, ideology and culture, religion, political belonging, and disability and/or their intersections. We conclude by suggesting that the decision to mobilize security is always a political choice.

1.1 Introduction

To speak of critique raises important questions about what the practice of criticism entails. When we critique, what are we doing? There are many possible answers to what it means to 'engage' in critique. But are there elements held in common across different perspectives that offer a critique of security? Moreover, why should we analyse our worlds through critique? What does critical analysis enable us to capture that we might otherwise miss? Why do we need to ask critical questions about security? What precisely do we gain?

Unfortunately, the term critique is often left undefined. Many times, it is referenced in academic work without any sense of how critique has shaped the analysis provided. It is also commonly confused with complaint and/or disagreement. By the end of this chapter you will see that critique may involve a complaint/disagreement but a complaint/disagreement is not necessarily critical. Similarly, critique is often pejoratively characterized as a mode of analysis used by radical idealists who do not understand how 'the real world' really works. As a consequence, in many contemporary political contexts, critical thinking is nearly entirely absent from security discussions and debates.

The principal aim of this chapter is to explain why we should engage in critique. To help you do so, we offer some guidelines on how to engage in critique and develop your critical thinking capacities. At the same time, we also outline some of the challenges that thinking critically can pose to us as analysts and global citizens. As Didier Fassin (2017, 13) notes, critique implies 'a questioning of a certain state of the world' connected to a 'dissatisfaction of what it is'. As such, critique arises from our embeddedness in our worlds and our connections to others. Sources of dissatisfaction can be found in the political, social, economic, or environmental aspects of our worlds. Our own dissatisfaction may be based on our political preferences, ethics, and/or morality. On the other hand, exposing the sources of problems that dissatisfy us may, paradoxically, also require us to attempt a 'distancing through intellectual operations' (Fassin 2017, 13). This distancing enables us to look afresh at what is familiar to us, including our own understandings, or even ourselves.

'Critique' has many different intellectual lineages that are impossible to cover here, even in passing. Thus, we offer a practical introduction to how to apply 'critique' to thinking about our worlds and their connections with security. At its simplest, **to apply 'critique' means to question and ask questions about our world(s)**. To do so, we start with a double move undertaken by all analyses informed by critique.

See **Zoom-in 1.1** on 'common sense'.

First, we must undertake the 'intellectual work of distancing [ourselves] from common sense' and de-familiarize ourselves with 'what we take for granted' (Fassin 2017, 17). As such, critique seeks to decentre predominant perspectives about our worlds and to look at them afresh. This is because how we perceive our world(s) shapes what we identify as problems and why, or what we can call **problem framings**. Problem framings, in turn, shape what we believe needs to be done. Problem framings also shape what we believe is possible to realize in light of the challenges that constrain the achievement of our goals. In other words, how we think about issues shapes how we will attempt to respond to them. Moreover, critique examines whether inequalities are natural and inevitable, refusing to accept that our worlds, or how we act in them, are beyond questioning.

ZOOM-IN 1.1 COMMON SENSE

Common sense comprises beliefs about the world that are said to be true and beyond questioning. These find expression in the form of maxims; for example, 'hard work pays off', 'racism is history', or 'markets are the most efficient way to distribute resources'. Yet, what various forms of critical analysis have shown is that common sense is in fact a highly variable set of beliefs about our worlds that work to help maintain the predominant order in any given society (see Chapter 3). Thus, rather than being beyond questioning, the tenets of common sense ought to be among the first things we investigate.

Second, a critical analysis **questions forms of domination and oppression by understanding them as forms of political, social, economic, and/or environmental injustice**. When critically analysing security, domination and oppression are forms of political violence. Forms of injustice are the conditions—institutional, material, and symbolic—through which people lose the power to exercise 'an effective voice' in living their own lives (Young 1990, 34). When people lose this ability, they are more likely to be subject to coercion. For example, structural racism, patriarchy, environmental degradation, and exploitative structures of economic distribution systematically prevent us from fully participating in the determination of '[our] actions or the conditions of [our] actions' (Young 1990, 38). Thus, economic structures, structural racism, patriarchy, and ableism are **forms of domination. Forms of oppression**, such as physical violence, material deprivation, segregation, exploitation, cultural diminishment, and/or marginalization, are how we can be systematically, and violently, prevented from interacting with others as equals (Young 2011). That is, oppression hinders us from being able 'to express . . . [our] feelings and perspectives on social life in contexts where others can listen' (Young 1990, 38). Oppression thus precludes the resolution of concerns raised by those subject to structures of domination.

See **Chapter 4** on political violence

Forms of oppression tend to be direct actions undertaken by people, states, and/or institutions against other people. Forms of domination are the structures that condition and shape how these actions are taken and justified. These structures, or orders, need not to be consciously and actively maintained. Often, they hide within what we take for granted and consider to be natural, such as gender roles, cultural predispositions, or economic outcomes. As we will see, this 'taken-for-grantedness' poses a challenge for determining the structures that are behind forms of domination and oppression made possible by security. Identifying these structures and what they do is precisely why we need to ask critical questions about security.

To ask critical questions about security is to ask *political* questions about security. In Section 1.2, we will see how, by being mindful of the **contingency**, **historicity**, **sociology**, and **transformative potential** of our worlds, we can begin to see how critique enables us to better understand what security does and how it does so. This means **never assuming that security thinking or practices are neutral, inevitable, or natural responses** (Huysmans 1998, 245). Instead, we should understand them as ways to govern people in our worlds. In Section 1.3, we discuss the key aims of critical perspectives. Adopting a critical perspective shows how security is **an important window into our worlds. Security shapes contemporary political thinking and justifies particular policies and practices, positioning them as necessary reactions to threats**. These forms of thinking and practices are connected to specific hierarchies in our societies; security, more often than not, reinforces them. Thus, in Section 1.4 of this chapter, we briefly introduce the key factors that work in conjunction with security and these hierarchies: **class**, **gender** and **sexuality**, **race** and **ethnicity**, **ideology** and **culture**, **religion**, **political belonging**, and **disability**. These factors, and **their intersections**, are where domination and oppression, and ultimately political violence made possible by security, are experienced. They also inform our own positionality vis-à-vis others as well as our own taken-for-granted assumptions about our worlds and how security shapes them.

See **Chapter 2** on the concept of security

See **Chapter 3** on socio-political orders and hierarchies

See **Chapter 4** on political violence

1.2 What is critique?

See **Box 1.1** for our approach to 'critical perspectives'

As noted above, we cannot offer a comprehensive overview of the intellectual traditions of 'critique' because of its rich history. At the same time, we would stress that to critique is more than to criticize ('for the sake of criticizing'), with all its negative connotations. 'Critique', from the ancient Greek work *kritikos*, is etymologically connected to distinguishing, deciding, judging, and estimating. In its European intellectual history, 'critique' has negative and positive meanings. We deploy a specific understanding of the term that emerges from the philosophy of Immanuel Kant in the late eighteenth century (Tonelli 1978). While problematic in many ways, Kant's view of critique centres on a **rigorous attitude** towards analysing the phenomena that surround us. Kant argued that critique also requires that we reveal **the reasons informing our 'judgements'** about them.

See **Zoom-in 1.2** on Kant and the ethico-political complexities of historical texts

Thus, to engage in critique requires **distancing and decentring ourselves from our worlds without leaving them**. As an attitude towards thinking, critique comprises four exercises to reflect upon our worlds. We believe that these can guide us as researchers and as global citizens to identify otherwise hidden dynamics that surround us and affect our worlds. As in any other form of analysis, critique, or 'being critical', requires a clear and rigorous explanation and application of its central tenets, whatever specific configuration they take. The strength of any critique rests in the empirical demonstration of specific forms of domination and/or oppression. This includes what these forms of domination and/or oppression are and how they affect our lives. Any critique must be conceptually, empirically, and/or normatively demonstrated. Facts never speak for themselves; we rigorously select and organize them to demonstrate an argument. Critique is an engagement, but it is not one that denies our own presence in the world, or where we are situated in relation to other worlds.

1.2.1 Contingency

Current conditions are not the only possible way of organizing the world. Likewise, our worlds, and how these are represented to us, are contingent; they do not have to be how they are. Contingency understands the present to be 'a product of human

ZOOM-IN 1.2 ON THE USES OF KANT (AND THE CANON)

While Immanuel Kant directly influenced the work of many philosophers who followed him and remains an important figure in Euro-Atlantic philosophical circles today, we need to cast a critical eye over his work. For example, Kant's 1798 *Anthropology from a Pragmatic Perspective* contains passages in which sexist, ethno-nationalist, and racist views co-mingle with a liberal defence of individual rights for white men (Shilliam 2021). How to best deal with such texts, both historical and contemporary, where the potentially emancipatory co-habits with domination and oppression is a pressing ethical and methodological question within security studies, and beyond (see Park 2013).

action, and thus implicitly, is the product of some actions among a larger range of possibilities' (Calhoun 1995, 35). It highlights that current conditions are a 'changing function of multiple variables' (Smith 1988, 11). Emphasizing the contingent character of socio-political and economic arrangements, rather than their essential nature, is necessary for distancing our thinking from the constraints of common sense, the taken-for-granted, and the goes-without-saying that underpin dominant views. The point is that the dominant view does not exhaust other possible ways to understand the worlds surrounding us, or act in them. This includes the fact that dominant views can obscure some of these worlds and what it is like to live in them. Likewise, we need to understand how our position within a socio-political order might shape how we view our world and other worlds. This is known as **reflexivity**. Therefore, viewing our worlds as contingent is also an invitation to engage with action. It is a recognition that our worlds could be different (see Section 1.2.4 on transformation).

*See **Box 1.2** for a discussion of reflexivity*

1.2.2 Historicity

Critical perspectives always question the historical conditions of emergence for specific identities, ideas, interests, institutions, and infrastructures, as well as the practices they inspire. This includes how groups of people are defined and treated. In doing so, critique searches to uncover the historical lineage of our actions by identifying how our present came to be through processes of continuity and change that produced contingent outcomes. Our worlds are shaped by history. It is from historical processes that we inherit words and ideas (e.g., security), identities (e.g., national identity), institutions (e.g., laws), events (e.g., colonization), interests (e.g., sustainable development), actions (e.g., humanitarian interventions), infrastructures (e.g., healthcare facilities), and conditions (e.g., climate change). But critique challenges the claim that historical arrangements are self-evident, natural, necessary, perennial, and/or unavoidable.

*See **Section 2.2** for a discussion of 'security' as a concept*

Critique also casts a discerning eye over claims of novelty. We are surrounded by proclamations that events are unprecedented (e.g., the attacks on 11 September 2001 in the United States). In making these claims, it is often argued that unprecedented events require new courses of action that are not permissible under existing socio-political arrangements (e.g., provisions in the Patriot Act in 2001 greatly decreased individual protections from state surveillance). Critique challenges the idea that anything is unquestionably novel by examining these claims more closely. Assuming novelty necessarily de-historicizes current conditions, missing how events in the present may be tied to the past. In doing so, claiming current conditions are novel can also divest those who may be responsible (in full or in part) from being held accountable for them.

*See **Box 2.1** for a discussion of the security–liberty balance*

1.2.3 Sociology

Critical perspectives recognize that individuals, groups, and institutions are connected to one another. These relationships can span across geographical locations and historical time periods. They can also take many forms. Understanding the

*See **Section 3.2** on socio-political orders and relations of power*

socio-political orders** shaping these relationships is crucial to understanding how different actors interact with one another and the outcomes these interactions generate (de Goede 2018). For example, in order to understand why a state chooses certain security policies, it may be useful to identify the key institutional players in its security decision-making processes. This enables us to see how a collection of different, if not conflicting, interests resulted in a decision, and the kinds of trade-offs made in the process. It also enables us to potentially pinpoint when a rationalization for the decision emerged and from where, including if this was provided post-hoc after a decision was reached. This is important because the reasoning behind security decisions is often a reflection of predispositions, ideas, identities, and/or interests rather than careful evaluations of potential courses of action.

Interactions among actors are also influenced by who they think they are and how they are seen by others. For example, the militarization of policing has changed how the police understand themselves and their role in the provision of security (Phillips 2018). It has also changed how they are viewed by others, including policymakers, the media, and the general public (Moule et al. 2019). A different emphasis can be applied to the various interactions, relationships, and connections among actors. Importantly, critical perspectives seek to avoid reifying individuals, groups, and institutions, as well as their relationships, when analysing security.

*See **Chapter 6** for more on the militarization of policing*

Reification (also known as commodification) literally means to 'turn into a thing'. We do this when we reduce the inherent complexity of something, or someone, down to a characteristic (or set of characteristics). This characteristic, or set of characteristics, is taken as a given that defines them and explains their behaviour. For example, we reify people as belonging to a 'race' when we reduce the complexity of people to our perceptions of the colour of their skin. We also reify the world we live in when we exclusively see the objects of our everyday lives—for example, clothes, food, technology—as things we obtain in exchange for money. Doing so hides the social relations these objects may have with us, how we are connected to other people through these objects, and how we impact upon the living conditions of others, and the environment, by consuming these objects (see Marx 1976 [1867]). For example, the clothes we wear may be produced in sweatshops in Bangladesh, Leicester, New York, or the Northern Marianas. Our new mobile phone may contain toxic and/or environmentally harmful components which have been extracted through unsustainable practices. Crops, which are turned into food, may rely on agricultural techniques that degrade soils as well as pesticides that pollute groundwater and poison insects and animals. Clothing, technology, and food production also rely on labour which may involve exploitative employment practices that prey on vulnerable individuals and communities. As such, by asking critical questions and avoiding reification, we can see how we are connected to others in complex ways.

*See **Chapters 14** and **18** for examples of these practices and how they relate to security*

1.2.4 Transformation

By highlighting the contingent, historical, and sociological embeddedness of our worlds, critical perspectives seek to find ways to transform societies into more just and humane socio-political orders. Critical perspectives offer different ways of identifying how societies are hierarchically structured and how these hierarchies are reflective of forms of domination and oppression that express themselves through identities, ideas, interests, institutions, and infrastructures. Transformation should not be confused with change. Change addresses symptoms rather than underlying forms of domination and/or oppression that shape the status quo. For example, the 1997 Ottawa Treaty established a global prohibition on the use of landmines because of the indiscriminate harm they can inflict on civilians. Despite this accomplishment, the Ottawa Treaty did not transform the underlying structures of oppression and domination enabling the use of violence against others (including civilians), the structures through which this violence is governed, or existing hierarchies in world politics; for example, China, Russia, and the United States refused to sign up to the treaty. Thus, while the Ottawa Treaty might be considered an important change, it did not lead to transformation by addressing the structural causes of conflict, or the incentives for states to resort to violence (Beier and Crosby 1998).

See **Section 3.3** on these five enablers of domination and oppression

Finally, critical perspectives must also be directed towards the institutions where analyses of our worlds are produced. These are institutions such as schools, universities, advocacy groups, think tanks, international organizations, media, and governments. Critical perspectives extend to all forms of knowledge production, examining their contingency, historicity, sociology, and transformative potential.

> BOX 1.1 'CRITICAL PERSPECTIVES' IN *SECURITY STUDIES: CRITICAL PERSPECTIVES*

We are using the term critical perspectives in this book to denote an understanding of security that highlights its contingent, historically situated, and sociological characteristics alongside an interest in transforming contemporary socio-political orders. More formally, it has been social theories and analytical approaches—for example, Marxisms, post-structuralism, feminisms, post-colonialism, decolonialism, queer theory, and new materialisms—that have shaped our own thinking about security. It is not necessary for you to be familiar with any of these to engage with this book. *Security Studies: Critical Perspectives* draws from various social theories while not being beholden to any one in particular. Moreover, we are keen for readers to develop their own perspective from the bottom up, rather than adopting a perspective neatly aligned with a theory from first principles.

This has been a conscious choice on our part to provide you with as broad a range of channels as possible to explore security. While attention to contingency, historicity, sociology, and transformation is consistent across the book, there will be places where there is an emphasis on different factors for different reasons. While we are aware that this may lead to some tensions, or disagreements, it aligns with our approach to expose our readers to different ways of asking questions to capture what security does. This may also lead some readers (and instructors) to feel that we have under-emphasized, or over-emphasized, certain aspects of security; for example, whether it is a condition of possibility or impossibility for living a life in common with others (see Section 2.4). However, the methodology and conceptual framework we offer aligns with different approaches to security (see the online resources for examples).

Doing so raises questions about what we think we know, how we know it, and why we believe it to be true. Moreover, critical perspectives are interested in how knowledge is shaped by the institutions in which we study/work and societies in which we live. Thus, with regards to our knowledge of security, we might wish to ask the following questions:

- How do institutions influence the security knowledge that is produced?
- What are the criteria for something counting as security knowledge? Whose voices and perspectives do these criteria exclude (if any)?
- How is security understood across different sites of knowledge production and how do these understandings shape research that is undertaken (e.g., what are the differences between the knowledge generated by a state military and a peace institute)?
- How has security been shaped by contingent historical events such as the development of the state in Europe, colonialism, and/or contingent cultural outcomes such as the European Enlightenment?
- How might we be oblivious to circumstances relevant to analyses of security because we may not have direct awareness or personal experience of specific forms of oppression and domination?

See **Sections 2.2** and **4.3** for more on the historical contingency and colonial lineages of security and legitimacy

1.3 Why do we need to approach security critically?

Without a doubt, security is a complicated concept and phenomenon. Within the field of security studies (keeping in mind security is also studied by other disciplines!), there has been much discussion since the end of the Cold War. Security was previously linked to state policies concerned with military and international affairs. From this perspective, security was about protecting the state and/or advancing the national interest. This is an association that still holds and is relevant today. However, despite objections from some (see Walt 1991), scholarly and policy definitions of security have extended beyond military defence to areas such as the environment, policing, finance, economics, health, and development and to 'levels' separate from the state (UNDP 1994).

See **Section 3.3** for how security shapes our political horizons

What do these definitions make possible politically? What do they emphasize and what do they ignore, whether by commission or omission? As we will see in Chapter 2, whether security is being defined as an objective and measurable achievement, or as a subjective experience and feeling, critical perspectives highlight that **'security' does something to our worlds and it is fundamental to how our worlds work**. As such, we are not going to provide you with a definition of security that you can apply across time and space. Rather, we will introduce you to ways of analysing how security functions in our worlds. In other words, **what does security do in a given context?** By taking account of the contingency, historicity, and sociology of security, you will be able to analyse how it shapes us and our worlds.

BOX 1.2 REFLEXIVITY

The starting principle of reflexivity is that 'while saying something about the "real world", one is simultaneously disclosing something about oneself' (Pels 2000, 2). Thus, reflexivity refuses to maintain the traditional analytic separation between things 'out there' and who we believe ourselves to be (Pels 2000, 2). The consequence is that it is important for everyone to think carefully about how their identities, interests, privileges, experiences, and relations with others shape how they view and interpret their worlds (England 1994). Reflexivity requires that we be conscious of:

- the underlying premises that might be shaping our worldviews;
- how our descriptions of the world contain political and normative content that is not neutral;
- the potential limitations of what we know and how we have come to know it.

However, **reflexivity is not the same as relativism**. On the contrary, reflexivity enables us to offer ethico-political judgements in the absence of 'objective' standards by thinking carefully about how our judgements are also informed by key factors we discuss in Section 1.4. One needs to be open and honest that our knowledge is situated, which is not always an easy admission to make. This refers to how our positional relationships within socio-political orders will shape what we accept as knowledge and common sense. It is not a concession that there are no objective situations and facts. An ongoing challenge for reflexivity is how to interact with positions unwilling to accept the connections between who we are and what may count as knowledge.

Asking critical questions about security can show us **how security governs people**. As such, security reveals core assumptions that underpin how our societies are organized. It demonstrates how a society understands itself and what its members may hold in common. Security can also reveal how societies are divided and how people are governed in terms of different categories generated by security. Security is a mobilization to counter a 'threat', or to protect those who are deemed to be under threat, according to these categories (see Chapter 2). As we will see throughout this book, security is an **essentially contested concept** and not just because scholars may disagree about what it is, or what it means. Rather, security is an essentially contested concept because **security is also a site of contestation about what is held in common**. Security brings people together while simultaneously separating them from others. Critical questions, in their many forms, are needed precisely because they highlight these contestations over security. By asking critical questions, the paradox that security often generates its own (hidden) insecurities becomes apparent.

See **Sections 1.4** and **3.2–3** on security and categorization

See **Section 3.4** on challenges and resistance to security

Security also shapes concrete practices and policies. These practices and policies 'do things' by producing specific security outlooks, spaces, and experiences, including political violence (see Chapter 4). What security does will vary. There are many reasons why. **First, not everyone can mobilize 'security' in the same ways, or for the same reasons** (Monsees et al. 2020). Generally, leading political figures and policy-makers within governments are more likely than civil society groups to be able to have their perceptions of threat treated as matters of security that require particular forms of mobilization. For example, when US president Richard Nixon declared a 'war on drugs' in 1973, it resulted in reconfigurations of the US legal system and policing apparatus, alongside widespread changes to the regulation of financial activity even beyond the United States. In sharp contrast, Extinction Rebellion has not yet been as successful in having its security claims regarding the catastrophic impacts of climate change stimulate widespread reconfigurations in states or the global economy. **Second, not everyone is affected by the mobilization of security and the forms of political violence it entails in the same ways, or for the same reasons.** This is a point dramatically emphasized within the #BlackLivesMatter movement: policing tactics such as 'stop and search' have different impacts on different communities.

See Section 2.4 on security as a political mobilization

See Chapter 5 on the global drug war

For more, see Chapter 18 on environmental security

See Chapter 4 for more on forms of political violence

Third, what security means and how it is mobilized often reflect the views of the most dominant groups in a given society. These views shape how security problems are framed and the actions taken to resolve them. Often, these problem framings and perceptions of threat connect to their potential impacts on the positions of the most privileged in a given society. To be clear, this is not to say security is an outcome of conspiracy, or necessarily the result of deliberately bad or self-interested intentions (although we can find many examples of the latter). Rather, it is to foreground that security is inextricably intertwined with how societies are ordered through relations of power. Often, the potential consequences of security are not consciously understood by those voicing genuine concerns. Thus, by asking critical questions, one can uncover and detail how power, privilege, and problem framings shape how security is articulated and practised. Critique is also concerned with the uneven effects of security, including political violence, on different people.

See Section 3.2 for more detail on relations of power

Fourth, security is often seen, or presented, as apolitical and amoral. It is to be understood as a technocratic exercise in countering dangers and threats (Cohn 1987). Not to do so would be imprudent, if not dangerous. Thus, from this perspective, security is beyond politics. Moreover, to question security can even be viewed as presumptuous because security 'experts' have access to information that others lack. For example, denying that drugs, rogue states, or migrants are security threats is thought by some to be akin to denying the influence of gravity on the physical world.

Critical perspectives challenge this view of security as an apolitical and amoral technocratic exercise. As we noted above, security (whether as a concept or practice) is never neutral, inevitable, or natural. **The decision to frame something as a security issue, and to mobilize security measures in response, is a political choice with ethical implications. It could *always* be otherwise.** This is not to say that security is always bad, or unnecessary. Nor is it to argue that risks and threats can always be ignored. Rather, we simply wish to make the following point: since security contributes to choices about what we share in common, how we should act in our worlds, and how we should act in 'the world', it should not be removed from the realm of debate, ethical reflection, and contestation (Robinson 2011). It is a deeply political practice. To deny its political dimensions is to do a disservice to ourselves and to others.

We live in societies in which security thinking is present and shapes our daily lives. It is this pervasiveness of 'security' in our worlds that was our motivation for this book. Given that security has a direct impact on how we live and how we are governed, we felt it should be subject to ongoing critique. It affects us. And it affects others. If we do not ask critical questions about security, we risk becoming complacent, if not complicit, in the face of injustice and the perpetuation of political violence. As critical thinkers and global citizens, we have a responsibility to scrutinize security more closely, notably by establishing the key factors that affect how security is mobilized and how security affects us by producing, reinforcing, implementing, and, at times, even challenging specific socio-political hierarchies.

1.4 Key factors for security, our worlds, and ourselves

Critical perspectives seek to ask questions about our worlds and ourselves. They also demand that we think about how best to ask these questions. The worlds we live in are complex. Thus, we should be suspicious of single-cause explanations of them. Indeed, we cannot ever fully comprehend and embrace the complexity all around us. However, we can use concepts and analytical tools to try to break this complexity down into smaller and analytically manageable parts. The concepts and tools that we use to do this are both a scholarly and political choice. As a scholarly choice, the decisions we make are connected to our ability to use certain methods of finding answers and to uncover evidence of what security does. As a political choice, the decisions we make necessarily prioritize certain kinds of question and ultimately a certain kind of understanding of our worlds. Thus, these choices always require justification.

In *Security Studies: Critical Perspectives*, we highlight class, gender and sexuality, race and ethnicity, ideology and culture, religion, political belonging, and disability to understand the effects of security. These ten factors individually, and at their intersections, shape forms of domination and oppression in our worlds. All are also deeply embedded in academic, media, and political debates regarding their relevance in contemporary societies *and* with respect to security. It is impossible to provide an extensive account of these debates here. Rather, we focus on these factors because we believe they are helpful to make better sense of how we witness and experience security daily.

Before briefly discussing these factors in more detail, we need to mention three things. First, these factors are often empirically intertwined. Within the academic literature, this is referred to as **intersectionality** (see Crenshaw 1990; Collins 2019). Intersectionality is a central feature across perspectives critical of security. No credible critical security analyst would ever claim that only one of these factors matters and that the others are irrelevant. However, specific analytical approaches (see online resources) may place a greater emphasis on a specific factor, and/or how some factors intersect with one another, than others. This is a choice that needs to be justified. Second, these factors can help us to understand the sources behind forms of domination and oppression as well as how different individuals, groups, governments, and organizations view the world. Sometimes, though, they may be less helpful. How particular issues are presented and experienced by us will affect the prominence of factors in our thinking. Third, these factors, how they are defined, and how they are applied can vary greatly. Thus, what we offer here are 'rule-of-thumb' definitions to help you grasp their importance in analysing what security does.

Class: This positions people in relation to others in terms of economic capital (i.e., wealth), but also other forms of socio-cultural capital that are not necessarily economic in nature. These could include levels of education, forms of tacit knowledge (e.g., how to communicate effectively in different social situations), pastimes, cultural awareness, accents, clothing, and food preferences. As sociologist Pierre Bourdieu (1979) has shown, socio-cultural capital positions and orders people by how this 'capital' is recognized, valued, and used in a society. Membership in a class (both via self-recognition and identification by others) stems from possessing and using such assets. Depending on the socio-political order and situation, these may provide advantages or disadvantages.

Gender and sexuality: We refer to gender as the result of social processes through which individuals and/or groups are assigned particular qualities or roles based on presumed associations with biological sex categorizations (e.g., male or female). Resulting hierarchies usually value the masculine over the feminine and associate a set of ascribed qualities to both (Butler 1990). For example, gender scholars have long demonstrated how politics and the public sphere (including security) are represented as 'masculine' spaces while the everyday and private realms are understood as 'feminine' (Massey 1996). By sexuality, we simply refer to how people are classified and placed into hierarchies in terms of their sexual preferences. Such classifications and hierarchies are then often mobilized to justify and enact policies that oppress individuals and groups (Sjoberg 2015, 450–451).

> See **Chapter 10** on how gender and sexuality affect security

Race and ethnicity: We refer to race as the process through which individuals or groups are *racialized*; that is, reified racially. Historically, this has principally been through claims regarding 'innate' biological and behavioural differences that were linked to skin colour. More recently, racialization has been undertaken through cultural, ethnic, and/or religious attributes that are said to reflect innate predispositions. While there are no biological races, racialization, the attribution of racial traits, and the consequences of these processes are very real. People continue to be categorized via race. Racialized categories contribute to hierarchies that lead to differences in treatment and are used to legitimize forms of domination and oppression (see Murji and Solomos 2005).

> See **Chapter 11** on how race and ethnicity affect security

Ethnicity refers to similar processes through which people are reified via practices said to indicate evidence of a common descent (e.g., language, geographical origins, cultural traditions, religion). Thus, ethnicity is a marker of difference (Elia et al. 2016). It can also be a strategy for recognition within socio-political orders defined by the 'saris, steel bands, and samosas' brand of multiculturalism where difference is acceptable so long as it is does not generate political demands (Troyna 1983).

Ideology and culture: Ideology is a set of beliefs that are grouped, more or less coherently, to form the guiding principles for a political movement, party, or organization.

Ideologies also guide our actions. They prioritize certain values over others. They promote a particular vision of a life in common and how society should operate. And they often identify other ideologies as competitors, if not threats, in a political struggle. Ideologies thus create hierarchies and provide ways of ordering the world. Associating oneself with a particular ideology, or being associated with a particular ideology by others, can have positive or negative effects, including the extension of privileges (e.g., being a Communist party member in the People's Republic of China) and marginalization (e.g., being associated with Antifa movements in the United States).

Following noted cultural theorist Raymond Williams (2011 [1958]), we understand culture to be what we hold in common. Thus, a culture may include a shared language, forms of education, food, dress, dance, arts, films, television, memes, music, stories, and jokes. But culture is more than practices, objects, and artefacts—it also encompasses shared modes of interpretation and/or feeling (Clarke et al. 1975). Like ideologies, cultures both produce and articulate worldviews. Worldviews shape our actions, prioritize certain things over others, and establish hierarchies.

Religion: This is any set of beliefs about life that rely on the worship of a transcendental power. Religion may be practised in highly organized systems incorporating a vast number of people or in smaller, loosely organized groups. Religious belief systems might influence ideologies and cultures (and vice versa). Similarly, religions can coalesce around political, ideological, or cultural movements, parties, and organizations. Larger religious belief systems usually possess a variety of interpretations (e.g., Christianity, Islam, Buddhism, etc.), making it difficult, if not impossible, to speak of 'a' religion. Like ideologies and cultures, religions guide the actions of individuals, groups, organizations, and governments. They do so by prioritizing certain values over others, by promoting a certain life in common over others, and often by painting other belief systems (including other religions) as profane or even existentially threatening.

Political belonging: This is an attachment to a political institution (such as the state) or a political expression of an attachment to a defined group. Political belonging structures relationships among individuals deemed to share these attachments and the institutions representing them, and those who do not. Citizenship is a good example of these two dimensions. You can be formally attached to a state as a citizen, yet still be considered potentially, or inherently, a threat to it because of your (ascribed) cultural background, disability, race, ethnicity, class, religion, ideas, or sexuality if you are perceived to be in opposition to the dominant understanding of that political attachment, or as potentially disloyal to it. The life in common that is structured by the conditions of political belonging in a state or political unit can thus be marked by the marginalization of individuals, or groups whose loyalty, and even humanity, is challenged on security grounds (see Guillaume and Huysmans 2013). This includes placing individuals and groups outside of legal protections offered to those whose political belonging is not in question.

See **Chapter 11** on citizenship and security

Disability: In 1976, the Union of Physically Impaired Against Segregation (UPIAS) argued that 'disability is something imposed on top of our impairments by the way we are unnecessarily isolated and excluded from full participation in society' (as quoted in McLaughlin 2020, 184). From this understanding, an impairment (which could be a disease, congenital condition, injury, or from aging) is not the cause of disability. Rather, disability results from socio-political inequalities and environmental obstacles that actively and passively exclude and/or marginalize those with impairments. Approaches to addressing exclusions generated by disability often individualize it by focusing on 'reasonable adjustments' rather than considering the broader structures behind the inequalities and obstacles that generate disabilities in the first place. It also calls into question whose bodies and capabilities are taken as the norm. Thus, the forms of political violence enabling disability for those living with impairments are often overlooked, including gross forms of insecurity from employment discrimination and higher risks of physical violence, sexual assault, and economic deprivation (Hollomotz 2013). Yet, disability is often used to portray those with impairments as physical threats (e.g., by right-wing eugenics movements) and economic threats (e.g., adopting draconian processes to prove disability in order to access state benefits).

All these factors, and their intersections, can be found throughout this book and the accompanying online resources. While they may not always be explicitly flagged in every chapter, it is important that they are present in your mind when you ask your own questions about security. While not always immediately visible, all have a presence in socio-political orders and the political violence that stems from these hierarchies.

1.5 Conclusion

The ability to engage in critique by asking questions is something that we acquire through practice. Critique is a concern with raising questions about how our worlds came to be as they are, the forms of domination and oppression that structure them, and how we have come to understand them as we do. When it comes to security, as we will see in Chapter 2, critical perspectives help us to identify how security is a political claim. Security is always a choice. It is not something natural, inevitable, or neutral. Furthermore, adopting a critical perspective allows us to be open to different worlds while better understanding how they are shaped by security. In other words, critique enables us to problematize the status quo, to ask relevant questions about it, and to find answers to our questions. Finally, while not being an engine for transformation on its own, critique offers multiple ways to identify and analyse how forms of domination and oppression create socio-political orders. Thus, by helping us to identify the sources of problems, critique offers the possibility of socio-political transformation.

Additional short introductions to theoretical approaches are available on the online resources to take your understanding of key theories further:
http://www.oup.com/he/Grayson-Guillaume1e.

Questions for further discussion

1. Identify a form of political, social, economic, or environmental injustice. Discuss how it encompasses different factors, or their intersections, discussed in Section 1.4. Do these factors help you understand who is affected by this injustice? If so, how?

2. How is a form of injustice you have discussed in Question 1 a form of domination and/or oppression? Discuss the possible identities, ideas, interests, institutions, infrastructures, and practices that contribute to the forms of domination/oppression you have identified. *See 3.3 about these enablers*

3. Identify a security issue, or any issue, presented as novel. Try to find relations with past issues. Discuss the implications of the 'novelty' framing for this issue.

4. How knowledge about security is produced matters to how we approach what security does. Select one of the questions in Section 1.2.4 and discuss the possible implications of where security knowledge is produced (e.g., governments, militaries, think tanks, or universities) on what is known about security.

5. Identify a security issue and discuss how policies to address it are presented as necessary. What are other possible ways one could approach the issue?

Further reading

TUHIWAI SMITH, LINDA. 2012. *Decolonizing methodologies: Research and Indigenous peoples*. 2nd ed. London: Zed Books.
This book examines the connections among the development of scientific thought, colonialism, racism, and the dehumanization of Indigenous peoples, including how Indigenous forms of knowledge and knowledge production continue to be discounted in the present day.

DAS GUPTA, TANIA, CARL E. JAMES, ROBERT C. A. MAAKA, GRACE-EDWARD GALABUZI, and CHRIS ANDERSEN. Eds. 2007. *Race and racialization: Essential readings*. Toronto: Canadian Scholars Press.
This book provides an overview of anti-racist thought and practice from around the world.

LOOMBA, ANIA. 2007. *Colonialism/Postcolonialism*. 2nd ed. New York: Routledge.
This book provides a historical and conceptual overview of colonialism and post-colonialism. Loomba is particularly good at situating colonialism and post-colonialism in their different contexts, illustrating connections to other global dynamics and theoretical outlooks.

GOODLEY, DAN. 2016. *Disability studies: An interdisciplinary introduction*. London: Sage.
This book introduces disability as a concept, how it intersects with other identity categories, and how one can challenge ableist practices in a global world.

SHEPHERD, LAURA J. 2008. *Gender, violence and security: Discourse as practice*. London: Zed Books.
Shepherd examines how gender violence and international security are connected and understood. Her case study is the United Nations Security Council Resolution 1325 on women, peace, and security. Her analysis demonstrates the limitations of the approaches offered and from where these limits arise.

References

Beier, J. Marshall and Ann D. Crosby. 1998. 'Harnessing change for continuity: The play of political and economic forces behind the Ottawa Process'. *Canadian Foreign Policy Journal* 5(3), 85–103.

Bourdieu, Pierre. 1979. *La distinction. Critique sociale du jugement*. Paris: Les éditions de minuit.

Butler, Judith. 1990. *Gender trouble: Feminism and the subversion of identity*. London: Routledge.

Calhoun, Craig. 1995. *Critical social theory: Culture, history, and the challenge of difference*. Malden, MA: Blackwell Publishing.

Clarke, John, Stuart Hall, Tony Jefferson, and Brian Roberts. 1975. 'Subcultures, cultures and class'. In *Resistance through rituals: Youth subcultures in post-war Britain*, edited by Stuart Hall and Tony Jefferson. London: Routledge.

Cohn, Carol. 1987. 'Sex and death in the rational world of defense intellectuals'. *Signs: Journal of Women in Culture and Society* 12(4), 687–718.

Collins, Patricia Hill. 2019. *Intersectionality as critical social theory*. Durham, NC: Duke University Press.

Crenshaw, Kimberlé. 1990. 'Mapping the margins: Intersectionality, identity politics, and violence against women of color'. *Stanford Law Review* 43(6), 1241–1300.

de Goede, Marieke. 2018. 'The chain of security'. *Review of International Studies* 44(1), 24–42.

Elia, Nada, David M. Hernández, Jodi Kim, Shana L. Redmond, Dylan Rodríguez, and Sarita Echavez. Eds. 2016. *Critical ethnic studies: A reader*. Durham, NC: Duke University Press.

England, Kim V. 1994. 'Getting personal: Reflexivity, positionality, and feminist research'. *The Professional Geographer* 46(1), 80–89.

Fassin, Didier. 2017. 'The endurance of critique'. *Anthropological Theory* 17(1), 4–29.

Guillaume, Xavier and Jef Huysmans. 2013. 'Introduction: Citizenship and security'. In *Citizenship and security: The constitution of political being*, edited by Xavier Guillaume and Jef Huysmans. London: Routledge.

Hollomotz, Andrea. 2013. 'Disability, oppression and violence: Towards a sociological explanation'. *Sociology* 47(3), 477–493.

Huysmans, Jef. 1998. 'Security! What do you mean? From concept to thick signifier'. *European Journal of International Relations* 4(2), 226–255.

Marx, Karl. 1976 [1867]. *Capital: A critique of political economy*. Volume 1. London: Penguin Books.

Massey, Doreen. 1996. 'Politicising space and place'. *Scottish Geographical Magazine* 112(2), 117–123.

McLaughlin, Janice. 2020. 'Disability'. In *Social geographies: An introduction*, edited by the Newcastle Social Geographies Collective. Lanham, MD: Rowman and Littlefield.

Monsees, Linda, Mike Slaven, Ákos Kopper, András Szalai, and Stefan Kroll [forum]. 2020. 'The politicisation of security: Controversy, mobilisation, arena shifting'. *European Review of International Studies* 7(1), 105–122.

Moule Jr, Richard K., Bryanna Hahn Fox, and Megan M. Parry. 2019. 'The long shadow of Ferguson: Legitimacy, legal cynicism, and public perceptions of police militarization'. *Crime & Delinquency* 65(2), 151–182.

Murji, Karim and John Solomos. Eds. 2005. *Racialization: Studies in theory and practice.* Oxford: Oxford University Press.

Park, Peter K. J. 2013. *Africa, Asia, and the history of philosophy: Racism in the formation of the philosophical canon, 1780–1830.* Albany, NY: SUNY Press.

Pels, Dick. 2000. 'Reflexivity: One step up'. *Theory, Culture & Society* 17(3), 1–25.

Phillips, Scott W. 2018. *Police militarization: Understanding the perspectives of police chiefs, administrators, and tactical officers.* London: Routledge.

Robinson, Fiona. 2011. *The ethics of care: A feminist approach to human security.* Philadelphia, PA: Temple University Press.

Shilliam, Robbie. 2021. *Decolonizing politics: An introduction.* Oxford: John Wiley & Sons.

Sjoberg, Laura. 2015. 'Seeing sex, gender, and sexuality in international security'. *International Journal: Canada's Journal of Global Policy Analysis* 70(3), 434–453.

Smith, Barbara H. 1988. *Contingencies of value: Alternative perspectives for critical theory.* Cambridge, MA: Harvard University Press.

Tonelli, Giorgio. 1978. '"Critique" and related terms prior to Kant: A historical survey'. *Kant-Studien* 69(1–4), 119–148.

Troyna, Barry. 1983. 'Multicultural education: Just another brick in the wall?'. *New Community* 10(3), 424–428.

United Nations Development Programme. 1994. *Human development report.* New York: Oxford University Press.

Walt, Steven M. 1991. 'The renaissance of security studies'. *International Studies Quarterly* 35(2), 211–239.

Williams, Raymond. 2011 [1985]. 'Culture is ordinary (1958)'. In *Cultural theory: An anthology*, edited by Imre Szeman and Timothy Kaposy. Oxford: Wiley-Blackwell.

Young, Iris M. 1990. *Justice and the politics of difference.* Princeton, NJ: Princeton University Press.

Young, Iris M. 2011. *Five faces of oppression.* Princeton, NJ: Princeton University Press.

2

Security

2.1	Introduction	18
2.2	Security: the history of an ambiguous term	20
2.3	Security as a threshold/security as a process	24
2.4	Security as a political mobilization	29
2.5	Conclusion	33

READER'S GUIDE

In this chapter we ask the question, 'what is security?'. We explore the history of security as a concept and practice that emerged out of the long nineteenth century. We show its inherent ties to colonialism and imperialism. We then suggest that security can be seen as an achievable threshold/goal whose progress can be measured, or as an ongoing process that is never complete. Either way, security is a form of political mobilization that acts upon our worlds through the prism of threats and risks, creating conditions of possibility and impossibility. We conclude that the ubiquity of security demands that we ask how it defines our relations with others and with ourselves in shaping socio-political orders. To ask 'what is security?' is ultimately to answer the question, 'what does security do?'.

2.1 Introduction

'What is security?' This question, and answers to it, are not as easy as we might think. First, what does it mean to be secure? Does security require being invulnerable? Relatively safe? Somewhat protected? Or merely subject to calculated risks? Second, what does security encompass? Physical harm? General well-being? Freedom from fear? Freedom from want? Third, at what level should security be applied? Individuals? Households? Ecosystems? Cultures and ways of life? Societies? Economies? States? Regions? The international system? Or the biosphere? Fourth, what policy domain is best positioned to provide security? The military and defence? The police? Economic development? Social welfare? Language, arts, and culture? Public health? The environment and natural resources? Or perhaps law and human rights? Are any of the categories mutually exclusive or are they interdependent? Are they competing demands or mutually reinforcing? Finally, is security a 'good' thing? Is it something that should be valued above everything else? Or should it be one consideration among many for individuals and societies?

These are important questions at the heart of security. They endure because **security is ubiquitous in our daily lives yet remains politically contentious**. We speak of national security, human security, health security, food security, social security, cyber security, environmental security, economic security, and so on. Security is embedded into the forms of policing we experience from 'security screening' at airports to security guards in schools. Security thinking also remains central to military defence. Against a narrow focus on the military and the state, there is a longstanding claim that security is best achieved through the well-being of individuals and taking action to free them from fear and/or want. This vision of security has been mobilized by non-violence movements, anti-nuclear groups, human rights organizations, the United Nations, and for periods of time even states such as Canada, Japan, Norway, and Thailand.

Despite this diversity, what security means is frequently assumed without looking more carefully at what security does when it is mobilized. Thus, security is often seen as being inherently 'good' without considering its potential consequences and costs. Moreover, although many actors invoke security similarly, we should not assume that they do so in the same ways, or for the same purposes. Critical perspectives are interested in how security 'makes things happen'. More precisely, they share the view that '[t]he abstract noun "security" is an umbrella term that both enables and conceals a very diverse array of governing practices, budgetary practices, political and legal practices, and social and cultural values and habits' (Valverde 2001, 90). So in asking 'what is security?', we are not going to provide a ready-made definition. Rather, we believe the best answer is to offer a series of analytical strategies that will enable you to uncover what security does to our worlds. These will allow you, as a security analyst, to understand in a given political context how security produces specific relations of power and hierarchies. With this capacity to analyse security critically, you will be equipped to tackle the significant political questions 'security' poses to us as global citizens.

See **Chapter 3** on relations of power and hierarchies

To put it more bluntly, the history of security is replete with practices that have made particular groups of people 'secure' by imposing insecurities onto others. The imposition of insecurity is often unacknowledged by those in positions of authority and can remain hidden in plain sight depending on one's vantage point. Therefore, we should pay attention to those groups, especially those we term security professionals (e.g., law enforcement officers, military personnel, security analysts, the security industry, *and* security scholars), for whom security is a stake in itself. It is a stake for these individuals and groups because security is linked to their interests beyond any underlying rationales for its mobilization.

See **Section 1.2.3** on the sociology of security

'Security' is not a universal term, experience, or set of policies. In every context, it has a history. In Section 2.2, we therefore start this chapter by presenting an overview of the recent histories of practices found under the auspices of 'security'. During the long nineteenth century, security gained prominence as a means to manage the uncertainties of political and social life. It emerged within socio-political and economic contexts shaped by the consolidation of the nation-state in Europe, the expansion and acceleration of European colonization, the disruptive emergence of capitalism, desires for public order, the ascendancy of 'scientific' racism, and the cross-fertilization of practices of state and empire building. As analysts, we need to uncover these strands and their connections to contemporary socio-political processes (Barkawi and Laffey 2006). Doing so demonstrates that the complementary, contestable, and contradictory dimensions of security have been apparent from the start. By seeing how different understandings of security lead to different forms of political mobilization, you can distinguish how these understandings produce different security outcomes for different groups of people.

> **Section 1.2.1** discusses the contingency of security

A first step towards this goal, as we see in Section 2.3, is to determine **whether security is being understood as a goal/threshold (with its achievement defined by fulfilling a set of criteria) or as an ongoing set of processes**. These two understandings are not necessarily mutually exclusive; however, they suggest different sets of questions. Nevertheless, both require that we look closely at **how security is mobilized and the consequences of security mobilizations**. The mobilization of security refers to how security depicts and acts upon people, interactions, events, places, and things that have been determined to be threatened, or threatening, by someone with the authority/capacity to do so. As we will see in Section 2.4, then, the focus on security as a mobilization is an important reminder that to speak or act 'security' is not neutral, innocent, inevitable, or natural. **To call upon security is a political choice.** There are always alternative ways to define problems and address them that do not require us to speak of security, deploy security thinking, or adopt security practices.

> **Section 1.2.2** has more on the necessity of historicizing and contextualizing security

The mobilization of security opens up political questions regarding why this problem framing is being used, how it shapes the understanding of a problem and its definition as a *security* 'problem', the interests behind its mobilization, and how it invites the use of particular resources to address a problem that has been identified as a 'security problem'.

> See **Section 1.3** on the necessity of critique

2.2 Security: the history of an ambiguous term

As Lucia Zedner (2009, 11) notes, when we hear the word security, there is a tendency to think of it as a universal condition with a shared understanding. Yet it has 'widely varying usages across jurisdictions deriving from differences in local history, social structure, and legal and political cultures' (Zedner 2009, 11). Given this diversity, we cannot possibly offer a thorough discussion of the historical development of a concept such as 'security' (for an erudite philological account, see Hamilton 2013). Nor can we discuss its myriad meanings. We can observe, however, its prevalence in many aspects of contemporary society. This prevalence is a catalyst to analyse security via critique so that we can uncover its contingency, historicity, sociology, and roles in fostering or inhibiting change and/or transformation.

> For more on critique, see **Section 1.2**

To understand how security has become embedded in our daily lives, it is useful to start by examining western Europe at the start of the long nineteenth century. This is because the period's legacies of violence have shaped the world up to the present day. This particular socio-political context is the time when what we would recognize as the modern security apparatus emerges in places such as France, Germany, and Britain. One of its distinguishing features was to differentiate the roles of the police and the military. This separation formalized the creation of inward-facing security tasks undertaken by the police and outward-facing security tasks managed by the military.

> **Chapters 6 and 7** also cover the functional differentiation of the police and military

In its inward-facing forms, security emerges as a means for identifying, calculating, and controlling socio-political dynamics said to be threats. There was a focus on phenomena believed to be detrimental to the collective health and well-being of the nation-state and its key elements (including the economy and society). Such threats included the urban poor and the criminal classes of the *Lumpenproletariat*, mental illness, communicable diseases, 'deviant' sexual practices, other groups (whether cultural, ethnic, racial, or religious), and political ideologies said to contain elements of Marxism, socialism, anarchism, syndicalism, and/or calls for the extension of political freedoms and equalities (including suffrage) and national self-determination.

> **Chapter 15** examines surveillance and data-veillance

In its external-facing forms within the demands posed by large-scale armed conflicts and state development, European countries began to incorporate forms of national conscription to replace mercenary and professional armies. This greatly increased state concerns over the security (i.e., health, education, and well-being) of their respective populations. This was not undertaken out of a sense of charity but rather to ensure a plentiful supply of high-quality soldiers, as illustrated by Chad McCail in Figure 2.1.

It is, however, impossible to disconnect what happened 'within' Europe and its development of security without accounting for the intensification and acceleration of European colonial expansion in Africa, Asia, Oceania, and North America. Furthermore, security was shaped by the reconfiguration of European imperialism in spaces such as the Indian subcontinent and those areas previously subject to colonization such as Latin America and the Caribbean. The literature on nineteenth-century colonialism highlights how the development of policing and military practices in the global north was closely tied to security innovations fostered by different kinds of imperial and colonial experiences, including slavery and the genocide of Indigenous peoples (Glenn 2015). Thus, security developed in the nineteenth century through the circulation of socio-political and economic logics, dynamics, and practices across metropoles and peripheries. The experiences of colonial and home rule cross-fertilized to produce new security models, strategies, techniques, and equipment. These processes have strong echoes, forming what Derek Gregory (2004) has called the 'colonial present'.

> See **Chapters 11, 14,** and **17** for further examples

Take the example of the circulation of security practices across post-colonial and metropolitan sites. From the mid-1940s to the 1960s, the Parisian police adopted counterinsurgency techniques developed in French colonies such as Algeria and French-Indo China (Vietnam) (see Blanchard 2011). These techniques included new forms

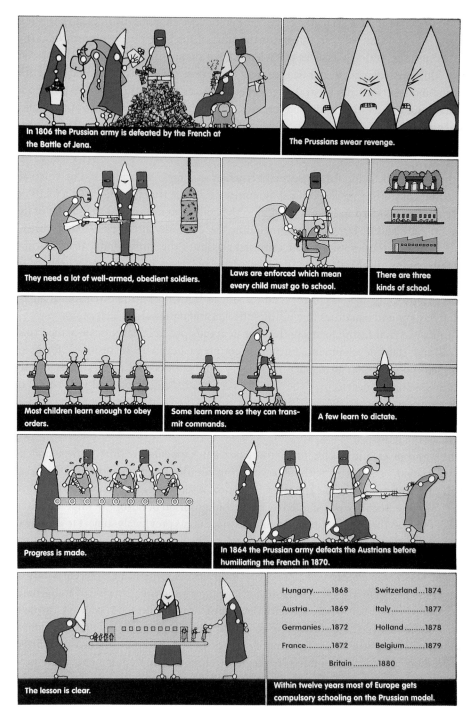

Figure 2.1 Chad McCail, 'Compulsory Education' (2008), 96 × 140 cm, screen print; www.chadmccail.co.uk/compulsory_education.html.

of intelligence gathering and the use of torture, internment, and forced deportations. In our 'colonial present', specific policing tools, such as COMPStat, a software package for tracking criminal activity hotspots pioneered in the 1990s by the New York Police Department, were used as counterinsurgency tools to manage the occupation of Iraq (Mitchell 2010). We can also find these connections in contexts where colonial dynamics might not appear obvious at first glance. For example, Brazil used opportunities offered by its peacekeeping operations in Haiti to develop counterinsurgency techniques and practices that have been incorporated domestically in the policing of 'favelas', poor areas within urban settings (Sanchez Nieto 2012). These modes of policing, first developed abroad, have deepened existing hierarchies and prejudices towards favela residents.

> See **Chapter 8** on counter-insurgency

In Table 2.1 we briefly summarize how the long nineteenth century has influenced how security has come to define the twenty-first century in relation to the different themes that are covered by this book.

These broader historical contexts are central to understanding how security has been constitutive of the different themes covered by the other chapters in this book. We will now turn to how experts and scholars conceptualize security.

Table 2.1 The effects of the long nineteenth century on security thinking and practices

Thematic chapters	Action	Tools	Example
• Policing • War and society • Terrorism and asymmetric conflicts • Identity and othering • Nationalism, racism, and xenophobia • Security and design • Weapons-systems	Direct exercise of violence by the state and/or its agents on groups deemed to be threatening.	Modernization of military and policing apparatus.	Peterloo Massacre (1819); Wounded Knee Massacre (1890); Amritsar Massacre (1919).
• Gender and sexuality • Health • Borders and mobilities • Prisons and camps	Practices of confinement used to rehabilitate or cure 'dangerous' individuals.	Establishment of new academic disciplines such as psychology, sociology, and criminology.	Establishment of state and/or privately operated prisons, asylums, and sanatoriums.
• Gender and sexuality • Nationalism, racism, and xenophobia • Health • Development • Digital, (in)security, and violence • Borders and mobilities • Prisons and camps	Establish norms/patterns for social and biological phenomena at the level of a population. Then identify and address unusual deviations from these norms/patterns.	Advancement of statistics and accounting. Pathologization and medicalization of 'deviant' social, gendered, and sexual behaviours/orientations.	Public health initiatives; public welfare systems; universal public education.

(Continued)

Table 2.1 *Continued*

Thematic chapters	Action	Tools	Example
• Development • Property, extraction, and accumulation • Digital, (in)security, and violence • Environment • Policing	Design spaces and systems that facilitate desired forms of activity and circulation (e.g., goods, people, finance) while preventing others.	Ascendancy of liberal political economy (ideological) and re-ordering of European societies (e.g., agrarian and industrial revolutions). Plunder from and continuous exploitation of imperial conquests and colonization to fund European and North American development; slavery.	Changes in urban planning from a concern with fortification (medieval) to openness (for commerce and trade). Growth of policing to deal with vagrants, the working poor, and criminal classes; exclusive property rights over the commons.
• Policing • War and society • Terrorism and asymmetric conflicts • Identity and othering • Nationalism, racism, and xenophobia • Digital, (in)security, and violence • Weapons-systems	Ongoing advancement in practices of hunting/ capturing individual trouble-makers/ security threats.	Experience of asymmetrical warfare in imperial wars. Experiences of slave ownership and the threat of marronage.	American slave catchers (1800s); Palmer Raids (1919); Aceh War (1873–1904); Anti-British National Liberation War (1948–60).

2.3 Security as a threshold/security as a process

Despite the diversity of historical pathways by which security has become predominant in contemporary societies, it is typical for analysts to attach themselves to a specific aspect of security. You will find a brief introduction to key analytical approaches to security and their associated research communities in the online resources. However, as a first step, it is useful to divide these views about security into two categories: (i) security as a **potentially achievable goal or threshold** and (ii) security as an **ongoing process** that will always be incomplete.

These two understandings are not mutually exclusive. Nevertheless, they help delineate the different things that security does. Moreover, they are united in their shared concern about what happens when security is mobilized as a political claim. In other words, they tell us something important about the implications of being defined as a threat or in need of protection.

2.3.1 Security as a threshold

Security is a goal or threshold when it is defined in reference to an outcome that might be achieved—that is, being secure in relation to someone and/or something. Security, in this sense, is based on an assessment of whether a specific set of criteria have been achieved. It could also be based on subjective feelings. To understand security in this way raises a series of interesting questions: what criteria determine when one is secure? Are these criteria and threats to them objectively determinable? There are many things that could bring security. Likewise, there are many things that might physically harm us (e.g., terrorist attacks and communicable diseases), cause costly disruptions (e.g., cyber-attacks and climate change), or be detrimental to our general well-being (e.g., street crime and environmental pollution), but not all might be considered security issues. Thus, to what extent do we believe (in)security can be objectively determined from a neutral vantage point? Is it inevitable that our sense of (in)security will be shaped by how subjective perceptions and interests influence what we believe needs to be secured (and from what?)? If so, is this necessarily a bad thing?

Some analysts argue that security is a goal or threshold that can be objectively determined in two senses. First, security is an objective state achieved when some end goal (e.g., physical safety, full employment, national security) is completed. Second, conceptualizing security as a threshold/goal that can be objectively determined also means that there are certain threats that 'objectively' matter more than others. For some, military and economic threats against states are what matter most. Others argue that it is physical, sexual, and economic threats faced by individuals within states that are objectively the most important security issues. Regardless of what is to be secured and how, to position security as an objectively determinable goal free of subjective influence is a choice that often tries to hide its political character. It is political because by invoking objectivity, one is seeking to affirm the priority of one's view over others without acknowledging one's positionality. Moreover, treating security as an objectively determinable goal has often been used to marginalize, and even disqualify, alternative perspectives of security. This does not mean that 'anything goes' when it comes to security. Rather, it is simply to note how appeals to objectivity can sometimes be used to shut down discussions of alternative ways of understanding and practising security and/or moving away from it. It raises the question of how anyone can be objective about security if being objective means removing yourself from the socio-political and economic contexts in which you live in order to evaluate the sources of insecurity, free of your shaped perceptions, subjective feelings, and interests, and how best to address them. Moreover, even if it were possible, would this level of detachment be desirable?

On the question of reflexivity, see **Box 1.2**

See **Section 3.3** for distinctions between the political and politics

Box 4.1 discusses non-violence as an alternative perspective

Viewing security as a subjectively determined threshold is to understand it as 'an existential state that varies not only according to objective risk but also according to extraneous factors such as individual sensitivity to risk and danger' (Zedner 2009, 16). To *feel* entirely, or partially, secure is an individual determination. It may be connected to knowledge of potential threats to one's own safety or be in complete ignorance of them. It can also be connected to culturally produced social anxieties and/or

See **Section 1.4** on the factors shaping our perceptions

Chapter 19 covers migration and security

individual perceptions of safety that hold in spite of the presence of many dangers. For example, research suggests that those most likely to view immigration as a security threat are those with the least amount of lived experience with minority groups and migrant communities (McLaren 2003). Similarly, some readers may feel entirely at ease in places that might otherwise be perceived as dangerous (e.g., due to high crime rates) because of their familiarity with the setting and its associated risks. Moreover, if (in)security is indeed shaped by subjective perceptions and interests (whether in full or to some degree), is it legitimate to derive security policies from them? More provocatively, if feelings of (in)security originate from broader social anxieties and concerns that may misconstrue and/or wrongly identify sources of harm, should they still be incorporated into how security is mobilized?

Now that we are more familiar with objective and subjective understandings of security as a goal or threshold, we can turn to three sets of questions. These questions are methodological and ethical. They are methodological because they determine how we build up our knowledge of security. These questions are also ethical because the means we use to determine what security *is* will have profound effects on ourselves and others. These include shaping how others are governed, how we are governed, how others behave, and how we behave towards others. The first question, then, is **how do we identify security goals, regardless of whether we see them as objectively or subjectively determined? Moreover, how do we determine the right means to achieve a security end?** While there are many possible answers, what is interesting is how these questions are often actively excluded from public discussion by limiting what can be considered security knowledge, who is able to produce knowledge of security, and how security can be provided. This is accomplished by over-relying on security professionals: practitioners embedded within, or connected to, the security apparatus of the state.

Questions of legitimacy and authority are covered in **Sections 4.3–4**

A second related set of questions thus concerns voice: **who, in a given context, can identify security threats (as an objective or subjectively derived set of criteria) and have these assessments taken seriously?** Does everyone have the same power and authority to do so? If not, who is vested with the legitimacy and authority to make claims about security goals? Moreover, if the power to voice security concerns is unevenly distributed, who speaks in the name of those deemed to be objectively or subjectively threatened? In other words, who can 'speak' security? The emergence of the concept of human security is a good example of this dynamic.

See **Section 5.3.1.1** for more details on the question of who can 'speak' security

In 1994, the United Nations Development Programme (UNDP) introduced 'human security' into security discussions as a means to provide 'people-centred, comprehensive, context-specific and prevention-oriented responses that strengthen the protection and empowerment of all people and all communities' around the world, but with an emphasis on lower-income states in the global south (United Nations, 2016, 6; Tadjbakhsh and Chenoy 2007). While providing funding to manage local human security issues in lower-income member states, it is important to explore who defines acceptable ways of living, whose challenges are deemed worthy of support, and how any decision potentially 'interconnects with the security of the global north' (Duffield 2010, 68).

A third set of questions focus on measurement. **Regardless of how we define security, how can we measure it? And if we are going to measure security, how will measurements be translated into an evaluation of the ability of particular courses of**

action to manage insecurities (Zedner 2009, 15)? Similarly, measurement also relates to questions about how to identify, assess, and evaluate the costs and benefits of particular courses of action in the pursuit of security. More importantly, we need to ask whether measurements and their guiding assumptions are even valid in the first place. For example, to counter the threat of terrorism, should liberal democracies strike a judicious balance between security and liberty?

The above questions regarding the determination of what constitute security goals, who can participate in this process, and how we evaluate these determinations highlight how security is dynamic. Security is contested; from these contests, security is shaped and reshaped while shaping and reshaping the worlds around it. In other words, security is a process.

> **Box 2.1** offers a discussion of the balance 'myth'

> See **Section 3.4** on challenges and resistance to security

> ### BOX 2.1 THE FLAWED LOGIC OF THE SECURITY–LIBERTY BALANCE
>
> Whether in the aftermath of the terrorist attacks of 11 September 2001, during the 1954–62 Algerian war, or through legal instruments such as the 2015 Australian Biosecurity Act, states have acted in ways (both *de facto* and *de jure*) that establish particular balances between security and liberty. The balance metaphor presumes the following chain of logic. First, in times of crisis liberty can only be protected by limiting it. Second, security can only be increased by limiting liberties. Third, once liberties have been curtailed and security has increased, it is possible for security to give way again to liberty. Limitations on liberty for the purposes of increasing security have included curbs on the freedom of movement, the right to due process, privacy, and basic human rights (including the use of torture and extrajudicial killing). The underlying logic of viewing security and liberty as a balancing act is highly problematic. Jeremy Waldron (2003) offers a substantial critique of its underlying assumptions. At its heart is a rejection of the idea that security and liberty can be 'measured' and compared with precision. We can sum up the concerns he raises in five questions:
>
> - How much licence do/should we give to the state so it can protect us?
> - Can individual liberties be reduced to a means to an end (i.e., diminishing liberties increase security and vice versa) rather than being inherently valuable in their own right?
> - To what extent does a reduction in our liberties via security disproportionally affect specific groups?
> - To what extent does the reduction of our liberties result in a reduction of our security *vis-à-vis* the state?
> - To what extent do security measures that are undertaken have symbolic or real effects?
>
> Moreover, the security–liberty balance rests on the assumption that security and liberty can be accurately measured and exchanged such that a judicious balance is maintained. Is this the case? And who decides what is considered judicious?
>
> Mark Neocleous (2007) goes even further in his critique of the liberty and security balance metaphor. He shows how in the classical liberalism of thinkers such as John Locke and Adam Smith the underlying motivation was not to protect everyone's liberties at all times but rather to protect the property rights of the wealthy. Neocleous highlights how the focus on the myth of the balance between security and liberty elides a more fundamental question about how the state's protection of liberties for all is more often about protecting the wealth and property of a smaller number of individuals.

2.3.2 Security as a process

Security may be a process for two reasons. First, we can recognize that security is an ongoing pursuit. In this sense, security 'is probably unattainable and at best impermanent' (Zedner 2009, 19). **Second, we can see security as a series of ongoing and evolving practices that are said and done.** These practices imbue people, interactions, things, spaces, and events with special qualities, including the status of being a threat and/or something that is threatened. This capacity of security has specific effects that we will detail in Section 2.4. The central point is that **security is an ongoing political struggle over what should be a security issue and/or best courses of action to take once something is identified as a security issue**. Meaning-making and productive processes are essential here.

Meaning-making processes establish how specific meanings are attributed to people, interactions, things, spaces, and events that make them security issues. As such, meaning-making processes are central to the relations of power and hierarchies that are shaped by security. Meaning can be established via many different routes including the specific language we use to describe things, cultural practices (such as celebrations and memorialization), and discourses (for instance, on race, gender, and religion).

As we indicated, an important question is 'who' can speak security and be listened to. Who is silenced? Who stays silent and why (Parpart 2020)? Security is a process through which particular meanings become established and connected to people, interactions, things, spaces, and events. These shared meanings enable particular courses of action as well as for these actions to be considered legitimate responses. They are also the site of challenges and contestation. Thus, in any given context, who is considered a legitimate 'speaker' of security? Are these speakers challenged in their processes of meaning-making? If so, how? By whom?

Productive processes are actions, interactions, things, spaces, and events that affect people. Primarily, these productive processes shape the ways in which people are able to understand and/or interact with each other through the prism of security. These processes contribute to political logics and dynamics informed by security in two ways. First, as we will see, they can contribute to the mobilization of security as an

> See **Sections 3.2–4** on relations of power and hierarchies and their relations to socio-political orders
>
> **Zoom-in 2.1** introduces the concept of discourse

🔍 ZOOM-IN 2.1 DISCOURSE

Discourse is a central concept and site of analysis; however, it has many different definitions. This leads to a great deal of confusion. We take discourses to be collections of words, ideas, forms of knowledge, and rules that coalesce into shared understandings of what a subject or topic area encompasses. Thus, we might speak of a drugs discourse, terrorism discourse, health discourse, or migration discourse. Discourses serve as guides to orientate our perceptions, behaviours, actions, and decision-making; they are how people and institutions tend to think, speak, and act in relation to particular things. Discourses are also important because they reveal what is taken for granted and naturalized within a given topic area (see Zoom-in 1.1), even where there may be disagreement. In other words, by analysing discourses, we may discover shared understandings held by different positions.

action and the justification of such a mobilization. For example, environmental factors, from climate change to pollution, are potentially shaping how security is mobilized to interpret phenomena and react to them. Their mere presence and effects may press upon us the need to declare them to be security issues and act accordingly. Or, on the contrary, it may be that we choose to treat them otherwise and deploy a different outlook (e.g., ecology, public health, global justice) to manage them.

Second, these processes can contribute to shaping our lives in multiple ways. Security 'does' something as actions taken under its auspices affect us (e.g., physical confinement measures in times of pandemics) or are affected by us (e.g., the complexity of passwords we use online). Spaces we inhabit (e.g., our streets), travel through (e.g., airports), and where we engage in communicative exchange (e.g., social media), as well as those that are imposed on us (e.g., migrant camps), are all governed by security in ways that affect our lives. Finally, objects are also imbued with 'security', from the presence of small arms in the communities in which we live to the urban design of streets.

Whether we primarily understand security as a goal that can be achieved, as an ongoing process that can never quite be reached, or as a combination of both, it should **always be considered relational and contextual** (Zedner 2009, 15). Security is a relation that exists among different people, institutions, things, spaces, events, and time periods. Security is contingent and has a history and sociology. Regardless of the character of these relationships, the important thing is that when mobilized, security brings different things together. In doing so, **security establishes connections, meanings, and productive processes that generate political outcomes**.

It follows that if security is relational, it must also be contextual. In other words, security relations will be different depending on where we live as well as how we are identified in different settings and by different actors. Security acts upon us differently depending on the relationships in which we are embedded (Pratt 2013). Thus, rather than trying to determine what security is and/or when it has been achieved, **we should be primarily concerned with what security 'does'**. In other words, a critique of security is always interested in what happens when the term 'security' is used, actions are taken in its name, and this is done so in relation to an event, situation, group, person, space, or time. When we know what happens, we can better see how security is a form of political mobilization.

2.4 Security as a political mobilization

Whether understood as a goal or process, security is a form of **political mobilization**. As a form of political mobilization, security classifies, identifies, and acts upon people, processes, things, spaces, and events through the prism of threats and risks. Security always makes a specific **political claim** about who (or what) is a threat and who (or what) is threatened. In this context, the term 'political' is in reference to the choice to frame something as a *security* issue: there are always alternative framings that could be used that might lead to a different set of responses (and outcomes). To accept, resist, or remain distant towards the mobilization of security is also a choice, albeit one often limited by circumstances. We are not always, if ever, entirely free to choose to do or act in accordance with what we think is just or fair, or even in ways that align with our minimum preferences. Nonetheless, while it may be important to assess the success or failure of any attempt to 'do' security, we should never lose sight of the fact that 'security' is always a 'political act' and therefore is 'neither innocent nor neutral nor inevitable' (Huysmans 1998, 245).

Any claim about security involves several actors. First, there is a claimant. This can be a group, institution, or individual who has the authority and legitimacy (i.e., perceived expertise and/or social role) within a given socio-political order to make a claim that something pertains to security. There may also be those who contest the connection(s) to security that are made. In other words, there is no guarantee that a security claim will be successful, even in cases where the claimant is an actor with significant authority and power. Security necessarily involves a political contest over what is prioritized as a security issue, why it is being prioritized, and how it is prioritized (e.g., through funding, agenda setting, awareness raising, or action plans). Finally, security can be a stake for what we have termed security professionals; that is, interest groups or individuals who are professionally defined, and who identify themselves, through the mobilization of security. Hyperbolic responses by security authorities to calls to defund the police are a good example of this.

Defunding the police is motivated by the view that police services are being asked to undertake too many tasks (e.g., first-line response to individuals in mental distress) and/or address issues that are manifestations of other forms of social deprivation (e.g., homelessness) to which they are ill suited. The point is to scale back public funding of police services to their core crime/public order functions. Resources could then be directed to other agencies (e.g., public health departments, parks and recreation agencies, social care, schools) who could address the underlying causes of crime and who are less likely to mobilize forms of violence in the name of security provision. Some police unions, as associations of security professionals, may resist defunding the police because their interests rest in maintaining resources that provide benefits for their members (e.g., jobs). Others may agree to implement changes in policing practices while still resisting this potentially transformative moment in policing as a whole.

Chapter 6 covers the roles of policing

See **Section 1.2.4** on transformation

Part of the reason why security is contentious is that it impacts upon the ability of ordinary people to go about their daily lives. For some analysts, security is a **condition of possibility** opening up new opportunities, freedoms, and spaces for action. For other analysts, security is a **condition of impossibility**. In this view, security not only closes down what people may be able to do but even undermines their position as holders of rights and statuses (including the status of a human being with rights). These two broad understandings are not mutually exclusive as security can be a condition of possibility for some but a condition of impossibility for others. What is important is that these conditions are often in tension (Nyman 2016). Different forms of domination and oppression mobilized by security reinforce hierarchies. The key question is whether mobilizing security can be a way to emancipate people 'from those physical and human constraints which stop them carrying out what they would freely choose to do' (Booth 1991, 319).

On the one hand, the political mobilization of security can be a condition of possibility. This means that security enables individuals and groups to move beyond insecurities that negatively impact upon their daily lives such as poverty, ill health, or violence. Mobilizing security addresses these issues by elevating their importance on policy agendas, drawing both attention and resources for addressing the causes and manifestations of insecurities. For example, contemporary counterinsurgency doctrine stresses that tackling under-development is an important element for defeating insurgencies. By freeing people from the constraints of destitution, one potentially undermines the political legitimacy of insurgent movements. As a result, many donor states over the past decade have changed how they distribute development aid, targeting regions that they believe are terrorist/insurgency strongholds. The hope is that by reshaping the socio-political order through development aid, the insurgency will end (Bell 2011). Concurrently, this redistribution of development efforts comes at the expense of those who formerly received aid to help to address economic inequalities.

> **Chapter 12** investigates the links between development and security

On the other hand, security establishes conditions of impossibility. For example, security creates in-groups seen as virtuous and out-groups who are argued to be a threat to in-groups. This framing enables various courses of action that would otherwise not be permissible. For example, in India a new citizenship bill introduced by the Hindu-nationalist Bharatiya Janata Party government in 2019 legally enshrined discrimination against Muslims. These measures reflected broader security discourses around 'the fifth column threat' posed by the presence of this long-established religious minority group within the country. As a condition of impossibility, as we see with the citizenship bill, security creates, maintains, and/or reinforces the exclusion of certain groups by entrenching specific hierarchies. Security also justifies exceptional measures to accepted norms that enable governments to ignore legally enshrined rights and protections (Fluri 2012). However, for some, being subject to the powers of the exception and conditions of impossibility is in fact the norm.

> See **Chapters 9, 10,** and **11** for different illustrations

> See **Section 4.3** on the notion of the exception

In creating conditions of possibility or impossibility, **security also marshals resources within a society**. These resources could be funding, laws, labour, and even knowledge production. While it is often the state and its agencies that retain a monopoly on catalysing security mobilizations, contemporary security issue management is also distributed across private and non-governmental actors (Loader 1999). The privatization of security provision has reproduced all of the same issues around transparency of security decision-making by the state. Privatization also adds the problem of establishing accountability for security decisions made by these actors and their broader social outcomes. Keeping this dispersion in mind, we will highlight how security can be mobilized.

First, there is the **material mobilization** of security. This can include human resources (e.g., military personnel, private security forces, paramilitaries, self-defence groups, experts, and cyber-defence analysts), economic resources (e.g., government budgeting/spending, redirecting civilian economic production towards security ends), and technological resources.

> For example, see **Chapter 17** om weapons-systems

Second, there is the **institutional mobilization** of security. Security institutions are formal organizations or informal arrangements which identify, manage, and coordinate responses to security situations. They are also the institutional frameworks that are designed to direct material mobilizations and give shape to specific security framings (like laws and regulations). Formal institutions can thus be the arrangements among agencies across all levels of government (from the local to national) as well as arrangements that extend beyond the nation-state to the regional (e.g., the Association of Southeast Asian Nations) and international levels (e.g., Interpol).

Informal institutions are arrangements that involve security coordination and information sharing among mixtures of public institutions and/or private providers. This could include anything from social media platforms that will share user data with counterterrorism organizations to criminal enterprises which run protection rackets.

> See **Zoom-in 2.1** on the concept of discourse

Finally, a security mobilization can be a **discursive mobilization**. A discursive mobilization seeks to impose a particular set of meanings on people, interactions, things, spaces, or events that connect to a security issue. These meanings then become the predominant framing which everyone (whether in agreement or disagreement) must work with (Campbell 1998). For example, when President George W. Bush addressed the people of the United States in the aftermath of 11 September 2001, he asked, and then answered, his own question about the motivation behind the attacks: 'why do they hate us? ... they hate our freedoms' (Bush 2001).

> For more representations of terrorism, see **Chapter 8**

Whether intended or not, this discursive mobilization presented terrorism as an irrational emotional act orchestrated by deviant actors. They were simply evil. Moreover, it established the highly gendered and racialized parameters upon which terrorism as a security issue continues to be understood and contested today (i.e., an act committed by irrational racial others). Our point here is not to justify or downplay a criminal act of political violence. Rather, it is to emphasize that discursive mobilizations are important because they establish the boundaries within which a security issue is understood (Hansen 2013). With 9/11, it was to place the violence outside of politics, and even outside of regular legal processes used to administer justice, by understanding it as an attack on a way of life. By establishing key terms that shape the framing, a successful discursive mobilization often requires all parties (even critics) to acknowledge (and work within) the predominant framing of a security issue in order to be understood and taken seriously.

Security as a political mobilization can take different forms and have different effects. Therefore, as security analysts, we need to be looking at who is able to mobilize security and how they are able to do so in a given context. This includes being sensitive to broader socio-political and economic relations that may shape security understandings and practices. It also means examining actors who are tasked with providing security (and to whom!), those who justify its mobilization, and those who contest mobilizations. Security provision has become the purview of many security professionals including the police, militaries, private security companies, and intelligence services, as well as other groups such as public health organizations, development organizations, schools, financial institutions, tech firms, airlines, and media companies.

2.5 Conclusion

Security has become ubiquitous in our contemporary worlds. Its ubiquity means that as global citizens, we need to ask how security defines our relations with others, our surroundings, the rhythms of our daily lives, and who we understand ourselves to be (Huysmans 1998, 231). Security always comes at a cost. As you will see in the thematic chapters and illustrative cases, costs are distributed unevenly within societies and around the world. Importantly, security 'sticks'. Institutions, practices, and ideas shaped by the mobilization of security are difficult to undo. **Security therefore has a political resilience and staying power not necessarily possessed by other modes of governance.**

Now that we have established the political relevance of security and the importance of approaching it critically, we need to provide the means by which to do so. More specifically, as we will see in Chapter 3, how can we analyse security **to better understand our worlds and how it shapes them?** As a political claim, security never arises in a vacuum. It is always embedded in a socio-political order that is articulated through relations of power reflective of key factors such as political belonging or disability. These relations of power produce hierarchies that are articulated through ideas, identities, interests, institutions, and infrastructures. These are the broader sites you will explore to identify security claims and what they do.

> **Section 1.4** discusses these different factors

Additional short introductions to theoretical approaches are available on the online resources to take your understanding of key theories further:
http://www.oup.com/he/Grayson-Guillaume1e.

Questions for further discussion

1. How would *you* define security? Does your definition have broader applicability beyond the contexts of your worlds?

2. What is a threat? Identify something that might be considered a threat from an 'objective' perspective and/or a 'subjective' perspective. Discuss how defining this issue as a threat might be problematic when devising a security policy to address it.

3. Who can 'speak' security in a given context is crucial. Identify a non-governmental group (whether a non-governmental organization, a think tank, or a social movement) and discuss what capabilities it has to 'speak' security even if it is not connected directly to the security apparatus of the state.

4. Identify a security issue of your choice. Specify and discuss the material, institutional, and discursive mobilizations that are connected to it as a security issue and how they shape what security does.

5. Pick a question from Box 2.1 and apply it to a concrete situation (e.g., pandemic restrictions, travel security measures, etc.).

Further reading

BUZAN, BARRY, OLE WÆVER, and JAAP DE WILDE. 1998. *Security: A new framework for analysis*. Boulder, CO: Lynne Rienner Publishers.
Arguably, this is the most influential book on security of the post-Cold War era. It advances the notion of securitization and posits how issues may become 'security issues' across various sectors (e.g., military, environmental, societal, etc.). By doing so, the authors established an adaptable albeit often misinterpreted framework that has shaped scholarly debates about the politics of security for the past three decades.

CAMPBELL, DAVID. 1998. *Writing security: United States foreign policy and the politics of identity*. New and revised ed. Minneapolis, MN: University of Minnesota Press.
Campbell's *Writing security* has been one of the most influential books reflecting on how security is a central process by which collective identities are constituted through the articulations of threats and danger. Identifying such articulations in the most 'rational' official security documents, Campbell demonstrates the significant impacts of security.

PUAR, JASBIR K. 2018. *Terrorist assemblages*. Durham, NC: Duke University Press.
This book explores how sexual exceptionalism (based on claims that a country has adopted permissive approaches to LGBTQ rights), the regulatory function of queer identities, and the rise of normative whiteness produce politically salient understandings of the bodies of terrorists and citizens. Thus, Puar shows how ideas about heterosexuality and homosexuality contribute to the war on terror.

THOMAS, CAROLINE. 2000. *Global governance, development and human security: The challenge of poverty and inequality*. London: Pluto.
This book was one of the first to critically analyse the intersections of human security and global development. While it has been two decades since it was published, its insights into the challenges posed by poverty and inequality to human security unfortunately remain pertinent.

JOHNSON, MICAIAH. 2020. *The space between worlds*. London: Hodder and Stoughton Ltd.
In a multiverse of 380 parallel realities, Cara is only alive in 8. This science fiction novel explores the politics of insecurity through its protagonist Cara, touching on themes of power, inequality, citizenship, and violence.

References

BARKAWI, TARAK and MARK LAFFEY. 2006. 'The postcolonial moment in security studies'. *Review of International Studies* 32(2), 329–352.
BELL, COLLEEN. 2011. 'Civilianising warfare: Ways of war and peace in modern counterinsurgency'. *Journal of International Relations and Development* 14(3), 309–332.
BLANCHARD, EMMANUEL. 2011. *La police parisienne et les Algériens (1944–1962)*. Paris: Nouveau monde éditions.
BOOTH, KEN. 1991. 'Security and emancipation'. *Review of International Studies* 17(4), 313–326.
BUSH, GEORGE W. 2001. 'Address before a joint session of the Congress on the United States response to the terrorist attacks of September 11'. 20 September. www.govinfo.gov/content/pkg/WCPD-2001-09-24/pdf/WCPD-2001-09-24-Pg1347.pdf (last accessed 17 February 2022).

Campbell, David. 1998. *Writing security: United States foreign policy and the politics of identity*. New and revised ed. Minneapolis, MN: University of Minnesota Press.

Duffield, Mark. 2010. 'The liberal way of development and the Development–Security impasse: Exploring the global life-chance divide'. *Security Dialogue* 41(1), 53–76.

Fluri, Jennifer. 2012. 'Capitalizing on bare life: Sovereignty, exception, and gender politics'. *Antipode* 44(1), 31–50.

Glenn, Evelyn N. 2015. 'Settler colonialism as structure: A framework for comparative studies of US race and gender formation'. *Sociology of Race and Ethnicity* 1(1), 52–72.

Gregory, Derek. 2004. *The colonial present*. Oxford: Blackwell Publishing.

Hamilton, John T. 2013. *Security: Politics, humanity, and the philology of care*. Princeton, NJ: Princeton University Press.

Hansen, Lene. 2013. *Security as practice: Discourse analysis and the Bosnian war*. London: Routledge.

Huysmans, Jef. 1998. 'Security! What do you mean? From concept to thick signifier'. *European Journal of International Relations* 4(2), 226–255.

Loader, Ian. 1999. 'Consumer culture and the commodification of policing and security'. *Sociology* 33(2), 373–392.

McLaren, Lauren. 2003. 'Anti-immigrant prejudices in Europe: Contact, threat perception, and preferences for the exclusion of migrants'. *Social Forces* 81(3), 909–936.

Mitchell, Katharyne. 2010. 'Ungoverned space: Global security and the geopolitics of broken windows'. *Political Geography* 29(5), 289–297.

Neocleous, Mark. 2007. 'Security, liberty and the myth of balance: Towards a critique of security politics'. *Contemporary Political Theory* 6(1), 131–149.

Nyman, Jonna. 2016. 'What is the value of security? Contextualising the negative/positive debate'. *Review of International Studies* 42(5), 821–839.

Parpart, Jane. 2020. 'Rethinking silence, gender, and power in insecure sites: Implications for feminist security studies in a postcolonial world'. *Review of International Studies* 46(3), 315–324.

Pratt, Nicola. 2013. 'Reconceptualizing gender, reinscribing racial–sexual boundaries in international security: The case of UN Security Council resolution 1325 on "Women, Peace and Security"'. *International Studies Quarterly* 57(4), 772–783.

Sánchez Nieto and W. Alejandro. 2012. 'Brazil's grand design for combining global South solidarity and national interests: A discussion of peacekeeping operations in Haiti and Timor'. *Globalizations* 9(1), 161–178.

Tadjbakhsh, Shahrbanou and Anuradha Chenoy. 2007. *Human security: Concepts and implications*. London: Routledge.

United Nations. 2016. *Human security handbook*. https://www.un.org/humansecurity/wp-content/uploads/2018/05/HS-Handook_rev-2015.pdf (last accessed 17 February 2022).

Valverde, Mariana. 2001. 'Governing security, governing through security'. In *The security of freedom: Essays on Canada's anti-terrorism bill*, edited by Ronald J. Daniels, Patrick Macklem, and Kent Roach. Toronto: University of Toronto Press.

Waldron, Jeremy. 2003. 'Security and liberty: The image of balance'. *Journal of Political Philosophy* 11(2), 191–210.

Zedner, Lucia. 2009. *Security*. London: Routledge.

3

Orders, power, and hierarchies

3.1 Introduction 36
3.2 Socio-political orders and relations of power 37
3.3 Hierarchies: identities, ideas, interests, institutions, and infrastructures 42
3.4 Challenging and resisting security 47
3.5 Conclusion 49

READER'S GUIDE

What does it mean to adopt a critical perspective to analyse security? In this chapter, we highlight that critical perspectives share a common concern with identifying and transforming forms of domination and oppression. To identify how security may be connected to domination and oppression requires uncovering the logics of the socio-political order in which a security mobilization takes place. To help, we discuss the different ways that we can conceptualize power and how power can (re)produce hierarchies through identities, ideas, interests, institutions, and infrastructures. We then illustrate how forms of domination and oppression made possible by security mobilizations can be contested and resisted.

3.1 Introduction

In Chapter 1, we discussed key elements required to analyse our worlds critically. In Chapter 2, we introduced how security can be conceptualized as a form of political mobilization. Now, we will explore what it means to critique security. To approach security critically, whether as a security analyst or a global citizen, can take different forms. Critical perspectives are shaped by different questions that can be asked about what security does. However, they share an interest in identifying and analysing forms of domination and oppression that flow through security mobilizations and political violence that arises from them. To map these connections requires that we are able to identify the characteristics of the socio-political order in which security is being mobilized.

See **Chapter 4** on political violence

Socio-political orders are structures that delimit what is acceptable, valuable, and possible in a given context. They shape forms of domination and oppression. This includes their related forms of political violence that are potentially present within a given context. Socio-political orders also shape the ability of group members to recognize domination and oppression as well as to live with, challenge, and/or resist them. Thus, socio-political orders produce and reproduce **relations of power**. What precisely constitutes power is an open question. Critical perspectives focus on different aspects of power. Power can directly coerce or deter. It also shapes how we think about the world(s) and ourselves (and others), and how we behave and even become ourselves. As such, security mobilizations have two fundamental political effects (see Huysmans 1998, 236–248).

The first effect is that a security mobilization makes an issue **politically salient** by framing it and imbuing it with political ramifications. Political saliency comes from identifying threats, or things that are threatened, that require our attention. The second effect is that a security mobilization performs an **ordering function**. Ordering places aspects of our worlds into categories that are arranged into hierarchies. **Hierarchies** reflect a ranking order of levels of threat and danger, or the importance of what should be protected. The political effects of saliency and ordering do not arise within a vacuum. They are contextually dependent. To provide further clarity on what it might mean to analyse security critically, Section 3.2 proceeds by introducing the concept of socio-political orders and how they are shaped by relations of power. This shows how the mobilization of security connects to relations of power. Furthermore, it reveals how security may reproduce, contest, or change these orders. Section 3.3 shows how the mobilization of security influences **hierarchies** enabled by **identities, ideas, interests, institutions**, and **infrastructures**. Looking at these enablers, we can see how the choice to mobilize security is 'predicated on the exclusion of other possibilities and actions' (Mouffe 2005, 17–18). In the final Section 3.4, we will discuss how security mobilizations and their hierarchies can catalyse **forms of contestation, challenge, and resistance**. Identifying resistance to security mobilizations is important but when most effective not entirely obvious.

> Security framing is covered in **Section 1.3**
>
> See **Section 2.3** on security as a process
>
> On the importance of context for analysing security, see **Sections 1.2** and **2.3**

3.2 Socio-political orders and relations of power

As we previously noted, two of the key dynamics of political saliency and order are who has the ability and legitimacy to 'speak' security as well as who can contest it. For example, outbreaks of communicable diseases (e.g., AIDS, COVID-19, Ebola) reveal how discourses of threats, dangers, and risks are forwarded and challenged by a variety of actors (e.g., the World Health Organization, national public health agencies, other governmental agencies, political actors such as presidents, ministers, and political parties, epidemiologists, practising physicians, private companies, interest groups, the media, and members of the public on social media platforms). To establish what is relevant to our analysis, and what questions we can

> We return to these questions in **Sections 4.3–4**
>
> See **Chapter 13** on the connections between health and security

ask about our societies through the prism of security, we need to determine the following:

- What are the socio-political orders within which security claims are made? And **why** is security mobilized?
- How do different relations of power facilitate **who can 'speak'** security?
- **Where, when**, and **how** are security claims made?

<aside>On the key tenets of critique, see **Section 1.2**</aside>

Asking these questions helps to determine **for whom** such security claims are made, **from what, for what purpose**, and **at whose expense**. These nine questions are a methodology for any critique of security. We will explore these in more detail in Chapter 5. For now, we will focus on the more general connections among security, socio-political orders, and relations of power.

A first step in analysing the contexts where security is mobilized is to identify the structures and logics of the socio-political order in which a security mobilization is taking place. **Socio-political orders are constituted by political, social, economic, cultural, religious, and environmental elements.** The distributions that constitute socio-political orders are shaped by key factors we identified earlier: class, gender and sexuality, race and ethnicity, ideology and culture, religion, political belonging, and disability. These elements are at the source of the laws, conventions, norms, beliefs, and expectations about what is desirable, fair, and legitimate. This includes institutions (e.g., forms of government, the family, legal systems), processes (e.g., elections, resource distribution, education), outcomes (e.g., access to political resources, the distribution of wealth, social mobility), and possibilities for change (e.g., positive, negative, incremental, or radical).

<aside>For definitions of these factors, see **Section 1.4**</aside>

Socio-political orders are also underpinned by systems of belief that can encompass religious understandings of any connections between the secular and sacred, frames of interpretation that derive from shared cultural understandings (e.g., stories, characters, events, and reference points that are held in common), shared languages, and political understandings of the boundaries of the socio-political order. These boundaries are both social (i.e., particular groups are 'inside' while others are 'outside') and spatial (i.e., an order is often bound to a particular territory). In sum, expectations, beliefs, boundaries, and outcomes generate specific forms of domination and oppression, as well as challenges to them that are frequently connected to the core factors we described in Chapter 1.

The structures that help to define socio-political orders are shaped by, and reflected through, relations of power. Relations of power refer to how capacities, resources, representations, and possibilities for action that confer benefits are distributed within a socio-political order. In this sense, power is not exclusively held by particular individuals or groups. As we will see, it also defines relations that join individuals and groups, as well as the potential effects of these relations. **Therefore, power is both a potential capability exercised by all parties in their relations with one another and that relation itself.** Structures within socio-political orders shape who is best able to leverage power capacities that are available to them, how this occurs, and how power affects the relations between individuals and groups. It also shapes how the exercise of power is resisted (Foucault 2019; Nandy 1987). Therefore, relations of power are contingent and contextual. They are a product of specific historical and sociological dynamics within a given socio-political order. In this sense, relations of power, and by extension socio-political orders, are not fixed: they are always subject to change and/or transformation. Nevertheless, because their operating structures are deeply embedded, socio-political orders tend to reproduce themselves, rather than change, over time. A key question then is when mobilized in a given context, how has security been shaped by, and helped to shape, a socio-political order? For example, in a racialized socio-political order, the logics that legitimize discrimination against racialized 'others' shape relations of power to maintain inequalities based on 'race'. We would therefore expect that security mobilizations by authorities within such a socio-political order would reproduce forms of racial inequality.

*Resistance is covered in **Section 3.4***

*See **Chapters 9** and **11** on questions of race and security*

Identifying relations of power is a particularly complex task and we will see how uncovering hierarchies can give us insight into them. The term 'power' is used in very different ways across the social sciences and humanities. Intuitively, we can understand relations of power as a connection among entities—individuals, a group(s) and an individual, an institution and individual(s) or group(s), states, and so on—where 'power' shapes the connection. While often undefined, there are at least four broad understandings of power (Digeser 1992). These understandings are not mutually exclusive. They are all likely present in any given context. We can place different emphases on aspects of power depending on the question we want to ask about security.

Short introductions to different critical security approaches can be found on the online resources

Following Peter Digeser (1992), the first two understandings of power are how we commonly think about it. First, power is the ability to make someone do something this person would not otherwise wish to do. We can think of this as the **power to coerce**. Power can also be the capacity to prevent someone else from doing something that this person would like to do (see Lukes 2005, 16–17, 22, 24). We can think of this as the **power to deter**. Both of these forms of power are likely present in a security mobilization when the dominant political motivation is to address an actual, or potential, threat identified in relation to a clearly defined source. For example, a country may be subject to airstrikes in order to coerce it into surrendering territory to an adversary. Or a police force may subject members of an ethnic minority group to intensive forms of scrutiny such as body searches in order to deter them from being present in particular parts of the city. It is easy to see how these forms of power link to oppression.

While links among oppression, coercion, and deterrence are important, they do not necessarily capture how power and domination work together to generate forms of oppression. Stephen Lukes (2005), via the work of Italian philosopher and politician Antonio Gramsci, identifies another type of power relation that concentrates on

> [how people can be prevented] to whatever degree, from having grievances by shaping their perceptions, cognitions, and preferences in such a way that they accept their role in the existing order of things, either because they can see or imagine no alternative to it, or because they see it as natural and unchangeable. (Lukes 2005, 28)

Here, we can see how security has the **power to shape our imagination** to consider alternatives to our current state of affairs. For example, despite proving to be a failure in terms of reducing the prevalence of drug use (up 30 per cent globally since 2009), associated medical harms, and overall rates of crime, the global war on drugs continues (see UNODC 2020). Even those who support the legality of some drugs (e.g., cannabis) will nevertheless agree that other substances (e.g., opioids or methamphetamine) should remain prohibited and subject to legal penalties, including imprisonment. These views hold despite long-standing evidence that while drug use is more prevalent in higher-income groups, those most impacted by drug policing are the most marginalized in any given society. These negative impacts include deaths linked to drug use from a lack of access to medical care and the socially corrosive impacts of imprisonment on families and communities (UNODC 2020, Booklet 5).

> We expand on these questions in **Chapter 5**

An analytic limitation shared across these three conceptualizations of power is their implied direction of travel. For all of them, A has power over B without B affecting A. What these understandings miss is how power, and in our case power via security, participates in the constitution of *both* A and B. That is, power constitutes both A and B as particular kinds of actors, how they act, who they understand themselves to be, and who they become through their interactions. Thus, the previous three conceptualizations do not consider how these relations are multi-directional. They also miss how those negatively affected by oppression and/or domination can also influence those who exercise it, either by reproducing these relations or resisting them. **Power, then, is also mutually constitutive:** the interactive processes through which multiple actors, their actions, representations, and the contexts within which they interact all form and shape one another. This constitutive view of power helps to delineate how historical and sociological contexts shape individuals, groups, institutions, interactions, and spaces in their relations with one another without reducing complex relationships to a single cause that imposes itself over all others.

> See **Section 3.4** for more on resistance

For example, counterterrorism agencies and terrorist organizations often deploy similar strategies and tactics against one another. This becomes part of a complex process where both sides attempt to make the other side act in ways that reinforce feelings of insecurity for their own group members. Terrorist organizations may attempt to make counterterrorism agencies over-react and deploy violence in ways that will draw new members to their cause. Likewise, the special measures at the disposal of counterterrorism agencies gain legitimation by ongoing acts of terrorist violence. By encouraging the threat of violence from the other side, counterterrorism agencies and terrorist organizations thereby reinforce their own *raison d'être* and perceptions of legitimacy held by group members and supporters. By taking a constitutive view of power, security analysts can gain crucial insights into how individuals, groups, and institutions define themselves in relation to one another. Similarly, power as mutually constitutive enables us to determine how actions and reactions involve investing them with meanings that seek to justify them relative to other possibilities.

> See **Chapter 8** on counter-terrorism

By adopting a more nuanced understanding of power and its forms, we can see how they both reflect, and help to produce, the political logics underpinning socio-political orders. For example, how consent for particular security actions is generated through fear and targeting groups who are otherwise stigmatized within a socio-political order becomes clearer. Similarly, relations of power shape and interact with class, gender and sexuality, race and ethnicity, ideology and culture, religion, political belonging, and disability to produce socio-political orders. For example, as initial national security rationales for the invasion of Afghanistan unravelled, US and NATO forces began to emphasize the promotion of gender equality as a justification. This played on existing prejudices about equality within predominantly Muslim societies, positioned women and girls in Afghanistan as helpless victims who needed to be 'saved', reinforced the notion of Western societies as being at the pinnacle of gender equality, and caused confusion when local women's groups made tactical concessions to local elites (see Singh 2020).

> **Chapter 9** explores the constitution of threat and its relation to the production of in- and out-groups

The connections we have outlined here are messy, highly variable, complexly interdependent, and often difficult to unpack. They do not readily lend themselves to single-cause explanations. Their contextual contingency also means it can be difficult to identify general conclusions. But this is absolutely fine! This messiness reflects the fact that socio-political orders are complicated. Moreover, our worlds, from the level of interstate relations down to our everyday lives, are always multidimensional. Our worlds are shaped by the influences of multiple socio-political orders that are shaped by different factors and co-exist at different levels from the intimate to the global (Enloe 2014 [1990]). These may reinforce or even undermine one another. As a security analyst, you cannot embrace all these factors, orders, or levels simultaneously. Therefore, when formulating specific questions about our worlds and security, you will need to make a choice about which dimension, or intersection, is most important to your analysis.

> See **Section 1.4** for details on these factors

> These nine questions are discussed in **Chapter 5**

To add to the challenge of formulating questions, socio-political orders are not always clearly visible to us. They do not always directly influence how actions are taken or decisions made, or how people react to the mobilization of security. However, they set the parameters within which security is mobilized. As such, the role of critical thinking is to make socio-political orders visible. Think, for example, of so-called 'natural disasters' such as tornadoes, floods, mudslides, and earthquakes. While the initial catalyst itself may be a result of natural phenomena over which we have no direct control, their impacts disproportionately affect marginalized communities. These harms are not accidental; those who are poorer and/or socially marginalized tend to live in places that are more vulnerable to these events because they cannot access and/or afford to live in safer areas. Thus, while the mudslide, flood, earthquake, or tornado may be the catalyst, socio-political orders and their associated forms of marginalization are what place particular communities in harm's way. To help us reveal these orders, we can demonstrate how the mobilization of security works with **hierarchies** that prioritize particular **identities**, valorize particular **ideas**, privilege particular **interests**, organize **institutions**, and design **infrastructures** that have particular effects. As such, some outcomes are more likely than others. Similarly, some individuals/groups are also more likely to do better from these outcomes than others.

> In **Box 3.1** you are given an opportunity to link security to an everyday object

> **BOX 3.1 URBAN SPACES AS SECURITY SPACES**

As security analysts, and as global citizens, we need to pay attention to how security may manifest itself in forms that are not immediately obvious. While some security mobilizations are readily apparent (e.g., the presence of armed guards or the wail of a police siren), security is often inconspicuous. Take the example (Figure 3.1) of a bench installed by Camden Council in London. To discourage 'anti-social' behaviours such as rough sleeping and loitering, the bench is functional, but uncomfortable, by design. As such, how might it reproduce hierarchies by mobilizing certain ideas about threats and safety? What is security doing here? What kind of space does it help to create? What types of hierarchies does this bench reproduce? How does it affect the experience of this urban space for business owners, shoppers, youth, and the poor (see Rosenberger 2020)?

Figure 3.1 Bench in Camden, London (from Wikimedia Commons: https://commons.wikimedia.org/wiki/File:Camden_bench.jpg).

3.3 Hierarchies: identities, ideas, interests, institutions, and infrastructures

Politics shapes our worlds through hierarchies. The term 'politics' or 'political' has different meanings. However, there are two dimensions to highlight. First, hierarchies are 'political' because they are structured by institutions and interactions which we associate with 'politics'. Politics can be defined as the struggle over the allocation and distribution of resources (e.g., military spending versus development aid). It can be institutional (e.g., an agreement to facilitate free movement within a grouping of countries) or symbolic (e.g., the recognition of past injustices). The aim of politics is to address issues that affect the organization of a life held in common by individuals and groups within a delimited unit such as a family, municipality, state, or intergovernmental institution (e.g., the United Nations). At the level of the state, the struggle to organize a collective life may be shaped by the regime type (e.g., democratic or authoritarian) and the contours of relationships among branches of the government. Politics is also influenced by the relations between the state and its citizens as well as citizens towards each other and non-citizens. Finally, the pursuit of a collective life held in common is also influenced by relations with other states as well as 'external' institutions such as regional and international organizations.

Second, these dynamics are 'political' because they are the visible expression of a larger socio-political order that materializes through 'politics' and a variety of practices that express different relations of power. Some critical perspectives will therefore explore how specific hierarchies in sites such as parliaments, courts, treaty negotiations, international organizations, or transnational security collaborations reflect these relations of power. Others will examine spaces that are less obvious. These include everyday sites like schools, workplaces, and homes as well as processes of production, consumption, and leisure that might ordinarily be considered apolitical (Grayson et al. 2009; Guillaume and Huysmans 2019).

We have already noted the political centrality of security to mobilizing material, institutional, and symbolic resources to manage perceived threats and protect those who are understood to be under threat or in danger. Critically analysing security therefore means identifying 'spaces' where security mobilizations occur and have effects. The goal is to see how security mobilizations reflect, and help to constitute, socio-political orders. These 'enablers'—identity, ideas, interests, institutions, and infrastructures—are where we can observe how a socio-political order becomes manifest through hierarchies. **A hierarchy is a structure in which some things are considered better than others and placed in a rank order.** The rankings within a hierarchy may concern explicit criteria and/or implicit assumptions. Hierarchies based on class, gender and sexuality, race and ethnicity, ideology and culture, religion, political belonging, disability, and their intersections are usually present, albeit with different effects and operations, across historical contexts.

See **Sections 2.4** on security as a political mobilization

There are two caveats to keep in mind. First, **these 'enablers' are often intertwined with one another.** Thus, we should have rationales for emphasizing different 'enablers'. Core factors also inter-relate with these 'enablers'. For example, one can understand ethnicity in terms of the hierarchies it expresses relative to identities, ideas, interests, institutions, and infrastructures. In some contexts, being identified as 'Indigenous' has been understood as posing a threat to the socio-political order (Hume and Walby 2021). Thus, measures have sought to assimilate and/or exterminate Indigenous peoples. Similarly, when it comes to ideas, Western knowledge is often prioritized over Indigenous forms of knowledge, even in less extreme socio-political orders. Being perceived as 'Indigenous' may also produce interests in terms of access to particular resources, or cultural inheritances granted by legal recognition of this status as well as challenges to them (Riggs and Augoustinos 2004). A set of institutions have been devised in various countries to govern Indigenous peoples, including multi-level governance arrangements, whose histories and outcomes are, at best, mixed. Finally, Indigeneity, as an ethnic status, connects to particular forms of infrastructure. For example, in some settler-colonial contexts such as Australia, Canada, New Zealand, and the United States, Indigenous peoples have higher rates of exposure to the penal system while not receiving the same levels of access to healthcare or education systems as others.

Second, **how security is mobilized through these 'enablers' can be reflective of its status as a claim or stake.** As we noted earlier, some groups, like security professionals, have a stake (i.e., consequences for themselves, their agency, and profession) in seeing security mobilized in ways that satisfy their interests. These interests would include resource allocations that prioritize their services over others and practices that enhance their status as security providers (e.g., inter-agency competition). We can concentrate on security as an interest and look to see how it is expressed through these 'enablers', or we can focus more on the content of the claim itself (see online resources). With these caveats in mind, we can turn to each of them individually.

> See **Section 2.3-4** on the role of security professionals

The first 'enabler' is **identity**. Identities are largely articulated in terms of hierarchies, which can be positive or negative. These relate to difference, with a rank ordering on the perceived degree of relative difference from an identity understood to be the 'norm'. Threats are understood to emanate from these degrees of difference. For example, this may be in terms of a threatening class (e.g., the proletariat), political belonging (e.g., non-citizens), or religion (e.g., religious minority group). The superiority of one's threatened identity is depicted in various ways using different characteristics from gender to race to disability.

> Questions related to identity are discussed in **Chapters 9, 10,** and **11**

When security is mobilized around identity, very often the point is to dehumanize difference as a characteristic of an 'inferior' other. Identities tied to forms of political belonging are articulated *vis-à-vis* differences that are 'external' to the expressed boundaries of belonging as well as 'internal' to it. These 'differences' can be raised by highlighting transnational connections. Therefore, formal membership within a country, most often by virtue of being a citizen of that country, does not necessarily confer symbolic membership in its political community in the minds of members. Because of ascribed differences in terms of religion, ethnicity, skin colour, gender, sexuality, ideology, culture, class, or disability, some citizens are therefore depicted as outside of, or opposed to, a political community and its 'real' members.

The forms that these hierarchies take, and the ways in which the mobilization of security acts upon them, are multiple and at times contradictory. Some, because of characteristics that are associated with their identity, may be subject to security measures to protect others. This kind of security dynamic can create paradoxical situations. For example, the free movement of citizens across national borders within the European Union (EU) co-exists with strict border management strategies to prevent unwanted forms of migration into the EU. These strategies include extra-territorial border arrangements with states in Eastern Europe and Africa who agree to detain suspected migrants before they can attempt to enter EU territory (Basaran 2010). Thus, free movement for some rests on practices that inhibit, and make illegal, the free movement of others.

> See **Chapter 19** on migration, borders, and security

The second 'enabler' that helps to enact hierarchies is **ideas**. 'Ideas' is a broad term that brings together ideologies (e.g., liberalism, fascism, humanitarianism, communism), socio-political concepts (e.g., multiculturalism, the welfare state, self-determination), and preferences shaped by ideologies and socio-political orders (e.g., capitalism is the best economic system). It also includes cultural traditions and belief systems such as religions. Whatever their form, ideas can justify the mobilization of security. Likewise, some ideas deploy security as a form of justification. For example, those who argue in favour of the Responsibility to Protect (R2P) often justify violations of state sovereignty that result from humanitarian interventions. They do so on the basis that these actions provide security to those facing direct harms within a state as well as security at the international level by containing problems (see Fishel 2013 for a discussion of the shortcomings of this perspective). Ideas can also serve as a background against which identities and interests are given meaning as threats or something in need of protection.

> Questions related to ideas are discussed in **Chapters 12, 14, 16,** and **20**

During what European politicians and media outlets called the 'refugee crisis' of 2015, the idea that all human beings have equal rights led some actors to contest how refugees were treated by EU authorities. Humanitarianism, as a moral sentiment (see Fassin 2012 [2010]), has been one of the sources to understand refugees and migration quite differently from the prism of security. Grassroots movements to help refugees in places like the 'Jungle' refugee camp in Calais, France catalysed 'new forms of community based on care and commitment towards refugees and other volunteers' (Sandri 2018, 77).

The third 'enabler' of hierarchies is **interests**. Interests connect to receiving a specific benefit as an individual and/or group. Interests can also be a concern with being involved in an activity. Interests can be multiple and potentially competing, both for an individual/group and across a socio-political order. For our purposes, interests are connected to how security is conceptualized (e.g., a threshold or process). Any conception of security will shape how an actor defines its interests. For example, the US National Security Strategy represents an official statement of the US government's national security interests. In the interim document issued by the Biden Administration in March 2021, one of the stated aims is to 'strengthen our enduring advantages and allow us to prevail in strategic competition with China or any other nation' (Biden Jr 2021, 20). Thus, we can clearly see how an interest in maintaining existing economic and technological advantages is perceived as a security issue. At the same time, the underlying conceptualization of security within the strategy is predicated on US predominance. Thus, it creates an interest in maintaining all forms of comparative advantage over China.

> **Section 2.3** covers differences between security as a threshold and as a process

But it is not always the case that an actor clearly articulates its interests. Likewise, an actor may not necessarily know what its interests are in a given situation. Adding a further layer of complexity, is an interest really an interest because an actor has identified it as such? Moreover, how can interests be scaled up such that we can say with any confidence that there is such a thing as *the* national interest? As we have seen in Chapter 2, to discuss interests opens up questions about how our understandings of ourselves, others, and our worlds are shaped by subjective perceptions. All interests, as subjectively understood benefits and concerns, are important because actors use them to justify particular courses of action among many other possible courses of action. Thus, to act in one's own interest is, in part, to act under the constraints of what we believe our interest dictates (Cohen et al. 2006). Nevertheless, the invocation of interests, particularly collective interests (e.g., the national interest), can also be a means of recasting particular interests that benefit a select few as collective. This enables the legitimation of actions through positive (i.e., this is in our interests and will produce benefits) and negative (i.e., this threatens our interests and we therefore cannot ignore it) framings.

> Questions related to institutions are discussed in **Chapters 6, 7, 8, 13, 19, and 20**

The fourth enabler is **institutions**. As we have noted previously (see Section 2.4), institutions are formal organizations, or informal arrangements, which identify, manage, coordinate, and undertake actions for some purpose in a socio-political order. Institutions can be formal arrangements at the local, national, regional, and international levels as well as those that cut across them. Institutions are also established practices, codes of conduct, and forms of law that are recognized as holding a regulatory function within and/or across a socio-political order. As such, institutions are influenced by their relations with other institutions. Collectively and individually, institutions shape imaginaries about the worlds we live in and invest individuals and groups with particular identities. Thus, institutions are important to the pursuit of a collective life held in common, including trust.

For example, with the signing of the Comprehensive Test Ban Treaty (1996), signatories agreed to stop testing nuclear weapons. To verify compliance with the treaty, the Comprehensive Nuclear Test Ban Treaty Organization (CTBTO) was formed. It is an institution tasked with identifying and verifying potential tests. Thus, to build levels of trust necessary for a prohibition on nuclear tests to hold among signatories while maintaining the capacity to identify potential nuclear testing events, the CTBTO exercises institutional oversight of a vast monitoring infrastructure. This global network of sensors enables it to distinguish nuclear tests from other forms of explosion and/or seismic activity. The CTBTO thus incorporates formal institutional structures alongside practices that perform a regulatory function.

> Questions related to infrastructures are covered in **Chapters 12, 14, 15, 16, 17, and 20**

The final 'enabler' that can help us identify and analyse political dynamics is **infrastructures**. Infrastructures are interfaces that bring together disparate elements to make actions possible. For example, electrical grids are an infrastructure that produce, regulate, and distribute electricity. Electrical grids are themselves composed of power stations, cables, wires, poles, and transformers. In turn, electricity is something that relies on this critical infrastructure but also enables other infrastructures, such as telecommunications, transportation, water supply, and waste management, to operate (see Larkin 2013, 329). Many devices, such as computers, require electricity to function. Yet computers are also part of the infrastructure that makes electricity possible by controlling the supply across different power grids and directing substations to control voltage levels. Moreover, electricity is dependent on other infrastructures to function as it requires different forms of energy connected to hydro-electric plants, wind farming, and coal, gas-fired, and/or nuclear power stations. However, we cannot understand electricity as an infrastructure by only paying attention to its material structures. We also need to take into account its institutional and discursive structures (see Badenoch and Fickers 2010). This means considering a range of factors from its modes of distribution, as either a publicly subsidized necessity or private good, to discourses around climate change and environmental sustainability that shape the forms of electrical production that take place in a society. Therefore, infrastructures are more than inanimate 'things'. They are also political constructs that materially, institutionally, and discursively produce hierarchies.

Infrastructures bring together material, institutional, and discursive elements that contribute to segregation and exclusion made possible through hierarchies within a socio-political order. For example, the Haussmann Boulevards in Paris, built during the nineteenth century, contributed to maintaining public order, even if their primary purposes were economic development and public health. By replacing smaller medieval streets characteristic of the city centre, Napoleon III hoped to make it more difficult for popular insurrections to barricade streets and thus control Paris (Choay 1969, 15–22). This technique continues to influence urban design in cities such as Naypyidaw, the new capital of Myanmar.

> **Chapter 16** returns to this question in relation to design and security

3.4 Challenging and resisting security

Thus far, we have seen how different socio-political orders (re)produce hierarchies through security by articulating political claims that shape, and are shaped by, different 'enablers'. But this is only one side of the equation. These 'enablers' can also comprise challenges and forms of resistance against security claims/practices. Therefore, critical perspectives are also interested in analysing how people react to security claims and their effects. By recognizing the multiple dimensions of power, a critique of security can determine how security is challenged and resisted, forming the possible basis for change or transformation. Some forms of challenge and resistance may be easy to identify, but they can also be less obvious. Identifying them may also be a matter of interpretation (Guillaume and Lemay-Hébert 2023). In this final section, we offer a series of key distinctions and pointers to help you to identify and analyse them.

Formal and direct forms of challenge and resistance are probably quite familiar to you. Protests, legal challenges, political advocacy campaigns, and even violence (from petty vandalism to armed rebellions) are ways of countering security claims. These activities seek to challenge and change security claims and how these are mobilized in very public and direct ways, blending strategic planning with emotion (Gould 2002). There is often a clear recognition by the parties involved of the stakes at play in undertaking these forms of resistance. For example, resisting war through avowedly non-violent protest nevertheless may involve acts of civil disobedience (e.g., refusing to serve in the armed forces, blockading arms factories, protesting outside of military bases). Non-violence itself is an idea that challenges the very core

> See **Box 4.1** on non-violence

of security thinking. Non-violence movements know what they are trying to resist and why. Likewise, authorities will seek to act upon and/or prosecute members for the very same reasons. The interplay of security claims, mobilizations, and reactions is an important dimension of the politics of security. By focusing on formal and direct forms of challenge and resistance, one can capture key aspects of the politics of security; however, this focus can also miss a great deal too, including how resistance movements themselves may reproduce forms of insecurity for their members (Eschle 2018).

There are also forms of challenge and resistance that are more **informal and/or indirect**. These are often less obvious to those whose security claims and mobilizations are being challenged as well as to outside observers. These types of challenge and resistance may seek to slow down, delay, and prevent aspects of security by adopting tactics that are not recognized as resistance by those in positions of authority. They are also less clearly connected to a conscious attempt to resist and bring about transformation; however, their cumulative effects may nonetheless do so. James C. Scott (1985) has referred to these as the 'weapons of the weak'. For example, simply raising concerns about the practical implementation of specific security practices may constitute a form of resistance in some contexts. Likewise, challenges arise via hyper-conformity, for example by inundating a security hotline with reports of fictious events that directly map onto official guidance regarding signs of suspected criminal activity. Other forms of challenge and resistance may be even less direct, manifesting themselves through everyday activities that 'grow out of the particular circumstances of the social place and the life experience of the people that do the resisting' (Johansson and Vinthagen 2016, 422). These may include:

- cultural forms like satire or the carnivalesque that undermine authority via humour;
- oral histories that preserve knowledge, stories, and ways of living;
- maintaining a language (e.g., the use of Basque during Franco's regime in Spain);
- music (e.g., hip hop), fashion (e.g., the keffiyeh), and dance (e.g., capoeira);
- participatory theatre (e.g., Theatre of the Oppressed);
- art (e.g., Dada or *Négritude* movements during the twentieth century);
- literature (e.g., the genre of magical realism offered coded critiques of military governments in South America during the 1970s);
- education curriculums and how they are delivered (e.g., Paulo Freire's *Pedagogy of the Oppressed*).

All can offer a counterpoint to security by raising awareness in an audience. This is by providing safe spaces, ways to cope, and means to accommodate security claims and mobilizations, as well as their effects. Awareness also provides new ways to speak about security and the wider socio-political order it sustains. Even if not overt or formal, one of the surest signs that a challenge, or form of resistance, is being taken seriously in a socio-political order is when it becomes a site for security intervention by the state and/or agents that seek to defend that order. These less than obvious forms are often deemed threatening because it is hard for a regime to understand precisely what these actions mean and whom they represent. This makes them difficult to control. Thus, what does not neatly conform (e.g., styles of dress like the 'Zoot suit' or more recently baggy trousers; see Entwistle 2015) is often perceived as posing a potential threat to the authority and legitimacy of underlying hierarchies that help to define a socio-political order. Having presented some of these forms of indirect challenge and resistance, it remains important that security analysts, and global citizens alike, should seek to avoid imposing intentions, and effects, that may be absent.

Critique pays particular attention to those who usually go unrecognized or are invisible as agents in power relations because prevailing assumptions are that they cannot deter, challenge, or resist security. By paying careful attention to challenge and resistance, we can see how security connects different actors, shaping both oppressors and the oppressed, as well as those who dominate and are dominated. By taking a broader understanding of power, we can see how security reproduces hierarchies underpinning forms domination and oppression that characterize a given socio-political order as well as how both are challenged and resisted.

> Authority and legitimacy are explored in **Sections 4.3–4**

3.5 Conclusion

Critique offers a series of steps to analyse what security does when mobilized and the effects it has on people and their worlds. As we have seen in this chapter, the first step is to consider how socio-political orders shape, and are shaped by, relations of power. Relations of power, in turn, are most apparent through the different hierarchies that constitute our worlds. In turn, security mobilizations often reproduce these hierarchies. By paying attention to identities, ideas, interests, institutions, and infrastructures, critical perspectives can identify security mobilizations and their effects. They can also uncover how mobilizations are challenged and resisted. As we will see in Chapter 4, one of the principal ways to reveal what security does to our worlds is to identify the forms of political violence that security makes possible and enacts in a given socio-political order via its hierarchies. We will show how political violence is a manifestation of harm that results from establishing, reproducing, and challenging hierarchies tied to security. As we will see, political violence can take multiple forms—it can be physical, psychological, material, and/or symbolic. It can also manifest itself in different ways. By tying security to power and the shape of socio-political orders, forms of injustice and violence that may not initially register become more readily apparent. Security mobilizations make possible the prevalence of domination and oppression.

Additional short introductions to theoretical approaches are available on the online resources to take your understanding of key theories further:
http://www.oup.com/he/Grayson-Guillaume1e.

Questions for further discussion

1. Identify key elements of the socio-political order where you live. How do they shape security practices?

2. How can we identify and analyse the four forms of power? Using a single example connected to security, demonstrate how each form of power exposes different dimensions of the broader socio-political order.

3. Within your own context, identify hierarchies related to identity, ideas, interests, institutions, and infrastructure (one for each).

4. Is there a national interest (when it comes to security)? What role does the national interest play in security discussions?

5. Drawing upon events from the past, present, or fiction (e.g., films, television, novels), provide three different examples of how security mobilizations can be resisted.

Further reading

SHAMS, TAHSEEN. 2018. 'Visibility as resistance by Muslim Americans in a surveillance and security atmosphere'. *Sociological Forum* (33)1, 73–94.
On the basis of her ethnographic fieldwork in Los Angeles, the author explores how Muslims negotiate daily living within a context in which they have been made a focus of attention by security authorities.

AMOORE, LOUISE and ALEXANDRA HALL. 2010. 'Border theatre: On the arts of security and resistance'. *Cultural Geographies* 17(3), 299–319.
This paper examines how artistic and creative interventions have been mobilized to contest border-security landscapes.

DAVIS, ANGELA Y. 2011. *Women, race, and class*. New York: Vintage Books.
In this extremely influential book, Davis critically investigates how women's liberation movements can encapsulate the racist and classist thinking of the prevailing social order.

SAID, EDWARD. 1994. *Culture and imperialism*. New York: Vintage Books.
How has imperialism become embedded in European culture? How did culture shape imperialism? These questions are covered by examining cultural and imperial practices from the late eighteenth century to the end of the twentieth century.

POPE, LUCAS. 2013. *Papers, please*. 3909 LLC.
In this award-winning video game, players undertake the role of a border guard in an authoritarian state. Gameplay requires one to implement increasingly draconian security measures while weighing one's growing disillusionment with the ruling regime against the imperatives of personal survival. Available for Windows, Linux, OS X, and iOS.

References

BADENOCH, ALEXANDER and ANDREAS FICKERS. 2010. 'Introduction. Europe materializing? Toward a transnational history of European infrastructures'. In *Materializing Europe: Transnational infrastructures and the project of Europe*, edited by ALEXANDER BADENOCH and ANDREAS FICKERS. Basingstoke: Palgrave Macmillan.

Basaran, Tugba. 2010. *Security, law and borders: At the limits of liberties*. London: Routledge.
Biden, Jr, Joseph R. 2021. *Interim national security strategy guidance*. March. www.whitehouse.gov/wp-content/uploads/2021/03/NSC-1v2.pdf (last accessed 17 February 2022).
Choay, Françoise. 1969. *The modern city: Planning in the 19th century*. New York: George Braziller.
Cohen, Dara Kay, Mariano-Florentino Cuéllar, and Barry R. Weingast. 2006. 'Crisis bureaucracy: Homeland security and the political design of legal mandates'. *Stanford Law Review* 59(3), 673–760.
Digeser, Peter. 1992. 'The fourth face of power'. *The Journal of Politics* 54(4), 977–1007.
Enloe, Cynthia. 2014 [1990]. *Bananas, beaches and bases: Making feminist sense of international politics*. Berkeley, CA: University of California Press.
Entwistle, Joanne. 2015. *The fashioned body: Fashion, dress, and social theory*. London: Polity.
Eschle, Catherine. 2018. 'Troubling stories of the end of Occupy: Feminist narratives of betrayal at Occupy Glasgow'. *Social Movement Studies* 17(5), 524–540.
Fassin, Didier. 2012 [2010]. *Humanitarian reason: A moral history of the present*. Trans. Rachel Gomme. Berkeley, CA: University of California Press.
Fishel, Stefanie. 2013. 'Theorizing violence in the responsibility to protect'. *Critical Studies on Security* 1(2), 204–218.
Foucault, Michel. 2019. *Power: The essential works of Michel Foucault 1954–1984*. London: Penguin.
Gould, Deborah. 2002. 'Life during wartime: Emotions and the development of ACT UP'. *Mobilization: An International Quarterly* 7(2), 177–200.
Grayson, Kyle, Matt Davies, and Simon Philpott. 2009. 'Pop goes IR? Researching the popular culture–world politics continuum'. *Politics* 29(3), 155–163.
Guillaume, Xavier and Jef Huysmans. 2019. 'The concept of "the everyday": Ephemeral politics and the abundance of life'. *Cooperation and Conflict* 54(2), 278–296.
Guillaume, Xavier and Nicolas Lemay-Hébert. 2023. 'Everyday resistance'. In *Oxford handbook of international political sociology*, edited by Stacie Goddard, George Lawson, and Ole Jacob Sending. Oxford: Oxford University Press.
Hume, Rebecca and Kevin Walby. 2021. 'Framing, suppression, and colonial policing redux in Canada: News representations of the 2019 Wet'suwet'en blockade'. *Journal of Canadian Studies* 55(3), 507–540.
Huysmans, Jef. 1998. 'Security! What do you mean? From concept to thick signifier'. *European Journal of International Relations* 4(2), 226–255.
Johansson, Anna and Stellan Vinthagen. 2016. 'Dimensions of everyday resistance: An analytical framework'. *Critical Sociology* 42(3), 417–435.
Larkin, Brian. 2013. 'The politics and poetics of infrastructure'. *Annual Review of Anthropology* 42(1), 327–343.
Lukes, Steven. 2005. *Power: A radical view*. 2nd edition. Basingstoke: Palgrave Macmillan.
Mouffe, Chantal. 2005. *On the political*. London: Routledge.
Nandy, Ashis. 1987. 'Cultural frames for social transformation: A credo'. *Alternatives: Global, Local, Political* 12(1), 113–123.
Riggs, Damien W. and Martha Augoustinos. 2004. 'Projecting threat: Managing subjective investments in whiteness'. *Psychoanalysis, Culture & Society* 9(2), 219–236.
Rosenberger, Robert. 2020. 'On hostile design: Theoretical and empirical prospects'. *Urban Studies* 57(4), 883–893.

SANDRI, ELISA. 2018. '"Volunteer humanitarianism": Volunteers and humanitarian aid in the Jungle refugee camp of Calais'. *Journal of Ethnic and Migration Studies* 44(1), 65–80.

SCOTT, JAMES C. 1985. *Weapons of the weak: Everyday forms of peasant resistance*. New Haven, CT: Yale University Press.

SINGH, SHWETA. 2020. 'In between the ulemas and local warlords in Afghanistan: Critical perspectives on the "everyday," norm translation, and UNSCR 1325'. *International Feminist Journal of Politics* 22(4), 504–525.

UNITED NATIONS OFFICE FOR DRUGS AND CRIME. 2020. *World drug report 2020*. https://wdr.unodc.org/wdr2020/en/index.html (last accessed 17 February 2022).

4
Political violence

4.1	Introduction	53
4.2	Political violence as an analytical concept	55
4.3	The political question of legitimacy	61
4.4	The political question of authority	64
4.5	Conclusion	67

READER'S GUIDE

What is political violence? In this chapter, we present a conceptual framework that identifies different forms of violence, their relation to security, and their political dimensions. We focus on four types of violence: physical, psychological, material, and symbolic. To determine the potential political dimensions of violence, we explore actors, intentions, structures, and its presence within socio-political orders. Two key questions then arise: (1) when is violence legitimate? and (2) who has the authority to exercise violence legitimately within a given socio-political order? We conclude that understanding how violence emerges from security mobilizations is important to understanding security.

4.1 Introduction

In France, there has been public outcry over the policing of the *gilets jaunes* protests (Chapter 6). In the United Kingdom, the Trident nuclear submarine programme has been renewed at a cost of GBP 10 billion while 31 per cent of children live in poverty (Chapter 7). In Guatemala, the Maya Genocide killed tens of thousands of civilians, mainly from Indigenous communities, under the auspices of a thirty-year counter-insurgency war (Chapters 8 and 9). Globally, it is estimated that over 40,000 women and girls are killed by a family member or intimate partner every year (Chapter 10). In Côte d'Ivoire, heated public debates arise over the identities of politicians with the implication that some are not true members of the national community (Chapter 11). During the COVID-19 pandemic, access to vaccines was highly differentiated depending on where one lived, despite pledges to ensure equitable global distributions and/or share vaccine production knowledge (Chapters 12 and 13). In the United Kingdom, adults with a disability or severe illness are almost three and a half times more likely to experience serious violence (Rosetti et al. 2016, 10). In Sierra Leone and Colombia, state authorities provide support to private companies to access communal property for the purposes of resource extraction, often without the consent of the affected communities (Chapter 14). Post-conflict reconstruction has begun to incorporate biometric systems into governance structures, raising questions about local consent for these systems, ownership of the data, and how it is used (Chapter 15). New technologies, like smartphones, make us increasingly visible to the security apparatus of the state (Chapter 16). In Waziristan, a drone launches a Hellfire missile at a compound, killing eight suspected militants (Chapter 17). Scientific consensus is that climate change is real, tied to human activity, and that the environmental costs will be disproportionately experienced (Chapter 18). Increasingly, states are using border walls to divert migrants into areas like deserts that are inhospitable to human life (Chapter 19). Prisons are dehumanizing spaces with little regard to the violence faced by prisoners (Chapter 20). In each of these examples, there is evidence of a potential harm from loss of privacy to loss of life. However, are all of these examples of political violence? How might they be tied to the critical analysis of security?

We argue that questions of political violence are essential to security. As we have discussed, critical perspectives see security as a political claim and mobilization that:

> Section 2.4 explains how security is a political mobilization

1. acts upon people, things, spaces, interactions, and events;

2. enables and is enabled by identities, ideas, interests, institutions, and infrastructures.

> Section 3.3 discusses these enablers

Security seeks to address something that an authority has determined to be a threat or under threat. In this context, **violence can be deemed political when it is legitimized and authorized from a security claim, as well as when it is an effect of a security mobilization that has emerged from a security claim**. For example, political violence may be present when:

- psychological harms are suffered because one's beliefs are continuously presented as threatening and dangerous by the dominant groups in society;
- a group is under the threat of genocide and influential states may (or may not) mobilize measures (e.g., sanctions, armed intervention) to protect them;
- a neighbourhood's critical infrastructure (e.g., roads, streetlights, schools, recreational spaces) has been allowed to decline and the area is subject to intensive policing because it is considered a dangerous place.

Security aims to counter threats understood to produce violence (e.g., a military invasion, genocide, gang activity). However, when mobilized, security obscures how these 'threats' may be the manifestation of political inequalities and/or perceptions of mistreatment connected to hierarchies. Thus, security mobilizations violently establish, maintain, or challenge hierarchies (in their existing forms). We have already seen that different conceptions of security may differ in how they analyse political violence. For some, security is a condition of possibility that limits these forms of violence,

> For an introduction, see **Section 2.3**

thus enabling change and even transformation. For others, security is a condition of impossibility that encourages political violence and underlying forms of domination and oppression. These two conceptions are not necessarily mutually exclusive, but they emphasize different dimensions of security in our worlds. The thematic chapters that follow explore these different dimensions.

In this chapter, we provide a conceptual framework that identifies different forms of violence, their relation to security, and their political dimensions (Section 4.2). The aim is to develop your capacity to determine what might be political about any given act of violence when security is involved. Our framework, largely inspired by the work of Johan Galtung, begins with classifying violence into four types: **physical, psychological, material**, and **symbolic**. This framework also identifies how acts of violence connected to security are political. First, who are the **actors** involved? Second, has the violence been **intentional or unintentional**? Third, is the violence an **isolated event or structurally embedded**? Finally, is the violence **manifest or latent**? We then discuss how the connections between security and violence can be political. First, we consider the **legitimacy** of the recourse to violence and how legitimacy is shaped by a Western-centric understanding that is limited (Section 4.3). Second, who has the **authority** to attach meaning to violence? More specifically, how is it that some acts of violence are categorized as political and others are not? What are the consequences of these categorizations (Section 4.4)?

4.2 Political violence as an analytical concept

In a security mobilization, how security legitimizes or delegitimizes violence is important. Likewise, we must pay attention to how security authorizes or prohibits violence. The political effects of security mobilizations connect to how relations of power and hierarchies create possibilities for forms of violence. For example, security can legitimize and desensitize the public to the violence enacted by security forces against certain groups based on their class, gender, sexuality, race, ethnicity, ideology, culture, religion, political belonging, or disability. At the same time, security can also serve to designate forms of violence to protect people based on these factors as politically relevant and thus worthy of mobilization. We see again how security can be both a condition of possibility or impossibility depending on how one is classified in a given context. Thus, it is important for security analysts and global citizens to understand how the mobilization of security produces violence and invests it with political meaning.

On the meaning-making power of security, see **Section 2.3.2**

Identifying the meanings attached to violence will uncover how security structures, relations of power, and hierarchies are established, or hidden by, these meaning-making processes. As we have seen, meaning-making is never neutral. The capability to identify, interpret, legitimize, delegitimize, authorize, and/or prohibit violence by establishing meanings that are broadly accepted is unevenly distributed within societies and across them. For example, in Canada, the National Inquiry into Missing and Murdered Indigenous Women and Girls (2019, Final report volume 1a, 55) noted that Indigenous women and girls represent 4 per cent of the female population but 24 per cent of the total number of female homicides. This disproportionate probability of being murdered has only very recently entered public discussions. While homicide is a criminal offence, the killing of Indigenous women and girls has not been understood as a security issue. The situation is so grave that the National Inquiry into Missing and Murdered Indigenous Women and Girls has argued it should be considered a genocide (2019, Supplementary Report—Genocide). Yet, the Canadian government has not implemented substantive measures to address the genocide. Thus, how violence becomes politically meaningful, as opposed to 'criminal' or 'pathological', such that it is elevated to the status of a security issue, is central here. Likewise, domestic assaults are another example. Frequently, violence against women and girls by men within the home is understood as a criminal act underpinned by specific pathologies attributed to the perpetrator (e.g., a controlling individual with a temper). However, if such acts of violence connect to existing hierarchies in a given socio-political order produced through gender inequalities and misogyny, are they exclusively attributable to individual responsibility? What prevents us from using 'security' as a way to give meaning to these issues to make them politically salient?

Violence, including the understandings attached to it, can also be 'productive' or 'constitutive' of who we are and how we are able to be ourselves (Rae and Ingala 2019, 1). The sustained violence against Indigenous women and girls, and the muted responses of the Canadian government and general public, certainly reflect myriad racial, class, and gendered inequalities these women face. The violence also contributes to self-understandings of how they are perceived by others and thus strategies adopted to cope individually and/or collectively (Flowers 2015).

On the connections between security and the environment, see **Chapter 18**

It is also important to keep in mind that violence can be productive of material harm to non-humans, for example through the environmental consequences of unsustainable economic practices, or conflict (Mehta and Merz 2015). This violence can occur through the exploitation of natural resources as 'regular' economic activity, as a driver of conflict, or for the purposes of sustaining a conflict. It can also arise from pollution including that which results from military materials, weapons, and ammunition (e.g., uranium-tipped munitions).

Chapter 14 *explores the relationships among security, natural resources extraction, and exploitation*

If political violence is not always obvious, particularly if it requires us to think anew about our own worlds and their underlying assumptions that guide us through them, how then can we identify it? To provide guidance on how one might link political violence to security, we suggest that the work of Johan Galtung is very helpful. On the one hand, Galtung offers a series of distinctions that helps connect security and violence. On the other hand, Galtung (1969, 169) conceptualizes violence as a **relation of power that influences actors, whether as perpetrators or as recipients.**

For more on Galtung's notion of violence, see **Zoom-in 4.1**

This relation of power will potentially shape the actions, emotions, feelings, health, thinking, and/or well-being of those committing acts of violence and those who are its recipients. As a rule of thumb, if we think of political violence as a prism to study security, we should focus on two things. First, what are the processes of meaning-making behind violence and how do they relate to security? Second, when security is mobilized or enacted, what does violence do to constitute, maintain, and/or challenge relations of power and hierarchies?

See **Section 3.2** *on relations of power*

> ### 🔍 ZOOM-IN 4.1 GALTUNG'S CONCEPT OF VIOLENCE
>
> From a normative perspective, Galtung (1969, 168) defines violence as an act that hinders or prevents someone from achieving their 'potential realizations'. This connects with our emphasis on forms of domination and oppression (Chapter 1). However, while Galtung's concept of violence offers a platform to think about the legacies of structural forms of violence, it is not perfect. Notably, his conception of violence does not always engage with how violence is shaped by factors like racialization or gender (see, for instance, Confortini 2006), even if their importance is formally acknowledged in his work (see Galtung 2019). Moreover, Galtung shies away from the question of whether political violence is necessary to counteract domination and oppression. Nevertheless, his thinking is a useful starting point to think about forms of violence that may not always be obvious.

We can place violence into four categories—physical, psychological, material, and symbolic—that can help us understand if they are political and their connections to security. To make sense of them, it is important to ask the following questions (see Galtung 1969, 169–172):

1. Who and/or what are the (potential) actors involved in the relation?
2. Is the violence intended or unintended?
3. Does the violence have a delimited effect or is it structural (and hence the effects may be wide ranging and/or take longer to achieve)?
4. Is the violence manifest (i.e., already occurring) or latent (i.e., has the potential to occur)?

These questions run parallel to our nine security questions presented in Chapter 5.

4.2.1 Four forms of violence

Violence can exist in different forms and have different effects. We can group these forms and effects into four categories: **physical, psychological, material**, and **symbolic**. These categories are not exclusive. For example, physical violence can have both physical and psychological harms. It can also have material effects, with physical and psychological harms contributing to material consequences (e.g., post-traumatic stress from a violent event may make it difficult for someone to remain employed). Physical and psychological harms can also have symbolic effects. For example, during the Troubles in Northern Ireland, 'door-step' killings, in which paramilitary groups would kill people inside their homes, were considered a particularly egregious form of violence. This is because the relationship encompassed multiple kinds of violence: the physical violence inflicted on bodies that resulted in losses of life; psychological violence caused by the trauma of the killings; and material violence against the victim's family and community. Moreover, door-step killings symbolized an intentional violation of the sectarian division of space between Catholics and Protestants as well as the sanctity of the household as refuge from the outside world (Feldman 1991).

In order to clarify a specific relation between security and violence and their effects, the form of violence is important. These are as follows.

Physical violence is the use or threat of physical force to constrain, brutalize, repress, damage, destroy, maim, or kill a target. It is what we commonly tend to think of as violence. Usually, physical violence encompasses actions against people (see below for non-humans and inanimate objects). This could include the use of force by the police, combat in war, criminal activities such as assault and extortion, or domestic abuse. But physical violence, and the examples above, are often understood as being caused by 'pathological' factors that can be isolated within individuals (e.g., bad people commit crimes), contexts (e.g., force was required to subdue a dangerous suspect who was resisting arrest), or institutions (e.g., the international legal system and the recourse to war). However, physical violence can also have structural dimensions (Galtung 1969, 169, 171). For example, prisons are spaces whose architectural design enables physical control. This creates possibilities for forms of physical and psychological violence as a part of their day-to-day operations—from strip-searches to the physical confinement and isolation from being detained in cells. Moreover, defining criminal behaviour and the processes through which guilt is determined, sentences applied, and punishments administered can relate to broader inequalities and hierarchies in a society. Thus, physical violence can also have structural dimensions (Sirleaf 2018).

Psychological violence is undertaken to damage the cognitive and/or emotional state of an individual or group of people. Psychological violence can be an effect of physical and structural violence. It can also be manifest and/or latent (Salter et al. 2018). For example, the constant noise of police helicopters above 'favelas' in Brazil has manifest psychological impacts on people who live in these areas. These include sleep deprivation from the noise to the fear of being killed by snipers who ride inside them (Adey 2010). Psychological violence can also be latent, stemming from the possibility that past acts of violence might occur at some point in the future. Lingering threats and uncertainties have significant psychological effects.

Material violence is connected to the material dimensions of our worlds. Material violence damages economic well-being as determined by employment, finances, and property ownership as well as economic capacity such as agricultural, industrial, and digital forms of production. It may also target built environments in which we live and work, such as homes, offices, factories, hospitals, schools, critical infrastructure (e.g., communication systems, power grids, and other utilities), government buildings, places of worship, cultural sites, and other public spaces (Coward 2008). Material violence can also be inflicted upon the natural environment, ecosystems, and climate. These forms of violence may be discrete (e.g., a bombing campaign targeting critical infrastructure). They can also be structural, such as the deterioration of city centres in the North American context during the late twentieth century due to processes of socio-economic segregation known as 'white flight'. Like any other

> Chapter 20 discusses the question of prisons and their architectural design

> On the links between the environment and security, see **Chapter 18**

forms of violence, material violence may be intentional, such as with the bombing campaign noted above. It can also be an unintended consequence resulting from some other action like the profligate use of fossil fuels contributing to global climate change.

Symbolic violence creates, reinforces, or challenges hierarchies and relations of power by deploying categorizations that contribute to the politics of stratification (Bourdieu and Passeron 1970). These categorizations are communicated through language, social institutions (like schools), and/or media where they are present in images, music, literature, video games, memes, and films. For example, categorizing the unemployed as 'unproductive', 'a burden on society', or a threat to general economic well-being produces symbolic violence. Such categorizations position the 'unemployed' as outside of 'proper' society and potentially as a threat to it. The consequences of symbolic violence can be material (e.g., a loss of welfare provisions), psychological (e.g., in terms of reduced feelings of self-worth), and even physical (e.g., an increased likelihood that one's body may be subject to coercive force by others or poorer overall health). Symbolic violence can often obscure the political stakes at play, such as the unequal distribution of resources (including opportunities) within a society (Harrits 2011). It can also have an effect on how people view themselves and who they are.

Another aspect of symbolic violence connects with the deployment of categorizations. Whether consciously or unconsciously, violence is also a form of communication in which the perpetrators, victims, and/or form of violence produce additional meanings beyond the violence itself. We can see this in the door-steps example above where physical violence was connected to demonstrating one's capacity to violate spatial orders that were symbolic of sectarian territorial control. Thus, symbolic violence both communicates and deploys categorizations in relation to existing distributions of power.

As you can see from these short treatments, even if we identify the form of violence, additional information is still required to uncover its political aspects and how these link to security. A further set of questions can help us to do so.

4.2.2 Identifying and demonstrating the relations between security and violence

To identify violence, we need to know the actors involved. By doing so, we can identify the hierarchies shaping how political violence is manifested through security as well as understand how an act of violence establishes, maintains, contests, and/or transforms these hierarchies. Our intuition might be to ask: 'who has committed violence and against whom?' However, potential actors can also be groups or institutions, both of which are composed of people (e.g., the state and its security apparatus, social movements, businesses, criminal networks, or religious organizations). As we have already hinted at above, these relations are not limited to human beings. They can also include non-humans, such as buildings, critical infrastructure, computer networks, flora and fauna, ecosystems, and even the biosphere.

After determining the different actors involved, we can try to determine if the violence is **intentional** or **unintentional**. In principle, we can distinguish:

(i) how one may intentionally use violence to attain an objective (e.g., killing the leader of a terrorist organization to disrupt its capacity to carry out attacks);

(ii) how violence can be an unintended consequence of some other set of decisions (e.g., the connection between abolishing gun controls and mass shootings); and/or

(iii) how violence is experienced by those who were not the intended targets (e.g., so-called collateral damage in contemporary warfare).

In practice, as hundreds of years of European jurisprudence can attest, it can be extremely difficult to determine unequivocally the intentions and motivations of actors (Sayre 1932). Regardless, the distinction remains an important political question. Whether violence is a means to an end, an end in itself, or an unintended outcome, intention is central to claims made about the legitimacy of violence and the authority to commit legitimate violence.

A third question is to ask if the violence is **isolated** or **structural**. Isolated violence refers to incidents in which violence is largely determined by the specificities of the situation. This might include the actors involved, their interpersonal relations, the immediate context in which they are interacting, and so on. For example, one might conclude that a drunken brawl outside of a nightclub is isolated physical violence. We would suggest that one should not do so without considering how this violence came to be. Assuming an act of violence is isolated might lead us to a premature conclusion by not taking into account the larger structures within which it took place.

Structural violence is violence whose conditions of possibility arise from wider hierarchies found within a socio-political order. For example, the overrepresentation of Māori in the New Zealand prison system (52 per cent compared to 15 per cent of the population) is indicative of structural violence (Ministry of Justice New Zealand 2021). Incarceration causes physical, psychological, material, and symbolic harms. These harms are enabled by institutionalized forms of racism that increase the probability of New Zealanders of Māori backgrounds being subject to arbitrary police intervention, getting charged with crimes when discretion can be applied, having access to good legal representation, being found/pleading guilty in courts, and receiving custodial sentences, in comparison to others in New Zealand engaged in similar activities.

> On prison systems and political violence, see **Chapter 20**

Finally, violence is **manifest** or **latent**. Some forms of violence and their harms are directly and immediately observable. In these instances, we can say that violence is manifest. For example, the coordinated bombing campaign of Gaza by Israeli forces in 2021, or the shelling of Ukrainian cities by Russia in 2022, are examples of manifest violence. However, in some cases, violence is a possibility but it has not yet emerged. Here we say that the violence is latent. For example, the global nuclear deterrence regime rests on a set of great powers having nuclear weapons that they *could* conceivably use.

In sum, these distinctions help answer the nine core security questions—who can 'speak' security, security for whom, security where, security when, security from what, why security, security how, security for what purpose, and security at whose

> We present and discuss these questions in detail in **Chapter 5**

expense—that can identify the sources and impacts of political violence. However, as we have alluded to above, these distinctions may be less clear in practice. Thus, it can be a challenge to research and analyse them. At the same time, we need to consider what we are including, what we are leaving out, our rationales for doing so, and how our preconceptions may be shaping our accounts. Moreover, we need to think about if, and how, our decisions might relate to specific hierarchies in which we are socially embedded. Being self-aware of how we might influence what we find is central to reflexivity.

For more on reflexivity, see **Box 1.2**

Shifting from questions that enable us to see the political dimensions of violence, we will now turn to two central political questions in relation to violence. These are:

1. under what conditions is violence legitimate?
2. who has the authority to commit (legitimate) violence?

There are many other political questions we can ask about violence and the mobilization of security (see Section 4.6); however, authority and legitimacy are central to uncovering their contingency, historicity, sociology, and possibilities for transformation. Moreover, they are excellent at exposing key challenges we face when examining security across diverse contexts.

4.3 The political question of legitimacy

Relations of power and their contestation extend beyond legislatures, summits, formal state policies, and street protests. Relations of power exist in any context with those who have the power to define security issues and those who do not. This power is important because it influences how we understand the worlds around us, frame problems, and prioritize particular issues over others. It also shapes which kinds of responses, including the use of violence, are determined to be legitimate or illegitimate. The question of the legitimacy of violence relates to two important premises about how security ought to be analysed: social contract theory and the rule of law. These are two premises that are eminently Western-centric in their origins and logic. For example, there are many contexts in both the global north and south in which one could argue that the rule of law is absent. There are also contexts where legitimacy comes from bonds formed by ethnic, linguistic, religious, familial, or nationalist affinities rather than governing structures. Moreover, there are many contexts in which security is not necessarily a public good provided by the state but rather is a private good provided by other actors through market forces (and in some contexts it is a combination of the two; see Leander 2005). Nonetheless, these two premises are central to understanding the connections between violence and security.

Chapters 2 and **3** discuss these questions

Legitimacy connects to social contract theory that comes from the political theorists of the European Enlightenment such as Thomas Hobbes, John Locke, and Jean-Jacques Rousseau. It encompasses assumptions shaped by the particularities of the European contexts of the time, alongside challenges to these predominant political assumptions posed by early encounters with societies of the 'New World'. It assumes that there is a specific form of social contract between 'governments', as embodied by the state, who can say or do 'security', and representative structures through which people grant governments this legitimacy. Internationally, this 'social contract' transposes to the level of an international society. Today epitomized by the United Nations (UN), legitimacy in international society is bestowed upon those actors who abide by, and uphold, its norms and rules.

Domestically, the rule of law is considered to be present when the exercise of security—usually by an executive branch of a government—is constrained by checks and balances emanating from other parts of the government—that is, the legislative and judicial branches—and/or from civil society. In other words, the assumption is that the state apparatus is subject to the law like any other individual or group in a society. Internationally, the international legal system (formal and customary) contains provisions about the legitimate use of force—from self-defence to the responsibility to protect (R2P)—which actors are supposed to follow. International legal frameworks accepted by state parties legitimize these provisions via their use within the UN system, as well as other international and regional intergovernmental organizations.

These two premises are important to keep in mind as many discussions hold them as unacknowledged and taken-for-granted starting points for understanding the politics of security. The Western-centric character of these two premises comes from their entry into legal and political theory within a European historical context grappling with an emerging and fragile relationship between people and their representatives (the state). Yet, from the seventeenth century onwards, through European colonial expansion, social contract theory and the rule of law became the predominant way to understand political dynamics in all contexts. This included regions outside of Europe, despite potential differences in social relations and histories (Mendoza 2017).

Social contract theory assumes that people in a territory have ceded part of their liberty to the state in return for protection and limited representation of their interests by some other actor or mechanism. Thus, representatives of the people and their agents have legitimacy to govern, including, in the classical formulation by Max Weber, via a monopoly over the *legitimate* use of violence (Weber 1994 [1919], 310). According to Charles Tilly (1985), the process of European state formation resulted in a trade-off between people and the state. On the one hand, people gained recognition as citizens with rights and were provided with security through the state's development of its police and standing military. On the other hand, by granting recognition and offering protection, the state gained legitimacy, as well as the fiscal, human, and material resources to wield coercion, in the name of the people. As Tilly notes, this often meant that the state operated as a 'protection racket', offering to keep people safe from harm while being a primary source of threat directly through its coercive apparatus or indirectly through its conflicts with other states.

Social contract theory, the rule of law, and the historical contexts in which they took hold as conceptual norms have led to a particular understanding of the

> **Chapter 6** discusses the distinction between police and the military; see also **Section 2.2**

political limitations that a state *should* have regarding *legitimate* violence. This connects to the idea of **the exception** (Agamben 2008). In normal times, the state ought to respect the rule of law when it wields its power. The exercise of violence is only legitimate when used in accordance with the law. Any violations of the law regarding the use of violence are illegitimate exercises of state power. The only time when a state may extend its use of violence beyond legal limits is during exceptional times, such as times of war, when an existential threat endangers the state and its people. Exceptional times should be limited in scope and duration. The expectation is that a temporary extension of state power will be rescinded once the situation has returned to normal. At the international level, the UN Security Council is able to authorize and legitimize the exceptional recourse to the use of force outside the agreed customary setting of self-defence. The responsibility to protect, which may violate the norm of sovereignty in order to intervene to stop crimes against humanity, is an exceptional measure that is also supposed to be limited in duration and scope.

On the question of the exception and the balance between liberty and security, see **Box 2.1**

The legitimacy of violence thus raises multiple political questions. But we want to return to two questions suggested earlier by our concern about the inherent provincialism in how legitimacy is often framed. First, what does the Western-centrism at the heart of questions regarding legitimacy do in terms of how we understand the connections between security and political violence? Second, how does the violence embedded in the rule of law and unequal social relations get reconciled in predominant understandings of political violence?

The 'exception', periods in which the arbitrary acts of a government go unchecked and unconstrained, may be more often the case than not, with some or many parts of a socio-political order being permanently positioned outside of legal protections. Moreover, being subject to exceptional acts by the state does not form a uniform distribution within societies. For example, social movements like #BlackLivesMatter have sought to raise awareness of the predominance of the exception on racialized minority groups, even in societies that understand themselves to be liberal democracies (Valdez et al. 2020). Internationally, social contracts and the rule of law assume that these arrangements are willingly entered into and not the result of coercion, through processes of conquest, colonization, or conflict. Moreover, we cannot assume that the decisions about the legitimacy of violence made in the name of an international society are free of special interests and are only concerned with upholding rules and principles for the sake of preserving order. Thus, in both sets of cases, assumptions about social contract theory lead to two fundamental problems.

First, they may impose a way of thinking about political relations underpinning the use of violence that is entirely inappropriate to the context. This can then lead to mischaracterizing, or even completely missing, the political dynamics at play in the mobilization of security. This is because evaluations are in relation to a completely different historical experience. Ultimately, these empirical errors become normative claims with political consequences. Thus, other ways of conducting politics and legitimizing violence are taken to be deviant from first principles without more careful consideration of how they may reflect different historical experiences and modes of thinking that developed in response to these experiences. Second, these assumptions assume that the law is a neutral and arbitrary technology that preserves order in a way that is outside of relations of power. While this may be the ideal to which legal systems aspire, and it is often the case that the presence of legal frameworks is better than its absence, the rule of law nevertheless has a very mixed history (Anghie 2007). For example, while international law may encourage the prosecution of those accused of war crimes, it has also justified imperial contest and the oppression of colonized peoples.

These concerns lead to our second question: how can we reconcile social contract theory and the rule of law with unequal social relations that may be at the heart of the connections between security and political violence? Our answer is that they cannot be reconciled. Thus, accounts that stress social contract theory and the rule of law have to downplay the political importance of inequalities to the exercise of violence. Even in contexts where a social contract holds and/or we can see the formalization of the rule of law, violence will still be structurally embedded in unequal social relations and hierarchies. The ideal of the 'social contract', where citizens each have an equal share of power in a society, has been demonstrated to be an inaccurate reflection of how societies are ordered based on the factors we identified at the outset of this book. Thus, socio-political orders inherently contain violence.

You can find a discussion of these different factors in Section 1.4

Getting back to the example of #BlackLivesMatter, the movement emerged as a reaction to forms of political violence, and their connections to security, committed against African-Americans by the state security apparatus and fellow citizens. Globally, the issue of femicide is a form of structural violence connected to other forms of inequalities that excuse gender inequalities and sexual violence, making women and girls more vulnerable to harm (Chapter 10). These two examples underscore that questions of legitimacy also ignore how the symbolic constitution of 'the people' deserving of protection is not free from specific hierarchies and forms of domination.

4.4 The political question of authority

To use legitimacy to frame the meaning assigned to violence—that is, as a legitimate response to a set of conditions—may tell us something about how an act of violence relates to the law, the state, regulatory frameworks, procedures, or even social conventions. Legitimacy and the question of authority are fundamentally connected. Thus, concentrating solely on legitimacy may hamper our ability to ask important political questions such as:

This opens up the question of challenging and resisting security; see Section 3.4

- Who has the authority to determine the legitimacy of violence in a given context?
- How is this authority shaped by contextual factors (including history, geography, and culture) that (re)produce specific hierarchies?
- Who must accept this determination and why must they do so?

There are always political questions related to what counts as the legitimate use of violence. These questions are relevant to domestic and international contexts as well as across a range of actors (e.g., the state and its agents, social movements, private interests). As we have shown above, the question of legitimacy does not help us to see other relations of power that may be at work when connecting security to political violence.

Authority is a central concern when exploring how political violence and security are related. It derives from the ability to determine what counts as legitimate or illegitimate violence, attribute a meaning to forms of violence, and evaluate its effects in our worlds. Authority is not a level playing field; some voices will carry more weight than others regardless of the evidence. Likewise, the ability to define violence as political as opposed to 'pathological' or 'criminal' or 'random' or 'senseless' is also linked to relations of power. The designation 'political' is extremely important for two reasons. First, from the perspective of meaning-making, the authority to designate forms of violence as political justifies them as meaningful acts within a political context and those who commit them as actors within a recognizable political dispute. At the same time, it can also delegitimize actors and the forms of violence they commit by failing to recognize the political dimensions connected to them. Framing matters because it sets out what is at stake, what are reasonable reactions, and how security is mobilized in response (Bakonyi 2015).

Second, authority has an ability to produce, maintain, and/or transform hierarchies and other structures that produce unequal outcomes through forms of violence. Following the analysis of Walter Benjamin (1996 [1921]), the question of authority is important because it draws attention to the conditions under which political violence relates to power. More specifically, Benjamin was concerned with how violence creates and contributes to new relations of power and how it can maintain pre-existing hierarchies and structures. In each case, there will be groups or individuals who benefit from the arrangements and those who do not. For example, the manifest structural violence experienced by Black, Asian, and minority-ethnic groups in the United Kingdom through policing reproduces and underwrites racial hierarchies in the country. The racial prejudices at the source of many police practices that involve the exercise of discretion, such as 'stop-and-search', disproportionately target racial minorities due to over-patrolling and/or racial biases (Vomfell and Stewart 2021). Thus, stop-and-search policies reproduce social stigmas against members of these communities as well as the perception that these communities are a threat to wider society.

This question of authority is also apparent when violence is characterized as a criminal or pathological act, rather than a product of political issues. The claim is that violence is an individual action outside societal influences, or a manifestation of forms of illnesses, and/or moral degeneration in the individuals who have commissioned and/or undertaken the violence. This characterization has two interesting dimensions. The first is that it presents itself as a largely descriptive claim. It describes how an act of violence relates to the law or expected norm, and its illegitimacy according to the law or expected norm. Second, whether used to criticize the actions of an individual, group, or state, this assumes that the law, itself a system of arrangements, institutions, people, regulations, and rules, is not shaped by relations

> **BOX 4.1 NON-VIOLENCE**
>
> The mobilization of security is a political choice. So too is the recourse to violence as well as the decision **not** to use violence. Non-violent resistance, civil disobedience, pacifism, and non-violence as principles have different histories and have been mobilized differently in our contemporary worlds. Some traditions of non-violence can trace their roots back to religious teachings, whether Hindu, Christian, Muslim, Jain, or Buddhist, to name but a few. Non-violence as a principle can also be a deliberate strategy for a political movement serving as its *raison d'être*, or a tactic adopted to navigate contestation and change.
>
> The logic of non-violence is that there is no efficacy in violence. Violence, even in the name of justice, simply reproduces domination and oppression (albeit potentially in different forms). Most famously, non-violent resistance has been associated with Mohandas Gandhi's movement against British imperialism in India, the civil rights movement in the United States (particularly followers of Reverend Dr Martin Luther King Jr), and the Iranian revolution of 1977–9. While not always successful in generating socio-political transformation in the face of domination and/or oppression, non-violence nonetheless possesses a particular kind of transformative potential.
>
> Primarily, non-violence refuses to accept the parameters of political disputes as set by violent actions. That is, non-violence will not concede that violence has an instrumental role to play in achieving objectives, or that the response to violence is violence. In strict versions, deliberately harming others—whether human or non-human—cannot ever be justified. Only by rejecting violence can there be socio-political transformations that eliminate domination and oppression. A key question is: how does non-violence delegitimize violence? Which particular acts, and committed by whom, are challenged? The political choice to use violence or to practise non-violence, how these choices are (de)legitimated, and by whom are important lines of inquiry for us as security analysts and as global citizens.

of power. This is not to say that particular acts of *political* violence are not criminal, or that crime and violence are not related. Rather, it is to say that criminal or 'abnormal' acts of violence may also be political while political acts of violence may also be criminal. The presence of criminality or 'normality' does not necessarily remove the political dimensions of violence. When security is involved, it is quite the contrary! Analytically, what matters are the forms of authority at work defining criminality and normality—these socio-political orders—and the political consequences of these designations.

For example, when pictures emerged of US soldiers abusing Iraqi prisoners at Abu Ghraib, the official narrative was that this violence stemmed from a few 'bad apples'. Less attention was devoted to the inherent brutality of the system in which both the prisoners and guards were embedded. As V. Spike Peterson (2010) notes, one of the US soldiers involved was immediately represented as deviant by US authorities because of her personal background. She also received extensive media attention because her actions fell outside of stereotypical gender expectations, even in a military context. Thus,

> On political violence and prisons, see **Chapter 20**

the political issues underpinning these systematic abuses such as cultures of violence in the military, the use of torture, and the dehumanization of prisoners were downplayed. Instead, the focus was on trying to connect the 'abnormal' individual qualities of the guards with the 'abnormal' acts of violence.

In sum, who authorizes violence, who possesses the authority to define what counts as (political) violence, what kinds of violence can be authorized, under what conditions violence is authorized, and how violence is authorized matter. These questions of authority and legitimacy shape what is politically salient for the mobilization of security. They also help us to understand how security politicizes or depoliticizes violence in a given context.

4.5 Conclusion

Forms of violence that are legitimized and authorized through the mobilization of security shape us. Some of us avoid the most adverse consequences of such mobilizations. Some of us, not necessarily by choice, benefit from them. The aim of this chapter was to demonstrate the centrality of political violence to analysing security critically. The relationships between violence and security are complex and multiple. They demand that we think about how violence is political and what political questions we can ask about violence. Doing so, we can better fulfil our roles as security analysts and as global citizens.

Now that we have set the key concepts and questions that contribute to perspectives critical of security, Chapter 5 will provide a basic methodology to analyse security. Then, the thematic chapters that follow will help you to think about the presence of security and political violence in our own lives and the lives of others.

Additional short introductions to theoretical approaches are available on the online resources to take your understanding of key theories further:
http://www.oup.com/he/Grayson-Guillaume1e.

Questions for further discussion

1. How does violence shape the meanings, actions, and identities of individuals and groups? Provide examples.
2. Is violence always unjustified? Under what conditions is it justified? What role does security play in making these evaluations?
3. How do relations of power create orders and hierarchies that enable forms of violence?
4. How can unintentional violence be political? Provide an example.
5. How can we challenge and/or resist violence?

Further reading

GOLDMAN, EMMA. 1910. 'The psychology of political violence'. In *Anarchism and other essays*. https://theanarchistlibrary.org/library/emma-goldman-anarchism-and-other-essays (last accessed 18 February 2022).

Emma Goldman was a prominent anarchist at the start of the twentieth century in the United States. She authored a series of important texts on class politics, political freedom, women's emancipation, and violence. Here she discusses the root causes of violence which she argues are a political reaction to the political violence of capitalism and government.

FANON, FRANTZ. 2001 [1961]. *The wretched of the earth*. Trans. Constance Farrington. London: Penguin Books.

Published just before his death, Fanon's book is based on his experiences as a clinical psychiatrist in Algeria during the War of Independence. *The Wretched of the Earth* is a call against the political violence of imperialism and colonialism as well as a reminder that decolonization is also a violent process. While *The Wretched of the Earth* immediately resonated with national liberation, revolutionary, and decolonial movements in Africa, Asia, and the Americas, its influence continues into the present.

ZVYAGINTSEV, ANDREY. 2014. Левиафан (*Leviathan*). 141 min. Non-Stop Production.

This fictional film set in a coastal Russian town tells the story of a family who impedes the urban regeneration ambitions of a corrupt local official. *Leviathan* demonstrates how physical, psychological, material, and symbolic violence manifest to reproduce hierarchies that are integral to the experience of insecurity. Gritty, visceral, and bleak; not a Netflix and chill film.

BOURKE, JOANNA. 2000. *An intimate history of killing: Face-to-face killing in twentieth-century warfare*. London: Granta Books.

By analysing archival material of correspondence from soldiers who fought in the First, Second, and Vietnam Wars, Bourke presents a troubling picture of the ease with which human beings can become socialized into violence in ways that do not distress them.

LIFTON, ROBERT J. 1986. *The Nazi doctors: Medical killing and the psychology of genocide*. New York: Basic Books.

How did physicians guided by the Hippocratic Oath become key perpetrators of the Holocaust? This is the question guiding Lifton's comprehensive study of the role played by doctors in Nazi Germany and the ways in which physical, structural, and symbolic violence became normalized within the profession.

A curated list of useful weblinks are available on the online resources to help take your learning further: http://www.oup.com/he/Grayson-Guillaume1e.

References

ADEY, PETER. 2010. 'Vertical security in the megacity. Legibility, mobility and aerial politics'. *Theory, Culture and Society* 27(6), 51–67.

AGAMBEN, GIORGIO. 2008. *State of exception*. Chicago, IL: University of Chicago Press.

ANGHIE, ANTONY. 2007. *Imperialism, sovereignty and the making of international law*. Cambridge: Cambridge University Press.

BAKONYI, JUTTA. 2015. 'Ideoscapes in the world society: Framing violence in Somalia'. *Civil Wars* 17(2), 242–265.
BENJAMIN, WALTER. 1996 [1921]. 'Critique of violence'. In *Walter Benjamin: Selected writing, volume 1. 1913–1926*, edited by MICHAEL W. JENNINGS. Cambridge, MA: The Belknap Press of Harvard University Press.
BOURDIEU, PIERRE and JEAN-CLAUDE PASSERON. 1970. *La reproduction. Eléments pour une théorie du système d'enseignement*. Paris: Les éditions de minuit.
CONFORTINI, CATIA C. 2006. 'Galtung, violence, and gender: The case for a Peace Studies/Feminism alliance'. *Peace & Change* 31(3), 333–367.
COWARD, MARTIN. 2008. *Urbicide: The politics of urban destruction*. London: Routledge.
FELDMAN, ALLEN, 1991. *Formations of violence: The narrative of the body and political terror in Northern Ireland*. Chicago, IL: University of Chicago Press.
FLOWERS, RACHEL. 2015. 'Refusal to forgive: Indigenous women's love and rage'. *Decolonization: Indigeneity, Education & Society* 4(2), 32–49.
GALTUNG, JOHAN. 1969. 'Violence, peace, and peace research'. *The Journal of Peace Research* 6(3), 167–191.
GALTUNG, JOHAN with Dietrich Fischer. 2019. *Johan Galtung: Pioneer of peace research*. Berlin: Springer.
HARRITS, GITTE S. 2011. 'Political power as symbolic capital and symbolic violence'. *Journal of Political Power* 4(2), 237–258.
LEANDER, ANNA. 2005. 'The market for force and public security: The destabilizing consequences of private military companies'. *Journal of Peace Research* 42(5), 605–622.
MEHTA, SAILESH and PRISCA MERZ. 2015. 'Ecocide: A new crime against peace?'. *Environmental Law Review* 17(10), 3–7.
MENDOZA, BRENY. 2017. 'Colonial connections'. *Feminist Studies* 43(3), 637–645.
Ministry of Justice New Zealand. 2021. Hāpaitia te Oranga Tangata. www.justice.govt.nz/justice-sector-policy/key-initiatives/hapaitia-te-oranga-tangata (last accessed 18 February 2022).
National Inquiry into Missing and Murdered Indigenous Women and Girls. 2019. *Reclaiming power and pace: The final report of the National Inquiry into Missing and Murdered Indigenous Women and Girls*. Ottawa. Government of Canada. www.mmiwg-ffada.ca/final-report (last accessed 18 February 2022).
RAE, GAVIN and EMMA INGALA. 2019. 'Introduction: The meanings of violence'. In *The meanings of violence: From critical theory to biopolitics*, edited by GAVIN RAE and EMMA INGALA. London: Routledge.
ROSETTI, POLLY, TAMAR DINISMAN, and ANIA MOROZ. 2016. *Insight report: An easy target? Risk factors affecting victimisation rates for volent crime and theft*. England and Wales: Victim Support. www.victimsupport.org.uk/wp-content/uploads/documents/files/VS per cent20Insight per cent20Report per cent20- per cent20An per cent20easy per cent20target.pdf (last accessed 18 February 2022).
SALTER, PHIA S., GLENN ADAMS, and MICHAEL J. PEREZ. 2018. 'Racism in the structure of everyday worlds: A cultural-psychological perspective'. *Current Directions in Psychological Science* 27(3), 150–155.
SAYRE, FRANCIS B. 1932. 'Mens rea'. *Harvard Law Review* 45(6), 974–1026.
SIRLEAF, MATIANGAI. 2018. 'Ebola does not fall from the sky: Structural violence and international responsibility'. *Vanderbilt Journal Transnational Law* 51(2), 477–554.

Spike Peterson, V. 2010. 'Gendered identities, ideologies, and practices in the context of war and militarism'. In *Gender, war and militarism: Feminist perspectives*, edited by Laura Sjoberg and Sandra Via. Santa Barbara, CA: Praeger.

Tilly, Charles. 1985. 'War making and state making as organized crime'. In *Bringing the state back in*, edited by Paul Evans, Dietrich Rueschemeyer, and Theda Skocpol. Cambridge: Cambridge University Press.

Valdez, Inés, Mat Coleman, and Amna Akbar. 2020. 'Law, police violence, and race: Grounding and embodying the state of exception'. *Theory & Event* 23(4), 902–934.

Vomfell, Laura and Neil Stewart. 2021. 'Officer bias, over-patrolling and ethnic disparities in stop and search'. *Nature Human Behaviour* 5(5), 566–575.

Weber, Max. 1994 [1919]. 'The profession and vocation of politics'. In *Weber: Political Writings*, edited by Peter Lassman and Ronald Speirs. Cambridge: Cambridge University Press.

5

Critical questions

5.1 Introduction 71
5.2 The global drug war 72
5.3 Nine security questions 73
5.4 Conclusion 84

READER'S GUIDE

Using the global drug war as an illustrative case study, we outline the nine different questions we can ask in relation to security: who can 'speak' security; security for whom; security where; security when; security from what; security how; security why; security for what purpose; and security at whose expense? Some of these questions help to determine the context within which security is being mobilized, while others enable us to precisely identify what security does within a given socio-political order. By asking our nine security questions about the global drug war, we are able to show how illicit drugs have been used as a pretext to reproduce racism, violence, and structural inequalities. As such, we conclude by restating the importance of not taking security thinking at face value.

5.1 Introduction

In previous chapters, we discussed what makes an analysis critical and how security links to power, hierarchies, and political violence. This chapter asks 'how can we unpack these complex dynamics?' More specifically, how can we identify the forms of power and hierarchies connecting different actors through the mobilization of security claims? What questions enable us to uncover and better understand how security might relate to political violence in a given context? What should we look for and pay attention to? What will help us to determine the impacts of security? In this chapter, we outline a methodology to analyse what security does in a given context.

In order to illustrate how to apply this methodology, we will deploy a single case for illustrative purposes throughout the chapter: the global drug war. For over six decades, drugs have been identified as such a dangerous threat that many states have declared 'war', both rhetorically and practically, to be the only legitimate counter-response. The 'war on drugs' has been multi-faceted, involving transformations in policing, legal regimes, medical practices, and incarceration, as well as contributing to a series of conflicts around the world. Yet, despite these efforts, the global drug war has been a failure on most counts, including its own.

In this chapter, we are going to use the example of the global drug war to think through how we might ask questions about security, the socio-political orders, relations of power, and hierarchies that it (re)produces or challenges, and the forms of violence that flow through it. The questions we pose are applicable to other security issues. The thematic chapters that follow this chapter, and the illustrative case studies you can find in the online resources, engage with some of these questions on their own terms. Thus, this chapter will help sharpen your skills to ask questions in relation to these different themes.

What is a methodology? For our purposes, a methodology encompasses ways to capture the contingency, historicity, sociology, and transformative potential of security. Thus, our methodology is a series of questions. Moreover, these questions can help us to better contextualize, situate, and ultimately analyse what security does by suggesting where we need to look for answers. Our nine questions, which we have briefly discussed in previous chapters, are:

- who can 'speak' security?
- security **for whom?**
- security **where?**
- security **when?**
- security **from what?**
- security **how?**
- security **why?**
- security **for what purpose?**
- security **at whose expense?**

These nine questions (and answers to them) enable us to identify what security does. In order to help you to apply this methodology such that you can uncover the meaning-making and productive processes of security, we will start with a depiction of what has come to be termed the global drug war (Section 5.2). This illustration will serve as the empirical thread to help you understand how to use the nine questions to problematize what security does (Section 5.3).

5.2 The global drug war

Drugs, substances that induce a physiological, neurological, and/or emotional change in the human body, including opium, cannabis, coca leaf, tobacco, and alcohol, have been known for millennia. However, it has only been for a little over a century that the production, distribution, and consumption of particular substances (known as illicit drugs/narcotics) have been framed as a security threat. Beginning with anti-opium laws in Australia, Canada, and later the United States at the turn of the twentieth century and culminating in the 1988 UN (Vienna) Convention, both national and international security infrastructures have been established to combat illicit drugs (Herschinger 2015). The UN Convention itself is one of the most highly ratified international treaties in history, with 191 signatories giving explicit consent to be bound to its stipulations, representing states from Afghanistan to Zimbabwe. Drugs have been considered such a dangerous threat that many states have declared a 'war on drugs', with some, like the United States, engaged in large-scale policing at home and armed interventions abroad (e.g., Afghanistan, Colombia, and Mexico) to disrupt drug networks for almost half a century. Yet, rather than preventing production, distribution, and consumption:

- globally, the value of the illicit drug industry is approximately 500 billion USD per year (May 2017, xi);
- hundreds of thousands die each year from consuming illicit drugs, drug-related crime, and drug policing;
- incarceration rates for drug offences have increased dramatically since the early 1980s (Penal Reform International 2021). This has been particularly evident in the United States, with members of otherwise marginalized groups disproportionately arrested and imprisoned for drug crimes (despite not producing, distributing, or consuming drugs at higher rates than other demographic groups).

*See **Chapter 20** for more on global incarceration rates*

These failures and inequalities have led to a broader questioning of prohibition in some jurisdictions with restrictions on certain drugs (e.g., cannabis) being relaxed (e.g., Canada, Portugal, and some US states). Nevertheless, there remains a consensus that substances such as heroin, cocaine, and methamphetamine require ongoing prohibition and extraordinary security measures, including the use of violence.

5.3 Nine security questions

In previous chapters, we identified nine questions that can help you to analyse the mobilization and enactment of security to understand what security does. We can group these nine questions into two broad categories: **contextual questions** and **understanding questions**. Both categories of questions have a different purpose. Their shared aim is to 'break down' the complexity of security in order to identify the sociopolitical orders, relations of power, hierarchies, and forms of political violence that are at work when security is mobilized and/or challenged. Using these nine questions, we can identify the contingency, historicity, and sociology of security in order to map its constitutive parts and what they do. This identification and analysis are crucial to reflecting upon the possibilities for challenging, resisting, or transforming security and broader socio-political orders.

*Reviewing **Section 1.2** can help to connect this back to the idea of critique*

All good questions demand answers that go beyond a 'yes' or 'no' based on pure description. This is why asking 'to what extent is x an example of y?' questions are unproductive. They already contain in their formulation an answer that invites pure description (i.e., x is y because it contains elements a, b, and c). For example, 'to what extent are drugs a security threat?' places the respondent in a position where the link between drugs and threat is already assumed. Thus, the way to answer the question is to list security threats that can be associated with drugs without further investigating how these associations have been derived. Probing questions, however, usually take two possible shapes with very different expectations about what purposes they will serve. These are 'why' and 'how possible' questions. Each has a role to play in trying to determine what security does (see Doty 1993, 298–299). Critical perspectives will tend to ask 'how possible' questions because they are concerned with how security is constitutive of meanings and productive effects, which reveal:

> For further discussion of what security does, see **Section 2.3.2**

(i) How socio-political orders shape what security does;

(ii) What type of relations of power are at work and how—through the hierarchies (re)produced by security; and

(iii) How these hierarchies are reproduced using political violence deployed through identities, interests, ideas, institutions, and infrastructures.

In other words, 'how possible' questions help us to see how our worlds are affected by the mobilization of security.

For example, if we were to ask the question 'why has there been a war on drugs?', Roxanne Doty's (1993) distinction between 'why' and 'how possible' questions is really important. The 'why?' question framing *potentially* presupposes that key parts of the question exist in a particular form and that these forms are unproblematic. Here war and drugs are assumed to be straightforward concepts and that there is an underlying problem with drugs to which war is an answer. All of these assumptions are tied to representations and meanings that are socially constructed and reproduced. For example, we know that drugs here refer to specific drugs that are 'dangerous' and since wars are usually fought between contending political entities, the term 'war' is being used somewhat metaphorically. However, without being socialized into these specific meanings and their underlying representations (e.g., cocaine and heroin are bad drugs; war is a mass mobilization to wage violence against an enemy; see Barkawi 2016), the question makes little sense.

In contrast, if, as Doty (1993, 298) contends, 'meanings are produced and attached to various social subjects/objects', then being sensitive to these meanings helps us to understand that questions are shaped by 'interpretive dispositions'. To return to our example, we know that the question concerns illicit drugs whose effects are considered socially corrosive and medically dangerous such that waging war is the only possible solution. Doty's main point is that we should not assume these things to be true from first principles. Therefore, asking how it became possible for these to be understood as true is also an important part of analysing security.

We will now turn to our nine questions within the contextualizing and understanding categories. As we noted, the aim of *Security Studies: Critical Perspectives* is to help you question what security does. Thus, by asking these questions you will be able to capture how the contingency, historicity, and sociology of security shape its practices, while identifying possibilities for transformation.

5.3.1 Contextualizing security

In any analysis of security, one needs a sense of the key coordinates to locate the sociopolitical orders in which it is operating. These include answering questions about the actors involved in a security mobilization, where security is being mobilized, when security is being mobilized, what security is mobilized against, and how security is being mobilized. Establishing these coordinates is crucial because they provide the context, including potential relations of power and hierarchies, that may be involved. A useful way to structure answers to these questions is to use the key factors we presented in Chapter 1 (i.e., class, gender and sexuality, race and ethnicity, ideology and culture, religion, political belonging, and disability). As we noted, these factors are intersectional. Thus, we need to be clear about the factors we are focusing on, why we are focusing on these factors, what we are not covering, and the limitations of whatever we find. This is another way to practise reflexivity.

*For discussions of the four ways of understanding power and the reproduction of hierarchies, see **Sections 3.2–3***

*Key factors are discussed in **Section 1.4***

*See **Box 1.2** for a discussion of reflexivity*

5.3.1.1 Who can 'speak' security?

Who is framing a particular issue as a security issue? Is it the government? A ministry? The military? The police? The media? Members of the public? Conversely, answers can also help determine who is in a position to contest a security claim and who is not. Answers can tell us whose representations and meanings are predominant, allowing us to determine who benefits from them and their broader consequences in a sociopolitical order. Key subsidiary questions are:

- who are the actors in the power relations shaping claims that something is a security issue?
- who agrees; who disagrees?

Section 3.4 discusses how security can be challenged and resisted

For example, during the negotiations over the 1961 Single Convention (a precursor to the 1988 UN Convention), the United States, Canada, Switzerland, Japan, the Netherlands, and the Federal Republic of Germany grouped themselves together as advanced pharmaceutical states with 'no cultural affinity for organic drug use'. On that basis, they demanded strict controls over illicit raw materials such as opium, coca leaf, and cannabis. At the same time, they strongly opposed restrictions over synthetic drugs like amphetamines and tranquilizers that were staples of their pharmaceutical sectors. These states worked together to establish a regulatory regime in which organic materials were placed under the most onerous schedules on the basis that these substances were not used in Western medicine and should be considered hazardous until scientifically proven to be otherwise. This was a virtual impossibility given the

Chapter 14 covers property, extraction, and accumulation

controls that constrained their use (Grayson 2008, 78–80). The end result reduced the amount of legal income that raw material states could earn from natural resource endowments in this sector. Thus, the Convention produced material violence (i.e., a reduction in income) through symbolic violence (i.e., notions of cultural affinity).

5.3.1.2 Security for whom?

In whose name is security mobilized? That is, who is to be protected via security? While these questions are simple, we must be careful here. Even if some security claims directly identify who should be protected, it does not mean that this is necessarily the case. Sometimes the 'who' might be a thing (e.g., critical infrastructure) or an ideal (e.g., democratic ways of life). One way to navigate claims about the positive aspects of a security mobilization is to examine who might benefit from it. These benefits can be professional recognition or receiving protection from a threat. Are these the benefits presented publicly? Similarly, who does not benefit from, or is harmed by, the mobilization? While we have to take into account the stated intentions behind security claims, it is important to be cautious about the conclusions we draw from them. By being cautious about security for whom, we can then see if the distribution of benefits reflects power relations shaped by key factors and which hierarchies the benefits help to reproduce.

> This relates to the question of 'security at whose expense?' discussed in **Section 5.3.2.3**

In relation to the global drug war, at the turn of the twentieth century early anti-opium laws specifically targeted Chinese migrant workers in New Zealand (1901), Australia (1905), Canada (1908), and the United States (1914). They did so in part as a reaction to fears that East Asian migration would overwhelm socio-political orders based on white supremacy in settler-colonial societies, or what was called the 'Yellow Peril' (see Lyman 2000). A 'moral panic' developed that opium consumption promoted an 'unnatural mixing' of the races. This was code for sexual relationships between women of European descent and racialized others. The belief was that these relationships would lead to moral degeneracy and threaten the 'natural' superiority of white races by 'polluting' the genetic pool. The fear was that other races were seeking to subvert the natural racial order by weakening white races. Securing the purity of a racialized community continued with successive rounds of anti-drug legislation well into the late twentieth century, often with the prohibition of specific drugs linked to uptakes in the presence of racialized others through patterns of migration (both into and within these countries; see Grayson 2008). Thus, from the start, the global drug war has also been a race war that has sought to maintain white supremacy in settler-colonial societies. It constructed meanings via forms of identification that reproduced inequalities and symbolic violence that would justify ongoing physical, psychological, and material violence against racialized communities.

> See **Chapter 9** on identity and othering and **Chapter 11** on nationalism, racism, and xenophobia

> See **Box 5.1** on jenkem

5.3.1.3 Where?

Where does security happen? What are the different spaces (e.g., borders, sovereign territories, battlefields, urban environments), specific locations (e.g., the streets of Jakarta or the Amazon basin), and scales (from the everyday to the global) where security is active and connects to other dynamics? Where are places that are affected by

BOX 5.1 THE GREAT JENKEM SCARE OF 2007

From media reports of salacious opium dens to the crazed antics of methamphetamine addicts, 'moral panics' have legitimized and justified treating drugs as a security issue for over a century. According to Stanley Cohen (2011, 1), a moral panic is:

> a condition, episode, person, or group of persons [that] emerges to become defined as a threat to societal values and interests; its nature is presented in a stylized and stereotypical fashion by the mass media; the moral barricades are manned by editors, bishops, politicians and other right-thinking people; socially accredited experts pronounce their diagnoses and solutions; ways of coping are evolved or (more often) resorted to; the condition then disappears, submerges, or deteriorates and becomes more visible.

One of the more bizarre examples of a moral panic was the Jenkem Scare of 2007. Reports began to circulate across regional media outlets in the United States that schoolchildren were getting high by breathing in human waste that had been fermented in jars. The practice was said to have originated among street-children in Zambia who inhaled methane for its hallucinogenic properties. One television station in South Bend, Indiana went as far as telling parents that they should 'wait up for [their children] at night and not let their kids go to bed until they have seen them and smelled their breath' (Cheatham 2007). In the end, jenkem was a hoax, cultivated by internet trolls connected to websites like 4chan. However, the moral panic it produced can be attributed to three factors. First, jenkem was presented as a threat to the well-being of children. Second, jenkem was represented as a practice associated with racialized others. Third, the connection to human waste invoked strong feelings of disgust, raising the fear that the effects of jenkem had to be incredibly pleasurable and powerful for anyone to contemplate using it.

security but remain hidden to many? How does security affect specific spaces? How does security connect and/or disconnect spaces, locations, and/or scales? As you can see, the 'where' question forces us to reflect on relations of power and the hierarchies that are (re)produced by security. What it means to mobilize security for the purposes of fighting crime will be very different in a public housing project as compared to an affluent gated community. The question 'where' therefore opens the exploration of a vast array of spaces, locations, and scales and how they are linked to people and/or objects.

Where we decide to look at the global drug war can tell us very different things about the security dynamics at play. For example, Kevin Lewis O'Neill (2016) has explored how the drug war has shaped the urban cityscape in Guatemala City. He uses the term 'narcotecture' to highlight two phenomena in particular. The first is an explosion in high-rise building developments with state-of-the-art security features to protect against the street violence fomented by the drug industry. These developments have become the preferred form of housing for the very wealthy as well as a means for cartels to launder money earned through the drug trade. In their design, cost, and clientele, these buildings are meant to keep people out and facilitate the mobility of residents in ways that are 'safer' (e.g., by offering helicopter pads and parking spaces for armoured vehicles). He contrasts these with the proliferation of drug treatment clinics run by Pentecostal groups in the older quarters of the city. Here colonial-era buildings are retrofitted with security measures to prevent 'patients', many of whom are admitted against their will, from leaving. In the old city, security measures keep people in. Thus, where we look, even in the same city, can tell us very different things about how security is mobilized and what it does within the global drug war. Primarily, we can see how security connects to the production of space and ways of preventing, and administering, forms of violence.

5.3.1.4 When?

When does security happen? Does it change depending on the time of day? In which socio-historical, political, economic contexts has a security mobilization occurred? How does security affect the relationships that people, goods, and spaces have with time? How have security practices evolved over time? What are the similarities or differences in security discourses and practices over time? As we have already seen, critical perspectives look at different temporal aspects—from claims of 'novelty' to the exploration of past examples to historicize security by identifying points of emergence, (dis)continuities, and transformation. 'When' is often linked to questions of 'where', helping to provide details of the context within which security mobilizations take place.

> See **Section 2.2** on the historicity of security and **Section 1.2.2** on the importance of historicizing

The question of when—that is, the historical period in which we decide to examine the global drug war—will draw our attention to very different kinds of security practices. In the nineteenth century, the global drug war is best captured by the Opium Wars (1839–42 and 1856–60) fought by Britain (and later joined by France) against the Qing dynasty in China. In order to address gross imbalances in trade, European powers (particularly Britain) farmed opium in their colonial possessions (like India) and then exchanged it for Chinese goods. To maintain a favourable balance of trade, European powers encouraged opium smoking in order to increase Chinese demand. This shows both the hypocrisy of anti-opium laws in other parts of the world and the active deflection of who was forcing drugs upon whom for profit and control. The opium trade was so fundamental to Britain and the global economy that Karl Marx (1858) identified it as a key commodity underpinning capitalism at the time. Seeing the deleterious effects of opium smoking and wishing to stop the practice, the Qing attempted to ban imports of opium into China. This led to two wars that China ultimately lost. In the aftermath, Britain and France received significant trading concessions, improved access to markets, and territorial concessions on the Chinese mainland. As a result, the Opium Wars continue to shape the thinking of the Chinese government on the sanctity of state sovereignty to this very day. Thus, if we are looking at the global drug war in the mid-nineteenth century, we see colonial powers using opium to subjugate China in order to generate wealth and maintain an economic system in which they disproportionately benefitted. The connections to physical, psychological, and material violence are readily apparent.

If we shift to the late twentieth century, after the ratification of the 1988 UN Convention, the United States implemented its annual certification procedure which assessed how well states around the world adhered to commitments made in light of the Convention. Any state deemed not to be taking sufficient measures to honour its commitments would then lose its eligibility for direct forms of US assistance (e.g., foreign aid) and face automatic 'no' votes from the US government for loan approvals in any multilateral development banks of which it was a member. The point is to coerce lower-income governments into dedicating resources to participate in the global drug war to a level demanded by the United States. For wealthier states, the concern is the potential reputational damage of being associated with bad actors, like North Korea, from inclusion on the list. For example, in government-level discussions over the decriminalization of cannabis in Canada at the turn of the twenty-first century, concerns were raised about being 'decertified' by the United States (Grayson 2008, 58). Here we can see how the threat of material and symbolic violence is shaping behaviours.

5.3.1.5 Security from what?

Another important question to ask when mapping a security mobilization is 'what is the source of the threat?' As discussed above in relation to 'for whom', what is being framed as a 'danger' or a 'threat' is not always readily apparent. Explicit designations can be rich with implicit sub-texts. These sub-texts need to be examined. Moreover, the framing of a threat may be reflective of identity politics that reproduce hierarchies tied to key factors like class, race, gender, and so forth. It is therefore important to look for underlying political dynamics that are not readily apparent at first glance. These need to be uncovered and analysed.

Most often, public officials justify a security-first approach to drugs based on medical risks, social effects, and the harms to specific groups. Thus, illicit drugs (such as heroin, cocaine, and methamphetamine) are presented as highly addictive and dangerous, directly leading to overdoses, death, crime, murder, and gang activity because of their chemical properties. Moreover, it is often argued that children and young people are the most in danger from the threats posed by illicit drugs, leading to, for example, harsher penalties for any drug-related activity that takes place in spaces frequented by children (e.g., school zones) or that directly targets children. However, drugs on their own are incapable of producing and distributing themselves. Likewise, drugs are incapable on their own of causing someone to consume them. Thus, as noted above, from the very first anti-opium laws, illicit drugs have been represented as something brought into imagined political communities by (racialized) others to weaken this community through moral, mental, and physical degeneration. This includes their association with:

- the fear of being overrun by racialized others at the start of the twentieth century;
- Communist infiltration during the Cold War;
- the spread of inner-city decay in the late twentieth century;
- contemporary Islamic insurgent groups in places like Syria, the Philippines, and Afghanistan.

Thus, illicit drugs are represented as the thin edge of a threatening racialized wedge. Here the productive power of security to catalyse forms of physical violence directly links to the meanings that particular drugs have and understandings of who is involved in drug activity.

5.3.1.6 How?

How is security mobilized? There are a wide range of possible answers, all of which can tell us something about the meaning-making and productive aspects of security. The ways in which security is mobilized, enacted, or challenged—for example, political speeches, legal texts, media coverage, military strategies, policing tactics, cultural artefacts, or personal practices—are not necessarily exclusive of one another. We may find that they are all present if we embrace the complexity of a specific event. If you were to focus on answering how this is achieved via security design or weapons-systems, you would most likely concentrate on specific objects (e.g., drones), or processes (e.g., ergonometric principles embodied within weapons-systems). If you were interested in borders and/or questions of mobility, you might look at how international relief organizations plan refugee camps, the type of criteria used at the border of a country to determine those who are too risky to be given permission to enter, and so on. The question 'how' therefore groups together a vast array of possible objects, processes, institutions, and events.

> **Chapter 16** covers security and design
>
> **Chapter 17** covers weapons-systems
>
> See **Chapter 19** on border practices
>
> **Chapter 20** examines camps

How security is mobilized and enacted within the global drug war involves a complex apparatus of measures that span across several different policy areas. These include:

- legal frameworks encompassing penalties for drug crimes, asset forfeiture laws that seize any assets that have been funded through criminal activity, and international regulatory regimes like the UN Convention;
- national medical regimes (including medical malpractice insurance for doctors) that have sought to reinforce claims that there are no medically legitimate uses for drugs like cannabis or psilocybin while making it difficult to run trials to challenge these claims and/or prescribe them;
- surveillance practices like wiretaps, infrared technologies (to capture the heat signatures of indoor grow operations), electricity monitoring, precursor chemical registries (for substances that can be used to manufacture illicit drugs), financial transaction reporting (to identify suspicious exchanges of money), informant networks (developed through awareness campaigns like 'how to tell if you live next door to a meth house' and encouraged by financial rewards), and sophisticated border control technologies to track airplanes, boats, and motor vehicle traffic;
- the use of foreign aid and development assistance (via the US certification procedure);
- policing strategies that take a zero-tolerance approach to low-level drug activity and policing techniques that adopt military tactics and equipment in civilian settings;
- military actions at home, as in 1981 when President Ronald Reagan rescinded the 'Posse Comitatus Act' enabling the US armed forces to assist in domestic counter-narcotics operations, and abroad (e.g., Plan Colombia or opium interdiction efforts by NATO in Afghanistan);
- media activity including government marketing campaigns (e.g., 'Just Say No!') and US Drug Enforcement Agency involvement in the entertainment industry to shape portrayals of the drug war and the agency (Secker 2019).

Thus, there are many possible ways to examine how security is mobilized and the political violence it makes possible, including the meanings attached to specific drugs/actors as well as particular regimes and practices.

5.3.2 Understanding security

The last set of questions we can ask about security relate to how security mobilizations are understood and experienced. These understandings and experiences cover those who enact security mobilizations, those for whom security is mobilized, and for those upon whom security is mobilized. Even with the concerns raised above by Doty (1993), 'why' questions help us to uncover the logics that key actors use to justify security mobilizations. 'For what purpose' questions take us beyond those logics to look at how these might have significant socio-political effects by reproducing relations of power, hierarchical structures, and forms of domination and oppression. 'At whose expense' questions force us to look very carefully at the costs of security. This is a question with two interconnected parts. The first captures the resources required to enact security mobilizations. These may be direct and material costs (e.g., through taxation systems), indirect and symbolic costs (e.g., a loss of privacy), or opportunity and institutional costs (e.g., money spent on fighter jets cannot be spent on social programmes). The key here is: who pays these costs and is this in proportion to any benefits received? The second is: who ends up being subject to the forms of political violence that security makes possible?

The contextual questions noted above can guide us to where we might find those for whom security is the experience of political violence. Moreover, by remaining sensitive to context, we can begin to see how costs travel across time and space. Or, to be blunter, asking these questions helps us to understand how it becomes possible that as security threats change, it tends to be the same marginalized groups of people (e.g., women, the working classes, ethnic, religious and sexual minorities, those with disabilities, and intersectional communities) who remain subject to the political violence of security.

5.3.2.1 Security why

Asking 'why security?' exposes the rationales underpinning security mobilizations as well as resistance to them. It can also help us to understand the very instrumental reasons why actors may frame issues as security issues. For example, it is obvious why the defence industry might have an interest in continuing to define security in ways that emphasize military threats and militarized solutions to situations like migration. However, 'why' should not be limited to the immediate and direct reasons offered by those who are mobilizing or challenging security. These do not suffice in and by themselves. Actors have a particular view of situations, of their own rationales, and of themselves. These are only one part, and often a small part, of the story. As such, the question 'why' relates to answering the question 'security for what purpose?' In order to identify the purposes to which security is mobilized, we need to connect to their underpinning security claims. This provides better insight into the effects of security on specific socio-political orders.

As noted above under 'security for whom?' and 'security from what?', why drugs are a security issue involves a shifting set of rationales provided by officials in which

> See the discussion of security as a threshold in **Section 2.3.1**

> See **Section 5.3.2.2** for a discussion of this question

different threats are explicitly and implicitly identified as justifications. For example, health and safety threats might be identified (from individual risks of overdosing and mental illness to public health risks associated with communicable diseases like HIV/AIDS), as well as social risks such as crime and violence associated with drug use and drug economies. More recently, within the US war on terror, illicit drugs have been connected to insurgent groups, shifting counter-narcotics into a form of counterinsurgency and counterterrorism. For perspectives critical of security it is also important to note the failures in the logics behind these security claims and mobilizations. For example,

> See **Chapter 13** on health and security

> See **Chapter 8** on terrorism and asymmetric conflicts for the insecurities that arise in these situations

- if the potential public health consequences of illicit drugs are a security threat, a logical response would be to legalize them so that medical authorities can establish quality controls over the substances themselves, restrict access to them, and engage in harm reduction practices that reduce the risks from drug use;
- if the global drug war, in part, is waged to deny a key funding source for insurgent groups, why not make drugs legal, create regulated production chains, and deny insurgents this lucrative source of income? Likewise, ending the war on drugs would enable a vast security apparatus and its capacity to divert towards other priorities like counterinsurgency operations.

There are many context-specific rationales provided for why the threats associated with drugs are at such a heightened level that 'war' is the only possible response. Critical perspectives can help us, as analysts and global citizens, to see whether these security rationales stand up to scrutiny, inside and outside of their logical propositions. Furthermore, we can closely examine meanings that enable security practices that do things to particular groups of people, even when the underlying rationales are suspect.

5.3.2.2 Security for what purpose?

This question links us back to our claim that security is a window into our societies that enables us to see how power and inequalities flow through them. Does security connect to broader socio-political orders that contribute to forms of oppression and structures of domination? What broader purposes does using security as the framework to understand complex socio-political, economic, or environmental issues serve? What purposes are served by mobilizing and enacting security in one way rather than others? What purposes are advanced when security actors, like the police or the military, prioritize certain approaches to security over others? If contemporary mobilizations of security connect to historical dynamics, what purpose is security serving: is it to maintain these dynamics or challenge them?

As has been suggested from answers to the security questions above, the global drug war, its practices, and their outcomes have reproduced a racialized socio-political order both locally (in many contexts) and globally in which marginalized groups (e.g., by ethnicity, class, religion, and/or gender) are subject to forms of political violence from the physical to the symbolic. Referring to wars fought by European settlers in North America against Indigenous populations that spanned over five centuries, Curtis Marez (2004) argues that drug wars are the continuation of the 'Indian Wars'. They take place in what are constructed as border zones (e.g., opium dens, inner cities, along state territorial boundaries) where majority-white populations come into contact with those they have racialized as the 'other'. The global drug war has accelerated in the wake of a decline in state social spending in many jurisdictions that has come with privileging market forces in the allocation of social goods. By criminalizing the poor, underrepresented groups, and foreigners, local manifestations of the global drug war have deflected attention away from underlying forms of structural political violence by reducing the causes of social issues to the influence of illicit drugs. Thus, the global drug war has further entrenched local and global inequalities anywhere it is waged.

5.3.2.3 Security at whose expense?

While there is nothing radical about being interested in how people and communities are affected by security mobilizations, critical perspectives ask 'security at whose expense?' to highlight the contingency, historicity, and sociology of security. This requires extending beyond crude cost–benefit analyses of security where disproportionate costs, whether borne by a group (e.g., Muslim women), a location (e.g., the global south), or dimension (e.g., the environment), are justified if who (or what) was intended to be secured is satisfied. For example, this is a logic that sees the environmental costs of nuclear weapons past, present, and future as justifiable insofar as nuclear weapons are perceived to be providing 'security' to a state and its citizens in the present. The second is to connect contemporary forms of inequality generated through security dynamics to forms of political violence that have been present in previous historical contexts. This gets to a question noted above: how is it possible that the same groups of people tend to benefit from security across time and space while others tend to pay the direct, indirect, and opportunity costs of security through their treasure and blood, even as understandings of security threats change? How is it possible for the same patterns that intertwine security with political violence and inequality to repeat themselves?

> See **Chapter 18** on security and the environment

The global drug war has inflicted costs on bodies. These embodied costs include deaths from drug economy-related violence and state counter-narcotics policing. For example, states with vibrant underground drug economies and aggressive counter-narcotics policing such as El Salvador, Mexico, and Brazil, have intentional homicide rates five to ten times the world average (World Bank 2021). Increases in incarceration rates around the world, particularly in the United States, correlate with the escalation of the global drug war in the 1980s. In many domestic contexts, the largest growth rates have been seen in racial-minority communities. In particular, it is women within these communities whose incarceration rates have dramatically increased. They often occupy the lowest rungs of drug enterprises, are given the riskiest jobs (like transporting drugs across international borders), and have very little knowledge of operations to exchange for sentencing deals with prosecutors (Sudbury 2005).

> **Chapter 20** offers further discussion of this increase

> See **Chapter 10** on gender and sexuality for more on the reproduction of gender inequalities via security

Beyond direct forms of physical violence, there are other costs. For example, in some jurisdictions in the United States, a criminal felony record removes voting eligibility. Thus, the drug war has disenfranchised large numbers of people. The financial costs of the global drug war are also high in terms of the overall resources dedicated to counter-narcotics policing. Drug war spending also siphons resources from tackling other crimes and security threats and/or those that could be used to address pressing social inequalities in areas such as unemployment, local development, education, health, and environmental issues. Thus, as police in the Philippines execute those suspected of drug use, citizens are prevented from voting in Florida because of a previous drug felony, and individuals are separated from their families while serving prison sentences for drug possession, marginalized communities disproportionately bear the costs of the drug war repeatedly. The global drug war has preserved gendered, racialized, classed, and sectarian socio-political orders locally and globally through forms of political violence.

5.4 Conclusion

See **Section 1.2** on critical perspectives and Zoom-in 1.1 on common sense

Chapter 9 analyses the role of such oppositions in identity construction

Taking the global drug war as an illustrative example, this chapter has presented nine questions to help you map, contextualize, and ultimately analyse what security does. Thinking critically requires you to question what is taken for granted or presented as 'it goes without saying'. One of the key features of security is that it reconfigures our worlds into sharp oppositions (e.g., friend–enemy, good–bad, safe–threat). Therefore, for some, there are clear security threats and clear ways to counter them. For those who see their worlds in terms of these sharp contrasts, to question these stark framings is at best counter-productive and at worst dangerously naive. Some may even go so far as to argue that certain people, places, and things are inherently security threats full stop—there is no need for discussion or debate!

Our point is not to deny that there are real dangers in our worlds. Rather, it is that we have a duty as global citizens not to take security thinking at face value. Whatever the threat drawn to our attention, is security the best approach to address it? To challenge security thinking with precision, we need to know what questions to ask in order to understand what security does and evaluate its consequences. To help, we have provided you with a series of questions to ask about security claims and the mobilization of security. In the thematic chapters that follow, our expert contributors will turn to specific security themes to show you in more detail how asking these questions reveals the stakes and consequences of using security thinking to navigate our worlds.

Additional short introductions to theoretical approaches are available on the online resources to take your understanding of key theories further:
http://www.oup.com/he/Grayson-Guillaume1e.

Questions for further discussion

1. What would happen if we reframed our nine 'security' questions as 'insecurity' questions (e.g., insecurity for whom; insecurity where)? Is the potential change in emphasis significant? If so, why?

2. Compare and contrast potential answers to the following two questions:

    a. Why have many governments around the world declared a war on terror?

    b. How did a war on terror become possible?

    Discuss the differences and similarities in the content of your answers.

3. Use the table below to connect examples from the discussion of the nine security questions to identities, ideas, interests, institutions, and infrastructure. Then link these to the potential forms of political violence generated.

Question	Identities	Ideas	Interests	Institutions	Infrastructures	Forms of violence
Question 1						
Question 2						
Question …						

4. Can you think of a film, television show, song, novel, poem, painting, photograph, or other cultural artefact that might help you answer one of the nine security questions in relation to a specific security mobilization?

5. 'The same communities disproportionately experience forms of insecurity regardless of the threat.' Discuss this statement in relation to two different security issues from two different periods.

Further reading

MOON, KATHARINE H. S. 1997. *Sex among allies: Military prostitution in US-Korea relations*. New York: Columbia University Press.
This book, based on ethnographic work in South Korea, explores the question of 'security at whose expense?' by examining the security consequences of the sex economy that has developed to service demand from US military bases in the country.

WEIZMAN, EYAL. 2012. *Hollow land: Israel's architecture of occupation*. London: Verso Books.
This comprehensive exploration of architecture and infrastructure design in Israel-Palestine shows how security is mobilized in ways that might not always be obvious and how buildings, highways, and housing projects can be used to subjugate groups of people. It thus innovatively engages with questions of 'security where' and 'security how'.

BOURGOIS, PHILIPPE. 2003. *In search of respect: Selling crack in El Barrio*. 2nd ed. Cambridge: Cambridge University Press.
This book provides an in-depth and harrowing ethnographic account of crack cocaine dealers in East Harlem, New York. By seeking to understand the logics and practices of a sub-population understood to be a threat, Bourgois uses the question 'security from what?' to show how forms of oppression can be reproduced by the oppressed, thereby contributing to the proliferation of insecurity and violence.

MISIRI, DEEPTI. 2014. *Beyond partition: Gender, violence, and representation in post-colonial India*. Urbana, IL: University of Illinois Press.
By asking questions related to 'security for whom?' and 'from what?', this book traces the cultural violence that has been generated by contending understandings of India post-partition. In particular, it shows how insecurities stemming from communal violence, terrorism, and state security practices are linked to forms of gender violence within communities.

BEHERA, NAVNITA CHADHA, KRISTINA HINDS, and ARLENE B. TICKNER. 2021. 'Making amends: Towards an antiracist Critical Security Studies and International Relations'. *Security Dialogue* 52(1), 8–16.

Who are critical perspectives for? This article draws attention to how critiques of security can reproduce forms of racial inequality. To avoid reinforcing racial hierarchies, it offers a series of practical steps to embed anti-racism into perspectives critical of security.

References

BARKAWI, TARAK. 2016. 'Decolonising war'. *European Journal of International Security* 1(2), 199–214.
CHEATHAM, KELLI. 2007. 'Police warn about new drug made from raw sewage'. *WSBT Local News South Bend*, 7 November. https://web.archive.org/web/20071109120038/http://www.wsbt.com/news/11077771.html (last accessed 19 February 2022).
COHEN, STANLEY. 2011. *Folk devils and moral panics*. London: Routledge.
DOTY, ROXANNE L. 1993. 'Foreign policy as social construction: A post-positivist analysis of U.S. counterinsurgency policy in the Philippines'. *International Studies Quarterly* 37(3), 297–320.
GRAYSON, KYLE. 2008. *Chasing dragons: Security, identity, and illicit drugs in Canada*. Toronto: University of Toronto Press.
HERSCHINGER, EVA. 2015. 'The drug dispositif: Ambivalent materiality and the addiction of the global drug prohibition regime'. *Security Dialogue* 46(2), 183–201.
LYMAN, STANFORD M. 2000. 'The "Yellow Peril" mystique: Origins and vicissitudes of a racist discourse'. *International Journal of Politics, Culture, and Society* 13(4), 683–747.
MAREZ, CURTIS. 2004. *Drug war: The political economy of narcotics*. Minneapolis, MN: University of Minnesota Press.
MARX, KARL. 1858. 'Free trade and monopoly'. *New York Daily Tribune*, 25 September. www.marxists.org/archive/marx/works/1858/09/25.htm (last accessed 19 February 2022).
MAY, CHANNING. 2017. *Transnational crime and the developing world*. Washington, DC: Global Financial Integrity. https://gfintegrity.org/report/transnational-crime-and-the-developing-world (last accessed 19 February 2022).
O'NEILL, KEVIN L. 2016. 'Narcotecture'. *Environment and Planning D: Society and Space* 34(4), 672–688.
Penal Reform International. 2021. *Global prison trends 2021*. www.penalreform.org/global-prison-trends-2021 (last accessed 19 February 2022).
SECKER, TOM. 2019. 'Contracts reveal for first time how the DEA exercises control over television, film productions'. *Shadowproof*, 28 May. https://shadowproof.com/2019/05/28/contracts-reveal-for-first-time-how-dea-exercises-control-over-television-film-productions (last accessed 19 February 2022).
SUDBURY, JULIA. 2005. 'Celling black bodies: Black women in the global prison industrial complex'. *Feminist Review* 80(1), 162–179.
World Bank. 2021. *Intentional homicides (per 100,000 people)*. https://data.worldbank.org/indicator/VC.IHR.PSRC.P5?end=2018&most_recent_value_desc=true&start=1990 (last accessed 19 February 2022).

6

Policing

Cédric Moreau de Bellaing

6.1 Introduction 87
6.2 Policing, violence, and the state 89
6.3 The professional organization of policing 92
6.4 Police and society 95
6.5 The police in the face of changes in crime and war 97
6.6 Conclusion 100

READER'S GUIDE

This chapter explores how police forces have become an integral part of our societies. It demonstrates how policing is connected to everyday relations of power and is reflective of socio-political orders. First, the chapter outlines the historical and social processes that led to the creation of police forces and their connections to the early development of the state in Europe. The chapter then explores the different ways police forces have been professionalized and the consequences of these differences for how police forces relate to the societies in which they are embedded. The chapter concludes by exploring some contemporary policing issues: police reforms, transnational crime, and the militarization of police forces.

6.1 Introduction

> Illustrative case studies on the topics explored in this chapter are available on the online resources to help take your understanding of policing further:
> http://www.oup.com/he/Grayson-Guillaume1e.

Policing is an institution which, for better or worse, is an integral part of our worlds and socio-political orders. Policing is an activity carried out by an organization, mostly but not necessarily public, that is tasked with managing disturbances to public order, preventing crime, and controlling behaviour, while having the legal power to use force as required. This means that policing links to everyday relations of power and is reflective of socio-political orders. The diversity in how policing is experienced and conducted in different contexts requires that we investigate what policing is, for whom policing is enacted, and how security is mobilized through it.

The national contexts where policing takes place can be very different. For example, France has two main security forces: the national police and gendarmerie. However, in the United States, there are nearly 18,000 different police forces, encompassing city, county, state, and federal levels. This correlates with 'how' police forces are organized and thus 'how' security may be enacted. For example, recruitment structures and controls determine 'who' can become a law enforcement officer and 'where'. In France, recruitment can be national, leading to situations where police recruited from rural areas are stationed in urban centres characterized by high levels of social diversity with which they have little experience. Conversely, in the United States, police may be from the local area but also exhibit local biases and potential prejudices. In the United States, some law enforcement roles are elected, as is the case with sheriffs, making the appeal of a candidate to a political constituency the main rationale for their legitimacy. 'How' security is enacted by police also differs because of the range of roles that a police force may undertake. These include public order functions, investigative work, intelligence gathering, and/or policing public disturbances such as protests. Therefore, is anything held in common between a police officer with a neighbourhood beat who may be trying to establish enduring relationships of trust with shopkeepers and residents and a member of an anti-gang squad who is tasked with undertaking 'hit-and-run' arrests of high-risk suspects?

The diversity of policing is not only linked to how its day-to-day operations are organized. It is also connected to the specific local and international contexts in which policing is undertaken. In most Western contexts, there is an assumption that security is a public good. The power and legitimacy of policing therefore derives from, and is supposed to be limited by, the rule of law. Yet, in other contexts, security, and policing, are private goods. Your own (in)security is dependent on your ability to purchase it. The absence of a clear policing apparatus dedicated to maintaining security as a public good is often seen as evidence of state failure. Yet the privatization of security is pervasive. The prevalence of private security companies that undertake policing functions raises questions about their relations with public authorities. The persistence of self-defence groups is also a challenge to understanding policing. In view of this rapidly sweeping diversity, does it still make sense to talk about policing in general?

Beyond differences in function, organization, missions, and professional culture, the presence of police institutions is characteristic of socio-political orders centred around the authority of the state. The absence of the police is generally understood as a lack. The systematic presence of multiple policing institutions is due to what Émile Durkheim (2007 [1893]) termed the progressive division of labour in societies. The composition of an institution of specifically trained professionals with the power to use force is a strong indication of the historical, social, and political transformations in socio-political orders as they become more differentiated. As the complexity of our lives in common increases, so does the complexity of the institutions that govern these lives.

Socio-political orders and relations of power are discussed in **Section 3.2**

The question of 'security how?' is introduced in **Section 5.3.1.6**

The question of legitimacy is discussed in **Section 4.3**

Box 6.1 *explores the privatization of policing*

Authority is covered in **Section 4.4**

> BOX 6.1 PRIVATIZATION AND POLICING?

The privatization of policing is regularly presented as an indication of a weakening of the state monopoly on legitimate violence. Yet policing as a private good that is directly paid for is often the reality in many countries. The increase in private security, defined as the protection of property, persons, and information by commercial actors, can be observed in many parts of the world (de Maillard 2017). Private security companies often undertake tasks that would ordinarily be the purview of public police forces (CoESS 2019). This can include the surveillance of private places open to the public (supermarkets, shopping centres, parking lots), patrolling public spaces, conducting investigations for certain categories of crime (e.g., theft), questioning individuals suspected of criminal activity, and using (lethal) violence when undertaking some of these tasks.

We need to reflect critically about the privatization of policing and what this means for security in a given socio-political order. First, is privatization really a novel phenomenon? The conduct of surveillance and policing activities by private groups dates at least from the nineteenth century. For example, the Pinkerton agency in the United States was routinely employed by corporations to monitor, disrupt, and violently harass unions. Second, the term 'privatization' encompasses very different realities: it can refer to the work of transnational firms such as G4S, which employs 546,000 people in 120 countries, as well as to the work of groups of voluntary citizens responsible for keeping public spaces peaceful and to the activities of bounty hunters in the United States. National contexts also differ greatly: while in Hong Kong, private forces outnumber public forces five to one, in Italy they outnumber their public counterparts six to one (Johnston 2007). Finally, privatization does not always follow the same logic: in Brazil, privatization developed under the impetus of the property-owning classes to protect their assets, while in South Africa, privatization under apartheid was due to the fact that public police forces were primarily deployed to control racially segregated townships (Jones and Newburn 2006). For all these reasons, some prefer to speak of the multilateralization (Bayley and Shearing 2001) or the pluralization (de Maillard 2017) of policing to provide a more nuanced understanding of security as a private good.

6.2 Policing, violence, and the state

Following the European historical experience, it may seem obvious that policing institutions should have emerged with the rise of the state. Yet, historically, the existence of the police in their contemporary forms should not be taken for granted. For a long time, inter-personal violence was largely regulated on the basis on social rules that informally codified when it could occur, its intensity, and the conditions under which it should stop. Public order did not presuppose a third-party bureaucratic authority: it relied upon the respect of these rules in a face-to-face relationship. This is the case, for example, of the social codification of rules around avenging wrongdoing. From this point of view, the emergence of institutionalized police forces must be historically understood as an internal transformation in societies that have progressively experienced the delegitimization of these traditional social relations of violence.

> We provide a short history and its connection to colonial spaces in **Section 2.2**

The first institutions similar to police forces, like those that emerged in Paris (1667), arose from the need to protect trade routes (Napoli 2003) and fight crime (Williams 1979). They were often the result of local initiatives that formed against a backdrop of growing urbanization and intolerance of disorder. This expectation of security for trade routes and fast-growing cities is only, however, indirectly related to how states developed in Europe. The emergence of the police can also be linked to processes of state building that extended existing chains of interdependence among individuals, social groups, and society into a larger space like the state (Elias 1975 [1939]). This extension raised expectations for bureaucratic regulations to guide behaviours, the maintenance of public order, and third-party dispute settlement procedures.

This is not to say that the introduction of policing succeeded in meeting these expectations. Police forces appear at a moment in history when European socio-political orders, especially in the nineteenth century, transitioned from status-based to class-based societies. Policing also emerges during an intensification of colonial expansion by European states, transforming itself through the occupation of colonized spaces. Within these contexts, professionalized police forces were asked to control, and often repress, emerging working-class movements around working conditions and democratic rights. They were also central to the brutal treatment of colonized populations and in some contexts, like with the westward expansion of the Canadian state, were central to imperial control of newly acquired territories. Thus, rather than being neutral arbitrators, very often the *raison d'être* of the police was to privilege one side over others as they contributed to the establishment of a particular socio-political order.

> How socio-political orders are reflected in specific hierarchies is discussed in **Section 3.3**

As state building increased, with different outcomes due to specific national trajectories (Bayley 1990), uncertainty concerning the role of police institutions became apparent. This ambivalence crystallized around the autonomy that police institutions should have in relation to political power. Gradually, this uncertainty dissipated. The police became important for the stability of political regimes because they developed an apparatus to conduct large-scale surveillance, could contain/repress various forms of dissent, and/or provided competence in security provision (for some). Therefore, they potentially generated legitimacy for state institutions more generally.

Police institutions thus have almost always been associated with political decisions from their inception. They were described as the 'armed arms of the state'. It was argued they should be seen as 'a relatively inert instrument, which is animated to respond mechanically to the commands of the state, itself in the service of the class interests of which it is the agent' (Brodeur 1991 [1984], 320). The police, in other words, represented the interests of dominant groups and implemented/maintained hierarchies that benefitted these groups. However, allowing the police to be autonomous also risked leaving them in charge of evaluating their own actions, including when violence was necessary. In this sense, the risk was the police would become a 'state within a state'. By escaping third-party control and accountability to political institutions in favour of maximizing their own interests, the police would be able to pursue their own ends by whatever means they saw as necessary (see Mann 1994).

The question of police interests has become an essential issue for political leaders and governmental officials into the present day, especially in situations of regime change: can the police be loyal to two successive—and opposed—political regimes? Is it possible to avoid a police purge when a dictatorship becomes a democracy? How should one build a police force after a long period of colonial domination? Should the main structures of the existing police forces be maintained, while only changing their missions and recruitment methods? These challenges have been encountered in many contexts including Northern Ireland, post-Apartheid South Africa, and in light of de-Baathification in Iraq.

In democratic regimes, this balancing act between the police as an instrument of the state and as an independent institution rests on the presupposition that in order to perform to a high standard, the police need a level of autonomy, which is usually referred to as 'police discretion' (Bittner 1979). This expression refers to the legal leeway that police are granted to provide law and order (Culp Davis 1975). In other words, it is claimed that police officers must have a certain degree of autonomy. Yet this autonomy is simultaneously a source of concern since it raises the question of its limits: how can the police be prevented from awarding themselves a level of permissiveness that is problematic (Napoli 2003)? As we will see, the professionalization of police forces has been one answer to this question. Yet, despite these efforts, police action is regularly criticized in terms of 'security for whom?' and 'at whose expense?', particularly with regard to certain social groups (defined, for example, by their economic status, their origin, the colour of their skin, their faith, and/or the political ideas they are promoting). In recent years, police violence against such groups has increasingly been discussed in places like the United States, the United Kingdom, Italy, France, India, and the Philippines. For example, Amnesty International estimated that over 7,000 people were killed in the Philippines by police and vigilante groups during a six-month period in 2016 (Amnesty International 2017). Nearly all of the victims were poor and lived in slums or informal settlements (Human Rights Watch 2017).

> These questions are introduced in **Sections 5.3.1.2** and **5.3.2.3**

6.2.1 Policing: a euphemism for political violence in social relations?

Police institutions assume a paradoxical position when it comes to political violence. On the one hand, they are often denounced as being systemically violent towards certain groups, as has been highlighted by the #BlackLivesMatter movement (Nelson 2000). On the other hand, some historical perspectives insist that the monopolization of violence by the state (via the police) has improved security for everyone by decreasing the levels of internal violence within states and by increasing public intolerance towards violence (Elias 1973 [1939]). In states where the division of labour has not led to a bureaucratized police force that is formally accountable to other governance structures, the question of the exercise of violence, and in whose interests the police operate, is even more pronounced.

The paradox of policing—public order via violence—becomes even clearer if we closely examine what it means to have a 'monopoly' on the legitimate use of violence and the processes that have concentrated this into the hands of the state and its agents. The process of monopolization does not simply consist in restricting the right to legitimately use force to the state and its agents. According to Norbert Elias (2017 [1989]), the process of monopolization has two distinct stages with major implications. First, law enforcement institutions with legal authorization to use force must initially compete with, and eventually replace, forms of traditional, local, and community-based violence that regulated social relations. The institutions of law and order thus gradually become preferable to cycles of revenge that shape traditional socio-political orders in ways that generate insecurity through their brutality and unpredictability. This is why one can say that the process of monopolizing violence brought order; there was a shift from a system shaped by violence committed among contending groups to one: the state (Simmel 1992 [1918]). Second, for a monopoly of violence to become socially embedded and accepted, it cannot solely benefit a small number of socio-economic groups. This monopoly must exist for the benefit of the wider socio-political community.

The recent case of the *gilets jaunes*, 'yellow vests', protests in France or the demonstrations against police brutality towards African-Americans in the United States are clear examples of reactions against police violence that is not perceived as legitimate. These movements demonstrate that even in democratic regimes the exercise of legitimate violence is a dynamic that is never really settled and reflects hierarchies that are present in the socio-political order. In spaces where divisions between the conduct of war and police regulation of crime is either more blurred or has never really taken place, the exercise of violence towards individuals and groups is usually done with greater brutality (Bat and Courtin 2012).

6.3 The professional organization of policing

Thus far, we have seen how the police and a particular understanding of policing emerged in Europe from the nineteenth century onwards. This was part of a process which gave law enforcement authorities a specific function in the management of public order. Interestingly, the term 'police' was originally used to designate both the order established to govern cities and the science of governing the state, including broader activities than those we associate with policing today. Our current understanding is the result of a long series of changes in governmental rationalities. From the eighteenth century onwards, the scope of police action began to diminish from this broader concern with governing public life as a whole 'to a subsidiary function of jurisdictional activity' (Napoli 2003, 68). The notion of 'administration' emerged to describe the public management of a socio-political order and provision of social goods (e.g., health, education, infrastructure) rather than police. Gradually, the notion of 'police' exclusively referred to the tasks of maintaining that order. This transition was accompanied by the increasing professionalization and specialization of police activity through its organization as a bureaucratic function of the broader 'administration' (Mann 1994).

This professionalization and specialization led police institutions to have their own division of labour. Across different countries, you can see how policing performs functions recognizable everywhere, but how policing is performed to provide security, for whom, by whom, and towards whom reflects national contexts. The question of the centralization of policing and its institutions is thus diverse. The management of the police, whether through ranks, procedures determining career advancement, performance review, or training systems, is different in states in which police forces are controlled by the central government (e.g., France, Denmark, Ireland, Senegal, and Japan) compared to contexts where it is largely decentralized and left to local or regional administrative levels (e.g., the United States, Brazil, Germany, and Belgium).

The antagonisms that run through societies at a given moment in their history are invariably reflected in the organization of police forces. This means, first, that the forms of specialization favoured in police institutions depend on state–society relationships and how political struggles are understood. For example, countries with a tradition of large-scale street protests tend to have forces specialized in maintaining public order, whereas political regimes with weak levels of social legitimacy will invest primarily in surveillance and intelligence police. Second, tensions in society, such as racism, inevitably find their way into policing institutions. The police largely mirror the hierarchies of the socio-political order in which they are situated.

> On security as a political claim and mobilization, see **Sections 2.3.2** and **2.4**

Professionalization is also a window to ask questions such as 'security how?' and 'by whom?'. We can find answers by examining how the relative autonomy of the police actually works in practice. Any police force possesses a clear chain of command, yet 'rank-and-file' police officers often benefit from much more autonomy than their commanding officers. This process, which Dominique Monjardet (1996) has termed 'hierarchical inversion', raises questions about the difficulty of reforming the police if any reforms can be easily ignored by the rank and file. To prevent excessive autonomy at the ground level, police forces have internal oversight bodies like 'internal affairs' divisions. Furthermore, training schools are often developed and centralized to ensure that police forces are organizations whose actions are guided by professional standards. Finally, police autonomy is also constrained by documentation, reports, and forms that provide an official record of the activities of officers. For example, Kevin Haggerty and Richard Ericson (2005) note that a Canadian police officer responding to a road accident is formally required to fill out a dozen documents to provide an account of the incident.

> The tension between reform and transformation is discussed in **Section 1.2.4**

Professionalization has also led to an increase in specialisms that reflect the range of tasks: patrolling, intelligence gathering, tactical units (i.e., SWAT), protest policing, anti-gang activities, counter-narcotics, cybercrime, and so on. These specialisms are also reflected in the specialized training courses that are in addition to basic training mentioned above. If it seems normal for police officers to be trained in academies or in schools, the situation was quite different in the nineteenth century and well into the twentieth, when the most highly regarded training was experience in the role.

It is now beyond the capacity of any officer to perform the full range of policing tasks undertaken by police forces. For example, protest policing is now a highly specialized role in countries such as Spain, Germany, and France. This has led to the further specialization of well-defined and distinct ranks and tasks—from front-line officers in charge of arrests to those using crowd-control weapons such as tear gas. A lack of training in protest policing can lead non-specialized units to face situations where they can rapidly lose control and escalate levels of violence, notably by employing dangerous forms of restraint and weapons (like stun grenades). As we will see, other dynamics such as the militarization of policing can lead to further issues.

Beyond the processes of bureaucratization and specialization, we need to ask if there is a common professional policing culture independent of specific contexts. In one of the first works on the subject, Jerome Skolnick (1966) attempted to sketch out the 'work personality' of the police. This referred to the characteristics shaping their relationships to the world, the public around them, their missions, and their 'clients'. Skolnick (1966) thus sought to identify the 'cognitive lenses' of the police. He came up with nine shared characteristics: a culture of suspicion; a sense of their own social isolation; a strong belief in the need for internal solidarity; the perception that they are not understood by the public; the imperative to exercise authority in their mission; an ambiguous relationship to morality; a narrow focus on police *force*; moral and political conservatism; and pressure to be efficient. This definition of a distinctive homogeneous professional culture among police officers has been one way that police work has been understood. It also explains rationales behind many attempts to reform police institutions to make them less alienated from the public.

Several studies have challenged this homogeneity hypothesis by highlighting the 'pluralism, or even . . . heterogeneity of the professional environment' of policing (Monjardet 1994, 396). This heterogeneity stems from continuous processes of specialization. The claim is that the differentiation of policing roles through specialization is so strong that there cannot be a homogenous culture within an institution in which multiple services, rationales, and modes of action compete with one another (Monjardet 1996). In other words, when we speak about policing, should we think of it in the plural and not in the singular? At the same time, heterogeneity does not mean that there are no shared standards used by police officers to judge or criticize the behaviour of their colleagues. As with any professional occupation, these professional norms are a set of rules collectively and implicitly recognized by a given social group. These rules depend largely on the kind of units, the tasks to be carried out, and the degree of autonomy of these services.

A common point, however, is that these rules are marked by a strong internal solidarity among police officers (i.e., the 'thin blue line'). Nevertheless, the professional norms that are structured by these rules play out differently in different parts of the police. For example, while norms may be embedded in official doctrines, they may be no more than informal 'rules of thumb' during patrols which are characterized by a high degree of autonomy. However, it is these norms that constitute the main source of control over police activity today, over and above any other mechanisms, whether internally or externally imposed. These are also the rules which are central to understanding the relations between police and a socio-political order, a mutually constitutive relation that is always hierarchical and which implies the potential recourse to (legitimate) violence.

6.4 Police and society

In liberal democracies, police institutions are usually caught between the requirements of public authorities and the expectations of the population. If a police institution concentrates on the guidelines set by public authorities, it will be considered insufficiently attentive to the population. This is, for example, how the intelligence gathering by the police in the Federal Republic of Germany during the 1960s was perceived or, more recently, the police management of the 'yellow vests' movement in France in 2018–19. If, on the contrary, a police force only concentrates on locally determined objectives, it is likely to be criticized for its potential clientelism. A clear example are US counties in which sheriffs are elected by the population.

What this tension highlights is the ongoing political struggle over the purpose of policing. Is the purpose to:

- protect the state?
- enforce the law?
- serve and protect the public by providing security (and if so, for whom, from what, and at whose expense)?

There have been many answers to these questions. Jerome Skolnick (1966) has argued that the police ensure the preservation of a socio-political order while the protection of the public is a secondary objective. For others, like Egon Bittner (1990), it is the power to use force that counts. This power has the effect of making the police the only institution in any state who can intervene in cases where there is 'something-that-ought-not-to-be-happening-and-about-which-someone-had-better-do-something-now' (Bittner 1990, 249). For Bittner (1990), law enforcement is secondary. It may justify how the police intervene, but it is not the primary reason why they do so. Why and how security is provided through police activity also differs whether we are examining community policing, which is based on the idea that police priorities must be agreed with local stakeholders (Skogan 2006), problem-orientated policing, which is based on situational logics of crime prevention (Goldstein 1990), or more repressive strategies dictated by broader political considerations (Crawford 2009).

Questions about the purposes of policing do not only concern democratic regimes. They also exist within authoritarian regimes, albeit in different forms. In authoritarian regimes, police autonomy is not as pronounced as in democratic regimes. The police exercise coercive violence with impunity at the exclusive service of ruling groups (e.g., by 'disappearing' political opponents). Similarly, states in which the monopoly of violence is systematically challenged see official law enforcement agencies co-exist with vigilante groups, some of which involve law enforcement officers (Fourchard 2018).

The differences between democratic and authoritarian regimes should not be assumed. Police in non-democratic regimes may exercise restraint in their actions (Brogden and Nijhar 2005). Likewise, democratic regimes may also have police forces that are extraordinarily violent. For example, in Brazil, 2020 marked the year with the highest number of people killed by the police since data started to be collected in

2013: 6,416 individuals were killed by on- or off-duty officers, an increase of almost 200 per cent from 2013 (Acayaba and Reis 2021). The state of Rio de Janeiro alone accounted for 1,245 victims, a figure higher than the total number of people killed (1,127) by the police in the entire United States that year (Police Violence Report 2021). These killings are reflective of structural violence and racialized hierarchies in the country that oppress particular communities. Close to 80 per cent of the victims in Brazil were of Afro-descent, while this population accounts for only 56 per cent of the total population (Acayaba and Reis 2021). This is similar to the United States. In 2021, 28 per cent of the people killed by the police were identified as Black, while representing 13 per cent of the total US population (Police Violence Report 2021).

> Structural violence is discussed in **Section 4.2.1**; on racialized hierarchies, see **Chapters 9 and 11**

6.4.1 Reforming police institutions and denouncing illegitimate police practices

If the police begin to lose their legitimacy in the eyes of those who they claim to serve and protect, what measures can be taken to reform them? How can this specific form of security mobilization can be challenged and resisted? Lawrence Sherman (1978) has shown that reforms of police institutions involve a set of steps:

> Challenging and resisting security is discussed in **Section 3.4**

- illegal practices committed collectively by officers are successfully denounced;
- the public revelation of these practices provokes a scandal;
- under political pressure, official commissions are organized to investigate these practices, and in some instances the police even contribute to these proceedings;
- conclusions from the investigations pave the way for police reforms through new legislation and/or changes to policing practices.

Numerous examples have been used to support Sherman's argument. For example, the Knapp Commission in the United States, launched in 1970 by the mayor of New York City, investigated the widespread culture of corruption in the city's police force. In the United Kingdom, the McPherson Commission, established after the racially motivated murder of Stephen Lawrence in 1993, exposed the multiple ways that the police resisted thoroughly investigating the murder and concluded that the Greater London Police was institutionally racist.

It would not be unfair to say that police forces only appear to be interested in reform in the wake of scandals. Thus, we can legitimately wonder if scandals actually transform policing practices and the social norms that guide police actions. Or, at best, do they simply catalyse changes at the margins? Often the public uproar and social movements which follow such scandals express the need to collectively re-examine the professional norms at work within police services that have allowed—or at least did not prevent—illegal or illegitimate actions by police officers such as the unnecessary use of (lethal) violence, institutionalized racism, and corruption. What is worth noting here is that public uproar happens only if there has already been a change in social relations with police institutions. In other words, illegal or illegitimate actions from some police officers will only trigger changes in an already changing socio-political order;

they are not a source of change. This also means that reform can fail or at least fall well behind the demands of the public and politicians.

For example, Dame Cressida Dick was appointed Commissioner of the Metropolitan Police Service (the Met) in London in 2017. As a women and openly gay senior officer who was also strongly supported by the rank and file, it was thought she would be able to push through reforms required in the wake of several scandals. These included a pattern of sexual relationships initiated by undercover officers with potential suspects, significant corruption investigations, the murder of Sarah Everard by a serving member of the force, and repeated examples of misconduct that indicated misogyny, racism, homophobia, and discrimination within the Met. She was forced to resign when the Mayor of London, Sadiq Khan, publicly announced he was not satisfied with the pace or extent of reform, as new scandals continued to emerge.

Governments regularly claim that police institutions are highly regulated through the existence of internal affairs divisions, external reviews, judicial controls, the media, and public oversight. More recently, surveillance technologies like body and vehicle cameras have been introduced to improve the monitoring of street-level activity by police forces. For example, in Brazil, after only two months of deploying cameras, São Paulo registered a 40 per cent drop in lethal incidents (Folha de São Paulo 2021). While not a panacea, there are specific ways in which surveillance and design can potentially underpin the rule of law.

> **Chapters 15 and 16** analyse surveillance and design in relation to security

However, the persistence of illegitimate practices by police raises numerous questions about the effectiveness of these oversight measures. Some point to the tendency to individualize bad behaviours without considering the organizational dimensions that make them possible. Others emphasize the fact that the very nature of policing is likely to excuse, or even encourage, illegitimate practices against marginalized communities. This critique has notably taken the form of social movements, with some calling for the defunding or even abolition of the police. In this case, as Charmaine Chua (2020, 130) has argued, the call for abolition is also a call for dismantling 'racism, patriarchy, homophobia, capitalism, and other structures of domination'. Her point is that we cannot distinguish police actions from the evolution of the socio-political orders in our worlds. Even from less maximalist positions, we are still left with the questions of whether changes to policing can lead to transformations in a socio-political order. More specifically, what are the conditions that would make the public and governments unwilling to condone the continuation of structural police misconduct against the specific social groups mentioned above?

6.5 The police in the face of changes in crime and war

Policing continues to evolve in light of new demands and challenges. How security is mobilized through policing is central to recent debates on its increasing similarity to warfighting. Some scholars argue that policing tactics (e.g., hit-and-run raids), rationales (e.g., the disruption of criminal networks), and technologies (e.g., the use of tanks, drones, and cyber-surveillance) are similar to contemporary counterinsurgency.

> **Chapter 8** covers counterinsurgency

For many, this is seen as a distressing development, reflecting a transformation in the role of policing (particularly where it has rested, even rhetorically, on notions having the consent of the population) as well as an escalation in the use of violence by the state and the risk of disproportionate application against some social segments of the population. However, the debate remains open as to the extent of these transformations and their consequences. In this final section, we will explore two connected areas from which these issues are discussed: the evolution of the fight against transnational organized crime and the perceptions of an increase of violence in policing social disorder.

6.5.1 Policing and transnational crime

From the 1990s onwards, with the acceleration of globalization, some argued that the structure of organized crime had become transnational (Williams 1994). This diagnosis raised calls for changes in policing. It was claimed that borders between nation-states were becoming less and less relevant for policing. This was because criminal organizations were understood to be engaging in activities across several countries, if not continents, and diversifying their operations to encompass both traditional pursuits (e.g., drug trafficking, car thefts, extortion, human trafficking) and new opportunities like terrorism, online fraud, illegal arms, weapons of mass destruction, and eco-crimes (e.g., illegally dumping contaminated materials across state borders). Many police forces, especially those services involved in criminal investigations, were thus reorganized, with new forms of international cooperation put in place to ensure information sharing and joint investigations. For example, Europol and Interpol have become prominent in managing a global policing network (Bigo 1996).

However, the impact of the globalization of criminal networks and police institutions has been a source of debate. Some have contested the novelty, and even the extent, of the transformations in organized crime, showing that some criminal networks such as the Mafia have always been transnational (see Varese 2011). Even if claims are overblown about the effects of the diversified portfolios of criminal organizations (Abrahamsen and Williams 2009), the idea that new policing methods and laws are required in response is entrenched. Nevertheless, transnational crime does not fundamentally challenge the division of labour established in the long nineteenth century regarding the roles of the police and the roles of the military (see Hufnagel and Moiseienko 2022). Crime remains conceived of as an internal matter to be managed by the police and criminal organizations are seen as having territories *within* states. What is potentially changing are the tactics and aesthetic adopted by police forces.

6.5.2 The militarization of the police?

Militarism is discussed in **Box 7.1**

There is a growing concern that policing is becoming increasingly militarized. During the long nineteenth century, the growing difference in military and police functions alongside the emergence of differentiated legal frameworks dedicated to crime and war reflected distinctions that began to be made between criminal and warlike forms of violence (Linhardt and Moreau de Bellaing 2013). This process was first centred on western Europe and North America, while many other spaces, particularly colonized territories, still experienced military and police institutions whose roles were blurred (Blanchard et al. 2017). More recently, three different developments suggest that this distinction born from the European/North American experience may not be as relevant today (Lemieux and Dupont 2005).

The first development, popularized in TV shows and films, concerns the evolution of the weapons, equipment, and tactics deployed by some police forces. A familiar example is Special Weapons And Tactics (SWAT) units in the United States (Kraska 2001). The first SWAT team was formed in Los Angeles in 1968 to counter the Black Panther Party and the concern that its doctrine of (armed) self-defence made it impervious to existing forms of policing. SWAT teams gradually developed into emergency intervention units, covering various forms of crime; these interventions involve heavily armed officers, equipped with hi-tech kit and military-grade weapons, who adopt military tactics to resolve situations where it is believed that there is the risk of armed resistance to arrest. Beyond the development of these specific units, some of which emerged in Europe in reaction to the terror attacks of the 1970s, there is a broader trend in the use of military-grade equipment, from weapons to armoured vehicles, for policing purposes. In the United States, researchers have established a strong correlation between a transfer of equipment worth 4.3 billion USD from the US military to law enforcement agencies (without charge on the condition that law enforcement would take over maintenance contracts) and fatalities during a period spanning 1997 to 2014 (Delehanty et al. 2017). As noted earlier, these fatalities are disproportionately found within the targeted social groups already mentioned, paving the way for an increasingly powerful critique of structural violence used to maintain the socio-political order.

Militarization also affects some of the core functions of the police, such as policing demonstrations. Police forces are borrowing a number of characteristics from the military, including the development of highly disciplined units that are isolated from others (Bruneteaux 1996). In France and Spain, the CRS (Compagnies Républicaines de Sécurité), the Gendarmerie mobile, and the UIP (Unidades de Intervención Policial) are cases in point. These units, highly recognizable by their protective equipment designed for riots, are specifically trained to face demonstrators and to make use of sub-lethal weapons (e.g., rubber-bullet guns, disruption grenades, tear gas) for the purposes of crowd control. Their development is also connected to stricter legislation that has increased penalties for offences and crimes committed during demonstrations.

Finally, the chain of command, whether in connection to protest policing or otherwise, has also been influenced by militarization, abandoning any pretence of policing by consent. Policing by consent refers to interconnections and relations between the police and society based on notions of trust and mutually vulnerability. This disconnect can, subsequently, lead to increasing levels of conflict and violence between police and the public (Waddington et al. 2009). In regard to demonstrations, for example, increasingly police no longer negotiate with organizers of demonstrations about the marching route that will be taken, where the demonstration will culminate, or the internal mechanisms by which organizers will control and police themselves. This lack of coordination, or even communication, can lead to an increase in violence and brutality.

6.6 Conclusion

> The elements of critique are detailed in **Section 1.2**

One of the tasks of critical perspectives is to denaturalize what appears to be self-evident in our daily lives. As we have seen, policing originated in a specific historical context and reflects larger social processes like specialization that have come with the development of the state as a governing unit. Taking into consideration this history enables us to revisit central political questions about what security does by looking at police institutions, their social functions, their missions, and their evolution.

As we have seen, policing is a contingent mobilization of security through specific kinds of units such as patrols and SWAT teams. It also involves different actors like elected local sheriffs and internal affairs units. It also undertakes different functions from settling disputes to policing protests. These multiple functions and mobilizations of security have evolved across time, spaces, and political configurations. They are strongly linked to how statehood is structured across specific socio-political orders and political regimes. The aim of this chapter was to help you to ask questions about how political violence is enacted by an institution with a (legitimate) monopoly on such violence. Specialization and professionalization, or the lack thereof, are two central processes that open up critical questions about policing, including what are the social processes that make it possible for violence to be applied writ large and disproportionately against specific social groups.

Questions for further discussion

1. The police are often the visible face of security in our everyday lives. When do you come into contact with the police? What do they actually do? Starting from your everyday experiences, reflect on the purposes of the police and how different people may see security differently through these interactions.

2. Can there be a police force without autonomy for its officers? How would different levels of autonomy affect everyday forms of interactions with the police?

3. Are the police an inherently violent institution? Reflect on the different specialisms and professionalization processes. Do they affect the enactment of political violence by the police? If so, how?

4. Are police institutions professional organizations like any other? As a professional organization, what makes the police a difficult organization to reform, or transform?

5. Are there still differences between the police and the military? Why and in which contexts might these differences matter?

To explore this theme further

SOUTHLAND. 2009–13. John Wells Production/Warner Bros. Production.
> In this fictional television series, members of the Los Angeles Police Department (LAPD) across different divisions—detective investigation, patrol, and so on—are followed during their daily activities. The series was designed to bring viewers closer to the challenges of policing in a very detailed way that avoids easy answers.

Line of Duty. 2012–. BBC/World Productions.
> This TV drama features the work of investigators from an internal affairs department in the UK. Although very fictionalized, the series does address the internal regulation of policing.

Mindhunter. 2017–19. Netflix Production.
> *Mindhunter* tells the story of the gradual incorporation of behavioural sciences within the FBI in its fight against crime, particularly in the hunt for what would later be called serial killers. This series is very well documented and directly engages with the issues of specialization and professionalization discussed in this chapter.

VAN MAANEN, JOHN. 1978. 'The asshole'. In *Policing: A view from the streets*, edited by PETER K. MANNING and JOHN VAN MAANEN. New York: Random House.
> This is an influential chapter on the relations between the professional activity of policing and the formation of policing judgements at the street level. Although dated, it remains a fascinating depiction for those wanting to understand police action.

LEHANE, DENNIS. 2008. *The given day*. New York: William Morrow and Company.
> Set in the early twentieth century, Dennis Lehane's novel explores the internal divisions in the Boston police force between patrol officers who are in the process of unionizing, the upper echelons of the police force, and local political elites. The book dramatizes the September 1919 police strike, which resulted in violence and deaths, and explores how the striking officers were accused of being deserters and Bolshevik agents.

References

ABRAHAMSEN, RITA and MICHAEL C. WILLIAMS. 2009. 'Security beyond the state: Global security assemblages in international politics'. *International Political Sociology* 3(1), 1–17.

ACAYABA, CÍNTIA and THIAGO REIS. 2021. 'N° de mortos pela polícia em 2020 no Brasil bate recorde; 50 cidades concentram mais da metade dos óbitos, revala Anuário'. *Globo.com*, 15 July. https://g1.globo.com/sp/sao-paulo/noticia/2021/07/15/no-de-mortos-pela-policia-em-2020-no-brasil-bate-recorde-50-cidades-concentram-mais-da-metade-dos-obitos-revela-anuario.ghtml (last accessed 26 February 2022).

Amnesty International. 2017. 'Philippines: The police's murderous war on the poor'. Amnesty.org, 31 January. www.amnesty.org/en/latest/news/2017/01/philippines-the-police-murderous-war-on-the-poor (last accessed 26 May 2022).

BAT, JEAN-PIERRE and NICOLAS COURTIN. Eds. 2012. *Maintenir l'ordre colonial. Afrique et Madagascar, XIXe–XXe siècles*. Rennes: Presses Universitaires de Rennes.

BAYLEY, DAVID. 1990. *Patterns of policing*. New Brunswick, NJ: Rutgers University Press.

BAYLEY, DAVID and CLIFFORD D. SHEARING. 2001. *The new structure of policing*. Washington, DC: US Department of Justice.

BIGO, DIDIER. 1996. *Police en réseaux*. Paris: Presses de Sciences Po.
BITTNER, EGON. 1979. *The functions of police in modern society*. Cambridge: Oelgeschlager, Gunn and Hain.
BITTNER, EGON. 1990. *Aspects of police work*. Boston, MA: Northeastern University Press.
BLANCHARD, EMMANUEL, MARIEKE BLOEMBERGEN, and AMANDINE LAURO. Eds. 2017. *Policing in colonial empires: Cases, connections, boundaries (ca. 1850–1970)*. Bern: Peter Lang.
BRODEUR, JEAN-PAUL. 1991 [1984]. 'Police: mythes et réalités'. *Les Cahiers de la Sécurité Intérieure* 6, 307–337.
BROGDEN, MIKE and PREETI NIJHAR. 2005. *Community policing: National and international models and approaches*. Portland, OR: Willan.
BRUNETEAUX, PATRICK. 1996. *Maintenir l'ordre*. Paris: Presses de Sciences Po.
CHUA, CHARMAINE. 2020. 'Abolition is a constant struggle: Five lessons from Minneapolis'. *Theory & Event* 23(5), 127–142.
COESS (Confederation of European Security Services). 2019. *2016–2017 European Monitoring Statistics from Monitoring and Alarm Receiving Centres*. www.coess.org/download.php?down=Li9kb2N1bWVudHMvZmYtZXVyb3BlYW4tbW9uaXRvcmluZy1zdGF0aXN0aWNzLTIwMTYtMjAxNy1maW5hbC5wZGY (last accessed 3 March 2022).
CRAWFORD, ADAM. 2009. *Crime prevention policies in comparative perspective*. London: Routledge.
CULP DAVIS, KENNETH. 1975. *Police discretion*. St. Paul, MN: West Pub. Co.
DELEHANTY, CASEY, JACK MEWHIRTER, RYAN WELCH, and JASON WILKS. 2017. 'Militarization and police violence: The case of the 1033 program'. *Research and Politics* 4(2), 1–7.
DE MAILLARD, JACQUES. 2017. *Polices comparées*. Paris: Montchrestien.
DURKHEIM, ÉMILE. 2007 [1893]. *De la division du travail social*. Paris: PUF Quadrige.
ELIAS, NORBERT. 1973 [1939]. *La civilisation des mœurs*. Paris: Press Pocket.
ELIAS, NORBERT. 1975 [1939]. *La dynamique de l'Occident*. Paris: Press Pocket.
ELIAS, NORBERT. 2017 [1989]. *Les Allemands. Lutte de pouvoir et développement de l'habitus aux XIXe et XXe siècles*. Paris: Seuil.
FOLHA DE SÃO PAULO. 2021. 'No 2° mês de câmeras "grava tudo", SP registra quera de 40 per cent na letalidade policial'. *Folha de São Paulo*, 6 August. www1.folha.uol.com.br/cotidiano/2021/08/no-2o-mes-de-cameras-grava-tudo-sp-registra-queda-de-40-na-letalidade-policial.shtml (last accessed 26 February 2022).
FOURCHARD, LAURENT. 2018. 'État de littérature. Le vigilantisme contemporain. Violence et légitimité d'une activité policière bon marché'. *Critique Internationale* 78, 169–186.
GOLDSTEIN, HERMAN. 1990. *Problem-oriented policing*. New York: McGraw-Hill.
HAGGERTY, KEVIN and RICHARD ERICSON. 2005. 'Les technostructures militaires du maintien de l'ordre'. In *La militarisation des appareils policiers*, edited by FRÉDÉRIC LEMIEUX and BENOÎT DUPONT. Saint-Nicolas: Presses de l'université de Laval.
HUFNAGEL, SASKIA and ANTON MOISEIENKO. Eds. 2022. *Policing transnational crime: Law enforcement of criminal flows*. London: Routledge.
HUMAN RIGHTS WATCH. 2017. '"License to kill": Philippine police killings in Duterte's "war on drugs"'. HWR.org, 2 March. www.hrw.org/report/2017/03/02/license-kill/philippine-police-killings-dutertes-war-drugs (last accessed 26 May 2022).

JOHNSTON, LES. 2007. 'Transnational security governance'. In *Democracy, society and the governance of security*, edited by JENNIFER WOOD and BENOÎT DUPONT. Cambridge: Cambridge University Press.

JONES, TREVOR and TIM NEWBURN. Eds. 2006. *Plural policing: A comparative perspective*. London: Routledge.

KRASKA, PETER B. 2001. *Militarizing the American criminal justice system: The changing roles of the armed forces and the police*. Boston, MA: Northeastern University Press.

LEMIEUX, FRÉDÉRIC and BENOÎT DUPONT. Eds. 2005. *La militarisation des appareils policiers*. Saint-Nicolas: Presses de l'université de Laval.

LINHARDT, DOMINIQUE and CÉDRIC MOREAU DE BELLAING. 2013. 'Ni guerre, ni paix: Dislocations de l'ordre politique et décantonnements de la guerre'. *Politix* 104, 7–23.

MANN, PATRICE. 1994. 'Pouvoir politique et maintien de l'ordre. Portée et limites d'un débat'. *Revue française de sociologie* 35(3), 435–455.

MONJARDET, DOMINIQUE. 1994. 'La culture professionnelle des policiers'. *Revue française de sociologie* 35(3), 393–411.

MONJARDET, DOMINIQUE. 1996. *Ce que fait la police. Sociologie de la force publique*. Paris: La Découverte.

NAPOLI, PAOLO. 2003. *La naissance de la police moderne. Pouvoir, normes, société*. Paris: La Découverte.

NELSON, JILL. Ed. 2000. *Police brutality: An anthology*. New York: W.W. Norton & Co.

Police Violence Report. 2021. https://policeviolencereport.org (last accessed 26 February 2022).

SHERMAN LAWRENCE W. 1978. *Scandal and reform: Controlling police corruption*. Berkeley, CA: University of California Press.

SIMMEL, GEORG. 1992 [1918]. *Le conflit*. Paris: Circé.

SKOGAN, WESLEY G. 2006. 'The promise of community policing'. In *Police innovation: Contrasting perspectives*, edited by DAVID WEISBURD and ANTHONY BRAGA. Cambridge: Cambridge University Press.

SKOLNICK, JEROME H. 1966. *Justice without trial: Law enforcement in democratic society*. New York: Wiley.

VARESE, FEDERICO. 2011. *Mafias on the move: How organized crimes conquer new territories*. Princeton, NJ: Princeton University Press.

WADDINGTON, DAVID, FABIEN JOBARD, and MIKE KING. Eds. 2009. *Rioting in the UK and France: A comparative analysis*. London: Routledge.

WILLIAMS, ALAN. 1979. *The police of Paris, 1718–1789*. Baton Rouge, LA: Louisiana State University Press.

WILLIAMS, PHIL. 1994. 'Transnational criminal organisations and international security'. *Survival* 36(1), 96–113.

7

War and socio-political orders

Victoria M. Basham

7.1	Introduction	104
7.2	Where is war?	105
7.3	How is war possible?	109
7.4	Who or what does war secure?	112
7.5	Conclusion: should we continue to wage and prepare for war?	115

READER'S GUIDE

In this chapter, we explore the relationship between war and society using three key questions: where is war, how is war possible, and what (or who) does war secure? Asking these questions enables a deeper understanding of the choices that societies make about why, when, and where to fight and prepare for war, how the choices of actors and their actions make war possible, and the benefits and costs to people's security that wars can bring about. Such questions can help us to evaluate whether we should continue to prepare and wage war, and for what purposes.

7.1 Introduction

> Illustrative case studies on the topics explored in this chapter are available on the online resources to help take your understanding of war and socio-political orders further: http://www.oup.com/he/Grayson-Guillaume1e.

War has undoubtedly played a significant role in human history. This is perhaps why we all intuitively have some sense of what war is. Some thinkers have even suggested that if you were to stop anyone, anywhere, and ask them what war is, they would be able to confidently describe war to you (Nordstrom 1998). Most studies argue that fighting and violence define war (Öberg 2019). However, reducing war to fighting means we risk overlooking practices and experiences central to how wars come about and are conducted. For example, during the 2001–21 war in Afghanistan, coalition military leaders prioritized 'winning the hearts and minds' of Afghan people through non-violent means, alongside fighting.

The tendency to define war as fighting has also led humanity to collectively condemn and attempt to curtail wars horrors through international laws and regulatory practices. Representations of fighting in war, both real and imagined, also saturate global popular culture, making war a source of entertainment (Stahl 2010). Whole libraries of books, museums, and many films and television shows tell stories about war that are primarily told from the perspective of fighting soldiers (Nordstrom 1998). This focus on those who fight wars has given rise to a tendency to see war as something that has always played, and therefore always will play, a fundamental role in human existence; to take it for granted. War's prevalence across time and space can lead us to think that we live in a perpetually violent world. Fascination with soldiers, violence, and aggression may lead us to assume that war is the outcome of our brutish and competitive 'human nature'. Even among those who see war as a subversion of our usually peaceful human nature—as something that arises over competition for resources—war is often assumed to be an unstoppable force.

See **Sections 1.2–3** on the importance of critique

When we make such assumptions about war, it perhaps becomes easier to see why states around the world see preparing for war and waging it as vital to their security. Strong warfighting forces, it is assumed, will make states and their populations more secure (Malešević 2010). However, what if we were to question this 'common consciousness' (Vitalis 2015, 5) around why we fight wars and adopt a perspective critical of war? What if we asked why states and societies constantly prepare for war and dedicate often considerable resources to it? What if, instead of asking what war is, we asked how war has come to play such an important role in our security, and what it does to our societies?

To these ends, we ask three key questions in this chapter. First, we will consider *where* we commonly come to understand war as being located to explore how this might shape our understanding of war as something that provides security. Second, we will think about which actors and practices make it possible to wage war in the first place. How can actors and their actions normalize war and preparing for it? Finally, we will ask what, or who, war actually secures. Depending on the answers, should war play such a significant role in global politics as a result? We concluded by suggesting that these questions highlight that war is the outcome of social and political choices. This means that making other choices—ones that could provide people with greater security—is possible.

These questions are introduced in **Sections 5.2.1.1–3** and **5.3.2.1–3**

On security as a political claim and mobilization, see **Sections 2.3.2 and 2.4**

7.2 Where is war?

Many people around the world have an especially 'intimate' and direct relationship with war (Parashar 2013), but we all live in societies shaped in one way or another by war's historical, legal, and institutional legacies, by ongoing political decisions about military necessity (Brighton 2019), and/or by the broader influence of the military and war on

Box 7.1 discusses militarism

societies, or what is often depicted as militarism. However, when we begin to look more closely at where war *is*—that is, where war can be seen and where our ideas about war come from—we may begin to think differently about why we wage and prepare for war.

Let me begin with an example. Close to where I live there is a railway line that is surrounded by barbed wire to stop people from getting onto the tracks, injuring themselves and other people, or damaging the railway. Barbed wire is something that the managers of the railway lines have used to secure property and people, just as politicians and militaries have used war to secure territory and people. Barbed wire is part of my local built environment and perhaps is where you live too. However, barbed wire is also a globetrotting technology of war.

The relations between design and security are discussed in Chapter 16

Barbed wire, first patented in the United States in 1874 by a farmer called Joseph Glidden, was initially designed to contain livestock. As farmers began to enclose their farms with barbed wire, violent disputes broke out between them. Cattle herders saw previous routes to grazing land and markets blocked by barbed-wire fences. Indigenous Americans were especially affected: barbed wire restricted their access to land and resources.

In 1901, barbed wire became widely used by British forces during the Anglo-Boer war both defensively, to secure railway lines as the main means of communication,

> ### BOX 7.1 MILITARIZATION
>
> The concept of militarization is often used by scholars who are interested in how war, and preparing for war, shapes societies. Enloe (2016, 18) argues that although it can take generations for a socio-political order to become 'militarized', militarization has taken hold once civilians come to see 'military solutions as particularly effective' to the problems that socio-political order faces, for instance policing issues (see Chapter 6). Enloe (2016, 18) argues that in socio-political orders that have come to see the 'world as a dangerous place', military force becomes a logical response to that danger. Exploring militarization means thinking about how people come to believe in such dangers and solutions, and how civilian life can become arranged in ways that support or normalize military objectives and ideas (Woodward 2005).
>
> In the context of a large-scale conflict like the Second World War, it is easy to understand how socio-political orders came to see the world as dangerous and that society should play a part in the 'war effort'. In the United Kingdom, for example, civilians were encouraged to 'make do' with and mend old clothes so that garment factories could be requisitioned to produce weapons. Supporting the war effort by 'making do' became a social virtue, though, not just a necessity of war. Some contemporary environmental campaigners have suggested we need to use this same solution born out of military need to reduce waste and over-consumption.
>
> It is important to note that the term 'militarization' has been criticized because it implies a unidirectional process where the military (or state) does the 'izing' to socio-political orders (Cowen in Bernazzoli and Flint 2009). Socio-political orders are not simply encroached upon by militaries, though. Instead, socio-political orders have come to organize *themselves* in ways that are conducive to preparing for and waging war (Geyer 1989; Howell 2018). It is therefore interesting to explore how socio-political orders have done this, and when and where military and civilian values align and diverge.

and offensively, to trap and capture Boer commandos. During these operations, large numbers of families were also trapped by barbed wire. Displaced from their homes, many were interred in concentration camps around South Africa, also surrounded by barbed wire, where many died from disease due to insanitary conditions and overcrowding. During the First World War, barbed wire was also used to trap enemies as well as to defend trenches. In the Second World War, barbed wire became a symbol of the Holocaust through its use at death camps where mass exterminations occurred.

When viewed through its military uses, something as mundane and ubiquitous as barbed wire makes war visible, giving expression to different forms of political violence. In the Anglo-Boer War, as in many wars since, barbed wire reconfigured an entire landscape. In doing so, it created displaced civilians and made them insecure. In concentration camps, barbed wire was not merely a material tool physically delimiting and enforcing specific hierarchies by allowing governments to control unarmed masses of civilians deemed hostile or a political threat (Netz 2004). Barbed wire is not just tool or an object; it is an infrastructure. Its use in war, and even beyond the battlefield, has profoundly reconfigured social and political relations (Woodward 2005). To answer the question 'where is war?', we therefore need to look at everyday life.

> What camps are and what they do is discussed in **Chapter 20**

> **Chapter 4** explores political violence and its different forms

> Infrastructure as an enabler is discussed in **Section 3.3**

7.2.1 Locating war and what counts as war

Where we think war happens can also shape what counts as war and how we make sense of it. Tarak Barkawi (2016, 199) argues that when scholars label something 'war', what they are usually describing are conflicts 'fought between nation-states, fought between regular armed forces'. The concept of war is therefore based largely on the experiences of countries in the global north and Eurocentric ideas of what constitutes 'proper' war. In contrast, conflicts primarily involving actors from, and located in, the global south are usually labelled differently. These are variously 'small Wars, insurgencies, emergencies, interventions, uprisings, police actions, or something other than war proper' (Barkawi 2016, 199).

Wars in South Asia, for example, are often labelled 'communal conflicts' and wars in Africa as 'ethnic conflicts' (Mamdani 2003, 133). Characterizing war in these terms—even ones that have occurred within Europe as with 'ethnic conflict' in the Yugoslav wars of the 1990s—can shape how we understand and react to them. These 'less-than-wars' can come to be seen simplistically as the inevitable outcome of 'ancient hatred' and as intractable problems (Campbell 1998). This can divert our attention from the more concrete economic, social, and political hierarchies within a political order that may have facilitated wars, making it harder for us to understand them (Baker 2018). It can also conceal the significant role that war has played in anti-colonial struggles and the capacity of war to generate, as well as destroy, social and political communities.

> **Chapter 8** discusses asymmetric conflicts

7.2.2 Sites of perpetual war?

How we come to see a country or a region's relationship with war also matters. As Nivi Manchanda (2020, 5) demonstrates, Afghanistan—its people and its culture past, present, and future—has come to be imagined in ways that have made it seem a like place of perpetual war, making it possible, or even common-sensical, to invade and bomb it. Afghanistan has become a place where war *is*. Manchanda (2020) shows, for example, how a selective reading of Afghanistan's history has led it to be constructed through the *idea* of the 'Graveyard of Empires'. Here, Afghanistan is depicted as a land of unassailable terrain and rugged warriors desensitized to hardship who are always ready for combat. As Manchanda (2020) points out, however, the British ostensibly won at least two of the three Anglo-Afghan wars, so the idea that Afghanistan is unconquerable, or that its warriors are undefeatable, is not borne out by the evidence. This myth nonetheless persists and characterizes Afghanistan as a warring and chaotic place, rendering it, as Manchanda (2020) argues, more legitimate to invade and bomb Afghanistan to secure other populations at the cost of Afghans. Similarly, Sherene Razack's (2004) analysis of the shooting of two unarmed Somalis, and the torture and killing of a sixteen-year-old Somali boy by Canadian peacekeepers in 1993, illustrates how Somalia was constructed as a place of chaos and disorder. This idea of Somalia was then used to explain away the violent behaviour of 'traumatized peacekeepers' subjected to the inherent violence of Somalia.

7.2.3 Securing civilization through war

Where we see war from is also important to how and where we think wars *should* be waged. Kyle Grayson's (2016) analysis of drones and targeted killing questions how it is that this mode of counterinsurgency and policing has made specific people, places, and things 'targetable' in order to ensure other people are secure. This idea, that some people in some parts of the world necessarily experience war's violence for other people's security, has a lengthy history. In 1899, for example, the British refused to sign the part of the Hague Declaration that explicitly prohibited the use of expanding bullets (known as 'dum-dums'). This was on the grounds that these weapons were necessary to use against African and Asian tribes as wars against them were different from 'civilized war'. Sir John Charles Ardagh, the British delegate to the conference on the Declaration, argued:

> in civilized war a soldier penetrated by a small projectile is wounded, withdraws to the ambulance, and does not advance any further. It is very different with a savage. Even though pierced two or three times, he does not cease to march forward, does not call upon the hospital attendants, but continues on, and before anyone has time to explain to him that he is flagrantly violating the decision of the Hague Conference, he cuts off your head. (Quoted in Mégret 2006, 293)

Scholars have also argued that there has been significant resistance, both moral and political, to seeing brutality in war as something that comes from *within* European politics and culture.

To take the example of the Holocaust, it is often explained as the outcome of an ahistorical 'evil' (Mamdani 2003). Zygmunt Bauman (1989) instead argues that a more credible interpretation of the Holocaust is as an organizational achievement of a bureaucratic society in which practices prized as 'civilized' were used to facilitate mass murder. Bauman points to how the Holocaust heavily relied on modern technologies and sensibilities such as the factory system, where instead of producing goods from animals and crops, in death camps like Auschwitz humans were the raw materials, and the end product was death. Bauman (1989, 18) points to how technological innovations such as the railroads simply shipped other forms of 'cargo'—human cargo—and argues that the 'truth is that every ingredient of the Holocaust—all those many things that rendered it possible were normal' within European cultures and societies. Bauman (1989, 105; author's emphasis) also argues that rather than being a culture of civility and peace, modern European culture is one of dehumanization, wherein soldiers are 'told to shoot *targets* which *fall* when they are *hit*' and company employees are 'encouraged to *destroy* competition', making it 'difficult to perceive and remember the humans' behind these technical terms. The Holocaust, when thought about this way, is not the outcome of an evil that pervades human nature but of arrangements within a socio-political order that were chosen and used for violence.

We can understand war similarly as an outcome of socio-political orders, including how they are governed. For example, war has been shaped by the development of *institutions* such as International Humanitarian Law or the 1948 Convention on the Prevention and Punishment of the Crime of Genocide. International laws and conventions provide guidance on the necessary conditions for wars to be legitimate, as well as measures that if undertaken are to be considered sufficient to divest perpetrators of violence from legal liability for outcomes, including the killing of non-combatants. War is thus embedded in legal regimes (as noted earlier) and institutional arrangements such as the International Criminal Court.

> On institutions as enablers, see **Section 3.3**

Thus, when we ask where war *is*, we can perhaps better understand how what we have come to know about war depends on how we see war in our own lives, on which conflicts are even defined as war, and on how some parts of the world come to be defined as 'warlike' and especially violent and others more peaceful. If some parts of the world are deemed to be places where war is more likely or even inevitable, this can lead us to overlook why wars have arisen there in the first place. It may mean that some states legitimize war and preparing for war as necessary for their security in the face of the insecurity that they assume that other states pose. It may lead us to think that we have no choice but to make people in other societies less secure by waging war there because we come to believe it is necessary to our own security.

7.3 How is war possible?

Shaw (2005, 40–41) has argued that most theories of war are defective because they have not considered 'what people actually do in war'. One of the most obvious roles that people play in war and preparing for war is not as soldiers or combatants but as a range of actors who engage in practices that make war possible. For example, Carol Cohn's (1987) seminal study of male defence intellectuals explored how, through gendered daily practices, they came to see nuclear weapons as rational, tough, and masculine. This led them to normalize, and prioritize, stockpiling and potentially using nuclear weapons for maintaining global security during the Cold War. Looking more closely at what people actually do in war and when preparing for war highlights how war is made possible by actors and their actions.

7.3.1 Gender, racialization, and war

Killing and injuring others, which is the main business of soldiering, is often normalized through the idea that war is fought on behalf of one's country or some other 'big cause'. Motivating people to fight and possibly die for a cause is not necessarily straightforward. Contrary to what many people believe, studies have shown that engaging in violence is very difficult (Collins 2008). Killing, after all, is something that people are raised to abhor and that is outlawed across the globe. Militaries and militia groups must therefore invest considerable resources—in the form of training (Grossman 1996) and other forms of socialization (Bourke 1999)—to convince otherwise law-abiding people that they should fight. This means it is important to pay attention to cultural, racialized, and gendered explanations for why certain people are expected to wage war and prepare for it, and in what ways.

> These different dimensions are discussed in **Chapters 9, 10, and 11**

Militaries across the world are overwhelmingly populated by men. Men have more often joined or been conscripted into militaries than women. In some countries, such as South Korea, it is still only men who are conscripted. This does not mean that women do not fight or have not fought. For example, an estimated 40 per cent of the Kurdistan Workers Party (PKK), who are fighting for an independent Kurdish state, are women. Nor does it mean that there are not considerable differences in how different men and women experience soldiering (Henry 2015). However, many scholars have demonstrated that gender norms and racialized logics normalize *expectations* about who makes the best soldiers. They have shown how soldiering and violence have come to be equated with manliness (MacKenzie 2015) and how racialized 'martial qualities' have come to be associated with certain ethnic groups (Streets 2004). These ideas have been used to motivate and cajole certain men to be warriors. There is nothing natural about men, or men from specific communities, fighting in war. However, cross-culturally gendered and racialized norms have determined, and continue to determine, the roles that people are *expected to*—and therefore often, but not always—play in war and preparing for war (Goldstein 2001).

> **Chapter 10** explores how security affects transgender people

The reliance of militaries on certain ideas about men's and women's roles in war can also be highlighted through tensions around the conscription of transgender people. In South Korea, for example, the government will only conscript people they consider to be 'able-bodied men' to serve for two years (due to the formally ongoing war with North Korea). Transgender people who identify as transmen but were assigned female at birth are not considered by the state to be able-bodied men. Therefore, they are exempted from military service. Transgender people who identify as transwomen but were assigned male at birth often find that they are conscripted because the state sees them as able-bodied men (Yi and Gitzen 2018). For the South Korean state, war continues to be something men should prepare for and perpetuate. Much like someone's sex at birth, the relationship between men and war is seen as inherent and unchangeable.

Nira Yuval-Davis (1997, 94) has argued that even though men and women have been mobilized in different ways within different militaries and armed groups, one of the most salient ideas surrounding war is of 'men as warriors and of women as worriers'. This leads to simplistic associations between men and the public business of war as well as between women and the private sphere of the home. Both can reinforce ideas about how men and women should act to support war. State actors, and not only military officers, are almost always men. More importantly, however, security settings are one where masculine traits, whether exhibited by men or women, continue to dominate and are prized over feminized ones (Cohn et al. 2005).

The normalization of men as warriors also conceals how men and women's labour can make war possible in different ways. For example, Maria Rashid (2020) points to how the Pakistan Army has over-relied on recruiting men from specific regions of Pakistan. Within these regions, the idea that a person's masculinity is secured through military service has become prevalent over time. This association motivates more men to enlist. Rashid (2020) shows how the wives of these men are expected to emotionally support their husbands and their military service, even if this is through mourning their deaths. Similarly, Victoria Basham and Sergio Catignani (2018) have highlighted the pivotal role that women are expected to play in the United Kingdom's defence by freeing up their husbands and male partners to engage in military training and war preparations by taking on increased domestic and caring labour in the home. Katherine Moon (1997) has also shown how significant women's sexual labour has been to maintaining strong security relations between states such as the United States and South Korea. A national sex work industry in South Korea developed in response to demand from American military bases established in the country in the aftermath of the Korean War, alongside a regulatory system for the industry implemented by the South Korean government to protect the health of American soldiers.

In instances where women are involved in armed struggles, even when for survival against state oppression, notions of 'proper' masculinity and femininity can still lead to expectations that they must behave in ways that do not challenge men's authority or the ideas of masculinity that are important to the identity of armed groups (Tambiah 2005). Often women's involvement in these struggles only offers them partial or fleeting experiences of gender equality (Tezcür 2020). However, others have shown the importance of the pleasure that women have taken in gaining power that they would not normally hold outside of war and how this has shaped their identities and their pursuit of violence (Mailänder 2015).

7.3.2 Agents and agency in war

How people's actions in war are remembered and recorded can also enable us to think more deeply about the relationship between war, militarized violence, and socio-political orders. Henrique Furtado's (2017) work on the Brazilian Truth Commission demonstrates how the specific ways in which the Commission engaged in 'truth-seeking' resulted in divergent characterizations of the violence that different actors perpetrated during Brazil's 'dirty war'. While the Commission rightly, and importantly, condemned the violence of state military and police actors who perpetrated systemic state terror, they depoliticized and victimized leftist militants, characterizing them as 'mere dreamers who fought for liberty and democracy in the past' (Furtado 2017, 316). In doing so, the Commission undermined the political nature of these militants' violence and how they sought to use violence to bring about radical social change. This matters because such characterizations can reinforce the idea that there is a natural relationship between state actors and violence, and in contrast non-state violence must be deviant and illegitimate. Whose contributions to war are seen as normal, whose contributions are valued, and whose are overlooked can therefore tell us something potentially important about what is being secured and how. It can prompt us to think more carefully about how the idea that war is vital to the security of states is reproduced through social and political practices. This may lead us to ask questions about war's supposed inevitability and about who is secured by war and its practices.

> See **Section 3.4** on challenging and resisting security

7.4 Who or what does war secure?

> All societies that maintain armies maintain the belief that some things are more valuable than life itself. (Billig 1995, 1)

For Michael Billig (1995), war is something that societies have come to value. In fact, they value it more than the lives of those they expect to die while waging it. Pointing to historical examples of wars fought for causes that we would consider absurd—such as defending chivalric honour—as well as to more contemporary rhetoric about the need to defend 'the nation', Billig suggests that wars are fought to secure states and the idea of 'nationhood', not to secure human life. The assumption that war provides states and populations with security is common, though. Militaries and soldiers are often revered in societies in ways that mean that 'military approaches to political problems gain elite *and* popular acceptance' (Kuus 2009, 546; my emphasis). Some scholars have argued that the idea that societies should organize themselves 'for the production of violence' (Geyer 1989, 79) has become so normal that when a country announces an increase to its military spending, typically it is a 'no brainer' because if the country's warfighting capacity has increased, so too will that country's security (Lutz 2014, 184). Although people do not often explicitly articulate that it is necessary to prepare for war or in states must maintain armed forces and weapons-systems in 'any great detail or as a clearly thought through set of rational principles' (McSorley 2014, 119), the assumption that strong militaries make us safe is widespread.

7.4.1 Why do we think war makes us secure?

But does war make societies more secure? If not, why do we think it does? After all, we know that war is profoundly destructive. In addition to direct deaths, it leads to the proliferation of sexual violence; disrupts agriculture and food supplies;

destroys infrastructure, places of education, cultural heritage, and worship; and disrupts public health and social care provision, policing and legal processes, politics, and much more besides. Why then do so many societies value war and preparing for it?

Scholars from different parts of the world have tried to address this question by asking how societies come to see war and preparing for war as a normal part of their society and politics. Some have focused on how military actors and war are represented in education. In Indonesian schools, for example, children's textbooks celebrate the heroism of Indonesia's soldiers but underplay or critique the role of its civilian politicians (Purwanta 2013). Similarly, Turkish textbooks inform children that all Turks are warriors and that the military is what makes Turkey a strong and competent country (Altinay 2004). Others have explored how across cultures—from Lebanon (Rey-García et al. 2020), Russia (Danilova 2015), Japan (Repo 2008), and Namibia (Öberg 2016) to Zimbabwe (Mpofu 2016), China (Lopes 2020), Pakistan (Rashid 2020), Denmark, and Sweden (Åse and Wendt 2018)—rituals of war commemoration and sacrifice have socialized generations of people into seeing war, and preparing for it, as fundamental to the identity and continuation of their socio-political orders.

War, and preparing for war, as we have already explored, are also represented as 'normal' parts of human existence in many forms of popular culture. Scholars have examined how films glamorize the US military and can legitimize the idea of the United States as the world's foremost military power (Weber 2006), or how depictions of the military and its soldiers in Sri Lankan advertising, theatre, film, and literature venerate war and those who fight it (de Mel 2007). Others have explored how nationalism and war have been celebrated in pop music in the Yugoslav region (Baker 2020) and through sport in Brazil (de Melo and Drumond 2017), or how nostalgia for war can be found in consumer habits in the United Kingdom (Tidy 2015). In these societies, and many others besides, scholars have explored how the 'production and circulation of popular culture' continues to play a significant role in making 'world politics what it currently is' (Grayson et al. 2009, 157), which is one where war and preparing for war are seen as normal.

7.4.2 Societal benefits and costs of war

In some societies, militaries, soldiers, and military practices are seen as a means for creating greater security *within* societies as well as protecting them from external threats. In some societies, enlisting in the military gives people access to educational and economic opportunities, and to medical and social services, that they would not otherwise have (Cowen and Gilbert 2008). Enlisting even allows some people to gain citizenship (Ware 2012).

However, in countries such as the United States where joining the military gives people access to some of these opportunities, certain socio-economic and minority-ethnic groups are over-represented in the armed forces. This means that the burdens and dangers of war fall disproportionately on poorer and non-white members of US society than on others. Some migrants also only receive citizenship after being killed during military service. Moreover, the US military's racial diversity can obscure systemic racism and how it leads to a lack of opportunities in civilian jobs that drives some people towards military service in the first place (Ray 2018).

In the United Kingdom, military veterans have received extensive government funding to provide activities for children excluded from schools to try to solve the political problems of both veteran unemployment and educating children who are considered to have behavioural problems. Such schemes are based on assumptions that military training and employment gives veterans skills that are useful in teaching. Engaging in military-style activities in educational settings often means young people lose out on formalized education, though, and some do not take exams. This can limit their future prospects while equipping them with skills that would be most valuable to a career in the military, potentially limiting their choices (Basham 2016).

More widely, when a country decides to increase its military spending to secure itself, this can lead to defunding or deprioritizing other spending needs (see Table 7.1). These can include services that might provide greater social security such as shelters, support for victims of interpersonal violence, or job training for the homeless. It can also lead to less investment in other initiatives such as tackling climate change, arguably the greatest source of insecurity for humanity.

In some socio-political orders, fears around conflict or criminal activity have led to popular and elite support for greater military involvement in societal activities. Saul Rodriguez (2018) argues that in Colombia fear generated by internal conflict has led to the embedding of pro-military attitudes in Colombian society, enabling civilian politicians to adopt militaristic approaches to countering a broad range of perceived threats to stability within the country. Cristina Rojas (2009, 229) argues that Colombia's pro-military socio-political order has undermined democracy and exacerbated economic

Table 7.1 A snapshot of UK military spending and costs of the military-industrial sector

Spending (2020)	59.2 billion USD
World rank (2020)	5th
Spending as a % of GDP (2020)	2.2
Spending as a % of GDP in other sectors (2020)	0.64 environmental protection 0.82 housing and community amenities 1.77 public order and safety
Austerity cuts to military spending 2010–18	7%
Austerity cuts to other sectors (2010–18)	44% family and children's welfare 23% protection (policing, fire services, courts, prisons, and public order and safety) 17% education

Sources: Tian et al. 2021; OECD 2021; Human Rights Watch 2019.

inequalities by engendering 'a citizenry less inclined to claim his or her rights politically and more prone to "voluntary obedience" in return for protection'.

Similarly, in Brazil, fear over violent crime, alongside the historic role that the military has played in governing, has normalized the Brazilian military's involvement in maintaining law and order. This meant that over time, 'crimes against public safety were transformed into crimes against national security' (Zaverucha 2000, 21). This has engendered a common narrative of a security crisis (also found in Mexico) that has justified the internal deployment of military forces to tackle drug trading and trafficking (Passos 2018). Militarized policing has done little, however, to address the extreme inequality and poverty that feeds criminality and violence in Brazil and that makes so many Brazilians insecure. Military forces have instead been deployed to residential areas, particularly socio-economically deprived favelas, where they have routinely used lethal violence against civilians, generating further insecurity (Wacquant 2008). Moreover, non-white Brazilians are disproportionately represented among those killed by armed military and policing forces (Cano 2010).

Thus, while Catherine Lutz (2014) suggests that increased military spending and other investments in war, and preparing for it, are often considered 'no brainers', scholars have suggested reasons for why it might not be the case that war, and preparing for war, provides security. War and preparing for war often generates *in*security, and can exacerbate inequalities and engender hierarchies between competing ideas of who, or what, should be secured and how.

7.5 Conclusion: should we continue to wage and prepare for war?

> We are quick to accept the facile and mendacious ideological veneer that is wrapped like a mantle around the shoulders of those who prosecute [war] . . . to give this kind of slaughter an historical inevitability it does not have. (Hedges 2002, 20)

The war correspondent Chris Hedges has called war a 'force that gives us meaning'. Although he is critical of the ways in which war is often depicted as an inevitability, he also suggests that its destructiveness can expose the value of life and having a life that has purpose. It is perhaps this human urge to make sense of death on a mass scale that leads us to think of war as primarily about fighting and as something that has always been, and always will be, part of the human experience. These things may lead us to assume that preparing for war makes our societies more secure.

In contrast, we have considered war, and preparing for war, as outcomes of social and political choices and practices. We have highlighted how important *where* we look for war is to how we understand it, and how socio-political orders can be characterized as spaces of war through the stories we tell about them. We have looked at how people are expected to behave in relation to war and war preparations and how their actions make war possible. We have highlighted how the choices we make about war, and the ways it is practised, can unevenly distribute (in)security across socio-political orders.

If we begin to think about war as something that is reliant on our social and political choices, rather than something that is inevitable, we can envision different forms of politics. The imperative to do so is vital. As Jairus Grove (2019, 2) argues, despite repeated warnings from the world's scientific community that our finite resources mean that humanity has long faced a choice between war and survival, those 'in a position to make a decision chose war'. Environmental degradation means that it is perhaps only by making different choices, by making sense of war in different ways than we have traditionally done, that we might yet avert the biggest threat to humanity's security, which may otherwise prove catastrophic for us all.

> **Chapter 18** concentrates on linking security to the environment

Questions for further discussion

1. How useful might it be to reorientate our discussions of war away from what it is towards asking where is war?

2. Does war become less 'normal' or 'rational' when we think about it through the lens of socio-political orders and lived experience?

3. What can we learn about war when we ask who fights and supports it?

4. Why might it be important to focus on actors profoundly affected by war but who have received less attention, such as children?

5. What is the biggest threat to the security of humanity? Can war and/or preparing for war address this?

Further reading

CONWAY, DANIEL. 2012. *Masculinities, militarisation and the end conscription campaign: War resistance in Apartheid South Africa.* Manchester: Manchester University Press.
Conway's analysis focuses on white men who objected to being drafted for compulsory military service in Apartheid South Africa. Drawing on a range of archival materials and interviews, Conway details the relationship between military conscription, conscientious objection, citizenship, and masculinities.

ENLOE, CYNTHIA. 2000. *Manoeuvres: The international politics of militarizing women's lives.* Berkeley, CA: University of California Press.
Enloe's accessible global analysis explores how women's lives are shaped by war and the scope and extent of just how much gendered labour it takes to sustain war and war preparations.

EDWARDS, LOUISE. 2016. *Women warriors and wartime spies of China.* Cambridge: Cambridge University Press.
Focusing on the lives of China's most famous women warriors and wartime spies, Edwards explores how these women have been commemorated in popular culture, and how popular and official representations of these women have evolved in line with China's shifting political values to glamorize war historically and in China today.

ORACZ, MICHAŁ and JAKUB WIŚNIEWSKI. 2014/2017 [video game/board game]. *This War of Mine*. Krakow: Galakta Games.

This War of Mine, available as a video and a board game, highlights that contrary to most depictions in popular culture, not everyone who experiences war is a soldier. It puts players in the position of civilians trying to survive war. Players have to make and find useful things, and solve various dilemmas and problems faced by real people in warzones.

SPIEGELMAN, ART. 2003. *Maus*. London: Penguin.

Maus tells the story of Vladek Spiegelman, a Jewish survivor of the Holocaust, and of his son, the author, coming to terms with his father's story. This graphic novel offers insights into how survivors experienced the Holocaust, the intergenerational trauma of war, and the perpetration of mass violence in war.

References

ALTINAY, AYŞE GÜL. 2004. *The myth of the military-nation: Militarism, gender, and education in Turkey*. Basingstoke: Palgrave Macmillan.

ÅSE, CECILIA and MARIA WENDT. 2018. 'Gendering the new hero narratives: Military death in Denmark and Sweden'. *Cooperation and Conflict* 53(1), 23–41.

BAKER, CATHERINE. 2018. *Race and the Yugoslav region: Postsocialist, post-conflict, postcolonial?* Manchester: Manchester University Press.

BAKER, CATHERINE. 2020. 'The defender collection: Militarisation, historical mythology and the everyday affective politics of nationalist fashion in Croatia'. In *Making war on bodies: Militarisation, aesthetics and embodiment in international politics*, edited by CATHERINE BAKER. Edinburgh: Edinburgh University Press.

BARKAWI, TARAK. 2016. 'Decolonising war'. *European Journal of International Security* 1(2), 199–214.

BASHAM, VICTORIA M. 2016. 'Raising an army: The geopolitics of militarizing the lives of working-class boys in an age of austerity'. *International Political Sociology* 10(3), 258–274.

BASHAM, VICTORIA M. and SERGIO CATIGNANI. 2018. 'War is where the hearth is: Gendered labour and the everyday reproduction of the geopolitical in the Army Reserves'. *International Feminist Journal of Politics* 20(2), 153–171.

BAUMAN, ZYGMUNT. 1989. *Modernity and the Holocaust*. Cambridge: Polity.

BERNAZZOLI, RICHELLE M. and COLIN FLINT. 2009. 'From militarization to securitization: Finding a concept that works'. *Political Geography* 28(8), 449–450.

BILLIG, MICHAEL. 1995. *Banal nationalism*. Los Angeles, CA: Sage.

BOURKE, JOANNA. 1999. *An intimate history of killing*. London: Granta.

BRIGHTON, SHANE. 2019. 'Critical war studies'. In *Routledge handbook of critical international relations*, edited by JENNY EDKINS. Abingdon: Routledge.

CAMPBELL, DAVID. 1998. *National deconstruction: Violence, identity, and justice in Bosnia*. Minneapolis, MN: University of Minnesota Press.

CANO, IGNACIO. 2010. 'Racial bias in police use of lethal force in Brazil'. *Police Practice and Research* 11(1), 31–43.

COHN, CAROL. 1987. 'Sex and death in the rational world of defence intellectuals'. *Signs* 12(4), 687–718.

Cohn, Carol, Felicity Hill, and Sara Ruddick. 2005. *The relevance of gender for eliminating weapons of mass destruction*. Stockholm: Weapons of Mass Destruction Commission.

Collins, Randall. 2008. *Violence: A micro-sociological theory*. Princeton, NJ: Princeton University Press.

Cowen, Deborah and Emily Gilbert. 2008. 'Citizenship in the "Homeland"'. In *War, citizenship, territory*, edited by Deborah Cowen and Emily Gilbert. New York: Routledge.

Danilova, Nataliya. 2015. *The politics of war commemoration in the UK and Russia*. Basingstoke: Palgrave Macmillan.

de Mel, Neloufer. 2007. *Militarizing Sri Lanka: Popular culture, memory and narrative in the armed conflict*. New Delhi: Sage.

de Melo, Victor Andrade and Mauricio Drumond. 2017. 'The military in Brazilian sport: A long and controversial presence'. In *Sport and militarism: Contemporary global perspectives*, edited by Michael L. Butterworth. Abingdon: Routledge.

Enloe, Cynthia. 2016. *Globalization and militarism: Feminists make the link*. 2nd ed. Lanham, MD: Rowman & Littlefield.

Furtado, Henrique. 2017. 'On demons and dreamers: Violence, silence and the politics of impunity in the Brazilian Truth Commission'. *Security Dialogue* 48(4), 316–333.

Geyer, Michael. 1989. 'The militarization of Europe, 1914–1945'. In *The militarization of the Western world*, edited by John R. Gillis. New Brunswick, NJ: Rutgers University Press.

Goldstein, Joshua. 2001. *War and gender: How gender shapes the war system and vice versa*. Cambridge: Cambridge University Press.

Grayson, Kyle. 2016. *Cultural politics of targeted killing: On drones, counter-insurgency, and violence*. Abingdon: Routledge.

Grayson, Kyle, Matt Davies, and Simon Philpott. 2009. 'Pop goes IR? Researching the popular culture–world politics continuum'. *Politics* 29(3), 155–163.

Grossman, Dave. 1996. *On killing: The psychological cost of learning to kill in war and society*. New York: Back Bay Books.

Grove, Jairus V. 2019. *Savage ecology: War and geopolitics at the end of the world*. Durham, NC: Duke University Press.

Hedges, Chris. 2002. *War is a force that gives us meaning*. New York: Public Affairs.

Henry, Marsha. 2015. 'Parades, parties and pests: Contradictions of everyday Life in peacekeeping economies'. *Journal of Intervention and Statebuilding* 9(3), 372–390.

Howell, Alison. 2018. 'Forget "militarization": Race, disability and the "martial politics" of the police and of the university'. *International Feminist Journal of Politics* 20(2), 117–136.

Human Rights Watch. 2019. *Nothing left in the cupboards: Austerity, welfare cuts, and the right to food in the UK*. New York: Human Rights Watch.

Kuus, Merje. 2009. 'Cosmopolitan militarism? Spaces of NATO expansion'. *Environment and Planning A* 41(3), 545–562.

Lopes, Helena F. S. 2020. 'Foreign friends and problematic heroes: Remembering a global World War Two in early twenty-first century Chinese cinema'. *Journal of War & Culture Studies* 15(1), 42–66.

Lutz, Catherine. 2014. 'The military normal: Feeling at home with counterinsurgency in the United States'. In *Violence and civilization: Studies of social violence in history and prehistory*, edited by Roderick Campbell. Oxford: Oxbow.

MacKenzie, Megan. 2015. *Beyond the band of brothers: The US military and the myth that women can't fight*. Cambridge: Cambridge University Press.

MAILÄNDER, ELISSA. 2015. *Female SS guards and workaday violence: The Majdanek concentration camp, 1942–1944*. East Lansing, MI: Michigan State University.
MALEŠEVIĆ, SINIŠA. 2010. *The sociology of war and violence*. Cambridge: Cambridge University Press.
MAMDANI, MAHMOOD. 2003. 'Making sense of political violence in postcolonial Africa'. *Socialist Register* 39, 132–151.
MANCHANDA, NIVI. 2020. *Imagining Afghanistan: The history and politics of imperial knowledge*. Cambridge: Cambridge University Press.
MCSORLEY, KEVIN. M. 2014. 'Towards an embodied sociology of war'. *The Sociological Review* 62(S2), 107–128.
MÉGRET, FRÉDÉRIC. 2006. 'From "savages" to "unlawful combatants": A postcolonial look at International Humanitarian Law's "Other"'. In *International law and its others*, edited by ANNE ORFORD. Cambridge: Cambridge University Press.
MOON, KATHERINE H. S. 1997. *Sex among allies: Military prostitution in US-Korea relations*. New York: Columbia University Press.
MPOFU, SHEPHERD. 2016. 'Toxification of national holidays and national identity in Zimbabwe's post-2000 nationalism'. *Journal of African Cultural Studies* 28(1), 28–43.
NETZ, REVIEL. 2004. *Barbed wire: An ecology of modernity*. Middletown, CT: Wesleyan University Press.
NORDSTROM, CAROLYN. 1998. 'Deadly myths of aggression'. *Aggressive Behaviour* 24(2), 147–159.
ÖBERG, DAN. 2016. 'Enduring war: Heroes' Acre, "the empty throne", and the politics of disappearance'. *Critical Military Studies* 2(3), 155–172.
ÖBERG, DAN. 2019. 'Ethics, the military imaginary, and practices of war'. *Critical Studies on Security* 7(3), 199–209.
OECD. 2021. *Government at a glance 2021*. Paris: OECD Publishing.
PARASHAR, SWATI. 2013. 'What wars and "war bodies" know about international relations'. *Cambridge Review of International Affairs* 26(4), 615–630.
PASSOS, ANAÍS M. 2018. 'Fighting crime and maintaining order: Shared worldviews of civilian and military elites in Brazil and Mexico'. *Third World Quarterly* 39(2), 314–330.
PURWANTA, HIERONYMUS. 2013. 'Militer dan konstruksi identitas nasional: Analisis buku teks pelajaran sejarah Sma masa Orde Baru' ['Military and national identity construction: analysis of high school history textbooks during the new order era']. *Paramita: Historical Studies Journal* 23(1), 88–102.
RASHID, MARIA. 2020. *Dying to serve: Militarism, affect and the politics of sacrifice in the Pakistan army*. Stanford, CA: Stanford University Press.
RAY, VICTOR. 2018. 'Militarism as a racial project'. In *Handbook of the sociology of racial and ethnic relations*, edited by PINAR BATUR and JOE R. FEAGIN. Cham: Springer.
RAZACK, SHERENE. 2004. *Dark threats and white knights: The Somalia Affair, peacekeeping, and the new imperialism*. Toronto: University of Toronto Press.
REPO, JEMIMA. 2008. 'A feminist reading of gender and national memory at the Yasukuni Shrine'. *Japan Forum* 20(2), 219–243.
REY-GARCÍA, PABLO, PEDRO RIVAS-NIETO, and NADIA MCGOWAN. 2020. 'War memorials, between propaganda and history: Mleeta Landmark and Hezbollah'. *Cultural Trends* 29(5), 359–377.
RODRIGUEZ, SAUL M. 2018. 'Building civilian militarism: Colombia, internal war, and militarization in a mid-term perspective'. *Security Dialogue* 49(1–2), 109–122.

Rojas, Cristina. 2009. 'Securing the state and developing social insecurities: The securitisation of citizenship in contemporary Colombia'. *Third World Quarterly* 30(1), 227–245.

Shaw, Martin. 2005. *The new Western way of war: Risk-transfer war and its crisis in Iraq*. Cambridge: Polity.

Stahl, Roger. 2010. *Militainment, Inc.: War, media, and popular culture*. New York: Routledge.

Streets, Heather. 2004. *Martial races: The military, race and masculinity in British imperial culture, 1857–1914*. Manchester: Manchester University Press.

Tambiah, Yasmin. 2005. 'Turncoat bodies: Sexuality and sex work under militarization in Sri Lanka'. *Gender and Society* 19(2), 243–261.

Tezcür, Güneş Murat. 2020. 'A path out of patriarchy? Political agency and social identity of women fighters'. *Perspectives on Politics* 18(3), 722–739.

Tian, Nan, Alexandra Marksteiner, and Diego Lopes da Silva. 2021. *Trends in world military expenditure 2020*. Stockholm: SIPRI.

Tidy, Joanna. 2015. 'Forces sauces and eggs for soldiers: Food, nostalgia, and the rehabilitation of the British military'. *Critical Military Studies* 1(3), 220–232.

Vitalis, Robert. 2015. *White order, black power politics: The birth of American International Relations*. Ithaca, NY: Cornell University Press.

Wacquant, Loïc. 2008. 'The militarization of urban marginality: Lessons from the Brazilian metropolis'. *International Political Sociology* 2(1), 56–74.

Ware, Vron. 2012. *Military migrants: Fighting for YOUR country*. Houndmills: Palgrave Macmillan.

Weber, Cynthia. 2006. *Imagining America at war: Morality, politics, and film*. London: Routledge.

Woodward, Rachel. 2005. 'From military geography to militarism's geographies: Disciplinary engagements with the geographies of militarism and military activities'. *Progress in Human Geography* 29(6), 718–740.

Yi, Horim and Timothy Gitzen. 2018. 'Sex/gender insecurities: Trans bodies and the South Korean military'. *Transgender Studies Quarterly* 5(3), 378–393.

Yuval-Davis, Nira. 1997. *Gender and nation*. London: Sage.

Zaverucha, Jorge. 2000. 'Fragile democracy and the militarization of public safety in Brazil'. *Latin American Perspectives* 27(3), 8–31.

8

Terrorism and asymmetric conflicts

Christian Olsson

8.1 Introduction	121
8.2 What is asymmetric conflict? What is terrorism?	122
8.3 Security, violence, and the struggle for political order	125
8.4 The relation between clandestine political violence and counterterrorism	127
8.5 Terrorism and counterterrorism: locating the political	129
8.6 Civilians caught between rival political orders	132
8.7 Conclusion	134

READER'S GUIDE

We ask the question of 'security for what purpose?' in asymmetric conflicts where rival political-military organizations, typically a government and a clandestine group, compete to institute and enforce a socio-political order. We highlight why parties to these conflicts often come to threaten individuals—be it through indiscriminate repression or clandestine political violence. We also show that the protagonists of such conflicts generally seek to define security in terms of the stability of their own socio-political order, thus potentially increasing levels of violence. It is in the context of such conflicts that we discuss the concepts of terrorism and counterterrorism.

8.1 Introduction

> Illustrative case studies on the topics explored in this chapter are available on the online resources to help take your understanding of terrorism and asymmetric conflicts further:
> http://www.oup.com/he/Grayson-Guillaume1e.

Terrorism and the asymmetric use of violence are often understood to pose specific kinds of security challenges that distinguish them from other forms of political violence like war. Their association with the deliberate targeting of civilians causes them to be perceived as illegitimate and particularly threatening. However, what is distinctive about them compared to other forms of violence? In particular, the link between asymmetry and 'terrorism' defined as the deliberate targeting of civilians must be questioned. Let's start with an example.

During the Algerian War of Independence, the Algerian Front de Libération Nationale (FLN) was accused of using violence against civilians. In response to these accusations, Ahmed Ben Bellah, the leader of the FLN, is alleged to have said: 'Give us tanks and aircrafts and we'd abandon terror' (Dudai and Baram 2004). This statement highlights a link between the intentional targeting of civilians and military asymmetry, or at least technological inferiority. It even comes close to admitting to the tactical use of 'terror'. However, the ethico-political problem is twofold. On the one hand, technologically advanced armies also intentionally target civilians, as with the aerial bombing of cities during the Second World War. Relatedly, guerrilla movements fighting overwhelmingly superior adversaries do not always kill civilians. For example, the 1920 Revolution Brigade who fought against the US military presence in Iraq after the invasion of 2003 refrained from targeting civilians. On the other hand, when conventional armies target civilians intentionally, it is rarely labelled as terrorism. This holds even when it is very vocally condemned in international fora as with the bombardment of hospitals in rebel held areas in Syria. George Bush Jr very explicitly claimed that the use of improvised explosive devices by Iraqi guerrillas was terrorism, even when it targeted US military forces rather than civilians. These are just some initial examples of how terrorism and asymmetrical conflict are still often conflated. Thus, when we speak of the threat of terrorism and asymmetric conflicts, we must ask: 'what precisely are we seeking security from?'

In the five sections that follow, you will see that that there are different answers. First, we look at how terrorism and asymmetric conflict are defined, showing that their definitions are contested and tied to how security professionals make sense of their worlds. Thus, rather than being purely analytical or descriptive terms, they shape security practices (Olsson and Bonditti 2016). Second, we consider how (accusations of) terrorism and asymmetric conflict emerge from rival claims to political authority over a territory and what this might tell us about security. Third, we will explore how clandestine political violence and counterterrorism are connected. Fourth, we will explore how it becomes possible for the political dimensions of clandestine violence to be simultaneously ignored and foregrounded by agents of counterterrorism. Finally, we conclude by highlighting the dynamics that create insecurities for civilians in asymmetric conflicts.

> Types of political violence are discussed in **Section 4.2.1**

> 'Security from what?' is presented in **Section 5.3.1.5**

> The question 'who can "speak" security?' is presented in **Section 5.3.1.1**

> On security as a productive process, see **Section 2.3.2**

> On security as a political mobilization, see **Section 2.4**; on authority and legitimacy, see **Sections 4.3–4**

> See also what war does to society in **Chapter 7**

8.2 What is asymmetric conflict? What is terrorism?

In the context of armed conflict, the adjective 'asymmetric' is often used to describe differences in military capabilities between opposing sides that are so uneven that the weaker party seeks to avoid direct combat (Arreguín-Toft 2001). Instead, the weaker party will seek to deploy elements of surprise, stealth, and local knowledge to reduce its strategic disadvantage. Asymmetric conflict then refers to situations in which non-conventional or irregular warfare is practised by the weaker side. But if we move beyond a focus on military power, one can identify a series of factors that could generate asymmetries that will shape a conflict:

- situational asymmetries between 'international forces' and 'local combatants' (implying different levels of willingness to make sacrifices to achieve victory);
- sociological asymmetries between bureaucratic organizations and (neo-)traditional or informal groups;
- numerical asymmetries between a single government and a coalition of non-state armed groups;
- legal asymmetries between sovereign states who hold a formally legal monopoly on the use of force and groups for whom the use of violence is considered illegal.

The underlying implicit assumption when a conflict is defined as asymmetric is that 'symmetric' wars are the norm in world politics. However, even war between 'like-units', typically sovereign states, are usually not symmetric since there are differences in technology, skill, and numbers that armies will seek to overcome or exploit. In this sense, all wars are dissymmetric: that is, all parties to war are likely (and expected) to seek to exploit strengths and weaknesses to their own advantage. This is, so to speak, part of the commonly accepted 'rules of the game' of war. The concept of asymmetry is therefore generally reserved to situations in which differences in capabilities are so big that they lead to fundamental disagreements on these 'rules of the game'; for example, on the question whether war is about avoiding, or seeking out, frontal combat. Since what defines a conflict as 'asymmetric' is open-ended, we will focus on armed conflicts between incumbents and challengers. More specifically, we explore conflicts between a government and non-state armed organizations, with the latter contesting the former's authority.

'Terror' or 'terrorism' is also a problematic term. Definitions abound but there is very little agreement on the core definitional elements beyond its vague association with forms of violence like suicide bombings (see Asad 2007). Terrorism generally refers to the indiscriminate killing of civilians for political gain. The term is mostly, if not exclusively, used in the discourses of official authorities in relation to non-state armed groups. The notion of state terrorism is sometimes used by scholars but rarely by governments (Goodwin 2006). Indeed, designating a recognized state as 'terrorist' would subvert long-standing diplomatic norms (Bull 2012 [1977]). Terrorism is also often defined by its focus on 'soft targets' (e.g., unarmed civilians) to cause harm or extort political concessions from governments (Hoffman 2017). As the target of the violence (presumably random civilians) and the audience to which terrorists make political demands (presumably the government) are different, it is frequently described as an indirect strategy. It is also commonly considered as a 'weapon of the weak' used to pressure stronger opponents.

'Terrorism' is often seen as an urban phenomenon based on the strategy of 'propaganda of the deed' (Hoffman 2017). This expression, coined by the anarchists of the nineteenth century, refers to the idea that attacks against symbols of authority have the power to galvanize the population against the state by highlighting its vulnerability. Furthermore, the strategy assumes that any security crackdown that follows such attacks will further undermine the government, especially if it is bloody and indiscriminate, creating a situation in which the revolutionary organization could seize power. The 'propaganda of the deed' implies a strong belief in the communicative power of physical violence.

> On authority and political violence, **see Section 4.4**

> On the necessity of critique, see **Sections 1.2–3**

'Terrorism' is obviously not a neutral or objective term (see Tilly 2004). The notion of terrorism has been used to describe anti-colonial forces such as the FLN in Algeria, diverse groups within the Palestinian national liberation movement, the African National Congress of Nelson Mandela, and the anti-Nazi resistance in Europe. All are groups that would describe themselves as freedom fighters and fiercely reject the terrorist label. The questions of who can 'speak' security and what security does are critical here. For example, while the Islamic State (IS) has never reclaimed the notion of terrorism to describe itself, it is vocally comfortable with being labelled this way by Western governments. Being perceived as the terrorizer of Western powers is worn like a badge of honour, proving its jihadist and anti-Western credentials to its target audiences.

Even the most basic definitional criteria of terrorism, like indiscrimination or arbitrariness, are difficult to apply in a consistent way. If terrorism is the systematic and indiscriminate use of physical violence against civilians for political gain, the nuclear bombing of Hiroshima and Nagasaki, or mass aerial bombing of cities under 'Shock and Awe' campaigns, would easily qualify. Rarely is the word used to describe these events. Thus, what determines the use of the terrorism is not its definition but what the word *does*. It justifies responses that would not otherwise be permissible. For example, in the past two decades states defined as liberal democracies have directly or indirectly been involved in the arbitrary and illegal detention and torture of terrorist suspects through rendition programmes. Perhaps even more importantly, the word itself delegitimates political options, such as negotiations, that could otherwise be viable in ending an armed conflict (Olsson 2019).

To avoid these conceptual problems, the term 'clandestine political violence' may be preferable. Clandestine political violence is a more precise term. It connects the use of violence to a type of actor (a would-be political authority) in a context marked by the relative control by incumbent political authorities. It directly connects to asymmetric wars in which violence is used as part of a conflict over the legal right to use violence. Thus, it sheds light on the importance of claims to 'legitimate' as opposed to 'terrorist' violence. That being said, not all organizations designated as terrorist are clandestine (Della Porta 2013). Indeed, they do not all systematically conceal their activities and whereabouts. For example, Hezbollah, a group considered by the United States to be a 'terrorist' organization, is the biggest political party in Lebanon and is ever-present in Lebanese political life (Berti 2011). Conversely, not all clandestine armed groups are labelled as terrorist.

8.3 Security, violence, and the struggle for political order

Asymmetric conflicts and clandestine political violence can provide us with insights into the question of 'security (and violence) for what purpose?' Usually these unfold in the context of struggles between rival socio-political orders (Baczko et al. 2018), between rival claims to define socio-political order on a same territory. The most frequent scenario sees state authorities and non-state challengers—alternatively called insurgents, rebels, or revolutionaries—championing different socio-political orders.

All socio-political orders seek to uphold ordering principles. Such principles typically answer questions such as: how is wealth to be allocated? On what basis are property rights to be granted and exchanged? How, and to what extent, is security to be guaranteed? For whom? From what? There are many possible answers to these questions. In rules-based societies, such ordering principles provide predictability and a normative framework allowing for the management of widely different interests (Funk 1972). Political authorities typically are organizations defining, enforcing, and guaranteeing these principles. This is ultimately what justifies these authorities laying a claim to a monopoly on the *legitimate* use of physical violence (Weber 1965). It is worth noting that states are not the only ones who can make this claim. Non-state armed groups, including criminal organizations, can also provide predictability and normative frameworks in the absence of (or in competition with) the state (Taussig 2003). When there are rival claims to exert political authority, each one will try to define its own normative order as what needs to be secured and the challenger as a threat. Political authorities are, as a last resort, often expected to use violence in such situations in 'defence' of their political order.

> Socio-political orders and hierarchies are explained in **Sections 3.2–3**

> **Section 4.3** covers the question of legitimacy

While political authorities provide, by enforcing ordering principles, a framework for social transactions throughout the polity, they also tend to favour the dominating groups. They are, however, likely to be seen as having societal value as long as they facilitate social transactions (e.g., education, rights, commerce) by providing a stable framework for them. Even highly exploitative or autocratic states, or rogue armed groups, might draw significant support from the populations over which they claim authority if the only alternative is seen to be a world of 'chaos' where predictability with regards to life expectancy, property, and social position is jeopardized. For example, Michael Taussig (2003) has shown that popular support for paramilitary squads that emerged in Colombian cities in the 1990s was based on mixed feelings of fear and relief towards the extra-judicial killings of known criminals. The enforcement of any rule was perceived as better than the existing set of unenforced rules.

Political authorities might themselves produce insecurity in areas in which they are challenged, especially during times of crisis. This to highlight the costs of challenging them. It is here that security and insecurity become tightly linked (Bigo 2006). Thus, it is not uncommon for authorities to offer protection from dangers for which they are actually the cause (Tilly 1985; Taussig 2003). Ultimately, a government may uphold its authority by becoming a threat to the political order it has instituted and still claims to safeguard (Olsson 2015). This is the logic that led Muammar Gaddafi and Bashar al-Assad to explicitly threaten to destroy their respective countries, Libya and Syria, during the so-called 'Arab Spring'. In their effort to safeguard the existing socio-political order, they were prepared to destroy material infrastructures and exert indiscriminate violence against most of their population, rather than face any challenge to these orders.

Whenever the ordering principles enforced by political authorities are said to be threatened, we are dealing with an attempt to mobilize security for the preservation of a political order. Any concrete definition of (in)security necessarily outlines the core ordering principles of a given socio-political order (see Lipschutz 1995).

On the one hand, security is a resource. Political authorities might mobilize the material, institutional, and discursive resources that security provides to present domestic opposition groups as a political threat by accusing them of destabilization. For example, in the wake of the so-called 'Arab Spring', there were attempts in Egypt, Libya, and Syria to stigmatize the opposition by linking it to Al-Qaeda, foreign intelligence services, or drug addiction. By mobilizing security in this way, politicians might succeed in delegitimizing the opposition and in justifying their own attempts to violently supress dissident voices. Should the opposition respond in kind, this might give rise to an asymmetric conflict between incumbents and challengers. In this context, as already discussed, the exclusive right to enforce a socio-political order also creates an exceptional capacity to undermine it. The powers to protect and to intimidate become intimately linked when political authority is contested (Bigo 2006).

On the other hand, maintaining security can become a constraint on political authorities. By claiming to protect the socio-political order, state authorities become vulnerable to accusations of not living up to this claim. It is not a coincidence that the first domestic reaction after the attacks of 11 September 2001 in the United States was to question the competence of its intelligence services and their leadership. Non-state armed political organizations can experience similar challenges when they impose their own political order and taxation system, policing, and administrative services on the territory they control. We can see this in Gaza after Hamas gained power in 2007 (Berti 2016), and in the parts of Colombia that were controlled by FARC (Fuerzas Armadas Revolucionarias de Colombia) at the beginning of the 2000s. Their day-to-day governance and security provision have generally not been perceived as aligning with their claims to be the defenders of their respective constituents.

Challenges to political authority present state governments with another dilemma. If they fight back by resorting to widespread violence, they implicitly recognize that their legitimacy is at best challenged, if not faltering. Moreover, this legitimacy risks being eroded through the use of violence (Olsson 2013). The more violence, the more a government risks undermining the ordering principles it claims to safeguard. Conversely, if governmental authorities do not respond in kind, they may lose both their legitimacy as security providers and their exclusive monopoly on the use of violence, to the point that other groups may become accepted as the legitimate monopoly of such use. This tension is at the heart of any asymmetric conflict and, as we will now see, between clandestine political violence and counterterrorism.

Section 2.4 examines security as a political mobilization

8.4 The relation between clandestine political violence and counterterrorism

If we are to understand the relationship between clandestine political violence and counterterrorism, we need to examine the actors that define the relationship: clandestine organizations and the state. These actors are inextricably intertwined. While the relationship between 'terrorism' and counterterrorism is often presented as one between a clear threat and a response to it, this is too simplistic for four reasons.

First, contemporary forms of clandestine political violence develop in the context of modern 'surveillance states' (see Foucault 2012 [1975]). Clandestine organizations are only clandestine in relation to a state that effectively controls its whole territory. As powerful and well-organized states are able to more fully control their territory, particularly urban 'population centres', armed oppositional groups are forced to go underground, to organize in a decentralized way, to restrict their interactions with non-members, and to recruit in closed circles (Sinno 2011). In rural and less bureaucratized states, armed groups tend to become less clandestine and more guerrilla-like with a centralized leadership, an ability to control a 'heartland', and close interactions with surrounding populations.

Second, the type of mass attacks associated with terrorism, generally planned to maximize civilian casualties, only makes strategic sense to the extent that the state is seen to be responsible for the life and well-being of its citizens. The very idea of the 'propaganda of the deed' is to expose the state's incapacity to do 'what it should'; that is, in most cases, to ensure the general well-being of its populations (e.g., physical security, health, employment, and education). As highlighted by Foucault, this understanding of security as a governmental preoccupation for the life of populations is distinctly modern since he locates its emergence around the eighteenth century (Foucault 2009 [1978]).

The third, the political challenge between parties to an asymmetric conflict, rarely starts with 'terrorist attacks'. Generally, there have been several cycles of confrontation involving opposition movements and police repression. These cycles typically lead to the emergence of splinter groups that detach themselves from the original opposition movements (Della Porta 2013). The multiplicity and rivalry between splinter groups can cause them to adopt increasingly uncompromising positions, including the advocacy of clandestine violence. For example, PIRA (Provisional Irish Republican Army) broke away from the original Irish Republican Army (IRA) three years after the beginning of the 1966 Republican parades commemorating the Éirí Amach na Cásca (Easter Rising of 1916). This was precipitated by some members of the IRA becoming dissatisfied by its responses to Unionist violence against Catholics following these parades (Bosi and Ó Dochartaigh, 2018). PIRA's advocacy of clandestine political violence caused British authorities to designate it as a 'terrorist' organization. As this case demonstrates, we are not dealing with a simple sequence in which terrorism triggers a government response in the form of counterterrorism. Rather, we see a gradual escalation between different incumbents and challengers over a longer period of time.

Finally, clandestine political violence and counterterrorism are also intertwined through counterterrorist policies that often escalate the use of violence on the part of the incumbents (Goodwin 2001).

8.4.1 Counterterrorism as war

Often counterterrorist policies, whether pursued by military interventions, harsher sanctions for terrorist crimes, or mass intelligence and surveillance, are conceived of through the prism of war. However, the war metaphor is inappropriate if one considers the clandestine group's use of violence (rather than the political order that they champion) to be the main threat (Howard 2002). As highlighted by Clausewitz (2010 [1832]), violence inevitably escalates in the course of war. Waging war on a clandestine group may undermine the political order it claims to institute; it will certainly lead it to resort to more violence.

For state authorities, there may be a difficult decision to make between destroying a clandestine organization—an objective that suppresses it as a political force but that is likely to push its remaining members to become even more violent—and finding a middle ground that simply de-escalates violence—an objective that might be successful in minimizing violence but that is likely to empower the organization politically. The path that is generally chosen by counterterrorist policies is to destroy the foe and risk retaliatory attacks on civilians.

For example, take the tactical decision to eliminate the senior political leadership of a 'terrorist group' through targeted killings. 'Decapitating' an armed organization not only may close doors to negotiation; it also makes it more difficult for the armed group to lay down its weapons as this requires a strong leadership. 'Decapitation' might furthermore fragment the clandestine organization and activate processes of ideological outbidding (or radicalization) among the remaining splinter groups (Della Porta 2013). The governmental objective, though, is invariably presented publicly as the unconditional protection of the population. There is, in other words, a tendency on the part of counterterrorist policies to misrepresent their underlying logic as one of violence reduction rather than of political struggle.

Take, as another example, and in spite of its many excesses, the Colombian government. It was astute enough between 2012 and 2016 not to completely destroy the FARC after a string of governmental military successes. Rather, it engaged in painstaking and controversial negotiations (Nussio and Ugarriza 2021). Had it destroyed the organization, the former FARC combatants would most likely have joined other groups, such as the Ejército de Liberación Nacional (ELN) or even drug cartels, as has happened with so many other defeated guerrilla organizations in South and Central America. Violence would have increased as a result. The Colombian government hence broke away from the counterterrorist rationale presiding over its security operations to engage—at least temporarily—in political negotiations. From this point on, FARC was no any longer considered a threat to the established sociopolitical order. Therefore, the government accepted the need to de-escalate its use of violence.

Similarly, the use of force in counterterrorism operations, particularly when it is viewed as excessively violent, has a tendency to drive parts of the population into the hands of the 'terrorists'. Random killings by incumbents generally increase the popularity of the political challengers (Kalyvas 2006). This was very powerfully illustrated during the Algerian War of Independence (1954–62). While the French army achieved significant tactical gains over the independence-seeking FLN, this came at a very high political cost. The French presence was largely rejected by Algerians in light of a counterterror campaign that included systemic intimidation, mass violence, and organized torture, as powerfully illustrated in *The Battle of Algiers* (1966), a film that was screened by the US Office of Special Operations and Low-Intensity Conflict in the lead-up to the invasion of Iraq (Gourevitch 2003). While the FLN was initially perceived negatively by most Algerians in 1954, by 1962 it was widely seen as a national liberation army as the result of the violence inflicted by the French (Horne 2012).

These adverse effects of certain types of counterterrorism have led some countries to develop alternative approaches to clandestine armed groups. The focus is on educational and cultural programmes, the social integration of 'at-risk groups', and the promotion of non-violent change, often under the moniker of 'de-radicalization' policies. One of the more famous examples is the British Prevent strategy launched in 2011. It claims to monitor, mentor, and ultimately safeguard 'vulnerable people' from joining terrorist groups through a multi-agency approach involving the police, faith-based organizations, schoolteachers, health professionals, and charities (Ragazzi 2017) Another focus concerns the mobilization of security and surveillance technologies. High-tech equipment is used to intercept communications, identify individuals on the move, detect suspicious behaviour, identify risky groups, and implement surveillance measures (see Bonditti 2004). This creates conditions in which authorities incarcerate on the basis of anticipated actions inferred from intelligence gathering as opposed to acts that have actually been committed (Aradau and van Munster 2007). These different types of action form conditions of possibility or impossibility through security. Both inform counterterrorism practices that target social groups deemed 'riskier' than others. For example, in the context of the fight against 'Jihadi terrorism', it is clear that Muslim minorities are subject to heightened counterterrorism measures. These measures reinforce the social stigma from which they already suffer in many contexts (Bigo 2010).

> On security as a condition of possibility or impossibility, see **Section 2.3**

8.5 Terrorism and counterterrorism: locating the political

> Political violence is discussed at length in **Chapter 4**

Terrorism is generally considered to be a specific type of political violence by authorities and analysts alike. Simultaneously, there is a tendency to downplay the role of political demands on the part of clandestine armed groups. For example, some analysts of terrorism delve into the psychology of perpetrators to identify signs of violent or otherwise deviant behaviour irrespective of political ideologies and contexts (Pearlstein 1991). This leads to a form of depoliticization of violence: the focus is put on individual idiosyncrasies rather than political demands. In a similar vein, some

> **Box 8.1** discusses (ir)rationality and clandestine political violence

authors have sought to explain 'terrorism' through poverty and dispossession, thus seeing economic inequalities as its root cause (Falk et al. 2011). While this may be the case at times, political violence is not necessarily a simple reaction to such inequalities. Most studies on Jihadis born and raised in the Middle East who engaged in high-profile attacks in Europe and the United States have been recruited from among the relatively wealthy, educated, and Westernized strata of their respective societies (Sageman 2014).

Regardless of motivations, it is important to keep the organized and collective nature of 'terrorism' in mind (Malešević 2017). This is ultimately what sustains the activity of clandestine armed groups in extremely adverse and hostile conditions. Even self-radicalized 'lone wolf terrorists' are also captured by this organizational

BOX 8.1 CLANDESTINE POLITICAL VIOLENCE AND THE QUESTION OF (IR)RATIONALITY

Explanations of terrorism are sometimes sought in the presumed psychiatric disorders of its perpetrators. The claim that irrationality, insanity, or 'mental disorders' lie behind political violence is, however, potentially ambiguous in its meaning and implications.

On the one hand, it has the potential of freeing the perpetrator of the charge of terrorism. This is the case when it is a psycho-legal assessment in the context of a trial. Indeed, the 'diagnosis' of insanity might in many legal systems contradict any charge of terrorism. It depoliticizes the incriminating act by denying that it flows from a political (rational) choice. The 'insanity defence' is therefore sometimes pursued by lawyers of terrorist suspects seeking to free their clients from any charge.

On the other hand, the 'charge of insanity' can also serve to accuse someone of pursuing a politically deviant agenda. It implies a pathologization of the politics behind the violence. Insanity here refers to wickedness and moral depravity rather than a disconnection between intent and action. Such rhetoric is frequent when it comes to references to 'Mad Mullahs' in the case of 'Islamic terrorism'.

The 'insanity defence' and the 'insanity charge' were played out against each other during the trial of far-right extremist Anders Breivik, the author of the 2011 mass shooting at Utøya in Norway. In 2012, he was convicted of mass murder and 'acts of terrorism' after having been recognized as 'sane' by psycho-legal experts. During the trial, Breivik actively refused to use the 'insanity defence' that could have freed him of any charge but that would have undermined his political agenda. In the media, however, he continued to be described as a 'sick mind' suffering from political paranoia and pathological racism long after his conviction. These descriptions were by no means meant to depoliticize or decriminalize his horrendous actions. They served to highlight the politically and criminally insane character of his 'terrorist acts'.

Of course, not all psychological readings of political violence go as far as to either demonize or deny any moral responsibility to terrorist suspects. By focusing on the role of psychological idiosyncrasies in predisposing individuals to political violence, however, they tend to disregard social, organizational, and political factors. This does not need to be the case. Authors like Olivier Roy have argued that the psychological factors that he claims to be involved in 'Jihadi terrorism' are themselves deeply political, shaped by power and socio-political orders (Roy 2017).

dimension: they appeal to, call for the creation of, imitate, or try to engage in a process of ideologically outdoing existing organizations. Personal biographies or psychological explanations, however relevant, cannot account for this. Ultimately, clandestine violence is political in that it emanates from identities, ideas, interests, institutions, and infrastructures that seek to contest existing power structures and to impose their own normative order (Malešević 2019).

> These different enablers are presented in **Section 3.3**

The political nature of clandestine violence is not just analytically important. It is also at the heart of wider political debates on violence. Indeed, clandestine political violence is generally addressed through a special regime of laws and practices based on the premise that because it is political, it is not ordinary criminal behaviour. There are roughly two positions taken on the legal ramifications. Both foreground the political nature of 'terrorism' but interpret it in different ways with very different implications.

The first can be classified as a traditional liberal stance. It argues that the political nature of armed violence ought to be considered a mitigating factor with regards to individual guilt (Moucheron 2006; Caesar 2017). While the violent means employed by such groups entail illegal acts, their motivations do not lie in personal gain, distinguishing these actions from 'ordinary criminal activity'. The objectives of these groups are deemed to be rooted in a principled vision regarding the common good. Disagreements about the collective good are at the heart of legitimate politics. The objectives pursued by these groups can therefore not be assumed from first principles to illegitimate, even though the means used might be intolerable.

> For more on this position, see **Section 4.3**

This is to a certain extent the understanding that prevailed under the British Emergency Provisions Act of 1973 in the context of the 'Troubles' in Northern Ireland. The act granted 'Special Category Status' to any IRA prisoner condemned for terrorist offences for more than nine months. The underlying assumption was that the political nature of nationalist violence mitigated the individual guilt of the perpetrators. 'Special Category' prisoners were accordingly given much more autonomy and rights to organize inside prisons than ordinary criminals. Wary of the message these 'terrorist privileges' might send to the British public, the British government revoked this special status in 1976. All prisoners convicted for terrorist acts were to be treated as ordinary criminals and deprived of the privileges they had previously enjoyed under the Act (Caesar 2017).

The second position on the legal ramifications of the political nature of 'terrorism' is more security-focused. According to this stance, 'terrorism' is political in the sense that it is a crime against the whole of the body politic, much like genocide. The political nature of terrorism here is an aggravating rather than mitigating factor. Terrorism destroys life, limb, and property, but also the political relations and basic trust that make it possible, or even desirable, to live together in a socio-political order. 'Terrorism' here is primarily political in the sense that it undermines democratic decision-making procedures that are the only source of legitimate politics. It is political because it seeks to undermine all forms of (democratic) politics. This is the interpretation of 'political violence' that tends to prevail in the contemporary fight against 'radical Islam'. It justifies exceptional practices, practices that are recognized to suspend established rules such as widespread wiretapping, random body-searches, racial profiling, preventative incarceration, systematic resort to solitary confinement in prison, and other measures that might not otherwise be tolerated. While the frequently used metaphor is of a balance between the benefits of liberty and the needs of security, Didier Bigo (2010) has shown that it often amounts to questioning the liberties of marginalized minorities to improve the security of the majority, thereby reinforcing existing hierarchies through security.

> The security-liberty balance is discussed in **Box 2.1**

It is interesting to note that counterterrorism, when it entails the use of force, is never presented as reflecting the political motivations of the incumbents. It is characterized as a technical rather than a political instrument. Since politics is generally seen as the domain of public debate, contingent choices, and human agency (Arendt 1998 [1958]), the description of counterterrorist repression as political would risk it being understood as arbitrary, contingent, and contestable. State violence legitimates itself by denying its own political nature. It justifies governmental decisions by invoking an independent legal order of self-referential rules rather than a world of contingent and contestable political agendas (Olsson 2013).

References to security in counterterrorism also play an important role with regards to depoliticization of its approach to law enforcement. Security is portrayed as the domain of necessity and requires taking definitive action in the face of existential threats to collective survival. If (normal) politics is about doing what one collectively wants, security is frequently framed as being about doing what one *must*. It is often perceived as being beyond (normal) politics (see Wæver 1995). To invoke security for a given course of action is a claim that there is no viable alternative, that one is acting under the constraints of necessity. The security rationale of counterterrorism in this sense also serves to depoliticize state repression, to conceal the underlying political choices that are made in the process of fighting terrorism. Yet, in the most basic sense, counterterrorist violence is political since it aims to enforce a socio-political order. Hard-line counterterrorist security postures also often obfuscate that this socio-political order might be what fuels clandestine political violence. It is not a coincidence that political hard-liners in Israel frequently present Palestinian violence as the mere expression of religious extremism and/or antisemitic bigotry (e.g., Netanyahu 1986). By doing so, Palestinian resistance is disconnected from what international law has unambiguously characterized as an ongoing illegal occupation of East Jerusalem, the West Bank, and Gaza (Weiss 2016).

8.6 Civilians caught between rival political orders

In many asymmetric conflicts, non-state armed groups are able to control territory. For example, we have seen this recently in the Democratic Republic of Congo, Somalia, Yemen, and Syria (Staniland 2012). For the civilians who inhabit contested territories potentially subject to changes in control, a fine line separates security from insecurity as they must constantly consider whose authority to endorse. To adhere to the order provided by one group in the conflict is to risk reprisals from other groups. Navigating this insecurity becomes a matter of life and death. Decisions taken will largely depend on uncertain predictions about the future outcome of the conflict.

> The question of authority is explored in **Section 4.4**

The uncertainty of these contexts can also help us to understand why they can become so violent. Kalyvas (2006) has highlighted that civilian populations are not only passive victims but also active participants in the targeting of other civilians in such situations. A significant portion of the violence against civilians in asymmetric conflicts arises from civilians denouncing other civilians as traitors, insurgents, threats, enemies, or government agents depending on who happens to control the territory. Claims are often based on broader societal hierarchies that do not necessarily correlate entirely with the political stakes between the political incumbents and its challengers.

The more territorial control an armed organization enjoys in a local area (whether that group be the state or a non-state actor), the more people will seek to increase their own security by engaging in denunciations. While this enhances the survival chances of the denunciators, it also, in theory, potentially reduces the likelihood of indiscriminate violence on the part of the newly established incumbents. This stems from the information they receive about 'threats' which enables them to more easily identify those who are 'in' or 'out' of the new socio-political order (Kalyvas 2006). Conversely, a situation in which the former incumbents (or insurgents enjoying territorial control) have to leave a territory may lead to a cycle of broader arbitrary reprisals against those believed to be disloyal but who are harder to accurately identify (Kalyvas 1999). The departing incumbent (or insurgents enjoying rebel control) will therefore likely be seen by the population as increasingly threatening. In contrast, the newly arriving authority may come to be seen as an unambiguous provider of security by imposing a stable set of rules that does not require indiscriminate violence to uphold order.

These dynamics highlight how easy it is for an organization to appear as a 'legitimate' security provider when it exercises significant levels of control of a socio-political order in a given territory. Where and when clandestine armed groups seize power, they generally become providers of governance, security, and policing. Conversely, where and when their hegemony is contested, they become a source of targeted actions and then random violence against civilians. This can clearly be seen in the way in which Taliban narratives on urban Afghans changed in 2021, as they took control of cities across the country. First, the Taliban described themselves as a force able to strike anyone, anywhere and anytime, who opposed them. As their control extended, their narrative shifted to one in which they were the protectors and defenders of fellow Afghans, irrespective of political beliefs, ethnicity, gender, or religious creed. On 17 August 2021, two days after the Taleban seized Kabul, Zabihullah Mujahid, their spokesperson who for years had claimed and threatened attacks on civilian and military targets in Kabul, including embassies, suddenly changed his tone: 'we want to assure the residents of Kabul for full security, for protection of their dignity and security and safety. . . . The security of the embassies is very crucial, of crucial importance for us' (Mujahid 2021). Asymmetric conflicts are ultimately sites where the contingency of power relations reveals the ambiguous nature of (in)security and socio-political (dis)order. To provide security or insecurity, and to establish order or threaten disorder, become two sides of the same coin.

8.7 Conclusion

In this chapter, we have shown how clandestine political violence and asymmetric conflict emerge from struggles between rival socio-political orders. Security is the core of these conflicts. Here, security refers to what aspects of collective life must be safeguarded for the sake of the polities' survival, even at the cost of some lives. More broadly, these conflicts order societies by defining what can be done in the name of security. This occurs as authorities blur the line between the criminal and the political enemy, the one who breaks the law of the land and the one who tries to impose a new law on the land. Clandestine political violence and asymmetric conflict hence generally borrow their representations from warfare and policing without being reducible to either of these categories (Olsson 2019). In fact, as highlighted by Walter Benjamin (2009), the violence that subverts the law always contains, even if only potentially, an alternative law waiting to be put into action. Similarly, the violence that upholds the law always also seeks to prevent the potential emergence of alternative socio-political orders.

Being attuned to contingency, historicity, sociology, and the possibilities for transformation highlights the potential fluidity of parties to asymmetric conflicts with regards to maintaining and undermining order. To put it more directly, asking critical questions reminds us of the fact that the incumbents of today might be the challengers of tomorrow, and vice versa. In many cases, yesterday's terrorists have been today's negotiating parties and tomorrow's power-holders. From the Continental Army of the 13 Colonies during the American revolutionary war to the African National Congress (ANC) in South Africa, or the Palestine Liberation Organization (PLO), examples abound of groups that were once considered 'terrorists' or 'insurgents' gaining access to legitimate authority (Connelly 2002).

> These core elements of critique are discussed in **Section 1.2**

In the case of Al-Qaeda and IS, the dynamics of clandestine violence are complicated by the fact that their most spectacular (but not necessarily most lethal) attacks are geographically remote from the targets of their political strategy for seizing power. Their strategy is highly internationalized and their audiences segmented. As such, their activities reflect trends that can also be observed in the field of counterterrorism. The globalization of the fight against terrorism and the transnational characteristics of clandestine political violence have their own independent drivers. However, they are also mutually reinforcing as each feeds off the actions of the other.

Questions for further discussion

1. In 1969, referring to the Vietnam War, US Secretary of State and National Security Adviser Henry Kissinger claimed: 'The conventional army loses if it does not win. The guerrilla wins if he does not lose'. What does this mean? Do you agree?

2. Regarding NATO forces in Afghanistan, the Taliban are reported to have said: 'You have the watches, we have the time'. How do different asymmetries affect the types of questions we can ask about security?

3. We often say that 'one's person terrorist is another's freedom fighter' to highlight the subjectivity of terrorism. Does this distinction still matter politically? If so, why?

4. The necessity for state actors to respect the rule of law is presented by some governments and even in popular culture (e.g., the TV series *24*) as hampering the fight against terrorism. At the same time, the rule of law is claimed by others to be the best weapon against clandestine armed groups. What do you think? Why?

5. According to most statistics, states are on average responsible for more civilian casualties in asymmetric conflicts than their non-state opponents. Why might this discrepancy matter politically?

Further reading

Arjona, Ana, Nelson Kasfir, and Zachariah Mampilly. Eds. 2015. *Rebel governance in civil war*. Cambridge: Cambridge University Press.
This edited volume deals with the way in which insurgent organizations interact with civilian populations when they manage to control territory. It shows how some groups manage to govern and provide public services to populations while at the same time fighting against the official government.

Galula, David. 1964. *Counter-insurgency warfare: Theory and practice*. New York: Praeger.
This book is considered a classic of counterinsurgency. It is written by a former French officer who participated in the Algerian War of Independence. It outlines an approach that is very different from the one that was implemented by the French in Algeria.

Khalili, Laleh. 2012. *Time in the shadows: Confinement in counterinsurgency*. Stanford, CA: Stanford University Press.
Laleh Khalili analyses the role of confinement in contemporary asymmetric wars, focusing on the post-9/11 'global war on terror' and the Israeli occupation of Palestine. She shows how civilians have been detained in camps and other facilities in diverse operations that highlight significant continuities with techniques of colonial control.

Pontecorvo, Gillo. 1966. *The battle of Algiers*. 120 min.
This movie revolves around the battle between the French military and clandestine cells of the FLN in the Algerian capital in 1958 during the Algerian war of liberation. Although opposed to the French presence, Gillo Pontecorvo has been criticized for giving the impression in the movie that the extreme methods used by the French military were ultimately successful. In reality, they participated in turning the majority of the Algerian population against the French presence and paved the way to Algerian independence in 1962.

Taussig, Michael. 2003. *Law in a lawless land: Diary of a limpieza in Colombia*. Chicago, IL: University of Chicago Press.
In this book, written as a diary, Michael Taussig recounts the two weeks he spent in a small town in Colombia's Cauca Valley where paramilitaries established their authority with the support of the police. The book describes what happens when a state tries to reclaim control over its territory with the help of paramilitary groups.

References

Aradau, Claudia and Rens van Munster. 2007. 'Governing terrorism through risk: Taking precautions, (un)knowing the future'. *European Journal of International Relations* 13(1), 89–115.

Arendt, Hannah. 1998 [1958]. *The human condition*. 2nd ed. Chicago, IL: University of Chicago Press.

Arreguín-Toft, Ivan. 2001. 'How the weak win wars: A theory of asymmetric conflict'. *International Security* 26(1), 93–128.

Asad, Talal. 2007. *On suicide bombing*. New York: Columbia University Press.

Baczko, Adam, Gilles Dorronsoro, and Arthur Quesnay. 2018. *Civil war in Syria: Mobilization and competing social orders*. Cambridge: Cambridge University Press.

Benjamin, Walter. 2009. *One-way street and other writings*. London: Penguin UK.

Berti, Benedetta. 2011. 'Armed groups as political parties and their role in electoral politics: The case of Hizballah'. *Studies in Conflict & Terrorism* 34(12), 942–962.

Berti, Benedetta. 2016. 'Rebel politics and the state: Between conflict and post-conflict, resistance and co-existence'. *Civil Wars* 18(2), 118–136.

Bigo, Didier. 2006. 'Protection: Security, territory and population'. In *The politics of protection: Sites of insecurity and political agency*, edited by Jef Huysmans, Andrew Dobson, and Raia Prokhovnik. London: Routledge.

Bigo, Didier. 2010. 'Delivering liberty and security? The framing of freedom when associated with security'. In *Europe's 21st century challenge: Delivering liberty*, edited by Didier Bigo, Sergio Carrera, Elspeth Guild, and R. B. J. Walker. London: Ashgate.

Bonditti, Philippe. 2004. 'From territorial space to networks: A Foucauldian approach to the implementation of biometry'. *Alternatives: Global, Local, Political* 29(4), 465–482.

Bosi, Lorenzo and Niall Ó Dochartaigh. 2018. 'Armed activism as the enactment of a collective identity: The case of the Provisional IRA between 1969 and 1972'. *Social Movement Studies* 17(1), 35–47.

Bull, Hedley. 2012[1977]. *The anarchical society: A study of order in world politics*. London: Palgrave Macmillan.

Caesar, Samantha A. 2017. 'Captive or criminal? Reappraising the legal status of IRA prisoners at the height of the Troubles under International Law'. *Duke Journal of Comparative & International Law* 27(2), 323–348.

Clausewitz, Carl von. 2010 [1832]. *On war*. Auckland: The Floating Press.

Connelly, Matthew. 2002. *A diplomatic revolution: Algeria's fight for independence and the origins of the Post-Cold War era*. Oxford: Oxford University Press.

Della Porta, Donatella. 2013. *Clandestine political violence*. Cambridge: Cambridge University Press.

Dudai, Ron and Daphna Baram. 2004. 'The second battle of Algiers'. *The Guardian*, 30 October. www.theguardian.com/world/2004/oct/30/comment# (last accessed 12 January 2022).

Falk, Armin, Andreas Kuhn, and Josef Zweimüller. 2011. 'Unemployment and right-wing extremist crime'. *The Scandinavian Journal of Economics* 113(2), 260–285.

Foucault, Michel. 2009 [1978]. *Security, territory, population: Lectures at the Collège de France, 1977–1978*. Houndmills: Palgrave Macmillan.

Foucault, Michel. 2012 [1975]. *Discipline and punish: The birth of the prison*. New York: Random House.

Funk, David A. 1972. 'Major functions of law in modern society'. *Case Western Reserve Law Review* 23(2), 257–306.

Goodwin, Jeff. 2001. *No other way out: States and revolutionary movements, 1945–1991*. Cambridge: Cambridge University Press.

Goodwin, Jeff. 2006. 'A theory of categorical terrorism'. *Social Forces* 84(4), 2027–2046.

Gourevitch, Philip. 2003. 'Winning and losing'. *The New Yorker*, 22 December. www.newyorker.com/magazine/2003/12/22/winning-and-losing (last accessed 17 February 2022).

Hoffman, Bruce. 2017. *Inside terrorism*. New York: Columbia University Press.

Horne, Alistair. 2012. *A savage war of peace: Algeria 1954–1962*. London: Palgrave Macmillan.

Howard, Michael. 2002. 'What's in a name? How to fight terrorism'. *Foreign Affairs* 81(1), 8–13.

Kalyvas, Stathis N. 1999. 'Wanton and senseless? The logic of massacres in Algeria'. *Rationality and Society* 11(3), 243–285.

Kalyvas, Stathis N. 2006. *The logic of violence in civil war*. Cambridge: Cambridge University Press.

Lipschutz, Ron D. Ed. 1995. *On security*. New York: Columbia University Press.

Malešević, Siniša. 2017. *The rise of organised brutality*. Cambridge: Cambridge University Press.

Malešević, Siniša. 2019. 'Cultural and anthropological approaches to the study of terrorism'. In *The Oxford handbook of terrorism*, edited by Erica Chenoweth, Richard English, Andreas Gofas, and Stathis N. Kalyvas. Oxford: Oxford University Press.

Moucheron, Martin. 2006. 'Délit politique et terrorisme en Belgique: du noble au vil'. *Cultures Conflits* 61(1), 77–100.

Mujahid, Zabihullah. 2021. 'Transcript of Taliban's first press-conference in Kabul'. 17 August. www.aljazeera.com/news/2021/8/17/transcript-of-talibans-first-press-conference-in-kabul (last accessed 11 March 2022).

Netanyahu, Benjamin. Ed. 1986. *Terrorism: How the West can win*. New York: Farrar, Straus, Giroux.

Nussio, Enzo and Juan E. Ugarriza. 2021. 'Why rebels stop fighting: Organizational decline and desertion in Colombia's insurgency'. *International Security* 45(4), 167–203.

Olsson, Christian. 2013. 'Legitimate violence in the prose of counterinsurgency: An impossible necessity?'. *Alternatives: Global, Local, Political* 38(2), 155–171.

Olsson, Christian. 2015. 'De la sécurité à la violence organisée: tropismes et points aveugles de « l'Ecole de Copenhague »'. *Études internationales* 46(2–3), 211–233.

Olsson, Christian. 2019. 'Can't live with them, can't live without them: "The enemy" as object of controversy in contemporary Western wars'. *Critical Military Studies* 5(4), 359–377.

Olsson, Christian and Philippe Bonditti. 2016. 'Violence, war and security knowledge: Between theoretical practices and practical theories'. In *International political sociology: Transversal lines*, edited by Tugba Basaran, Didier Bigo, Emmanuel-Pierre Guittet, and R. B. J. Walker. London: Routledge.

Pearlstein, Richard M. 1991. *The mind of the political terrorist*. Wilmington, DE: Scholarly Resources Inc.

Ragazzi, Francesco. 2017. 'Countering terrorism and radicalisation: Securitising social policy?' *Critical Social Policy* 37(2), 163–179.

Roy, Olivier. 2017. *Jihad and death: The global appeal of the Islamic State*. London: Hurst.

Sageman, Marc. 2014. *Understanding terror networks*. Philadelphia, PA: University of Pennsylvania Press.

Sinno, Abdulkader H. 2011. *Organizations at war in Afghanistan and beyond*. Ithaca, NY: Cornell University Press.

Staniland, Paul. 2012. 'States, insurgents, and wartime political orders'. *Perspectives on Politics* 10(2), 243–264.

TAUSSIG, MICHAEL. 2003. *Law in a lawless land: Diary of a limpieza in Colombia*. Chicago, IL: University of Chicago Press.
TILLY, CHARLES. 1985. 'State formation as organized crime'. In *Bringing the state back in*, edited by PETER EVANS, DIETRICH RUESCHEMEYER, and THEDA SKOCPOL. Cambridge: Cambridge University Press.
TILLY, CHARLES. 2004. 'Terror, terrorism, terrorists'. *Sociological Theory* 22(1), 5–13.
WÆVER, OLE. 1995. 'Securitization and desecuritization'. In *On security*, edited by RONNIE D. LIPSCHUTZ. New York: Columbia University Press.
WEBER, MAX. 1965 [1919]. *Politics as a vocation*. Minneapolis, MN: Fortress Press.
WEISS, PETER. 2016. 'International law and the occupied territories'. *Palestine-Israel Journal of Politics, Economics, and Culture* 21(3), 96–101.

9

Identity and othering

Melody Fonseca Santos

9.1	Introduction	139
9.2	Conceptualizing identity	142
9.3	Predatory identities	143
9.4	Alternative identity practices: relationality between/within differences	149
9.5	Conclusion	151

READER'S GUIDE

In this chapter we explore the relationship between identity, difference, and (in)security. If identity is primarily conceived of in relation to difference, we ask whether it must inevitably lead to 'othering' and violence. We then show how identity can be understood relationally such that difference need not be understood as inherently threatening. We conclude by exploring the possibilities that are generated when we view identity and difference as a relation that is shaped by a logic of 'both-and' rather than 'either-or'.

9.1 Introduction

Illustrative case studies on the topics explored in this chapter are available on the online resources to help take your understanding of identity and othering further: http://www.oup.com/he/Grayson-Guillaume1e.

Let us start with three vignettes about identity and how it can impact our daily lives. These vignettes also highlight that while central to the meaning-making and productive aspects of security, identity is nevertheless an extremely complicated social dynamic.

In 2016, Colin Kaepernick, an American football player for the San Francisco 49ers, started sitting down, and then kneeling, during the playing of the US national anthem before National Football League games. Kaepernick knelt specifically as a protest against racial injustice and police brutality that has generated fear and insecurity in African-American communities. In doing so, he tapped into previous protests such as Tommie Smith and John Carlos raising black-gloved fists (to symbolize Black Power) on the medal podium at the 1968 Olympics in Mexico City, or all-star baseball player Carlos Delgado's refusal to stand for the playing of 'God Bless America' during games to show his opposition to the invasion of Iraq in 2003. Kaepernick's actions also inspired the Black Lives Matter movement. Nevertheless, 'taking the knee' reignited a contentious debate about 'us' and 'them' within the United States, bringing into the open imaginaries of borders, migration, citizenship, and security. Given that the national anthem evokes institutions, ideas, and values central to American society, Kaepernick's protest was viewed by many, including President Donald Trump, as 'anti-American'. At the end of the season, Kaepernick became a free agent. Despite impressive levels of performance on the field, no team has been willing to sign him.

In 2013, the Dominican Republic Supreme Court withdrew Dominican citizenship from thousands of residents of Haitian decent born in the Dominican Republic since 1929. After an intense debate, the Dominican government has recently begun to reverse this decision by returning citizenship to a small number of those who had it revoked. However, the government has also claimed that it will build a border wall to guard against 'security threats' from the outside. Here we can see how citizenship and immigration laws can be used to delimit rights and responsibilities within a state depending on who is deemed a threat and who is considered worthy of protection. By extension, whether someone is deemed a threat or worthy of protection is related to who is considered to be inside, or the outside, of the political community.

Just as certain bodies can be perceived as threats to a community, so too can ideas. Recently, a group of French intellectuals signed a manifesto arguing against 'decolonial ideology' (https://manifestedes90.wixsite.com/monsite). The signatories considered decolonial thinking to be an import from the United States that destabilizes French society by imposing feelings of guilt about its colonial past. They positioned decolonial thinking as a menace to purportedly 'universal' republican values of liberty, equality, and fraternity. For these intellectuals, these values are threatened by any discussion of race and identity, which they believe inherently causes social fragmentation. Within French society, they claim that racial and identity politics have been driven by radical political movements that adopt decolonial praxis such as the Parti des Indigènes de la République (PIR).

These three vignettes demonstrate some of the ways that the domestic and the foreign are constructed through different social imaginaries and discourses of danger. These constitute the boundaries of an imagined collective 'self', and who can 'speak' security or against it. Thus, we can see how security relies on identity practices to help mobilize security. Identity practices are practices that enable a person, or a group, to establish or challenge who they are and who they are not in relation to difference (i.e., in juxtaposition to something that is not 'us'). More often than not, when these practices are connected to security, they become an exercise of othering. Othering transforms difference into the figure of an 'other' who is deemed to be inferior and, more importantly, dangerous. Thus, how does othering relate to security? How does the practice of othering lead to political violence?

Identity is a complex social construction. Identities are dimensions of our lives we subjectively use to make sense of ourselves, our actions, and those of others in the worlds around us; they are ways that we instil a sense of belonging. They provide us with a sense of security by telling us who we are, our place in our worlds, and where we should be rightfully positioned in relation to other individuals and groups—these underpin what is known as 'ontological security', a sense that one is secure in the knowledge of their world and how it works. Subjectively felt identities are also shaped by discourses, practices, debates, tensions, and conflicts about what they are for 'us' as a collective. The idea that this 'us' is being challenged and might change, or is in the process of changing, generates various anxieties. Who is the source of change? An intruder? A stranger to the community? A traitor? Someone who is a threat to 'us'? Why is there change? Just to be different? To divide 'us'? To destroy 'us'? When these questions shape security discourses and practices, our very existence may be called into question. In these circumstances, security is often mobilized in order to preserve a particular understanding of an identity, community, and/or way of life.

As security analysts and global citizens, we should ask the following when identity claims are used to mobilize security:

- Whose identity must be secured?
- From what?
- For what purpose?
- At whose expense?

Our everyday decisions are marked by tensions between our subjective identities (i.e., who we believe we are), how they are a part of socio-political orders, our understandings of them, and how they relate to security. But is every identity practice a security act and if so, why? Does identity always require difference? How are identity and practices of othering related to the legacies of colonialism, imperialism, racism, classism, patriarchy, heteronormativity, ableism, and other systems of domination and oppression? Must the relationship between identity and difference lead to othering? If so, are there ethical choices to be made in relation to the distance we place between ourselves and the other as well as the meanings we attach to difference?

To help you reflect on these questions, this chapter starts by introducing a set of concepts to analyse identity and othering in relation to security (Section 9.2). Identity practices are discussed. We provide a series of questions that can be asked about how identity relates to security. These questions will help you understand how identity can be conceptualized and its relation to difference. In Section 9.3, we engage with Arjun Appadurai's (2006) concept of 'predatory identities'. Here we see how identity practices built on nostalgic discourses of sameness, unity, nation, and empire project and construct an otherness understood as a threat to security. In Section 9.4, we introduce alternative identity practices that might decouple identity from notions of threat, while building upon difference and heterogeneity. This has

> On security as a mobilization, see **Section 2.4**

> **Chapters 10** and **11** discuss racism, patriarchy, and heteronormativity

been called deep relationality or *cosmopraxis* (Tickner and Querejazu 2021). We conclude with how these alternative practices of identity can disrupt traditional and predatory perspectives of security.

9.2 Conceptualizing identity

There are many different approaches to what identity *is* and what it does. For some, identity is primordial. This means that identity is an inherent characteristic that is fixed, unchanging, and independent of socio-political processes. Historically, national and ethnic identities have often been seen as primordial. However, other perspectives see identity as a social construct, developed through discourses and practices of representation. These practices occur at the individual and collective level. They often imply a complex inside/outside view of belonging based on the idea that only certain identities are rightfully part of a given socio-political order.

When thinking about identity as a social construct, it is common to see multiple elements to our own identity (as a Self) such as our gender, race, ethnicity, and class. Chances are that if you think about your own identity, different elements will come to mind. It may be very difficult to decide if only one (and which one) defines you. And how you define yourself might vary depending on the context. You might then be persuaded to see identities as multiple, contextual, contingent, and intersecting. Moreover, upon reflection, you may feel that these multiple elements are as connected to qualities that you believe that you *are not* as qualities you believe that you *are*. And who you believe you are (and are not) may change over time!

> On contingency, historicity, reification, and intersectionality, see **Section 1.2**

Despite this complexity, contingency, and multiplicity, identities *do* things that have significant security consequences within, and across, socio-political orders, including influencing who is understood to rightfully belong within a socio-political order and who does not. In the sections that follow, we will suggest different ways we can conceptualize identity as a social construct in which difference plays an important role in the construction of the Self. In doing so, we will be able to ask better questions that can help us to understand how identity and difference connect to security.

9.2.1 Identity/difference

One helpful way of conceptualizing identity is to be sensitive to how it relies on ideas of difference to give it meaning. David Campbell (1998, 9) argues that identity is 'an inescapable dimension of being . . . identity—whether personal or collective—is not fixed by nature, given by God, or planned by intentional behaviour. Rather, identity is constituted in relation to difference'. This view of identity enables us to look at security and other forms of state policy as ways of establishing and enforcing difference by distinguishing an imagined self (i.e., the domestic, the accepted, the normal) from the imagined Other (i.e., the foreign, the unacceptable, the abnormal).

Taken at face value, this understanding of identity raises an important question: can we (or a state actor) simply pick and choose our identities like we pick and choose what to wear each morning? For William Connolly (1991, 64), the answer is no: '[m]y identity is what I am and how I am recognized rather than what I choose, want, or consent to'. His point is that within a socio-political order our identities are interconnected with what others recognize and are potentially prepared to accept as our defining characteristics. This can be in relation to the validity of the identity claim (e.g., do you have evidence to support your claim that you are a citizen?) and/or its social legitimacy (i.e., is it socially acceptable to be identified in a particular way?). Likewise, we also must recognize the identities claimed by others. In this sense, identity/difference is a mutually constitutive practice whose power is dispersed across sets of relations that include people, ideas, and institutions. As such, Connolly argues that converting identity and difference into an 'Otherness' that mobilizes security is not inevitable. However, it is also not unusual. As Connolly (1991, 64) suggests, 'identity requires difference in order to be, and it converts difference into otherness in order to secure its own self-certainty'.

> Relations of power are discussed in **Section 3.2**

While the basis of differences assumed among selves and others may be blurry, the role of security is to maintain clear distinctions. Furthermore, identity practices, and the processes that establish and maintain identity/difference, are always partial and limited, and subject to contexts of domination and oppression. More broadly, critical perspectives, as we will see in Section 9.4, reveal how security influences identity practices as well as offering potential means to challenge, resist, disrupt, change, and even transform them. For many critical perspectives, our relationships with others should take an open approach that enables their multiple dimensions to be discovered through processes of mutual recognition rather than overlaying our own anxieties or fears onto them (Inayatullah and Blaney 1996, 65–66). This requires a willingness to engage in dialogue with others. By doing so, it is argued that opportunities will also arise for an internal dialogue about 'who we are' as our ideas about others inform our ideas about ourselves (Guillaume 2002). Thus, difference can potentially be positive and affirming rather than necessarily leading to a sense of insecurity.

9.3 Predatory identities

Security mobilizations tend to perceive identity and difference in binary terms with clear distinctions between the Self and Other. Here the Self is inherently good and under threat. In sharp contrast, the Other is an enemy that embodies negative characteristics in complete opposition to the Self. Binary thinking can help us to understand the identity practices of the nation-state. States regularly deploy narratives about who is considered a threat, who is an ally, which geographic spaces are secure/insecure as a result, and why security needs to be mobilized against an Other (Campbell 1998). For example, in Barbados, in the late 2000s, migrants from Guyana were subject to anti-immigrant sentiment and a focal point for political debates about the desirability of free movement provisions under CARICOM (Caribbean Community; see COHA 2009). While these concerns have encompassed traditional economic anxieties (i.e., 'they are stealing our jobs'), they have also incorporated social anxieties (e.g., 'they

> **Chapter 11** discusses the place of nationalism in security

are stealing our single men'). Underlying anti-Guyanese positions has been an understanding that they embody ethnic differences that pose a threat—most Guyanese migrants are of Indo-Caribbean descent in contrast to Barbados which is predominately Afro-Caribbean (over 90 per cent of the population).

Given these identity practices, their relations to security often appear enduring and deeply embedded into our worlds. How might we transform them, particularly if identity practices seem to shape every possible relationship by seeking to define and fix who we (and others) are? Must all identity practices be fixed and reifying rather than contingent and contextual? Must a secure sense of our own identity require us to negate the existence of other identities?

Arjun Appadurai has proposed the term 'predatory identities' to refer to 'those identities whose social construction and mobilization require the extinction of other, proximate social categories, defined as threats to the very existence of some group, defined as we' (Appadurai 2006, 51). Predatory identities provide a hierarchical and racialized way to understand the self vis-à-vis the other that often rely on logics first established under colonialism. A predatory identity can work in several different ways and be defined through a variety of factors (e.g., gender, race, sexuality, disability, and their intersections). Here we consider three forms of identity practice that generate predatory identities: exterminating, converting, or containing the Other (Fonseca and Jerrems 2012).

> On the impact of coloniality and the importance of Frantz Fanon, see **Box 9.1**

Predatory identities can produce forms of political violence like genocide whose objective is to completely eliminate the other. Extermination can be performed by a state or groups that claim a responsibility to defend national identity from those framed as a threat to it. The Jewish Holocaust, the Maya genocide in Guatemala during the 1970s and 1980s, and the Tutsi genocide in Rwanda in 1994 were acts of political violence enabled by (among other factors) an essentialist perception of the identity of the Self and understanding the mere existence of the Other as a security risk.

> Property rights, development, and security are discussed in **Chapters 12** and **14**

If we take the Maya genocide as an example, we can see how colonial legacies, white supremacy, land redistribution and property rights, and conceptions of development informed security practices in the context of the Cold War (Casaús Arzú 2019). Guatemala experienced a civil war from 1960 until 1996. With the support of the United States, the Guatemalan government claimed to be defending the established capitalist order against communist ideas highly popular in Indigenous peasant communities. Yet, for decades, the Guatemalan economic, political, and military elite built an anti-Indigenous narrative through processes of othering that framed Indigenous communities as the primary threat to Guatemala's progress. Thus, the mere existence of Indigenous peoples was presented as a threat to the development of the true Guatemalan nation. Racist theories were used to establish the Indigenous Other as biologically and culturally inferior (Casaús Arzú 2018). Security mobilizations (e.g., counterinsurgency campaigns) were undertaken to preserve a racialized order, in which people considered to be from white and *mestizo* backgrounds were privileged and protected. With most rural communities in Guatemala identified as

> ### BOX 9.1 FRANTZ FANON AND THE 'COLONIALITY OF BEING'
>
> '"Look, a Negro!" It was an external stimulus that flicked over me as I passed by. I made a tight smile.
> "Look, a Negro!" It was true. It amused me.
> "Look, a Negro!" The circle was drawing a bit tighter. I made no secret of my amusement.
> "Mama, see the Negro! I'm frightened!" Frightened! Frightened! Now they were beginning to be afraid of me. I made up my mind to laugh myself to tears, but laughter had become impossible'. (Fanon 1986 [1952], 84)
>
> It is with these words that Frantz Fanon began his reflection on the lived experience of being a Black man in France in the 1940s and 1950s. He took this as an opportunity to challenge the legacies of racist essentialism. In turn, his work provides us with an opportunity to think about how our identities still remain tied to coloniality. Fanon was one of the most influential Caribbean thinkers of the twentieth century. A trained psychiatrist, philosopher, and writer from Martinique (a non-independent country in the Caribbean with the formal status of *Territoire d'outre-mer* of France), Fanon enlisted with the French armed forces during the Second World War. There, he experienced the racism of the French army and the French population he helped to liberate. He relocated to Algeria in the mid-1950s and fought for its independence until his death at thirty-six years old. A result of this experience is his second major work, *The Wretched of the Earth* (2005 [1961]).
>
> Decolonial thought has forwarded the concept of the 'coloniality of being'. This refers to the lived experience of all colonized subjects that is constituted through colonialism and its impact on language, culture, and representation (identity). The coloniality of being draws our attention to identities and techniques employed to dominate, contain, and/or convert those who have been subject to colonialization, even after the formal institutional relationship has ended. For Fanon, the 'being' (i.e., the colonizer) will always have the advantage of naming, of giving back to the non-being (i.e., the colonized) his disrupted identity. In this sense, Fanon saw the continuation of non-being as the product of an anti-Black world. It is hidden away. Violence is the norm. At the same time, it is a space from which resistance can emerge.
>
> Fanon also argued that the liberation—not formal independence—of a colonized people should be carried out through a national and popular process with an international dimension, which he called a national consciousness, 'which is not nationalism'. For Fanon (2005 [1961], 179), '[t]his question of national consciousness and national culture takes on a special dimension in Africa. The birth of national consciousness in Africa strictly correlates with an African consciousness'. Fanon's work critically engages with the relationship between security and the self that is performed by white and colonial subjects to better understand how this produces non-white and colonized subjects. As such, the other is a creation of the self, and its reproduction is based on co-dependency.

being both peasant and Indigenous, the war against communism meant exterminating Indigenous communities.

Predatory identities may also be performed by attempting to convert the Other into the Self through acculturation. This process, practised by governments in colonial and post-colonial settings, is also rooted in racist theories that consider the Other to be backward, inferior, and undesirable. However, instead of pursuing the Other's extermination through mass killings or genocide, the ambition is to destroy languages, social structures, cultural artefacts, religions, belief systems, and ways of living that are present across different layers of societies. The purpose is to destroy worlds. Nevertheless, because this often occurs in the absence of physical violence, conversion can be harder to identify and challenge.

These intertwined methods of conversion include various practices that go from national policies on racial mixing and immigration to policies of racial segregation. For example, during the nineteenth century in Mexico, assumptions from scientific racism about the superiority of whites were challenged by the cosmic race narrative. This narrative argued that mixing among white, Indigenous, and Black populations was key to the betterment of the human race. This proposal privileged *mestizaje*—mixed people—as an alternative to white supremacy. However, the cosmic race narrative also essentialized *mestizaje* by stripping away the political violence that facilitated their emergence. They did not emerge as a community from harmonious mixing but rather came from a context of violent conquest, colonialism, and the systematic rape of Indigenous and African women. The cosmic race narrative also reinforced white supremacy since those who exhibited features closer to whiteness remained privileged within its idealized socio-political order (Sue 2013; Moreno Figueroa and Saldívar Tanaka 2016). Similar whitening policies took place in Brazil with so-called 'racial democracy'. From the end of the nineteenth century into the first decades of the twentieth century, Brazilian governments developed immigration laws encouraging white European immigration. These policies were rooted in Social Darwinism and aimed to whiten Brazilian society through racial mixing (FitzGerald and Cook-Martin 2014).

A third practice upheld by predatory identities is the containment of the Other. Containment is manifested through the politics of space and how spatial logics are informed by hegemonic imaginaries about the Self and Other (Harvey 1990). These policies include city planning that physically divides zones so that individuals racialized as non-whites are kept away from whiter and wealthier communities (Outtes 2003). As has been studied extensively, variables such as race, class, disability, and gender affect infrastructure policies, access to education, health outcomes, and security in cities all around the world, from Brasilia to Tokyo. The politics of space, and spatial relations, may also include regional politics that silence and/or erase the histories of non-white communities, driving them away from where they have lived and, thus, suppressing their history and identity (Appelbaum 1999).

Within a nation-state, predatory identities are most likely to be performed by those who disproportionately benefit from the current structure of the socio-political order. These benefits contribute to a sense of being superior to others. Yet Appadurai (2006, 53) suggests that predatory identities exhibit an 'anxiety for the incompleteness' that comes from the fear of the loss of identity in the face of the appearance of other identities. This anxiety operates in different ways. It is felt by those fearing that proximity to the Other will bring heterogeneity, placing the purity of one's identity at risk. Paradoxically, it is also felt by those who fear that proximity will homogenize their identity. Sameness, difference, heterogeneity, and homogeneity change in meaning depending on how predatory identity is mobilized in a given socio-political context.

For predatory identities, difference is considered a threat as it may change the identity of the Self. These threats may be perceived as coming from foreign countries. For example, Western representations of Muslim and Arab countries have historically positioned them as inferior to the West through a series of knowledge production practices that Edward Said (1978) has called 'Orientalism'. As identities are not fixed, the identification of the Other changes. However, this Other is considered at best a stranger and at worst an existential threat.

If we return to the Kaepernick vignette from the start of the chapter, his actions opened a double framing of identity and difference within US society. There is nothing more 'American' than objecting to racial violence, some would say. Kaepernick's actions thus follow a long history of civil disobedience in the face of discrimination. For others, there is nothing more un-American, and therefore foreign, than repudiating the symbolic objects that represent 'America' (referring to the national anthem). Objects, therefore, become an emotionally laden artefact linked to certain values which represent, at the same time, proximity to particular identities. In this case, it is the anthem's proximity to whiteness. Thus, the perception was that Kaepernick had chosen to abandon his political community by rejecting what identifies and unites 'the American self'. He thus became a potential threat to its identity.

For more on civil disobedience and security, see **Box 4.1**

The interrelation of emotions and identities is discussed in **Box 9.2**

But there are other dynamics. For example, in France, second- and third-generation migrants from former French colonies have begun to claim their own version of French identity within a society that tends to exclude them and not recognize them as legitimate members. Part of their claim criticizes the dominant political imaginary that sees republican values (e.g., liberty, equality, fraternity, separation of church and state) as universal while ignoring their connections to French colonial practices. Their claims, shared by the PIR, include challenges to the current use of some republican values such as atheism as they are used to exclude individuals (e.g., practising Muslims) from mainstream French society. This process of othering is usually accompanied by identity practices that are informed by a security framing that represents Muslims as a danger to French society, with a particular emphasis on the threat of religiously inspired (domestic) terrorism.

Chapter 11 discusses connections among religion, citizenship, and security

Predatory identities are also present beyond the nation-state. For example, the Apartheid regime in South Africa, which was largely condemned around the world, benefitted from the economic and military support of successive American, British, and Israeli administrations. This support stemmed from an unease over the perceived politics of anti-Apartheid groups (i.e., Marxist), tacit acceptance of the racialized socio-political order in South Africa (i.e., it would be hard to believe that similar support would have been offered to a Black-minority state

➔ BOX 9.2 IDENTITY AND THE CULTURAL POLITICS OF EMOTIONS

Sara Ahmed is a feminist scholar and activist of British-Australian Pakistani descent. She focuses on studying the intersections of feminist theory, queer theory, and critical race studies. Her scholarship and activism are an example of situated and intersectional critical knowledge production. Drawing on feminist and queer perspectives (see Chapter 10), Ahmed explores the intersectionalities of identity in *The Cultural Politics of Emotions* (2004). In this work, Ahmed engages with the 'emotional turn' in the social sciences and humanities. Since the 1980s, emotional aspects and regimes of sentiments have been considered important elements of discourse, identity, security, and politics.

In her analysis, Ahmed problematizes the emotional turn by seeking to understand how the political culture of a particular place is articulated through emotions such as pain, hatred, fear, disgust, and love. Ahmed emphasizes that a hegemonic understanding of identity is constructed through the imposition of a 'correct way' of managing emotions vis-à-vis those bodies/subjectivities whose emotions are 'incorrect'. We find two key examples in Ahmed's work.

First is her analysis of hatred. For Ahmed, hatred is not a direct dislike of someone. Hate is the product, or consequence, of a love relationship. But what is a love relationship? A love relationship occurs between a hegemonic element of a society/community—in her analysis, the white population—that loves its nation—a nation that has constructed itself as a white nation. A perceived threat to this nation (e.g., immigration, the transformation of traditional values, etc.) makes the identity of the hegemonic white population insecure. The insecurity of their identity is seen as damaging to their subject of love (the nation). Their reaction is to defend what they love. Therefore, the construction of political hatred is presented as a direct consequence of a love relationship. Ahmed's work thus explores how the cultural politics of emotions creates insecurities that generate political violence.

Ahmed provides a second example in *The Promise of Happiness* (2010). Here, she analyses how acts of happiness come from social pressures that push individuals towards specific experiences, objects, or behaviours. These objects of happiness allow Ahmed to explore the bodies and subjectivities of unhappiness: for example, 'feminist killjoys', but also the melancholic immigrant, who cannot access the pre-established canon of happiness and whose presence prevents the consummation of longed-for happiness. In this way, the Self's perception of the unhappiness of the Other becomes a 'threat' to the Self's happiness. Ahmed's work has been valuable for further exploring colonial and post-colonial modes of government. It has provided a cutting-edge perspective on how emotions affect our socio-political orders, locally and globally.

oppressing a white-majority population), and, in the case of Israel, the sense of sharing a similar internal security problematic to which others were unsympathetic. In turn, Apartheid governments in South Africa provided clandestine security support (including undertaking military operations) in Rhodesia (now Zimbabwe) in aid of its white-minority government. More recently, Canadian governments have intervened in the international passport regime to demand that passports issued by Indigenous communities that see themselves as sovereign entities (e.g., the Haudenosaunee) are not recognized by other states. And while many states have condemned the use of 'black sites' to detain and torture suspects in the war on terror, some turned a blind eye to 'rendition flights' that transported suspects to these sites using their airspace and/or that refuelled in their territories. These episodes call into question the idea of post-racial contemporary global order in which European imperial and colonial history (Césaire 2001 [1955]) has been left behind. Thus, predatory identities can serve to maintain the status quo and forms of domination and oppression even when they may not be directly connected to processes of othering.

Finally, physical borders are spaces in which identity practices and security intertwine to produce political violence. For example, the demands of a global capitalist system, the impetus to relocate production sites to least expensive location, and global value chains produce complex patterns of migration. In border areas, we may observe the constant mobility of workers (e.g., along the Mexico–US border). Returning to an earlier example, the government of the Dominican Republic has withdrawn citizenship for hundreds of thousands of Dominicans of Haitian descent who settled across border areas during the first decades of the twentieth century when the shortage of labour in the Dominican Republic encouraged relocation. It was in these areas that Haitians initially settled, became regularized, and had children who were born and raised as Dominican citizens. However, decades later, they are portrayed as foreigners who are threats to proper Dominican citizens. Thus, their own Dominicanness is being denied. The roots of this othering practice can be found in Dominican anti-Haitian racism. In the Dominican Republic, racism is fixed to hegemonic identity practices that privilege white and *mestizo* communities on the logic that Europeanness is superior to 'Africanness'. This identity practice also portrays an ideal of identities that need to be secured (i.e., white and *mestizo*) against threatening identities (i.e., Black; specifically, Haitian).

Given the different ways of performing predatory identities, it can feel like these are the only possibilities for relationships between the Self and the Other. However, there are different ways to engage with difference. Next, we will see how alternative identity practices and relationality can provide a different account of human/human and human/non-human connectivity.

9.4 Alternative identity practices: relationality between/within differences

As we have seen, identity practices are complex exercises of power that articulate who we understand ourselves to be and our place in the world. Our identity practices intertwine ethics with political practices while affecting our sense of belonging to a particular community. So far, we have seen how security framings establish a (threatened) inside from a (threatening) outside. In light of Connolly's (1991, 64) suggestion that 'some differences must be converted into otherness', two important questions remain:

1. Must identity and difference be shaped by binary thinking that makes the other a threat?
2. If not, what are the alternatives?

If we see identities as relational, we can move beyond the binary thinking (i.e., sameness vs. difference) encouraged by predatory identities. Identity and difference—or differences—are acknowledged to represent a relationship in which the other, even if absent, remains an interlocutor who influences who we believe ourselves to be. As Amaya Querejazu (2021, 33) argues, 'everything is related and nothing exists in isolation'. Thus, instead of understanding identity and difference as an 'either-or' logic (i.e., we are *either* this *or* that), we can use a relational 'both-and' logic. If we do so, we can see how identities and differences arise and transform through relationships they have with each other (Guillaume 2002; Trownsell et al. 2021; Tickner and Querejazu 2021, 396).

For example, for centuries, enslaved Black populations in the United States were considered non-human. Post-emancipation, alongside their freedom and citizenship (as Americans), formerly enslaved people were also given legal recognition as human beings within US society. However, social recognition as both human and American by the white majority did not take place. This was because in the political imagination underpinning the US socio-political order, Blackness was conceived as the opposite to human, with humanity exclusively connected to whiteness. Thus, to be a proper American was to be white; it seemed impossible to be both simultaneously. Therefore, from an either-or logic, one was either American or Black and thus either human or non-human.

A relational approach underpinned by a 'both-and' logic potentially better captures the complexities and contingencies of identity. For example, W. E. B. Du Bois (1897) proposed the concept of 'double consciousness' to understand the identity practice of post-emancipation African-Americans in the United States. For Du Bois, they (him) were both Black and American: not a mix of both, but both selves/subjects (among many other identities) simultaneously. Being both Black and American were parts of an indivisible Self, carrying multiple histories within their identity. Du Bois' 'double consciousness' reflects that encounters between the Self and the Other do not produce a synthesis or a hybrid identity. Instead, encounters 'give sense to [our] existence as complexity and contradiction' (Querejazu 2021, 33).

On Du Bois and the colour line, see **Box 11.1**

Knowing, understanding, and feeling yourself from a 'both-and' logic requires simultaneous inseparability. We should not separate ourselves from the different relations that produce and reproduce our identity, for it is impossible to do so. This impossibility implies that we can be multiple things simultaneously (e.g., Asian, Western, Australian, Christian, and transgender). Moreover, as Querejazu (2021, 34) argues, though we are many things simultaneously, we might perform or use certain identity features depending on the context.

Now, let us consider the broader implications. First, an identity practice is also a form of knowledge. We get to know who we are, just as we learn about who is the

Other. We produce a particular knowledge account of the encounter between 'us' and 'them'. Second, consider that an identity practice is a way of being—we identify ourselves and the Other by being who we are. Both processes occur concurrently and imply a way of being and feeling. Andean Indigenous cosmogonies have called this *sentipensando*; that is, being, while feeling, while knowing, while doing (Tickner and Querejazu 2021, 398; see also Escobar 2014). Although this conceptualization appears abstract, you can see how this works if you think about your own identity practices. Your way of being in this world generates certain feelings. How you understand the links between your way of being and feeling comes from the knowledge of yourself that you are constantly producing. This knowledge is always connected to what you do and how you do it.

As we have seen, identity/difference relationships are leading to othering. However, this exercise does not always have to be predatory. Moreover, if we move away from a binary understanding of identity/difference towards one that is relational, our understandings of ourselves and others potentially become less antagonistic.

While predatory identities assume the existence of an antagonistic other who must be exterminated, converted, or contained, a relational approach opens the possibility for the co-production of difference. In their work, Arlene Tickner and Amaya Querejazu (2021) propose the term 'deep relationality', or *cosmopraxis*, that would allow us to move from identities formed through binaries to finding spaces for managing conflict and promoting cooperation. *Cosmopraxis* implies 'co-being, coexistence, and complementarity as basic principles of existence' (Tickner and Querejazu 2021, 393). Co-being, co-existence, and complementarity provide the possibility of non-hierarchical and non-binary understandings of ourselves and others. Similarly, *cosmopraxis* is a way to understand ourselves (as humans) in relation to other non-human entities without assuming differences that do not exist (e.g., for hundreds of years it was thought that only humans felt pain) or reproducing hierarchies that have led to great ecological harms (Tickner and Querejazu 2021, 393).

> Relations between humans and non-humans within environmental security are explored in **Chapter 18**

Thus, *cosmopraxis* would suggest that identity need not necessarily lead to othering. A relational approach moves beyond othering since it considers similarity and difference as 'complementary opposites bound together as an inseparable whole' (Trownsell and Tickner 2021, 27). Therefore, it is possible to recognize differences without engaging in practices of othering.

9.5 Conclusion

In this chapter, we discussed different ways of thinking about identity, difference, and othering. We showed how all three inform our imaginaries about security/insecurity. We showed the problems when identity and difference are seen as binary oppositions. As such, there are other ways to study the dynamics of identity that are more accepting of difference. As mentioned earlier, we cannot escape the presence of the Other in the Self. Likewise, a relational approach to identity offers possibilities for co-being, co-existence, and complementarity. This is not to say that a relational approach eliminates conflict that may be generated by difference. On the contrary, conflict is recognized as a feature of relationality; however, by seeing the interconnections between the Self and Other, a relational understanding of identity is far less likely to understand difference as an existential threat. Rather, difference is just as much a part of who we are as it is a means of distinguishing ourselves from others.

Throughout this chapter, we have sought to question the perception that the relationship between identity and difference must lead to othering in terms of predatory identities. Predatory identities require an Other who is absolutely different to the Self. They portray this Other in binary terms and deploy practices of extermination, conversion, or contention. In this sense, predatory identities mobilize security because the Other is seen as an inherent threat. As a consequence, they perceive relationships between different subjects, entities, and states as antagonistic. Considering the Other as a threat to the Self can lead to political violence in order to reinforce who may legitimately belong to the community and who cannot. Furthermore, we have shown how political violence can also occur against those identities whose status as human and/or citizen is contested.

From relational perspectives informing understandings of identity like *cosmopraxis*, difference is an essential part of our identity and shapes the whole that constitutes us. Moving beyond binaries acknowledges that there are always traces of the Other within the Self, as well as how our identity discourses and practices build upon one another.

Questions for further discussion

1. What are different ways that one can identify oneself? How would they be connected to security framings?

2. What identity practices in your social context are potential predatory identities?

3. Are there identity practices within your social context that establish a positive relationality between differences? How would they be sources to move away from security framings?

4. What does deep relationality imply when it comes to distinctions made between human beings and 'nature'?

5. How might we turn identity from being a source of conflict into being a source of respectful co-existence?

Further reading

CAMUS, ALBERT. 1942. *L'Étranger* [*The stranger*]. Paris: Éditions Gallimard.
   This text exposes the problem of estrangement. The main character, Meursault, becomes a stranger who does not share the values of his political community. He is physically present but does not belong.

CROFT, STUART. 2012. *Securitizing Islam: Identity and the search for security*. Cambridge: Cambridge University Press.

Securitizing Islam analyses the impact of security on Islam and Muslims in the United Kingdom after 9/11. It shows how security practices within British society rely on othering Islam and Muslim populations.

DÍAZ, JUNOT. 2007. *The brief wondrous life of Oscar Wao*. New York: Riverhead.
This novel explores the everyday identity practices of a young Dominican man living in New York. It introduces the reader to the complexities of migrant and diasporic identities that are entangled with gender, race, and class. It also shows how the complementarity and the simultaneity of identity/difference work.

GONZÁLEZ VILLASEÑOR, ARTURO. 2014. *Llévate mis amores* [*All of me*]. 90 min. Acanto Films, Pimienta Films, Universidad Autónoma Metropolitana.
This documentary tells the story of Las Patronas, a group of women in Veracruz, Mexico, who feed thousands of Central American migrants who cross through Mexico to the United States on the top of the train La Bestia. It serves as an example of how a relational approach to difference may result in the desecuritization of border zones.

YATES, PAMELA. 2011. *Granito: How to nail a dictator*. 104 min. Skylight Pictures.
Granito shows the work undertaken to prove that the Guatemalan state was involved in the Maya genocide. It demonstrates the state's responsibility, confirming that the extermination of the 'Indigenous Other' was tied to predominant understandings of a socio-political order and its framing through security.

References

AHMED, SARA. 2004. *The cultural politics of emotions*. London: Routledge.

AHMED, SARA. 2010. *The promise of happiness*. Durham, NC: Duke University Press.

APPADURAI, ARJUN. 2006. *Fear of small numbers: An essay on the geography of anger*. Durham, NC: Duke University Press.

APPELBAUM, NANCY. 1999. 'Whitening the region: Caucano mediation and "antioqueño colonization" in nineteenth-century Colombia'. *The Hispanic American Historical Review* 79(4), 631–667.

CAMPBELL, DAVID. 1998. *Writing security: United States foreign policy and politics of identity*. 2nd ed. Minneapolis, MN: University of Minnesota Press.

CASAÚS ARZÚ, MARTA E. 2018. *Guatemala: Linaje y racismo*. Guatemala City: F&G Editores.

CASAÚS ARZÚ, MARTA E. 2019. *Racismo, genocidio y memoria*. Guatemala City: F&G Editores.

CÉSAIRE, AIMÉ. 2001[1955]. *Discourse on colonialism*. New York: New York University Press.

COHA (Council on Hemispheric Affairs). 2009. '"Barbarian first" policy flogs Guyanese in Barbados'. 5 August. www.coha.org/barbadian-first-policy-flogs-guyanese-in-barbados (last accessed 14 June 2022).

CONNOLLY, WILLIAM E. 1991. *Identity/difference: Democratic negotiations of political paradox*. Ithaca, NY: Cornell University Press.

DU BOIS, W. E. B. 1897. 'Strivings of the Negro People'. *Atlantic Monthly* 80, 194–198.

ESCOBAR, ARTURO. 2014. *Sentipensar con la tierra: nuevas lecturas sobre desarrollo, territorio y diferencia*. Medellín: UNAULA.

FANON, FRANTZ. 1986 [1952]. *Black skin, white masks*. London: Pluto Press.

FANON, FRANTZ. 2005 [1961]. *The wretched of the earth*. New York: Grove Press.

FitzGerald, David Scott and David Cook-Martin. 2014. *Culling the masses: The democratic origins of racist immigration policy in the Americas.* Cambridge, MA: Harvard University Press.

Fonseca, Melody and Ari Jerrems. 2012. 'Why decolonise International Relations Theory?'. Working paper presented at the British International Studies Association Annual Conference. www.academia.edu/2140460/Why_Decolonise_International_Relations_Theory (last accessed 11 March 2022).

Guillaume, Xavier. 2002. 'Foreign policy and the politics of alterity: A dialogical understanding of international relations'. *Millennium: Journal of International Studies* 31(1), 1–26.

Harvey, David. 1990. 'Between space and time: Reflections on the geographical imagination'. *Annals of the Association of American Geographers* 8(3), 418–434.

Inayatullah, Naeem and David L. Blaney. 1996. 'Knowing encounters: Beyond parochialism in International Relations Theory'. In *The return of culture and identity in IR Theory,* edited by Yosef Lapid and Friedrich Kratochwil. Boulder, CO: Lynne Rienner Publishers.

Moreno Figueroa, Mónica G. and Emiko Saldívar Tanaka. 2016. '"We are not racists, we are Mexicans": Privilege, nationalism and post-race ideology in Mexico'. *Critical Sociology* 42(4–5), 515–533.

Querejazu, Amaya. 2021. 'Why relational encounters?' *International Studies Perspectives* 22(1), 31–34.

Outtes, Joel. 2003. 'Disciplining society through the city: The genesis of city planning in Brazil and Argentina (1894–1945)'. *Bulletin of Latin American Research* 22(2), 137–164.

Said, Edward. 1978. *Orientalism.* New York: Pantheon Books.

Sue, Christina A. 2013. *Land of the cosmic race: Race mixture, racism, and Blackness in Mexico.* Oxford: Oxford University Press.

Tickner, Arlene B. and Amaya Querejazu. 2021. 'Weaving worlds: Cosmopraxis as relational sensibility'. *International Studies Review* 23(2), 391–408.

Trownsell, Tamara and Arlene B. Tickner. 2021. 'Differing about difference: An introduction'. *International Studies Perspectives* 22(1), 26–31.

Trownsell, Tamara A., Arlene B. Tickner, Amaya Querejazu, Jarrad Reddekop, Giorgio Shani, Kosuke Shimizu, Navnita Chadha Behera, and Anahita Arian. 2021. 'Forum. Differing about difference: Relational IR from around the world'. *International Studies Perspectives* 22(1), 25–64.

Turits, Richard L. 2002. 'A world destroyed, a nation imposed: The 1937 Haitian massacre in the Dominican Republic'. *Hispanic American Historical Review* 82(3), 589–635.

10
Gender and sexuality

Jennifer Hobbs and Laura McLeod

10.1	Introduction	155
10.2	Gender, sexuality, and security	158
10.3	Intersectionalities	160
10.4	The everyday	162
10.5	Transformative politics	164
10.6	Conclusion	166

READER'S GUIDE

This chapter explores the relevance of gender and sexuality for understanding how security/insecurity are distributed in the world. We look specifically at the following critical questions: security for whom, where, how, and at whose expense? To do so, we utilize three key feminist concepts: intersectionality, the everyday, and transformation. In using these concepts, we argue that gender and sexuality help us gain a critical perspective of security/insecurity by revealing both new areas of study, as well as helping us to see traditional security topics in a new light.

10.1 Introduction

> Illustrative case studies on the topics explored in this chapter are available on the online resources to help take your understanding of gender and sexuality further: http://www.oup.com/he/Grayson-Guillaume1e.

When we think about security, we often start from the same place: the activities of state actors, police, militaries, and policy elites. By virtue of who is most likely to hold these positions of power and authority, feminist and anti-racist scholars have pointed out that this 'mainstream' perspective could also be dubbed the 'malestream' or the 'whitestream', given that it tends to over represent the experiences of men and/or white people

(Sjoberg 2018, 51; Denis 1997). In this chapter, we highlight the unequal distribution of insecurity and violence in the world by choosing a different starting point for thinking about security. We focus on two dimensions of security that are frequently ignored by mainstream perspectives of security: gender and sexuality. In doing so, we invite you to join us in thinking about dimensions of security that are often hidden in plain sight.

There are several ways to consider the relationship between gender, sexuality, and dimensions of security. Scholars have taken a range of approaches to doing so. Typically, we act and talk as if gender and sex are the same thing, and that there are only two genders/sexes—men and woman, male and female. We often think that these two groups of people have certain physical characteristics (e.g., male genitalia refers to a penis and testes; women have breasts and vaginas). Furthermore, we often assume that men/women have certain social characteristics too. For example, we associate manliness and masculinity with strength, bravery, decisiveness, and being 'the person in charge of the barbecue', while we associate women and femininity with emotional intelligence, beauty, nurturing, and being the person who 'keeps track of the household chores'. There is a lengthy set of associations we often make between gender, sex, and sexuality without ever really thinking about it: from assuming gay men are 'camp', meaning effeminate, and similar to women, or that lesbian women are 'butch', meaning masculine, and similar to men. In all of these ways, in society we tangle gender, sex, and sexuality together and presume we know what we are talking about.

When you read the above descriptions, you may well have thought that these characterizations seem sexist, homophobic, and transphobic. After all, women are also strong, brave, decisive, and able to manage barbecues. Men are emotionally intelligent, nurturing, and capable of remembering to clean the bathroom and provide childcare. Not all lesbians are butch, not all gay men are camp, and plenty are both at the same time. Trans and non-binary peoples, and those living outside of the Western gender binary, remind us that not all women have vaginas and not all vagina owners are women (for an overview of other gender systems, see Picq 2020 and O'Sullivan 2021). Our ideas about gender and sexuality—that men and women are the only genders, and that each gender has particular bodies, characteristics, and abilities—have been used for centuries to enact and justify the oppression of women and those who do not fit into this gender binary.

In this chapter, we understand gender and sexuality as referring to the ideas we hold about certain social roles, bodies, and identities. We also understand gender and sexuality as dynamics of power, an axis through which security and insecurity are distributed. Gender and sexuality have consequences when we think about security. They form part of the unequal distribution of insecurity and violence we see in the world. Thinking about gender and sexuality as power dynamics, as well as descriptors of people, can help us to see not only who is made secure/insecure, but why, how that might be, and at whose expense.

We offer this understanding of gender and sexuality because we should all want to know how security works differently for gendered and sexualized populations. Thus, we need to ask critical questions about gendered and sexualized experiences of security. Of course, not everyone will agree with the stance we take on gender, sex, and

*The importance of critical questions is explored in **Section 1.3**; on socio-political orders and hierarchies, see **Section 3.3***

sexuality in this chapter. In offering you a feminist approach, we are not attempting to offer *the* definitive feminist approach to security, but instead *a* feminist approach to security. Feminisms are plural with specific positionalities, contexts, nuances, agreements, tensions, and disagreements (see Kemp and Squires 1997). But all feminisms would agree that we need to uncover the logics and hierarchies that underpin security and how they are intertwined with gender and sexuality.

Chapter 5 offers nine critical questions that serve as a starting point for uncovering questions about the logics and hierarchies that underpin security. When we think about security in relation to gender and sexuality, we want to apply these questions to 'security' as a concept and *also* to 'gender' and 'sexuality'. For example, what do we mean by gender and sexuality? Where do these terms come from? Who do they refer to? How do 'gender' and 'sexuality' inform security—and to whose benefit and expense?

See **Box 10.1** on the scholarship behind these terms

BOX 10.1 SCHOLARSHIP ON GENDER, SEXUALITY, AND INSECURITY: FOUR DECADES ON

Over the last forty years, scholars—particularly feminist and queer security scholars—have made important contributions to the relevance of gender and sexuality to thinking about security. Researchers have shown how gender and sexuality can reveal previously 'hidden' forms of insecurity that people experience, often making us look at more traditional security practices in a new light. For example, peacekeeping operations are often thought about as practices which can enhance the security of communities who are threatened by armed conflict. However, feminist researchers have pointed out that peacekeeping operations, which are overwhelming staffed by men, often face endemic problems of sexual exploitation and abuse committed by military personnel against local women (Karim and Beardsley 2016). Here we can see that paying attention to gender and sexuality can help us to see new facets of insecurity and reveal dynamics of security practices we might previously have ignored.

In addition to showing that gender and sexuality are important factors in deciding who is made secure and insecure in the world, scholars have also shown that gender and sexuality also impact the way we think—and therefore attempt to 'do'—security (see Section 2.2.2 for more on security as a process). For example, Carol Cohn's work (1987) shows how military communities responsible for nuclear strategy during the Cold War relied heavily on sexualized and gendered language and metaphors to express their ideas; this made certain types of thought (for example, thinking about nuclear disarmament as a policy strategy) not only hard to talk about but hard to even think about. Scholars have argued that understandings of gender and sexuality affect the way we think and practice security in a number of areas; from how we represent Islamic terrorists as perverse sexual others, and so justify violence against them (Puar and Rai 2002); to our gendered ideals of 'beauty' and how they can create support for wars (Nguyen 2011). This shows us that gender and sexuality matter to understanding what the idea of security can *do* in the world, and how it can affect people.

Throughout the remainder of this chapter, we offer you lots of examples to encourage you to think about the relevance of gender and sexuality for understanding what security does to and for various different people. But we start with one specific case—the assault and killing of Muhlaysia Booker. Muhlaysia's death was the result of several logics of violence and oppression that position trans women, and trans women of colour specifically, as vulnerable to gendered violence. In looking at one woman's death, we can start to see the potent impact gender and sexuality have on security. By utilizing an ethic of questioning and curiosity, we show how the life and death of Muhlaysia Booker highlight patterns of political violence and insecurity.

After discussing how Muhlaysia's life and death show us much about the connections between gender, sexuality, political violence, and security, we go on to introduce three key concepts that help us to think about some of the critical questions introduced in Chapter 5. We begin by showing how the concept of intersectionality can help us think about security for whom, and at whose expense. We then look at the concept of the everyday to think about questions of where and when security happens. Finally, we explore the concept of transformative politics to think about what the concept of security *does*, and how it shapes the world we live in. Throughout this chapter we argue that thinking about gender and sexuality is vital to understanding security—but thinking about gender and sexuality also requires us to change the way we think *about* security.

> Intersectionality is introduced in **Section 1.4**

> Transformation is discussed in **Section 1.2.4**

10.2 Gender, sexuality, and security

'Our time to seek justice is now. If not now, when?' This powerful question was posed by a woman called Muhlaysia Booker to a rally in South Dallas, Texas in April 2019 (Booker, quoted in Smith 2019). Muhlaysia was twenty-two years old at the time, and the rally had been organized in her support after she had been the subject of a violent transphobic assault (cbsnews 2019). At the rally, Muhlaysia called for justice for herself and all trans women who have been the victims of transphobic violence (Ear Hustling Podcast 2019). She was clear that her attack was not an isolated incident. 'This time it is me', she told the crowd, 'but the next time it is someone else. Someone close to you' (Booker in Ear Hustling Podcast 2019). One month later, Muhlaysia Booker was found fatally shot on a Dallas street (Dart 2019). Police believe her murder to be unconnected to her previous assault.

There are many questions that press upon us in the grief of Muhlaysia Booker's assault and murder. These questions are fundamentally about the intersections of security and gender. One of the primary ways we understand security is to be secure against physical harm. When we think about security, we are often concerned about who is and who is not being harmed in a given socio-political order. Muhlaysia Booker was not secure against physical harm. And her insecurity was not due to an isolated incident of personal violence. In May 2019, when Muhlaysia was murdered, she became the fourth trans person to be killed in the United States that year (Human Rights Campaign 2019). In 2019, at least twenty-six trans people were

> Types of political violence are discussed in **Section 4.2.1**

either murdered or had their deaths ruled as suspicious. By July 2020, the number of trans lives lost had already reached twenty-eight for that year (National Center for Transgender Equality 2020). The rate of violence against trans people is especially high for trans women of colour. In the United States, four out of five of all anti-transgender homicides are committed against trans women of colour (Human Rights Campaign Foundation 2020, 3).

Clearly, there is a pattern of violence in which Muhlaysia's assault and murder are included. What happened to Muhlaysia Booker has happened, and is happening, to some people much more than others, based on a person's gender. The same is true of sexuality, too. Looking for connections between gender, sexuality, and security helps us to think about *who* is secure and insecure in the world. Often, we can see that women, girls, and LGBTQI+ individuals are subject to violence based on their identity. For example, several countries around the world count femicide, the killing of women and girls as a result of their gender, as a hate crime. In Mexico, femicides have increased at a rate of 137 per cent between 2015 and 2020 (Vivanco 2020). Worldwide in 2012, the Organization for Security and Co-operation in Europe (OSCE) estimated that 43,600 women and girls were killed by a family member or intimate partner. This this almost four times the number of people killed by terrorism in the same year (11,133), even though we might assume terrorism to be a bigger security problem (OSCE 2017, 7). In many countries around the world, having same-sex relationships is still illegal. In some countries, expressing your sexual identity can result in imprisonment or death if you are LGBQ. As these examples show us, your gender and your sexuality can have a significant impact on the risk of violence, and resulting levels of insecurity, that you experience.

Muhlaysia Booker's assault and murder, and the examples above, all point to ways gender and sexuality can affect a person's direct, physical security, and risk of violence. But if we think about violence in broader terms than purely physical violence between individuals, we can start to gain a fuller picture of how both gender and sexuality help to distribute security unequally among populations. Physical forms of political violence are made possible by structural political violence. Acknowledging structural violence is important for thinking about *how* and *why* people of certain genders and sexualities are more insecure than others. In this chapter, we use structural violence to refer to less physical forms of violence, such as psychological, material, and symbolic violence. For example, discrimination against trans women may lead to forms of material violence; such as exclusion from health and medical services. Symbolic violence, such as sexist narratives in media and advertising, can lead to material violence, like women being paid less than men as they are considered less valuable in the workplace. These different types of structural violence are often connected to direct physical violence, too. If you are an LGBTQI+ youth who is made homeless by an unaccepting family (material violence), you may also be put at greater risk of physical violence as a result of sleeping on the streets. Thinking about these different types of violence and how they are connected can help us to think more deeply about why and how different groups of people are made to be insecure through violence that stems from negative understandings of certain genders and sexualities.

> Political violence is defined in **Section 4.2**

This book offers you nine questions to start thinking critically about security (see Chapter 5). Within this chapter, we use this critical methodology of questioning in conjunction with a specifically feminist curiosity. The concept of 'curiosity' as a research device has been pioneered by feminist scholar Cynthia Enloe, who challenges us to always question the things that we take for granted, or assume are 'natural', 'tradition', or 'always' (Enloe 2014, 3). Within this chapter, we build on the work of curious feminists to develop a curiosity specifically about the relationship between gender, sexuality, security, and political violence. It is a feminist curiosity and ethic of questioning that leads us to think about Muhlaysia Booker's heart-breaking assault and murder as being intimately connected to the politics of security. A feminist curiosity requires us to ask: what is the role of gender and sexuality in making people safe/unsafe? And, as Muhlaysia Booker asked in relation to justice, how do we address the unequal distribution of insecurity? Thus, how can we transform the current, unequal distribution of security?

For the remainder of this chapter, we employ three concepts—intersectionality, the everyday, and transformative politics—that prompt us to approach security with a critical curiosity about gender and sexuality. We use these concepts to think about how our understandings of security, along with our security practices, rely on ideas about gender and sexuality. We also use these concepts to analyse what security *does* in the world, both in terms of the gendered and sexualized meanings it produces and the effects of security practice on people of different genders and sexualities.

10.3 Intersectionalities

Our first concept is intersectionality, in particular between gender, sexuality, race and how it illuminates the politics of security in our worlds. Kimberlé Crenshaw (1991) is credited with coining the term intersectionality to describe how racism experienced by Black women is also inflected with misogyny. The understanding that racism and sexism do not operate separately is widely reflected in literature from feminists of colour, who have also introduced other axes of oppression into the discussion, such as class and disability (Moraga and Anzaldúa 1981; Collins and Bilge 2016). Intersectional feminist analyses push us to recognize ways in which different types of domination and oppression are reliant upon each other. This means recognizing that there is no way to understanding 'race' without also thinking about 'gender'; no way to understand 'disability' without thinking about 'sexuality', and so on. Taking intersectionality seriously as a concept can help us to critically explore security, as this section argues, by thinking more deeply about whom security is provided for, and at whose expense.

An intersectional feminist analysis of security requires us to look at how different groups have different experiences of security and insecurity. How are these experiences dependent upon multiple, interrelated relationships of power? We've already discussed what this might mean briefly when thinking about Muhlaysia Booker. The attack on Muhlaysia Booker, in conjunction with the numerous attacks worldwide, show us that while all trans people are vulnerable to transphobic violence, they are not *equally* vulnerable to it. Trans people of colour are at a greater risk of experiencing violence than their white counterparts (Dinno 2017; Xavier et al. 2005). While women in general are more likely to suffer intimate partner violence than men, disabled women are at even greater risk (Office for National Statistics 2020). Taking an intersectional understanding of gender and sexuality shows us that people and communities are not homogenous. For example, while the LGBTQI+ community may share some experiences of (in)security related to their sexuality, there is still a wide divergence of experiences. A poor gay white man living in Poland is likely to have different experiences of (in)security than an affluent bisexual Black woman living in Japan. Thinking about gender and sexuality from an intersectional position in relation to security can help us think even more deeply about who is insecure, and exactly why they might be more vulnerable to violence. Intersectionality can help us to identify the multiple and intersecting forms of oppression that will impact a person's lived experience of security.

To illustrate this further, let's look at the example of LGBTQI+ migration in more detail. There are many countries in the world where certain forms of LGBQ sexuality and gender expression specifically are criminalized. There are also many other countries where LGBTQI+ people are persecuted through disproportionate application of more general laws. This shows that there are specific factors related to discrimination and persecution that drive the migration of LGBTQI+ people. But more general drivers of forced migration, such as armed conflict and natural disasters, may also have specific impacts on LGBTQI+ communities. The loss of homes and community spaces may expose LGBTQI+ folks to harassment and violence. They may face difficulties accessing support and relief efforts which are often designed for heterosexual families and cisgender people (Gorman-Murray et al. 2017; Yamashita 2012). Something like accessing an emergency shelter may be very difficult for trans folks, as emergency accommodation is often sex-segregated by 'male' and 'female'. Trans and non-binary folks may be subject to harassment, violence, or denial of services if they are perceived as being in the 'wrong' space. Even once a person has made the difficult journey across countries, LGBTQI+ refugees often report facing discrimination, violence, and non-acceptance from both refugee communities *and* their host countries as a result of their gender and/or sexuality (Nathwani 2015).

Looking at gender and sexuality from an intersectional perspective can help us to think then about who is insecure. It can also help us to think more deeply about *why* they are insecure. For example, anti-homosexuality laws in many formerly colonized countries were introduced by European colonial governments, where sex between men was also illegal 'back home' (M'Baye 2013; Asante 2020). Prior to the advent of colonialism, some cultures believed in the existence of more than two genders. As such, they did not discriminate against or punish same-sex relationships—or make the same connections between sex and identity as we do in Western discourses of sexuality (Driskill et al. 2011). The idea of 'the homosexual' as a type of person, and a deviant type of person, was often introduced by Western colonial powers, establishing homophobic legacies that continue to discriminate against LGBTQI+ folks to this day.

An intersectional perspective can also help us think about how hierarchies articulated through security are layered. For instance, some feminists and women in western Europe and North America have critiqued some forms Islamic dress, such as the burqa and niqab, as a threat to women's rights and their security. It is argued that to dress in this way reinforces patriarchal forms of structural violence (Hoodfar 2001). French law bans face coverings, such as the niqab and burqa, in public places as these garments are deemed an actual threat to the French ideal of a secular state. However, some Muslim feminists and others have pointed out that being forced to cover your body is one thing; but a woman freely choosing how to express her own religious beliefs is quite another. They argue that the oversexualization of women's bodies in public spaces is a threat to women's rights and that prohibiting women from freely choosing to wear a garment is a threat to religious freedom. We can see here how different conceptions of what needs to be secured can be the source of different understandings of security as a condition of possibility or impossibility. Laws that are designed to 'secure' historically situated French ideas about women's rights actually produce political violence directing at some Muslim women, criminalizing their choices and restricting their access to public spaces.

> On security as a condition of possibility or impossibility, see **Section 2.3**

We can see that gender and sexuality are clearly important in understanding who is insecure and why. Moreover, we can see that security practices rely on understandings of gender and sexuality that change across time and space. This shows us that who is secure/insecure is linked to where and when this (in)security is happening. Thinking about intersectionality helps us to see more clearly who is insecure, why they might be secure/insecure, and at whose expense security is achieved.

10.4 The everyday

Our second concept is the everyday. You are probably quite familiar with this term as it is widely used, but for feminists 'the everyday' refers to a specific political space and type of experience. When feminists discuss the everyday—people's daily lives, relationships, and practices—they are drawing attention to the ways in which we often prioritize exceptional events and 'high' politics when we think about security. Feminists point out that (in)security is not produced only in intense and disruptive moments in international politics like a military invasion. It occurs during people's daily lives. The structures of (in)security that exist in the world are perpetuated and challenged in small moments, as well as big ones. (In)security affects not only the corridors and hallways of power but also how much food people can afford to buy for their families, the ability to safely joke about their government in public, or whether they show affection to their partner in the street. Thinking about the everyday is not simply about describing everyday matters, but rather involves theorizing the conceptual, analytical, and empirical implications of the 'everyday'. This helps us to think further about how security is achieved and what security does in/to the world. How are security practices dependent upon ordinary, even mundane, everyday interactions? What are the impacts of national security policies on the everyday lives of people?

One place where we can identify some interesting impacts of national security policies on the everyday lives of people is by looking at the airport, and in particular issues around surveillance at the airport (Salter 2008). If you have ever flown internationally, you may well have been asked to step through a full body scanner. These scanners can identify the presence of concealed items, both externally and internally, and their introduction needs to be understood as part of a post-9/11 climate of fear around terrorism and air travel (Patel 2012).

These scanners are not fool proof. In the United States, for example, current scanners used by the Transportation Security Administration (TSA) struggle to process certain forms of loose clothing, such as types of religious dress; medical implants and prosthetics; and thick and curly hair. Trans people may also have difficulties with full body scanners, which often use either a 'male' or 'female' prototype to compare scans to (Clarkson 2019, 624). This can cause problems for trans folks at airports as their bodies may indicate an 'anomaly'. This means that people wearing religious clothing, disabled persons, racial minorities, and trans people may have to undergo additional searches—such as invasive strip searches, disclosing intimate details to airport officials, and even showing their genitalia to airport security staff (Waldron and Medina 2019). The design of airport scanners therefore places some people at risk of material, physical, and psychological violence; it can cause people to miss flights, require invasive and traumatizing searches that may constitute physical assault, and lead to people feeling dehumanized and humiliated.

The inability of airport scanners to effectively process afro hair, medical implants and prosthetics, religious dress, and the bodies of trans people shows that these screening technologies were designed with some bodies in mind and not others. The 'normal' body that these technologies were designed to work for illustrates that part of the reason we are insecure to different degrees is because of our restrictive ideas about exactly 'who' the subject of security is. These scanners also reveal much about whose expense 'security' is achieved at. These screening practices are premised on the assumption that they make some of us secure by weeding out 'dangerous' people. But some of us are much more likely than others to attract suspicion of being 'dangerous'. There is a clear pattern here to those who are represented as a possible threat and who might be made insecure in follow-up screening practices. It is those of us who wear non-Christian religious forms of dress, have afro hair, are trans, are disabled, and/or have long-term health conditions that are flagged up as being possibly dangerous. The security of some of us is premised upon the *insecurity* of the rest of us.

At this point, you might be thinking that for many people in the world, air travel is still very much a luxury, or flat out inaccessible. We are concerned here primarily with the security practices that happen at the airport—forms of surveillance—that we take for granted in our daily lives. Looking at airports as an example shows us how these everyday forms of security practice are interwoven with gendered and sexualized ideas about 'who' is a threat to security and who is not. But we do not have to travel all the way to the airport to witness the importance of everyday experiences, practices, and spaces to security.

On surveillance and security, see **Chapter 15**

As feminists have pointed out, simply being at home can be a space of insecurity for women in particular. The World Health Organization (WHO) estimate that globally, around one in three women will be subjected to either physical and/or sexual violence at the hands of an intimate partner (WHO 2021b). Between 641 and 753 million women have been subjected to violence from an intimate partner at least once since they were fifteen years old (WHO 2021a, xii). The staggering scale of this violence against women means that for half of the world's population, a prime site of violence and subsequent insecurity is happening in the most mundane and everyday of spaces; our kitchens, bedrooms, and living rooms.

The same is true of everyday public spaces. Simply walking down the road can be a space of insecurity for women and LGBTQI+ people. In India, 79 per cent of women report facing harassment and abuse in public spaces; in Sao Paulo, 97 per cent of women report always, or sometimes, changing their walking routes to avoid harassment and violence (ActionAid 2016). In addition to the streets, school and work can be sites of insecurity for people of marginalized genders and sexualities. In Mexico, 67 per cent of people surveyed reported experiencing harassment and assault at school based on their sexuality or gender identity (Baruch-Dominguez et al. 2015). In the United Kingdom, 68 per cent of LGBT workers report experiencing sexual harassment at work (Trades Union Congress 2019). This shows us that it is not only everyday *practices* but the actual daily *spaces* we inhabit in our lives that are a prime site where security and insecurity are acted out and costs are imposed on some people more than others.

This leads us back to our feminist curiosity with the 'everyday'. A feminist analysis of people's everyday lives and practices—such as simply being at home—shows us that practices of security show up in our daily lives, as do the inequalities that these practices produce. Security is not an abstract public policy. It is experienced through people's everyday lives. Feminist perspectives thus stress the importance of resistance to security for the purposes of transformation in different venues.

10.5 Transformative politics

> Transformation is introduced in **Section 1.2**

Throughout this chapter, we have alluded to the importance of transformation, which is our third concept. Transformation is not a simple synonym for change. We use transformation to refer to the ways we can challenge underlying relations of domination and oppression. Feminists seek to transform the way that we ask questions about security as well as a normative ambition to alter the policies, structures, practices, and processes that inform security logics and security practices. This normative ambition is central as it enables the political rationale for the coming together of 'feminist', 'security', and 'studies' (Basu 2013, 457). A feminist transformation challenges us not just to manage the types of insecurity and violence generated by gendered and sexualized hierarchies of power. Rather, for feminists, transformation means we need to challenge the deep roots of these forms of power by rethinking our understanding of key terms such as security, insecurity, gender, and sexuality.

Asking questions about intersectionality and the everyday enables us to have a different viewpoint about the world—and equipped with this viewpoint, transformation can be sought. Recognizing that gender and sexuality are interwoven with a range of intersectionalities that are shaped by dominant forms of coercive militarized and police powers allows us to ask different questions about security (Agathangelou 2017, 740). For example, how do women experience social transformation in conflict-affected societies—can women experience empowerment as well (Yadav 2017)? How is gendered insecurity experienced in Indigenous communities, and what are the relationships between security and identity (Stern 2005)? How can we make sense of the role of women soldiers in torture (Richter-Montpetit 2016, 94)? In what ways can we understand women and LGBTQI+ communities as agents for change?

But a feminist stance is more than simply transforming the questions we ask about our worlds. A feminist perspective is also concerned with transforming how we tackle forms of political violence that we may face. Before her death, Muhlaysia Booker made a rallying call for justice. Underpinning this call was a radically transformative set of ideas about gender and sexuality and its relationship to political violence. Instead of accepting transphobic violence as being 'ordinary' and 'normal', we are asked to recognize that there are powerful social and political structures that sustain and enable them. That is, there are a set of gendered and sexualized power relations that need to be challenged to enable transformation.

Sections 4.3–4 discuss how legitimacy and authority are connected to political violence

For example, political settlements and peace negotiations are often imbued with the promise of a peaceful future for conflict-affected societies. However, from our feminist perspectives, we can see that these negotiations are rarely transformative. Typically, the focus is on negotiating with armed actors in violent conflicts, a focus which frequently excludes women from negotiations that shape their post-war lives. Indeed, many peace processes fail to meaningfully include women at all, such as the Bosnian peace process during the 1990s (Lithander 2000). As a result, the final peace agreement was not 'gender-just'. This means that there was no redistribution of power and opportunities or access for people of all genders. In the case of Bosnia and Herzegovina, this has meant that gendered hierarchies and reactionary conservatism are built into the post-war society (Björkdahl 2012, 307–308). More problematically, limited attention is paid to gender and its intersections with sexuality, class, disability, and race, which inevitably means that 'peace' tends to imply a 'return' to pre-war social relations. This can reinforce—or worse, create—social, political, and economic exclusions (Wibben 2020, 117). There are important ethical questions about who we should include in the peace process and what topics should be covered.

To be clear, this is not simply about adding women or LGBTQI+ folks to our existing security practices and ways of 'doing' security—we need to go beyond tokenistic inclusion if we want to really transform our world. In a UN study, Radhika Coomaraswamy (2015) observed that the international community had developed many projects that seek to include women in peace processes. However, these programmes were 'extremely narrow', often aiming 'just to bring a female body to the table' (Coomaraswamy 2015, 40). The result is that these peace processes fail to act as a 'comprehensive process within society that is inclusive, diverse, and reflective of the interest of the whole society' (Coomaraswamy 2015, 40). As we have noted, a feminist and critical perspective demands transformation: simply including certain bodies is not enough. Rather, we need to transform the issues and topics discussed and how they are discussed.

A feminist concern with transformation means that we no longer accept the notion that issues around gender and sexuality can be dealt with 'later'. 'Later' is a way to dismiss or marginalize the importance of making these issues central to the process.

The 2012–16 Colombian peace process provides us with an interesting example of how we can better include diverse voices. The official process included LGBTQI+ voices responding to their specific insecurities. The unprecedented inclusion of LGBTQI+ voices in negotiations opened up historic dialogues between LGBTQI+ communities and military and civil society groups. The internal conflict in Colombia since 1948 has meant that intolerance for gender diversity in Colombia has been life threatening, with LGBTQI+ persons persecuted, attacked, forcibly displaced, or killed as a result of their gender identity and sexual orientation (Bouvier 2016, 13). It was not uncommon for sexual violence against LGBTQI+ individuals to be inflicted as a form of 'corrective violence' or social cleansing (Bouvier 2016, 13). The final peace deal offered specific recognition to women, LGBTQI+, Afro-Colombian, and Indigenous groups as politically marginalized communities whose inclusion is vital to a stable peace. In other words, it takes a step towards acknowledging the political violence faced by individuals and seeks to improve their security.

10.6 Conclusion

We have drawn upon feminist ways of thinking to critically question the relationship between gender, sexuality, security, and violence. As Jamie Hagen (2017) notes, even feminist security studies have paid limited attention to the insecurities of women's sexual orientation or gender identities. How we research security may reveal our positionality and forms of privilege, such as 'cisprivilege', a potential advantage for individuals who identify with the sex/gender assigned to them at birth (Hagen 2017, 126). We hope that we have begun to address this gap by highlighting the relevance of thinking about gender, sexuality, and feminism in all matters of security. Concepts such as intersectionality, everydayness, and transformation have long been relevant to feminist analyses of security. Using these concepts in conjunction with a focus on gender, sexuality, and security helps us to shine a light on people, practices, and places that are often otherwise overlooked when we think about security. Gender and sexuality can thus help us gain a clearer and better insight as to what security does to our worlds, and how it affects people's lives. Gender and sexuality can help us to think about *who* is secure/insecure and at *whose* expense; *why* people might be more or less secure as a result of their gender and sexuality; and *when* and *where* we can locate security/insecurity along with security practices.

We have therefore shown you that not only do gender and sexuality open up new things for us to think about (e.g., understanding anti-trans violence as political violence or thinking about the home as a site of insecurity) but they also help us to think anew about more traditional, or conventional, security topics (like migration and peace processes). We hope you come away from this chapter with a sense of how gender and sexuality are relevant to *all* our thinking about security. Asking different questions and focusing on the importance of an intersectional analysis of everyday experiences opens up a genuinely transformative way of thinking about security. And it can help us get closer to answering Muhlaysia Booker's demand for justice: if not now, when?

Questions for further discussion

1. Are misogyny, homophobia, and transphobia political forms of violence; and if so, why?
2. Are gender and sexuality always relevant to thinking about security; and if so, why?
3. What 'everyday' experiences of in/security can you identify in your own proximity?
4. How does intersectionality challenge the way we think and talk about security?
5. Pick a space you inhabit every day (the home, the street, the university, etc.). How do your experiences of this space challenge traditional ways of thinking security and political violence?

Further reading

HARTMAN, SAIDIYA. 2019. *Wayward lives, beautiful experiments: Intimate histories of social upheaval.* London: Serpent's Tail.
Saidiya Hartman shows how Black girls, women, and queers in the US navigate profound insecurities in their everyday lives. Hartman's book shows us the importance of everyday experiences in understanding how and why people are made insecure, and how they resist and rebel against structures of insecurity.

JENKINS, BARRY. 2016. *Moonlight.* 111 min. London: Altitude.
Moonlight follows Chiron as a young boy, a teenager, and finally an adult as he grows up in an impoverished neighbourhood in Miami. The film depicts Chiron navigating various forms of (in)security throughout his childhood, reflecting on Black masculinity and the effects homophobia, racism, and racialized poverty have upon Chiron's security, identity, and life.

POLLOCK, MICA. Ed. 2008. *Everyday antiracism: Getting real about race in school.* New York: The New Press.
This edited collection offers a series of essays which reflect on anti-racism in the classroom, and how educators and students can work to facilitate anti-racist discussions. While not explicitly about 'security', this set of essays is useful in thinking about how patterns of insecurity can affect us in the everyday space of the classroom. The book offers useful resources to educators and students to think about how we can attempt to tackle the insecurity of racism within the classroom.

ADICHIE, CHIMAMANDA NGOZI. 2006. *Half of a yellow sun.* London: Fourth Estate Limited.
Set during the 1967–70 Nigerian-Biafran War, this novel focuses on the intertwined relationships between the main characters to show how their lives are torn apart by war. The novel explores themes of colonialism, gendered and sexualized violence, and the everyday insecurities created by war.

O'NEILL, EIMHEAR. 2017. *Wave goodbye to dinosaurs.* 59 min. Belfast: Fine Point Films.
A documentary focusing on the Northern Ireland Women's Coalition, a cross-community party formed in 1996 by local women who were frustrated about the failure to include women's voices in the peace process. The coalition won seats at the negotiating table that led to the 1998 Good Friday Agreement, and fought to include their policies on human rights, equality,

and inclusion in the agreement. The documentary not only shows the positive impacts that a more inclusive peace process can have but also, crucially, highlights the ways that in/security is both personal and mundane, and that this is relevant to how we think about political violence.

References

ActionAid. 2016. 'Fearless: Women's rights organisations key to ending violence against women and girls in our rapidly urbanising world'. actionaid.org.uk/sites/default/files/publications/safe_cities_for_women_may_2016.pdf (last accessed 30 January 2022).

Agathangelou, Anna. M. 2017. 'From the colonial to feminist IR: Feminist IR studies, the wider FSS/GPE research agenda, and the questions of value, valuation, security, and violence'. *Politics & Gender* 13(4), 739–746.

Asante, Godfried Agyeman. 2020. 'Anti-LGBT violence and the ambivalent (colonial) discourses of Ghanian Pentecostalist-Charismatic church leaders'. *Howard Journal of Communications* 31(1), 20–34.

Baruch-Dominguez, Ricardo, Cesar Infante-Xibille, and Claudio E. Saloma-Zuñiga. 2015. 'Homophobic bullying in Mexico: Results of a national survey'. *Journal of LGBT Youth* 13(1–2), 18–27.

Basu, Soumita. 2013. 'Emancipatory potential in feminist security studies'. *International Studies Perspectives* 14(4), 455–458.

Björkdahl, Annika. 2012. 'A gender-just peace? Exploring the post-Dayton peace process in Bosnia'. *Peace & Change* 37(2), 286–317.

Bouvier, Virginia. 2016. *Gender and the role of women in Colombia's peace process*. New York: UN Women.

Cbsnews.com. 2019. 'Texas transgender woman seen in videotaped attack found dead'. 20 May. www.cbsnews.com/news/transgender-woman-killed-in-dallas-muhlaysia-booker-texas-transgender-woman-attack-video-last-month-shot-dead-Sunday (last accessed 30 January 2022).

Clarkson, Nicholas. 2019. 'Incoherent assemblages: Transgender conflict in US security'. *Surveillance & Society* 17(5), 618–630.

Cohn, Carol. 1987. 'Sex and death in the rational world of defense intellectuals'. *Signs* 12(4), 687–718.

Collins, Patricia and Sirma Bilge. 2016. *Intersectionality*. Cambridge: Polity Press.

Coomaraswamy, Radhika. 2015. *Preventing conflict, transforming justice, securing the peace: A global study on the implementation of United Nations Security Council Resolution 1325*. New York: UN Women.

Crenshaw, Kimberlé. 1991. 'Mapping the margins: Intersectionality, identity politics, and violence against women of color'. *Stanford Law Review* 43(6), 1241–1299.

Dart, Tom. 2019. 'Muhlaysia Booker: An advocate against trans violence is mourned in Texas'. *The Guardian*. 21 May. www.theguardian.com/us-news/2019/may/21/muhlaysia-booker-trans-woman-death-texas-dallas-mourns-activist (last accessed 30 January 2022).

Denis, Claude. 1997. *We are not you: First Nations and Canadian modernity*. Peterborough: Broadview Press.

Dinno, Alexis. 2017. 'Homicide rates of Transgender individuals in the United States: 2010–2014'. *American Journal of Public Health* 107(9), 1441–1447.

Driskill, Qwo-Li, Chris Finley, Brian Joseph Gilley, and Scott Lauria Morgensen. Eds. 2011. *Queer Indigenous Studies: Critical interventions in theory, politics, and literature*. Tucson, AZ: University of Arizona Press.

Ear Hustling Podcast. 2019. *Muhlaysia Booker speaks out at rally from Transgender Dallas attack Ear Hustling podcast.* 21 April. www.youtube.com/watch?v=nV6uiZW6x2k&ab_channel=EarHustlingPodcast (last accessed 30 January 2022).

Enloe, Cynthia. 2014. *Bananas, beaches and bases: Making feminist sense of international politics.* 2nd edition. Berkeley, CA: University of California Press.

Gorman-Murray, Andrew, Sally Morris, Jessica Keppel, Scott McKinnon, and Dale Dominey-Howes. 2017. 'Problems and possibilities on the margins: LGBT experiences in the 2011 Queensland floods'. *Gender, Place & Culture* 24(1), 37–51.

Hagen, Jamie. 2017. 'Queering women, peace and security in Colombia'. *Critical Studies on Security* 5(1), 125–129.

Hoodfar, Homa. 2001. 'The veil in their minds and on our heads: Veiling practices and Muslim women'. In *Women, gender, religion: A reader,* edited by Elizabeth Castelli and Rosamond Rodman. Basingstoke: Palgrave Macmillan.

Human Rights Campaign. 2019. 'HRC mourns the loss of Muhlaysia Booker'. 20 May. www.hrc.org/news/hrc-mourns-the-loss-of-muhlaysia-booker (last accessed 30 January 2022).

Human Rights Campaign Foundation. 2020. 'Dismantling a culture of violence: Understanding anti-transgender violence and ending the crisis'. https://hrc-prod-requests.s3-us-west-2.amazonaws.com/files/assets/resources/Dismantling-a-Culture-of-Violence-010721.pdf (last accessed 30 January 2022).

Karim, Sabrina and Kyle Beardsley. 2016. 'Explaining sexual exploitation and abuse in peacekeeping missions: The role of female peacekeepers and gender equality in contributing countries'. *Journal of Peace Research* 53(1), 100–115.

Kemp, Sandra and Judith Squires. Eds. 1997. *Feminisms.* Oxford: Oxford University Press.

Lithander, Anna. 2000. *Engendering the peace process: A gender approach to Dayton—and beyond.* Stockholm: Kvinna till Kvinna.

M'Baye, Babacar. 2013. 'The origins of Senegalese homophobia: Discourses of homosexuals and transgender people in colonial and postcolonial Senegal'. *African Studies Review* 56(2), 109–128.

Moraga, Cherríe and Gloria Anzaldúa. Eds. 1981. *This bridge called my back: Writing by radical women of colour.* Watertown, MA: Persephone Press.

Nathwani, Nishin. 2015. *Protecting persons with diverse sexual orientations and gender identities: A global report of UNHCR's efforts to protect Lesbian, Gay, Bisexual, Transgender, and Intersex asylum-seekers and refugees.* United Nations High Commissioner for Refugees. www.unhcr.org/uk/publications/brochures/5ebe6b8d4/protecting-persons-diverse-sexual-orientation-gender-identities.html (last accessed 30 January 2022).

National Center for Transgender Equality. 2020. 'Murders of transgender people in 2020 surpasses total for last year in just seven months'. 7 August. https://transequality.org/blog/murders-of-transgender-people-in-2020-surpasses-total-for-last-year-in-just-seven-months (last accessed 30 January 2022).

Nguyen, Mimi Thi. 2011. 'The biopower of beauty: Humanitarian imperialisms and global feminisms in an age of terror'. *Signs* 36(2), 359–383.

Office for National Statistics. 2020. 'Domestic abuse victim characteristics, England and Wales: year ending March 2020'. www.ons.gov.uk/peoplepopulationandcommunity/crimeandjustice/articles/domesticabusevictimcharacteristicsenglandandwales/yearendingmarch2020#disability (last accessed 30 January 2022).

OSCE. 2017. 'Combating violence against women in the OSCE region: A reader on the situation in the region, good practices and the way forward'. www.osce.org/files/f/documents/e/2/286336.pdf (last accessed 30 January 2022).

O'Sullivan, Sandy. 2021. 'The colonial project of gender (and everything else)'. *Genealogy* 5(3), 67–76.

Patel, Tina Girishbhai. 2012. 'Surveillance, suspicion and stigma: Brown bodies in a terror-panic climate'. *Surveillance & Society* 10(3/4), 215–234.

Picq, Manuela L. 2020. 'Decolonizing indigenous sexualities: Between erasure and resurgence'. In *The Oxford handbook of global LGBT and sexual diversity politics*, edited by Michael J. Bosia, Sandra M. McEvoy, and Momin Rahman. New York: Oxford University Press.

Puar, Jasbir K. and Amit Rai. 2002. 'Monster, terrorist, fag: The war on terrorism and the production of docile patriots'. *Social Text* 20(3), 117–148.

Richter-Montpetit, Melanie. 2016. 'Militarized masculinities, women torturers, and the limits of gender analysis at Abu Ghraib'. In *Researching war: Feminist methods, ethics and politics*, edited by Annick T. Wibben. London: Routledge.

Salter, Mark. Ed. 2008. *Politics at the airport*. Minneapolis, MN: University of Minnesota Press.

Sjoberg, Laura. 2018. 'Feminist security and security studies'. In *The Oxford handbook of international security*, edited by Alexandra Gheciu and William C. Wohlforth. Oxford: Oxford University Press.

Smith, LaVendrick. 2019. '"Our time to seek justice is now": Transgender woman speaks for first time since Oak Cliff attack'. *Dallas News*. 20 April. www.dallasnews.com/news/crime/2019/04/20/our-time-to-seek-justice-is-now-transgender-woman-speaks-for-first-time-since-oak-cliff-attack (last accessed 30 January 2022).

Stern, Maria. 2005. *Naming security—constructing identity: 'Mayan-women' in Guatemala on the eve of 'Peace'*. Manchester: Manchester University Press.

Trades Union Congress. 2019. *Sexual harassment of LGBT people in the workplace: A TUC report*. www.tuc.org.uk/research-analysis/reports/sexual-harassment-lgbt-people-workplace (last accessed 30 January 2022).

Vivanco, José Miguel. 2020. 'Opinion: Mexican government paralyzed in the face of a wave of femicides'. *Los Angeles Times*. 3 March. www.latimes.com/opinion/story/2020-03-03/opinion-mexico-government-femicides (last accessed 30 January 2022).

Waldron, Lucas and Brenda Medina. 2019. 'When transgender travellers walk into scanners, invasive searches sometimes wait on the other side'. *ProPublica*. 26 August. www.propublica.org/article/tsa-transgender-travelers-scanners-invasive-searches-often-wait-on-the-other-side (last accessed 30 January 2022).

Wibben, Annick. 2020. 'Everyday security, feminism, and the continuum of violence'. *Journal of Global Security Studies* 5(1), 115–121.

World Health Organization. 2021a. *Violence against women prevalence estimates, 2018*. www.who.int/publications/i/item/9789241564625 (last accessed 30 January 2022).

World Health Organization. 2021b. 'Violence against women'. 9 March. www.who.int/news-room/fact-sheets/detail/violence-against-women#:~:text=Estimates%20published%20by%20WHO%20indicate%20that%20globally%20about,Most%20of%20this%20violence%20is%20intimate%20partner%20violence (last accessed 30 January 2022).

Xavier, Jessica, Marilyn Bobbin, Ben Singer, and Eearline Budd. 2005. 'A needs assessment of transgendered people of colour living in Washington, DC'. *International Journal of Transgenderism* 8(2–3), 31–47.

Yadav, Punam. 2017. *Social transformation in post-conflict Nepal: A gender perspective*. London: Routledge.

Yamashita, Azusa. 2012. 'Beyond invisibility: Great East Japan disaster and LGBT in Northeast Japan'. *Focus* 69. www.hurights.or.jp/archives/focus/section2/2012/09/beyond-invisibility-great-east-japan-disaster-and-lgbt-in-northeast-japan.html (last accessed 30 January 2022).

11
Nationalism, racism, and xenophobia

Philippe M. Frowd

11.1	Introduction	171
11.2	Nationalism, racism, and xenophobia	172
11.3	Global security dynamics and the politics of belonging	177
11.4	Conclusion	183

READER'S GUIDE

In this chapter, we analyse the security implications of nationalism, racism, and xenophobia through their many interconnections. We specifically tackle the question of 'security for whom?' and 'security at whose expense?' to examine these categories' reliance on dynamics of inclusion and exclusion. In asking these questions, we are better able to examine the transnational facets of populist nationalism, the role of race as a global structure, and the often violent exclusions inherent in nationalism and citizenship.

11.1 Introduction

> Illustrative case studies on the topics explored in this chapter are available on the online resources to help take your understanding of nationalism, racism, and xenophobia further:
> http://www.oup.com/he/Grayson-Guillaume1e.

Nationalism, racism, and xenophobia are intimately connected to questions of security and political violence. They shape who mobilizes them, against whom, and how these are mixed into broader social systems such as statehood, warfare, and citizenship. The three concepts we examine here also refer to certain common elements: the management of identity and difference, the definition of communities, and the

On identity/difference and security, see **Chapter 9**

creation and often violent policing of real and imagined boundaries. Perhaps the most important element is the fundamental 'createdness' or imagined nature of nationalism, racism, and xenophobia—and how they remain stubborn and violent despite this. Nationalism is perhaps the most morally ambiguous of the three concepts discussed in this chapter, precisely because it includes diverse forms of community that provide meaning, such as nation, state, and diaspora. Nationalism can foreground common identity and social cohesion but also exclusion and rejection. Nationalism then constitutes and legitimizes hierarchies as racism and xenophobia do. Racism is almost universally condemned as a form of prejudice enabling rejection, discrimination, and even violent elimination. While racism as personal prejudice is easy to identify and critique, racism as a bigger and more pervasive social system is more resilient and adaptive—it also has deep impacts on institutions that affect who is secure and who is not secure. Xenophobia is closely related to racism but centres more obviously on negative views of human differences, whether it is those with another citizenship, culture, or religion. All three help to constitute and legitimize hierarchies within socio-political orders.

> On security as a meaning-making process, see **Section 2.3.2**

> Socio-political orders and hierarchies are discussed in **Section 3.3**

This chapter begins by providing a thematic explanation of each concept, then describes the links across them in more detail. It then moves on to a main analytical section that is orientated around three themes: nationalism and its transnational facets in an era of resurgent populism, racism as a structure of global politics with impacts on insecurity at a range of levels, and finally citizenship and the risks posed to it—and rights more broadly—by xenophobia. The chapter concludes with some reflection on how to make race in particular a more prominent concept in questions of whose security, security for what purpose, and at whose expense.

> These questions are presented in **Sections 5.3.1.2** and **5.3.2.2-3**

11.2 Nationalism, racism, and xenophobia

Nationalism, racism, and xenophobia are ideologies whose effects are visible in the world. They are also attitudes we can observe. Nationalism, racism, and xenophobia have multiple overlaps. Like security itself, the most benign nationalism and the most aggressive racist mobilization both function through categorization and distinction to shape socio-political orders. Nationalism, racism, and xenophobia as ideologies and as practices are inextricable from distinctions we make between self and other, which are in turn reflected onto key political issues: who belongs or not, who is worthy of security or not, and who has access or not to material, institutional, and/or symbolic resources (from access to land to the recognition of cultural or linguistic identities). The socio-political organization of our world into one of sovereign states is the most striking expression of the validity of nationalism, racism, and xenophobia for understanding our global life at face value. All three are central to the very existence of political communities in various forms, from minority representation to settler-colonial states. All are also used to justify and legitimize security mobilizations that authorize forms of political violence against those deemed not to belong and/or who are not worthy of being considered human.

> On security as a political mobilization, see **Section 2.4**

11.2.1 **Nationalism**

Nationalism is the belief that a nation as a coherent group identity (ethnic, linguistic, territorial, etc.) can be defined and should be protected, promoted, and/or made the basis of political institution and belonging, such as the state and citizenship. These characteristics make it perhaps the most ambiguous of the three terms covered in this chapter. Before delving into this ambiguity, we should note that it has much in common with the concepts of racism and xenophobia: nationalism delimits who belongs (or not) and it is just as arbitrary and subject to reinterpretation as the other concepts. The question of who is excluded from a nation or 'race' varies throughout history in unexpected ways and has been justified in shifting ways such as biology or culture. Thus, it is hard to predict who will fall on the right or wrong side of the divide.

For more on the contingency and historicity of concepts, see **Sections 1.2.1–2**

The Enlightenment vision of European nationalisms reflects this ambiguity very well. On one hand, the creation and centralization of European states began in part through national projects enabling greater centralization into the states we know today (e.g., Germany, Italy). Yet these projects reveal the limits of nationalism and the exclusions that are built into it. One need only to look at the resilience of minority languages in Spain or the persistent economic differences between northern and southern Italy to see the limits of nationalist state-making projects.

Across Africa, there is a notable contrast between the shape and organization of pre-colonial states and societies compared to the 'artificial' borders and states imposed, or shaped, in negotiation with colonial powers. But why, then, do Africans have national attachments today? The colonial encounter explains this partially, but nationalism is not simply a European project. Rather, it is a persistent form of 'imagining' community (to paraphrase Benedict Anderson's influential 1983 book). The essentially constructed ideal of the nation is common to all these cases, with the continuous meaning-making and productive processes giving it shape and existence (through education or historical narratives). These forms of imagined national attachment and belonging have real implications for security and insecurity. For example, in Mauritania, efforts to emphasize the country's Arab character have often come at the expense of African ethnic groups deemed 'Black' (see Frowd 2018)—highlighting the overlap between language, racialization, and nationalism.

Nationalism's double-edged character means it can animate movements for liberation as well as obscure racist political mobilization. On one hand, we can look at movements that Adom Getachew (2019) identifies as 'anticolonial nationalism' in the post-colonial world during the middle of the twentieth century. Getachew points to the strategic use of nationalism as a tool of resistance in an emerging global south, through which bonds of solidarity also emerged. The broader politics of the Third World in the Cold War period centred on a rejection of (and occasionally pragmatic relation towards) superpower rivalry—articulated in part around the struggles of newly decolonized nation-states.

On the other hand, 'nationalism' as a set of ways of speaking about the world can often be a code for racism or a cover for xenophobia. The term 'white nationalism', for instance, is typically used by groups who could simply be described as white *supremacists*.

Here, the exclusionary and potentially violent ramifications of who is 'in' the nation, and therefore who is 'out' of it, are clear: a racist 'ethno-state' of the type that many white supremacist groups desire would be built on a violent approach to those who do not belong. This is a live security concern. For example, US and British law enforcement agencies consider the threat from right-wing extremists of various kinds to be among the most pressing facing these countries (Pilkington 2020).

Discussions of nationalism must also be attentive to what we could call 'civic nationalisms'. This approach is portrayed by its defenders as a less ethnic or racialized vision of belonging. Some strains of contemporary nationalisms in minority regions such as Scotland, Québec, and Catalonia typically arise in these discussions. In these regions, existing as part of pluri-cultural states, nationalism may be a device for the formation of attachments to a very loose sense of the 'nation' that is multi-ethnic and multi-cultural but united by linguistic concerns or a distinct welfare model. Support for European Union (EU) membership in Scotland after the UK-wide EU referendum in 2016 certainly added fodder to a broad Scottish nationalism. Similarly, divergences in welfare-state and environmental regulation models have been emphasized by Québec nationalists to distinguish the province from the rest of Canada.

These civic discussions around national identity and belonging often include discussions of security policy, and more specifically where priorities may diverge from those of the national/federal state. Scotland, for instance, is home to the bulk of the submarines that form the United Kingdom's nuclear arsenal. Drawing attention to the costs of the nuclear arsenal, Scottish nationalists have pointed to the gap between existing threats to Scotland and the UK's national security policy (Neal 2017). These ethical distinctions between different forms of nationalism are crucial for the question of *who* is to be secured and at whose expense. For instance, the idea of citizenship as the basis of national belonging is a modern phenomenon that grants rights. However, it is also built upon the same structures of power which run through all other modern projects: classism and sexism, to name but two. Xavier Guillaume (2014) shows that citizenship, as a formal structure of political belonging, is bound up with religion, migration, colonial legacies, and more. Seeing the intersections of these factors is therefore crucial. Think, for example, of someone formally a citizen of a country who is constantly deemed potentially disloyal, and a security threat, to this country because of their gender, sexuality, religion, ethnicity, or ideological orientation. The place of the veil, as a religious garment, in France is a case in point. Some French women, whose parents or grandparents originate from former colonies in North Africa, are deemed a threat to the French Republic because they adorn a Muslim religious garment, from the hijab to the burqa or niqab. Despite being French citizens like any other, these women and girls are deemed threatening to constructed French 'universal' values such as secularism (Fernando 2014).

11.2.2 Racism

Everyday definitions of racism tend to highlight prejudice in behaviours and beliefs, especially when these are explicit in an individual's speech or actions. Yet racism—like nationalism—is a systemic and structural question. We should therefore pay attention to racist *effects* which may be indirect or filtered through other inequalities that generate insecurity, rather than simply intentions or explicit appeals to racial prejudice. Far from diluting the meaning of racism, this way of thinking about it as a systemic concern allows us to see its structural impacts and global inflections.

Racism can operate at a global level, as the early twentieth-century scholar W. E. B. Du Bois pointed to when he spoke of the 'color line' in *The Souls of Black Folk* (1903). Du Bois' argument is that race is a key phenomenon (like state sovereignty) in structuring the world order itself. Looking beyond recent history, we may wish to ask ourselves, as Adam Hochman (2019) does: is race modern? In his essay of the same name, Hochman (2019, 648) identifies that a concept of race 'appears to have emerged for the

On Du Bois and the colour line, see **Box 11.1**

 BOX 11.1 W. E. B. DU BOIS ON THE 'COLOR LINE'

W. E. B. Du Bois popularized the concept of the 'color line' in his writings around the turn of the twentieth century. He used this term to understand racism in the United States, but also the role of race in global contexts, including its linkages to imperialism and global hierarchies. Du Bois was aware and took into account the context of ongoing violent colonial conquest in Africa (Appiah 2015). Du Bois paints a vision that might be familiar to us: an increasingly connected world in which opportunities for advancement are rationed on lines we might today call racist. Du Bois' vision of the colour line is certainly a 'progressive' one, in the sense that *progress* in education and economics enables the line to be transcended. Du Bois' vision is clearly intersectional (Section 1.4) as he understands different hierarchies—economic hierarchies and global racial structures—to be connected together. In his 1899 book *The Philadelphia Negro: A social study*, Du Bois frequently describes the color line as facilitating economic hierarchy. Elsewhere in the book, Du Bois highlights how there is no natural basis to race, pointing instead to environmental factors and instances of successful cross-racial collaboration. These ideas, for the time, were radical in a world in which race was seen as a crucial—perhaps *the* crucial—form of identification and geopolitical organization. Du Bois' later work (1925), moving beyond the US specific context of racialization, makes explicit the links between racism, colonialism, and economic hierarchy.

In his 1925 *Foreign Affairs* essay 'Worlds of color', Du Bois gestures to the socially determined idea of race as something we learn, describing how the working classes of the 'white' world are 'born' into a 'spiritual world' associating whiteness with civilization, preventing them from wanting 'universal democracy for all men' (1925, 442). For Du Bois, what he calls the 'color problem' and the 'labor problem' are infinitely intertwined, with racism underpinning the economic insecurity of labour: 'the oligarchy that owns organized industry owns and rules England, France, Germany, America, and Heaven. And it fastens this ownership by the Color Line' (1925, 444). In short, the colour line as envisioned by Du Bois is not just a form of geographical distinction linked to biological ideas of race. It is a critique of colonialism and economic imperialism, and who gets to be secure, civilized, and modern. Our analysis of race and its multiple intersections with citizenship, violence, nationalism, and borders has a lot to gain from a pithy phrase from Du Bois which tells us so much about power and its distribution in our worlds.

first time at around the middle of the fifteenth century, in Spain', before what we might unambiguously call the modern era. Hochman's argument therefore takes a strong stance against the idea of race as anything other than a fiction that emerges from our prevailing beliefs and practices.

This argument echoes leading critical race theorist David Theo Goldberg (2002), who posits that while race is often defined in relation to biological characteristics, it is principally a historically defined and fluid concept. Hochman's (2019, 649) emphasis on 'racialized groups' focuses our attention on this historically specific creation of race and how it is associated with certain group characteristics. Race is therefore only 'real' so long as we treat it as such.

Race, like the other concepts discussed in this chapter, is a construct that nonetheless has powerful real-world effects. While it can be justified in relation to biological or territorial phenomena such as skin colour or geography, race is fluid. Race is also fundamentally what we make of it any given time. Ascertaining who counts as 'white', for instance, has varied considerably throughout history. If we examine the history of immigration to the United States, the inclusion of Italian and Irish populations into the dominant group of 'white' Americans was gradual and by no means guaranteed by skin colour or geographic origin.

Noel Ignatiev's (1995) book *How the Irish became white* shows how racism is not biologically fixed, but rather contextual. The book details how a group who were the victim of colonial oppression in their ancestral land became part of the dominant racial group in a new American home. The story of this process in the nineteenth century, which often transpired in the slums of major US cities on the east coast, is one of tensions between African-Americans (both freeborn and freed) and Irish immigrants. It is also a story in which Irish immigrants were perceived as a threat to the 'Anglo-Saxon' race, with religion and class strongly intersecting to present their presence as a danger (Kelly 2018). Race, therefore, is a 'social fact'; that is, it is something we agree on and which determines our behaviour but does not pre-exist our society. It is not handed down to us from anywhere, and we can make and remake it through our ideas and interactions (and changes in these). If race is the outcome of a social process, then the concept of 'racialization' to describe this process appears particularly helpful to understand how certain people become subject to certain ideas about the group to which they belong, or are attributed specific traits, that make security mobilizations possible. This also points back to race as a system, with racialization therefore a shorthand to refer to its origins and its effects, including effects that produce insecurities for some and not others in a socio-political order.

11.2.3 **Xenophobia**

The roots of the word xenophobia suggest a *fear* (phobia) of the other (xeno)—typically of an outsider or foreigner. It is closely linked to nationalism and racism but functions somewhat differently. As we have seen in this chapter, none of the three concepts in discussion is entirely extricable from the others, though they do emphasize rather different aspects of the central question of belonging and otherness. Xenophobia is linked to a question of identity, and more specifically one that foregrounds fear and the rejection of difference. While nationalism might highlight positive attachments, xenophobia is orientated around suspicion and rejection of an 'other' (see Chapter 9). The 'other' in question may be unclear, or defined in terms that involve ethnic, national, racial, religious, or cultural markers. Xenophobia, like the other concepts studied here, is constructed and arbitrary. It can emerge from everyday phenomena or small practices. One example of this is the use of ethnic classifications on state identification documents in some countries.

Xenophobia has a fundamental link to culture, and goes beyond a simple suspicion of those who lack formal membership of the national society. A fellow citizen who looks different or worships differently may experience xenophobia while a foreigner who 'fits in' may not. This association with culture is precisely what brings xenophobia into the same realm of meaning as racism.

Culture is increasingly a proxy for race, especially as the public understanding of racism has moved away from a crude naturalistic view of race as a biological fact. Rather than the scientific racism typical of the early twentieth century, xenophobia is grounded in insecurity in the face of otherness whether it is religious, cultural, or linguistic. Martin Barker's (1981) argument in *The new racism* is precisely that questions of nationalism and culture are bound together and find traction in populist discourse. Xenophobia is at its core about the designation of an 'Other' who may not, in fact, be racialized as much as 'othered' in such discourses. Here, the focus is on key characteristics, for instance between Africans during recent xenophobic violence in South Africa. While the apartheid system of white supremacy in South Africa is referred to as a clearly racist policy, violence enacted today by Black South Africans against African 'others' is typically labelled in media and scholarship as 'xenophobic violence' (Mosselson 2010). This may be because there is no 'colour line' being crossed, but also because the differences that are considered salient differ from the characteristics of 'race' and relate to the outsider-ness of non-citizens. While Nicholas De Genova (2008, 46) contests the concept of xenophobia as 'psychologistic and one-dimensional', due to its emphasis on *phobia* (irrational fear), such an emphasis on mindsets can be useful as subjective is an important element in security mobilizations. The concept of xenophobia effectively foregrounds the relations of fear, disgust, and rejection that make racism tick, while authorizing and legitimizing potential violence that arises from security mobilizations.

> Security as a subjective threshold is covered in **Section 2.3.1**

11.3 Global security dynamics and the politics of belonging

The three concepts above are fundamentally intertwined. They are ways of distinguishing, classifying, and creating hierarchies that underpin security practices. This is principally done in terms of who is deemed to belong, who is a member of the privileged group, and who is an object of fear (or not). Nationalism, racism, and xenophobia are

> **Chapter 3** discusses socio-political orders, hierarchies, and their links to security

fundamental to security and relations of power more generally because they shape the state's sovereign power to define who is a citizen, who is to be deported, and who is (to be) protected—these all rely on systems of categorizations that are tied to national belonging, suspicions of foreigners, and histories of race.

11.3.1 What are the transnational facets of nationalism?

We have seen that nationalism contains multiple ethical possibilities: depending on its form, it can justify the liberation and self-determination of a people, as well as endorse the harshest forms of exclusion. For whom or what does nationalism provide security? Examining visions of the national self in relation to migrants can be an illustrative exercise. Social debates about how to accommodate refugees can reflect the strong overlaps between nationalism and the forces of racism in security policies. The case of refugee supports in Sweden is instructive here in showing us how, in a country with a liberal reputation, tolerance and right-wing nationalism can form an uneasy co-existence. Emma McCluskey (2019) shows how the 'hypernationalist' Sweden Democrats represent the blurring of nationalism with darker forces, pointing to their recent history of fascist appeals. This is within the context of a broader rise of what we could call 'ethno-nationalist populism' (Bonikowski 2017) in Europe. This nationalism has clear consequences seen in the actions of states and individuals. In eastern Europe, for instance, vigilantism has become a major concern when it comes to migration, with people joining violent groups pledging to protect borders from migrants at the height of the exodus of people from Syria in 2015 (Germanova et al. 2016).

> The broader question of 'security for whom?' is presented in **Section 5.3.1.2**

The rise of nationalist populist political movements around the world represents one manifestation of contemporary nationalism. Slogans such as 'take back control' (Brexit) and 'America First' (Trump) imply a rejection of what are seen as globalized forms of political authority. They are put forward by those who see national sovereignty and security as having been degraded by international cooperation and integration. Here, nationalism, racism, and xenophobia are self-reinforcing as it is the 'structures of inequality, sexism, and xenophobia that have enabled the "post-truth" policies of politicians like Trump' (Crilley and Chatterje-Doody 2019, 168). The contemporary security politics of much of the political right is also focused on reasserting forms of 'nation' in an era of globalization.

In India, resurgent Hindu nationalism has produced greater insecurity for Muslim citizens while in China, a growing ethnocentrism around the Han majority has gone hand in hand with the repression of minorities such as the Uyghurs. In each case, these nationalisms rest on limited, partial visions of who fits within the nation. Politicians of the populist nationalist variety typically critique what they see as a 'transnational community that is both foreign and hostile to the sense of national, regional, and local identity of the people' (Abrahamsen et al. 2020, 99).

In the West, many of these rhetorical appeals hark back to antisemitic ideas about disloyalty, global finance, and a sinister cosmopolitanism. Belief in the nation, and its sovereignty, is in turn linked to hostility to immigration as well as free trade and the liberal 'elites' who are seen to favour them. National borders become tools for the reassertion of coherent national sovereignty and national identity to secure a clearly delineated national community—with violent consequences (see Jones 2016) for those who seek to circumvent them.

Despite their efforts to recentre the state, the paradox of these forces of resurgent nationalism is that they are themselves transnational and interlinked. The international dimensions of this 'New Right' (Abrahamsen et al. 2020) are worth pursuing to better understand a form of contemporary nationalism that is more complex than a simple will to close national boundaries to outside influence.

One of the most consistent principles found across diverse right-wing movements in North America and Europe today is a focus on 'Western civilization', particularly the need to secure it from attacks, both external and internal. More than a simple rhetorical play in arguments about education and popular culture, these claims about civilization tie into political claims about integration and otherness. Societal debates about the place of Muslims in Western societies have also tended to be accompanied by a rise in Islamophobic attacks. In some cases, resurgent nationalism may even veer towards xenophobia as a more culturally acceptable version of outright racist appeals. The accusation of racism may be politically charged and taboo in ways (e.g., anti-Black racism in the United States or antisemitism in Germany) that make xenophobia against foreigners, even if they are not explicitly racialized people, able to gain traction in public debates. David Haekwon Kim and Ronald R. Sundstrom (2014) analyse the discourse of German anti-Islam campaigns and find that they rely on 'civic ostracism' in which anti-racist language is explicitly repurposed to justify bigotry.

Nationalism has transnational dimensions that push against security policy, too. Think, for example, of the idea of an 'Anglosphere' which has been resurgent in the aftermath of the Brexit referendum of 2016. This disparate geographical space, typically restrained to the five chiefly British settler-colonial nations of Canada, New Zealand, Australia, the United States, and the United Kingdom, is what Vucetic (2011) identifies as a racial construction. The broadly white, settler connotations embedded in ideas of common language and governance are not only cultural but also institutional. These countries are, for instance, the proverbial 'five eyes' of the intelligence-sharing network of the same name. Since the UK's withdrawal from the EU's space of free movement, the idea of a CANZUK space of exchange and (mostly white) immigration and security infrastructure has emerged as a potential alternative basis for mobility rights. This link between nationalist thinking and security institutions finds even more direct expression in contemporary Europe, where right-wing parties in Austria and Italy have entered government and sought control of ministries with security responsibilities—mainly to harden policing and immigration policy (see Schultheis 2019).

11.3.2 How do race and racism structure global politics?

Race is a powerful way of organizing our world, whether we recognize how it manifests itself or not. Visions of international security as a form of 'order' have, as their flipside, an image of disorder that is inspired by the metaphor of the state of nature found in much classical liberal political theory. This mythical state of nature is inspired by accounts of 'first contact' conveyed by Europeans in the sixteenth and seventeenth centuries, which relayed the supposedly savage, pre-social societies of Indigenous peoples in the Americas. Errol Henderson (2013) identifies this legacy as well as twentieth-century thinking about race as instrumental factors in shaping how world politics is understood and practiced. We should also see race as an ongoing structuring force in world politics itself, of which a global 'colour line' is one of many manifestations. Debra Thompson (2013, 139) argues that race is central to the global socio-political order, showing how it was 'born in the transnational realm and bred to be central to discourses of modernity, empire and capitalism'. Race therefore stretches well beyond domestic histories and political concerns. We therefore need to focus on this concept's implications for (in)security globally.

We discuss this 'encounter' in Section 4.3

Race structures world politics and security in ways reminiscent of the 'colour line' (from Du Bois) mentioned earlier. This 'line' takes a clear geographical level when it comes to security issues such as international military and humanitarian interventions. These interventions, typically carried out by Western states in the global south, are often justified with reference to a conception of the 'failed' or 'fragile' state which has become a central term in the discourse of international donors such as the World Bank. This label is typically applied to states in the global south that are seen as lacking sufficient capacity to govern and protect their populations.

The vision of state failure obscures the historical role of racist forms of imperialism and colonialism (see Jones 2008). In some cases, intervention is discussed as intended to prevent state failure. This was the justification for France's military intervention in Mali in 2013. This operation sought, in France's account, to prevent jihadists overrunning the Malian army but also drew on longstanding French military presence across its former sphere of colonial influence in the region. While overt racial appeals are uncommon in the justification of military interventions, these interventions often reproduce pre-existing racial hierarchies about who can govern and who has the right to intervene. Think, for instance, of the US intervention in Afghanistan after the 9/11 attacks, justified in part by perceived cultural differences. Laura Shepherd (2006) describes how race and gender intersected in the US portrayal of veiled women living under Taliban authority to reinforce the vision of this enemy as a barbarian and oppressive one.

The structuring power of race blurs the lines between the global and the local. The circulation of policing knowledge and equipment is one such way that the violence meted out to foreign and domestic 'others' merges. The 'boomerang' effect of colonialism through which policing practices from the colonies return 'home' is visible in a broader trend of military practices being integrated into domestic policing (see Jensen 2016; O'Reilly 2017). The US Department of Homeland Security runs a programme through which US police forces can receive surplus military equipment. Surplus from the war on terrorism, driven by its own forms of racialization of the Arab/Muslim 'other', becomes repurposed in majority-Black US cities like Ferguson, Missouri in the repression of protest. Paramilitary forms of policing applied to Black protestors in towns like Kenosha, Wisconsin in 2020 testify to the spread of military style violence (or at the very least its aesthetic) to

See Section 2.2 on the historical contexts of this dynamics

internal populations. If we focus on processes of racialization, we can understand how the sources of (in)security of the external and internal other quickly begin to resemble each other.

In connecting global and local, racism also relates to insecurity at the personal level. The war on terrorism has operated along racialized lines in which everyday forms of policing make individuals insecure not only in terms of exposure to physical violence but also in terms of uncertainty in access to services. Efforts to 'counter violent extremism', typically in Western states, are underpinned by cultural understandings of who is capable or likely to carry out terrorist violence. This identification of 'latent violence' has specific impacts on individuals. Think, for instance, of the ten-year-old boy reported to British counterterrorism authorities for referring to his 'terraced' house, which was misunderstood as 'terrorist' house (BBC News 2016). This is part of a broader effort within counterterrorism in the UK and beyond that seeks to anticipate threats and detect early signs of religious radicalization. This has resulted in the reproduction of entire 'suspect communities' from which the risk of terrorism is seen as greater (see Heath-Kelly 2012). Asking the question 'security for whom?' pushes us to see how the burden of suspicion here falls on specific racialized communities, who are targeted by security practices that seek to focus on 'risk' but end up generalizing cultural and racial tropes.

*See **Box 7.1** on militarism*

***Chapter 8** covers terrorism and counterterrorism*

*Forms of political violence are discussed in **Sections 4.2.1–2**; see also **Section 2.3.1***

11.3.3 How do we decide who belongs and who doesn't?

Questions of racism, nationalism, and xenophobia are fundamentally about classification, difference, and hierarchies of belonging. Citizenship (and non-citizenship) is a key category around which we see the concrete effects of these systems of categorization and difference play out. Barry Hindess (2000) has argued that citizenship is a global system which, in dividing the global population and making it governable, contains a 'conspiracy against the foreigner' (2000, 1490). Nowhere is this clearer than in the ways that global borders function to include and exclude.

Work on borders and migration as sites of security has explicitly highlighted how mobility and migration have been framed and understood by policy-makers with reference to anxiety about outsiders (see Bourbeau 2011). Maggie Ibrahim (2005) understands crackdowns on migration as underpinned by a 'racial discourse', using the example of the portrayal of arrivals of irregular migrants to Canada. If language is crucial to how we understand political phenomena, Ibrahim reminds us that these ways of speaking are indelibly tainted by ideas about blood and belonging.

*For more on borders, see **Chapter 19***

Racial ideas are central to border controls, and Alpa Parmar (2020) shows us that race can be obscured even as it animates public policies. Parmar (2020, 184) highlights how something like the UK government's crime statistics are categorized by country 'without any nuance or breakdown of the figures, the link between nationality and criminality was thus magnified, fuelling cultural racism based on stereotypes of offending'. We must be careful, however, to recall that xenophobia towards non-citizens is neither a latent, pre-existing condition nor indelibly linked to being considered an outsider. As Georg Löfflmann and Nick Vaughan-Williams (2017, 208) argue:

> [a] tautology is potentially emerging whereby governments' justification of tougher border security ends up shaping the very opinion polls that they purport merely to be responding to, which in turn feeds securitised cultures of hostility and starves cultures of hospitality.

On security as a frame and a mobilization, see **Sections 2.3.2** *and* **2.4**

Security is a power imaginary that creates frames and connections. Modes of representing non-citizens and the ways insiders must relate to them, whether it is in descriptions or statistics, directly shape the insecurities of those who 'belong' as well as the forms of insecurity experienced by those who do not.

Far from just being a legal category, citizenship is about belonging and status which are often racialized and identity-laden. The question of belonging is fundamental to security at an individual level, including for one's sense of personal security and continuity. Think, for instance, about how the lack of formal status (e.g., legal identity papers) is most often felt by foreigners and racialized people. States' anxieties about immigration and belonging have typically targeted these populations, whether through medical screening of immigrants in the late nineteenth century or DNA testing of immigration applicants today. Xenophobic policies like these have taken the human body to be a reliable yardstick in determining who is allowed in and who is not. It is helpful to recall Jairus Grove's (2019) discussion of the importance of blood in international politics: it is important in a literal sense to determine who belongs and who gets citizenship, but also in a *metaphorical* sense (e.g., inheriting citizenship 'by blood'). Contemporary immigration practices that measure or scan the human body to discover truths about eligibility and belonging (such as biometric scanning at airports) all operate within this logic, assuaging the insecurities of some at the expense of others who typically lack citizenship.

The different key factors behind such hierarchies are outlined in **Section 1.4**

Citizenship as a legal category provides a sense of national identification but also gives uneven protection, with race (intersecting with class, religion, culture, and more) a key factor in shaping that uncertainty. Citizenship gives one rights and obligations and, crucially, membership in a political community that has a sense of permanence. This is reinforced by the sense of achievement that comes with gaining citizenship, often after passing a test and proving loyalty and integration in other ways. However, citizenship is not the guarantee we think it is. Just as easily as a citizen can be made, a citizen can also be 'unmade' (Nyers 2006) or deprived of the rights they took for granted.

Citizenship is one way that states create hierarchies within a supposedly binary legal category: think, for instance, of the diverse categories of British Citizen, British Overseas National, and so on, and the differential rights attributed to each. Recent debates in Europe about removing citizenship from convicted terrorists show this, especially as these policies target those who have (or could access) citizenship of another state—typically immigrants or their children. The removal of citizenship as a policy tool is the subject of proposals in a range of countries, such as France. Similarly, debates in countries such as Côte d'Ivoire about the 'true' nationality of politicians—often around eligibility for election—show that citizenship cannot be taken for granted and is often contested. This is meaningful to our broader discussions of nationalism, race, and xenophobia. Why else would some citizens be given due process of law, and others not? Peter Nyers' (2019) *Irregular citizenship* draws on the case of radical preacher Anwar al-Awlaki, one that reflects how this US citizen was killed by a drone strike in Yemen by his own government. While he was not tried for any crime, and had US citizenship by birth right, his citizenship played second fiddle to his role as a racialized national security risk living away from US soil.

Citizenship is supposed to confer rights and obligations. Crucially, this includes membership in a political community. Citizenship can also be a process which challenges security claims and mobilizations through what Hannah Arendt (1966) has termed the 'right to have rights'. Here, citizenship can sponsor counter-claims and counter-mobilizations against security. For example, Anne McNevin (2006) illustrates how persons made illegal resist this status by making visible their (hidden) integration into the daily political economy of cities in countries like France. This is to offset nationalistic, racialized, and xenophobic forms of othering. By challenging how their presence is shaped by security mobilizations that frustrate their own attempts integrate and be productive members of their host societies, illegalized migrants produce a powerful counter-narrative. Citizenship is therefore a place of meaning-making and productive processes that can offset the framing power of security (see Guillaume and Huysmans 2013).

> On challenging and resisting security, see **Section 3.4**

11.4 Conclusion

This chapter has shown that there are tight interconnections between nationalism, racism, and xenophobia, and how security questions like 'security for whom?' and at 'whose expense?' can inform our questionings about them. This is at both a conceptual level and in terms of the social practices in which we see these phenomena at work. Each relates to who belongs and who does not, whether this is refracted through biological, cultural, or national categories. These categories are not simply ideological; they are materially real and shape access to resources, treatment given by the state, insecurities felt, and opportunities given. When we consider their security ramifications, we are necessarily confronted with their ambiguity: for example, can there be 'national security' without nationalism? Can policing be devoid of forms of xenophobia or racism? Can a 'war against terrorism' avoid the trap of racialization if its object is so often defined culturally and geographically? As we have seen, security as a concept brings together multiple scales: collective, societal, individual, global, and more.

The concepts at the heart of this chapter were illustrated through three areas of contemporary security politics. First, we examined nationalism through the resurgence of populism and its deep ties to xenophobic politics which have clear (in)security effects: not only the insecurities that give rise to them but also those instilled in those who bear the brunt of ethno-populist appeals such as migrants, non-citizens, and those perceived as 'globalists'. Second, we saw the role of race as a global and structuring phenomenon with particular emphasis on the types of foreign policy and policing practices it enables. Far from being a question of individual prejudice, race is part of the infrastructure of our world and its security politics. Third, the chapter turned to the question of how decisions about citizenship and belonging go beyond the legal and formal categories to which we tend to associate them. Rather, they are intimately tied to forms of racialization, anxiety about others, and a sense of what the nation should be. As such, citizenship takes on a bodily and biological dimension that makes it a question of race in many contexts.

The study of security is a plural and interdisciplinary engagement. As seen in the other chapters of this book—as well as this one—critical questions about security come from a multitude of disciplinary and ethical positions. Our discussions of nationalism, race, and xenophobia in relation to security stand to benefit from greater engagement with work such as critical race theory. David Moffette and William Walters (2018) highlight an 'absent presence' of race in studies of security, showing that the field is genuinely concerned with issues shot through by race but often without naming it directly. Work on migration, citizenship, terrorism, and more can benefit greatly from what Charles W. Mills (2015, 204) calls 'recognition of the way [the] world has been whitened in both fact and representation'. Of the three concepts discussed in this chapter, race—with its varying intersections—has the widest analytical purchase and critical potential for showing how our worlds, and their categories of analysis, remain inextricable from fluid, yet persistent, hierarchies and classifications central to the dynamics of contemporary security.

Questions for further discussion

1. How do nationalism, racism, and xenophobia link to political violence? What are the specificities of how each of these phenomena relates to it?

2. If nationalism, racism, and xenophobia rest on socially constructed forms of identity and difference, to what extent can shifts in social attitudes mitigate the insecurity they cause?

3. Think of those who are excluded from political communities because of racism and xenophobia. What political strategies exist for them? How viable is citizenship as an end goal?

4. States are often said to rely on foundational myths about nationhood and values for their coherence. Can these myths be non-violent, or do they necessarily further insecurity?

5. The 'Global War on Terrorism' has highlighted the dependence between security practices and race. Is this relationship unique to Western counterterrorism?

Further reading

ADAMSON, FIONA B. 2020. 'Pushing the boundaries: Can we "decolonize" security studies?'. *Journal of Global Security Studies* 5(1), 129–135.
    This survey-like article assesses contemporary efforts in security studies to grapple with the colonial as well as questions of race and its attendant concepts (such as civilization, empire).

ANDERSON, BENEDICT R. 2006. *Imagined communities: Reflections on the origin and spread of Nationalism*. Rev. ed. London: Verso.
> An essential book in which Anderson develops his idea of the nation as an 'imagined political community'. Imagination here refers not to the artificiality of identity but rather the forms of political organization and collectivity nationalism enables.

ERIKSSON BAAZ, MARIA and JUDITH VERWEIJEN. 2018. 'Confronting the colonial: The (re)production of "African" exceptionalism in critical security and military studies'. *Security Dialogue* 49(1–2), 57–69.
> Eriksson Baaz and Verweijen argue that an image of 'passivity and backwardness' is reproduced through how terms such as 'security' and 'militarism' are selectively applied to understand African societies.

GOLDBERG, DAVID T. 2002. *The racial state*. Malden, MA: Blackwell Publishers.
> This book draws a clear link between dynamics of race and the foundations of the modern state—and by extension the political theories on which such state-building projects have rested. Its key contribution is not only to theorizing the state but also to seeing it as cementing forms of racial ordering.

MAYBLIN, LUCY. 2017. *Asylum after empire: Colonial legacies in the politics of asylum seeking*. New York: Rowman & Littlefield International.
> Mayblin applies a post-colonial lens to European policies around asylum and refugees. Her argument contests the notion that there is a novel 'wave' of non-Western asylum-seekers, as well as the categories of humanity on which much of the political and policy edifice of asylum policy is built.

References

ABRAHAMSEN, RITA, JEAN-FRANÇOIS DROLET, ALEXANDRA GHECIU, KARIN NARITA, SRDJAN VUCETIC, and MICHAEL WILLIAMS. 2020. 'Confronting the international political sociology of the New Right'. *International Political Sociology* 14(1), 94–107.

ANDERSON, BENEDICT R. 2006 [1983]. *Imagined communities: Reflections on the origin and spread of Nationalism*. Rev. ed. London: Verso.

APPIAH, KWAME A. 2015. 'Race in the modern world: Problem of the color line'. *Foreign Affairs* 94(2), 1–8.

ARENDT, HANNAH. 1966. *The origins of totalitarianism*. San Diego, CA: Harcourt Inc.

BARKER, MARTIN. 1981. *The new racism: Conservatives and the ideology of the tribe*. Frederick, MD: Aletheia Books.

BBC News. 2016. 'Lancashire "terrorist house" row "not a spelling mistake"'. 20 January. www.bbc.com/news/uk-england-lancashire-35354061 (last accessed 10 February 2022).

BONIKOWSKI, BART. 2017. 'Ethno-nationalist populism and the mobilization of collective resentment: Ethno-nationalist populism'. *The British Journal of Sociology* 68(1), 181–213.

BOURBEAU, PHILIPPE. 2011. *The securitization of migration: A study of movement and order*. London: Routledge.

CRILLEY, RHYS and PRECIOUS CHATTERJE-DOODY. 2019. 'Security Studies in the age of "post-truth" politics: In defence of poststructuralism'. *Critical Studies on Security* 7(2), 166–170.

DE GENOVA, NICHOLAS. 2008. 'Inclusion through exclusion: Explosion or implosion?'. *Amsterdam Law Forum* 1(1), 43–51.

Du Bois, W. E. B. 1925. 'Worlds of color'. *Foreign Affairs* 3(3), 423–444.
Du Bois, W. E. B. 1967 [1899]. *The Philadelphia Negro: A social study*. New York: Schocken Books.
Du Bois, W. E. B. 2007 [1903]. *The souls of Black folk*. Oxford: Oxford University Press.
Fernando, Mayanthi L. 2014. *The Republic unsettled: Muslim French and the contradictions of secularism*. Durham, NC: Duke University Press.
Frowd, Philippe M. 2018. *Security at the borders: Transnational practices and technologies in West Africa*. Cambridge: Cambridge University Press.
Germanova, Miroslava, Boryana Dzhambazova, and Helene Bienvenu. 2016. 'Vigilantes patrol parts of Europe where few migrants set foot'. *The New York Times*. 11 June. www.nytimes.com/2016/06/11/world/europe/vigilante-patrols-in-parts-of-europe-where-few-migrants-set-foot.html (last accessed 10 February 2022).
Getachew, Adom. 2019. *Worldmaking after empire: The rise and fall of self-determination*. Princeton, NJ: Princeton University Press.
Goldberg, David Theo. 2002. *The racial state*. Malden, MA: Blackwell Publishers.
Grove, Jairus V. 2019. *Savage ecology: War and geopolitics at the end of the world*. Durham, NC: Duke University Press.
Guillaume, Xavier. 2014. 'Regimes of citizenship'. In *Routledge handbook of global citizenship studies*, edited by Engin Isin and Peter Nyers. London: Routledge.
Guillaume, Xavier and Jef Huysmans. 2013. 'Introduction: Citizenship and security'. In *Citizenship and security: The constitution of political being*. London: Routledge.
Heath-Kelly, Charlotte. 2012. 'Reinventing prevention or exposing the gap? False positives in UK terrorism governance and the quest for pre-emption'. *Critical Studies on Terrorism* 5(1), 69–87.
Henderson, Errol A. 2013. 'Hidden in plain sight: Racism in international relations theory'. *Cambridge Review of International Affairs* 26(1), 71–92.
Hindess, Barry. 2000. 'Citizenship in the international management of populations'. *American Behavioral Scientist* 43(9), 1486–1497.
Hochman, Adam. 2019. 'Is "race" modern? Disambiguating the question'. *Du Bois Review: Social Science Research on Race* 16(2), 647–665.
Ibrahim, Maggie. 2005. 'The securitization of migration: A racial discourse'. *International Migration* 43(5), 163–187.
Ignatiev, Noel. 1995. *How the Irish became white*. New York: Routledge.
Jensen, Ole B. 2016. 'New "Foucauldian Boomerangs": Drones and urban surveillance'. *Surveillance & Society* 14(1), 20–33.
Jones, Branwen Gruffydd. 2008. 'The global political economy of social crisis: Towards a critique of the "failed state" ideology'. *Review of International Political Economy* 15(2), 180–205.
Jones, Reece. 2016. *Violent borders: Refugees and the right to move*. New York: Verso.
Kelly, Brian. 2018. 'Gathering antipathy: Irish immigrants and race in America's Age of Emancipation'. In *Rethinking the Irish diaspora: After the gathering*, edited by Johanne Devlin Trew and Michael Pierse. Basingstoke: Palgrave Macmillan.
Löfflmann, Georg and Nick Vaughan-Williams. 2017. 'Narrating identity, border security and migration: Critical focus groups and the everyday as problematic'. *Critical Studies on Security* 5(2), 207–211.
McCluskey, Emma. 2019. *From righteousness to far right: An anthropological rethinking of Critical Security Studies*. Montreal: McGill-Queen's University Press.

McNevin, Anne. 2006. 'Political belonging in a neoliberal era: The struggle of the Sans-papiers'. *Citizenship Studies* 10(2), 135–151.

Mills, Charles W. 2015. 'Unwriting and unwhitening the world'. In *Race and racism in international relations: Confronting the global colour line*, edited by Alexander Anievas Nivi Manchanda and Robbie Shilliam. London: Routledge.

Moffette, David and William Walters. 2018. 'Flickering presence: Theorizing race and racism in the governmentality of borders and migration'. *Studies in Social Justice* 12(1), 92–110.

Mosselson, Aidan. 2010. '"There is no difference between citizens and non-citizens anymore": Violent xenophobia, citizenship and the politics of belonging in post-Apartheid South Africa'. *Journal of Southern African Studies* 36(3), 641–655.

Neal, Andrew W. Ed. 2017. *Security in a small nation: Scotland, democracy, politics*. Cambridge: Open Book Publishers.

Nyers, Peter. 2006. 'The accidental citizen: Acts of sovereignty and (un)making citizenship'. *Economy and Society* 35(1), 22–41.

Nyers, Peter. 2019. *Irregular citizenship, immigration, and deportation*. London: Routledge.

O'Reilly, Conor. Ed. 2017. *Colonial policing and the transnational legacy: The global dynamics of policing across the Lusophone community*. London: Routledge.

Parmar, Alpa. 2020. 'Borders as mirrors: Racial hierarchies and policing migration'. *Critical Criminology* 28(2), 175–192.

Pilkington, Ed. 2020. '"It is serious and intense": White supremacist domestic terror threat looms large in US'. *The Guardian*. 19 October. www.theguardian.com/us-news/2020/oct/19/white-supremacist-domestic-terror-threat-looms-large-in-us (last accessed 10 February 2022).

Schultheis, Emily. 2019. 'How the far right weaponized Europe's interior ministries to block refugees'. *The Atlantic*. 14 March. www.theatlantic.com/international/archive/2019/03/europe-interior-minister-kickl-far-right/584845 (last accessed 10 February 2022).

Shepherd, Laura J. 2006. 'Veiled references: Constructions of gender in the Bush administration discourse on the attacks on Afghanistan post-9/11'. *International Feminist Journal of Politics* 8(1), 19–41.

Sundstrom, Ronald R. and David Haekwon Kim. 2014. 'Xenophobia and racism'. *Critical Philosophy of Race* 2(1), 20–45.

Thompson, Debra. 2013. 'Through, against and beyond the racial state: The transnational stratum of race'. *Cambridge Review of International Affairs* 26(1), 133–151.

Vucetic, Srdjan. 2011. *The Anglosphere: A genealogy of a racialized identity in international relations*. Stanford, CA: Stanford University Press.

12

Securing development; developing security?

Maria Stern

12.1	Introduction	188
12.2	Securing development; developing security?	190
12.3	Asking critical security questions	194
12.4	Conclusion: the question of political violence	201

READER'S GUIDE

In this chapter, we critically examine the politics of development and its relation to security. We specifically pose the questions: 'security for whom and from what?' and 'security when and where?' An exploration of the stakes of these questions ('security at whose expense?') is woven into the analysis of these overarching security questions. By posing these questions and following the lines of critique that they open up, we draw attention to connections linking development, the mobilization of security, political violence, and harm.

12.1 Introduction

Illustrative case studies on the topics explored in this chapter are available on the online resources to help take your understanding of development and security further: http://www.oup.com/he/Grayson-Guillaume1e.

> Development and security are inextricably linked. A more secure world is only possible if poor countries are given a real chance to develop. Extreme poverty and infectious diseases threaten many people directly, but they also provide a fertile breeding ground for other threats, including civil conflicts. Even people in rich countries will be more secure if their Governments help poor countries to defeat poverty and disease by meeting the Millennium Development Goals.
> (United Nations 2004, vii)

Are security and development inextricably linked? If so, how, when, according to whom, and to what effect? How can we think about development through the prism of security? What kinds of security logics are at play in 'development' efforts, and imaginaries such as that of former United Nations Secretary General Kofi Annan? How can we make sense of his words? To set the stage for this chapter, let us try to follow his logic.

Surely, we can agree that for people to survive and to thrive, immediate and even long-term threats such as extreme poverty, malnutrition, illness, environmental degradation, and direct violence must somehow be mitigated. *If* a child cannot venture far from her house to gather firewood or to help her mother grow the food she needs to survive for fear of sexual violence, buried land mines, stray bullets, drone attacks, bombs, or being forced to become a child soldier, then her chances of surviving and indeed thriving are indeed poor. *If* this same child is refused education, lives in an area where the soil is poisoned or infertile, and where even the most basic healthcare and medicines are unavailable, her life will be precarious. *If* the country in which she resides lacks the infrastructure, publicly allocated resources, functioning and accountable institutions, and governing structures to ensure her health and safety, then this lack of 'development' at the state level surely impacts her 'life chances' (Duffield 2010). Furthermore, *if* such misery perpetuates, or produces, armed conflict and political violence that stem from the unequal distribution of all sorts of resources (material, symbolic, etc.); and *if* conflict and political violence transgress the geographical scale within which they occur because people migrate, conflict in one place influences conflict in another, or such conflicts disrupt the core business of corporations upon which 'rich countries' depend, then we could perhaps agree that 'people in rich countries will be more secure if their Governments help poor countries to defeat poverty and disease'.

In following these logics, Annan's statement makes good sense. Read this way, development, understood as 'a multidimensional undertaking to achieve a higher quality of life for all people', depends on a level of security (United Nations 1997, 1–2). Security, in this sense, is understood as a knowable and measurable threshold with an identifiable end-goal, such as survival in the face of such threats and prospering according to certain ideas about 'quality of life'. Clearly, however, there are many ways of understanding the linkages between security and development, and, consequently, making sense of statements like Annan's.

Perhaps you are already uncomfortable with the framing and some of the assumptions about security and development embedded in Annan's statement; or, in the example we crafted above to help make sense of his words: why is the 'subject' of security and development in our example depicted as a girl? Where is her agency? What are the other threats alluded to and against whom/what? What is a 'rich' country? How can we *know* that poverty leads to violence, and so on? As established in Chapter 4, we can also ask how political violence might be enabled by connecting security and development in this way. Might, for example, the idea that poverty is a breeding ground for violence set the stage for violent exclusions of people fleeing violent conflicts and seeking asylum in the global north?

See **Chapter 18** on environmental security

Migration is discussed further in **Chapter 19**

On security as a threshold, see **Section 2.3.1**

On gender and security, see **Chapter 10**

In this chapter, we further explore some possible ways of critically thinking about development through the lens of 'security'. We highlight how the mobilization of security via development may aim to address forms of political violence but can also (re)produce them. We ask the following security questions in relation to a generalized account of the theme of development: security for whom, security from what, security where, and security when? In answering these questions, we will explore some of the possible stakes (security at whose expense?) that emerge. There are of course many, many more.

> These different questions are discussed in **Sections 5.3.1.2–5** and **5.3.2.3**

12.2 Securing development; developing security?

In this section, we provide a cursory overview of the major storyline that characterizes the logics of and changes in development thinking and practice. This is to equip you with some of the contextual knowledge required to critically evaluate development through the prism of security.

12.2.1 Development? The dominant storyline

> On the historicity of security, see **Section 2.2**
>
> Questions of legitimacy and authority are discussed in **Sections 4.3–4**
>
> **Chapter 11** covers the links between citizenship and security

Development usually refers to the process through which the underdeveloped state 'becomes' developed (that is, becomes a state as it is 'supposed to be') following the model of the modern liberal state that, so the story goes, prevailed in post-war Europe. In this model, the state is understood as the necessary foundation for freedom, justice, democracy, and the good society. Modern state sovereignty—which posits that there is no higher authority than the state, and that the state enjoys supreme authority within a specific territory—remains the guiding principle. The familiar reasoning is as follows: if the state is not 'secure', then political order unravels, and ultimately citizens, and all other possible 'referents of security', are imperiled.

Enlightenment ideas about freedom, improvement, and progress were central to this way of thinking. However, development has taken on different meanings over time and in different contexts. Two main currents prevail. The first focuses on global sustainable poverty reduction, either centring vulnerable communities and people, or the state as an actor which shall provide poverty relief for its population in a sustainable manner. The second is the merging of development with counterinsurgency, the prevention of violence and conflict, and the building of (certain versions of) liberal peace. While ideas about the interlinkages between security and development have long been central in policy and academic spaces, the contours and content of these discussions have, of course, changed (Hettne 2010). Let us then revisit a brief history of 'development' before we return to how it has been seen to relate to security.

> Economic development is outlined in **Box 12.1**

The explicit policy goal to 'develop' often newly independent countries by those states that were deemed to be already 'developed', including former colonial powers, accompanied the demise of the formal colonial period after the end of the Second World War. Indeed, development of the so-called 'Third World' through intervention and aid became a key strategy in the Cold War. The global superpowers of the

BOX 12.1 ECONOMIC DEVELOPMENT

Development, according to the 'West' during the Cold War, meant helping newly independent states to achieve economic growth through 'modernizing' their economies and social structures (see O'Brien and Williams 2020; Rostow 1962). Indeed, it was assumed that economic growth, measured by Gross National Product (GNP), would eventually lead to social, political, and infrastructural growth of the state as a whole, which would render it stable and 'secure'. More important, such states were more likely to become allied with the 'West'. It was also a strategy echoed by the Communist bloc but for different political purposes (Friedman 2015). Development thus became a key strategy for state building in post-colonial societies (Stern and Öjendal 2010).

Unfettered belief in modernization through 'development' as a quick route to escape 'underdevelopment' followed suit. However, the post-colonial world in the 1960s and 1970s did not achieve this modernist dream; instead, social and political problems proliferated. According to dominant understandings, the debt crisis of the 1980s made it clear that the development of the 'Third World' required more stringent oversight by the international community. An era of strict structural adjustment programmes designed by intervening countries and the International Monetary Fund (IMF) ensued, governing how developing states would organize their economies. Aid was conditional upon following these austere guidelines. The development state, so the story goes, had failed in its development. The overall development strategies in the 1980s were therefore characterized by the extreme dismantling of state institutions and authority in line with neoliberal economic logics and Cold War security logics.

time—the United States of America and the Soviet Union—vied for influence. The terminology of the 'Third World' was used to refer to those countries not (yet) aligned with the Western or Eastern blocs in the Cold War, but soon came to denote poor countries that were not 'economically' developed. This is not to say that development in this sense was a novel phenomenon. Ideas about development were foundational to colonial rule and imperialism from the late eighteenth into the late nineteenth and twentieth centuries (Desai and Potter 2014). French, British, and Dutch colonial policies in particular moved away from pure exploitative practices to put 'more emphasis on development on humanitarian grounds for native colonial communities' (Craggs 2014, 4). These policies, known as 'trusteeship', were strongly paternalistic towards racialized populations deemed to be 'child-like' and thus were used to justify Western supervision (Craggs 2014, 4).

In the 1990s, international development policies were designed to stabilize the economies of developing countries through strong international governance. The problem of underdevelopment, it was reasoned, was internal to developing countries. They needed help to build the state institutions, skills, and the political will required for 'good governance' and state building (Hettne 2010). Accordingly, development was not only driven by the state elites with the backing of the donor community but also served to constitute the post-colonial state. Such states, so the story goes, were in need of democratization, the instalment of the rule of law, Security Sector Reform (SSR) access to free and globalized markets, and the building of legitimate state institutions.

Zoom-in 12.1 outlines Security Sector Reform

ZOOM-IN 12.1 SECURITY SECTOR REFORM

Security Sector Reform (SSR) refers to policies which directly connect public security sector reforms in 'developing' countries with their capacity to fully develop. SSR is directly modelled on Western models of good governance in terms of accountability, transparency, and prudential management which are supposed to reflect the legitimacy and authority of the state (see Sections 4.3–4). For example, SSR concentrates on shifting the military away from policing to external defence while ensuring that police agencies adopt human rights norms and anti-corruption regulations. SSR starts from the assumption that war and policing should be separate (see Barkawi 2016). It also assumes that security is a public good despite the fact that it tends to be provided by private actors in most countries (see Abrahamsen and Williams 2006).

These key elements of state building would eventually engender security and peace, as well as development.

Development, however, was not only the purview of states. Ideas about human security, human development, and human rights clamoured for attention in international governmental and non-governmental organizations alongside state-centric economic models. Indeed, the concepts of human development and human security were presented as more or less synonymous. In addition to providing a framing for development efforts aimed at directly benefitting people in vulnerable positions, the notion that developing, conflict-ridden, and often corrupt states were incapable of providing basic human development, security, and rights to their citizens also became a strong legitimizing factor for humanitarian interventions in line with the Responsibility to Protect (R2P) norm. The US-led global War on Terror following the terrorist attacks against the United States on 11 September 2001 furthered the call for the building of stable democratic institutions in the developing world. The idea was to help so-called 'failed' states from fostering conflict and acting as 'breeding grounds' for terrorism and other dangerous things (Woodward 2017). The notion of states as 'failed' alludes to their (supposed) lack of success in following the blueprint for development set by the intervening parties.

Despite its state-centric-ness, development thinking and practice has changed. Indeed, it has been forced to change considering the clear global nature of problems and issues, not the least those related to global climate change, and pandemics such as COVID-19. Furthermore, the prominence of new donors (most notably China) and development cooperation between countries in the global south (referred to as South–South cooperation) add to the growing recognition that for sustainable development to occur, one must disrupt the simplistic binary between the developing and developed world (see Eriksson Baaz and Parashar 2021; Lisimba and Parashar 2021). The UN agenda 2030 clearly drives home this point in its seventeen Sustainable Development Goals (United Nations, n.d.).

The notions of a 'global north' and a 'global south' have thus begun to replace simplistic traditional notions about 'developed' and 'underdeveloped' societies (Rutazibwa and Shilliam 2018, 4–5). These terms denote that relations of power between the

On human security, see **Section 2.3.1**

On questions of health and the environment, see **Chapters 13** *and* **18**

'North' and the 'South' transgress territorial boundaries; there is a 'North' in the South and a 'South' in the North (Rutazibwa and Shilliam 2018, 4–5). It has become abundantly clear, for example, that poverty, disenfranchisement, marginalization, and the breakdown of state functions and institutions also exist in countries typically deemed to be 'developed', which allows us to speak of the global south existing in the United States or in Sweden as well as in Mozambique or Indonesia (see Eriksson Baaz and Parashar 2021).

12.2.2 Security development?

What of the connections between security and development? As noted earlier, the complex and pressing problems that societies face in today's globalized world have prompted both policy makers and academics to explore the interconnections between security and development as well as between poverty and conflict. Attention to these interconnections has also become an integral part of security policies and development assistance policies globally. Indeed, the now familiar notion of sustainable development and its connections to peace, human rights, and security accompanied the advent of the UN's Millennium Development Goals (2000–15) and more recently its 2030 Agenda for Sustainable Development.

The term 'security–development nexus' emerged in the early 2000s as a way of capturing this complexity. Donor countries and actors in humanitarian interventions emphasized how to best implement 'security' and 'development' in receiving countries. The general idea is that coordination among development and security sector actors best promotes peace, security, development, and good governance. For example, there is an increasing emphasis on humanitarian intervention as well as peacebuilding and state-building missions (Öjendal et al. 2021). In many instances, such as in the NATO-led mission in Afghanistan, military actors have either worked alongside development agencies or taken charge of promoting development, including gender equality, as a tool of counterinsurgency (Manchanda 2020). These connections and practices orientated to the prevention of conflicts are not new (see Hettne 2010; Stern and Öjendal 2019). However, since the 1990s, references to the connections between security and development have become prominent in most security policies of 'Western' states and international aid organizations (Duffield 2001), as well as at international bodies such as the United Nations and the European Union (see European Parliament 2016).

Despite the seeming certainty with which development has been incorporated into overarching security concerns (see Berger and Weber 2009), the term security–development nexus does not have a fixed meaning but has come to refer to a range of different things (see Stern and Öjendal 2010). These include how the complexity of problems, as we outlined in Section 12.1, are understood as *produced by* and as *productive of* insecurity and underdevelopment and/or poverty.

On security as a process, see **Section 2.3.2**

The security–development nexus can also refer to the actual practices and forms of knowledge production undertaken by states, international organizations, think tanks, and/or non-governmental organizations to devise holistic approaches and craft policy tools to address this complexity. One of these meanings also refers to the idea of a desirable threshold for attaining security and development that are promised by these practices and policy tools. Furthermore, these diverse meanings, framings, and types of mobilization also echo the different ways that security and development are seen to be interlinked, including how either security or development is the catalyst for the other.

Security and development are thus concrete elements of global governance. Take situations in which peacebuilding operations are established to promote state building, which has become firmly established in state and international policies as a way to tackle the security and development problems identified in 'developing' or so-called 'fragile' states (e.g., Paris and Sisk 2009). It has become increasingly clear, however, that peacebuilding efforts often do not work even when measured against their own parameters for success (Öjendal et al. 2021). For example, the long-standing peacebuilding missions in the Democratic Republic of the Congo (DRC) and Cambodia have not been able to stem violence, provide security, or end poverty for a large majority of the population. Various reasons are offered. Differences can be found in explanations for the 'failures' of these efforts as well as how to best identify remedies to provide security and ensure sustainable development in complex situations. Given this complexity, what questions should we ask about how connections are being established between security and development?

12.3 Asking critical security questions

Now that we have a sense of the narrative around development and how it may connect to security, or even how it *is* a security issue, we can begin to think critically about what security claims do politically. In this section, we do so by asking the following security questions: 'security for whom and from what?' and 'security when/where?' Asking these questions helps us see how security is mobilized in the crafting and enactment of development policies, or security-development/peacebuilding initiatives, and the security logics that underpin them. This helps render visible the hierarchies these logics reproduce, the forms of violence they enable, and the forms of knowledge that they privilege (see Kothari 2006; Ndlovu-Gatsheni 2020). Importantly, if we do not pose such questions about how security is mobilized in relation to development, then we might miss recognizing how violence and harm 'flow through' these imaginaries and the socio-political orders (such as racist and gendered coloniality) that underpin them and that they, in turn, reproduce and uphold. Ultimately, then, asking these questions allows us to explore the question 'security at whose expense?'

12.3.1 Security for whom and from what?

Clearly, the developing state looms large as the referent object of security in the mainstream story of development. The state—and how it is envisioned in its potential future guise—is the sovereign key actor and 'guarantor' for development. 'Development' is often measured in economic terms and in how well the state 'reforms' itself in the image of the 'West'. This story tells us that for the state to be secured, it needs to be developed, with strong state institutions, including robust and legitimate military and police forces. According to this line of thinking, state stability is key to security and development. These are understood as conditions of possibility for each other and as thresholds. According to this logic, the state does not pose a threat to 'its' people but, instead, should be their protector. The state therefore enjoys a monopoly over the use of legitimate violence and force in both domestic and international environments. The police provide 'internal' security and order. The military guard borders and the defend the nation from external threats.

> The question of legitimacy is discussed in **Section 4.3**, its relation to police forces in **Chapter 6**

An important aspect of this view is the connection between the state and national identity. According to this logic, the modern state requires that national identity—the 'we-ness' of the nation-state—is both overarching and ultimately comes first in the hierarchy of identities found within the state. In this sense, national identity predominates and ultimately incorporates all other political identifications. Any challenges to its hegemony cannot be tolerated. If the hegemony of the idea of the state is challenged through claims to other identifications (such as ethnic, national, and religious group belonging) and attendant calls for the re-distribution of resources, political representation, and so on, then the internal order and security of the state is challenged and national security measures must be taken.

> National identity and its links to security are discussed in **Chapters 9 and 11**

Why might the mobilization of security claims about development in which the state is the referent object/subject of security be problematic, even if the ultimate subjects to be secured are people? What does the mobilization of security according to this security logic do? To find answers, we need to ask questions about power and knowledge, and to notice how this narrative invests security elites and security actors with the power to determine when something, or someone, is a security threat.

We may then recall that in many cases worldwide the state is equated with the interests of the ruling elite. Furthermore, colonial rule and its accompanying political ordering continues to mark the political makeup of many so-called 'developing' states. Colonial powers divided territories along lines that reflected their interests and reach. These borders and boundaries often poorly reflected the political and cultural identities of the people living in these territories. In many instances, unequal distribution of resources and political influence contributed to the production of conflict and inequality between peoples living within and across state borders. This was arguably the case in Rwanda, providing the conditions of possibility for genocide in 1994 (Prunier 1995).

The developing nation-state—as it is currently drawn and imagined—can therefore be seen as an ill-fitting unit for developing the 'life chances' of the people residing within its borders (Duffield 2010; Nandy 1995). Surely, how well ruling elites address different people's needs in different socio-political orders will vary. Yet, in policies and strategies that focus on the state, the situation of those most vulnerable can become obscured. And, what vulnerable people may deem as dangerous to their well-being (be it the police, sexism, classism, racism, religious intolerance, the lack of functioning infrastructure, poor access to healthcare, etc.) may remain unrecognized as a valid security threat, if their voices are heard at all: who can 'speak' security indeed? What

> On who can 'speak' security, see **Sections 2.3.2, 2.4,** and **5.3.1.1**

might we learn about how people invest security and development with meaning if we were to pay attention to people who feel threatened by the state's security sector?

Further, critically posing questions about the subject of security allows us to query how a ruling elite, vested with the monopoly over the (legitimate) use of force and the authority to decide who and what is a threat, can be—and often is—invested in a particular political order that can entrench discriminatory and even violent hierarchies of belonging (see Krogstad 2012). We can also probe how imaginaries about modern state sovereignty enabling violence in all of its different forms are written into the concentration of power.

Following this line of critique, we may consider how in many contexts globally, state-building and peacebuilding projects fostered through external intervention occur amidst various forms of violence (see Öjendal et al. 2021). For instance, armed conflicts, skirmishes, parallel claims to legitimate socio-political order, and state repression emerge alongside peacebuilding, state-building, and targeted development efforts, even in the aftermath of peace agreements. Continuing political violence in Colombia after the 2016 peace accords certainly comes to mind (Rodriguez 2018). In this case, we can question how the mobilization of security for or through development can both reproduce and entrench such violence, making the 'peace' that holds for a few look and feel much more like violence for many (Georgi 2022).

Let's take another example. In the aftermath of peace agreements, the Eastern DRC has been, and continues to be, the site of many armed conflicts between the national armed forces (the FARDC) and different armed group as well as among these groups. It is also a site of peacebuilding and state-building interventions. The donor community (e.g., the European Union, the UN, and the USA) has espoused the belief that development depends upon 'peace and stability' and, vice versa, that people need to be protected by the state (Arnould and Vlassenroot 2016). Consequently, much funding has been directed at SSR, including strengthening the FARDC. The FARDC, however, has also been implicated in violence against civilians (e.g., direct violence, including sexual violence, extortion, etc.), as well as against those who are suspected of aiding, or belonging to, different armed groups (Eriksson Baaz and Stern 2013). Furthermore, some FARDC commanders have provided 'development' for the communities in which they are stationed (e.g., through the planting of crops, support of small businesses) as a mechanism for advancing military goals, including counterinsurgency by winning the 'hearts and minds' of these community members.

*SSR is covered in **Zoom-in 12.1***

These peacebuilding and state-building interventions are premised on the idea that the developing state needs help in 'learning' how to self-govern responsibly, or at least to respect and safeguard the 'human security' of its citizens. According to such security logics, the lack of good governance (as determined by those intervening) is the biggest threat to development. In this sense, the greatest peril to the *potentially* developed state is indeed the state itself. Following this line of reasoning, we can then critically interrogate the notion of responsible or 'good' governance. How does it emerge out of an ideal notion of a developed, 'Western' democratic nation-state? If it does, what might this mean? Indeed, as students of security, we may recall that those states that aim to help developing states evolve to be more like them are also riddled with violence, injustice, and divisions between a 'global north' and a 'global south' within their own borders. Insights into these relations of power would give us tools to probe these contradictions, as well as the paternalistic rationales that are arguably crafted out of colonial, universalizing, and racist discourses that produce harmful effects.

Critique might also help us understand how external intervention is seen as the condition of possibility for the development of national state sovereignty in the 'target' state (see Öjendal et al. 2021). We would therefore take notice of how certain imaginaries of global order may be reproduced through such interventions (see Jabri 2013; Ndlovu-Gatsheni 2013). We may also note how this global order is premised on certain states having the power and the means to intervene and 'teach', 'guide', or 'assist' developing states in good governance and ultimately legitimate a certain form of state sovereignty, which in practice means infringing on the 'developing' state's own sovereignty (Duffield 2010). Öjendal and his co-authors (2021, 278) argue, for instance, that

> the . . . 'need' for external assistance, protection, intervention and statebuilding—claimed to be the solution to war, violence and state 'failure'—constructs de facto peacebuilding as a device that sorts able states/regimes from those less able and in need of 'fixing' or 'building', while still responsibilising the target society for its own inevitable failure.

Seen this way, development and its accompanying peacebuilding, state-building, and stabilization projects are a 'vehicle of rule that reproduces forms of colonial and imperial order' (Öjendal et al. 2021, 278). This vehicle exports a 'Western' centric worldview, reproduces differentials in global power structures, and reinscribes violent practices, such as settler colonialism, 'robust' military intervention, and the exploitation of the global south in the global political economy. It also perpetuates coloniality and the political violence attached to it in the global north and the global south (Nandy 1995; Ndlovu-Gatsheni, 2013). Indeed, critically probing development and security as a technique of governing helps us to ask questions about how the mobilization of security in the name of development may pave the way for people to be bombed, or starved, in the name of humanitarian military intervention and state building (Manchanda 2020). Asking 'security development for whom and from what?' also helps us to query if, and how, efforts to build institutions aligned with the needs of particular societies are thwarted because they do not follow the universalizing blueprints drafted by external development actors.

Moving away from the state as the explicit referent object/subject of security, let's turn now to the gendered subject of security and development that I depicted in the introductory paragraphs to this chapter and that figures as the symbolic reference for many development programmes worldwide. Why might a reliance on the stereotype of the racialized, poor, uneducated, potentially disabled girl, or the aspirational 'empowered' girl, be problematic, especially given the growing global recognition of the nefarious workings of sexism? What kinds of questions might emerge from critically probing these stereotypes (Hickel 2014; Skalli 2015)? How do racialized and gendered stereotypes about specific groups and their associations with poverty and disability sustain development or humanitarian practices (see Gill and Schlund-Vials 2014)?

Critique and relations of power are outlined in Sections 1.2 and 3.2

Let us re-examine the stereotype of this imagined vulnerable girl in need of development and security. This stereotype builds on a host of interrelated assumptions that underpin the workings of both sexism and racism. It thus enables the mobilization of security in certain ways and hinders others (see Eriksson Baaz and Stern 2013; Parashar 2016). First, it reinforces the notion of the feminine as 'passive', in need of masculine protection, always already vulnerable (read: vulnerable to sexual assault), lacking in agency, and so on. This notion silences or at least muffles how women in developing states articulate their insecurities and enact their agency. Second, this stereotype also combines gendered logics with racist ones, such that Brown and Black feminine bodies are assumed to be threatened by brutal and uncivilized Brown and Black masculine ones—be they individual brutal bodies or political ones in the form of a corrupt, 'uncivilized', and 'undeveloped' culture, or in the guise of a 'failed' state. Third, a white saviour narrative latches onto this depiction of racialized femininity. In this narrative, 'white', masculine bodies (both individual ones and political ones, such as 'civilized', 'developed' states in the 'North/West') must save these 'poor victims' from the dangers inherent in their own lack of agency and their circumstances—be it through militarized humanitarianism (McCormack and Gilbert 2021) or more traditional development strategies. Fourth, the underlying gendered and racialized logics that render this stereotype intelligible (McClintock 1995) also cast 'developing' states as symbolically feminine (e.g., passive, emotional, unruly, and/or in the throes of an inferior barbaric masculinity) and the intervening actors who aim to help them develop and avoid these threats as rational and 'civilized'.

On gender and security, see **Chapter 10**

Attention to how gender/race are mobilized in such ways raises questions about how violent practices such as humanitarian assistance to support military strategic goals gain moral purchase as true, just, and, well . . . humanitarian, despite the direct and indirect violence they may wreak on individuals and communities (see Fassin 2012 [2010]). For example, the insecurity of women and girls at the hands of the Taliban was successfully mobilized to legitimize massive US spending on military aid and active combat in the country. Relatedly, we may then query how such gendered and racist logics underpin discriminatory practices in 'host' countries. Does fear of the dangerous, bestial, rapist Other who is personified by young men seeking asylum, for example, facilitate the transformation of migration into a security claim? Does this recast asylum seekers, refugees, and migrants as inherent threats to society and to (Western) women (see Gray and Franck 2019)? How do imaginaries of security and development enable the criminalization, detention, and death of vulnerable migrants?

On migration, criminalization, and the detention of migrants, see **Chapters 19 and 20**

These questions are discussed in **Sections 5.3.1.3–4**; *the question whether security is a process, or a threshold, is presented in* **Section 2.3**

12.3.2 Security when/where?

Much can also be learnt from how development is geographically and temporally envisioned and enacted. This spatiotemporal analysis of the where and the when (see Sections 5.3.1.3–4) concentrates on ideas about the timing of development and security as a process, or a threshold to be passed. It also speaks to where development and security are to take place.

Let us begin with asking the question of 'when?' By asking 'when', we would have to note that in the predominant narrative about development, nation-states are to be invented, established, secured, and evolved along a linear trajectory of 'progress', following the path forged by Europe (see Chakrabarty 2007, 7; Bhambra 2009). In this narrative, 'developed' countries inhabit a time more advanced than 'developing' countries, a time very much connected to a specific reading of the heritage of European Enlightenment (Stern 2011).

This imaginary was central to nineteenth- and twentieth-century colonialism, with its ideas about child-like, backward, and effeminate societies that required the governance, rule of law, political ordering, and development that only offered by colonial powers. The violent establishment and maintenance of these unequal power relations in all their forms, and the ordering effects these had, and continue to have (Nandy 1995), were linked to colonial powers' economic and geopolitical interests. Despite a formal end to most forms of colonialism, the temporal imaginary at work in development shows this continuous presence of colonial mentalities. This coloniality which informs contemporary global socio-political orders imbues 'development' with meaning, enables particular development practices (e.g., reforming public sectors according to 'international' standards), and serves as the condition of possibility for mobilizing security when these temporal expectations are not met.

Reading development thorough security, we can notice how development (and practices of peacebuilding, state building, and stabilization) are set up to 'fail'; the developing state is inherently cast as unable to be fully developed and sovereign in the precise temporal mirror image of its intervening actors. We can thus ask how global power imbalances are infused with violent and persisting colonial logics when ideas of development or human security are mobilized. How do dominant ideas about development cooperation render much South–South cooperation invisible? What are the implications of being represented as always before and behind the more powerful intervening actors? How do these relations of power and their consequences affect the lives and deaths of people to be 'developed'? And finally, how might agents of these 'developing' states or groups challenge or resist such relations of power (see Eriksson Baaz and Stern 2017)?

By exploring the political work undertaken by the idea of perpetual and inherent temporal failure that is written into the very notion of development (see Cowen and Shenton 1995), we can query how 'failure' acts as a central component of efforts to secure development and/or develop security. If, for instance, the developing state is fundamentally incapable of governing itself in a 'good' manner, then it *already* and *always* poses an inherent threat to itself as a potential (yet never fully realizable) state, its people, 'international society' (European Council 2008), and the socio-political order in the 'West/North'. This temporal reflection enables us to consider how *spatial* notions are at work; that is, how the 'where' is inherently connected and constructed through the 'when'. The geopolitics of where conflict-ridden, non-ordered spaces exist is usually linked to the developing world, through 'new wars', dangerous religious extremism, terrorism, corruption, illegal migration, and so on. It is also 'where' these issues are set in contradistinction to an idea of a 'here' that is 'developed' and in which prosperity will continue.

The evocation of the precarity of women and girls in the global south repeats this temporal narrative. For instance, as it is cast in numerous policy declarations, gender inequality emerges as a threat to the progress that women and girls have—at least seemingly—attained in the North, but that does not yet exist in the seemingly backwards, underdeveloped South. As Stern and Öjendal (2010, 17) note:

> [what] the promise of security, the dominant logics of development tell us, depends upon a successful (and sure-footed) march towards progress and modernity and the forms of modern life that inhere in this trajectory.

This includes equal rights, protection from gendered violence, and opportunities for women and girls. Accordingly, these 'unenlightened' spaces must be taught how to achieve gender equality in order not to pose a threat to the security of women and girls. This is done through varied development programmes and projects, many of which reproduce the gendered stereotypes noted above (see, e.g., www.sida.se/en/sidas-international-work/gender-equality). Additionally, we can query how these temporal assumptions also inform the mobilization of security in cases where claims are made that 'such' people and cultures might drag 'Western/Northern' countries back into the past with respect to gender equality via cultural/religious influences embedded through migration. What these claims fail to consider is how these measures may also be hiding ongoing structural violence towards women and girls in 'our' spaces.

Where, in this dominant storyline, should development–security take place? First, development happens elsewhere, to the (security) benefit of those who are to be developed by an already developed actor. Second, development and security must occur at every level of the developing state for the security of the developing actor to be ensured. The underdeveloped and threatening elsewhere is clearly set in opposition to spaces located in the 'West/North', developed states (e.g., Japan or South Korea), and/or global society, as Kofi Annan's words that introduced this chapter make very clear. To recap: the basic reasoning is that poverty, chaos-disorder, disease, religious fundamentalism, and so on lead to different forms of violence. These include terrorism, armed conflicts, gender-based violence, ecological disasters, pandemics, and so on. This violence and disorder, we are told, can, and will, spread across the globe and into the societies of the 'North/West'. Therefore, security–development efforts must be directed towards these developing societies. According to this reasoning, insecurity and underdevelopment only occur within an imagined geopolitical map of developing states and must be contained. This can be achieved by making sure 'we' are surrounded by 'a ring of well-governed countries' that can serve as a buffer or by stemming migration (European Council 2008, 7).

By being attentive to the 'where' and 'when' of security as well as their connections, we can see that this reasoning underpins security *and* development strategies worldwide, including those of the European Union, Australia, Canada, the United Kingdom, the United States, and Sweden. We can also see how these connections provide a strong rationale for the kinds of peacebuilding and state-building strategies deployed by the NATO-led mission in Afghanistan and which are at the heart of the UN system. We can then call attention to how security and development combined in practice can readily lead to situations in which development problems are only addressed through the lens of security policies. For example, this includes how poverty is treated as relevant 'only' as a cause of conflict to reasoning about immigration policies that informs domestic counterterrorism.

> Counter-terrorism is discussed in **Chapter 8**

12.4 Conclusion: the question of political violence

We began this chapter with a set of generally accepted propositions about the interrelations between security and development. At face value, many of these make a good deal of sense. They appeal to a generalized notion of a global ethical stance that strives for people's sustained well-being and the mitigation of danger. Yet, as Stern and Öjendal (2010, 7) note:

> the power of definition over 'development' and 'security' also implies power to define not only the relevant field of interest, but also the material content of practices, the distribution of resources, and subsequent policy responses.

When we place some of these propositions under critical scrutiny, possible connections between them and different forms of political violence emerge. This chapter has followed some of these forms and how they connect to how development is framed/enacted via security mobilizations.

Questions for further discussion

1. In 'Western' countries, development is often associated with countries and regions outside of Europe or North America. Yet connections between 'development' and 'security' are also found in the 'global north' as well as the 'global south'. Identify how critically interrogating 'development' is also relevant in the 'West'/'North'.
2. Whose knowledge and experience matters in how we imbue development with meaning and how we design and implement development policies?
3. How does security work in shaping who and what matters in how development is designed and implemented?
4. What forms of political violence occur in the name of development (and security development)? Whom/what is most affected?
5. How can we recognize and seek to prevent and redress such forms of political violence?

Further reading

DUFFIELD, MARK. 2007. *Development, security and unending war: Governing the world of peoples*. Cambridge: Polity Press.

Drawing on decades of experience working with development in Ethiopia, Mozambique, and Afghanistan, Mark Duffield has written the go-to book for insight into how development governs and polices people and their 'life chances'.

DESAI, VANDANA and ROBERT B. POTTER. Eds. 2014. *The companion to development studies*. 3rd edition. London: Routledge.

This volume provides an excellent critical overview of the academic field of development studies as well as its central questions and debates.

RUTAZIBWA, OLIVIA and ROBBIE SHILLIAM. Eds. 2018. *Routledge handbook of postcolonial politics*. London: Routledge.

This handbook provides an excellent overview of the 'coloniality' of politics, including security and development.

STERN, MARIA and JOAKIM ÖJENDAL. Eds. 2010. 'Special issue on the security–development nexus revisited'. *Security Dialogue* 41(1).

The articles in this special issue critically address the interconnections between security and development and offer the reader a series of top analyses on central concerns when both terms come to work together.

SPEAR, JOANNA and PAUL WILLIAMS. Eds. 2012. *Security and development in global politics: A critical comparison*. Washington, DC: Georgetown University Press.

This book offers an explicit and fruitful conversation on key issues between 'security' experts and 'development' experts.

References

ABRAHAMSEN, RITA and MICHAEL C. WILLIAMS. 2006. 'Security reform sector: Bringing the private in'. *Conflict, Security & Development* 6(1), 1–23.

ARNOULD, VALERIE and KOEN VLASSENROOT. 2016. 'EU policies in the Democratic Republic of Congo: Try and fail?' London: Security in Transition.

BARKAWI, TARAK. 2016. 'Decolonising war'. *European Journal of International Security* 1(2), 199–214.

BERGER, MARK and HELOISE WEBER. 2009. 'War, peace and progress: Conflict, development, (in)security and violence in the 21st century'. *Third World Quarterly* 30(1), 1–16.

BHAMBRA, GURMINDER K. 2009. 'Postcolonial Europe, or understanding Europe in times of the Postcolonial'. In *The Sage handbook of European studies*, edited by CHRIS RUMFORD. London: Sage Publications.

CHAKRABARTY, DIPESH. 2007. *Provincializing Europe: Postcolonial thought and historical difference*. Princeton, NJ: Princeton University Press.

COWEN, MICHAEL and ROBERT SHENTON. 1995. 'The invention of development'. In *Power of development*, edited by JONATHAN CRUSH. London: Routledge.

CRAGGS, RUTH. 2014. 'Development in a global-historical context'. In *The companion to development studies*, edited by VANDANA DESAI and ROBERT B. POTTER. 3rd edition. London: Routledge.

Desai, Vandana and Robert B. Potter. Eds. 2014. *The companion to development Studies*. 3rd edition. London: Routledge.

Duffield, Mark. 2001. *Global governance and the new wars: The merging of development and security*. London: Zed Books.

Duffield, Mark. 2010. 'The liberal way of development and the development–security impasse: Exploring the global life-chance divide'. *Security Dialogue* 41(1), 53–76.

Eriksson Baaz, Maria and Maria Stern. 2013. *Sexual violence as a weapon of war? Perceptions, prescriptions, problems in the Congo and beyond*. London: Zed Books.

Eriksson Baaz, Maria and Maria Stern. 2017. 'Being reformed: Subjectification and security sector reform in the Congolese armed forces'. *Journal of Intervention and Statebuilding* 11(2), 207–224.

Eriksson Baaz, Maria and Swati Parashar. 2021. 'The master's "outlook" shall never dismantle the master's house'. *International Politics Reviews* 9, 286–291.

European Council. 2008. *Report on the implementation of the European security strategy: Providing security in a changing world*. Brussels: The European Union.

European Parliament. 2016. *EU policy coherence for development: The challenge of sustainability*. Brussels: Directorate-General for External Policies.

Fassin, Didier. 2012 [2010]. *Humanitarian reason: A moral history of the present*. Berkeley, CA: University of California Press.

Friedman, Jeremy. 2015. *Shadow Cold War: The Sino-Soviet competition for the Third World*. Chapel Hill, NC: The University of North Carolina Press.

Georgi, Richard. 2022. Peace that antagonizes: Reading Colombia's peace process as hegemonic crisis. *Security Dialogue*. https://doi.org/10.1177/09670106221084444.

Gill, Michael and Cathy J. Schlund-Vials. Eds. 2014. *Disability, human rights and the limits of humanitarianism*. Farnham: Ashgate.

Gray, Harriet and Anja Franck. 2019. 'Refugees as/at risk: The gendered and racialized underpinnings of securitization in British media narratives'. *Security Dialogue* 50(3), 275–291.

Hettne, Björn. 2010. 'Development and security: Origins and future'. *Security Dialogue* 41(1), 31–52.

Hickel, Jason. 2014. 'The "girl effect": Liberalism, empowerment and the contradictions of development'. *Third World Quarterly* 35(8), 1355–1373.

Jabri, Vivienne. 2013. *The postcolonial subject: Claiming politics/governing others in late modernity*. London: Routledge.

Kothari, Uma. 2006. 'An agenda for thinking about "race" in development'. *Progress in Development Studies* 6(1), 9–23.

Krogstad, Erlend G. 2012. 'Security, development, and force: Revisiting police reform in Sierra Leone'. *African Affairs* 111(443), 261–280.

Lisimba, Alpha. F. and Swati Parashar. 2021. 'The "state" of postcolonial development: China–Rwanda "dependency" in perspective'. *Third World Quarterly* 42(5), 1105–1123.

Manchanda, Nivi. 2020. *Imagining Afghanistan: The history and politics of imperial knowledge*. Cambridge: Cambridge University Press.

McClintock, Anne. 1995. *Imperial leather: Race, gender, and sexuality in the colonial contest*. London: Routledge.

McCormack, Killian and Emily Gilbert. 2021. 'The geopolitics of militarism and humanitarianism'. *Progress in Human Geography* 46(1), 179–197.

Nandy, Ashis. 1995. *Violence and development*. Triere: Universitat Triere.

Ndlovu-Gatsheni, Sabelo J. 2013. *Coloniality of power in postcolonial Africa: Myths of decolonization*. Dakar: Codesria.

Ndlovu-Gatsheni, Sabelo J. 2020. *Decolonization, development and knowledge in Africa: Turning over a new leaf.* London: Routledge.

O'Brien, Robert and Marc Williams. 2020. *Global political economy: Evolution and dynamics.* 5th ed. Basingstoke: Palgrave Macmillan.

Öjendal, Joakim, Jan Bachmann, Maria Stern, and Hanna Leonardsson. 2021. 'Introduction: Peacebuilding amidst violence'. *Journal of Intervention and Statebuilding* 15(3), 269–288.

Parashar, Swati, 2016. 'Feminism and postcolonialism: (En)Gendering encounters'. *Postcolonial Studies* 19(4), 371–377.

Paris, Roland and Timothy D. Sisk. Eds. 2009. *The dilemmas of statebuilding: Confronting the contradictions of postwar peace operations.* London: Routledge.

Prunier, Gérard. 1995. *The Rwanda crisis: History of a genocide.* New York: Columbia University Press.

Rodriguez, Saul M. 2018. 'Building civilian militarism: Colombia, internal war, and militarization in a mid-term perspective'. *Security Dialogue* 49(1–2), 109–122.

Rostow, Walt W. 1962. *The stages of economic growth: A non-communist manifesto.* Cambridge: Cambridge University Press.

Rutazibwa, Olivia and Robbie Shilliam. Eds. 2018. *Routledge handbook of postcolonial politics.* London: Routledge.

Skalli, Loubna H. 2015. 'The girl factor and the (in)security of coloniality: A view from the Middle East'. *Alternatives* 40(2), 174–187.

Stern, Maria. 2011. 'Gender and race in the European security strategy: Europe as a "force for good"?' *Journal of International Relations and Development* 14(1), 28–59.

Stern, Maria and Joakim Öjendal, 2010. 'Mapping the security–development nexus: Conflict, complexity, cacophony, convergence?'. *Security Dialogue* 41(1), 5–29.

Stern, Maria and Joakim Öjendal. 2019. 'Peace through security-development: Nebulous connections, desirable confluences?'. In *The causes of peace: What we now know*, edited by Niklas Bård, Vik Steen, and Asle Toje. Oslo: Nobel Institute.

United Nations. 1997. *Agenda for development.* New York: United Nations.

United Nations. 2004. *A more secure world: Our shared responsibility. Report of the Secretary General's high-level panel on threats, challenges and change.* New York: United Nations.

United Nations. n.d. *Transforming our world: The 2030 agenda for sustainable development.* https://sdgs.un.org/2030agenda (last accessed 20 February 2022).

Woodward, Susan L. 2017. *The ideology of failed states: Why intervention fails.* Cambridge: Cambridge University Press.

13
Health

Sara E. Davies and Jessica Kirk

13.1	Introduction: health in the context of security	205
13.2	Health security: origin story	207
13.3	Health as security: who, what, how, and for what purpose?	208
13.4	Global health as security: non-Western experiences	216
13.5	Conclusion	218

READER'S GUIDE

We examine the increasingly prominent representation of health as a security issue, exploring its history, its two most common approaches, and the impacts of mobilizing security in this field. Specifically, we engage with the key questions of security from what, security for whom, security for what purpose, and at whose expense throughout the chapter. This discussion allows us to better grasp the different ways security can be mobilized, what these differences mean in practice, and how inequalities and hierarchies are reproduced within this field, with devastating consequences, for the health and well-being of people across the world.

13.1 Introduction: health in the context of security

> Illustrative case studies on the topics explored in this chapter are available on the online resources to help take your understanding of health further:
> http://www.oup.com/he/Grayson-Guillaume1e.

What is health in the context of security? If we turn to the United Nations (UN) Security Council, we see a narrow understanding of the relationship between health and security. While the Security Council has not provided a definition of health security, it has adopted resolutions that address particular health 'crises' that may impact on international peace and security including:

- the impact of HIV/AIDS on peace operations and conflict situations (Resolutions 1308 [2000] and 1383 [2011]);
- the impact of Ebola outbreak in West Africa on regional and even international security (Resolutions 2177 [2014] and 2439 [2018]);
- the impact of COVID-19 pandemic on possible conflicts and global inequalities (Resolutions 2532 [2020] and 2565 [2021]).

> On security as a threshold, see **Section 2.3.1**

In these resolutions, security remains, primarily, an ill-defined threshold in reference to the protection of states and individuals from specific diseases that may impact on the regional or international social, political, and security context. Yet, it is interesting to note that preventable infectious diseases that kill large numbers of populations every year, such as lower respiratory infections and diarrhoeal disease, have not been discussed by the Security Council. Likewise, neither have other health issues like access to healthcare, mental well-being, environmental pollution, or malnutrition.

Within the UN system, the World Health Organization (WHO), the leading international health organization, defines global (public) health security as the:

> activities required to minimize the danger and impact of acute public health events that endanger people's health across geographical regions and international boundaries. (WHO n.d.)

The WHO argues that health and security are linked only under certain conditions: a public health event—an infectious disease endemic or biochemical accident, but not enduring health inequality, for example—that endangers people's health across geographic regions and state borders. This narrow understanding of health and security is the subject of much debate, as we will discuss in this chapter. The stakes in these debates encompass very different answers to key questions like who decides the definition of 'health security', what gets defined as a threat, and whose security is represented.

> These questions are covered in **Sections 5.3.1.1–5**

In the first section of the chapter, we present the 'origin' story of health security that has led to the contemporary practices we see today in the WHO and UN Security Council. In the second section of the chapter, we present the different approaches to health security—namely, human security and national security—and consider why security is mobilized to respond to health issues. As we will see, the focus here is on public health events and their location (regions and borders). But what about the protection of 'people's health'? And whose health is to be protected?

> 'Security for what purpose?' is discussed in **Section 5.3.2.2**

In the final section of the chapter, we examine who are the 'peoples' to be protected from the dangers of health security. The COVID-19 pandemic reveals that despite a rapidly emerging global public health threat endangering everyone, with some more exposed to harm than others, the response was not equitable and reinforced existing hierarchies. We then conclude by examining the consequences of this experience for the future framing of health security.

> On socio-political orders and hierarchies, see **Sections 3.2–3**

13.2 Health security: origin story

Is health security concerned with the protection of the state or the protection of humans? In the 1990s, health security emerged at the same time as human security. The ambition was for health security to use diplomacy and development assistance programmes to advance a reconceptualization of security that promoted the health of individuals and their right to access essential medicines, sanitation, and universal health care (Thomas 1989). At the time, global health diplomacy was not only the protection of trade routes and peacekeepers from disease but also a global public good that could redress health imbalances in financing, services, and rights (Davies 2010).

However, at the same time, the construction of 'biosecurity' was emerging in foreign policy discourses and associated terms such as 'threat', 'emerging', 'infectious', 'cross-border contamination', 'defence', 'strategic security', and 'diplomacy' (McInnes and Lee 2006; Enemark 2007). During this decade, health security was conceptualized as *both* a universal human rights-centred public good *and* a threat mitigation practice that identified pathogenic risks (mostly infectious) to defend and protect the 'normal' political sovereign order (Davies 2010).

The human rights-centred appreciation of health sought to prioritize individuals as the 'referent object' that states needed to take responsibility to secure. Individuals had a right to health that included the right to be protected from infectious disease outbreaks, as well as protection from preventable diseases like maternal mortality and childhood diarrhoeal diseases. 'Who' should be secured is quite different to the 'normal' political order that positions the state as the primary referent object of security. In this framing, it is the state's economic, political, and military resources that should be secured. As such, the threshold for what type of health event may threaten a state will differ from what threatens an individual and, moreover, what threatens states with different levels of income, borders, and health systems.

This common but differentiated history of health security—is it for emancipation, enlightenment, or control (Youde 2016)?—has led to some advocating caution as to if/when health and security should 'meet'. Security engagement in the health space and health engagement in the security space does not change the 'rules of the game'. The terms on which health security is 'sold' to states and international organizations is often to protect the state—its troops, its trade, and its borders. Moreover, it appears that health security is sold to protect 'some' states more than others. An example of this is the Ebola outbreak in West Africa in 2013–15.

There is no doubt that this outbreak posed a significant risk to health, trade, travel, and socio-economic security. Between 15,000 and 20,000 people died from the disease; thousands also suffered discrimination, socio-economic disruption, political violence, and, for survivors, (possibly) long-term physical disability from the viral infection. Ebola spread from Guinea (December 2013) to Liberia (March 2014) and Sierra Leone (May 2014). It was not until an infected individual collapsed after exiting a flight from Liberia into Lagos, Nigeria (a highly connected global city of 21 million people) that the WHO mobilized to declare the outbreak an international public health

> On human security, see **Section 2.3.1**. The connections between development and security are discussed in **Chapter 12**

emergency concern on 8 August 2014. By then, over 1,000 people had died. It then took until 18 September for the UN Security Council to adopt Resolution 2177 to support the creation of a coordinated international emergency response to the outbreak. By then over 3,000 people had died. The debate afterwards mostly centred on whether health security 'worked' in this case and if so, for whom?

On the one hand, the UN Security Council had never supported an international mission to assist countries to respond to a disease outbreak event. The mission mobilized international medical teams in cooperation with local health teams to build local treatment centres on an industrial scale. On the other hand, the disease was circulating in the region months before August and September 2014. It was not until this disease crept closer to international flights and, possibly by extension, a city in a high-income country, that the international community recognized this health crisis as an international security risk that required action.

As the above example reveals, security framing mobilizes resources, diplomatic leverage, and money. For some, this is the attraction to link health and security. The Ebola outbreak also clearly shows how security produces hierarchies in specific international institutions by deploying ideas about what is a global health threat and when action is required (or not). These hierarchies are also a reflection of how health politics is shaped by infrastructures and policies that are considered to be 'low politics', most of the time, in most states.

Healthcare is a high-cost endeavour. Healthcare systems and research are expensive. 'Ramping up' the importance of health to ensure continued funding and infrastructures can be achieved by associating them with security of the state and the international system. But is this necessary? And is it desirable? Below, we consider the specifics of how, for who, and for what purpose health security is employed. Paradoxically, health as security provides the potential to challenge narrow, statist underpinnings of security that place emphasis on borders, militaries, and economies; yet, security language towards health issues can also uphold narrow statist approaches.

> On security as a political mobilization, see **Section 2.4**

> On hierarchies (re)produced through security, see **Section 3.3**

13.3 Health as security: who, what, how, and for what purpose?

The history of health security demonstrates that there are multiple ways to conceptualize the health as security relationship. Two approaches are especially prominent in global health governance, national security policies, and public and academic debates. These are human security and national security. Applying the questions outlined in Chapter 5, including whose security, from what, how, and for what purpose, shows that these two approaches offer very different answers. Each provides a different claim about why security mobilizations are a necessary, and even desirable, way to address health issues. And, crucially, at the heart of both are assumptions about what security means and does, as well as what it *should* mean and do.

> On security as a concept, see **Chapter 2**

13.3.1 National security

The predominant approach to health security is national security. Here, diseases are understood as a threat to the state. More specifically, disease is a security threat to the concerns and functions of the state, namely its military capability, its internal functioning, its relations with other states, and its population. Yet while this basic overview provides clear answers to the questions of 'whose security?' (i.e., the state's) and 'security from what?' (i.e., disease), it is crucial to recognize that this approach focuses on specific linkages between disease and national security.

While typically considered a 'non-traditional' security threat, health is often linked to more orthodox understandings of national security connected to military capability and the possibility of interstate violence. Militaries have often noted disease as a potential challenge to their 'operational performance'. The basic thrust of this argument is as follows: diseases native to a battlefield, or in a state of outbreak at the time, can infect a state's military forces operating in the vicinity. The US Department of Defence, for example, has insisted that communicable diseases pose a significant problem for the 'medical readiness' of the military and could even threaten operational defeat itself (US Army Medical Research and Development Command 2019).

Beyond its impacts upon the state's ability to act vis-à-vis the military, disease has also been portrayed as a traditional military threat. As the labelling of 'biological weapons' implies disease can, and does, occupy a position in some state's arsenal, even if such weapons are now legally prohibited by the 1972 Biological Weapons Convention. Despite this prohibition, it is possible that states could develop and use biological weapons. States' biosecurity programmes, after all, involve cultivating and storing dangerous pathogens, exploring dissemination techniques, and modelling catastrophic events. All of these are justified as defensive, as they help to respond to biological attacks. Yet this creates a 'biosecurity dilemma', where no one can be certain that these programmes are defensive rather than offensive (Enemark 2017, 3). However, for most state leaders and national security strategists, the more pressing threat lies in non-state actor use of biological weapons, or 'bioterrorism'. A clear articulation of this shift in threat-perception is found in the US government's 2009 *National Strategy for Countering Biological Threats*. It asserts that the threat of biological attack no longer derives primarily from other states, but 'fanatics' who have 'expressed interest in developing and using biological weapons against us and our allies' (USNSC 2009, i).

Chapter 17 discusses weapons-systems

While this 'guns, bombs, and terror' understanding of security has garnered a significant amount of attention (Price-Smith 2009, 192), it has also had the effect of revealing the vulnerability of states to naturally occurring infectious diseases. Here the answer to the 'security from what?' question is the 'dark side' of globalization where the emergence of a dangerous pathogen in one part of the world can quickly spread to another, while (economic and political) impacts are felt everywhere. Typically, naturally occurring disease is understood as a threat to the state in three ways due to its effects on: the population, critical infrastructure, and state stability.

The first refers to the Hobbesian idea that the state's very purpose is to protect its citizens, including 'from pathogenic forms of predation' (Price-Smith 2009, 11–12). The second is captured by Andrew Lakoff's (2008, 36–37) concept of 'vital systems security', which understands the state functioning through intricate networks of infrastructure, people, and technology such as the economy, bureaucracy, energy distribution, communications, and transportation. Anything that disrupts these structures threatens the functional existence of the state. Outbreaks disrupt all of them: workers fall ill, quarantine, or become fearful of workplaces, and at worst, die, while normally stable patterns of consumption and supply can become volatile.

The threat to state stability follows from the first two, but is particularly prominent in relation to 'weak' or 'fragile' states. Already fragile state structures will collapse under the weight of an outbreak, as infrastructure crumbles, health systems break down, populations panic, and turn against leaders (Price-Smith 2009, 89–114). Yet this idea often takes on a particular form, especially in Western states. Here, national security is not threatened by the state's own collapse but by the collapse of others. This aligns with arguments around 'failed' or 'fragile' states, where a distant state's apparent inability to deliver basic services and functions to its citizens is argued to facilitate the proliferation of regional and/or global security threats such as transnational crime, environmental degradation, terrorism, 'destabilizing' refugee flows, and the 'spillover' of conflict (Petersen 2002, 68). Disease is thus portrayed as a threat to national security through its apparent causal relationship with other security threats.

Given this understanding of the connections between health and security, it should come as little surprise that the responses typically offered by national security proponents involve practices to survey and contain outbreaks before they reach the state, as well as preparing national defences through pharmaceutical stockpiles. The WHO's cornerstone policies of health security, the *International Health Regulations*, reflect this perspective. Their aim is to:

> prevent, protect against, control, and provide a public health response to the international spread of disease in ways that are commensurate with and restricted to public health risks, and which avoid unnecessary interference with international traffic and trade. (WHO 2005, 1)

The WHO focuses on building core state capacity in disease surveillance and outbreak response, requires states to report any possible disease 'events', and enables the WHO to declare a 'public health emergency of international concern'. Crucially, the goal is not to prevent disease outbreaks or treat endemic diseases. Rather, security practices are implemented for the purposes of stopping infectious diseases from spreading internationally.

This focus draws criticism. The emphasis on identifying and halting the spread of disease outbreaks is not truly an abstract, universal approach to 'health security'. It prioritizes one type of security—national security—in one location—primarily high-income states. The bulk of policy discussion and practice surrounding national security approaches tends to focus upon a narrow set of threats: emerging or re-emerging infectious diseases, HIV/AIDS, and bioterrorism/biological weapons (Rushton 2011, 782). While these are not solely concerns of high-income states, they are typically framed in ways that reflect Western perceptions of threat. In particular, they reflect concerns of the increasing connectedness of the 'global north' with the 'developing' world, or the 'global south' (Wenham 2019). Endemic diseases, those more likely to directly threaten the populations and structures of 'developing' states, are typically missing from these discussions unless they suddenly threaten to cross borders or have wider implications (Rushton 2011, 783). Access to essential drugs, disability support, mental health, and sexual and reproductive health are missing from these high-level security discussions.

Health security conceptualized and practised through national security imperatives thus reproduces hierarchies and their resulting inequalities. Some diseases (and those who suffer from them) matter and are placed into the realm of security, where global resources and attention are plentiful. Others are relegated to being issues of development or public health, and are left for individual states or aid organizations to deal with on their own. For example, before the internationally recognized outbreak of Ebola in 2014, the disease had fallen into the category of 'neglected tropical disease' and was viewed as a troubling but endemic problem in central Africa (Nunes 2016). Its appearance in West Africa was not treated with urgency until it became possible that it might spread outside of the region.

See Chapter 3

Another criticism is that these arguments do not always add up. For the most part, studies have found that these threats are often over-exaggerated. Disease does not exist in a causal relationship with state failure. At most, it is a facilitator of internal instability, which is a far greater threat to an internal population than states outside of it (Price-Smith 2009). Militaries are not as susceptible to disease, or as dramatically undermined by it, as is claimed (see, for instance, Petersen 2002). Bioterrorism, moreover, is a far more complex endeavour than many terrorist organizations are capable of undertaking, requiring access to biological materials and the capability (and facilities) to weaponize them (Koblentz 2009). Thus, there is a crucially subjective element to this representation of health security. Health and disease are not 'objectively' national security issues but are positioned as such due to the concerns of powerful states, the role of key security actors, and the organizations that rely on their cooperation (see Weir 2014).

13.3.2 Human security

National security may be the predominant approach to health security, but alternatives do exist. The most prominent of these is human security. Health, as Jeremy Youde and Simon Rushton (2014, 1) note, lies at the heart of human well-being. It is thus already at the core of the human security approach. Human security emphasizes security for the individual, with their life and well-being as paramount. It sees health *as* security. Health, after all, directly affects the two major 'freedoms' that constitute human security: freedom from fear and freedom from want. Health is not only central to well-being but also directly contributes to an individual's economic, social,

*On security as a threshold, see **Section 2.3.1***

and personal livelihood. However, the precise relationship between disease and human security can differ, depending upon what is emphasized. This then shapes answers to the questions of 'security from what?', 'security why?', and 'security for what purpose?'.

> These questions are discussed in **Sections 5.3.1.5** and **5.3.2.1–2**

Generally, in terms of 'security from what?', the human security approach, in contrast to national security, focuses on the threat of disease *and* poor health. What the threat is, however, is less important than how it is understood as a threat. For human security advocates, disease and ill health are understood as threatening in two ways. First and most immediately, disease poses a direct threat to life. As Taylor Owen (2005, 38) illustrates, '[it] is communicable disease, which kills 18,000,000 people a year, not violence, which kills several hundred thousand, that is the real threat to individuals'. Intertwined here are two concerns: the harm caused to individuals' lives and the capacity to do this on a massive scale. The latter denotes the heightened global significance of the former; it is not merely the threat to one person's life that concerns human security scholars. Rather, it is the fact that this happens on a scale that signifies deep inadequacies in global systems of development and entails different forms of political violence towards individuals beyond direct physical violence.

> On the different forms of political violence, see **Section 4.2.1**

Second, disease and ill health cause indirect harms. Health is crucial for ensuring an individual's social, economic, and political security. Ill health directly entwines with poverty, creating a 'feedback loop' (McInnes and Lee 2012, 143). Ill health 'triggers a vicious spiral of impoverishment' by temporarily disrupting an individual's employment, adding sudden costs for treatment, and/or permanently damaging an entire family's economic position through the loss of income (Ogata and Sen 2003, 99). Disease also has detrimental effects upon social and political communities, particularly by reversing women's advances in education and economic empowerment (see O'Manique and MacLean 2010, 467–472), and by undermining trust in political authority (see Shisana et al. 2003, 149).

These slight variations in emphasis of '(human) security for whom?' manifest themselves in different types of projects. The first concentrates on the direct threats to life that stem from disease. This approach has resulted in public and private partnership financing projects such as the Global Fund to Fight AIDS, Tuberculous, and Malaria, or the Gates Foundation-founded GAVI Alliance. These projects have had some (limited) success in reversing incident and mortality rates. The second type of project, in contrast, has led to broader, and more development-orientated, initiatives, such as improvements to water and food access and attempts to strengthen health systems as a whole. The UN Millennium Development Goals (now the Sustainable Development Goals) are such an example. Despite these differences, however, these practices share a common answer to the question of 'security how'. For human security proponents, security is achieved through addressing the 'chronic and complex insecurities commonly faced by individuals and societies' through targeted and holistic interventions aimed at underlying inequalities and structural problems (Caballero-Anthony 2008, 509–510).

Yet human security's successes have been somewhat limited and controversial. As numerous scholars of global health have noted, human security has failed to gain significant traction within global health security and its governance, with the latter continuing to prioritize state-level security even as human security criticizes the effects (Davies 2010, 26, 145, 155; Rushton 2011, 791–793). The rationales vary, yet tend to follow—if not explicitly adopt—Roland Paris' (2001) critique of human security as unmanageable in practice, or as 'little more than a slogan' (McInnes and Lee 2012, 146). The practices of human security, moreover, have been criticized by other human security advocates and those that dispute the security framing entirely as being inadequate and dominated by Western philanthropist actors. In particular, projects focused on health threats are often criticized as neglecting those diseases and health concerns which do not have high mortality rates, but are nevertheless endemic and/or impact economic, political, and social dynamics. In practice, this can lead to 'vertical' and 'parallel' health systems, where funding and assistance are provided for specific health concerns while the capacity to deal with others is diminished. An example of this can be found in West Africa in 2014, where specific programmes had been established to combat the prevalence of HIV/AIDS and improve immunization rates, yet there had been little investment in strengthening the health system—including healthcare worker wages and safety equipment—essential to respond to the Ebola outbreak (Benton and Dionne 2015, 227–228).

Despite these issues, human security remains an influential approach to understanding health as security. It is often used as the normative yardstick against which other understandings of health as a security issue are compared, with scholars highlighting human security as what global health security *ought* to be (see Heymann 2015). Its emphasis on systemic inequalities and their manifestations in everyday forms of harm is seen by proponents as the only way to justly solve global health problems and ensure health for all (see Thomas 1989). Others have used arguments from human security to critique specific practices, such as the inability of the WHO and other global actors to recognize the unique insecurities of women during the Ebola outbreak (see, for instance, Davies and Bennett 2016). It thus continues to operate as both a practical approach to global health security and a critical alternative to national security framings.

13.3.3 Why (health) security? For what purpose?

Ultimately, meaning-making and productive processes have a crucial role in health security. Even when we might recognize diseases and health concerns as objectively threatening, they are not inherently *security* issues. Rather, they are represented as such, with these representations underpinned by the assumptions, perceptions, and interests of those able to claim security. Indeed, many of those diseases and health issues most responsible for death and suffering—diarrheal diseases, malnutrition, noncommunicable diseases, poor mental health, pollution, and heat stress—are rarely found in national security agendas or the resolutions of the UN Security Council. Considering the criticisms noted above, why is security still perceived as a suitable form of political mobilization for health? What does it mean to bring security logics into health?

> On security as a process, see **Section 2.3.2**

For many proponents of health security, both national and human, the foremost reason for employing security is that it mobilizes attention and resources that are desperately needed but otherwise unavailable. Security is a condition of possibility enabling actions that otherwise are seen as excessive: the use of the military and police, dramatic increases in expenditure, the loosening or bypassing of regulations constraining pharmaceutical development, and the tightening or introduction of laws and policies that control population movement and behaviour. In some circumstances, this has been life-saving. As Stefan Elbe (2006, 131–132) points out in relation to HIV/AIDS, representing the disease as a global security concern mobilized state action where it was either lacking or actively denied.

> On security as a political mobilization, see **Section 2.4**

The deployment of the military has been beneficial in both historical cases of influenza pandemics, in the 2014 Ebola outbreak, and more recently in the COVID-19 vaccination drive, as their 'operational self-sufficiency, capacity to rapidly mobilize, and independent medical capabilities' mean they can fill crucial gaps in emergency response such as hospital building, logistics, supply chains, and even health provision (Watterson and Kamradt-Scott 2016, 158). The mobilization of security during the 2014 Ebola outbreak also led to the funding and approval of vaccines that had long been dismissed as unprofitable for pharmaceutical companies but were now viewed as 'magic bullets' in the fight against the disease (Roemer-Mahler and Elbe 2016). These advances proved crucial for COVID-19 vaccine preparedness (Branswell 2022).

Beyond material mobilization, security is also perceived as useful for its discursive mobilization, namely in producing a political environment in which particular actions become acceptable. Human security advocates, for example, have argued that only a security framing, with its emphasis on life, death, harm, and well-being, can encourage the kind of dramatic transformation necessary to solve global health issues (see Caballero-Anthony 2008). By representing current hierarchies and inequalities as threatening to life, efforts can be made to transform these. Security can thus be emancipatory. This, however, requires an approach to security that is currently absent in the rhetoric and practice of key actors.

> Transformation and emancipation are discussed in **Section 1.2.4**

Some have taken the middle ground and argued that the predominant approach to health security—national security—can be used instrumentally to achieve some political good, namely changing the views of key actors who have expressed scepticism towards multilateral cooperation and aid (Youde 2016). Security framing, however, comes with pre-set practices and logics. Framing health as a threat places it within the remit of security actors such as the military and intelligence organizations who typically operate with one purpose: to protect state institutions. Health also becomes a way in which security is framed, to the point where some authors have noted the 'medicalization' of security (see Box 13.1).

> On security as a frame, see **Section 1.3**

Elbe (2006, 139) notes that when a disease is represented as a security threat the body containing it is also deemed threatening, with extreme responses justified. Security invokes an 'us versus them' mentality. Fears of contagion have led to violations of rights and liberties, both within states and between them. It has also led to resource hoarding and refusals to share public health goods to protect all vulnerable populations. For example, HIV-positive individuals have been denied work,

> **Chapter 9** discusses the logics of 'us versus them' dynamics

BOX 13.1 MEDICALIZATION OF SECURITY

Much of the discussion surrounding the health–security nexus has considered the relationship in one direction: the introduction of security to global health. Some recent contributions are exploring what happens when health (or the language and practices of medicine) is brought into security. For some, the answer to this is the 'medicalization' or 'pharmaceuticalization' of security (see Elbe 2014). This argument tends to have three components.

First, non-medical security problems are increasingly defined in medical terms, either through the problem itself being described as a medical one or medical language being used to understand it. As health problems are increasingly considered issues of security, issues of security are also being considered through their health dynamics. Indeed, security itself starts to be viewed as health. Protecting the nation thus progressively includes protecting the 'immunological ecosystem', or the health and well-being of the population (Wald 2008, 57–58), notably from the infected Others (see Chapter 9).

Second, medical professionals are increasingly becoming security actors, beyond just their involvement in global health. US presidents have started to add global health advisors to the National Security Council. Foreign policy and national security think tanks increasingly employ medical and/or public health professionals to consider the health dimensions of security policy. Counter-radicalization programmes in the United Kingdom are framed as mental health interventions. Rather than a siloing of expertise, it is blended across security issues.

Finally, security practices increasingly include what we term 'medical countermeasures': pharmaceuticals, vaccines, and the more 'social' public health measures such as quarantines and movement control. National security policy now includes the development, procurement, and stockpiling of medical equipment and pharmaceuticals, or the creation of pandemic preparedness plans. Elbe (2014) refers to this as the 'pharmaceuticalization' of security, how our everyday life, and even our own bodies, become part of the security–health nexus' remit.

housing, and free movement, as well as being subjected to dehumanizing treatment (such as forced testing and public disclosure of illness) and physical violence. Extensive use of surveillance and police access to privacy data has been justified to track individuals violating COVID-19 'stay-at-home' orders in Australia, China, South Korea, and the United Kingdom. These practices are not limited to the 'contagious', they may be applied to anyone deemed 'risky', and this categorization may be discriminatory.

In 2009, after Mexico declared an outbreak of a new subtype of H1N1 influenza, Mexican citizens were denied entry into other states within the country and some were even forcibly quarantined in other countries despite negative test results (Enemark 2017, 122–123). The protection of state institutions during health crises may 'justify' the abrogation of human rights and civil liberties. Public health measures may even adopt such approaches to achieve health security. This draws us closer to the most crucial issue regarding the mobilization of security in health: its reproduction of wider inequalities within societies, but also between the 'global north' and 'global south', the wealthy and the poor, and men and women.

> See **Chapter 15** on surveillance and data

> Questions of authority and legitimacy are discussed in **Sections 4.3–4**

13.4 Global health as security: non-Western experiences

The protection of 'people's health' raises the question: which people? It may appear that the 'natural' answer is everyone. However, as we noted, the tragic Ebola outbreak in West Africa did not register as an 'international' event until months later. The risks to 'people' across three countries—Guinea, Liberia, and Sierra Leone—were not perceived as a health security issue until those risks moved closer to 'people' in Europe and the United States. Thus, whose health security is to be protected? More recently, the COVID-19 global pandemic has dramatically illustrated how even when everyone is threatened, not all are protected. The potential threats from COVID-19 did not lead to the same forms of security mobilization. Moreover, potential forms of political violence that were induced by these mobilizations were unevenly distributed.

The outbreak of the SARS-CoV-2 virus was declared by the WHO to be a 'public health emergency of international concern' in January 2020, and was then declared a pandemic in March 2020. By the end of 2020, the spread of the virus around the world had already led to millions of deaths and millions suffering from 'long COVID' health complications (Groff et al. 2021). As the virus spread around the world it developed different strains, posing a higher danger to some regions (i.e., Sub-Saharan Africa, Latin America, and Asia) in 2021 than 2020. All people face risk of disease from this virus, but not all bear the same risk. Some individuals face a higher risk of death from COVID-19 due to age, pre-existing conditions, and/or an inability to be vaccinated due to compromised immune systems. Healthcare workers face a higher risk of infection due to exposure to higher viral loads when patients arrive ill. Not all communities can afford to socially distance in crowded, urban housing or in situations where sanitation is shared. And not everyone has the luxury of working from home or avoiding public spaces, and many rely on non-contractual jobs paid on a daily basis. Thus, the risk of infection intersects with race, gender, ethnicity, and class (Sze et al. 2021).

Domestic health systems do not have the same capacity to manage large numbers of patients arriving in need of intensive care support, often including continuous supply of oxygen and intubation. Even when 'security' is mobilized, not everyone has the capacity to deliver it. Not all health systems provide free medical care. This means some people die or become incapacitated due to differential access to healthcare, despite COVID-19 having been deemed an international or domestic security issue. Many will recall seeing images of people having to purchase their own oxygen tanks in Brazil, Indonesia, and Myanmar; and some individuals in the United States have described a genuine fear that they have recovered from COVID-19 disease to face unaffordable hospital expenses for the treatment and care they received (Blumenthal et al. 2020). While health security is supposed to protect everyone, COVID-19 highlighted how the risk of infection and death is not determined by biology alone and reflected pre-existing hierarchies within socio-political orders.

Public health measures necessary to contain the outbreak, especially public lockdowns, mask wearing, and social distancing, were often enforced, sometimes violently, through the security apparatus of the state, as necessary and exceptional measures. Between 2020 and 2021, countries adopted forms of lockdown such as school and business closures, curfews, and travel restrictions as a health security measure. In some locations, such as Wuhan, China, millions were placed in complete lockdown, with strictly enforced restrictions that meant being unable to leave their place of residence and relying on community workers to deliver food and medications.

In these lockdown situations, security measures undertaken highlighted how security does not apply to all equally and does not affect everyone similarly. Access to digital technology, online bank accounts, or home delivery for food supplies is not equally distributed across groups in socio-political orders. Many have had to manage living during lockdown restrictions while also trying to access cash, food, and (sometimes) information about the public health measures. The outbreak has also revealed how pre-existing gender and racial divides were exacerbated by the pandemic and the security measures that were imposed (Foster 2020).

In Australia, for example, when the state of Victoria lifted its 112-day lockdown in 2020, women had carried out the majority of care roles at home and accounted for 61 per cent of all job losses due to COVID-19 (see Equity Economics 2020). Prior to the pandemic, more women than men were employed in casualized labour in retail jobs. At the onset of the COVID-19 lockdown these retail jobs were deemed 'non-essential', and the 'non-essential' (non-food) retail industry was affected more than men's equivalent casualized labour employment industry—building and construction. These job losses will have a long-term effect on women and their families. Before COVID-19 women earned (on average) two thirds of men's wages in Australia. In Victoria, the lockdown also led to an increase in the number, frequency, and severity of domestic violence against women and girls, exacerbating difficulties in finding help and support (Pfitzner et al. 2020).

Health security as a global security concern was linked, even prior to the onset of COVID-19, to the unequal distribution of power in global health and its links to systemic forms of racism. Research into infectious diseases is a good example of this (Guinto 2019). The majority of drug and vaccine research and production is located in global north pharmaceutical and academic institutions, specifically in Europe and North America, and cater to the government of global health security concerns of the global north (see Elbe 2018). Western scientists study disease outbreaks in remote 'tropical' locations and publish their findings in prestigious global north journals. Pharmaceutical companies determine investment according to profit maximization rather than mortality and morbidity. The infamous example is that research funding into male pattern baldness is higher than research funding into malaria (Solon 2013).

The COVID-19 pandemic has revealed racial and economic inequality at its most harmful when health security is unequally distributed. When COVID-19 vaccine clinical trials began in 2020, the WHO director-general recommended that distribution needed to be equitable and that healthcare workers and most vulnerable groups around the world should be prioritized for vaccine access. Despite this recommendation, the United States, quickly followed by European countries, not only put export limits on the supplies of vaccine production and distribution but also supported pharmaceutical companies—who received investment and indemnity protection from governments—in keeping the intellectual property over any vaccine produced. These actions limited the ability to mass-produce low-cost vaccines quickly. Oxford University's AstraZeneca was the only vaccine where researchers insisted that the intellectual property would be shared (Euronews 2021).

Mass vaccine purchasing is expensive. For most countries, vaccine purchases on this scale means debt. The unequal global distribution of COVID-19 vaccine access and production between 2020 and 2021 has been described as an example of ongoing comfort in the West with a globalized capitalist economy that produces gross inequalities. As such, the political economy of vaccine production, distribution, and access is a contemporary example of resource extraction, racial discrimination, and colonialism (Bump et al. 2021). Thus, as a multi-faceted mobilization of security, responses to COVID-19 also reflected the broader global socio-political order.

13.5 Conclusion

Health security is a two-edged sword in theory and practice. 'Health' implies a focus on individual well-being, while security tends to favour one principal unit—the state. The power of health security frameworks is indisputable. Health security language can increase economic and political attention; it may even attract attention long enough to reveal the underlying socio-economic problems that require equal investment (Patterson 2018). Associating health with security can also produce immense risk. At the onset of the COVID-19 pandemic, securing communities from the spread of the virus required lockdowns that meant, for too many individuals, secondary risks of exposure to violence at home, food insecurity, and poverty. Despite having been deemed a global security threat, restoring health security has seen the privileging of some over others, with 'security' highlighting pre-existing socio-political orders and hierarchies as well as forms of political violence experienced by some more than others.

After three decades of health security discussion, diplomacy, and research, does the arrival of COVID-19 'vindicate' one or more of the health security perspectives we presented in the second part of this chapter? With the COVID-19 outbreak ongoing as we are writing, we will need to study the human rights impacts of health becoming a security issue before, during, and after this pandemic. Which security frames mobilized individual and, occasionally collective, states' response to COVID-19? When were WHO recommendations followed and when were WHO recommendations not suitable for all circumstances and all individuals? What has been the direct impact of COVID-19 on human rights, and the indirect impact of COVID-19 on rights fulfilment? What will happen as climate change and exposure to new pathogens through human encroachment into other ecosystems generate additional health challenges from heat stress to new diseases? A health security claim that is normative still requires continued critical attention to understand how the claim works or fails at the national, regional, and international levels. Continuous investigations into the lived experiences and consequences of the COVID-19 pandemic will reframe health security perspectives in profound ways.

Questions for further discussion

1. Should health be considered a security issue? Do the benefits outweigh the negatives?
2. What public health events, other than infectious disease outbreaks, might catalyse the mobilization of security? And what rationales might be used to justify these mobilizations?
3. Does it matter if global health research is located in the global north?
4. Is it as important to look at the social and economic impacts of a public health event as the health impacts?
5. How have responses to COVID-19 been informed by security?

Further reading

BÜYÜM ALI MURAD, KENNEY CORDELIA, KORIS ANDREA, and LAURA MKUMBA. 2020. 'Decolonising global health: If not now, when?'. *BMJ Global Health.* doi: 10.1136/bmjgh-2020-003394.
The origins of the study of global health have a colonial history and methodology that continues to produce and reproduce inequalities. This article illustrates how the COVID-19 pandemic has revealed public health prejudices and exploitation of Black, Indigenous, and People of Color (BIPOC) across the world in the name of public health practices and norms.

DAVIES, SARA E. 2008. 'Securitizing infectious disease'. *International Affairs* 84(2), 295–313.
One of the earliest articles published on disease as a security issue and its effects on global health governance mechanisms. Davies traces the process through which Western states and the WHO securitized infectious disease, crucially locating this in the relationship between the global health body and member states.

DIONNE, KIM Y. and FULYA FELICITY TURKMEN. 2020. 'The politics of pandemic othering: Putting COVID-19 in global and historical context'. *International Organization* 74(1), 213–230.
Blaming others for pandemics is an old practice that can be traced back historically. This article presents a long-ranging view of how pandemic 'othering' and blame is not new. Pandemics create opportunities for social marginalization but they also, more often than not, provide the perfect excuse to enact long-held political agendas to attack marginalized groups.

HERRICK, CLARE. 2016. 'Global health, geographical contingency, and contingent geographies'. *Annals of the American Association of Geographers* 106(3), 672–687.
Herrick argues that the study of global health has been dominated by the perspectives of political science and medical anthropology and could be better served by more engagement with arguments from health geography, which emphasize spatial logics and the dynamics of globalization.

WENHAM, CLARE and DEBORAH B. L. FARIAS. 2019. 'Securitizing Zika: The case of Brazil'. *Security Dialogue* 50(5), 398–415.

This article critically engages with the notion that Zika became a security issue in Brazil. Wenham and Farias argue that Zika was not considered a security issue based on the virus itself, or the number of people infected, but due to a concern with where the outbreak was occurring.

References

BENTON, ADIA and KIM YI DIONNE. 2015. 'International political economy and the 2014 West African Ebola outbreak'. *African Studies Review* 58(1), 223–236.

BLUMENTHAL, DAVID, ELIZABETH J. FOWLER, MELINDA ABRAMS, and SARA R. COLLINS. 2020. 'Covid-19: Implications for the health care system'. *New England Journal of Medicine* 383, 1483–1488.

BRANSWELL, HELEN. 2022. 'Why Covid-19 vaccines are a freaking miracle'. *STAT*, 14 February. https://www.statnews.com/2022/02/14/why-covid-19-vaccines-are-a-freaking-miracle (last accessed 21 February 2022).

BUMP, JESSE B., FRAN BAUM, MILIN SAKORNSIN, ROBERT YATES, and KAREN HOFMAN. 2021. 'Political economy of Covid-19: Extractive, regressive, competitive'. *British Medical Journal* 372. doi: 10.1136/bmj.n73.

CABALLERO-ANTHONY, MELY. 2008. 'Non-traditional security and infectious diseases in ASEAN: Going beyond the rhetoric of securitization to deeper institutionalization'. *The Pacific Review* 21(4), 507–524.

DAVIES, SARA E. 2010. *Global politics of health.* Cambridge: Polity Press.

DAVIES, SARA E. and BELINDA BENNETT. 2016. 'A gendered human rights analysis of Ebola and Zika: Locating gender in global health emergencies'. *International Affairs* 92(5), 1041–1060.

ELBE, STEFAN. 2006. 'Should HIV/AIDS be securitized? The ethical dilemmas of linking HIV/AIDS and security'. *International Studies Quarterly* 50(1), 119–144.

ELBE, STEFAN. 2014. 'The pharmaceuticalisation of security: Molecular biomedicine, antiviral stockpiles, and global health security'. *Review of International Studies* 40(5), 919–938.

ELBE, STEFAN. 2018. *Pandemics, pills, and politics. Governing global health security.* Baltimore, MD: Johns Hopkins University Press.

ENEMARK, CHRISTIAN. 2007. *Disease and security: Natural plagues and biological weapons in East Asia.* London: Routledge.

ENEMARK, CHRISTIAN. 2017. *Biosecurity dilemmas: Dreaded diseases, ethical responses, and the health of nations.* Washington, DC: Georgetown University Press.

EQUITY ECONOMICS. 2020. *Gender-based impacts of COVID-19.* https://static1.squarespace.com/static/539fdd0de4b09fc82dfddd08/t/5f57ccb9607469267f1fb88f/1599589607729/Gender-Based+Impacts+of+COVID-19-2.pdf (last accessed 9 January 2022).

EURONEWS. 2021. 'Global COVID vaccine inequality "becoming more grotesque every day," WHO warns'. 22 March. www.euronews.com/2021/03/22/global-covid-vaccine-inequality-becoming-more-grotesque-every-day-who-warns (last accessed 9 January 2022).

FOSTER, LUCY. 2020. 'Are countries doing enough to support women through the pandemic?'. *World Economic Forum.* 20 October. www.weforum.org/agenda/2020/10/covid19-employment-gender-gap-policy (last accessed 9 January 2022).

GROFF, DESTIN, ASHLEY SUN, ANNA E. SSENTONGO, M. BA DJIBRIL, NICHOLAS PARSONS, GOVINDA R. POUDEL, ALAIN LEKOUBOU, JOHN S. OH, JESSICA E. ERICSON,

Paddy Ssentongo, and Vernon M. Chinchilli. 2021. 'Short-term and long-term rates of postacute sequelae of SARS-CoV-2 infection: A systematic review'. *JAMA Network Open* 4(10), e2128568. doi: 10.1001/jamanetworkopen.2021.28568 (last accessed 21 February 2022).

Guinto, Renzo. 2019. '#DecolonizeGlobalHealth: Rewriting the narrative of global health'. 11 February. www.internationalhealthpolicies.org/blogs/decolonizeglobalhealth-rewriting-the-narrative-of-global-health (last accessed 9 January 2022).

Heymann, David L. 2015. 'The true scope of health security'. *The Lancet* 385(9980), 1884–1887.

Koblentz, Gregory D. 2009. *Living weapons: Biological warfare and international security.* Ithaca, NY: Cornell University Press.

Lakoff, Andrew. 2008. 'From population to vital system: National security and the changing object of public health'. In *Biosecurity interventions: Global health and security in question,* edited by Andrew Lakoff and Stephen J. Collier. New York: Columbia University Press.

McInnes, Colin and Kelley Lee. 2006. 'Health, security and foreign policy'. *Review of International Studies* 32(1), 5–23.

McInnes, Colin and Kelley Lee. 2012. *Global health and international relations.* Cambridge: Polity Press.

Nunes, João. 2016. 'Ebola and the production of neglect in global health'. *Third World Quarterly* 37(3), 542–556.

O'Manique, Colleen and Sandra J. MacLean. 2010. 'Pathways among human security, gender, and HIV/AIDS in Sub-Saharan Africa'. *Canadian Journal of African Studies* 44(3), 457–478.

Ogata, Sadako and Amartya Sen. 2003. *Human Security Now.* www.resdal.org/ultimos-documentos/com-seg-hum.pdf (last accessed 31 January 2023).

Owen, Taylor. 2005. 'Conspicuously absent? Why the Secretary General used human security in all but name'. *St. Anthony's International Review* 1(2), 37–42.

Paris, Roland. 2001. 'Human security: Paradigm shift or hot air?' *International Security* 26(2), 87–102.

Patterson, Amy S. 2018. *Africa and global health governance: Domestic politics and international structures.* Baltimore, MD: Johns Hopkins University Press.

Petersen, Susan. 2002. 'Epidemic disease and national security'. *Security Studies* 12(2), 43–81.

Pfitzner, Naomi, Kate Fitz-Gibbon, and Jacqui True. 2020. *Responding to the 'shadow pandemic': Practitioner views on the nature of and responses to violence against women in Victoria, Australia during the COVID-19 restrictions.* Victoria, Australia: Monash Gender and Family Violence Prevention Centre. https://bridges.monash.edu/articles/report/Responding_to_the_shadow_pandemic_practitioner_views_on_the_nature_of_and_responses_to_violence_against_women_in_Victoria_Australia_during_the_COVID-19_restrictions/12433517 (last accessed 10 January 2022).

Price-Smith, Andrew T. 2009. *Contagion and chaos: Disease, ecology, and national security in the era of globalization.* Cambridge, MA: MIT Press.

Roemer-Mahler, Anne and Stefan Elbe. 2016. 'The race for Ebola drugs: Pharmaceuticals, security and global health governance'. *Third World Quarterly* 37(3), 487–506.

Rushton, Simon. 2011. 'Global health security: Security for whom? Security from what?' *Political Studies* 59(4), 779–796.

Shisana, Olive, Nompumelelo Zungu-Dirwayi, and William Shisana. 2003. 'AIDS: A threat to human security'. In *Global health challenges for human security,* edited by Lincoln

Chen, Jennifer Leaning, and Vasant Narasimhan. Cambridge, MA: Harvard University Press.

Solon, Olivia. 2013. 'Bill Gates: Capitalism means male baldness research gets more funding than malaria'. *Wired*. 14 March. www.wired.co.uk/article/bill-gates-capitalism (last accessed 9 January 2022).

Sze, Shirley, Daniel Pan, Clareece R. Nevill, Laura J. Gray, Christopher A. Martin, Joshua Nazareth, Jatinder S. Minhas, Pip Divall, Kamlesh Khunti, Keith R. Abrams, Laura B. Nellums, and Manish Pareek. 2021. 'Ethnicity and clinical outcomes in COVID-19: A systematic review and meta-analysis'. *E-Clinical Medicine* 29 (100630). https://doi.org/10.1016/j.eclinm.2020.100630

Thomas, Caroline. 1989. 'On the health of international relations and the international relations of health'. *Review of International Studies* 15(3), 273–280.

US Army Medical Research and Development Command (MRDC). 2019. *Military Infectious Diseases Research Program (MIDRP)*. https://mrdc.amedd.army.mil/index.cfm/program_areas/medical_research_and_development/midrp_overview (last accessed 9 January 2022).

US National Security Council (USNSC). 2009. *National Strategy for Countering Biological Threats*. Washington, DC: White House. www.hsdl.org/?view&did=31404 (last accessed 9 January 2022).

Wald, Priscilla. 2008. *Contagious: Cultures, carriers, and the outbreak narrative*. Durham, NC: Duke University Press.

Watterson, Christopher and Adam Kamradt-Scott. 2016. 'Fighting flu: Securitization and the military role in combating influenza'. *Armed Forces & Society* 42(1), 145–168.

Weir, Lorna. 2014. 'Inventing global health security, 1994–2005'. In *Routledge handbook of global health security*, edited by Jeremy Youde and Simon Rushton. Abingdon: Routledge.

Wenham, Clare. 2019. 'The oversecuritization of global health: Changing the terms of debate'. *International Affairs* 95(5), 1093–1110.

World Health Organization. 2005. *International health regulations*. 2nd ed. www.who.int/publications/i/item/9789241580410 (last accessed 9 January 2022).

World Health Organization. n.d. 'Health security'. www.who.int/health-topics/health-security#tab=tab_1 (last accessed 21 February 2022).

Youde, Jeremy. 2016. 'High politics, low politics, and global health', *Journal of Global Security Studies* 1(2), 157–170.

Youde, Jeremy and Simon Rushton. 2014. 'Introduction'. In *Routledge Handbook of Global Health Security*, edited by Jeremy Youde and Simon Rushton. Abingdon: Routledge.

14

Property, extraction, and accumulation

Caitlin Ryan

14.1	Introduction	223
14.2	Classifying land as 'open' for extraction	226
14.3	Accumulating territory through accumulating property	228
14.4	Securing processes of extraction in order to secure accumulation	233
14.5	Conclusion	235

READER'S GUIDE

In this chapter, we consider how property is 'made' into an object of security through various forms of violence. We show how violence makes possible different forms of extraction, which in turn become sites that can be 'secured' through a material mobilization of security. Through examples of plantations and mines, we demonstrate how property shows us how security is mobilized, and how capital has historically depended on the protection of 'property rights' not only through appeals to the 'rule of law' but also through violence.

14.1 Introduction

Illustrative case studies on the topics explored in this chapter are available on the online resources to help take your understanding of property, extraction, and accumulation further:
http://www.oup.com/he/Grayson-Guillaume1e.

It might be easy to take the notion of 'property' as a pre-given. After all, not only is the Western philosophical tradition full of references to relations between individuals, property, and the state, but our own notion of it is also often derived from things that are not abstract—like bicycles, computers, cars, and houses (and the land they sit on). We probably also have a good understanding of the legal rights we have over our property. It is perhaps less common to think about the notion of extraction—such as (but not limited to) mining for metals, or drilling fossil fuels. Once we start thinking about it, we probably have similar assumptions about extraction as we do about property—for instance, that extraction is governed by sets of regulations, and that there are certain rights to property that govern who owns the products of extraction. The seemingly 'settled' nature of property makes it hard to see how this notion of property came into being through violent forms of extraction and accumulation.

This chapter critically considers the political violence steeped in the relations between property, extraction, and accumulation by considering 'security for what purpose?' and 'security at whose expense?'. As a starting point, I want to emphasize the relationality of both property and security. By this, I mean that the meaning of property, like the meaning of security, is always relational—it defines and constitutes the relations between what is inside/outside, and of what is included/excluded from rights and protection. Security is often related to property as a claim to the 'right' of states, companies, and individuals to have security *of* property—the purpose of security is thus assumed to ensure a right to maintain one's property, and in particular, to extract or accumulate value from it. In this sense, security is often mobilized to protect existing property rights (as defined under a specific socio-political order) and/or the security of some form of property itself (representing a material interest). The mobilization of security in defence of property and property rights should thus be considered in terms of how it consolidates and entrenches dominant political and economic hierarchies.

> These two questions are presented in **Sections 5.3.2.2-3**

> On security as a relational process, see **Section 2.3.2**

> Socio-political orders and hierarchies are discussed in **Chapter 3**

What questions might come to mind security forces forcibly removing 'peasants' from land they are farming in order to make way for an agribusiness plantation, or 'Mine police' removing informal miners from an industrial scale mine run by a multinational company? Some initial questions might be 'who owns the property?' or 'who has the rights to the mine?' From these questions, we might focus on the security forces, which leads to a bigger question: 'how are security regimes implicated in securing property rights and thus in securing extraction?' By security regimes, I am broadly referring to 'sets of principles, rules, [logics], and norms that provide a foundation for security [practices]' (Cronin 2010).

In order to consider the elements that will help us to find an answer, it is useful to ask a more foundational question. If security regimes are invoked to secure property rights (and thus the possibility to extract value from property), then it is also worth considering how violence (including structural and latent violence) is implicated in the very making of property rights in the first place. This is another way of complicating the first 'simple' question of who owns the property. For example, we might learn that the peasant farmers are part of a movement to undo hundreds of years of consolidated land-holdings by settler-colonizers and that the contemporary eviction of peasants to make space for a plantation has a historical precedent in a colonial conquest. Or, we might learn that the multinational mining conglomerate is headquartered in the former colonial power, and that granting the mining licence displaced hundreds of local miners. Thus, we would begin to see that it matters how property has come to be defined in particular ways, how it has come to be an object of security, and how this

> Different forms of political violence are discussed in **Chapter 4**

enables a distinction between who can, and who cannot, claim a right to extract value. Typically, the relation between security and property is framed wherein property is an object of security. This framing leaves out critical questions of how this came to be in the first place.

Thinking about property is significant for understanding the mobilization of security because it also provides a clear example of both the material and institutional mobilization of security for the protection of dominant interests and in service of perpetuating inequalities and hierarchies. The mobilization of security in relation to property does two (interrelated) things.

On security as a political mobilization, see **Section 2.4**

First, it claims a right to have secure property rights. Second, it enacts the protection of property itself (as a material thing to be secured). Rather than assume that property is a 'natural' or 'neutral' object of security, it is worth considering how a meaning of property derived from the Western philosophical and legal tradition became dominant through capitalist expansion, which relied on two key and interlinked processes: colonialism and slavery. Colonial expansion and the transatlantic slave trade are both reliant on 'making property' through practices like making new territories into the property of imperial powers and making humans into property. In turn, these forms of property—both land and people—enable expansive extraction of both labour and resources, which in turn enables a previously unthinkable accumulation of wealth. As capitalism as a mode of production expands and shifts, the forms of property and sites of extraction also change.

Thinking about how security regimes are implicated in securing property and the right to extraction allows us to consider continuities as well as differences—temporally and geographically. Thus, in this chapter we consider the relations between property, extraction, and security regimes across two particular forms of property and sites of extraction: plantations and mines. The aim is not to provide a wholesale history of plantations and mines but rather to think through plantations and mines to illuminate the questions of how property becomes an object of security, and how this enables extraction. Both plantations and mines vary enormously in their forms and scope across different places and in different moments, but they also offer some continuity. First, they enable us to consider how claims to property enable extraction. Second, they can reveal how security regimes are implicated in securing the rights of extraction and property for 'some' at the expense of 'others', and how this protects hierarchies of power and entrenches dominant interests.

A brief example may help to illustrate this in less abstract terms. A report entitled 'Martial mining' published by the London Mining Network (Selwyn 2020) illustrates the co-constitution of mining sites and global militarization insofar as nearly every material object used by security forces depends on mineral extraction. Here we can see the mutual dependence between transnational mining companies and the transnational arms trade. Arms manufacturers depend on the continued and un-impeded availability of raw materials so they can transform them into weapons-systems, fighter jets, tanks, guns, bullets, communication and surveillance systems, and so on. In turn, security forces that 'secure' sites of exaction are customers of arms manufactures—this is not merely for the weapons they may carry, but for the systems of surveillance

Weapons-systems are discussed in **Chapter 17**

they deploy against theft and sabotage. The report by the London Mining Network demonstrates the outsized share of the some of the world's most commonly mined resources goes to the arms industry, which in turn enables the sites of extraction to become sites of violence rendered through the logics of property and security. The section that follows begins to discuss these dynamics by focusing on how claims to property rights rely on the discursive mobilization of security.

14.2 Classifying land as 'open' for extraction

Sometimes, claims to secure a 'right' to property are deployed through material and/or symbolic violence. To illustrate how violence can be used to (re)make property for the purpose of extraction, I turn now to a place that can tell us much about these processes. Sierra Leone, and in particular, the Northern Region where I have worked with local communities to co-produce research, was a prime target for agribusiness investment deals in the post-2008 'land rush'. The Sierra Leone Investment Promotion Agency (SLIEPA) and other agencies within the Government of Sierra Leone classified over 3 million hectares of land (out of a total area of 7.4 million hectares in Sierra Leone) as 'unused' or 'underused' and thus available for large-scale agribusiness investment. The government does recognize the property rights of 'land-owning families' but, on its webpage, SLIEPA encourages potential investors that these land-owning families are eager to lease the 'unused' parts of their land for long-term projects (fifty years or more).

On material and symbolic violence, see Section 4.2.1

Within Sierra Leone, rights and social relations bound up in claims to be from a 'land-owning' family are complex, and do not fit neatly into an individualized understanding of land ownership—for instance, families are made-up of an extended lineage, and could be composed of dozens of households. A group of 'elders' of the land-owning families make decisions about land, including how to allocate use-rights for each farming season amongst the whole community, and land cannot be sold. Use-rights extend to people who do not belong to the extended family, and there are rules about what they can extract from the land (such as the seasonal crops they plant) and what they cannot (such as products from trees on the plot). While this is a very brief explanation, it should help us to see that there are differences between this system of land governance, and perhaps more familiar views of private property and their associated understanding of property as exclusive and transferable.

With the promotion of agribusiness, the Sierra Leonean state aims to facilitate investment in the form of large-scale plantations on land leased from multiple land-owning families. This investment is promoted through networks of international investors, international institutions, national politicians, local chiefs, and other powerful individuals, as well as by appealing directly to the land-owning families that these companies will 'bring development'. In promoting the eagerness of land-owning families to lease their land, SLIEPA frames the land as being 'owned' but also empty. Using this framing of 'emptiness' aims to justify shifting the 'rights of extraction' from local peasant farmers to multinational agribusiness companies.

On the connections between development and security, see Chapter 12

However, my experience within these communities has demonstrated how this claim of 'emptiness' is false. When asked, communities with some of their land under lease to an oil palm plantation will describe their land differently. Here, we will turn to a visit to one particular village for an example. During this visit, members of the community met under their largest mango tree to talk to me. From our position under the tree, a small patch of the community's own native oil palm was visible. To get to the village, we took our motorbike through alternating patches of the company's plantation, and farmland still under cultivation by the village. The ways in which the community understands their land were multiple. They described it in terms of what they produce on it, like rice, cassava, mango, garden eggs, groundnuts, oil palm, millet, hot pepper, cucumber, yam, corn, Benne seed, and banana. They also talked about their land in relation to what it 'gives' without cultivation, such as firewood, medicinal herbs, and materials for building and housekeeping.

Moreover, beyond 'extraction' they described their land by narrating the village's history and its relation to the national history of Sierra Leone, as one of the most important and famous anti-colonial leaders came from the area. Many people of the village are his descendants, and their pride in this lineage is intimately tied to their pride in the land itself. Finally, in addition to talking about their ancestors, they described the land in terms of the complex social relations tied up in it. Understandings of belonging, kinship, obligation, and power cannot be untangled from the land itself. In light of the company plantation occupying much of the community's land, some described the land in terms of what has been lost as a result of the plantation, or in relation to the process through which the lease was negotiated and signed. Such descriptions of what the community has 'now' are dominated by 'lack', 'shortage', 'absence'—there is a lack/shortage/absence of land, food, firewood, medicinal herbs, cash from selling surpluses, consent, understanding, acceptance, and consensus.

This brief snapshot from subsistence farms in northern Sierra Leone illustrates how the right to extract value from land is contested through two different claims about what form of 'using' land is most legitimate. For the national government, and investing companies, subsistence farming is proof of the owners' lack of capacity to extract the full potential value. This is also often framed in terms of needing to make Sierra Leoneans more 'food secure' by increasing the productivity of the land. This illustrates the mobilization of security through claims of rights to property in ways that protect hierarchies and advance the dominant economic interest of some, at the expense of others. However, if we maintain a view of land as embedded within a complex array of social relations, and providing a range of uses that are not monetized, then the question of 'extraction' can be seen differently, along with the question of security, wherein security as a member of a community, or the availability of non-monetized resources such as water, firewood, and medicinal herbs, also matters.

This raises important questions about the role of violence in privileging the extraction rights of an agribusiness plantation. There is a great deal of material and structural violence insofar as people face increased food insecurity and decreased economic opportunities from selling extra crops. In some communities the clearing of land for the plantation destroyed many tree crops. Moreover, in most communities I visited, reports of physical violence—by police securing the plantation, or violent conflicts in the community over the plantation—were extremely rare; however, people spoke of high tensions. Therefore, violence may be latent. Finally, aside from a loss of extraction value, there is symbolic violence in the de-valuing of farmers knowledge and expertise through the promotion of an agribusiness plantation as the superior form of farming.

> On latent violence, see **Section 4.2.1**

In this example we can see contesting views over what land is—either as an object to be secured in order to ensure 'efficient' production or as a socially embedded source of resources as well as belonging and legitimacy. We also can see contestation over how extraction is governed and how regimes of security are implicated. The rights of the agribusiness companies to extract value from the land are guaranteed by complex legal processes that privilege international and national elites over subsistence farmers. In Section 14.3, we turn to consider how this example of plantation agribusiness in Sierra Leone fits within wider dynamics of how property comes into being through contestation.

14.3 Accumulating territory through accumulating property

What is revealed about security when we consider the (contested) processes through which 'meanings' of property have been imposed and applied to 'make' property? Here, security is mobilized to determine who can and cannot claim rights to property, and what kinds of socio-political orders are made through claiming property rights. We can illustrate some of that contestation through considering how 'private property' was given meaning in relation to land, and how this made it possible to 'make' land into private property.

First, we need to establish what precisely the 'dominant' notion of property entails and how a dominant view of property as an object of security has developed. It is important to acknowledge that the dominant view of property 'we' have is not the only view, and that this view of property came to be through the expansion of global capitalism and colonialism. This dominant view of property treats property as a matter of exclusive rights (if it is 'mine', it cannot also be yours) that entitles the owner to extract value from it and transfer it. For instance, if we think in relation to land, as Nicholas Blomley (2003, 121) points out, property rights are relational—'being held against others' and this 'bundle of rights includes the power to exclude others, to use, and to transfer'. We might think of, for example, a 'No Trespassing' sign posted on a gate—this is a property claim that explicitly aims to exclude others. The sign indicates that the land beyond the gate is for the exclusive use of the person(s) who posted the sign and implicitly makes a claim that they are the only ones who can transfer that ownership. This view of property contributes to the meaning making that it must be secured—typically through legal claims and/or actions of ownership (e.g., maintenance). In some contexts, these legal claims include the right to exclude 'trespassers' through enclosure, force, and/or threat of force.

To support this view of property, we could turn to classical liberal philosophy (Hobbes, Locke, etc.), particularly how European practices of turning land into 'productive' property justified imperial conquests in the New World. Alternatively, we could approach exclusion in a much more material way by thinking about hedges. In eighteenth-century England, there was a concerted (and violent) effort to turn 'the commons' (i.e., land open to use by all members of a community) into private property (Peluso 2017). In an excellent historical study, Blomley (2007) demonstrates how the extensive use of hedges that demarcated (new) property boundaries provided a material barrier that prevented people from accessing land previously held in common. As such, hedges made it possible to turn the commons into private property.

This is useful for further illustrating how this form of property made a material and symbolic claim on who could (and who could not) legitimately extract value from the land. This precise means of making private property and enforcing a regime of extraction rights was not universal, but the spread of enlightenment thinking about 'making' and enforcing private property rights circulating this underlying idea of property as individualized, exclusive, and, crucially, an object of security. With increased colonial expansion particularly within settler colonies in the Americas, the boundaries between who could and who could not claim property rights and associated rights of extraction became increasingly racialized (Bhandar 2018). The interrelated expansion of the Atlantic slave trade—which fuelled the global expansion of European empires—further racialized the question of which humans could be made into property (Yusoff 2018).

In order to tie together the questions of how property is made, how it became a right to be secured, and who is included and/or excluded from rights to extraction and accumulation, we turn first to the logics of *terra nullius* and *res nullius*. These are one aspect of what made it possible to 'claim' land as empty and transform it into a site of extraction. We can then consider how this property becomes a means of accumulation

> These logics are presented in detail in **Box 14.1**

 BOX 14.1 THE LOGIC OF *TERRA NULLIUS*

Despite the enormous differences in different eras and spaces of colonialism across the Americas, Oceania, Africa, and Asia, the logic of *terra nullius* was widely deployed for 'rationalizing' the accumulation of land by colonizing powers. As part of processes of conquest and cession, references to *terra nullius* (land without owners) and its associate, *res nullius* (things without owners), helped make colonial expansion possible. Making a claim that land was 'without owners' was not meant to deny the presence of Indigenous people, but rather that their relationship to land was outside the bounds of law and property. This depended on claims that Indigenous people were outside the bounds of civilization, and thus outside the bounds of law (Bhandar 2018, 96). I refer here to *terra nullius* and *res nullius* as logics, rather than concrete legal doctrine, in order to recognize the debate over their historical use. I follow the line of argument developed by Laura Benton and Benjamin Straumann (2010) who suggest that the question of 'when' or 'whether' these become doctrines of colonizing powers is significantly less useful than thinking about *how* they are used, both by the legal scholars of the age and by colonial agents 'on the ground'.

through slave labour. While this may seem irrelevant to contemporary forms of property and extraction, we can see evidence of the application of the logics of *terra nullius* in both contemporary plantations and mining operations.

In particular, for the question of how property is 'made' into an object of security through violence, thinking about *terra nullius* and *res nullius* as logics that are part of wider sets of discourses and practices of colonization is extremely helpful in illustrating the violence imbued in them. They are applied in shifting, uneven, and scattered ways, while similarly claiming to take the appearance of 'doctrine' through 'scattershot' references to Roman law (Benton and Straumann 2010, 29). As an arbitrary and shifting application of legal doctrine is deployed to make it seem as though 'civilized' regimes of property rights are being brought into a 'legal void', we can begin to see how violence in this colonial form of 'property making' is structural and latent.

As Robert Nichols (2018) and Brenna Bhandar (2018) point out, refusing to acknowledge that previous inhabitation or use by Indigenous groups was ownership provides a 'way out' for colonizers and imperialists to avoid recognizing the loss experienced by Native peoples. If Native peoples did not previously have a conception of land as property, then they had no *a priori* legal claim to the land, and what they experienced was not theft. Nichols (2018) therefore offers an alternative formulation both to the Marxist theorization about accumulation by dispossession, and the anarchist formulation of 'property as theft'. Instead, Nichols proposes that in settler colonies, 'theft is property'.

To put it another way, through severing the social and ecological relations between Native people and land, Native dispossession was a mode of property-generating theft—property comes into being through colonialization as a form of theft. The scale of this property-generating theft was enormous, and was used to accumulate additional wealth—both for European empires and settlers throughout the 'New World' by removing Indigenous peoples from land and covering the landscapes in various forms of plantations. For these plantations to generate wealth, they needed labour. Property thus also comes into being through slavery, where the 'self' was made into property. As Calvin Warren (2018, 100) claims, 'the self as something that is supposed to remain immaterial and invisible [was] transformed into materiality'.

In the discussion of colonial expansion, we can see how land and people are made into property and, in turn, how some people are deemed to have a legitimate claim to property in land or people. Once land is 'made' into private property, it then becomes situated in a socio-political order that allows it to be secured. The making of land into property for the purpose of extraction, and particular the making of land into plantations as a site of extraction, has changed since the time of colonial expansion, but we can still see the logics of *terra nullius* at work.

This is evident in processes of expanding industrial agriculture through 'land grabs' wherein land becomes dis-embedded from social relations, and 'secured' as an object for 'useful' and 'efficient' extraction of value, as we saw with the example from Sierra Leone. Starting in 2008, with the global food crisis, there was a sudden and rapid acceleration in the acquisition of enormous tracts of land for industrial agriculture and the growing of crops for biofuels (Edelman et al. 2013). Many of these deals were facilitated by national governments and involved a complex array of investors and agribusiness companies (Wolford et al. 2013). These actors framed the deals as being for 'unused' or 'underused' land. Here, they also drew on the language of the World Bank, which has typically treated agriculture in Africa as 'underdeveloped' and characterized by low productivity and weak capacity to utilize land fully (World Bank 2009).

On the surface, then, these deals 'look' desirable—willing investors with diverse portfolios from all over the globe including government pension funds, wealthy entrepreneurs, and a host of other speculators, partnered with agribusiness giants. They made promises to increase global food security and combat climate change by growing feedstock for biofuels (such as palm oil and jatropha). Their target was 'unused' land in 'underdeveloped states'. This makes it appear as through the land is the property of no one. Therefore, using it to address global problems, while meeting World Bank objectives of facilitating foreign direct investment in developing states, appears legitimate. Of course, such things are never as simple and win-win as they are made to appear. Many non-governmental organizations and researchers have documented losses that people experience when their land is 'transformed' for agribusiness plantations.

Why would the classification and naming of land matter for how it becomes an object to be 'secured'? Security is mobilized in a discursive sense because in order to 'secure' land for investment, or to become a site of extraction, it first needs to be dis-embedded from its present uses. The classification of land as 'unused', or as 'wasteland', legitimizes land deals by positing the populations on that land as 'undeserving' or 'unable' to take advantage of its productive capacity. In the context of a biofuels project in India, Jennifer Baka (2013, 410) writes:

> On security as a discursive mobilization, see **Section 2.4**

> classification techniques and entrenched conceptions of wastelands construct these lands as empty, unproductive spaces available for development. In so doing, they obscure the existing land-use patterns and in this case, owners of the lands.

Using language that frames land as either empty, or inhabited by people that don't know how to 'use' land productively, makes it seem as though there are vast tracts of land that are not only available for investment but that investment is the most correct option for adequate extraction, productivity, and development. In her book *The Will to Improve*, Tania Murray Li (2007) argues that this intersection of capitalism and development is a striking feature in Indonesia, and that this intersection stretches over two centuries—from Dutch colonization and the New Order's modernization to present-day investment and development projects. This suggests we should consider the labelling of land as 'available' for extraction within a longer historical trajectory of how land is made into property, and how this relates to wider processes of turning property into an object of security. From there, it becomes easier to see how security regimes are implicated in securing rights to extraction.

However, this still leaves questions about the relation between property and extraction when we move beyond extracting value from the land through agriculture, to extraction of what sits under the surface of the land. To illustrate this, we can turn now to an example where there is contestation over the rights of extraction. The questions at stake relate to claims to ownership of minerals and 'who has a right to extract value from minerals and oil?' Many states that are rich in natural resources have laws that claim the natural resource wealth to be the exclusive property of the state. For example, in Sierra Leone, families might own land in the diamond-rich Eastern Region, but the state controls all rights to the diamonds in that land (Fanthorpe and Maconachie 2010). These rights are sold to miners, who can claim diamonds they mine, through purchasing mining permits and paying taxes to the government for every diamond that is found.

> On the connections between the environment and security, see **Chapter 18**

There are also disputes over oil rights in the Andean States of Bolivia, Peru, and Ecuador (Bebbington et al. 2008). Through international institutions, these states have been put under enormous pressure to privatize their oil resources. There are counter-claims by Indigenous groups that the oil belongs to the people (not even the state), and that it should either not be extracted at all, or that it should only be extracted if it provides for the economic development of the people (Riofrancos 2020). These are only two examples of contemporary sites of extraction. It is important to note that there is not a singular view of who (if anyone) can claim legitimacy to extract value from natural resources.

Security is also discursively mobilized in the debate over rights to claim natural resources as property and the rights to extract value from them. For example, Indigenous groups in Andean states may claim that no one should have a right to extract oil. This stems from a relational worldview in which the extraction of oil is form of violence against the earth, and that in the context of ongoing climate catastrophe, extraction is unjustifiable (Riofrancos 2020). In claiming that natural resource wealth should go to the state, governments mobilize a discursive claim to security as well—not in the traditional state sense of security, but in terms of economic security and national sovereignty—and in particular the right of the state to protect its natural resources from neo-colonial exploitation (Pellegrini 2018). In Sierra Leone, the state may make claims to control and regulate the extraction of mineral wealth in reference to the horrors of its civil war when the illicit sale of diamonds provided a source of funding for rebels during the conflict (Fanthorpe and Maconachie 2010).

In examining contemporary forms of extraction and their underlying property rights claims, it is helpful to consider the history of extraction. Both Achille Mbembe (2017) and Kathryn Yusoff (2018) argue that we need to be aware of the degree to which the slave trade also needs to be understood in extractive terms. Mbembe (2017, 40) sees this as a process where 'African people are transformed into living minerals from which metal is extracted'. Similarly, Yusoff (2018, 71) argues that:

> what is apparent is that the slave and the mineral are recognized in regimes of value, but only so much as they await extraction. Both these modes of extracting value—as property, and properties generate surpluses.

This leads us to Section 14.4, where we consider how securing property rights and the right to extraction mobilizes material and institutional security regimes.

14.4 Securing processes of extraction in order to secure accumulation

In Section 14.3, we saw how security is mobilized discursively through claims of rights to property and rights to extraction. We also saw how these claims are made in ways that produce and uphold dominant relations of power and hierarchies. In this section, we consider how political violence is deployed to 'protect' the property rights and extraction rights claims, and what this can tell us about the linkages between property, extraction, and security.

Throughout this section, we draw on the questions of 'security for what purpose?' and 'security at whose expense?' to argue that the purpose of contemporary security regimes at sites of extraction are to protect the economic interests of investors, thereby entrenching dominant interests. This often comes at the expense of people living adjacent to sites of extraction as well as the wider expanse of global security because of the linkages between mining and (global) militarization (Dunlap and Jakobsen 2020). The political violence at sites of extraction can be categorized as physical and material, where violence is generally intended, isolated, and manifest. However, the products of extraction that such political violence enables, contributes material goods to wider processes of global militarization, where violence is more structural, and also more latent (though also manifest). However, before moving to sites of extraction as sites of political violence, it is useful to discuss a particularly extreme historical example of how political violence was used to ensure property rights—that of slave patrols in the United States.

If we draw on the classification system for political violence from Chapter 4, we can see slave patrols as cutting across most of the classification system. Slave patrols had multiple symbolic purposes as well as their 'practical' objective of ensuring that escaped slaves—as property—were returned to their owners. The violence of slave patrols was absolutely intended. The violence was also both isolated and structural insofar as there was immediate violence used against anyone thought to be an escaped slave, as well as a deep structural violence wherein only people who looked like they *could* be slaves were stopped, and anyone who looked like they *could* be a slave would expect to be stopped (see Warren 2018). The system of slave patrols was legitimized to uphold the system of slavery, not only through the capture of escaped slaves (or indeed free men and women as well) but also through re-affirming that 'Blackness' was equated with a lack of self-hood. The violence of slave patrols was also clearly both manifest and latent and the violence was not only physical, but also psychological in terms of its assertion of Blackness with a lack of self-hood, and symbolic because it treated Black bodies as 'mere' property.

The existing scholarship on slave patrols and their role in creating Black subjects in the United States is invaluable for many reasons. Here, I draw on it to point to the historically deep and terrible relationship between security, property, and violence. Capital has historically depended on the protection of 'property rights' not only through appeals to a 'rule of law' but also through violence, and in particular though violence directed at people deemed to be 'outside' the bounds of protection. People outside of the bounds of protection have been placed there because they have been deemed to be less valuable than the potential value that can be extracted. Or, in the case of slave patrols, it is also because the violence being committed is understood as directed against people deemed to be non-human. This allows us to move to a discussion of how violence is used to protect rights to extraction and, in turn, how extraction itself fuels the militarization that drives an unequal geopolitics of violence.

As I showed in Section 14.3, sites of mining extraction are sites of contestation. The high value of extractives along with the social mobilization against exploitative and ecologically damaging mining practices means that extractives companies invest heavily in securing extractive sites. The means of protection varies considerably across different kinds of mine sites. For example, the security 'demands' on an open-pit cobalt mine are different than a shaft mine for gold, or the spread-out mining that takes place for alluvial diamonds. There are also differences based on the relations between the mining operators and the state—namely, there is less protection offered by the state to small and artisanal-scale miners than to large-scale industrial mines, which may be protected by some combination of the military, special mining police, and private security forces. However, there is a degree of commonality across sites of extraction. This commonality is that claims to extraction rights are often protected through violence or the threat of violence, and in turn, that people who are violently excluded from the benefits of extraction, or who suffer the 'slow violence' of ecological damage and loss of livelihoods, may mobilize violence against the mining operation. The institutional and material mobilization of security at mine sites protects the rights to property and extraction of powerful interests, at the expense of those at the political and economic margins.

I will illustrate this with two examples—the first discusses extractive sites where political violence is prevalent or latent. I follow this with a discussion of 'green militarization' where political violence is deployed by the state and international actors to prevent any extraction. This may seem counter to the logics of the rest of the section, but it goes to show how violence and property are linked by preventing Indigenous people from using forest resources in the name of 'global conservation'. It thereby illustrates another way some people are deemed ineligible to make property rights claims.

Across mine sites in the Americas, Africa, and Asia, we can identify forms security governance that bring together public and private security forces, particularly in places where companies perceive a limited capacity of the state to protect the company's extractive operations (Hönke 2013). In turn, as Jana Hönke and others (e.g., Geenen and Verweijen 2017) have pointed out, these companies claim to be contributing to improving 'governance' by training state security forces as well as by engaging in corporate social responsibility (CSR). While engaging in CSR may seem to be the opposite of violence, it is also interpreted as a means of silencing the dissent of social movements by presenting images of the companies as 'good social actors' (Engels 2018).

Social movements that challenge extractives companies are sometimes pitted against other local people who are employed by the companies. In their landmark study of social movements and extraction sites in Ecuador and Peru, Anthony Bebbington and his co-authors (2008) found that social movements that framed their activities around putting an end to exaction were subject not only to violent repression by the state and the mining company, but also a counter-movement by (local) employees. Similarly, in examining gold mining companies in the Democratic Republic of the Congo, Sara Geenen and Judith Verweijen (2017) found that social mobilization by artisanal-scale miners against the company had not led to violent responses from the state and private security forces protecting the mine, but that local power brokers who were aligned with the company were able to fragment the social movements.

Here, violence is both manifest and physical, as well as being structural and material. The operations of large-scale mining are protected from 'intrusion' by artisanal-scale miners. This occurs through isolated instances of physical violence aimed at keeping artisanal-scale miners out of the company's operations, and in turn produces material violence through the depravation of livelihoods for artisanal-scale mining. Furthermore, it lays the groundwork for more structural and latent forms of political violence, because the state, as well as local elites, serve the interests of the company. This situation leaves locals with few avenues for redressing their grievances.

While the securing of mining operations dictates who can profit from extraction and how, the militarization of conservation efforts seems entirely unrelated to the dynamics noted earlier. However, such 'green militarization' supports the argument that political violence around property and extraction serves as a means of determining the purpose of security and at whose expense it is generated. At first glance, conservation efforts wherein new national parks are established in the global south may seem like the precise opposite of establishing new sites of extraction and divorced from questions of property and extraction. However, much like mining sites, they represent spaces of (often violent) exclusion for Indigenous people.

We can see this, for example, in UN-led initiatives to create protected forests where logging is prohibited, or in the establishment of national game parks where there is no extraction of any resources. Security is mobilized discursively—as a claim to 'secure' forests or animals for conservation, but also materially and institutionally through preventing Indigenous communities from entering. In both examples, Indigenous forest communities are expelled, often though violent displacement (Marijnen and Verweijen 2016). In the name of 'global conservation', they are prevented from continuing to use the natural resources they have depended on for generations. Similar to the example from Sierra Leone earlier, this relies on representing these communities as 'incapable'. The difference is that rather than being framed as being incapable of extracting the full value form their land, they are framed as being 'incapable' of using it sustainably, despite generations of evidence to the contrary.

14.5 Conclusion

To conclude, I want to again raise the question of how security regimes are implicated in securing property and the rights to extraction. Throughout the chapter, we considered how property is 'made' into an object of security through various forms of violence, and how this makes possible different forms of extraction—from extracting value on contemporary plantations for agribusiness, to extracting value from the theft of Indigenous land, and the use of slave labour. There are multiple forms of violence at work in the way property is made, the kinds of extraction that are made possible, and the relations that determine who can, and who cannot, extract value from property. We also considered how security regimes are implicated in securing the actual operations of extraction, such as at mine sites. I want to conclude with one final example, which should demonstrate just how clearly security regimes are implicated in securing property and the rights to extraction.

It is necessary to consider how the securing of mining sites connects these mines to the wider expanse of global security because of the linkages between mining and (global) militarization. If we return to the example of the report by the London Mining Network from Section 14.1, we are reminded of the mutual constitution of security and (mineral) extraction. This report should raise some deeply important and uncomfortable questions—how can we challenge militarization without also challenging mines as sites of extraction? If we challenge the security regimes at sites of extraction, are we also challenging some of the world's most powerful arms dealers? More importantly, what is at stake if we don't raise these challenges?

In addition to providing some of the clearest examples of how security regimes are implicated in securing property rights and rights of extraction, we can see the physical, material, and symbolic violence that is at once structural and isolated in effects, and both manifest and latent. The question of the link between militarization and extraction therefore also emphasizes the relationality of property and security in their constituting of who is inside/outside and secure/insecure. Returning as well to the questions of 'security at whose expense?' and 'security for what purpose?', we are left with uncomfortable answers—if the purpose of securing mine sites is (at least in part) for the purpose of manufacturing weapons, which can in turn be used to secure mine sites, then the question of 'security at whose' expense becomes very important indeed.

> **Chapter 9** discusses the process of othering

Questions for further discussion

1. How can we see different forms of violence (physical, material, symbolic) enacted through the classification of different forms of property?

2. What kind of relationship exists between historical processes that made land into private property and processes that made people into property? How is violence (and what forms?) implicated in these processes?

3. How can we think about claims of a 'right to extraction' through the mobilization of security as political questions of inclusion/exclusion, and types of hierarchy?

4. How can we see different forms of violence enacted through the 'securing' of rights to extraction?

5. What connections draw together the securing of sites of extraction, and the securing of sites of conservation?

Further reading

BHANDAR, BRENNA. 2018. *Colonial lives of property: Law, land, and racial regimes of ownership*. Durham, NC: Duke University Press.
In this ground-breaking analysis, Bhandar traces how ideas about who could claim land as property relied on racialized definitions of citizenship in Canada, Australia, and Palestine.

DUNLAP, ALEXANDER and JOSTEIN JAKOBSEN. 2020. *The violent technologies of extraction: Political ecology, critical agrarian studies and the capitalist worldeater*. Basingstoke: Palgrave Macmillan.
The authors critique the idea and practices of 'extractivism' and the ways in which it is exacerbating climate catastrophe, environmental destruction, and the violent displacement of people from their land.

NICHOLS, ROBERT. 2018. 'Theft is property! The recursive logic of dispossession'. *Political Theory* 46(1), 3–28.
In this article, Nichols upturns the anarchist claim that 'property is theft' to illustrate how the dispossession of Native people turned land into property through theft.

SELWYN, DANIEL. 2020. *Martial mining*. London: London Mining Network. https://londonminingnetwork.org/wp-content/uploads/2020/04/Martial-Mining.pdf (last accessed 10 March 2021).
This report details both the militarization of mine sites and the interconnected network of arms manufacturers who rely on multinational mining companies.

HOFFMAN, DANNY. 2018. *Yellow woman*. 15 min. www.youtube.com/watch?v=zlGO1wH3RcU (last accessed 12 January 2022). See also Hoffman's 2019 article 'Yellow woman: Suspicion and cooperation on Liberia's gold mines'. *American Anthropologist* 121(1), 1–11.
This short film shows processes of extraction used by artisanal-scale miners who are mining for gold in Liberia, and offers a view of extraction on a different scale, but where rights and claims to extraction still create cleavages of inclusion/exclusion.

References

BAKA, JENNIFER. 2013. 'The political construction of wasteland: Governmentality, land acquisition and social inequality in South India'. *Development and Change* 44(2), 409–428.

BEBBINGTON, ANTHONY, DENISE HUMPHREYS BEBBINGTON, JEFFREY BURY, JEANNET LINGAN, JUAN PABLO MUÑOZ and MARTIN SCURRAH. 2008. 'Mining and social movements: Struggles over livelihood and rural territorial development in the Andes'. *World Development* 36(12), 2888–2905.

BENTON, LAUREN and BENJAMIN STRAUMANN. 2010. 'Acquiring empire by law: From Roman doctrine to Early Modern European practice'. *Law and History Review* 28(1), 1–38.

BHANDAR, BRENNA. 2018. *Colonial lives of property: Law, land, and racial regimes of ownership*. Durham, NC: Duke University Press.

BLOMLEY, NICHOLAS. 2003. 'Law, property, and the geography of violence: The frontier, the survey, and the grid'. *Annals of the Association of American Geographers* 93(1), 121–141.

BLOMLEY, NICHOLAS. 2007. 'Making private property: Enclosure, common right and the work of hedges'. *Rural History* 18(1), 1–21.

CRONIN, BRUCE. 2010. 'Security regimes: Collective security and security communities'. In *Oxford research encyclopedia of international studies*. Oxford: Oxford University Press. https://doi.org/10.1093/acrefore/9780190846626.013.296 (last accessed 12 January 2022).

DUNLAP, ALEXANDER and JOSTEIN JAKOBSEN. 2020. *The violent technologies of extraction: Political ecology, critical agrarian studies and the capitalist worldeater*. Basingstoke: Palgrave Macmillan.

EDELMAN, MARC, CARLOS OYA, and SATURNINO M BORRAS. 2013. 'Global land grabs: Historical processes, theoretical and methodological implications and current trajectories'. *Third World Quarterly* 34(9), 1517–1731.

ENGELS, BETTINA. 2018. 'Nothing will be as before: Shifting political opportunity structures in protests against gold mining in Burkina Faso'. *The Extractive Industries and Society* 5(2), 354–362.

FANTHORPE, RICHARD and ROY MACONACHIE. 2010. 'Beyond the "crisis of youth"? Mining, farming, and civil society in post-war Sierra Leone'. *African Affairs* 109(435), 251–272.

GEENEN, SARA and JUDITH VERWEIJEN. 2017. 'Explaining fragmented and fluid mobilization in gold mining concessions in eastern Democratic Republic of the Congo'. *The Extractive Industries and Society* 4(4), 758–765.

HÖNKE, JANA. 2013. *Transnational companies and security governance: Hybrid practices in a postcolonial world*. London: Routledge.

MARIJNEN, ESTHER and JUDITH VERWEIJEN. 2016. 'Selling green militarization: The discursive (re)production of militarized conservation in the Virunga National Park, Democratic Republic of the Congo'. *Geoforum* 75, 274–285.

MBEMBE, ACHILLE. 2017. *Critique of Black reason*. Durham, NC: Duke University Press.

MURRAY LI, TANIA. 2007. *The will to improve: Governmentality, development, and the practice of politics*. Durham, NC: Duke University Press.

NICHOLS, ROBERT. 2018. 'Theft is property! The recursive logic of dispossession'. *Political Theory* 46(1), 3–28.

PELLEGRINI, LORENZO. 2018. 'Imaginaries of development through extraction: The "History of Bolivian Petroleum" and the present view of the future'. *Geoforum* 90, 130–141.

PELUSO, NANCY L. 2017. 'Whigs and hunters: The origins of the Black Act, by E.P. Thompson'. *The Journal of Peasant Studies* 44(1), 309–321.

RIOFRANCOS, THEA. 2020. *Resource radicals*. Durham, NC: Duke University Press.

SELWYN, DANIEL. 2020. *Martial mining*. London: London Mining Network. https://londonminingnetwork.org/wp-content/uploads/2020/04/Martial-Mining.pdf (last accessed 10 March 2021).

WARREN, CALVIN. L. 2018. *Ontological terror: Blackness, nihilism, and emancipation*. Durham, NC: Duke University Press.

WOLFORD, WENDY, SATURNINO M. BORRAS, RUTH HALL, IAN SCOONES, and BEN WHITE. 2013. 'Governing global land deals: The role of the state in the rush for land'. *Development and Change* 44(2), 189–210.

WORLD BANK. 2009. *Awakening Africa's sleeping giant: Prospects for commercial agriculture in the Guinea savannah zone and beyond*. Vol. 1. Washington, DC: World Bank. https://doi.org/10.1596/978-0-8213-7941-7

YUSOFF, KATHRYN. 2018. *A billion black Anthropocenes, or none*. Minneapolis, MN: University of Minnesota Press.

15
Digital, (in)security, and violence

Rocco Bellanova

15.1	Introduction	239
15.2	Imagining the digital, imagining violence	241
15.3	Critically questioning security and surveillance	246
15.4	How local–global tensions matter	249
15.5	Conclusion	251

READER'S GUIDE

Our lives and societies have become largely digital. So too have many security practices. Digitization has led to an increase in surveillance. In this chapter, we explore the connections between security and surveillance in the order to discover how (in)security and violence are fostered by the digital. To do so, we need to understand the digital in terms of datafication, computation, and materiality. These enable us to critically explore security through society and technology and tensions between the local and the global, while asking questions about the growing role of IT companies in our worlds.

15.1 Introduction

> Illustrative case studies on the topics explored in this chapter are available on the online resources to help take your understanding of digital (in)security and violence further:
> http://www.oup.com/he/Grayson-Guillaume1e.

The digital is ubiquitous in our everyday lives. The digital shapes our social interactions, our public institutions, and private companies. The digital informs our lives when we use a phone or a computer, when we connect to the internet, or when we swipe a card to use public transport. Moreover, the digital is part of our experience of security and international politics. For example, many public authorities around the world cross-check our fingerprints against a biometric database to decide whether we are granted permission to cross a border. International agreements channel the transfer of personal data across diverse jurisdictions as well as between private and public actors. Blockbuster movies and series such as *Enemy of the State* and *Black Mirror* have established popular culture tropes about the power of drones and algorithmic systems. These cultural products emphasize how digital technologies allow states to carry out mass surveillance and exert violence through kinetic strikes at a distance. Political debates about harmful content online—be it hate-speech, disinformation, or terrorist propaganda—raise concerns about the responsibility of social-media platforms to police their users' behaviour. New forms of cooperation between IT companies and public authorities raises the question of who defines what counts as violence—be it an image or bits of software—and thus what constitutes a security threat that requires remedial forms of action.

> On borders and security, see **Chapter 19**

It is impossible to understate the importance of the digital in contemporary security practices. Yet, defining the *digital* is challenging. Digital's seemingly ubiquity risks presenting it as a never-ending theme of materials, practices, and sites. As noted earlier, the digital can potentially relate to just about any possible form of insecurity or security practice. To keep ourselves focused, we will show the importance of questioning our very understanding of the digital. This will open up new perspectives on security, surveillance practices, forms of violence, and insecurity. In its most technical sense, the digital refers to signals, pulses, and/or other forms of data used by computers that are conveyed in binary code (usually 0s and 1s). As the Oxford English Dictionary notes, the origins of the word stem from digits (i.e., numbers) which itself finds its origins in the Latin word for finger (i.e., *digitus*). From its technical definition and etymological origins, we can see three important features of the digital—its relation to *datafication*, its connection to *computing*, and its *materiality*.

Focusing on these three features permits us to better recognize how the digital shapes (in)security in practice, and how it promotes, implements, and/or reinforces specific forms of violence and domination. For example, datafication is at the core of modern statecraft—techniques for counting things and people allow authorities to maintain control over a population at a distance, imposing and collecting taxes that can be used to reinforce their military power (Scott 1998). At the same time, showcasing the development of computing permits us to emphasize the key role of security imaginaries in shaping what is now called the *digital age*. Notably, US defence projects played a key role in coupling the digital with computing from the Second World War onwards (Edwards 1996). One of the first instances of the term 'digital' relates to the development of targeting technologies to shoot down enemy aircraft (Ceruzzi 2012, 1–2). Finally, insisting that digital things are material runs counter to the 'illusion of immateriality' (Kirschenbaum 2004, 110) that envelops the digital. Modern digital technologies require socio-material infrastructures to function, including wires, servers, phones, and computers.

In this chapter, we investigate the relations among the digital, (in)security, and violence. While unable to provide an exhaustive analysis, we offer some conceptual suggestions on how to study what the digital does to security (and the other way round). We also suggest that focusing on the digital (understood as datafication, computation, and materiality) allows us to ask questions about the 'how', 'when', and 'where' of security. Engaging with these questions often requires bringing together a constellation of literatures that—despite their differences—challenges traditional scholarly understandings of the actors and practices that shape the worlds we inhabit (Bellanova et al. 2020).

> These questions are presented in **Sections 5.3.1.3, 5.3.1.4,** and **5.3.1.6**

For example, exploring the links between the digital and security has often been done in relation to questions regarding surveillance (Bauman et al. 2014). Surveillance is understood as the capacity of some actors to closely control and intervene on the behaviour of other actors (Lyon 2007, 14). At the heart of such questions is an assumption about the transformative role of digital technologies. That is, digital technologies do not just strengthen or challenge existing state power (e.g., think about the use of malicious software to spy on senior members of government), but also give way to new relations of power (Mayer et al. 2014). Special attention has been given to data-driven practices, such as profiling systems designed to flag those who may pose a security risk. This body of research highlights how the surveillance rationales underpinning security initiatives have a significant impact on individual and collective liberties while increasing the roles played by private actors in what had previously been a public policy domain (Amoore and de Goede 2008).

> Relations of power are discussed in **Section 3.2**

In this chapter, we will introduce some key concepts that will allow you to ask further questions about how the digital, (in)security, and violence are connected. We begin with some perspectives on how to study practices of security and surveillance. We consider the digital in terms of datafication, computing, and materiality. We then highlight how the digital and security may facilitate specific forms of violence, how these are enacted, and towards whom.

15.2 Imagining the digital, imagining violence

We may be familiar with images showing how the digital relates to security and surveillance practices. For example, we see the aftermath of drone strikes based on algorithmic-driven analysis of various data sources including location data transmitted by mobile phones (Heller 2013). Public and secret surveillance programmes allow authorities to track social relations captured by digital means (Bigo 2019). Cyberattacks aim at hampering the everyday functioning of military and civilian infrastructures (Dunn Cavelty 2013). Thus, the digital is at the core of old and new security practices carried out by public and private actors.

It is also a site of insecurity for people, institutions, and companies alike. Despite the rhetoric of 'targeted killing', a drone strike nevertheless is an act of violence, understood as the use of kinetic force upon people (Chamayou 2013). This example can push us to think deeper about the various roles of the digital. For example, the decision-making behind a drone strike may involve data-driven inferences about who should be targeted, where, and when. In these cases, powerful actors mobilize digital technologies to claim that their use of violence is based on an objective assessment of an imminent threat and is thus legitimate (Emery 2020). At the same time, the circulation of video footage made with digital cameras or smartphones can cast a light on the consequences of a drone strike and its victims.

Other images—especially those relating to digital surveillance, or cybersecurity—may have less direct relation to common understandings of physical violence and coercive force. For example, the algorithmic identification of potential suspects based on the automated analysis of financial or travel data covers millions of people, but only a few will face further investigation, be subject to personal searches, have their transactions denied, or be prevented from entering a country. In other words, these forms of surveillance mostly remain out of sight, with the majority of those under surveillance unaware of the fact that they are being watched (de Goede and Wesseling 2017). The fact that these data already exist in a digital format is what makes large-scale surveillance practices acceptable to public authorities. Moreover, if a security measure is not perceived, it is unlikely to be considered coercive. Hence, this raises the question of 'what counts as violence' (Amoore and de Goede 2014, 496) in a digital age (see Chapter 4).

Embracing the perspective of those groups who are targets for less visible forms of data surveillance can become a way to investigate how the digital—understood as datafication and computing—may strengthen racist biases despite claims to objectivity. For example, Louise Amoore and Marieke de Goede (2012) argue that the commercial data harvested by public authorities for border security and financial surveillance feeds into mechanisms that create people and behaviour as implicitly risky and thus more likely to experience violent actions by state authorities. Many algorithms (which are formulas for decision-making that adapt in real time through machine learning) are based on assumptions that use the predominant group in a socio-political order as the norm. While public authorities and companies claim that they are pre-empting violent attacks and thus increasing the security of our societies, those individuals and groups that end up being frequently targeted due to biases (e.g., racial, gender, class, disability) inscribed into the algorithms will actually see their everyday insecurity increase. This is because those with 'high-risk' profiles are flagged as potential threats and/or routinely stopped and searched.

Coming back to the three facets of the digital—datafication, computation, and materiality—can help us establish relations between violence and insecurity. Notably, it expands our questions beyond direct forms of physical violence to make connections to other forms of violence. Take, for example, the power that datafication lends to some actors. As Ulises Mejias and Nick Couldry (2019, 3) note, 'datafication combines two processes: the transformation of human life into data through processes of quantification, and the generation of different kinds of value from data'. When we think about the digital in terms of datafication, we can identify diverse forms of violence at play. First, processes of datafication predate the digital, and are inter-connected with statecraft, security, and violence. We can see this in the history of statistics and its relation to the capacity of states to maintain a standing army or identify abnormal behaviours (Scott 1998).

On forms of violence, see **Section 4.2.1**

Currently, the introduction of biometric technologies legitimizes existing forms of governance and the acts of violence that they entail. For example, the use of biometrics to manage large numbers of refugees exposes them to new forms of insecurity, as the data of already vulnerable individuals is shared with authorities who see them as potential threats (Lindskov Jacobsen 2017). Beyond exposing forms of physical violence, datafication also casts a light on other violent dynamics. Consider how logics of quantification can support the identification of some neighbourhoods as more insecure than others. This can affect decisions about whether to prioritize public services and private investments in these areas or to look elsewhere, with the potential perverse effect of further marginalizing the inhabitants.

Thinking about the digital in terms of datafication also emphasizes the political economy in which relations between the digital and violence take place. This is evident in those cases where data-driven security, or surveillance practices, require the active cooperation of public and private actors. Indeed, as controversies surrounding mass-surveillance programmes have highlighted, even powerful public actors need companies to provide data for governmental databases as well as the software and infrastructure necessary to process diverse datasets. For example, documents about US secret surveillance programmes—leaked and published in leading news outlets from 2013 onwards—illuminate the crucial role played by major IT companies in providing the US National Security Authority with datasets (Bauman et al. 2014). A few years later, in 2018, several Google employees went public with their discontent towards a company project—called MAVEN—which would enhance target recognition and acquisition capabilities for US military drones (Suchman 2020).

Weapons-systems are discussed in **Chapter 17**

To say that the digital involves computing may sound like an obvious observation. The large diffusion of algorithmic systems across public and private spheres, and in different security contexts (Amoore and Raley 2017), has made us more aware of the crucial role of computation in our societies. Here, research on algorithmic power, particularly the question of whether algorithms have the ability to do things on their own, or simply empower those that have the resources to deploy them, suggests that supposedly objective calculations can be turned into forms of discriminatory targeting and actions (Eubanks 2018).

For example, Marieke de Goede (2012, xxi) shows that the tracking of terrorist finance, notably when supported by algorithmic systems, transforms security into a 'speculative' practice. Here, a violent action is taken to pre-empt the mere possibility that something may happen, rather than countering a confirmed threat. In concrete terms, this security worldview can push financial actors to deny their services to already marginalized people who—according to algorithmic speculation—may pose a threat at some point in the future. These security practices can deprive targeted people of essential services in our societies.

Furthermore, a focus on the digital as computing requires us to consider how computation works in practice and what it requires. Beyond abstract rationales and the imaginaries that computing may support, computation is also a concrete activity. Algorithmic systems require the existence of data in a digital format, but also their preliminary organization and classification. The creation and curation of datasets are practices that remain open to the introduction of various bias. Any dataset applies a series of assumptions that shapes how the collected information is interpreted and organized. Think, for example, how a question like 'what is your sex?' with a set of options (e.g., male, female, prefer not to say) reflects a view of gender as a binary that is informed by particular biases. Therefore, the use of seemingly objective databases is prone to further discrimination rather than its eradication (Chun 2021). Ultimately, the fact that datasets used for machine learning may include important bias can, in fact, aggravate specific forms of violence. First, it is difficult to identify and expose the biases underpinning machine learning unless one has access to the underlying coding. Second, the supposed objectivity of machine learning provides legitimacy for the violence that it enables, thus making it politically difficult to critique.

> Gender, sexuality, and security are discussed in **Chapter 10**

Finally, a more comprehensive approach to the digital requires attention to its material dimensions and those that it reshapes. Digital technologies are material things. They also create material relations. For example, to listen to our favourite podcast on our smartphone, we need software (e.g., a podcast app) and some hardware (e.g., a smartphone). There is, in other words, a material dimension to take into consideration if we want to play the podcast. At the same time, being able to listen to a podcast with our phone and some earbuds reshapes our understanding of what we can do with a (smart)phone.

When it comes to the relation between the digital and security, this can be somewhat more difficult to grasp in practice. As mentioned earlier, we may not perceive the material existence of a security technology, as we are familiar only with some 'security devices' (Amicelle et al. 2015) like CCTV cameras or body scanners. Many others like the algorithmic systems that flag travellers for secondary screening are less obvious. One site where the materiality of the digital becomes evident are borders. The digitalization of borders is explicit and even promoted by public and private actors (Broeders 2007). Intended to facilitate circulation, digitalization enables coercive force to materialize suddenly without warning (Pallister-Wilkins 2016). For example, border checkpoints have automated gates that will open (or not) after the scanning of your passport and the cross-checking of the information contained therein. You may need to you have your fingerprints collected, or be required to enter a body scanner to detect concealed objects. Capturing the material dimensions of the digital often means retracing and unpacking invisible data infrastructures that underpin high-tech surveillance measures and inform security decisions. The fragile materiality of data infrastructures casts a light on those forms of violence and insecurity that they may trigger. For example, as discussed in Box 15.1, the very existence of a biometric

> Border spaces are discussed further in **Chapter 19**

 BOX 15.1 BIOMETRICS AND THE WAR IN AFGHANISTAN

Figure 15.1 captures the stakes of relations among the digital, violence, and insecurity. We see a US soldier 'utiliz[ing] a biometric enrolment and screening device on an Afghan man' in 2014. The Afghan man seemingly accepts that his retinas are being scanned. This might have been the first scan for enrolment onto a programme managed by the US Department of Defense, or an identity check. If it was the latter, with his biometrics already stored in a database, the scan would cross-match them for the purposes of verifying his identity.

Figure 15.1 Picture released by the US Department of Defense, www.defense.gov/Multimedia/Photos/igphoto/2001128445 (last accessed 17 November 2021).

This picture hints at different relations among the digital, security, and violence. For example, the use of biometrics in the context of military operations has been promoted to assert 'identity dominance' (Woodward 2005, 30). Identity dominance refers to the ability of those who wish to govern a population to register people in ways that facilitate their political and societal objectives. For example, the provision of important services might be limited to those individuals who are already identifiable. Joseph Pugliese (2010, 90) argues that such configurations of the digital and security facilitated 'the assimilation of biometric technologies into the biopolitical configuration of US empire, war and bodies'. This then produced forms of physical, symbolic, and structural violence. Indeed, in this image, the ambition to achieve identity dominance showcases how the deployment of biometrics is closely linked to warfare and conflict, bringing together actors in relations of physical and symbolic domination.

After the retreat of US troops from Afghanistan, this image suggests additional ways to think about the relations among the digital, (in)security, and violence. News about the Taliban regime being able to use the data infrastructure built by US authorities circulated immediately after their arrival in Kabul in August 2021. While this does not mean they can access all the data collected and stored by the US military during its period of occupation, this image reminds us that there are several databases in the country that 'had not yet achieved the level of function they were intended to' but that 'they still contain many terabytes of data on Afghan citizens that the Taliban can mine' (Guo and Noori 2021, n.p.). In sum, the socio-material system established by US forces to achieve identity dominance risks becoming available to their former adversary, because of its very materiality. If used by the Taliban, the system offers an additional tool to govern and control the population.

database of Afghans, launched and used by US military during their twenty-year occupation, is now in the hands of the Taliban regime. What are the security consequences for those whose data is contained within?

15.3 Critically questioning security and surveillance

Some concepts can help us to map how the digital relates to (in)security and violence. A focus on the digital invites us to consider the diversity of security and surveillance practices surrounding us and affecting our lives. Notably, digital technologies are ubiquitous in our worlds. Determining how this affects our societies is paramount, not least when it comes to (in)security and violence. Indeed, while we have already seen that digital technologies are at the heart of warfare practices such as drone strikes, we should not lose sight of how the digital brings security together with surveillance practices (Salter 2010). At the same time, the growing relevance of digital technologies to security mobilizations should catalyse consideration of how best to make sense of the relationship between society and technology. More particularly, how does the processing of digital data—their continuous production, storage, and analysis—potentially lead to violence (Huysmans 2014)?

Security often happens in unexpected places and moments. In other words, focusing on digital technologies highlights how security is not only a matter of conflicts among states. Following the overlap between security and surveillance, we can see that the 'where of security' has changed, and this is even the case with 'national security'. For example, in the aftermath of the 9/11 attacks, exchanges between security and surveillance logics have catalysed legislators around the world to see a growing number of 'categories of information . . . [as] relevant for security agencies to monitor' (Salter 2010, 193). As controversies concerning the use of high-tech tools by US and other national intelligence agencies have highlighted, when and where digital data becomes relevant to security does not follow pre-defined legal and geopolitical partitions. Questioning the ambition of governments to carry out digital mass surveillance requires studying how the 'when' and 'where' of security are negotiated in specific instances. In practice, it means retracing what matters in these negotiations. For example, will automated systems be used, (how) will human rights be respected, and what institutional oversight will be adopted? We also need to identify who are the main actors involved into these data-driven security practices—be they security authorities, citizens, companies, and so on.

Focusing on how the digital facilitates the convergence of security and surveillance raises questions about 'security at whose expense'. The increasing use of digital data processing at the core of security practices raises questions concerning fundamental rights, in particular privacy and data protection. Much of the political debate that has accompanied major counter-terrorist initiatives in the last twenty years has evoked the 'security–liberty balance' (Zedner 2009). This metaphor assumes any decrease in freedom for individuals leads to an increase in security. This is used to justify data-driven

---

Security 'when?' and 'where?' are presented in **Sections 5.3.1.3–4**

The question of 'security at whose expense?' is covered in **Section 5.3.2.3**

The security–liberty balance is discussed in **Box 2.1**

measures that clearly affect the existing rights of individuals, and is open to challenge (Neocleous 2007).

Importantly, when we focus on how some security practices affect some people and communities more than others, we can question the supposed objectivity of digital technologies. As mentioned above, data processing practices are not free from bias. In fact, algorithmic systems—to a large extent—are expected to discriminate in order limit the scope of decision-making they are required to undertake. Hence, we can question security and surveillance by analysing how discriminatory biases have been inscribed into a given algorithmic system (intentionally or unintentionally). Furthermore, we can highlight how its use eventually may harm or make some people more vulnerable to violence in ways that are disproportionate to any gains from increased efficiencies in identifying potential suspects.

As such, we must remain aware of the diverse relations between technology and society. Take, for example, debates about so-called autonomous weapons; that is, algorithmically driven machines able to select and kill targets (Asaro 2012). These technologies illustrate a series of questions about how the digital reshapes the performance of security, notably regarding the issue of who is responsible for the physical violence that follows. A closer look at autonomous weapons shows how humans and non-humans are deeply entangled (Suchman 2020). Raising questions about the actual who of security allows us to advance accountability for security actions as well as consider the relations between society and technology that shape our worlds. If we are to explore these relations, a focus on the digital adds new units of analysis. In practice, this means analysing how non-human actors (e.g., digital things such as algorithms, or spyware) participate in security practices with the capacity to influence how human actors (police officers, or soldiers) act (Leander 2013). In turn, this reveals how these security entanglements may create novel forms of insecurity for our societies, whereby many of us live in close relation with other technologies. For example, while smartphones potentially provide many benefits, they can also be a vector to spread malware or capture personal data about us.

> **Chapter 17** explores the composition of weapons-systems
>
> Questions of authority and legitimacy are outlined in **Sections 4.3–4**

As such, focusing on the study of security as practice is a promising approach to unpack the 'how' of security. Anthony Amicelle and his co-authors (2015, 302, italics in original) suggest we should adopt an 'analytics of devices . . . to study security as "security practices = actors' social dispositions + *socio-technical characteristics of devices* + context"'. Their approach seeks to identify the elements that comprise a security practice enabled by technologies, and then the relations between them. Notably, this can cast a light on questions such as 'security for whom?'

> For more on 'security how?', see **Section 5.3.1.6**
>
> This question is discussed in **Section 5.3.1.2**

Security initiatives often become a means to conduct surveillance that would not otherwise be permissible on specific communities. Similarly, security initiatives may reflect and consolidate hierarchies that shape the social dispositions of security actors as can happen when predictive crime systems encourage police to target members of marginalized communities who are already subject to disproportionate levels of policing. We can also analyse security as practice by focusing on the creation of novel relations of power, especially when data-driven technologies are involved.

For example, de Goede (2018, 25) shows how counterterrorism financing relies on 'a security chain' of 'commercial data'. This chain begins with the data output of financial transactions and then moves through a series of computational practices to become the 'basis for intervention by police and potential prosecution'. From this perspective, the computational facet of the digital foregrounds how technical decisions (e.g., how data are stored, exchanged, and analysed) can influence the relations between actors. Do these decisions give private companies a privileged position in relation to other institutions, thus affecting whom (or what) should benefit from security?

Returning to the materiality of the digital, the infrastructural underpinnings of data-driven security practices are also important. An infrastructural perspective advances questions about the when and for what purpose of security. Infrastructure reveals the political dimensions of the seemingly mundane components that enable something to work, hold together, or fall apart (McFarlane and Rutherford 2008). When focusing on the relation between the digital and (in)security, infrastructures thus participate in defining when a security practice takes a given form and acquires a specific purpose. Examining infrastructures can also help us to understand when they do not function as expected, while still operating and potentially feeding into novel forms of insecurity (Pollozek and Passoth 2019). Moreover, infrastructures are fragile and thus we should not forget that even powerful ones require constant maintenance in order to function (Bellanova and Glouftsios 2022).

> Infrastructure as an enabler is presented in **Section 3.3**; questions of 'security when?' and 'for what purpose?' are discussed in **Sections 5.3.1.4** and **5.3.2.2**

Attention to infrastructures raises important insights into the when of security. For example, research on the maintenance of large-scale data infrastructures to manage migration shows that they contain an 'uncertain and, at least sometimes, disrupting agency', and that controlling it becomes a preliminary, and yet constant, purpose that influences 'govern[ing] international mobility' (Glouftsios 2021, 454). In this sense, (in)security does not only happen when an algorithmic decision is made or a drone strike takes place, but begins when the required infrastructures are put in place. (In)security is continuous as the same infrastructures are kept in place through maintenance.

Insisting on the materiality of the digital also allows us to counter the idea that the digital is disembodied. Yes, security analysts may only see the outcomes of data analysis on a screen, but these data-points refer to actual people. Feminist perspectives on the relation between society and technology therefore insist that disembodiment is not an automatic effect of the digital but a design choice to make some people or relations invisible (see also Chapter 16). In this respect, Lucy Suchman (2020, 175) notes that '[a] feminist sensibility . . . directs attention to how difference is enacted as an integral constituent of technologies of militarism, and with what consequences for the differential valuation of lives'.

This approach contributes to crucial questions such as security for whom and at whose expense. Unpacking drone warfare, and focusing on a specific attack killing multiple people, Lauren Wilcox (2017, 13) charts the 'the embodied and embodying nature' of a security practice in which the digital plays a crucial role. Wilcox (2017, 24) shows how 'drone assemblages incorporate modes of embodiment from algorithmic, visual, and affective technologies that enable the individualization of gendered, racialized targets'. From this perspective, studying relations among the digital, (in)security, and violence requires asking how seemingly objective, or neutral technologies in fact reconfigure who is considered a security threat, who is to be made more secure, and who is at risk of being violently obliterated.

15.4 How local–global tensions matter

Relations among the digital, (in)security, and violence occur around the world. Thus, we need to study local contexts and how the digital brings them into global relations (Appadurai 1990). This helps us ask questions about security where, for whom, and at whose expense. For example, a drone strike in Afghanistan brings together different spaces: the place hit by the missile, the military command centre that has ordered the strike, the place from where the operator flies the drone, and the foreign airbase where the drone is stationed. The same kinetic strike highlights that violence can be exerted at a distance insofar as some actors are visible (and thus targetable) while others operate from very remote, or well protected, locations (Bousquet 2018). Who benefits from this security practice, and who pays the price for it?

Whether through drone strikes, surveillance architectures, data-capture, or digitization, multiple local contexts are brought into global relations. These diverse contexts are far from equal, with the expected increase of security of some turning into a visceral decrease in security for others. In sum, the local–global tensions are at the core of the relations among the digital, (in)security, and violence. It is thus important to grasp the specific ways in which datafication, computing, and materiality are performed in different contexts. What relations of power are produced, for example, as in the case of online terrorist content moderation? To best understand relations connecting the digital, we need to capture their specificities and retrace their legacies, notably with regard to datafication and materiality, while remaining attentive to how these are also shaped by global dynamics.

See **Box 15.2** for a discussion of online terrorist content moderation

To do so, post-colonial perspectives help by raising important questions, especially since the historical experience of colonialism shapes global–local tensions (Seth 2013). Identifying tensions can help us to better 'recognize and problematize colonial histories and practices and their continuing influence on surveillance in modern life' (Newell 2019, 716). For example, Simone Browne's (2015, 16) work develops the notion of 'racializing surveillance'. This concept refers to 'a technology of social control where surveillance practices, policies, and performances concern the production of norms pertaining to race', while empowering those that conduct surveillance to define who has the right to exist and belong and under what conditions (Browne 2015, 16). Take, for example, the use of facial-recognition software to detect known and potential suspects. Both the decision to deploy this kind of system in specific sites and the handling of cases of misidentification can lead to criticism. Notably, the 'training' of facial-recognition software involves datasets that generate misidentifications that have racists underpinnings like the inability to distinguish among members of racial minority groups. Use of this software can thus generate (in)security for some groups. Moreover, deploying a system that will produce much higher rates of false-positives among some

BOX 15.2 ONLINE TERRORIST CONTENT MODERATION

Following the attacks in France (2015) and New Zealand (2019), several governments and companies have identified online terrorist content as a major security threat and are developing practices to prevent/remove this content. Notably, leading IT companies have been very active at international level. In 2017, the Global Internet Forum to Counter Terrorism was launched. This is an 'NGO designed to prevent terrorists and violent extremists from exploiting digital platforms . . . [f]ounded by Facebook, Microsoft, Twitter, and YouTube' (https://gifct.org/about). This kind of initiative institutionalizes specific relations among the digital, (in)security, and violence building upon previous practices of monitoring users' content (Gillespie 2018).

One of the mechanisms at the core of the Global Internet Forum to Counter Terrorism is the so-called Hash Database. Whenever the online moderation services of an associated platform label a given digital object as terrorist content, it algorithmically extracts from this object a unique string of characters. This string is then stored in a common repository—the Hash Database—to which all other associated platforms have access. Companies run the same algorithm on the digital objects uploaded by users, and automatically compare whether the resulting string of characters matches one already stored in the common repository. If this is the case, the object is—in principle—not uploaded or immediately taken down, without the need to check its actual content. This is because somebody else in the same company, or an associated one, has already labelled it as terrorist content (Gorwa et al. 2020). Thus, this practice brings together companies that are otherwise expected to be competitors to form a 'content cartel' (Douek 2020).

This system is far from fool-proof. Even minor modifications of the digital object (such as slightly cropping an image) generate files that the algorithm will turn into novel strings of characters. It also reconfigures relations of the digital, (in)security, and violence in ways that emphasize the power relations embedded in those content moderation decisions in which the actual content is not even assessed but eliminated by the surveillance practice. Hence, a rather simple form of computing becomes the pivotal point of various power dynamics that are largely indifferent to the presence, or absence, of violence in the digital objects being circulated because the focus is on the string.

communities than others sends the message that these groups do not deserve the same levels of security. Therefore, it reinforces racial hierarchies initially established under colonialism. As mentioned earlier, violence occurs during data collection and curation. Decisions about data quality and the data used to train algorithmic systems have far-reaching discriminatory effects on specific groups (Benjamin 2019).

Post-colonial approaches also strengthen our politico-economic perspective on security practices, with some speaking of the emergence of 'data colonialism'. For example, Jim Thatcher and his co-authors (2016) argue that the big data imaginary of endless progress and shared benefits promoted by companies and governments is dangerous. Against this digital frontierism, they propose 'the metaphor of data colonialism . . . [that] has the advantage of highlighting the power asymmetries inherent in contemporary forms of data commodification' (Thatcher et al. 2016, 992). In other words, when we think of the digital in terms of datafication, we can also question how turning people and their lives into digital data facilitates the extraction and appropriation of information that empowers some actors to the detriment of others.

For example, platforms that provide digital services ultimately see humans and their online activities as resources to be exploited. If we engage with data colonialism in a less metaphorical way, we can better understand how many digital data practices aim to secure a specific ideology—capitalism. Couldry and Mejias (2018, 337) note that '[d]ata colonialism combines the predatory extractive practices of historical colonialism with the abstract quantification methods of computing'. They thus insist that '[u]nderstanding Big Data from the Global South means understanding capitalism's current dependence on this new type of appropriation that works at every point in space where people or things are attached to today's infrastructures of connection'. While the internet may still be presented as a tool for fighting oppression and contesting the status quo, the fact that it is actually mediated by some actors—especially IT platforms—gives these actors a unique opportunity to extract valuable (data) irrespective of the content of the communication. This mechanism feeds company business models, but also underpins forms of oppression and structural violence. Indeed, the design of critical digital services—like online search engines—allows for the reproduction of existing (racial) stereotypes by incentivizing inaction and reactive remediation. Thus, the reproduction of many stereotypes through online platforms are not addressed because the expectation is that they will not bother most users (Noble 2018).

Finally, a post-colonial approach to data practices also draws attention to the political economy that supports the materiality of the digital. For example, the anatomical analysis of an Alexa device carried out by Kate Crawford and Vladan Joler (2018) reveals the colonial legacies of its production model that exploits the labour and the environment of people living in the global south. Many (big) data practices would not be possible without this exploitation. These devices are dependent on obtaining rare earths, metals, and hydrocarbons at low prices and promoting a consumer culture that quickly abandons devices for the latest upgrade, generating unnecessary waste (Pickren 2014).

15.5 Conclusion

How can we study the multiple relations among the digital, (in)security, and violence? To identify some avenues to address this question, we have explored our understanding of the digital. As Benjamin Peters (2016, 93) notes, '[a]s digital techniques continue to saturate the modern world, we increasingly find the keyword digital, understood in its most conventional sense, slouching past its prime'. We have shown the benefits of analysing the digital through three elements: datafication, computing, and materiality. From this perspective we can investigate relations among the digital, (in)security, and violence, from highly visible drone strikes to less obvious forms of algorithmic surveillance.

We have also offered some conceptual lenses that help us critically question security and surveillance. Notably, we have demonstrated how the digital can renew key questions for security, such as security for whom, security where, security from what, security when, security for what purpose, security at whose expense, and security how. Notably, we have drawn attention to the 'who' of security to ask who should be accountable for the diverse forms of violence produced by the digital and the worlds that are produced when society and technology are entangled in security practices. Furthermore, we have investigated the tensions between the local and global that underpin the relations between the digital and security. Beyond identifying asymmetries in the capacity to exert violence enabled by the digital, we can also grasp the political economy of extracting value from the datafication of people and the role of private companies in defining what counts as violence, and what forms of discrimination are tolerated.

Questions for further discussion

1. Identify a security issue and its relations to the digital. How do datafication, computing, and materiality allow us to understand the production of insecurities?

2. What forms of violence are most often depicted in pop culture representations of online surveillance? Are there forms of violence that are made invisible?

3. Compare differences in how the same security practice is experienced across diverse local contexts.

4. Are there other examples of how data colonialism affects the security of marginalized groups?

5. Think about a concrete case in which a leading IT company made a decision about what counts as violence. What diverse (in)security implications did this decision have for various actors?

Further reading

AMOORE, LOUISE and MARIEKE DE GOEDE. Eds. 2008. *Risk and the war on terror*. London: Routledge.
A pioneering collection of works foregrounding the emergence of new security logics and practices and their reliance on data-driven technologies.

BENJAMIN, RUHA. 2019. *Race after technology*. Cambridge: Polity.
This powerful work unpacks the racist worldviews underpinning many algorithmic systems and how data-driven technologies foster discrimination and domination through their claims of objectivity.

BOUSQUET, ANTOINE. 2018. *The eye of war: Military perception from the telescope to the drone*. Minneapolis, MN: University of Minnesota Press.
An innovative work that examines contemporary high-tech military practices through a sociotechnical analysis of how weapons and perception devices have shaped each other and informed military violence.

EDWARDS, PAUL N. 1996. *The closed world: Computers and the politics of discourse in Cold War America*. Cambridge, MA: MIT Press.
An enticing study of the diverse roles of computing in relation to the post-Second World War US politics and pop culture.

KANTAYYA, SHALINI. 2020. *Coded bias*. 85 min. 7th Empire Media, JustFilms/Ford Foundation. This documentary reveals the structural dysfunctions of facial-recognition software and the racist and discriminatory bias at its core. Thus, it raises awareness about how seemingly neutral algorithmic systems can affect social justice.

References

AMICELLE, ANTHONY, CLAUDIA ARADAU, and JULIEN JEANDESBOZ. 2015. 'Questioning security devices: Performativity, resistance, politics'. *Security Dialogue* 46(4), 293–306.

AMOORE, LOUISE and MARIEKE DE GOEDE. Eds. 2008. *Risk and the war on terror*. London: Routledge.

AMOORE, LOUISE and MARIEKE DE GOEDE. 2014. 'What counts as violence?'. In *Global politics: A new introduction*, edited by JENNY EDKINS and MAJA ZEHFUSS. London: Routledge.

AMOORE, LOUISE and RITA RALEY. 2017. 'Securing with algorithms: Knowledge, decision, sovereignty'. *Security Dialogue* 48(1), 3–10.

APPADURAI, ARJUN. 1990. 'Disjuncture and difference in the global cultural economy'. *Public Culture* 2(2), 1–24.

ASARO, PETER. 2012. 'On banning autonomous weapon systems: Human rights, automation, and the dehumanization of lethal decision-making'. *International Review of the Red Cross* 94(886), 687–709.

BAUMAN, ZYGMUNT, DIDIER BIGO, PAULO ESTEVES, ELSPETH GUILD, VIVIENNE JABRI, DAVID LYON, and R.B.J. WALKER. 2014. 'After Snowden: Rethinking the impact of surveillance'. *International Political Sociology* 8(2), 121–144.

BELLANOVA, ROCCO and GEORGIOS GLOUFTSIOS. 2022. 'Controlling the Schengen information system (Sis II): The infrastructural politics of fragility and maintenance'. *Geopolitics* 27(1), 160–184.

BELLANOVA, ROCCO, KATJA LINDSKOV JACOBSEN and LINDA MONSEES. 2020. 'Taking the trouble: Science, technology and security studies'. *Critical Studies on Security* 8(2), 87–100.

BENJAMIN, RUHA. 2019. *Race after technology*. Cambridge: Polity.

BIGO, DIDIER. 2019. 'Beyond national security, the emergence of a digital reason of state(s) led by transnational guilds of sensitive information: The case of the Five Eyes Plus network'. In *Research handbook on human rights and digital technology*, edited by BEN WAGNER, MATTHIAS C. KETTEMANN, and KILIAN VIETH. Cheltenham: Edward Elgar.

BOUSQUET, ANTOINE. 2018. *The eye of war: Military perception from the telescope to the drone*. Minneapolis, MN: University of Minnesota Press.

BROEDERS, DENNIS. 2007. 'The new digital borders of Europe'. *International Sociology* 22(1), 71–92.

BROWNE, SIMONE. 2015. *Dark matters*. Durham, NC: Duke University Press.

CERUZZI, PAUL E. 2012. *Computing: A concise history*. Cambridge, MA: The MIT Press.

CHAMAYOU, GRÉGOIRE. 2013. *Théorie du drone*. Paris: La fabrique éditions.

CHUN, WENDY H.K. 2021. *Discriminating data: Correlation, neighborhoods, and the new politics of recognition*. Cambridge, MA: MIT Press.

COULDRY, NICK and ULISES A. MEJIAS. 2018. 'Data colonialism: Rethinking big data's relation to the contemporary subject'. *Television & New Media* 20(4), 336–349.

CRAWFORD, KATE and VLADAN JOLER. 2018. *Anatomy of an AI system*. New York: AI Now Institute and Share Lab.

DE GOEDE, MARIEKE. 2012. *Speculative security: The politics of pursuing terrorist monies*. Minneapolis, MN: University of Minnesota Press.

DE GOEDE, MARIEKE. 2018. 'The chain of security'. *Review of International Studies* 44(1), 24–42.
DE GOEDE, MARIEKE and MARA WESSELING. 2017. 'Secrecy and security in transatlantic terrorism finance tracking'. *Journal of European Integration* 39(3), 253–269.
DOUEK, EVELYN. 2020. *The rise of content cartels*. New York: Knight Institute/Columbia University.
DUNN CAVELTY, MYRIAM. 2013. 'From cyber-bombs to political fallout: Threat representations with an impact in the cyber-security discourse'. *International Studies Review* 15(1), 105–122.
EDWARDS, PAUL N. 1996. *The closed world: Computers and the politics of discourse in Cold War America*. Cambridge, MA: The MIT Press.
EMERY, JOHN R. 2020. 'Probabilities towards death: Bugsplat, algorithmic assassinations, and ethical due care'. *Critical Military Studies*. doi.org/10.1080/23337486.2020.1809251.
EUBANKS, VIRGINIA. 2018. *Automating inequality*. New York: Picador.
GILLESPIE, TARLETON. 2018. *Custodians of the internet: Platforms, content moderation, and the hidden decisions that shape social media*. New Haven, CT: Yale University Press.
GLOUFTSIOS, GEORGIOS. 2021. 'Governing border security infrastructures: Maintaining large-scale information systems'. *Security Dialogue* 52(5), 452–470.
GORWA, ROBERT, REUBEN BINNS, and CHRISTIAN KATZENBACH. 2020. 'Algorithmic content moderation: Technical and political challenges in the automation of platform governance'. *Big Data & Society* 7(1), 1–15.
GUO, EILEEN and HIKMAT NOORI. 2021. 'This is the real story of the Afghan biometric databases abandoned to the Taliban'. www.technologyreview.com/2021/08/30/1033941/afghanistan-biometric-databases-us-military-40-data-points (last accessed 11 March 2022).
HELLER, KEVIN JON. 2013. '"One hell of a killing machine": Signature strikes and international law'. *Journal of International Criminal Justice* 11(1), 89–119.
HUYSMANS, JEF. 2014. *Security unbound: Enacting democratic limits*. London: Routledge.
KIRSCHENBAUM, MATTHEW. 2004. 'Extreme inscription: Towards a grammatology of the hard drive'. *TEXT Technology* 13(2), 91–125.
LEANDER, ANNA. 2013. 'Technological agency in the co-constitution of legal expertise and the US drone program'. *Leiden Journal of International Law* 26(4), 811–831.
LINDSKOV JACOBSEN, KATJA. 2017. 'On humanitarian refugee biometrics and new forms of intervention'. *Journal of Intervention and Statebuilding* 11(4), 529–551.
LYON, DAVID. 2007. *Surveillance studies: An overview*. Cambridge: Polity.
MAYER, MAXIMILIAN, MARIANA CARPES, and RUTH KNOBLICH. 2014. 'The global politics of science and technology: An introduction'. In *The global politics of science and technology: Vol. 1*, edited by MAXIMILIAN MAYER, MARIANA CARPES, and RUTH KNOBLICH. Heidelberg: Springer.
MCFARLANE, COLIN and JONATHAN RUTHERFORD. 2008. 'Political infrastructures: Governing and experiencing the fabric of the city'. *International Journal of Urban and Regional Research* 32(2), 363–374.
MEJIAS, ULISES A. and NICK COULDRY. 2019. 'Datafication'. *Internet Policy Review* 8(4), 1–10.
NEOCLEOUS, MARK. 2007. 'Security, liberty and the myth of balance: Towards a critique of security politics'. *Contemporary Political Theory* 6(2), 131–149.
NEWELL, BRYCE C. 2019. 'Introduction: Decolonizing surveillance studies'. *Surveillance & Society* 17(5), 714–716.
NOBLE, SAFIYA U. 2018. *Algorithms of oppression: How search engines reinforce racism*. New York: New York University Press.
PALLISTER-WILKINS, POLLY. 2016. 'How walls do work: Security barriers as devices of interruption and data capture'. *Security Dialogue* 47(2), 151–164.

Peters, Benjamin. 2016. 'Digital'. In *Digital keywords: A vocabulary of information society and culture*, edited by Benjamin Peters. Princeton, NJ: Princeton University Press.

Pickren, Graham. 2014. 'Political ecologies of electronic waste: Uncertainty and legitimacy in the governance of E-waste geographies'. *Environment and Planning A: Economy and Space* 46(1), 26–45.

Pollozek, Silvan and Jan Hendrik Passoth. 2019. 'Infrastructuring European migration and border control: The logistics of registration and identification at Moria hotspot'. *Environment and Planning D: Society and Space* 37(4), 606–624.

Pugliese, Joseph. 2010. *Biometrics: Bodies, technologies, biopolitics*. London: Routledge.

Salter, Mark B. 2010. 'Surveillance'. In *The Routledge handbook of new security studies*, edited by J. Peter Burgess. London: Routledge.

Scott, James C. 1998. *Seeing like a state*. New Haven, CT: Yale University Press.

Seth, Sanjay. 2013. 'Introduction'. In *Postcolonial theory and international relations*, edited by Sanjay Seth. London: Routledge.

Suchman, Lucy. 2020. 'Algorithmic warfare and the reinvention of accuracy'. *Critical Studies on Security* 8(2), 175–187.

Thatcher, Jim, David O'Sullivan, and Dillon Mahmoudi. 2016. 'Data colonialism through accumulation by dispossession: New metaphors for daily data'. *Environment and Planning D: Society and Space* 34(6), 990–1006.

Wilcox, Lauren. 2017. 'Embodying algorithmic war: Gender, race, and the posthuman in drone warfare'. *Security Dialogue* 48(1), 11–28.

Woodward, John D. Jr. 2005. *Using biometrics to achieve identity dominance in the global war on terrorism*. Santa Monica, CA: RAND.

Zedner, Lucia. 2009. *Security*. London: Routledge.

16

Security and design

Mark Lacy

16.1	Introduction	256
16.2	The visibility of security	258
16.3	Design and invisible wars	261
16.4	Design, security, and war: critical perspectives	263
16.5	Conclusion	268

READER'S GUIDE

This chapter addresses the different ways that design is used to shape security and war. While we often think about security politics as outcomes of specific interests or ideas, this chapter begins to illustrate how it is also the case that security policies, and related forms of political violence, are made possible by the various products imagined and manufactured by designers. The chapter goes on to show how the ideas and approaches of designers are being used to generate new perspectives and questions on security problems in a time of rapid technological change and transformation.

16.1 Introduction

Illustrative case studies on the topics explored in this chapter are available on the online resources to help take your understanding of security and design further: http://www.oup.com/he/Grayson-Guillaume1e.

In this chapter, we introduce an aspect of our existence that we might not think about in relation to security: design. Simply put, human beings design *things*: they imagine, plan, experiment, and then they make objects that change how we live and how we experience this thing called life. Design involves creating objects (tools, clothing, vehicles, buildings, technologies) that do not currently exist.

Design can involve improving the way the object functions (the technical or practical question)—but it can also involve questions of how the object should look (the aesthetic question). As this chapter shows, objects of design can be important elements, even infrastructures, in the production of the complex, messy, dividing, protecting, and controlling security landscapes that all humans (and possibly all *life*) inhabit. These are the environments of security that provide safety for some in a community—and control, policing, and insecurity for others. Individuals and groups experience and understand the discourses of 'security' and its hierarchies in different ways. They are also impacted differently by national and international security policies. These discourses and practices of security are often made possible by the objects of everyday life that we often ignore–or that have been deliberately designed to be camouflaged or invisible. Moreover, as we will see, there is more to design and security than these 'material' aspects of social and political life.

> Infrastructure as an enabler is discussed in **Section 3.3**

> See **Box 16.1** for more on design

Design might first appear to us as something on the margins of security but it is vital to everyday practices that 'produce' and maintain order and hierarchies of power inside states. Design is also important for security politics and in the ways technologies of war are designed in order to police and produce geopolitical 'orders'.

> **Sections 3.2–3** cover orders and their related hierarchies

BOX 16.1 DESIGN

Human beings design *things*. They imagine, plan, experiment, and they make objects that change how we live. The search for security has been shaped and transformed by the tools, vehicles, buildings, and weapons that result from our imagination and ingenuity. Design involves imagining and creating objects that do not currently exist and devising ways for these products to become real. Design is an encompassing process that questions and seeks to rethink not only what we produce or why it is produced, but also how we produce it. New types of production needed to be designed to enable the production of new weaponry during the Second World War, from the Plexiglas nose cone of the B-17 bomber to the overall assembly of the B-29 (Margolin 2013).

Design thus not only involves questions of ergonomics (i.e., how to efficiently produce an object that can effectively achieve its function with comfort), but also aesthetics (i.e., what the object looks like). A designer might want an object to be effective but also to 'look good' so that it is desirable. Sometimes groups, from specific sub-cultures like punks or goths, to formal sub-organizations like air units or marines, will use objects as symbols of their community. Design also helps objects and practices emerging from the security sphere to enter the civilian sphere, and vice versa. Think about that yellow Humvee you may have seen on the road. Design is therefore a process which thinks, produces, and evaluates the things and practices that are at the heart of security and its place in our worlds.

Of course, the 'best-made plans' of security might contribute to the production of more geopolitical *disorder*. These domestic/international aspects of design and security have been vital in making the worlds that we inhabit. In many ways, the techniques and technologies of security and design raise key questions:

- how is 'power' deployed to produce order and hierarchy in society?
- who designs the world we live in—and for what purpose?
- how do different understanding of threat lead to different designs for security technologies around the world?

In this chapter we examine how ideas of design and security become more complex and diverse in light of different states, actors, technologies, and security objectives in the twenty-first century. We then look at how two different groups of security professionals are responding to this complexity. In particular, we will see how two very different approaches to security and design are engaging with complex problems of global politics in a moment that some argue is a time of radical technological and geopolitical change. The first is the work of 'critical design' which focuses on our understanding of security in the broadest sense—encompassing all aspects of life, society, technology, ecology, and policy. The second is the 'military design' movement focusing on questions of war in the twenty-first century.

Critical design provokes the question *how* should we explore the security future that some are attempting to design for 'us'? The emergence of military design, for its part, raises the question of *where* can 'critical' ideas emerge on security and war? And what does it mean to be 'critical' of the practices of security and war? Should we 'reform' or transform war—or should we oppose all war and militarism in the twenty-first century?. As you will see, these two approaches to design leave us with unsettling questions but, as this book illustrates, vital to thinking critically about society and security is never being satisfied that you have arrived at the final answer that means our work is done. We should always be questioning (and re-examining) the worlds around us and our understandings of security politics.

16.2 The visibility of security

Thinking about security and design often begins with the idea that many aspects of life are objects of security for politicians and policy-makers tasked with creating order and control in their states. As more and more aspects of life become objects (or subjects) of security, these new 'objects' of security help produce the landscapes or environments of security in which people live. For example, one of the famous examples of urban planning and security is the idea that Paris was redesigned in the nineteenth century by planners, such as Georges-Eugène Haussmann, with security and policing concerns at the forefront of tactical thinking about the management of the city. As the German cultural and political thinker Walter Benjamin (2002, 165) suggested in 1938:

> The real aim of Haussmann's works was the securing of the city against civil war. He wished to make the erection of barricades in Paris impossible for all time. With the same purpose, Louis Philippe had already introduced wooden paving. Nonetheless, the barricades played a role in the February Revolution. Engels gave some thought to the technique of barricade fighting. Haussmann intended to put a stop to it in two ways. The breadth of the streets was to make the erection of barricades impossible, and new streets were to provide the shortest route between the barracks and the working-class areas.

The design of new wide boulevards was an element in the production of a new security and policing environment. Paris was viewed by policy-makers as a city troubled by revolutionary movements that could bring disorder and the political and policing desire was to make it difficult for protestors to shut down the city, an objective that continues to be a part of urban protests as seen with the anti-vaccination blockade of Ottawa in 2022. Large boulevards were meant for police, and possibly the military, to control the city more freely and in increasingly 'efficient' ways. However, we should also be careful not to reduce these plans in Paris to questions of policing. Haussmann wanted to design a city for more 'positive social purposes' by offering parks and open spaces, creating healthier environments for the people of Paris (Sennett 2018, 32). Thus, his design was for a city that created new possibilities for health and security for some—but new types of control and policing for others.

Designing security in the city is about trying to control the circulation of individuals and groups in societies that have become increasingly 'mobile' in the modern age, implicitly or explicitly categorizing and hierarchizing them. One of the most visible (and mundane) attempts to manage circulation securely are traffic lights. But there are also less obvious attempts to control circulation. Park benches can be designed with questions of 'public safety' and security in mind; benches are often designed to deter people sleeping on them in parks. Some exclusive buildings in cities have studs on the floors of entrances and doorways in order to prevent homeless people sleeping there (Savičić and Savić 2012). These design tactics are all about policing and maintaining the hierarchies of economic and political power in society, often justified in terms of defending individuals and communities from a threat. Security and design are often concerned with what is called 'deterrence by denial' by security professionals. Designers and policy-makers use design innovations to deter an actor from doing something. For example, 'anti-terror' concrete bollards are deployed to deter cars from being used to drive into people on pavements (Mars and Kohlstedt 2020).

States often claim to be taking measures to protect all citizens, transforming everyday life to make the safest form of life possible. But inside the project of securing territory can be a concern with more narrow objectives: protecting a particular group or set of interests. Indeed, it could be argued that much of design is ensuring separation

We provide a concrete discussion of this case in **Box 3.1**

and distance between different groups in society, from gated communities to innovations in what some describe as 'defensive architectures' (Graham 2011). Indeed, thinking about security designs reveals the tactics for 'ordering' society that produce hierarchies that often remain invisible and/or unquestioned.

> **Chapter 3** explores these questions in detail

Visibility is a vital aspect of security and deterrence. The 'secure' city is designed to become as transparent as possible. This is to enable police (and citizens) to see what is present so that it can be controlled. Control enables order, authority, and power to be maintained. Some would argue that one of the most vital transformations of security and everyday life during the last 200 years has been the streetlight (Virilio 2000, 2). The streetlight transformed the world. Lighting up streets meant that people would have less chance of being attacked in the dark. Thus, the economic and social 'life' of a city could extend into the night. Paris became the 'city of light', an amazing vision of consumerism *and* increasingly transparent to the gaze of the police. Streetlights—these products of imagination and design—deployed across a city transform the security environment.

At the same time, the project to produce visibility and transparency has also worked to make being under the light difficult for some groups like unhoused individuals as it draws unwanted attention from authorities. Visibility enhances the power of states and police in a way that can be dangerous for those individuals and groups constructed as a 'threat' in the politics of national security. This was dramatically illustrated by the various bureaucratic measures used in Nazi Germany to police, control, and murder Jewish people, tactics used by states around the world to make individuals and groups 'disappear' (Bauman 1991).

Thinking about security and design begins with thinking about 'the everyday'. It can involve the seemingly banal questions of park benches through to the more complex and sophisticated design innovations to prevent terrorist attacks (Low and Maguire 2019). We are potentially being transformed into objects of security and economic power. For example, think about the role of smart phones during the pandemic as a technology of surveillance *and* health/security. At the same time, urban environments are becoming smart or 'sentient' cities (Shepard 2011). Even our bodies are potentially subjected to security design. Andrew Bickford (2020) provides evidence that there is an interest in designing performance enhancement technologies that will produce new types of soldier. In the twenty-first century we might not simply be designing new objects or buildings, but redesigning 'life'.

> **Security professionals** are explored in **Section 2.2**

> **These enablers** are discussed in **Section 3.3**

How far would you go to alter yourself and your city in the search for security? Is the world becoming a 'homogeneous' securitized planet where everywhere looks the same? Or, are there different approaches, innovations, and effects in security and design? How is everyday security connected to the different political projects, values, and priorities of states and/or security professionals? Perhaps more importantly, how can we direct our questions to the security 'experts' about how they are working on problems that emerge from a rather narrow and limited understanding of what security problems actually are for different people and communities? Do these understandings of security create identities, ideas, interests, institutions, and/or infrastructures that reinforce hierarchies that prioritize the security of some over others? To what extent might design serve to challenge how security and design are enmeshed in one another? We shall now turn to how war and design are interlinked to advance our critical questioning of these issues.

> Challenges and resistance to security are analysed in **Section 3.4**

16.3 Design and invisible wars

War and design are intimately connected. Simply put, whoever has the best designed kit, the most efficient weapons, and the best logistics to support troops is often the most effective and successful during war. Audrey Kurth Cronin (2020) has examined the implications of military innovation that is 'closed' compared to when military innovation is 'open'. The nuclear revolution in the twentieth century was 'closed' due to the resources and expertise needed to research and develop this type of weaponry. However, in the 'information revolutions' of the twenty-first century, the use and development of new technology is far more open. For example, the 'costs to entry' are far lower in an age of 'cyber' and 'drones'. As Cronin (2020) suggests, a broad range of actors—including those with fairly limited resources—can get hold of technologies that have the potential to enhance their capability and capacity. In the 'worst-case' scenario, these actors might develop destructive capabilities that matches states without being subject to the same logic of deterrence.

> Weapons-systems are examined in **Chapter 17**

In a fascinating account of the history of the Kalashnikov (the AK-47), Cronin (2020) examines the design process that resulted in the assault rifle that became the 'weapon of choice' for terrorists, organized crime, and insurgents. One of the key points that Cronin (2020) makes is that the original design of the AK-47—a process that involved a contest in the Soviet Union—emerged from a concern about having a relatively light weapon that might lack the destructive capacity of other weapons but enabled soldiers to carry more ammunition (and not worry about kickback). The gun was designed to be simple to use and durable, composed of resilient and interchangeable components that were 'ideal for lightly armed, highly mobile troops, travelling long distance' (Cronin 2020, 140). It was fast, easy to use, and required limited training.

The weapon was viewed as technologically unimpressive by militaries in the West. Yet, it became widely used around the world, becoming a symbol of insurgent power. Cronin (2020, 61) points to studies that suggest that the circulation of the AK-47 was an element in the increasing failure of states around the world to manage local insurgencies. The Soviet Union also faced unintended consequences from the AK-47 in the war in Afghanistan in the 1980s when the weapon they designed was turned against them. As this example illustrates, a focus on design calls conventional understandings about world politics into question. We often think of history being shaped by politicians, policy-makers, and generals or the disruptive events of the global economy. But the world can also be transformed by the objects we design and create (Salter 2015, 2016). Once in circulation and 'out in the wild', these objects can produce unintended consequences not imagined by policy-makers and designers.

The AK-47 is a powerful symbol of military design. But many more 'mundane' elements of the 'war-machine' are the product of design decisions that result from the increasingly organized and well-funded bureaucracies (and corporations) tasked with research and development of military 'kit'. The design of war might range from the seemingly banal—such as the soles on boots to protect feet for longer periods in difficult conditions—through to the latest innovations in military hardware in an age of drones and robots.

The popular image of military design products is of quality, efficiency, and durability—and the production of symbols and images that are attractive to people both inside and outside the military. This results in styles that filter into civilian consumer products (Adams 2020). While building identity and community is a vital part of military culture and design, becoming *invisible* is an essential part of military tactics. In a variety of situations, the objective is to be able to see your enemy in increasingly 'granular' detail while at the same time being invisible to the 'vision machines' (e.g., cameras, drones, and satellites) of your opponent. Being hidden, or camouflaged, may even influence how soldiers fight in a battlefield. Camouflaged uniforms—a product of late nineteenth- and early twentieth-century amateur designers, but now a product of industrialized and heavily funded research and development—encourage soldiers to 'hunt' rather than to fight their opponents (see Guillaume et al. 2016). With the design of war increasingly concerned with making terrain contours visible, another primary object of design and war is secrecy, camouflage, and invisibility—war has become hunting and hiding in an increasingly transparent planet (Bousquet 2018).

The development of war has involved vast resources and expertise tasked with the job of making the military machine as efficient as possible. There are many commentators that point out that war—and the preparation for war—has been a vital source of social and technological progress in society. Projects of national defence and security have produced many innovations from the emergence of new medical procedures through to revolutions in information communication technologies (MacMillan 2020, 38).

In the twenty-first century, sources of technological and scientific innovation come from a range of organizations and locations. This change in the sources of innovation emerges from the sheer range of technologies and sciences (from robotics to AI to quantum computing) that are potentially transforming socio-political orders. At the same time, technological innovation emerges in a context that some would describe as 'neoliberalism' where there is a focus on the public sector taking a 'backseat' in areas where it is believed that the private sector will be more dynamic and efficient. Even if a state wanted to fund research and development, there are simply too many spaces of innovation across the planet, from boardrooms to labs and design hubs of Apple, Google, or Tencent.

In the United Kingdom, for example, the Defence Evaluation and Research Agency (DERA) was the part of the Ministry of Defence. It worked on many of the challenges discussed above like ensuring military kits were fit for purpose, researching, and advising on the new technological possibilities of war, and so on. During the 1990s, it was divided into two organizations: the Defence Science Technology Laboratory (DSTL) and QinetiQ, a commercial firm focusing on both military and civilian technologies. The creation of QinetiQ could be viewed as a way of turning the expertise

> The connections between war and society are analysed in **Chapter 7**

and innovation of the state-funded military sector into a profitable economic venture. Or, it might be viewed as a means of limiting the state's role in defence technology while maintaining control of essential areas in a world that was becoming too technologically complex to stay ahead in all areas of innovation in the 'open system' described by Cronin (2020, 12).

One way of understanding 'great power politics' and technological competition in the twenty-first century is that we now have multiple actors (from commercial technology businesses to different states and emerging 'peer competitors') trying to design the future of war across a growing number of technologies and spaces of scientific innovation. One of the primary areas of competition is an 'arms race' in AI, an arms race that will potentially have radical and diverse impacts on all aspects of economy, science, society, and war, but also might result in 'post-human' design creativity and innovation (Kania 2017, 6; Payne 2022).

Some argue that Chinese state is funding and supporting innovation in AI in a way that will outpace the progress that will emerge from technology companies in the West. The counter-argument is that innovation in the 'neoliberal' West will ultimately prove to be superior and more dynamic. But the broader question is this: where will innovation in the design of war emerge from in the twenty-first century? Who will be designing the future of war? Are we able to see how war might be changing? Or is it emerging in the invisible spaces of labs and workshops beyond scrutiny and debate? In terms of the questions introduced in Chapter 5, who is designing the future possibilities for security/war and for what purposes (geopolitical plans and strategic visions)? And, do the designers know what the possible risks are from the new technologies that are being imagined and manufactured?

16.4 Design, security, and war: critical perspectives

Following on from the questions raised earlier, we next examine how different groups are using design thinking to raise questions about the desire for individual, community, national, and planetary security through new technologies, economic policies, and geopolitical strategies. Both perspectives introduced here raise questions about how we think about security in a complex world. They also prompt us to think about who should be shaping the technologies, strategies, and policies that aim to deliver or produce security 'for whom?', and 'at what expense?' Unfortunately, there are no easy solutions to these serious problems. Indeed, the perspectives here raise even more difficult and uncomfortable questions. But central to this book is the idea that we need to ask questions about our worlds to seek change, if not transformation.

We discuss transformation in **Section 1.2.4**

16.4.1 Security through critical design

What does it mean to think critically about design and security? On one level, thinking critically about security and design is about making the invisible *visible*. Critical designers draw attention to the often invisible innovations that attempt to redesign the worlds we live in—from the seemingly banal (transparent bin bags in train stations intended to deter the use of bins for bombs) to the tools of 'surveillance capitalism' that make our everyday activities the subject of increasingly intimate and granular surveillance (Zuboff 2019). We could examine how designers themselves are used by policymakers in the development of specific projects, such as 'designing out' insecurity and terrorism from everyday life in the UK (Lacy 2008). Designers are most well placed to produce 'visualizations' and 'materializations' of the issues and debates that security and design render invisible. And they can do so in a way that is often more accessible to citizens in the public sphere: a powerful image or object can generate more traction than an academic text (Lacy and Weber 2011).

> Socio-political orders are presented in **Section 3.3**

The problem of security and design is not just about the use of design as a brute instrument of power and control, enforcing the violent policing of unequal socio-political orders. It is also a broader problem. Global citizens confront worlds where 'development' is creating a multitude of social and ecological threats, vulnerabilities, and insecurities. Global citizens are confronted with worlds where new technologies are being designed and produced to transform our planet, how we live on it, and what we may become. As the science fiction writer William Gibson has suggested:

> These connections are examined in **Chapters 12, 14,** and **18**

> the strongest impacts of an emergent technology are always unanticipated ... We're increasingly aware that our society is driven by these unpredictable uses we find for the products of our imagination. (Gibson 2011)

What technologies will you be using in 2035, or 2067, or even 2099? Will it just be a constant process of upgrading the latest smartphone? Or will we be dealing with new possibilities in biology, technology, and politics? Will we see the emergence of new products and technologies that radically change all aspects of life, from how we work to how we love? Can we have enough critical distance towards technology when the pace of change makes critique difficult? And, following Gibson's point, what could these unintended consequences be? How can we begin to explore them? And who is, or should be, identifying what the unintended consequences are and the social, political, ecological, and human dangers that they may be connected to?

> For more on critique, see **Section 1.2**

There are 'critical designers' exploring ways to think about the worlds that designers and technologists might be creating. For example, in books such as *Design noir: The secret life of electronic objects* (2001) and *Speculative everything: Design, fiction and social dreaming* (2013), Anthony Dunne and Fiona Raby have developed an approach to design that can be described as 'critical design' or 'design for debate' (Sterling 2019). On the one hand, critical design is about encouraging people to think about the values and political desires of design, often through the creation of provocative objects deployed in exhibitions at the Museum of Modern Art, New York or the Centre Pompidou, Paris. An example of their work is a project on how robots might become part of everyday life (Geisler 2017). How will consumers want the various robots that might fill our worlds to look? How might we *not* want them to look? How will our cultural values and anxieties shape these machinic futures? Should robots be made to look 'friendly' and 'welcoming', or should we maintain distinctions and separation between the human and the 'inhuman' robot? What type of robotic futures are being imagined? And who will be shaping robotic futures? For what ends?

In the video 'Designs for an overpopulated planet: Foragers', Dunne and Raby (2009) explore the future of food in a world experiencing population growth and climate change (see Chapter 18). Through an exploration of radical possibilities in food production, 'Foragers' is about exploring possibilities beyond anything usually found in the public sphere in order to raise provocative questions about how we will produce and consume food—in ways that might challenge our values and ideas in radical ways (Dunne and Raby 2013, 151). How far would you be willing to change the 'traditional' diet you have grown up with in order to challenge the ecological consequences and inequalities of global food production and ensure food security? What should future food look (and taste) like to become acceptable to consumers? What have been the planetary consequences of our 'modern' (or Western diet) in terms of ecology, inequality, and health? These interventions are more than speculations or 'design fictions'—Dunne and Raby's work emerges from detailed research and consultations with a range of 'experts' in the areas they explore. You can see the various projects they have developed at the website: http://dunneandraby.co.uk/content/projects.

Chapter 14 discusses food production and the question of property rights

Questions of health and environment are assessed in **Chapters 12** and **18**

This concern with 'the future' in the work of Dunne and Raby emerges from the view that the 'experts' shaping technologies to make the world more secure might reflect a narrow view (or 'fiction') of what society should be like, what it means to be secure, what risks or costs are acceptable, and what it means to live a 'good life'. The 'experts' of security and technology offer a specific window into how our political imaginations are shaped. They may also be shielded from certain realities and from reflecting on the unintended consequences of a policy, or the ethical consequences of a scenario (on nuclear weapons, see Cohn 1987).

On security as a frame, see **Section 1.3**

Critical designers are concerned with investigating emerging issues to uncover the potentially negative consequences of technology, policy, and design before they become reality. We live in a time where there are a growing number of movements that are trying to shape debates about future technologies and policies that might emerge from our imaginations and technological innovation. For example, the Campaign to Stop Killer Robots has been using provocative short films to raise awareness about how AI might transform war (Payne 2022). The challenge of global politics in the twenty-first century is that we are dealing with the ethical and political problems of the past, present, and *future*: in this crowded space of global challenges, critical designers can use their provocative and often startling work to draw attention to what these accelerations feel like so that we can ask questions about them.

As Dunne and Raby (2013) admit themselves, however, critical design can also have its dark side. It may bring into our worlds possibilities that were best left unimagined. For example, it can desensitize us to certain transformations, like biotechnologies, by 'paving the way for a greater acceptance' (Dunne and Raby 2013, 51). Imagination and creativity are not only forces of critique; they can also be dangerous. As we explore the dark side of technology and politics, we might create dangerous new possibilities, a new type of terrorist attack, or a new use for an existing technology to be used by governments to control citizens.

On the question of lethality and incapacitation in weapons-systems, see **Box 17.1**

The point Dunne and Raby are making is that it is both necessary and possible to contribute to the creation of debates that will make people aware of what might be on the horizon and to the political and legal processes that will place pressures on governments and corporations as they explore new possibilities. We might not know for certain what is being imagined by the technologists trying to create and shape the future. However, what the critical designers do is to try to show us—drawing on what is possible or realistic in terms of science and technology—what futures might be on the horizon and what the intended and unintended consequences might be of new technologies or policies. Simply put, Dunne and Raby are using design to explore the questions of 'why' security and 'at whose expense?' when security is mobilized to design a life in common that is more secure, more efficient, and/or 'new and improved'.

16.4.2 The future of war and the military designers

What will future wars look like? Confronted with new technologies (e.g., drones, AI, and cybertechnologies), new actors (e.g., rising great powers and new types of non-state actors), new tactics (e.g., hybrid warfare and lawfare), and new 'terrains' (e.g., from the impacts of climate change to the militarization of the cyberspace), policy-makers, military planners, and security professionals are invited to reimagine and redesign war. Key questions then include: what types of wars will be fought, what types of wars will be supported, and how will support be generated and mobilized? Furthermore, what types of soldiers and equipment will militaries need in these coming ages of new wars? Should we only denounce the potential political violence induced by design, as discussed earlier, or do we need to rethink how war is thought about, planned for, and operationalized? Idealistically, how can we prevent violence? Less idealistically, how can we prevent more violence than should be necessary in a time of war?

A group that has been grappling with these questions is the 'military design' movement, a group of scholars inside and outside the military who are interested in using ideas from the design world to help rethink war in the twenty-first century (Beaulieu-Brossard and Dufort 2017; Peterson 2021; Zweibelson 2019). Military designers ask: is the traditional military able to respond to the emergence of new tactics (such as the use of social media), technologies (the use of robots), and actors (criminal hackers used by states)? You can get an introduction to the military design approach, by a weapons-system designer, in the 'Military design 101 masterclass' available online (Zweibelson 2021).

Chapter 17 explores weapons-systems in depth

Many of the key players in the military design movement experienced the wars in Iraq and Afghanistan—and the experience left them questioning how wars were being 'designed' by policy-makers and bureaucrats. Simply put, military designers draw on designers who work on a range of problems outside the military world—in the tech world, in architecture, and in urban planning—to find techniques to disrupt what can be a very traditional and conservative military imagination. One view, for example, is that unlike in the lead up to the Second World War, US military forces will not have the luxury of 'warm-up periods' to develop tactics and weapons when facing new threats (Peterson 2021). So, how do we prepare for war in new terrains (such as space), using new technologies (such as AI), and techniques (the use of social media) when we have not experienced or used them before on the battlefield?

The interest of the military designers is not with designing new 'science fiction' tools for future war. Rather, the interest is in using the *processes* used by designers as they begin to think differently about emerging problems in order to create concepts and processes that can challenge the structure of the organization seeking to solve a problem (or the very understanding of the problem itself). The tactics and techniques being used against your armed forces or police might not be the one you have prepared for—especially during a time of disruptive technological change (see Galeotti 2022). Military designers draw on contemporary design methodologies (e.g., Dorst 2015) to show how traditional approaches, or 'frames', can limit the creation of solutions to complex problems. In doing so, they demonstrate how a number of design techniques can be drawn upon to challenge the traditional approaches of military organizations built for an age of industrial war rather than a time that has been described as 'liquid warfare' (Demmers and Gould 2018).

One of the key influences in the emergence of the 'military design' movement was the work of Shimon Naveh in the Israel Defence Forces during the 1990s. Naveh is considered the founder of military design. His work pioneered design applications in security contexts and developed an alternative mode of thinking and acting in war called 'Systematic Operational Design Theory'. Activists and scholars consider Naveh's approach to design and security as reinforcing forms of control and violence against Palestinians in the Occupied Territories (Weizman 2007). Naveh, on the other hand, sees his approach as minimizing the damage and harm to Palestinians during urban conflict (Feldman 2007). Of course, there is an ambiguity in Naveh's vision, and at the heart of 'military design'. A military might want to minimize harm for legal and ethical reasons, or it might want to minimize harmful images that result from an event or tactic, but it still produces forms of violence. One of the most well-known examples of Naveh's attempt to disrupt conventional military thinking was a creative solution to the problem of urban conflict and policing proposed by one of his students (see Weizman 2007).

> Forms of political violence are examined in **Chapter 4**

The urban battlespace is a congested terrain leaving soldiers vulnerable and exposed. Enemies may have the advantage of knowing the environment and being able to hide and surprise. Moreover, it puts civilians at the centre of combat due to the chaotic nature of urban fighting. Naveh and the students thought to redesign urban warfare tactics by elaborating tactics and reflecting on weapons which would facilitate the Israeli infantry improving its manoeuvrability and reducing its losses by moving through buildings. This literally meant walking through walls by destroying them or blowing them up, to avoid the treacherous, booby-trapped, and ambush-prone streets that the enemy expected them to travel on (Weizman 2007; Weizman with Watkins 2014).

Despite having been used in Palestine, we need to be cautious not to overstate the significance the use of 'military design' by the military in Israel (Feldman 2007). As noted, Naveh sees his approach as minimizing the damage and harm done to Palestinian civilians. However, how we understand this question of harm and political violence depends on the socio-political orders and the hierarchies that are set in a militarized occupied space such as Palestine. This also shows the tensions between the aim of military designers to make certain tactics more 'acceptable' or 'ethical' without considering what is generating conflict. Thus, it is a stretch to see military design as transformative.

> For more on transformation, see **Sections 1.2.3 and 3.4**

This leaves us nonetheless with a range of questions for which there are no easy answers. Should military designers' attempt to minimize harm in war be viewed as problematic? Are they simply perpetuating what they seek to minimize because they contribute to strategies and tactics that support a politics of security that some would argue creates unnecessary forms of violence? Or, is it possible to engage in critique from within the 'war-machine'? There are discussions about these difficult questions in military thinking and the problems of 'transgressive creativity' in military organizations and 'reflexive' military practices (Oberg 2018; Danielsson 2020). Even if the broader politics of security is problematic, should attempts to minimize harm through creative tactics be viewed as 'improvement' in the conduct of war? How do we negotiate between these competing perspectives on war and insecurity? What to do with the work of those who seek to 'improve' or change war if we consider it still ultimately contributes to its perpetuation? Is non-violence, pacifism, and resistance to the war-machine the only legitimate course of action?

> Non-violence is discussed in **Box 4.1**

Engaging with military design makes this question inescapable. It recalls divisions over 'reform vs. revolution' or 'realism vs. idealism' that have long been part of political disagreements about security politics. Military designers will argue that we need to think creatively about how war can be fought differently (to 'reform' war); critical designers will argue we need to find creative alternatives to war and security. Some will argue that the positions are mutually exclusive and exist in radically different worlds. Others might argue there are points where the different positions can meet and converge. But each position we take has potential risks and costs. What we need to do as students of security is to examine these different risks and costs, recognizing that the impacts of those risks and costs will be experienced differently depending on who and where you are as well as how security has been designed. These are unavoidable questions if we are to re-imagine the future of war.

16.5 Conclusion

In many ways we are left with more questions than we began and these are questions for which there are no simple answers. From military design, we are seeing a move towards new tactics and technologies in war that are focused on minimizing harm in response to a new generation of conflicts. For critical design, these tactics might be examples of problematic design that support a problematic politics of security that perpetuates forms of violence despite, or precisely because of, their novelty or 'creativity'.

The emergence of military design may reflect a broader reconfiguration in how security and war are being thought about in the twenty-first century considering types of conflict described as 'grey zone' conflicts or hybrid, liquid, and ambiguous wars

(Galeotti 2022). What security means and what security does are not 'fixed', timeless, and universal. The place of security professionals and what they do in the world becomes a pressing factor when we reflect upon the future of war. Are we seeing signs of change emerging from *inside* the war-machine? Or, are we perpetuating domination through security, only framed and presented differently? Critical design itself is not outside of these questions. The dangers of asking certain questions about the future of security, society, and technology could unleash possibilities that were previously 'unthought of' or 'unimagined'.

In this chapter, we have raised an important question central to the politics of security: do we know who is 'designing security'? Where is it being designed and for what purpose? What are the technologies, tactics, and objects which will inform how security is mobilized and what security does? Who will design the tactics that contest, challenge, and resist how security technologies and policies are being imagined and produced? How do newly designed technologies challenge our security and freedom?

Taking the use of design by Dunne and Raby as inspiration, how can we produce our own 'critical design' to create, or intervene, in debates and discussions about emerging technologies? How can we produce alternative imaginaries about our future worlds? These are hard questions. Thinking about design and security is often about revealing aspects of everyday life and global politics that may be invisible to us and this invisibility may be an intentional element of a design. The 'fog' of what could be the future of war/security, and the difficulties in imagining or discerning a different horizon, requires a plurality of perspectives that will exceed the ethical, political, and strategic capacities of all the 'legacy' viewpoints we have used thus far to make sense of the world (Austin and Leander 2020). Thinking about design multiplies the questions we ask about the worlds we live in. We must allow these questions to 'mutate' given the changing economic, ecological, technological, and political conditions of the worlds they find themselves in.

> On the historicity of security, see **Sections 1.2.2** and **2.2**

> The balance between security and freedom is analysed in **Box 3.1**

Questions for further discussion

1. Can you think of a security design, object, or infrastructure used in everyday life that is largely unnoticed, or leads to particular people, places, or things being rendered invisible?

2. What are the hierarchies underpinning security design? Who are the designers and why does this matter to the politics of security?

3. Considering the inevitability of AI and robots in the provision of security and warfare, how would you want a peacekeeping robot to be designed? Would it look different than one designed for warfighting? What ethical, technological, and aesthetic concerns would you think are important for the design of robots used in security and war?

4. Using your creative and imaginative skills, what will a 'smartphone' be able to do in ten years from now? How might these new capabilities transform security or war?

5. How are infrastructures (such as cities, airports, stadiums, etc.) designed to provide security? How have they evolved over the past century? How might they evolve in the future? How are they also sources of insecurity? Towards whom and how?

Further reading

DORST, KEES. 2015. *Frame innovation: Create new thinking by design.* Cambridge, MA: The MIT Press.
>This is a book used by members of the 'military design' community that provides a range of case studies (some that are on issues of crime and security—but not all of them) to show how new 'frames' can be developed by organizations as they deal with complex contemporary problems.

DUNNE, ANTHONY and FIONA RABY. 2013. *Speculative everything: Design, fiction and social dreaming.* Cambridge, MA: The MIT Press.
>This is a fascinating overview of the history of the radical designers who have used design to think critically about the 'dark sides' of the modern world. This book provides insight into how Dunne and Raby use 'critical design' to explore future economic, social, and technological problems.

CRONIN, AUDREY KURTH. 2020. *Power to the people: How open technological innovation is arming tomorrow's terrorists.* Oxford: Oxford University Press.
>This book shows how 'products' of security and war such as Kalashnikovs, drones, and artificial intelligence can be used by non-state actors in ways that create complex problems for states and militaries. The book concludes with a discussion of how to manage the proliferation of 'dual-use' technologies in a time of technological acceleration and geopolitical transformation.

SENNETT, RICHARD. 2018. *Building and dwelling: Ethics for the city.* London: Penguin.
>The book provides a richly detailed insight into the way we have designed all aspects of urban life—and how the city has transformed the possibilities for how we can live with other people. The book concludes with a discussion of an 'ethics for the city' in neoliberal times of inequality, ecological change, and new technologies of control.

BICKFORD, ANDREW. 2020. *Chemical heroes: Pharmacological supersoldiers in the US Military.* Durham, NC: Duke University Press.
>While there is currently great interest in drones, robots, and AI, this book takes us into an area that will likely increase in importance in coming years—the US military's attempt to 'design' super-soldiers that will be created using performance enhancement technologies for future battlefields viewed as a 'dangerous pharmacological environment'. This 'molecular militarization' raises important (and troubling) ethical questions about the possibility of attempts to 'redesign' human beings in coming decades.

References

ADAM, MARK. 2020. 'How the bomber jacket formed and subverted subculture,' *High Snobiety.* www.highsnobiety.com/p/bomber-jacket-history-guide (last accessed 12 February 2022).

AUSTIN, JONATHAN and ANNA LEANDER. 2020. 'Designing-with/in world politics: Manifestos for an international political design'. *Political Anthropological Research in International Social Sciences* 2(1), 83–185.

BAUMAN, ZYGMUNT. 1991. *Modernity and the Holocaust.* Cambridge: Polity.

BEAULIEU-BROSSARD, PHILIPPE and PHILIPPE DUFORT. 2017. 'Introduction. Revolution in military epistemology'. *Journal of Military and Strategic Studies* 17(4), 1–20.

BENJAMIN, WALTER. 2002. *The arcades project.* Cambridge, MA: Harvard University Press.

BICKFORD, ANDREW. 2020. *Chemical heroes: Pharmacological supersoldiers in the US Military.* Durham, NC: Duke University Press.

BOUSQUET, ANTOINE. 2018. *The eye of war.* Minneapolis, MN: University of Minnesota Press.

COHN, CAROL. 1987. 'Sex and death in the rational world of defense intellectuals'. *Signs* 12(4), 687–718.

CRONIN, AUDREY KURTH. 2020. *Power to the people: How open technological innovation is arming tomorrow's terrorists.* Oxford: Oxford University Press.

DANIELSSON, ANNA. 2020. 'Knowledge in and of military operations: Enriching the reflexive gaze in critical research on the military'. *Critical Military Studies* 20(1), 1–20.

DEMMERS, JOLLE and LAUREN GOULD. 2018. 'An assemblage approach to liquid warfare: AFRICOM and the "hunt" for Joseph Kony'. *Security Dialogue* 49(5), 364–381.

DORST, KEES. 2015. *Frame innovation: Create new thinking by design.* Cambridge, MA: The MIT Press.

DUNNE, ANTHONY and FIONA RABY. 2009. 'Designs for an overpopulated plant: Foragers'. http://dunneandraby.co.uk/content/projects/510/0# (last accessed 13 February 2022).

DUNNE, ANTHONY and FIONA RABY. 2013. *Speculative everything: Design, fiction and social dreaming.* Cambridge, MA: The MIT Press.

FELDMAN, YOTAM. 2007. 'Dr Naveh, or, how I learned to stop worrying and walk through walls'. *Haaretz*, 25 October. www.haaretz.com/1.4990742 (last accessed 12 February 2022).

GALEOTTI, MARK. 2022. *The weaponisation of everything: A field guide to the new way of war.* New Haven, CT: Yale University Press.

GEISLER, THOMAS. 2017. 'Is design ready for the robots?'. *Damn*, 61. www.damnmagazine.net/2017/03/21/readiness-robots (last accessed 12 February 2022).

GIBSON, WILLIAM. 2011. 'The art of fiction, No.211'. *The Paris Review*, 197. www.theparisreview.org/interviews/6089/the-art-of-fiction-no-211-william-gibson (last accessed 12 February 2022).

GRAHAM, STEPHEN. 2011. *Cities under siege.* London: Verso.

GUILLAUME, XAVIER, RUNE S. ANDERSEN, and JUHA A. VUORI. 2016. 'Paint it black: Colours and the social meaning of the battlefield'. *European Journal of International Relations* 22(1), 49–71.

KANIA, ELSA. 2017. 'Battlefield singularity: Artificial intelligence, military revolution and China's future military power'. *Centre for a New American Security*, 28 November. www.cnas.org/publications/reports/battlefield-singularity-artificial-intelligence-military-revolution-and-chinas-future-military-power (last accessed 12 February 2022).

LACY, MARK. 2008. 'Designer security: Control society and MoMA's SAFE: Design takes on risk'. *Security Dialogue* 39(2–3), 333–357.

LACY, MARK and CYNTHIA WEBER. 2011. 'Securing by design'. *Review of International Studies* 37(3), 1021–1043.

LOW, SETHA and MARK MAGUIRE. Eds. 2019. *Spaces of security: Ethnographies of securityscapes, surveillance and control.* New York: New York University Press.

MACMILLAN, MARGARET. 2020. *War: How conflict shaped us.* London: Profile Books.

MARGOLIN, VICTOR. 2013. 'The United States in World War II: Scientists, engineers, designers'. *Design Issues* 29(1), 14–29.

MARS, ROMAN and KURT KOHLSTEDT. 2020. *The 99% invisible city: A field guide to the hidden world of everyday design.* London: Hodder and Stoughton.

OBERG, DAN. 2018. 'Warfare as design: Transgressive creativity and reductive operational planning'. *Security Dialogue* 49(6), 493–509.

PAYNE, KENNETH. 2022. *I, WARBOT*. London: Hurst.
PETERSON, NOLAN. 2021. 'Inside Project Galahad: How the 75 ranger regiment used "creative destruction" to prepare for the contemporary battlefield'. *Black Rifle Coffee Company*, 6 January. https://coffeeordie.com/project-galahad (last accessed 12 February 2022).
SALTER, MARK. Ed. 2015. *Making things international 1: Circuits and motion*. Minneapolis, MN: University of Minnesota Press.
SALTER, MARK. Ed. 2016. *Making things international 2: Catalysts and reactions*. Minneapolis, MN: University of Minnesota Press.
SAVIČIĆ, GORDON and SELENA SAVIĆ. Eds. 2012. *Unpleasant design*. Belgrade: G.L.O.R.I.A.
SENNETT, RICHARD. 2018. *Building and dwelling: Ethics for the city*. London: Penguin.
SHEPARD, MARK. Ed. 2011. *Sentient city: Ubiquitous computing, architecture and the future of urban space*. Cambridge, MA: The MIT Press.
STERLING, BRUCE. 2019. 'Design fiction: New Dunne and Raby interview'. *Wired*, 28 August. www.wired.com/beyond-the-beyond/2019/08/design-fiction-new-dunne-raby-speculative-design-interview (last accessed 12 February 2022).
VIRILIO, PAUL. 2000. *A landscape of events*. Cambridge, MA: The MIT Press.
WEIZMAN, EYAL. 2007. *Hollow land: Israel's architecture of occupation*. London: Verso.
WEIZMAN, EYAL with KATIE WATKINS. 2014. 'Al Jazeera's rebel architecture: episode 3, "The architecture of violence"'. *Al Jazeera*, 2 September.www.archdaily.com/543538/al-jazeera-s-rebel-architecture-episode-3-the-architecture-of-violence (last accessed 12 February 2022).
ZUBOFF, SHOSHANA. 2019. *The age of surveillance capitalism*. London: Profile Books.
ZWEIBELSON, BEN. 2019. 'The multidisciplinary design movement: A frame for realizing industry, security, and academia interplay'. *Small Wars Journal*, https://smallwarsjournal.com/jrnl/art/multidisciplinary-design-movement-frame-realizing-industry-security-and-academia-interplay (last accessed 12 February 2022).
ZWEIBELSON, BEN. 2021. 'Military design 101 masterclass'. www.youtube.com/watch?v=zCL-LGDA-HA (last accessed 12 February 2022).

17

Weapons-systems

Mike Bourne

17.1 Introduction 273
17.2 What are weapons and what do they do? 275
17.3 Does the manner of violence matter? 279
17.4 How are weapons controlled? 282
17.5 How is weapons-politics entangled with other forms of violence and security? 284
17.6 Conclusion 286

READER'S GUIDE

In this chapter, we engage with weapons-systems as a central aspect of the question 'security how?' We also engage with security 'for whom?', 'from what?', and 'at whose expense?' We show how particular assumptions about weapons as technologies have excluded critical questions about how power and violence combine in, and through, weapons-systems and their control. At stake are the range of issues that are downplayed when killing and destruction are assumed to be inherent to security and when tools of violence are not recognized as political.

17.1 Introduction

Illustrative case studies on the topics explored in this chapter are available on the online resources to help take your understanding of weapons-systems further: http://www.oup.com/he/Grayson-Guillaume1e.

The connections joining weapons, security, and violence emerge with a flash of light, a muzzle flare, or a mushroom cloud. In a shooting, kinetic energy drives a projectile into flesh and bone, the bullet moves on, maybe expanding, or tumbling, but always releasing energy into the body. A cavity opens and collapses as the energy dissipates, having crushed soft tissue and splintered bone. A bloody event. Or, there is a blinding double flash of light and a mushroom cloud, or a squadron of bombers carpet bombing a city. And yet much security discussion about weapons loses sight of physical destruction and harm. It forgets the wounded bodies, destroyed cities, scorched earth, and raging fires as it sanitizes and legitimizes political violence of all types. It also tends to downplay the wider political, cultural, and economic relations in which the production, use, and control of weapons is situated, given meaning, and set in motion. Instead, weapons are engaged as a resource, 'a neutral tool of security and violence explained by other rational choices.

Weapons are a central and pervasive aspect of the material, institutional, and discursive mobilizations of security. The power to kill and injure is constituted and connected to the ordering of sovereignty and international security through weapons. It is common to think of security as being about defending against war and physical violence, usually by countering threat with threat, or characterized by global arms races between superpowers (Glaser 2000). Such understandings are shaped by thinking about weapons as the material resources that states or people need to deter, or defend against, the violence of others. Likewise, part of the rationalization of the state is the monopolization of (legitimate) violence enacted both through the threat of violence and its control.

> On security as a political mobilization, see **Section 2.4**. Authority, legitimacy, and their connection to political violence are discussed in **Sections 4.3–4**

As such, weapons have long been both a tool and a measure of power. Most prominent are nuclear weapons, possessed by only nine states: the United States of America (1945), Russia (1949), the United Kingdom (1952), France (1960), China (1964), India (1974), Israel (undeclared), Pakistan (1998), and North Korea (2006), many of which are modernizing their nuclear forces. The estimated total of 13,150 nuclear warheads (FAS 2021), mostly held by the United States and Russia, represents a significant reduction in numbers from Cold War highs (70,300 in 1986). Contemporary warheads, however, are many times more destructive.

In contrast to nuclear weapons held by a small number of states, most states possess major conventional arms (tanks, military aircrafts, etc.), and all possess small arms and light weapons (SALW). In 2020, global military spending reached a new high of nearly 2 trillion USD (Lopes Da Silva et al. 2021), and the top 100 arms companies sold 420 billion USD worth of weapons in 2018 (Fleurant et al. 2019). These figures give a sense of inter-state weapons-politics and the preparation and potential for war, but much is lost when these weapons are assumed to be the mere tools of rationally directed instrumental physical violence (see Section 4.1.1). Rather than resources and tools, we will explore the role of weapons-systems in security politics as a way in which violence of all types is constituted.

Weapons are full of all the forms of violence Galtung (1969) asks us to consider, and are central to the ways in which that violence is enacted on some bodies, spaces, and times and not others. They are thus a way of addressing critical questions of 'how security?', 'for whom?', 'from what?', and 'at whose expense?'. Section 17.2 engages with understanding weapons as neutral tools, and shows how questioning this can open new ways of engaging violence. It does this through exploring what weapons are, and how seemingly technical issues are always political. Indeed, part of the argument put forward is that by being attentive to technologies we are not excluding political,

> These different questions are covered in **Sections 5.3.1.2, 5.5–6, and 5.3.2.3**

social, ideological, and other human factors as an explanation of violence, but rather that all of these things come together in and through weapons.

Understanding weapons as technologies, then, does not merely mean the technical functioning of the device, or the kind of things that an instruction manual or advert would note like the calibre, range, accuracy, or rate of fire of the weapon itself and the requirements of its use (though these are part of the picture). Rather, it means considering the range of forms of violence that are enabled and legitimized. Weapons-politics, then, reveals what we might think of as lethal legitimations: the legitimation of killing, the preparation for killing, and the distinctions (racial, colonial, gendered, religious, class, civilizational) that allow us to take for granted that killing is inherent to security.

We will pose three questions about security and violence that arise through weapons-politics:

- Does the manner of violence matter?
- How are weapons controlled?
- How is weapons-politics entangled with other forms of violence and security?

Rather than viewing weapons as the mere tools of top-down power, order, and security (see Chapter 3), we will progress from the conduct of physical violence, to the political and legal practices of politics about weapons, and then into the wider forms of violence, domination, and threat that are mutually reinforcing with physical violence. Across these questions we see that weapons-systems are the materialization of violence of all types.

17.2 What are weapons and what do they do?

It might make sense to begin a discussion of weapons with some definitions. But definition is a slippery process. As a way of including or excluding things from consideration, it is an inherently political act. The definition of weapons is always connected to what is considered to be violence, and is central to the conduct and legitimation of violence. You may come to the subject already knowing what is a weapon (e.g., a gun, a missile) and what is not (e.g., marshmallows, carrots, and pillows), but there is a wide middle ground of ambiguous objects that can be *used* to inflict bodily harm even if they were not *designed* to do so.

Many weapons are not produced in factories geared for war. Perhaps, the most emblematic are Improvised Explosive Devices, created from repurposed junk and electronics (e.g., boxes, wires, batteries) and homemade explosives without a standardized industrial design. Accounting for up to two-thirds of US soldiers killed or wounded in Iraq and Afghanistan, such weapons trouble any sense of technological, or civilizational, superiority of Western high-technology military power (Grove 2016). Similarly, many things that would be considered weapons are designed not to kill but to incapacitate in some manner. So-called non-lethal (or less lethal) weapons such as tear gases or water cannons are tools of the violence (legitimized as 'force') that underlies the state. However, by enabling violence without killing, they also make military action and police use of force more 'legitimate' even when used in the governing of populations (de Larrinaga 2016).

> On security and design, see **Chapter 16**

> Lethality and incapacitation are explored in **Box 17.1**

> **Chapter 6** discusses this question from the angle of policing

BOX 17.1 LETHALITY AND INCAPACITATION

Weapons kill, but they are not designed solely to optimize killing. For instance, many weapons and ammunition are optimized to have a 'stopping power', echoing international legal and ethical principles that the aim is to 'weaken' enemy forces, and put out of combat their combatants. The aim is to stop an enemy, supposedly with the minimum suffering necessary to that task—though death may often result. This, of course, is often framed through highly racialized notions of civilization. The condemnation and banning of expanding 'dum-dum' bullets, which expand inside the body on impact and leave larger disabling injuries, limited itself to Western warfare but not to colonial warfare against 'savaged' others. Similar colonial histories and emphasis on disabling an enemy prefigure contemporary trends towards the development of less lethal technologies that are designed to incapacitate rather than kill; for instance, tear gases diminish fighting capacity both through the tear response and by forcing the wearing of gas masks. While such gases are now banned in war after the shocks of the First World War, they are permitted 'domestically' in law enforcement purposes such as crowd control. A wider range of weapons are designed to minimize death by disabling, temporarily or permanently, intentionally or unintentionally (see Section 4.2), people in policing and war contexts: Acoustic weapons (sound cannons) used by the US military in Iraq in 2004 were first developed and used for policing crowd control such as the Occupy Wall Street demonstrations; electric shock weapons (taser guns) evolved from cattleprods into weapons for police and military use. These forms of political violence intimately connect disability with the use of force by the military or militarized police, but also with how political violence is thought of by security professionals (Castrodale 2019). Whether designed to kill or incapacitate, or even to be a weapon (see also Chapter 16), weapon-systems invite us to reflect upon the types of hierarchies—racialized, class, ideological, and so on—that are articulated through disability.

Rather than resolve the question of 'what is a weapon?' by relying on design or lethality, perhaps we should operate only with a generic common-sense definition that some things definitely are weapons. Yet even then, it is difficult to offer a clear dividing line between what is and what is not a weapon. Knives are a case in point. Debates on gun control often include a view that firearms are not the problem since violent crime would otherwise be conducted with knives (Kleck 1991)—a view disputed by evidence showing the lethality of criminal violence is related to the weapons used (Zimring 1972)—or the claim that the 1994 Rwandan genocide was committed with machetes not guns (though this obscures the degree to which machetes were imported and distributed for this purpose, and the ways in which firearms were central to the organization of this violence).

However, this common-sense definition often implies that a resolution can be achieved with attention paid to the 'wrong hands' using said object. There are two further problems with doing that. First, any characterization of whose hands are 'the wrong hands' is inevitably an ethico-political claim. For example, the inventor of the AK-47, a gun used to kill hundreds of thousands, invoked patriotic pride and the competitive nature of international politics to legitimize his life's work, noted he never personally shot at anyone, and dismissed any ethical responsibility for more distant consequences (see Kalashnikov 2006, 151). Second, it is deeply reductive. Is what makes something a weapon simply the intention and character of the hands that wield it? There is a common-sense intuition at work here but this seems to replace one problem with another by moving the focus to a different part of the constitution of violence.

Perhaps the key is to connect this to violence. After all, by defining weapons, we are looking to identify the tools of political violence. Remembering Galtung's (1969, 169) claim that violence, conceived as influence, requires 'an influencer, and influence, and a mode of influencing', then weapons may be whatever constitutes the latter. Galtung works this through the most obvious case of personal violence—violence visited upon a person's body (object) by another (subject) using a particular tool or technique (action)—by looking to the effects on the body (crushing, tearing, piercing, burning, poisoning, or 'evaporation') and on the physiology (denial of air, water, food, or movement) (Galtung 1969, 174).

If we consider weapons to be whatever constitutes the mode of action (e.g., a tool, technique, etc.) weapons can be a range of things from fists to guns to nuclear weapons as well as techniques (e.g., strangulation, starvation, siege). On this foundation, Galtung (1969) outlines direct physical violence but also structural violence. Yet this conceptualization is already far wider than the commonplace notion of what a weapon is, as it includes chains, prisons, and 'brain-washing' (Galtung 1969, 174).

In addition to Galtung's typology numerous other acts and objects can be counted as weapons—rape, for instance, or computer code when used to create 'cyber-weapons'. Perhaps we should welcome this broadening of what we consider a weapon since it enables us to register and engage with politics that occurs with and through a range of tools and techniques of violence. Certainly, the 'wrong hands' argument now seems reductive since Galtung's trinity is reduced to the 'subject'. However, we are still left with the problem of the common-sense assumptions about technology that underlie many of the problems of working out what weapons are through definitions or typologies.

The first common-sense assumption about weapons, which underlies the 'wrong hands' argument, is summed up in the US National Rifle Association (NRA) mantra that 'guns don't kill people, people do'. This is often invoked to oppose calls for enhanced gun laws in the wake of tragic mass shootings. Yet, even this truism relies on the political force of a commonplace assumption: it must be people and not tools that explain things and thus give us ethico-political purchase on violence. This, in part, is what is known as an 'instrumental' account of technology. The technological object is just a neutral tool; it does what its possessor desires save for malfunction or accident.

Yet, even this truism is not true in and of itself. Its meaning has changed over time. When first coined, it was not a claim of universal truth mobilized to cut off legislative change and demonstrate indifference to suffering; it was an appeal to people to act responsibly—to not to be careless with inherently dangerous weapons (e.g., not leaving them loaded and accessible to small children). More importantly, though, the assumption of the inherent neutrality of 'tools' is problematic. The 'instrumental'

On Galtung's notion of political violence, see **Section 4.2** *and* **Zoom-in 4.1**

On prisons, see **Chapter 20**

What constitutes a weapon is also explored in **Chapters 10** *and* **15**

notion of technology is deeply depoliticizing. Much security discourse adopts the position of the rational calculating actor deploying military force as a crucial tool in the pursuit of power and security. Weapons are thus encountered as a resource to be used in the pursuit of other goals. Nothing more.

But if that claim is questionable then its reverse is equally problematic. Here we can move from the NRA to MAD. Mutually Assured Destruction (MAD) was the dominant version of the concept of deterrence applied to nuclear weapons that shaped so much of the Cold War period that it too has come to be taken for granted. The logic is elegant and appealing. In a situation with two (or more) nuclear armed states, the sheer destructive force of the weapons themselves means that no political goal can be achieved through the use of force. The costs so greatly outweigh the benefits that war becomes irrational (see Freedman 2004). The claim that leaders will be cautious and avoid war because of something inherently dangerous in the weapon is why this perspective's proponents can be referred to as 'technological determinists': the nature of the technology determines the character of the relations of which it is part (though notably, this view is often reserved only for nuclear weapons and no other technologies).

> To consider how MAD shapes the socio-political order and political violence, see **Sections 3.2** and **4.2.2**

A third claim, however, recognizes the ambiguities we have highlighted thus far. It concentrates on how these ambiguities may be provisionally settled, distributed, and productive (Rappert 2005). Here weapons-politics works through these ambiguities rather than only arising once they are defined away. To pursue this argument, we need to fundamentally shift how we see weapons and other technologies. They are not simple objects that *then* get associated with particular meanings and political relations. Rather, they *are* the set of relations that constitute them. Relationality is a larger consideration at the heart of the Science and Technology Studies (STS) academic field. Take a B-52 bomber: What is it? An aircraft. What does it do? It flies and it bombs. This seems obvious, but it omits more fundamental questions about how we understand the actions of flying and bombing, and thus how these are connected to identities, ideas, interests, institutions, and infrastructures.

> These enablers are presented in **Section 3.3**

For example, what is a bomber without a pilot (i.e., someone trained to pilot a plane to deliver a nuclear payload)? What is it without the specific idea of bombing that is guiding the US Air Force (on the idea of bombing, see Lindqvist 2001)? What is it without the interests articulated in the National Security Strategy of the United States? Or, what is it without infrastructure like air traffic control, guidance systems, or fuel supply networks? Surely to be a B-52 is to be a particular combination of all of these things. This foregrounds action in a way that does not require locating agency within either the subject or the tool, but as an effect of them both. As Bruno Latour (1999, 182) notes, flying, and we could add bombing, 'is a property of the whole association of entities that includes airports and planes, launchpads and ticket counters. B-52s do not fly, the US Air Force flies'. In connection with bombing, missile guidance systems are also reflective of a range of political decisions, personal beliefs, material components, and scientific processes that had to be 'engineered' to come together to produce accuracy in missiles (Mackenzie 1990). Such an approach views weapons not as static objects that can be defined separately from their security politics, but as 'assemblages' of relations and processes conjoining the social and the technical (Bourne 2012).

Understanding weapons as processes and relations foregrounds the connected ways they are made and made 'legitimate' (Bousquet et al. 2017). In weapons-politics meaning-making processes of legitimation occur in several overlapping ways: by default, by discourse, by law, and by use. By default, weapons are deemed legitimate by assuming they are tools. Through discourse, weapons are categorized into 'conventional' arms—which reinforces the default—while terminology like 'weapons of mass destruction' or 'inherently indiscriminate' weapons casts a different light. Through law and other national and international agreements, categorizations gain definition and operational efficacy. Through the use of categorizations, distinctions get blurred or mobilized in different ways to legitimate or criticize particular forms of violence. Thus, while it is important to ask what makes some weapons 'illegitimate' this question gains its importance from the default assumption that without certain features, or meanings, weapons are assumed to be legitimate.

For more on legitimacy, see **Sections 2.3.2 and 4.3**

The argument here is that even when there is not an explicit politics singling out particular types of weapons, weapons are political. The title of this chapter is 'weapons-systems': weapons are not just single objects (guns, missiles, tasers) but systems: sets of relations and processes that extend in multiple ways to incorporate things that we more easily recognize as *political*. These would include hierarchies, rationalities (and thus choices), identities, values, aims; and *violence* such as killing, maiming, excluding, disempowering, and dominating. We therefore use the term weapons-systems to reflect what we might also call weapons-politics (the hyphen is important as it conjoins the two). Weapons are a coming together of multiple processes and things that are always political in some sense. Weapons-politics is not just a separate issue *upon which* politically important distinctions are drawn, they are the process of enacting those distinctions and making them meaningful. This is explored in the next three sections through three key questions: (1) does the manner of violence matter? (2) how are weapons controlled? and (3) how is weapons-politics entangled with other forms of violence and security?

Security as a political claim and mobilization is covered in **Sections 2.3.2 and 2.4**

We present how to approach violence politically in **Chapter 4**

17.3 Does the manner of violence matter?

Does it matter *how* we kill and die, or wound and suffer wounding? As Elaine Scarry (1985, 67) argues, 'reciprocal injuring is the obsessive content of war', not a mere consequence or an 'accidental and unfortunate entailment of human injury' that just happens. By forgetting the bodies, places, and environments that are injured, accounts of war and violence that foreground rational calculations ignore the contingency embedded into the question 'security how?' This forgetting is not incidental to physical violence and is connected to other forms of violence.

The question 'security how?' is explored in **Section 5.3.1.6**

One might wonder whether the manner of killing and wounding really matters? Surely, what matters is whether or not someone dies, and who dies according to the international legal and ethical distinction between combatants and non-combatants. Indeed, the distinction between who may and may not be legitimately killed in war plays out in weapons-politics where characterizations of some weapons as 'inherently indiscriminate' (and thus unable to be used without contravening this principle) were mobilized to de-legitimate anti-personnel landmines, chemical weapons, biological weapons and currently in the politics of autonomous weapons (killer robots). But while the questions of who kills, and who is killed, are centrally important to addressing questions of security for whom and at whose expense, the ways in which weapons-politics shapes other characteristics of physical violence are less common. Indeed, the manner of violent death and injury has tended to arise only in the context of debate on whether some weapons are more objectionable than others. The military historian Martin Van Creveld (1989, 72) thus noted that '[t]aking an "objective" view, it is not clear why the use of high explosive for tearing men apart should be regarded as more humane than burning or asphyxiating them'.

The answer, for some, is to explore the processes through which some types of weapons have *come to be* viewed as inherently worse than others. Richard Price (1997), for instance, argues that while the physical effects of chemical weapons are awful, similarly harmful technologies are not banned or viewed in the same way. In such analysis the answer lies not with the weapon itself but with the historical processes shaping values, norms, and ways of understanding the weapon—processes through which 'taboos' on particular weapons (or more limited taboos on their use) are constructed. Certainly, the meanings (positive or negative) that have become associated with particular categories of weapons are crucially important in understanding why some weapons are banned and others are deemed legitimate. It is equally important to note that these meanings are not simply the recognition of some inherent property of the weapon. However, there are a number of aspects of what we might call the 'manner' of killing that this does not capture.

Some weapons are constructed as being 'inherently' worse than others. Indeed, in the history of weapons-politics there has long been recognition of this possibility, albeit codified with a high degree of ambiguity. For instance, the Martens Clause, a rather vague aspect of many international humanitarian law treaties from the Hague Convention of 1899 onwards, is a blanket provision applying to any action or weapon in war not covered by other treaties. It claims that they are subject to the standards of international law relating to 'the usages established between civilized nations ... the laws of humanity and the requirements of the public conscience' (Preamble to the Hague Convention II 1899). This reference to unspecified principles of 'humanity' and 'public conscience' not only creates space for very wide interpretation or dismissal of the clause but also has contextually been used to justify the use of these more inhumane actions or weapons towards those deemed 'uncivilized' in colonial or counter-insurgent wars.

More concrete mobilizations of the principle, however, have led to some weapons being deemed 'inhumane' by virtue of causing either 'unnecessary suffering' or 'superfluous injury'. This is closely connected to the norm of proportionality. Weapons that cause more suffering than necessary to achieve legitimate military aims are deemed to be 'inhumane'. Successful mobilization of this distinction contributed to bans on incendiary weapons like napalm, blinding lasers, and dum-dum bullets. Indeed, such a characterization of both biological and chemical weapons (combined with being 'inherently indiscriminate') led—eventually—to those categories of weapons being prohibited. Similar arguments have been made about nuclear weapons (such as by the International Court of Justice in 1996).

Of course, such effects are not only part of the politics of making physical violence more 'civilized' through legal restraints but also of the design of weapons, with the history of bullet design shaped by different goals and measures of 'lethality' and 'stopping power' that were formed through a range of scientific, racial, and imperial framings of the utility of violence (Shah 2019). Indeed, one of the key factors that emerges in such debates is whether weapons are likely to cause permanent disability or just temporary effects. The perception that non-lethal weapons avoid lasting harms feeds into their legitimation.

We might also think about the forms of targeting as part of how weapons-systems constitutes the manner of killing. Targeting is a practice of seeing and representing that cannot be reduced to accurately distinguishing between combatants and non-combatants—as if such distinctions are neutral and objective. Rather, the manner in which targets are produced is deeply cultural, political, and technical (Suchman et al. 2017).

For example, in 'signature' drone strikes the target is not a known 'terrorist' or 'militant'. Rather, an individual is identified a target by their behaviours and wider 'pattern of life' (e.g., locations, associations, and everyday movements) (Wilke 2017). Such targeting tends to reify, combine, and act upon racialized and gendered distinctions to determine who can be targeted. Most infamously, during the occupation of Afghanistan, this was through the generic category of 'Military Age Males' (Allinson 2015). Indeed, in drone strikes, and throughout military history, targeting has assembled a wide range of cultural and scientific practices particularly related to different mobilizations of vision (Bousquet 2018). Increasingly, these are argued to blur seemingly given distinctions, as the human and machine are configured as human-machine. Thus, technologies of vision and violence are intimately connected such that seeing and killing are entangled.

The manner of violence also relates to its spatial and temporal organization. For instance, drone strikes have been argued to create a global battlespace, an 'everywhere war' (Gregory 2011). There is therefore a growing blur between policing and war as similar technologies, logics, and practices migrated from war to urban policing (Davis 2019) and border control.

Similarly, in relation to temporality, the nature of weapons technology shapes the time for politics. Early arms control theorists noted that weapons developments in the 1950s 'inhumanly compressed the time available to make the most terrible decisions' and further concentrated nuclear decision-making in the hands of a few (Schelling and Halperin 1961, 3). Currently, developments of hypersonic weapons (that fly beyond Mach 5 and are manoeuvrable in flight, enabling them to reach their targets long before any sonic boom alerts defences) raise concerns about the possibility of political decision-making in both nuclear and conventional war.

Indeed, the development of autonomous weapons-systems may give human personnel very limited capacity to exercise oversight over artificial intelligence kill decisions given that speed is central to the advantages they supposedly offer. Speed is only one dimension of the ordering effects of weapons-politics, with others including omnipresent twenty-four-hour surveillance of armed drones, or the ways in which drone strikes and the everywhere war enable legal notions of 'self-defence' as justification for the use of force to be reconfigured as 'pre-emptive self-defence'.

Overall, then, the manner of violence and killing connects the act of killing or inflicting bodily harm with a much wider political terrain. Weapons-systems contribute to the effects of violence on bodies, shifting practices of targeting, and the spatial and temporal arrangements of physical violence.

17.4 How are weapons controlled?

Weapons-systems conceived as mere instruments become the resources of power projection, deterrence, and a defining feature of international order as questions of who is most powerful or of polarity often rely on measures of military power. Weapons-politics is concerned not only with the incidence and conduct of physical violence, and the ways in which other forms of violence shape physical violence, but also with attempts to control violence by controlling weapons. Here, we encounter the politics that is explicitly about weapons. This includes restricting how weapons spread but regulating who possesses certain types of weapon (non-proliferation), and the ways in which states may agree to limit their weapons-systems to preserve a balance or reduce tension (arms control). It also encompasses the ways in which the reduction or abolition of some weapons is pursued (disarmament). This too is deeply entangled with structural and symbolic violence.

> On the question of legitimacy, see **Section 4.3**

The monopolization of the legitimate use of force is central to what it is to be a state, including gaining and exercising sovereignty. The ability to determine how and when force is used—and the power to successfully claim that this is legitimate—is central to many notions of 'order' whether in the domestic sphere or internationally. Why, then, would any state also seek to place limits on the use of force and the tools of violence? What can such attempts really achieve? Here we must remember our earlier distinction between instrumental and determinist accounts of technology, since these have been formative of assumptions about the *possibility* and *purpose* of limiting the use of physical violence.

Early arms control theorists in the 1950s, for example, were keen to distance themselves from what they saw as the inherent naivete of the pursuit of general and complete disarmament during inter-war years. They did so on the basis of a distinction between disarmament and arms control. Disarmament was cast as a utopian idea based on a misconception. For some of the inter-war disarmament negotiators, war had become anachronistic, and weapons were at best a legacy, and at worst, a potential cause of future conflict (Noel-Baker 1958). In contrast, early Cold War arms control scholars argued that weapons were a mere symptom, not a cause, of political tension. Thus, the management of arms (arms control and non-proliferation rather than disarmament) meant maintaining a prudent balance (Bull 1961).

The dismissal of disarmament (as being based on a dangerous error of attributing casual power to mere instruments) haunts the debate on disarmament to this day as much as it did when it was articulated amid rising faith in the stabilizing effects of nuclear deterrence. While pursuing prudent arms control to stabilize and manage deterrence forms much of what we know about nuclear weapons-politics, it also led many to criticize arms control as an inherently conservative legitimating practice that reinforced the nuclear arms race and the threat of mass destruction.

Weapons-politics is always partly a question of what makes changing the nature and distribution of violence possible or impossible. Certainly arms control (and arms reduction—disarmament by another name) has produced a number of trade-offs. In essence, these are that:

- some states can possess nuclear weapons—as permitted by the 1968 Nuclear Non-Proliferation Treaty—but others should not;
- some weapons deemed excessively injurious, inherently indiscriminate, are largely prohibited—with varying degrees of success if we look at biological or chemical weapons or anti-personnel landmines;
- other 'conventional' arms are regulated in a complex of national and multilateral controls that place often weak restrictions on their trade, but very few on their use or development.

However, these trade-offs are not—as we have noted—merely the logical outgrowth of the technical capacities of weapons. Rather, they result from enacting restraint through political bargains, changing norms, changing meanings, and shifting security agendas.

Cold War-era arms control operated largely within the terms of dominant understandings of weapons (i.e., they provided stability by making nuclear war unthinkable and inducing caution in states) and assumed a managerial role in maintaining a rather precarious balance. Increasingly, however, arms control and disarmament have also been cast as pursuing more transformational humanitarian goals (e.g., landmine bans, arms trade regulation, etc.). What is interesting here is that this has taken the practice of negotiating deals outside of the framework of managing military capabilities. Indeed, it has achieved a degree of success through challenging the ways in which weapons are assumed to be mere instruments and how weapons-politics was framed in terms of strategic balancing rather than bodily harm and suffering.

For example, the negotiation of bans on anti-personnel landmines, cluster munitions, and even nuclear weapons achieved success by reframing weapons away from a situation where instrumentality and military necessity were assumed to a focus on the bodily, humanitarian, and environmental consequences of their use. In each case, victims were brought into the negotiations to make present the harm caused in rooms otherwise full of military experts and diplomatic personnel. This is not to say that such people experienced a Damascene conversion but that it shifted the conversation and the burden of proof.

While such measures are often cast as a victory for notions of humanitarianism and human security, or indeed of moral progress, many scholars also point out that prohibitions and disarmament commitments for 'indiscriminate' or 'inhumane' weapons reflect the self-identification of the West as civilized military powers engaged in the civilizing of warfare. This civilizational politics was present in the nineteenth-century colonial practices of arms control. It was inherited and reproduced in nuclear weapons control and humanitarian arms control today (Cooper 2018). Indeed, even within seemingly progressive moves towards disarmament, the voices and experiences of some states and communities are often diminished to the role of victim on display (Mathur 2020). This rearticulates post-colonial power relations even when non-Western actors (such as the Pacific-island states) exercise some agency in utilizing these civilizational discourses and assumptions of 'responsible' Western nuclear weapons possession to argue for nuclear test bans and the Treaty on the Prohibition of Nuclear Weapons (see Bolton 2018).

> On the connections between security and post-colonial power relations, see **Section 2.2**

The power of Western states to dominate the practice of arms control is most clearly revealed by what is excluded. For instance, practices of humanitarian arms control exclude the majority of conventional weapons from significant regulations. They do not cover the regulation of firearms owned by civilians in powerful states, the procurement and development of major conventional arms, or new high-technology weapons (like hypersonic weapons). At times, these have been on the agenda but were blocked by powerful states (often the United States of America). Similarly, while the agreement of a global Arms Trade Treaty in 2013 was seen by many as a sign of progress in establishing a degree of responsible control over this multi-billion-dollar trade, its effectiveness in controlling transfers of weapons to where they are misused is diminished by being framed in terms of national export controls assessing whether there is an 'overriding risk' that the particular weapons will be used in crimes against humanity. This has been shown to be amenable to manipulation. For example, the United Kingdom, which exports large quantities of arms to Saudi Arabia while it is engaged in war crimes in Yemen, can claim that it conducted such an assessment and, later on, deny responsibility because it did not know that breaches of international humanitarian law were occurring, or that any breaches were isolated incidents or accidents (Stavrianakis 2020). Overall, then, the control of weapons—even when cast in terms of progress—is always also a space where sovereign power and global asymmetries are rearticulated and reinforced.

17.5 How is weapons-politics entangled with other forms of violence and security?

> The notion of militarism is discussed in **Box 7.1**

Different modes of physical violence formed through weapons and the politics of their control connect to a wider set of structures and cultures of violence that shape the processes of weapons-politics. One way to engage this is to think in terms of 'militarism':

> a set of attitudes and social practices which regards war and the preparation for war [or more broadly organized political violence] as a normal and desirable social activity. (Mann 1987, 35)

This includes play and war games but also science and culture—and many of the strategies of legitimation outlined earlier such as fantasies of precision, domination, civilizational discourses, and so on (Mann 1987; Bourke 2014). In diverse ways, then, war and the preparation for it become normalized, seen as inevitable, natural even. This is, partly, framed in terms of the infamous 'military-industrial complex' US President Eisenhower warned of in 1961 whereby companies that design and produce weapons, and military institutions that order, deploy, and use them become a powerful conjoined lobby.

In the twenty-first century, according James Der Derian (2000), this has taken the form of a Military-Industrial-Media-Entertainment Network (MIME-NET). MIME-NET has been central to the emergence of the idea of 'virtuous wars' that presented as 'surgical' through the use of precision-guided munitions. It would be a mistake, then, to see the structural and symbolic violence connected to weapons-politics as solely consisting in the self-interest of powerful defence companies and military officials. Rather, the cultural legitimation of direct violence is how weapons-politics makes the world into its own image.

Similarly, the history of science and technology is shaped by weapon research and particularly the form and extent of the funding dedicated to it. For example, most of the (dramatically expanded) US government funding for science in the early Cold War came from the Department of Defense (Moore 2013). Different forms of government support encouraged or inhibited 'innovation' in weapons-systems by scientists, a dynamic that continues (Evangelista 1988). Certainly, there have been many spin-offs and wider benefits to technologies originally developed in national security and military laboratories or funded by them from weather prediction to the internet or the Global Positioning System (GPS).

But another effect is a structuring of science that means that particular modes of organization, and forms of knowledge, become prioritized. Further, as Kyle Grayson (2016) shows, the logics and values of science and war fighting doctrine in relation to drones are also embedded in values and assumptions derived from capitalism. Speed, adaptability, flexibility, and efficiency—for instance—all connect in extended networks of experts, private companies, think tanks, and maintenance contracts that come to constitute contemporary high-technology war. Of course, scientists and engineers have also led some influential movements to pursue disarmament (e.g., the Pugwash conferences), and sometimes disavow weapons-related research, as in the case of Google workers protesting against involvement in the US Department of Defence's Project Maven which develops artificial intelligence for use in increasingly autonomous weapons-systems. Nevertheless, science and military developments are inextricably linked.

Ultimately, weapons-systems are the materialization of the most extreme and explicit processes of political violence. The crux of this, of course, is about who kills and who dies. The taken-for-granted distinction at work in this question—between combatant and non-combatant—and similarly those between legitimate and illegitimate violence, war and terrorism, defence and policing are not static or isolated from

*See **Chapters 3 and 4***

wider relations of power, order, and violence. Indeed, weapons-politics is pervasive in the way these distinctions are enacted and shift. The carrying of a weapon can be decisive in making the distinction between combatant and non-combatant (both in practices of targeting and in international law). The production of a soldier (or indeed an armed police officer) involves training not just in the use and maintenance of weapons but also through an emotional re-tuning to overcome any aversion to killing (Protevi 2008). Conversely, the ethico-political distinction between intentional killing and accidental casualties legitimizes some weapons and delegitimizes others. The pervasive assumption that security must rest on the threat, use, and control of direct physical violence can thus be opened up to critical reflection by exploring the ways in which this is made through weapons-politics.

17.6 Conclusion

The politics of weapons draws its legitimacy from claims about security and vice versa. Similarly, the politics of violence and security draws its legitimacy from claims about weapons. The dominant understanding, though, remains that weapons are mere tools—the servants of rational decision in the 'threat, use and control of military force' (Walt 1991, 212). As such, most weapons are deemed to be 'conventional' arms—with only those that have become designated as 'inherently indiscriminate' or 'excessively injurious' being prohibited.

*Questioning neutrality is a key attribute of critical thinking; see **Section 1.2***

In this chapter we, have shown that this can be called into question. One of the major effects of viewing weapons as neutral tools is that much is forgotten, and must be forgotten, to sustain this position. What is forgotten are the processes of making weapons (through definitions, conceptualizations, and the cultural practices of science and militarism as well as material production), making them legitimate (through law, discourse, and asymmetric global power relations), and making them kill (through targeting, training, emotion, etc.). These processes reveal how weapons are imbued with power and violence even when they are not being used. Moreover, the ambiguities of weapons reveal assumptions about violence and the ways in which lethal legitimations are entangled with (rather than just attached to) weapons. Weapons-systems make particular forms of violence possible and legitimate by being part of ethico-political distinctions that are drawn, blurred, and broken. Critically questioning security requires some engagement with the supposed inevitability of killing and maiming when security is mobilized. As such, security is shaped, at least in part, through weapons-politics.

Questions for further discussion

1. How does security politics reflect weapons-politics?
2. How are weapons-systems connected to direct physical violence? How are they connected to other forms of violence?

3. What makes weapons-systems legitimate or illegitimate? Why does the question of legitimacy matter in specific socio-political orders?

4. What, if anything, can arms control and disarmament achieve? How are these achievements, or lack thereof, representative of specific hierarchies?

5. In what ways are weapons-systems connected to wider assumptions and cultures of security and violence?

Further reading

MACKENZIE, DONALD. 1990. *Inventing accuracy: A historical sociology of nuclear missile guidance*. Cambridge, MA: The MIT Press.
This is a classic text in STS as well as a fascinating empirical case of how developments in nuclear missile guidance systems affected and were shaped by Cold War weapons-politics. In this way it troubles assumptions of technological progress as being inevitable, and somehow separate from, or determining, politics.

BOUSQUET, ANTOINE. 2018. *The eye of war: Military perception from the telescope to the drone*. Minneapolis, MN: University of Minnesota Press.
The eye of war provides a compelling and intricate history of the connection between weapons and perception in the practice of targeting. This history shows how perceptual technologies and cultures have created many aspects of the manner (speed, space, etc.) of contemporary killing. The wider cultural politics of targeted killing can be engaged through reading Kyle Grayson's 2016 book: *Cultural politics of targeted killing: On drones, counterinsurgency, and violence.* London: Routledge.

RAPPERT, BRIAN. 2006. *Controlling the weapons of war: Politics, persuasion and the prohibition of inhumanity*. London: Routledge.
This is an excellent in-depth engagement with humanitarian weapons-politics that works through how the ambiguities of what weapons are and what they do are contested and settled. It explores how the complexities of what constitutes acceptable violence is entangled with the challenges of devising and enforcing prohibitions.

EDEN, LYNN. 2003. *Whole world on fire: Organizations, knowledge, and nuclear weapons devastation*. Ithaca, NY: Cornell University Press.
The theme of forgetting highlighted in the chapter was partly inspired by this book which shows how the exclusion of knowledge of fire storms fed into the rationalization of nuclear war and led to a larger nuclear arsenal than its war planning required. It is also an important text in thinking through how organizational routines and technologies are co-constituted with important political effects.

KUBRICK, STANLEY. 1964. *Dr Strangelove: Or how I learned to stop worrying and love the bomb*. 94 min. Columbia Pictures.
This movie speaks of the rationalities of nuclear war and deterrence, and engages nuclear weapons through compelling satire. Films have been made or shown by campaigning non-governmental organizations during diverse UN arms control processes, such as the 2017 short film *Slaughterbots* that highlights issues of lethal autonomous weapons-systems, or the 2005 film *Lord of war* (loosely based on a famous arms dealer).

References

Allinson, Jamie. 2015. 'The necropolitics of drones'. *International Political Sociology* 9(2), 113–127.

Bolton, Matthew. 2018. 'The "-Pacific" part of "Asia-Pacific": Oceanic diplomacy in the 2017 treaty for the prohibition of nuclear weapons'. *Asian Journal of Political Science* 26(3), 371–389.

Bourke, Joanna. 2014. *Wounding the world: How military violence and war-play invade our lives*. London: Virago.

Bourne, Mike. 2012. 'Guns don't kill people, cyborgs do: A Latourian provocation for transformatory arms control and disarmament'. *Global Change, Peace, and Security* 24(1), 141–163.

Bousquet, Antoine. 2018. *The eye of war: Military perception from the telescope to the drone*. Minneapolis, MN: University of Minnesota Press.

Bousquet, Antoine, Jairus Grove, and Nisha Shah. 2017. 'Becoming weapon: An opening call to arms'. *Critical Studies on Security* 5(1), 1–8.

Bull, Hedley. 1961. *The control of the arms race: Disarmament and arms control in the missile age*. London: Weidenfeld and Nicolson.

Castrodale, Mark A. 2019. 'Disabling militarism. Theorising anti-militarism, dis/ability and dis/placement'. In *Manifesto for the future of critical disability studies. Volume 1*, edited by Katie Ellis, Rosemarie Garland-Thomson, Mike Kent, and Rachel Robertson. London: Routledge.

Cooper, Neil. 2018. 'Race, sovereignty, and free trade: Arms trade regulation and humanitarian arms control in the age of empire'. *Journal of Global Security Studies* 3(4), 444–462.

Davis, Oliver. 2019. 'Theorizing the advent of weaponized drones as techniques of domestic paramilitary policing'. *Security Dialogue* 50(4), 344–360.

De Larrinaga, Miguel. 2016. '(Non)-lethality and war: Tear gas as a weapon of governmental intervention'. *Critical Studies on Terrorism* 9(3), 522–540.

Der Derian, James. 2000. 'Virtuous war/virtual theory'. *International Affairs* 76(4), 771–788.

Evangelista, Matthew. 1988. *Innovation and the arms race: How the United States and the Soviet Union develop new military technologies*. Ithaca, NY: Cornell University Press.

Federation of American Scientists (FAS). 2021. *Status of world nuclear forces*. https://fas.org/issues/nuclear-weapons/status-world-nuclear-forces (last accessed 24 November 2021).

Fleurant, Aude, Alexandra Kuimova, Diego Lopes Da Silva, Nan Tian, Pieter D. Wezeman, and Siemon Wezeman. 2019. *The SIPRI top 100 arms-producing and military services companies, 2018*. www.sipri.org/publications/2019/sipri-fact-sheets/sipri-top-100-arms-producing-and-military-services-companies-2018 (last accessed 27 November 2021).

Freedman, Lawrence. 2004. *Deterrence*. London: Polity.

Galtung, Johan. 1969. 'Violence, peace, and peace research'. *The Journal of Peace Research* 6(3), 167–191.

Glaser, Charles L. 2000. 'The causes and consequences of arms races'. *Annual Review of Political Science* 3, 251–276.

Grayson, Kyle. 2016. *Cultural politics of targeted killing: On drones, counter-insurgency, and violence*. London: Routledge.

Gregory, Derek. 2011. 'The everywhere war'. *The Geographical Journal* 177(3), 238–250.
Grove, Jairus. 2016. 'An insurgency of things: Foray into the world of Improvised Explosive Devices'. *International Political Sociology* 10(4), 332–351.
Hague Convention. 1899. *Preamble: Convention (II) with respect to the laws and customs of war on land and its annex: Regulations concerning the laws and customs of war on land.* https://ihl-databases.icrc.org/ihl/INTRO/150 (last accessed 21 February 2022).
International Court of Justice. 1996. *Legality of the threat or use of nuclear weapons: Advisory opinion of 8 July 1996.* www.icj-cij.org/public/files/case-related/95/095-19960708-ADV-01-00-EN.pdf (last accessed 23 February 2022).
Kalashnikov, Mikhael with Elena Joly. 2006. *The gun that changed the world.* Translated by Andrew Brown. Cambridge: Polity.
Kleck, Gary. 1991. *Point blank: Guns and violence in America.* New York: Aldine De Gruyter.
Latour, Bruno. 1999. *Pandora's hope: Essays on the reality of science studies.* Cambridge, MA: Harvard University Press.
Lindqvist, Sven. 2001. *A history of bombing.* Trans. Linda Haverty Rugg. London: Granta Books.
Lopes Da Silva, Diego, Nan Tian, and Alexandra Marksteiner. 2021. *SIPRI fact sheet: Trends in world military expenditure, 2020.* www.sipri.org/publications/2021/sipri-fact-sheets/trends-world-military-expenditure-2020 (last accessed 27 November 2021).
MacKenzie, Donald. 1990. *Inventing accuracy: A historical sociology of nuclear missile guidance.* Cambridge, MA: The MIT Press.
Mann, Michael. 1987. 'The roots and contradictions of modern militarism'. *New Left Review* 162, 35–50.
Mathur, Ritu. 2020. *Civilizational discourses in weapons control.* New York: Palgrave Macmillan.
Moore, Kelly. 2013. *Social movements, American scientists, and the politics of the military: 1945–75.* Princeton, NJ: Princeton University Press.
Noel-Baker, Philip. 1958. *The arms race: A programme for world disarmament.* London: Atlantic Books.
Price, Richard. 1997. *The chemical weapons taboo.* Ithaca, NY: Cornell University Press.
Protevi, John. 2008. 'Affect, agency and responsibility: The act of killing in the age of cyborgs'. *Phenomenology and the Cognitive Sciences* 7(3), 405–413.
Rappert, Brian. 2005. 'Prohibitions, weapons and controversy: Managing the problems of ordering'. *Social Studies of Science* 35(2), 211–240.
Scarry, Elaine. 1985. *The body in pain: The making and unmaking of the world.* Oxford: Oxford University Press.
Schelling, Thomas and Morton Halperin. 1961. *Strategy and arms control.* New York: The Twentieth Century Fund.
Shah, Nisha. 2019. 'Ethical dispositions designing the injuries of war'. *Critical Studies on Security* 7(3), 201–218.
Stavrianakis, Anna. 2020. 'Requiem for risk: Non-knowledge and domination in the governance of weapons circulation'. *International Political Sociology* 14(3), 233–251.
Suchman, Lucy, Karolina Follis, and Jutta Weber. 2017. 'Tracking and targeting: Sociotechnologies of (in)security'. *Science, Technology & Human Values* 42(6), 983–1002.

VAN CREVELD, MARTIN. 1989. *Technology and war: From 2000 B.C. to the present*. New York: The Free Press.

WALT, STEPHEN M. 1991. 'The renaissance of security studies'. *International Studies Quarterly* 35(2), 211–239.

WILKE, CHRISTIANE. 2017. 'Seeing and unmaking civilians in Afghanistan: Visual technologies and contested professional visions'. *Science, Technology & Human Values* 42(6), 1031–1060.

ZIMRING, FRANKLIN, 1972. 'The medium is the message: Firearm caliber as a determinant of death from assault'. *Journal of Legal Studies* 1(1), 97–123.

18

Environment

Madeleine Fagan

18.1	Introduction	291
18.2	How should we think about the environment and security?	294
18.3	Three approaches to environment and security	296
18.4	Conclusion: environmental insecurities	303

READER'S GUIDE

In this chapter, we explore the implications of treating the environmental crisis as a security issue. We engage directly with the questions of security for whom, where, and at whose expense. By exploring these questions we gain critical purchase on how claims about the environment and security make visible, and securable, particular worlds while obscuring others, and rendering them insecure. Thus, we can see how attempts to secure the environment are connected to symbolic violence that generates other forms of political violence.

18.1 Introduction

> Illustrative case studies on the topics explored in this chapter are available on the online resources to help take your understanding of the environment further:
> http://www.oup.com/he/Grayson-Guillaume1e.

We are living in a period of unprecedented environmental change. The stable climatic conditions that have allowed human life to flourish are now threatened by our own (in)actions. Measurements in 2016 by the World Meteorological Organization indicated this was the hottest year on record (WMO 2019). Extreme weather events are increasing in frequency and duration. In 2020, there were wildfires in the Arctic and Australia (Bulletin of the Atomic Scientists 2020). The northern hemisphere recently had its hottest summer on record (National Centers for Environmental Information 2020). Record-breaking floods are becoming the 'new normal', threatening human life, infrastructure, and agriculture (UNEP 2020). We face biodiversity loss of a scale so great it has been termed the 'sixth great extinction' (Kolbert 2016). The delicate ecological balance required to support life on earth is under threat. Rising sea levels threaten the habitability of atoll states such as Kiribati (Storlazzi et al. 2018). They also place densely populated delta regions at increased risk of flooding, forcing people to leave their homes and livelihoods and destroying crucial food production.

As we approach surpassing the 2°C threshold for 'safe' global warming above pre-industrial temperatures, the spectre of the 'runaway' heating of the earth emerges. Above 2°C, atmospheric tipping points that control the feedback mechanisms regulating the stable earth system we have inhabited since the last ice age (over 11,700 years) will be passed. The scale of human impact on the planet has led many earth systems scientists and geologists to argue that we have created a new geological epoch in which we are now living: 'The Anthropocene'. This marks changes to the planet and its systems which cannot be reversed (Crutzen 2002).

> *The Anthropocene is discussed in **Box 18.1**.*

In some ways, it is clear that the scale of the challenges we now face is a security issue of the highest order. Environment and climate as threats have featured in the national security policies of a number of Western states, including the United Kingdom and the United States (Cabinet Office 2009; White House 2006), the European Union Global Strategy (European Union External Action Service 2016), and NATO's Strategic Concept (NATO 2010). There is an argument that framing environmental problems in terms of threats to security is the only way to attract the resource and scale of change needed to address them (Campbell 2008). Indeed, for activists such as Greta Thunberg, talk of extinction, emergency, urgency, and risk are central to mobilizing action on climate change (Thunberg 2019).

> *On security as a political mobilization, see **Section 2.4***

However, what is meant when it is claimed that the environment is a security issue is not always clear. When the term 'environmental security' first came to prominence in the 1980s, it was in the context of the Cold War and the military-strategic thinking prevalent at the time. The environment was considered a security issue insofar as it posed a potential threat to the national security of states, understood in traditional terms of military capability and resources (for a similar logic, but concerning health). To cast this in terms of political violence, these early interventions were concerned with the physical violence of war.

> *Chapter 13 examines the connections between health and security in detail*

> *The concept of political violence is discussed in **Chapter 4***

In the 1990s, the broadening of the concept of security to consider risks other than war, and its deepening to consider the security of entities other than the state, shifted the terms of debate around environmental security. Most influentially, environmental security became understood through the emerging framework of human security in which the survival and flourishing of individuals and communities, rather than the state, was the focus (UNDP 1994). Environmental change, it was argued, posed far more of a threat to individuals than to the state. Moreover, environmental threats could not be considered in isolation from issues of welfare, justice, peace, sustainable development, and inequality which made some people more vulnerable than others (Barnett 2001).

> *On broadening security, also see **Section 1.3***

BOX 18.1 THE ANTHROPOCENE

The Anthropocene has been proposed to describe a new epoch in the geological timeline, marked by the impact of humans on the structure of the planet. Clark, Crutzen, and Schellnhuber (2004, 1) define it as 'a new geologic epoch in which mankind has emerged as a globally significant—and potentially intelligent—force capable of reshaping the face of the planet'. Our current geological stage is the Holocene epoch, which began around 11,650 years ago and has been characterized by the warm and stable planetary conditions following the last ice age. In contrast, the Anthropocene is characterized by instability, tipping points, and feedback loops that make planetary conditions unpredictable and change non-linear.

There is debate about when (and if) the shift from the Holocene to the Anthropocene took place. In order for a new geological epoch to be formally accepted into the geological timeline, there must be evidence of a distinctive trace in rock layers that can be found occurring globally at the same time. Usually this is the first appearance of a fossil species, but for the Anthropocene the geological marker proposed is made by the radionuclides created and spread worldwide by the nuclear bomb tests in the early 1950s (http://quaternary.stratigraphy.org/working-groups/anthropocene). This date also reflects the 'great acceleration' in a number of socio-economic and earth-system measures.

Some authors argue that the Anthropocene in fact started much earlier, with the dip in atmospheric CO_2 in 1610 caused by the large decline in human numbers and the regeneration of forest due to the deaths of Indigenous people in the Americas as a result of colonization (Lewis and Maslin 2015). Other suggestions are the start of the Industrial Revolution, the advent of subsistence settlement, animal domestication, and cultivation agriculture (see Autin and Holbrook 2012). Clearly, the different starting dates proposed have different political implications in terms of who is responsible and what worlds are made visible (see Yusoff 2019).

In the social sciences and humanities, it is the challenge that the Anthropocene poses to the human/nature distinction and the interconnected and planetary perspective that it requires which have received most attention. According to Crutzen and Stoermer (see Rudy and White 2013, 128), the insertion of the human into the geological means that there is no 'natural' nature anymore; humans have impacted on it everywhere. Therefore, the advent of the Anthropocene puts into question one of the key organizing logics of modernity upon which much security thinking is built: the separation between human and nature (see Walker 2005).

Since the late 1990s, with advances in environmental science, the expansion of earth-system science, and the adoption of ecological thought by a number of security scholars, the terms of debate have shifted once again. Ecological security approaches start from an understanding of humans and nature as deeply interconnected in complex ways. They argue that securing humans from the effects of environmental change, or securing the environment from the effects of humans, no longer makes sense in the age of the Anthropocene.

Clearly, then, the link between the environment and security is a complex one. In this chapter, we will analyse the different political implications of each formulation of environmental security and to illustrate what is at stake in the debates around this issue.

To do so, we will first introduce a number of questions to consider when assessing claims about environmental security. We will then go on to outline the development of debates in the literature on security and environment to show how understandings of both 'environment' and 'security' have changed and become contested. Throughout, we offer examples of how these questions can be used to open up more detailed analyses of the different approaches to environmental security briefly discussed earlier.

18.2 How should we think about the environment and security?

Hierarchies in security are presented in Section 3.3

The environmental challenges noted in Section 18.1, while often planetary in their scope, affect different people and different places very differently. The types of political violence they enact are not the same everywhere or for everyone. The policies implemented to mitigate their effects affect people and places differently. The structural violence of economic inequality means that privileged citizens of wealthy countries are likely to have the resources to relocate, shield themselves from extreme weather events, access secure food supplies, and benefit from the use of military force to secure scarce resources.

Chapter 14 explores natural resources in more detail

For example, placing caps on industrial production—seemingly essential to slow down the rate at which CO_2 is being released into the atmosphere—has different implications for industrialized states in the West, who have already benefited from the release of more than their 'fair share' of CO_2, than it does for industrializing, or newly industrialized, states such as China who may want to 'catch up'. It means something else again for former colonies whose populations were exploited and enslaved to enable the industrial revolution, and where many extractive industries on which the global north relies—and their associated waste and by-products—are located. The way in which the environment and security are related then depends on *who* we are and *where* we are.

The questions 'security for whom?' and 'where?' are presented in Sections 5.3.1.2–3

Understandings of environmental security also depend on what we think 'counts' as a security issue, what kinds of political violence are considered important, and the problem to which environmental security needs to respond. Rather than focusing on planetary climatic changes, the earth system, complex webs of ecological interaction, and the advent of the Anthropocene, thinking about environment and security could start with the air pollution that kills an estimated 7 million people each year, mainly in low- and middle-income countries. Or the auctioning off of Indigenous lands in Ecuador for oil industry development. Or the threat to ancestral burial grounds, sites of historic importance, and the regional water supply posed by construction of the Dakota Access Pipeline through the Standing Rock reservation in the United States. Or the implications of the reliance by the West on oil and gas supplies controlled by undemocratic regimes.

The different forms of political violence are discussed in Section 4.2.1

Each of these starting points would lead to very different approaches to linking environment and security. Each is concerned with different types of political violence. For example, the symbolic violence which has led to the devaluing of nature, the direct physical violence associated with war, the structural violence which renders particular groups vulnerable to dangerous air pollution, and the symbolic and structural violence necessary to render Indigenous claims invalid.

Linking environment and security then might mean very different things to different people and those meanings can be contradictory. For Indigenous people living close to oil pipelines, environmental security might mean resisting the destruction of marginalized identities and ways of life. For a wealthy state, environmental security might mean ensuring access to sufficient oil supplies to sustain a petro-dependent lifestyle and economy. For resource-rich low-income states, environmental security might mean developing environmentally damaging extractive industries to fund essential infrastructure projects to achieve economic 'development'. For conservationists, environmental security might mean protecting the biodiversity of ecosystems threatened by these projects.

The links between security and development are discussed in **Chapter 12**

These understandings are contradictory. Each focuses on one particular type, site, or agent of violence. In doing so, they potentially obscure others. This points to an important paradox. In seeking security in relation to an issue, identity, idea, interest, institution, or infrastructure, something, or someone else, is usually rendered insecure. Being aware of different types of political violence, their locations, and likely perpetrators can reveal these insecurities.

These enablers are discussed in **Section 3.3**

Often different starting points are the result of linking security to different 'referent objects'; that is, they emerge as a result of different answers to the question of *what are we trying to secure*? Attempts to secure 'the environment' itself are likely to look rather different to attempts to secure 'the state' from possible environmental threats, and different again from attempts to secure 'humans', or particular traditions or ways of life, from those same environmental threats. Importantly, separating out referent objects in this way, and in particular seeking to separate out humans from nature or the environment, is on many readings itself a problematic practice. Particularly, in some bodies of Indigenous thought, the separation of human from nature is itself a violent practice which invalidates and obscures Indigenous life-worlds.

Socio-political orders are explored in **Section 3.2**

The question of what we are trying to secure goes hand in hand with the question of what we think it needs to be secured from; that is, *security from what*? Environmental security discourses might be about extreme weather events threatening lives and livelihoods for example, which produces the environment itself as a threat. They might be about security threats from climate-induced migration, producing dispossessed and marginalized people as a threat. They might be about conflict over scarce resources, producing 'traditional' threats to the state from other political communities. Or, they might be about the human threat to the habitability of the planet.

This particular question is discussed in **Section 5.3.1.5**

Chapter 19 explores links between migration and security

These different ideas about what needs to be secured, and from what, mean that claims about environmental security are *political claims*. In very simple terms, they have winners and losers. In short, securing one thing often means rendering another insecure. The stakes of winning and losing at the politics of environmental security can sometimes be seen very obviously, as in disputes over oil pipelines, access to scarce resources, or disagreements about which states should bear responsibility for reducing carbon emissions. Framing climate-induced migration as a security threat might

Security as a political claim is discussed in **Sections 2.3.2 and 2.4**

make the citizens of wealthy states feel more 'secure', but in doing so it renders those potential migrants deeply insecure.

The stakes, however, are sometimes a little more opaque. Claims that we need to secure the environment, keep fossil fuels in the ground, protect natural spaces, or 'save the Amazon!' similarly render marginalized people (made) dependent on extractive industries (often by the very constituencies calling for the protection of the environment) vulnerable and insecure. Sometimes the political stakes of claims about environmental security are even less easy to spot. This happens when security discourses present some things as 'natural', 'normal', or outside the scope of discussion.

> **Chapter 14** explores the connection between extractive industries and security

For example, the assumption that 'we' are something separate from 'nature' or 'environment' such that one can be secured from the other is put into question both by Indigenous perspectives and by the concept of the Anthropocene (Fagan 2016). In answer to the question of 'what does security do?', the consequences of this assumption include the marginalization of alternative (e.g., Indigenous) ways of viewing the world and the continued naturalization of a particular understanding of the human (associated with autonomy, mastery, and individualism) which has deemed those who do not fit its criteria as less human and thus insecure (see Fagan 2019).

> **Chapter 9** discusses some of these alternative ways of viewing

The question of what or who needs to be secured and from what threat is not a simple one to answer. It might even be the case that security is the wrong way to respond to global environmental change. We suggest that the way in which we formulate the *problem* to which environmental security is the response is of central importance for critically analysing discourses of environmental security. We will show how the different starting points sketched out above direct us to certain answers about who or what is threatened, who or what is doing the threatening, and the kinds of measures that might be appropriate in response to the threat. We will ask you to think about the concrete political consequences each of these formulations of environment and security. Who do they make visible? Whose lives and livelihoods do they assume are important? What histories and inequalities do they obscure and/or perpetuate?

18.3 Three approaches to environment and security

18.3.1 Environment, conflict, and security

Early links between the environment and security focused on how environmental issues impacted on the traditional concerns of security such as violent conflict, the state, and national security. This framing is still central to current governmental discourse on security and climate change (Selby and Hoffmann 2014). As the environment started to be linked to security in the context of the Cold War, the primary concern among Western academics and policy makers was with securing access to essential resources such as oil required to sustain their militaries and the oil-hungry lifestyles of their citizens. Natural resources then became framed as a national security issue—this is sometimes called 'energy security'.

More recent iterations of this theme have pointed to the ways that extreme weather events can directly impact on traditional national security if military bases are vulnerable to those events (Busby 2007). The prospect of 'traditional' security concerns emerging as a result of climate change can also be seen in the example of territorial disputes over the shifting landscape of the Arctic. As the Northwest Passage becomes navigable for the first time in recorded history and the ice retreats over Arctic lands, states with strategic interests in the region such as Canada and Russia have attempted to claim territory and increase their military presence (Campbell 2008).

However, the late 1980s and 1990s saw a shift of emphasis in the linking of environment and security. The *Brundtland Report* published in 1987 highlighted concerns about more general environmental trends such as water scarcity, climate change, and food shortages which were becoming compounded by population growth. It warned that this environmental degradation posed a 'threat to national security', and was potentially a 'source of conflict', mostly in the global south (United Nations 1987, I,2,22; III,11,I). As the global population approached 6 billion in the 1990s, a number of authors argued that population growth and the increasing scarcity of resources such as water, food, forests, and arable land would cause violent conflict in the developing world (see Klare 2001). More recently, some have argued that the conflict in Darfur should be considered a resource war of this type (Welzer 2012).

These approaches offer slightly differing accounts of who, or what, is to be secured. Resource war arguments focusing on the energy security of the West are most straightforward: developed, Western states require access to oil to sustain their militaries. The potential need to engage in armed conflict to secure this poses a direct threat to national security. Resource scarcity of this type also poses threats to Western economies and ways of life (Campbell 2008). However, the potential for widespread civil unrest and conflict in the developing world as a result of scarcity is also argued to pose threats both within and beyond directly affected countries. Political and regional instability, state failure, spill-over conflict, and mass migration are argued to be likely outcomes which impact security on a global scale (UNSG 2009).

A number of studies, however, have indicated that no simple link can be drawn between environmental change and violent conflict (see Homer-Dixon 1999). For these authors, the evidence suggests that environmental scarcity is always linked to other, non-environmental, factors when associated with violent conflict. For example, scarcity can lead to decreased economic productivity, thus contributing to relative-deprivation conflicts, causing further economic decline, and potentially violent conflict. These approaches sometimes describe the environment as a 'threat multiplier', where environmental problems are just one part of a more complex situation. Such an approach has been applied to analyses of the ongoing war in Syria. In 2016, the head of the UN Office for Disaster Risk Reduction argued that the drought of 2008–11 was partially responsible for pushing more of the population into cities, thus exacerbating existing tensions (Rowling 2016).

The route linking the environment and conflict thus begins to look so tortuous that some authors have argued that conceiving of the environment in terms of security threats is not only inaccurate but also counterproductive. In an influential critique, Daniel Deudney (1990) argued that the nature of the challenges posed by environmental change were so different from traditional security concerns of interstate violence that the security framework was the wrong way to approach them. Neither the type of threat posed by environmental degradation nor the responses required fit neatly into traditional state- and military-based security thinking. A national security framing tends to imply military rather than political analyses of and solutions to the problem of environmental change As Simon Dalby (2009, 4) argues, militaries are not well suited to dealing with environmental degradation: 'They are designed, equipped, and trained to break things and kill people, not nurture trees, breed fish, clean river beds, or install solar panels'.

In terms of 'what does security do', a national security framing tends to lead to military, rather than political, approaches to the problem of environmental change. Assuming that population growth will inexorably lead to scarcity and conflict bypasses the political decisions and structural violence that contribute to these outcomes. Peluso and Harwell (2001) show, for example, that it is the inadequate distribution of returns from extraction which leads to conflict rather than environmental issues themselves. A number of authors have also argued that it is in fact resource abundance, rather than scarcity, which is linked to conflict (see Collier and Hoeffler 2005). If we approach environmental conflict as a distributional problem, then sustainable development, or a critique of the capitalist global economy, might be more appropriate frame than security (Dalby 2002).

See **Chapter 14** on natural resources

For many authors critical of the traditional environmental security discourse, environmental crises are not a threat national security, but to dominant structures of production and consumption as well as to modern narratives of growth and progress. To engage effectively with environmental change, we need to think beyond the state and the military and possibly also beyond security. In the following sections, we will introduce two approaches to the environment and security that seek to address these issues.

18.3.2 **Human security**

From a human security perspective, it remains useful to make environmental issues security ones, but only as part of a reorientation away from securing the state and towards securing people. Jon Barnett's (2001, 5) *The Meaning of environmental security* argues for a focus on the human as referent object with the aim of 'making people central' to environmental security discourse.

To return to my opening questions of the different problems to which different understandings of environmental security respond, human security approaches see the problem as the harm done to human life, core values, and practices by environmental degradation (see McDonald 2013). Environmental change, it is argued, more obviously threatens individuals than it does the state or international system. So, for example, rather than viewing climate-induced migration as a threat to the stability of the destination state, a human security approach would see the threat as directed towards those people forced to relocate. The human replaces the state as the referent object of security. Movements such as 'Insulate Britain' are a good example of this kind of approach. As Cameron Ford (2021) argues:

> this is not about protecting polar bears and whales. As important as those things are, it's about creating socially useful, government-funded jobs that protect us . . . [it is] about morality towards our kids and those already suffering in the Global South.

In practice, very often human security approaches are concerned with the lives and communities of marginalized people most vulnerable to climate change. A human security approach seeks to make visible the ways in which vulnerability is not evenly distributed but rather depends on, and intersects with, other forms of insecurity such as poverty, hunger, and weak governance structures. The United Nations Development Programme report of 1994 codified an approach to human security which included environmental security as one of seven interconnected threats, alongside economic security, food security, health security, personal security, community security, and political security. Among the concerns highlighted by the report were access to clean water, land degradation and deforestation, pollution, and the effects of global warming (UNDP 1994). This interconnected approach means the connections linking environment and security are understood differently to traditional approaches. Whereas vulnerability to the effects of environmental change might be seen from a traditional security perspective as creating tensions which could *lead* to insecurity and conflict, for human security approaches environmental stresses on communities are the *result* of intersecting insecurities (Elliott 2015), and uneven forms of structural violence.

In response, a human security approach seeks to minimize that vulnerability and 'enhance adaptive capacities' in the developing world (McDonald 2013, 46). It is closely linked with the notion of sustainable development and enabling communities to develop in resilient ways through a focus on environmental management and natural resource governance. Decreasing vulnerability means enabling individuals and societies to better adapt to the impacts of environmental change (see Adger 2000). The human security agenda then is often focused on ways in which existing structures can be made to better serve a broader range of interests—through commitments to welfare, peace, and justice (Barnett 2001).

However, a human security approach is not without its critics. The focus on building resilient communities is often paired with continued reference to national security, for example in the argument that in more resilient societies environmental pressures are less likely to lead to social unrest and violence (Elliott 2015). Human security is thus tasked both with increasing the security of the marginalized and vulnerable populations which are its primary focus, and, through this, with stabilizing the international system produced as threatened by those vulnerable communities.

This is problematic because the security and development of vulnerable communities can become instrumentalized as a means towards the security of more powerful states or the international system (Duffield and Waddell 2006). Assuming that enhancing development and adaptive capacity in marginalized and vulnerable communities

Chapter 12 explores this theme further; see also **Section 2.2** on the history of security

can simultaneously contribute to international peace and stability does not leave space to consider that the 'international security' from which more powerful states benefit is reliant on the continued vulnerability of some people and places. The idea that the solution to insecurity lies with enhancing adaptive capacity, or sustainable development, *within* vulnerable communities risks obscuring the structural violence and power relationships which *make* certain people and places vulnerable and insecure.

Similarly, as Peter Dauvergne (2016) has argued, modes of consumption in the North impact on the lives of marginalized people growing the crops used in the North or facing disruptions caused by the mines, oil wells, and pipelines required for that consumption. The rising sea level threatening the existence of small island states cannot be overcome by supporting the adaptive capacities of their populations. It is likely that their populations can only be made secure by far-reaching reforms to the ways of life in developed states that contribute to climate change, with the associated economic insecurity in those states that this might entail, or through a rethinking of the foundational links between territory and population which would rescue their populations from the status of climate refugee. As these arguments demonstrate, unless we bring to light the ways in which the security of some is reliant on the insecurity of others, then attempts at adaptation and resilience building will only ever go so far.

On this reading, simply supporting the development of vulnerable communities so that they can better cope with the challenges of environmental change is insufficient. A number of authors have argued that the scope and scale of environmental challenges means that we need instead to seek structural change and a radically new way of thinking about the relationships between humans and the natural world. This is the starting point for approaches to the environment and security that can loosely be grouped under the title 'ecological security'.

18.3.3 Ecological security

Ecological approaches to security focus on the close ties between the human and non-human world, tracing the implications of understanding the biosphere (i.e., the entire global ecological system and the non-living elements with which it is connected) in terms of the complex interdependence of ecosystems. For ecological security, the security of individuals, and of ecosystems, are intertwined. As Dalby (2009, 100) argues, 'we are part of nature, it's part of us'. The ecological security agenda is correspondingly broad, encompassing relations between human societies, nature, pests, disease, demographic change, and economic modes of production. It encourages us to think holistically about the ways in which the environment is woven into the structures of the modern world including states, economies, violence, domination, and the separation of human and nature (Fagan 2016).

There are a number of key themes drawn from ecological thought which are taken up in the ecological security literature. The first is an intrinsic valuing of the non-human sphere (see Plumwood 2002) and a move away from anthropocentrism. This contrasts with the human security perspective which sees the environment as important to the extent that humans 'rely on its functioning for their survival' (Floyd 2010, 8).

The second is an understanding of humans and nature as inextricably interconnected and an understanding of the human as embedded in a broader ecological context (Pirages 2013). The third, drawing on earth-system science, emphasizes the *planetary* interconnectivity of human and natural phenomena conceived in terms of the biosphere and the various planetary processes that determine its stability or otherwise.

It is this interconnected, planetary biosphere which is most often the referent of security for ecological security. More specifically, it is the maintenance of its equilibrium in the face of threats associated with political, economic, and social structures (McDonald 2013). A focus on the biosphere means 'thinking about the whole rather than the parts' (Barnett 2001, 111) when it comes to security. Thus, for many ecological security authors, the ideas of balance and equilibrium between humans and the ecosystem of which they are a part are key.

In concrete terms one way to think about the security of the biosphere is through the notion, drawn from earth-system science, of a 'safe operating space' for humanity (Rockström et al. 2009). This approach focuses on nine interdependent processes that regulate the stability of the earth system: climate change, chemical pollution, ocean acidification, stratospheric ozone depletion, the biochemical flow boundary (nitrogen and phosphorus flows to the biosphere and oceans), global freshwater use, change in land use (e.g., deforestation), biodiversity loss and extinction, and atmospheric aerosol loading.

For each of these processes there is a boundary that marks the maximum allowable impacts within which humanity can operate safely. Once a boundary is transgressed, the possibility of abrupt, non-linear global environmental change emerges including the melting of polar ice sheets, extreme storms, and mass extinctions of wildlife (Rockström and Klum 2015). In 2009 when they introduced the concept, Rockström and his co-authors suggested that three of the boundaries had already been transgressed—climate change, the rate of biodiversity loss, and changes to the global nitrogen cycle. By 2015, researchers had added land-system change to the list of boundaries already crossed (Steffen et al. 2015) (see Figure 18.1).

A focus on a 'safe operating space' offers a very different way to think about security. For the approaches discussed earlier, the environment is seen to pose a threat to the security of the state, the international system, communities, economies, or individuals. An ecological approach overturns this framework, suggesting that these very political, economic, and social structures are the things which threaten the security of the biosphere, and the human as part of it. That is, some ways of life threaten the very thing that they rely upon. Rather than seeking to protect these ways of life, the imperative according to ecological security thinkers is to 'fundamentally rebalance the relationship between people and the natural environment' (McDonald 2013, 48).

For a number of authors, such an ecological sensibility requires far-reaching change; the maintenance of a safe operating space for humanity is not something that can be achieved within current economic and political structures. Dalby (2020) suggests that it is in tension with the growth dynamics at the heart of the global economy and with statist forms of political organization and analysis.

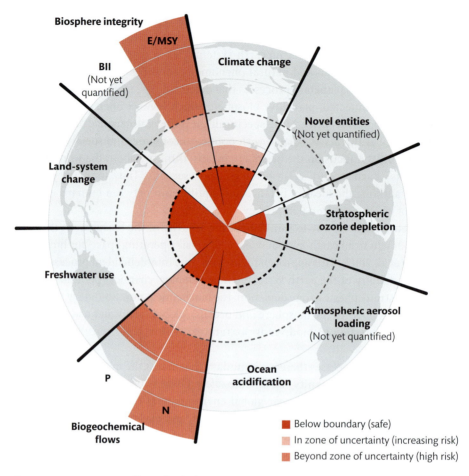

Figure 18.1 Estimates of how the different control variables for seven planetary boundaries have changed from 1950 to the present. The darker shaded polygon represents the safe operating space (Steffen et al. 2015; www.stockholmresilience.org/research/planetary-boundaries/the-nine-planetary-boundaries.html).

Moreover, as a number of authors have argued, since environmental degradation is a product of our current socio-political order which has understood nature as a resource for human domination and consumption, we may need to think outside of our current political, economic, social, and cultural structures in order to deal with it (Fagan 2016). On this reading we cannot secure the current global economy or the dominant socio-political order at the same time as seeking to secure the planet or biosphere; ecological security requires a radical overhaul of our ways of life in contrast to more traditional forms of environmental security which seek to secure them. For some, this means that security is no longer an appropriate way to approach ecological problems at all because it is too bound up in logics of the state, growth, capitalism, individualism, and the devaluing of nature and alternative ways of life. As Dalby (2009) argues, security secures precisely the consumer society that is part of the problem.

Movements such as Extinction Rebellion mirror a number of the themes found in ecological security approaches—the 'war' with which they are concerned is 'between profit and life', with that life understood as an intricate web of human and non-human stretching backwards and forwards across generations (Extinction Rebellion 2021).

Rather than seeking to secure a dominant way of organizing the world, a significant body of work in this area uses ecological insights about interconnection as a prompt to instead make visible other ways of viewing the world (see Whyte 2018). Such an approach highlights the symbolic violence done by the continued separation of the human and nature which devalues alternative ontologies and in turn obscures the physical, psychological, and material violence done to Indigenous and other marginalized communities.

Native or Indigenous cosmologies, for example, frequently start with a conception of living within ecosystems, 'denying . . . opposition, dualism and isolation' (Allen 1996, 243) and instead emphasizing connection and relation between the human and the natural world rather than seeing it as a resource (LaDuke 1999). Similar perspectives offer accounts in which the human and nature are not separate from but integral to one another:

> **Chapter 4** discusses these forms of violence and their consequences

> our truth . . . in a majority of Indigenous societies, conceives that we (humans) are made from the land; our flesh is literally an extension of soil. (Watts 2013, 27)

When we are sensitive to the presence of these perspectives, ecological renewal, the meaning attached to the natural world, the different and overlapping timescales that human and natural processes inhabit, local and community-based knowledge of ecological processes, different understandings of time, history, and obligations to past and future generations, and the power relations that have marginalized these other understandings all become of central importance.

18.4 Conclusion: environmental insecurities

As we have seen, the environment and security can be linked in a number of very different ways. Each makes different assumptions about what kinds of political violence are important. For traditional environmental security approaches, the focus is on the direct physical violence of war. Human security shifts the focus of political violence from the state to the individual level, and identifies the structural violence—from poverty, patriarchy, and underdevelopment for example—which render some individuals vulnerable to environmental degradation. Ecological security maintains this concern with structural violence but goes further and highlights the role of symbolic violence—in particular around the separation of human and nature—in obscuring the complexity of the planetary challenges we face and making some types of structural, physical, and material violence invisible.

Each of these approaches to environmental security has political implications in terms of both whose interests are served and what issues, places, and problems are made visible. Each approach reveals a very different world: the world of access to oil to fuel massive militaries for state security; the world of a subsistence farmer facing the intersecting threats of flooding or drought, poverty, weak state institutions, and political instability; the world of planetary crisis and the 'sixth great extinction'. Each approach seeks to secure not only different referent objects, but also the world it reveals. A focus on one of these worlds as a security issue might directly threaten one of the others; it is important to look for what is being made insecure when security claims are made.

A consideration of the effects of symbolic violence is one route into this kind of critical appraisal of security claims that asks what security 'does'. As we saw in this chapter, the 'worlds' made visible or otherwise are made so by deploying particular categorizations of environment, security, human, and nature. They each enact symbolic violence through reproducing particular hierarchies via these categorizations. For example, categorizing a disaster as 'natural' obscures the structural conditions that render particular groups more vulnerable to it than others. Linking the environment and security enables climate migrants to be framed as security threats. Equating the environment and the natural renders the non-human (and those humans classed as closer to nature) mute and without agency. The reluctance among certain authors in this area to adopt a 'security' lens with which to address problems of environmental degradation can also be understood as a concern about the symbolic violence done by the category of security, as we saw in early critiques of the environmental security agenda.

This is not to suggest that we can somehow do without these kinds of categorizations. As the challenge of moving beyond the human/nature distinction that emerges around ecological security indicates, this would be difficult (and probably not very useful). Instead, thinking in terms of the different worlds made visible or invisible by the different security approaches that we have looked at in the chapter illustrates how all attempts at representation and making sense enact symbolic violence. That is, practices of sense-making create hierarchies. In order to critically analyse the different approaches to environment and security, we need to be attuned to the different ways in which each perpetuates violence.

Questions for further discussion

1. Whose interests are served by the different varieties of environmental security described in the chapter?
2. Is security a useful lens through which to think about environmental degradation?
3. Are 'the human' and 'the environment' separate?
4. Can non-humans cause, or be subject to, political violence?
5. What kinds of violence are done by describing environmental degradation as a security issue?

Further reading

Bonneuil, Christophe and Jean-Baptiste Fressoz. 2017. *The shock of the Anthropocene*. London: Verso.
  Bonneuil and Fressoz offer seven histories of the Anthropocene, which illuminate the political choices, responsibilities, processes, and institutions which have led to it. Their approach is interesting because they show the contingency of particular events, the myriad resistances to environmental destruction, and the paths not followed.

Dalby, Simon. 2009. *Security and environmental change*. Cambridge: Polity.
  Dalby offers an accessible and comprehensive guide to the key debates in environmental security, informed by an ecological approach. He argues that rather than framing the environment as a security threat, environmental change instead requires us to rethink what we mean by security.

Ghosh, Amitav. 2016. *The great derangement: Climate change and the unthinkable*. Chicago, IL: University of Chicago Press.
  Ghosh's book offers a different route into questions about rethinking dominant modes of political, social, and economic organization raised by ecological security approaches. Ghosh shows how it is not only explicit security discourses but also broader cultural elements such as the structure of the novel that perpetuate an 'imagination failure' which limits our ability to engage with the climate crisis.

Yusoff, Kathryn. 2019. *A billion black Anthropocenes or none*. Minneapolis, MN: University of Minnesota Press.
  This short book offers a critical analysis of the Anthropocene which reveals the links between race, colonialism, slavery, and geology. Yusoff shows the political stakes involved in different starting points for the Anthropocene through the lens of critical race studies.

Nixon, Rob. 2011. *Slow violence and the environmentalism of the poor*. Cambridge, MA: Harvard University Press.
  Nixon introduces the concept of environmental degradation as 'slow violence' to describe gradual and invisible violence with no clear perpetrator, rooted in inequality. He shows how this kind of violence, as experienced overwhelmingly by people in the global south, is very easily ignored and yet has calamitous repercussions.

References

Adger, W. N. 2000. 'Social and ecological resilience: Are they related?'. *Progress in Human Geography* 24(3), 347–364.

Allen, Paula G. 1996. 'The sacred hoop'. In *The ecocriticism reader: Landmarks in literary ecology*, edited by Cheryll Glotfelty and Eric Fromm. Athens, GA: University of Georgia Press.

Autin, Whitney J. and John M. Holbrook. 2012. 'Is the Anthropocene an issue of stratigraphy or pop culture?' *GSA Today* 22(7), 60–61.

Barnett, Jon. 2001. *The meaning of environmental security: Ecological politics and policy in the new security era*. London: Zed Books.

Bulletin of the Atomic Scientists. 2020. *Closer than ever: It is 100 seconds to midnight. 2020 doomsday clock statement.* https://thebulletin.org/doomsday-clock/2020-doomsday-clock-statement (last accessed 9 January 2022).

Busby, Joshua. 2007. *Climate change and national security: An agenda for action.* New York: Council on Foreign Relations.

Cabinet Office. 2009. *The national security strategy of the United Kingdom: Update 2009. Security for the next generation.* https://assets.publishing.service.gov.uk/government/uploads/system/uploads/attachment_data/file/229001/7590.pdf (last accessed 9 January 2022).

Campbell, Kurt. Ed. 2008. *Climatic cataclysm: The foreign policy and national security implications of climate change.* Washington, DC: Brookings Institution Press.

Clark, W. C., P. J. Crutzen and H. J. Schellnhuber. 2004. 'Science for global sustainability'. In *Earth systems analysis for sustainability*, edited by H.J. Schellnhuber, P.J. Crutzen, W. C. Clark, C. Martin, and H. Hermann. Cambridge, MA: MIT Press.

Collier, Paul and Anke Hoeffler. 2005. 'Resource rents, governance, and conflict'. *The Journal of Conflict Resolution* 49(4), 625–633.

Crutzen, Paul. 2002. 'The Anthropocene: Geology by mankind'. In *Coping with global environmental change, disasters and security: Threats, challenges, vulnerabilities and risks*, edited by Hans G. Brauch, Úrsula Oswald Spring, Czeslaw Mesjasz, John Grin, Patricia Kameri-Mbote, Béchir Chourou, Pál Dunay, and Jörn Birkmann. Berlin: Springer.

Dalby, Simon. 2002. *Environmental security.* Minneapolis, MN: University of Minnesota Press.

Dalby, Simon. 2009. *Security and environmental change.* Cambridge: Polity.

Dalby, Simon. 2020. *Anthropocene geopolitics: Globalization, security, sustainability.* Ottawa: University of Ottawa Press.

Dauvergne, Peter. 2016. *Environmentalism of the rich.* London: MIT Press.

Deudney, Daniel. 1990. 'The case against linking environmental degradation and national security'. *Millennium: Journal of International Studies* 19(3), 461–476.

Duffield, Mark and Nicholas Waddell. 2006. 'Securing humans in a dangerous world'. *International Politics* 43(1), 1–23.

Elliott, Lorriane. 2015. 'Human security/environmental security'. *Contemporary Politics* 21(1), 11–24.

European Union External Action Service. 2016. 'Shared vision, common action: A stronger Europe. A global strategy for the European Union's foreign and security policy'. Brussels: European Union External Action Service.

Extinction Rebellion. 2021. 'Why we rebel'. https://extinctionrebellion.uk/the-truth/about-us (last accessed 9 January 2022).

Fagan, Madeleine. 2016. 'Security in the Anthropocene: Environment, ecology, escape'. *European Journal of International Relations* 23(2), 292–314.

Fagan, Madeleine. 2019. 'On the dangers of an Anthropocene epoch: Geological time, political time, and post-human politics'. *Political Geography* 70(1), 55–63.

Floyd, Rita. 2010. *Security and the environment: Securitisation theory and US environmental security policy.* Cambridge: Cambridge University Press.

Ford, Cameron. 2021. 'Insulate Britain: "Stand with us against UK government or face end of civilisation"'. *Open Democracy.* 16 November. www.opendemocracy.net/en/opendemocracyuk/insulate-britain-stand-with-us-against-uk-government-or-face-end-of-civilisation (last accessed 9 January 2022).

HOMER-DIXON, THOMAS. 1999. *Environment, scarcity and violence*. Princeton, NJ: Princeton University Press.
KLARE, MICHAEL. 2001. *Resource wars: The new landscape of global conflict*. New York: Henry Holt.
KOLBERT, ELIZABETH. 2016. *The sixth extinction: An unnatural history*. London: Bloomsbury.
LADUKE, WINONA. 1999. *All our relations: Native struggles for land and life*. Cambridge, MA: Southend Press.
LEWIS, SIMON L. and MARK A. MASLIN. 2015. 'Defining the Anthropocene'. *Nature* 519(7542), 171–180.
MCDONALD, MATT. 2013. 'Discourses of climate security'. *Political Geography* 33(1), 42–51.
National Centers for Environmental Information. 2020. 'Global climate report: August 2020'. 14 September. www.ncdc.noaa.gov/sotc/global/202008 (last accessed 9 January 2022).
North Atlantic Treaty Organization (NATO). 2010. *Active engagement, modern defence: Strategic concept for the defence and security of the members of the North Atlantic Treaty Organization*. www.nato.int/nato_static_fl2014/assets/pdf/pdf_publications/20120214_strategic-concept-2010-eng.pdf (last accessed 9 January 2022).
PELUSO, NANCY and EMILY HARWELL. 2001. 'Territory, custom and the cultural politics of ethnic war in West Kalimantan, Indonesia'. In *Violent environments*, edited by NANCY PELUSO and MICHAEL WATTS. Ithaca, NY: Cornell University Press.
PIRAGES, DENNIS C. 2013. 'Ecological security: A conceptual framework'. In *Environmental security: Approaches and issues*, edited by RITA FLOYD and RICHARD A. MATTHEW. London: Routledge.
PLUMWOOD, VAL. 2002. *Environmental culture: The ecological crisis of reason*. London: Routledge.
ROCKSTRÖM, JOHAN and MATTIAS KLUM, with PETER MILLER. 2015. *Big world, small planet: Abundance within planetary boundaries*. London: Yale University Press.
ROCKSTRÖM, JOHAN, WILL STEFFEN, KEVIN NOONE, ÅSA PERSSON, F. STUART CHAPIN III, ERIC LAMBIN, TIMOTHY M. LENTON, MARTEN SCHEFFER, CARL FOLKE, HANS J. SCHELLNHUBER, BJÖRN NYKVIST, CYNTHIA A. DE WIT, TERRY HUGHES, SANDER VAN DER LEEUW, HENNING RODHE, SVERKER SÖRLIN, PETER K. SNYDER, ROBERT COSTANZA, UNO SVEDIN, MALIN FALKENMARK, LOUISE KARLBERG, ROBERT W. CORELL, VICTORIA J. FABRY, JAMES HANSEN, BRIAN WALKER, DIANA LIVERMAN, KATHERINE RICHARDSON, PAUL CRUTZEN, and JONATHAN FOLEY. 2009. 'Planetary boundaries: Exploring the safe operating space for humanity'. *Ecology and Society* 14(2), 32ff.
ROWLING, MEGAN. 2016. 'Stop ignoring costs of smaller disasters: U.N. Risk Chief'. *Reuters*, 21 January. www.reuters.com/article/us-climatechange-disaster-risks-idUSKCN0UZ12U (last accessed 9 January 2022).
RUDY, ALAN and DAMIAN WHITE. 2013. 'Hybridity'. In *Critical environmental politics*, edited by CARL DEATH. London: Routledge.
SELBY, JAN and CLEMENS HOFFMANN. 2014. 'Rethinking climate change, conflict and security'. *Geopolitics* 19(4), 747–756.
STEFFEN, WILL, KATHERINE RICHARDSON, JOHAN ROCKSTRÖM, SARAH E. CORNELL, INGO FETZER, ELENA M. BENNETT, REINETTE BIGGS, STEPHEN R. CARPENTER, WIM DE VRIES, CYNTHIA A. DE WIT, CARL FOLKE, DIETER GERTEN, JENS HEINKE, GEORGINA M. MACE, LINN M. PERSSON, VEERABHADRAN RAMANATHAN, BELINDA REYERS, and SVERKER SÖRLIN. 2015. 'Planetary boundaries: Guiding human development on a changing planet'. *Science* 347(6223), 736–746.

Storlazzi, Curt D., Stephen B. Gingerich, Ap van Dongeren, Olivia M. Cheriton, Peter W. Swarzenski, Ellen Quataert, Clifford I. Voss, Donald W. Field, Hariharasubramanian Annamalai, Greg A. Piniak, and Robert McCall. 2018. 'Most atolls will be uninhabitable by the mid-21st century because of sea-level rise exacerbating wave-driven flooding'. *Science Advances* 4(4). DOI: 10.1126/sciadv.aap9741

Thunberg, Greta. 2019. 'Speech to the UN Climate Action Summit 2019'. www.youtube.com/watch?v=KAJsdgTPJpU (last accessed 9 January 2022).

United Nations. 1987. *Report of the World Commission on Environment and Development: Our common future.* Oxford: Oxford University Press.

United Nations Development Programme (UNDP). 1994. *Human Development Report 1994.* Oxford: Oxford University Press.

United Nations Environment Programme (UNEP). 2020. 'How climate change is making record-breaking floods the new normal'. 3 March. www.unenvironment.org/news-and-stories/story/how-climate-change-making-record-breaking-floods-new-normal (last accessed 9 January 2022).

United Nations Secretary General (UNSG). 2009. *Climate change and its possible security implications. Report of the Secretary General.* 11 September. https://digitallibrary.un.org/record/667264?ln=en (last accessed 31 January 2023).

Walker, R.B.J. 2005. 'On the protection of nature and the nature of protection'. In *The politics of protection*, edited by Jef Huysmans. London: Routledge, pp. 189–202.

Watts, Vanessa. 2013. 'Indigenous place-thought and agency amongst humans and non-humans (First woman and sky woman go on a European world tour!)'. *Decolonization: Indigeneity, Education and Society* 2(1), 20–34.

Welzer, Harald. 2012. *Climate wars: What people will be killed for in the 21st century.* London: Polity.

White House. 2006. *The National Security Strategy of the United States of America.* www.comw.org/qdr/fulltext/nss2006.pdf (last accessed 9 January 2022).

Whyte, Kyle P. 2018. 'Indigenous science (fiction) for the Anthropocene: Ancestral dystopias and fantasies of climate change crises'. *Environment and Planning E: Nature and Space* 1(1–2), 224–242.

World Meteorological Organization (WMO). 2019. 'WMO confirms past 4 years were warmest on record'. 6 February. https://public.wmo.int/en/media/press-release/wmo-confirms-past-4-years-were-warmest-record (last accessed 9 January 2022).

Yusoff, Kathryn. 2019. *A billion black Anthropocenes or none.* Minneapolis, MN: University of Minnesota Press.

19

Borders and mobility

Benjamin J. Muller

19.1	Introduction	309
19.2	Identity: whose security?	313
19.3	Surveillance, ID technology, and the virtual border: where is security?	316
19.4	Deadly deterrence: when enhanced security leads to insecurity	318
19.5	Conclusion	320

READER'S GUIDE

Borders and bordering practices are presented as essential to security. Conversely, forms of mobility are framed as threats, and in the process mobile actors are regularly rendered precarious and dehumanized. How should we understand borders as spaces of contestation? To what extent are borders and mobility about the production and negotiation of belonging and precarity, sometimes violently, along hierarchies of class, gender, race, sexuality, Indigeneity, and territoriality? In this chapter, we focus on territorial sovereign borders and demonstrate the extent to which borders, bordering practices, and boundary making are framed as 'belonging' and mobility well beyond territoriality.

19.1 Introduction

Illustrative case studies on the topics explored in this chapter are available on the online resources to help take your understanding of borders and mobility further: http://www.oup.com/he/Grayson-Guillaume1e.

Migrants clinging to a perilous raft, drifting across the Mediterranean Sea, are left to perish while nearby commercial vessels choose not to intervene. Lost souls find themselves wandering through the Sonoran Desert in North America's southwest, disorientated from the oppressive heat and severe dehydration. Suddenly, the migrants scatter to seek shelter from the oppressive gaze of Department of Homeland Security drones. Migrants flee Haiti to the shores of the United States and forgotten paths, far away from ports of entry along the Canadian border, seeking refuge from political and economic instability aggravated by persistent climate disasters, only to face a violent rebuke from the state and a fundamental denial of their humanity and the colonial legacy that sent them north.

Unfortunately, migrants die trying to cross borders. Migrants find themselves in dangerous and precarious geographies, traversing barren washes, dangerous mountain passes, high seas, and fortified areas on the outer periphery of nation-states. If migrants successfully thwart these natural and national impediments to their mobility, they are regularly detained within crowded refugee camps or incarcerated in private or state-run detention facilities. These examples, and countless others, tell a story of insecurity, precarity, and dehumanization. They frame mobility as a threat for which borders are represented as an imperfect but practical solution, or as what Mountz (2020) refers to as the contemporary death of asylum itself.

One can also consider a rather different experience. From January to May 2008, I was a visiting research fellow at the Border Policy Research Institute at Western Washington University in Bellingham, Washington. Approximately 60 kilometres from the Canadian border, Bellingham is a relatively easy commute by automobile from much of the populated suburban communities surrounding Vancouver, British Columbia, Canada. During my five months as visiting fellow, I crossed the Canada–US border between three and four days per week, totalling between six and eight crossings per week over the course of twenty weeks. My research fellowship also coincided with the commencement of the Western Hemisphere Travel Initiative (WHTI), a US policy that made passports and other approved identity documents mandatory for successful crossing of the US border (see Muller 2010a). In part because of this new policy, and my interests in the changes to US border security and the management of the Canada–US border, I enrolled in the binational government-trusted traveller programme: NEXUS.

A bilateral programme designed to speed up border crossing for 'low risk, pre-approved travellers', NEXUS is run jointly by the Canada Border Services Agency (CBSA) and the U.S. Customs and Border Protection (CBP) (Government of Canada 2021). Applicable at both land crossings and airports, NEXUS provides expedited clearance, and over time has become reliant on self-serve kiosks that, among other things, match the biometric data of the individual with the NEXUS pass. To obtain the pass, an 'interview' is conducted by officials from both Canada and the US. In both cases, security and the pre-assessment of your risk profile is the objective, but it differs dramatically how, when, for whom, and so on. In the US interview, risk assessment is related to your personal travel history, political affiliations, personal history, and even ethnic background. This example shows how identity and security become intermeshed, as identity is framed as an essential part of the risk assessment. In sharp contrast, the Canadian interview focused on the commercial aspects of mobility:

restrictions on purchasing amounts, limits on controlled substances, and duties owed. This experience, and the NEXUS programme itself, speaks to contemporary trends with mobility and borders, wherein the 'treasures' of the modern welfare state are prized and protected, while those hoping to gain access are pre-assessed, profiled, and made precarious.

This chapter considers the security politics of borders and mobility. We expect many of the questions about borders and mobility to focus on national border agencies, ports of entry, immigration and refugee policies, legal regimes, practices of detention, deportation, and perhaps even recognition of or adherence to international laws and norms surrounding asylum. Within these contexts, the question of security is relatively straightforward: the resilience of the territorial sovereign state is premised on its monopoly of legitimacy, authority, and violence. Mobility is one among many potential threats faced by the state, and that threat is met at the border.

Chapter 20 explores the question of detention in more detail

See **Box 19.1** on territoriality

BOX 19.1 TERRITORIALITY

As a principal way to view and understand political space, territoriality is a key organizing principle: it portrays geographic political space as 'a series of blocks defined by state territorial boundaries' (Agnew 1994, 55). Borders are the lines and limits of the domestic politics contained within these geographic spaces that are defined territorially. The story of sovereignty's emergence, as the governing principle of territorial politics, remains contested (see Walker 1993, 168). However, the Treaty of Westphalia of 1648 has become a mythical account in many scholarly fields, beyond an historically accurate depiction, to designate how states practice domestic politics autonomously from the influence and interference of other states (Osiander 2001).

Behind the idea(l) of the so-called Westphalian order are specific notions of authority and legitimacy (see Sections 4.3–4) which privilege the dominance of the territorial state as the dominant unit of global politics. This idea(l) of a Westphalian order also concerns the location and limits of the political community in terms of identity (citizenship) and difference (others) (see Chapters 9 and 11). Borders, and mobility, are therefore central issues in the construction of a modern political imagination as it confronts the maintenance of the territorial limit of politics—the territorial state border—and the continuity of identity of the political community. The question of borders and the bodies that cross them is a central question in analysing security insofar as the territorial sovereign state dominates the security imaginary behind the state. This is what John Agnew (1994) calls the 'territorial trap'. The trap, to some extent, precludes nuanced, heterogenous, and complex scales such as local and global for the sake of elegant simplicity of domestic and international, inside and outside, us and them. As noted in this chapter, one way to distinguish the border from bordering practices is the extent to which practices of bordering speak to strategies of political violence through the mobilization of security, notably through othering difference (see Chapter 9), which leads to the inclusion and exclusion of individuals and groups that are not necessarily aligned with an imagined territoriality and sovereign border.

> These different questions are discussed in **Sections 5.3.1.1-3** and **5.3.2.3**
>
> **Chapter 10** discusses gender and queer identities; **Chapter 18** discusses climate crises; **Chapters 9** and **11** discuss political belonging
>
> see **Section 2.3.2** on security as a political claim
>
> On the distinction between security as a threshold and a process, see **Sections 2.3.1-2**

When speaking of mobility and borders, where is security enacted? By whom is security enacted and with what consequences? These questions allow for more nuanced stories that move one from a vision of borders and mobility as inherently in tension to one that problematizes such simplistic accounts. Instead, we should scrutinize the conditions under which mobility is prompted, be that due to the persecution of queer identities, climate crises, shared historical and territorial claims, or specific challenges for women and children, to consider the breadth of security and insecurity that is far from the territorial border.

The extent to which migrants, and mobility itself, are made precarious and even dehumanized should also be exposed and critiqued, as should the central role of security, as a political claim, within these formulations of borders and mobility. The security and insecurity of mobile actors is as much a part of the narrative and focus of analysis as the border policies, law enforcement agencies, and security strategies. It is also worth noting that similar dynamics are present in non-state scenarios. Challenging socio-economic borders, ageist divides, and even aesthetic and intellectual boundaries are regularly framed as contrary to the status quo, and pejoratively disruptive. As such, security is understood as the preventative actions undertaken to manage the insecurity and danger posed by people crossing borders.

Security, as a political claim, is also present in bordering practices and boundary making that exist far from the sovereign borders of a given territory. Here, security is a threshold and a process; it is about the capacity to perform bordering practices and boundary making, as well as managing and controlling the integrity of the border (i.e., to make the border a barrier to unwanted inflows and permeable to desired inflows). Yet, in empirical terms, one cannot prove that borders are effective, and as such an endless process of boundary making is necessary to serve the interests of security. Walls are built at borders, and still, borders remain porous. Endless fortification leads to further dissatisfaction and gives rise to perceptions of the persistence of insecurity. In terms of borders, and the impractical and imperfect question of effectiveness, measuring the immeasurable leads to a proliferation of strategies that are inevitably unsatisfactory. More checkpoints, walls, surveillance, drones, biometric identification cards, and so on cannot solve the alleged problem of insecurity or control. There will still be those who cross borders, challenge boundaries, undermine bordering practices, and inhibit attempts at boundary making.

What may appear to be straightforward questions provide productive avenues for analysis. Perhaps most obvious, by taking security as a contested concept, the security of mobility itself, and those who are mobile, is called into question, drawing attention to how the security of mobility may at times be at odds with the security of the state (as noted earlier). In this chapter borders and bordering practices are understood as more than lines that demarcate sovereign jurisdictions. For example, consider the demarcations of urban spaces that often follow and reinforce socio-economic class, ethnicity, in some cases even gender identity; or the spatial and intellectual lines drawn to separate Indigenous and non-Indigenous peoples. By asking where security is enacted, what is being secured, by whom, and the consequences of these security mobilizations, we can consider how borders and mobility reproduce forms of violence set out in Chapter 4. The politics of borders is manifest in enhancing and removing privilege and precarity, movement and stasis, the status quo and resistance, often along the lines of class, gender, race, social norms, and practices.

Security in terms of bordering is unsatisfying in its unattainability. However, this serves the interests of those promoting bordering and boundary making, as the demand for borders is always growing, expansive, and never achieved. This chapter prompts us to understand that although borders and mobility are often connected to the borders of sovereign states, they can also be present well away from those charged spaces, or, as Nick Vaughan-Williams puts it, the border may be 'not where it's supposed to be' (Vaughan-Williams 2012, 15). It also seeks to raise our awareness of precarious mobilities (for a great example of this, look at the Undocumented Migrant Project and the related Hostile Terrain 94 participatory art project: www.undocumentedmigrationproject.org/hostileterrain94).

Considering how identity is connected to security opens many of the categories of violence described in Chapter 4 and raises the question 'whose security?' These categories allow us to unpack the ways in which we might critically analyse borders and mobility, and specifically what or who is made secure and what or who is rendered insecure and precarious. It is not just whose security is important, but also how security is exercised (or, one might argue, abused), and at what cost. Finally, the alleged unintended consequences of violence are questioned by reframing them as intended and intentional. Most notably, the doctrines of deadly deterrence exercised by states and non-states regularly take advantage of perilous borderland geographies, which through a discourse of unintended consequences regularly permit the state to evade responsibility for intensely precarious and even deadly forms of mobility.

> We elaborate on this question in **Section 5.3.1.2**

19.2 Identity: whose security?

Political theorist Wendy Brown's influential *Walled borders, waning sovereignty* (2014) contends that the increasing prevalence of border walls is not a sign of the resilience of sovereign power, but an indication of sovereignty's fragility. Along similar lines, many others have highlighted that although border walls are globally prolific, this represents a more complicated story about the ways in which sovereignty is increasingly under threat, scrambling to assert its ever-diminishing monopoly over violence, legitimacy, authority, and certainly the control of mobility (see Jones 2012; Vallet 2014). Although much of this literature speaks of sovereign borders, borders of various sorts, and bordering practices, have similarly proliferated. These range from the demarcation of socio-economic classes to sexual orientation, race, and even what Paolo Virno (2004) refers to as 'ways of being'.

Coinciding with state responses to the COVID-19 pandemic, and the deep inequities exposed by these responses, such measures were accompanied by the bordering of urban spaces, occupational practices, healthcare, and vaccination strategies. This coincided with an intensification in police violence, corresponding calls to defund the police (see Maynard 2020), the mobilization of Black, Indigenous, and People of

> Legitimacy and authority are covered in **Sections 4.3–4**

Colour (BIPOC) groups such as Black Lives Matter (www.blacklivesmatter.ca) and Indigenous Lives Matter such as 'Idle No More' (https://idlenomore.ca), and challenges to state reinforced heteronormativity, such as the 'Rainbow Railroad' (www.rainbowrailroad.org). Not unlike the 'strugglefield' (Tazzioli 2015) of borders and migration, these examples of bordering and the responses and resistance to them represent similar dynamics to what Peter Nyers refers to as 'un/making citizenship through anti/deportation' in which the irregular is faced off against the regular, those whose subjectivity is rendered more and more precarious, and those whose rights and subjectivity is more consolidated (Nyers 2019). Although nation-state borders and the migrants attempting to traverse these fortified borderlands are the exemplars of this making/unmaking of (ir)regularity, similar phenomena are present in our urban landscapes, in our schools, at our workplaces, in our colleges and universities, as well as in our popular culture, our aesthetics and architecture, and so on (see Muller et al. 2016). Like the tensions between extending and/or protecting the rights and privileges of the welfare state to those migrating from elsewhere, the spaces and practices associated with privilege that equally rely on class, gender, and race bear witness to the violence of borders and bordering.

> **Chapter 11** explores the links between citizenship and security

Long before President Donald Trump embarked on the construction of a massive border wall along the southern US frontier with Mexico, various strategies located at a distance from the border were at play and serving to secure identity. Asking the question 'whose security?' releases a wave of compelling and complex issues surrounding borders and mobility that are otherwise not analytically captured. These issues can expose the extent to which security, or insecurity, involves actors and institutions other than the state, migrants, and/or other mobile bodies. At times, securing specific notions of identity, interests, institutions, and infrastructures may serve the overall strategy to 'secure the border', but in doing so also consistently contribute to the production of migrants as precarious. In other words, asking about whose security can expose racist and exclusionary practices that enhance borders and undermine mobility, but appear to be doing something altogether different. It is important to expose this production of precarity as well as opening space for the migrants' own stories.

The US border state of Arizona enacted bills in the state Senate and House during 2010 that were instrumental in the story of borders and mobility, as well as security and violence. However, these legislative changes had nothing to do with border agents, the Department of Homeland Security, drones, surveillance, immigration policy, or other high-tech security and surveillance capabilities that were also proliferating during this same period. As noted in Chapter 4, violence can take many forms. In the case of the state of Arizona, some observers argued that conservative legislators managed to control both bodies and minds (Amster 2011). Basically a 'show us your papers' law, Senate Bill 1070 (SB1070) enabled law enforcement officers to request identity documents from anyone. The request was largely based on racial profiling and appealed to a logic of 'attrition through enforcement' (Amster 2011). Controlling the minds of students became manifest in House Bill 2281 which imposed a ban on the teaching of ethnic studies in public schools in the state of Arizona, in which approximately

50 per cent of the students were Hispanic (Amster 2011). Although more conventional security strategies along the physical border continued, posing questions about who and what is being secured, and taking seriously different types of violence, draws our analytical gaze to changes to public school curriculums and enhanced law enforcement powers that are essential aspects of border and mobility stories in the US–Mexico borderlands of the early decades of the 2000s.

Asking questions about who is being secured, from whom, and how forms of violence are manifest therein helps us to unpack the way in which mobility is itself framed as a security issue. If we don't ask these questions, we are left to examine border security policies, immigration and asylum laws, and facts and figures about the numbers of Border Patrol agents, or the ballooning budget of Customs and Border Protection, or FRONTEX, which most definitely tells a story about borders and mobility. However, it is by no means a complete story, and it might even be misleading. The question of 'whose security?' brings us in direct contact with identity and its role in questions of security and the exercise of violence.

The question of identity is often at the heart of conversations about mobility and borders. Recognizing the spread of market forces, sovereignty has little to say when it comes to global trade and commerce. Coincidentally, such spheres are relatively hollow in terms of the conventional bundle of issues, practices, traditions, rituals, and so on generally associated with identity (see Donnan and Wilson 1999). Although branding and consumptive habits have a role to play, the sovereign state remains a key contributor to identity. The maintenance of national mythologies and origin stories, or what Eric Hobsbawm and Terence Ranger call 'the invention of tradition' (Hobsbawm and Ranger 1992), is often most evident at the border.

Those living in the borderlands often reject the differentiations between us and them, mobile and inactive, friend and enemy, determined by borders and their management of mobility. This presents a sharp contrast between the common conceptions of border security that applaud exclusionary practices and limitations on mobility, and how integral mobility and more hybrid identities are to borderland identities. Again, the question 'whose security?' troubles the analysis, highlighting the nuances and the identities that thrive in the uncertain spaces of the borderlands.

Secondary inspection is a common practice at most borders. This involves directing those at the Port of Entry to more involved and sometimes invasive search and inquisition beyond the initial queries one encounters at the border. The reasons behind this decision are usually connected to risk assessments and profiling. Rates of secondary inspection at ports of entry, quantities of daily border crossings, and numbers of Customs and Border Protection agents deployed provide a narrative of borders and mobility and the experience of security and violence that is not incorrect. However, such accounts fail to engage the way in which language policies, school curriculums, and profiling that rests on narratives of racial purity are equally relevant in comprehending how borders and mobility are negotiated. To this end, asking about where security is helps uncover the extent to which sovereign borders emerged as a pre-eminent site of security after the events of 11 September 2001.

19.3 Surveillance, ID technology, and the virtual border: where is security?

In response to the events of 11 September 2001 and the US-led Global War on Terror that followed, perceived terrorist threats momentarily closed borders and dramatically slowed global travel. Although there was no connection between the events perpetrated on 11 September 2001 and border security or migration policy, the events nonetheless led to global changes to the international passport regime and created new norms in both border and mobility management. The new regime became heavily reliant on surveillance, biometrics, and artificial intelligence (AI). The response to 'where is security?'—or perhaps more correctly, 'where is insecurity?'—caused many policy-makers and media commentators to point to the border. As a result, a host of repressive and exceptional tactics were deployed. Yet, these measures only served to entrench the perception that borders are an insecure space. This was further entrenched by narratives of threat, danger, risk, and uncertainty that unleashed a constellation of strategies to manage mobility.

Eager to return to some sort of 'new normal', citizens were more than willing to accept the changes with little public debate and deliberation (not unlike the situation surrounding government responses to COVID-19; see Cooke and Muller 2021). The use of identification technologies, such as biometrics, an intensification of surveillance, and the pre-assessment of mobility in all its forms, was motivated by a model of 'governing through risk' (Aradau and van Munster 2016; Muller 2010b). These innovations changed borders and mobility in qualitative ways, transforming the border from a barrier into a 'sorting' mechanism. When asking where security is, the answer that increasingly emerged was wherever complex forms of surveillance and identification technology is present; its absence came to be equated with insecurity.

In the years following 11 September 2001, mobility was framed as a security issue in deeply problematic ways. By drawing on surveillance tactics and identification technologies, these problematic understandings were amplified. Preoccupied with deploying surveillance and biometrics to verify that 'you are who you say you are', these technologies also assess risk and sort individuals. Thus, borders and technologies became part of an apparatus that assigned worth, differential opportunities, levels of access, and forms of prevention that could accelerate or disrupt movement. In what David Lyon (2002) refers to as 'social sorting', intensifying pre-existing social categories of gender, race, and class (Beauchamp 2009; Browne 2015) are used to differentiate and classify. Asking questions about who is being secured, from whom, where, and for what purpose yet again provides a more nuanced account of this important development in borders and mobility. In terms of where, in much the same way that Afghanistan and subsequently Iraq were US-led answers to the question 'where is insecurity?', the border itself also emerged as a space of insecurity. As a result, it was thought to be in need of almost limitless security resources. Like the war on drugs, the war on terror defined the 'where' as external, frustrating opportunities for self-reflection. To reiterate, the question 'where is security?' can help to reinforce the state's own narrative and lay blame at an external and existential enemy, threat, or danger that might be foiled by border security or foreign interventions.

The growing reliance on surveillance technologies, biometrics, and AI has grown to satisfy seemingly insatiable tendencies to securitize all forms of mobility at national borders. While Chapter 15 deals directly with issues of technology, these issues are germane to the conversation here. The ways that all those entering border spaces are framed as suspicious, and as such insecure, is a key impact of these developments. Furthermore, as research has shown, the use of these technologies amplifies existing biases and limited conceptions of race, gender, and class, disproportionately impacting women, children, Indigenous peoples, people of colour, and those identifying as non-binary (see Kruger, Magnet, and Van Loon 2008; Beauchamp 2009; Magnet and Rodgers 2012; Browne 2015). Whether national or not, borders of all kinds have served to manage and punish difference(s). The implementation of surveillance and identification technologies has led to an intensification of differentiations on the basis of race, gender, and socio-economic class.

Asking what or who is being secured takes us to the database, the algorithm, and the question of enrolment. While the technology facilitates physical forms of security in the service of managing mobility at the border, questions of what constitutes security, and security from what or whom, noticeably change. For undocumented migrants, the fact that they are not enrolled in many of these systems in and of itself renders them less secure. For the mobile bodies who have a choice, the decision not to enrol can be framed as a category of suspicion, expanding what is insecure when it comes to mobility and the border, and as a result also expanding what is precarious. For those fleeing political persecution of any kind, but especially if related to identity, be that to escape ethnic cleansing or leaving regimes that persecute people who identify as LGBTQI+, the collection of personal data may be uncomfortable and possibly perilous.

Thus, with these technologies, we need to recalibrate questions of security and insecurity, highlighting the extent to which enrolling personal data into systems that may allow tracking and tracing presents serious challenges to the security of the individual refugee claimant. Those seeking asylum from violence are often confronted with different types of violence as they encounter the border virtually. The automation of pre-assessment and preclearance of migrants and asylum seekers not only speaks to a proliferation of borders but also demonstrates the proliferation of violence that accompanies it. Posing the question 'where is security?', we begin to see that rather than the border, it becomes the database, the information technology expert, the private corporation maintaining personal records and developing border automation, and so on, all engaged in often divisive bordering practices. The adherence to the 1951 Refugee Convention by a particular state, or the number of asylum seekers accepted annually, may capture little in the way of the pervasive insecurity for undocumented migrants who are left vulnerable to the proliferation of surveillance and identification technologies (see Molnar and Gill 2020).

> Gender, sexuality, and security are covered in detail in **Chapter 10**

19.4 Deadly deterrence: when enhanced security leads to insecurity

Whether it is the dangerous mountain passes of Waziristan, the unbearably hot Sonoran Desert, or the high seas of the Mediterranean, throughout the world, many of those whose mobility is not encouraged face inhospitable geographies. Border walls may be erected and fences festooned with barbed wire, yet it is often the natural environment that is most impenetrable. To understand the security politics of borders, we need to be aware of the role of geography, among other issues and factors, rather than perceiving it as something outside of the security frame. Identifying how violence is exercised unintentionally, or perhaps intentionally, in these hostile environments, we should unpack the array of policies contributing to deterrence via death, as well as the range of non-state actors who intervene to facilitate and protect and mobile bodies that traverse these harsh spaces. Most importantly, we should question the intentional violence that masquerades as unintentional. This will show that the perilous paths taken by migrants may in fact be an intentional exercise of violence that weaponizes the environment against them.

Sadly, in the case of territorial border security, the death of migrants may not be a failure or an unintended violence. By asking questions about whose security, where, when, and at whose expense, we can consider deeper questions about borders and mobility. The most obvious: to what extent is the death of migrants a policy failure? In other words, the power of the state may be the power to kill, rather than a failure to maintain life (Mbembe 2019; Sandset 2021). Whether it is the case that the policies themselves lead to deadly outcomes, there are examples that show that analysing security and violence rather than policies or institutions will yield a more political engagement with borders and mobility.

> On the concept of necropolitics, see **Box 19.2**

Deaths in the Mediterranean Sea and the Sonoran Desert are just two examples of the way deterrence via death has become a dominant state model of mobility and border management. In the case of the European Union (EU), research has focused on the sharp contrast between the EU's alleged commitment to humanitarianism and human rights when it comes to current member states and its outsourcing of more nefarious practices to some of its neighbours (Ataç, Rygiel, and Stierl 2017; Mutlu 2011; Squire 2017, 2020; Stierl 2016, 2018, 2019; Vaughan-Williams 2012). The EU's willingness to work with Turkey and states in the Balkans, as well as to provide funding for more restrictive, surveillance-led border and migration management in Sub-Saharan Africa (Frowd 2014, 2018, 2021), indicates a deterrent-driven strategy. Thus, the EU, much like the US, Australia, and other actors, is willing to use the deadly terrain of seas, deserts, and mountain passes as an essential aspect of its border and mobility strategy in the knowledge that this leads to increased mortality among migrants. In terms of the US southern border, recovering and accounting for human remains has become an essential part of social movements that challenge the state to accept that its deterrent

BOX 19.2 NECROPOLITICS

Michel Foucault (1995 [1975]; 1997 [1975–6]) argues that state power has grown in complexity over the past few centuries to be much more than the straightforward power to exercise corporeal punishment on the state's subjects, or conscript them for military service (and as such potential death for the state). Instead, we have witnessed a shift towards what he terms biopolitics, where the state power is manifest more and more in the management of maintenance of life (bio-) rather than the capacity and legitimacy to kill; while the state has the power to kill, it also has the power to let live. Connected to the historical emergence of the analytical category of 'population' in the eighteenth century, the state's biopolitics is notably expressed in the management of public health. Sanitation, eating habits, infant mortality, moral recidivism, and a host of other categories that constitute what we know as 'population' emerge as the domains of life over which the state has power.

Writers such as Hannah Arendt, Walter Benjamin, Giorgio Agamben, Roberto Esposito, and Achille Mbembe, and many others, have asked beyond the state's power over life, or the management of the population, what of the management of death? In practice, the violent and often deadly politics of border enforcement, particularly when it comes to some of the most vulnerable categories of mobility, such as asylum seekers and refugees, undocumented migrants, and the like, appear to illustrate what Mbembe terms necropolitics. Necropolitics, as Mbembe argues, emerges when we can identify in a state's practices 'the *generalized instrumentalization of human existence and the material destruction of human bodies and populations*' (Mbembe 2019, 68; original emphasis). Whether in the Sonoran Desert along the Mexico–US border, the Mediterranean shores of Greece, the eastern borders of Turkey, or mountain passes of Kashmir, necropolitics can be a helpful, although dark, concept for the security analyst to unpack critically the state's intentional disregard for the human lives of migrants at its borders. In fact, necropolitics helps us to unpack to what extent these actions are not simply indifference but malfeasance, and to begin to understand the related constellations of power, security, and political violence.

strategy contributes directly to migrant deaths, and as such is morally indefensible (Martínez et al. 2021). Being critical of security practices opens space for activism and intervention on behalf of the migrants and the deceased, most poignantly demonstrated by the work of a variety of scholars and initiatives along the US–Mexico border, including the Colibri Project and the Undocumented Migrant Project (www.undocumentedmigrationproject.org).

Asking questions about whose security, where and how that security is exercised, at what costs, and who suffers, particularly in the context of deadly deterrence strategies, further exposes the differential experience of mobility and borders. The differential experience of violence by mobile subjects highlights the ways in which the border continues to be 'a colour line' (Du Bois 1994)that frames racialized people as perpetual outsiders (Walia 2021). By asking straightforward questions about security and violence, we can expose what simple policy analysis is unlikely to uncover: the ways

On Du Bois and the colour line, see **Box 11.1**

in which the border acts as a sorting filter for mobility, enabling the mobility of some while hindering, and even exterminating, others.

Despite heightened levels of interconnectivity around the world and greater levels of migration and mobility for ever larger numbers, we must not lose sight of accompanying re-bordering strategies. The desperation of states to manage migration in highly differential ways has encouraged policies and strategies that invoke deterrence and 'corral' strategies (Boyce and Chambers 2021). These rely on forms of surveillance, checkpoints, and walls to force some forms of mobility towards hostile natural environments (i.e., deserts and oceans). Furthermore, deterrence and corral strategies are accompanied by policies that criminalize various forms of mobility. Thus, Mountz (2020) has suggested, we now bear witness to the death of asylum itself. These approaches are often not separate from the border strategies targeting mobility that contribute to increased deaths among migrants.

These strategies in the United States, EU, Australia, and elsewhere fit within what Miller (2019) refers to as an 'Empire of Borders', in which similar strategies and similar border industrial corporate interests pursue similar tactics with similar technologies and materials. Policy analysis and institutional accounts are unlikely to capture the role of the so-called 'border industrial complex' (Miller 2019) that has emerged around the world, serving the security interests of powerful states, and forms of capitalist mobility, while criminalizing, detaining, and disrupting unwanted movement. Different than the filtering function of the virtual border that is served by surveillance and identification technologies, these overtly destructive strategies focus on how border security is leveraged against mobility with promises of death and incarceration. The diversity of mobility is carved and corralled along class lines, according to gender and sexual identity, disempowering Indigenous claims of the right to traverse borders, and maintaining the border as a line of segregation. By asking questions about security and violence, we can unpack this differential sorting of mobility by the border, which policies, laws, and norms conceal by design.

19.5 Conclusion

As noted earlier, Nick Vaughan-Williams has observed that today, 'the border is not where it is supposed to be' (Vaughan-Williams 2012, 15). Asking key security questions helps to verify this claim. It also enables us to shed light on the array of issues associated with borders and mobility that are essential, but take place well away from the physical border itself. The border and the mobilities that are encountered there expose the difficulty in maintaining neat and tidy visions of the political. As a result, both the border and mobility come to be framed as insecure, dangerous, and risky. We must analyse the different tactics, relationships, and exercises that occur at the border and that are shaped by how security is defined, framed, and understood. Enhanced local law enforcement strategies, private contractors who enrich employment opportunities in borderlands, non-governmental organizations who work to uncover human remains analysing DNA or facilitate rescue in the Mediterranean, and public school curriculums may have as much or more to do with how borders emerge and mobility is managed as visa policies or biometric screening. In some cases, by appealing to an identity that is said to be under threat, the border and the mobility encountered there is subject to security logics, contributing to greater amounts of insecurity and danger, which in turn are used to justify continuing to mobilize security.

With the introduction of surveillance and identification technologies, the relationship between mobility and borders is understood in terms of filtering and sorting. Emphasizing Vaughan-Williams' point, as borders become virtual, they are as likely to be found when opening a bank account, renting an apartment, buying airline tickets online, or registering at university as at an official physical checkpoint that serves as a passage between two states. Finally, the border takes on its most brutal function as security and insecurity reach a zenith, leading to deadly strategies in the name of deterrence. In all these cases, the subject position of the mobile bodies reflects how authorities and societies define different forms of migration in different ways, associating them with varying levels of danger, insecurity, and risk. We should unpack these processes and uncover the politics embedded in these strategies, making visible the breadth of both the border and mobility well beyond the line in the sand.

Questions for further discussion

1. Regarding the framing of migration as a security issue, what do you believe is being secured? What is rendered insecure in the process?

2. Why has the narrative of borders as impermeable dominated over narratives of borders as porous?

3. Differentiation is often at the heart of borders and bordering practices. To what extent has the increasing reliance on surveillance and identification technologies in a range of bordering practices and boundary making led to more intensified differentiations based on gender, race, and class? Why might this be the case?

4. How does thinking critically about security challenge our assumptions about the alleged permanence and necessity of territorial borders?

5. Can you imagine a politics without borders? What are the challenges to thinking about this? What would such a political imagination mean for our understanding of mobility and violence?

Further reading

The border chronicle. www.theborderchronicle.com (last accessed 1 March 2022).
   This incredibly timely, accessible resource provides rich accounts of borders, migration, bordering practices, the impact of identification and surveillance technologies, and the so-called 'border industrial complex', with a geographic focus on the Mexico–US border. It presents a broad array of disciplinary perspectives and aligns with a critical, humanitarian approach to borders and mobility.

KING, THOMAS and NATASHA DONOVAN. 2021. *Borders*. Toronto: Harper Collins.
A graphic novel adaptation of Thomas King's short story, 'Borders', this story of an Indigenous boy and his mother crossing the Canada–US border to visit his sister raises compelling questions about identity, belonging, Indigeneity, and the artificial but nonetheless violent nation-state border from an Indigenous perspective.

DÍAZ-BARRIGA, MIGUEL and MARGARET E. DORSEY. 2020. *Fencing in democracy: Border walls, necrocitizenship, and the security state*. London: Duke University Press.
Although theoretically complex, this text provides a strong, critical, contemporary account of the relationship between the proliferation of border walls, the politics of deadly deterrence, and the accompanying amplification of security politics in the context of borders and mobility.

NYERS, PETER. 2019. *Irregular citizenship, immigration, and deportation*. London: Routledge.
Focused on the centrality of deportation and anti-deportation in contemporary citizenship and immigration politics, Nyers concentrates on the making and unmaking of citizenship that enables both deportation and anti-deportation, in the contested terrain of border governance, state politics of control, and the politics of rights and recognition. Generative and somewhat hopeful, this text provides an account of resistance and alternatives to the security politics that contribute to the endless escalation of border security.

WALIA, HARSHA. 2021. *Border and rule: Global migration, capitalism, and the rise of racist nationalism*. Black Point, Nova Scotia: Fernwood Publishing.
A political activist, critical account of the colonial, racist, and capitalist context of contemporary borders and mobility. While drawing on a wide range of theoretical and historical work, this is a relatively accessible source that provides a strong example of activist scholarship.

References

AGNEW, JOHN. 1994. 'The territorial trap: The geographical assumptions of International Relations theory'. *Review of International Political Economy* 1(1), 53–80.

AMSTER, RANDALL. 2011. 'Arizona bans ethnic studies and, along with it, reason and justice'. *Huffpost*, 25 May. www.huffpost.com/entry/arizona-bans-ethnic-studi_b_802318 (last accessed 1 March 2021).

ARADAU, CLAUDIA and RENS VAN MUNSTER. 2016. 'Governing terrorism through risk: Taking precautions, (un)knowing the future'. *European Journal of International Relations* 13(1), 89–115.

ATAÇ, ILKER, KIM RYGIEL, and MAURICE STIERL. Eds. 2017. *The contentious politics of refugee and migrant protest and solidarity movements: Remaking citizenship from the margins*. London: Routledge.

BEAUCHAMP, TOBY. 2009. 'Artful concealment and strategic visibility: Transgender bodies and U.S. state surveillance after 9/11'. *Surveillance & Society* 6(4), 356–366.

BOYCE, GEOFFREY A. and SAMUEL N. CHAMBERS. 2021. 'The corral apparatus: Counterinsurgency and the architecture of death and deterrence along the Mexico/United States border'. *Geoforum* 120, 1–13.

BROWN, WENDY. 2014. *Walled states, waning sovereignty*. New York: Zone Books.

BROWNE, SIMONE. 2015. *Dark matters: On the surveillance of blackness*. Durham, NC: Duke University Press.

COOKE, THOMAS and BENJAMIN MULLER. 2021. 'Why we need to seriously reconsider COVID-19 vaccine passports'. *The Conversation*, 19 May. https://theconversation.com/why-we-need-to-seriously-reconsider-covid-19-vaccination-passports-159405 (last accessed 1 March 2022).

DONNAN, HASTINGS and THOMAS M. WILSON. 1999. *Borders: Frontiers of identity, nation and state*. New York: Berg.

DU BOIS, W. E. B. 1994. *The problem of the Color Line at the turn of the twentieth century: The essential early essays*. New York: Fordham University Press.

FOUCAULT, MICHEL. 1995 [1975]. *Discipline and Punish: The birth of the prison*. New York: Vintage Books.

FOUCAULT, MICHEL. 1997 [1975–6]. 'Society must be defended'. In *Lectures at the Collège de France 1975–1976*. New York: Picador.

FROWD, PHILIPPE M. 2014. 'The field of border control in Mauritania'. *Security Dialogue* 45(3), 226–241.

FROWD, PHILIPPE M. 2018. 'Developmental borderwork and the International Organization for Migration'. *Journal of Ethnic and Migration Studies* 44(10), 1656–1672.

FROWD, PHILIPPE M. 2021. 'Borderwork creep in West Africa's Sahel'. *Geopolitics*. DOI: 10.1080/14650045.2021.1901082

Government of Canada. 2021. 'NEXUS'. https://cbsa-asfc.gc.ca/prog/nexus/menu-eng.html (last accessed 1 March 2022).

HOBSBAWM, ERIC and TERENCE RANGER. Eds. 1992. *The invention of tradition*. Cambridge: Cambridge University Press.

JONES, REECE. 2012. *Border walls: Security and the War on Terror in the United States, India, and Israel*. London: Zed Books.

KRUGER, ERIN, SHOSHANA MAGNET, and JOOST VAN LOON. 2008. 'Biometric revisions of the "body" in airports and US welfare reform'. *Body & Society* 14(2), 99–121.

LYON, DAVID. Ed. 2002. *Surveillance as social sorting: Privacy, risk, and digital discrimination*. New York: Routledge.

MAGNET, SHOSHANA and TARA RODGERS. 2012. 'Stripping for the state'. *Feminist Media Studies* 12(1), 101–118.

MARTÍNEZ, DANIEL E., ROBIN C. REINEKE, GEOFFREY BOYCE, SAMUEL N. CHAMBERS, SARAH LAUNIUS, BRUCE E. ANDERSON, GREGORY L. HESS, JENNIFER M. VOLLNER, BRUCE O. PARKS, CAITLIN C. M. VOGELSBERG, GABRIELLA SOTO, MICHAEL KREYCHE, and RAQUEL RUBIO-GLODSMITH. 2021. *Migrant deaths in Southern Arizona: Recovered undocumented border crosser remains investigated by the Pima County Office of the Medical Examiner, 1990–2020*. Tucson, AZ: University of Arizona Press. https://sbs.arizona.edu/sites/sbs.arizona.edu/files/BMI%20Report%202021%20ENGLISH_FINAL.pdf (last accessed 1 March 2022).

MAYNARD, ROBYN. 2020. 'Police abolition/Black revolt'. *Canadian Journal of Cultural Studies* 41(Fall), 70–78.

MBEMBE, ACHILLE. 2019. *Necropolitics*. Durham, NC: Duke University Press.

MILLER, TODD. 2019. *Empire of borders: The expansion of the US border around the world*. London: Verso.

MOLNAR, PETRA and LEX GILL. 2020. *Bots at the gate: A human rights analysis of automated decision-making in Canada's immigration and refugee system*. International Human Rights Program, University of Toronto. https://ihrp.law.utoronto.ca/sites/default/files/media/IHRP-Automated-Systems-Report-Web.pdf (last accessed 1 March 2022).

MOUNTZ, ALISON. 2020. *The death of asylum: Hidden geographies of the enforcement archipelago.* Minneapolis, MN: University of Minnesota Press.

MULLER, BENJAMIN J. 2010a. 'Unsafe at any speed? Borders, mobility and "safe citizenship"'. *Citizenship Studies* 14(1), 75–88.

MULLER, BENJAMIN J. 2010b. *Security, risk and the biometric state: Governing borders and bodies.* London: Routledge.

MULLER, BENJAMIN, THOMAS N. COOKE, MIGUEL DE LARRINAGA, PHILIPPE M. FROWD, DELJANA IOSSIFOVA, DANIELA JOHANNES, CAN E. MUTLU, and ADAM NOWEK. 2016. 'Collective discussion, ferocious architecture: Sovereign spaces/places by design'. *International Political Sociology* 10(1), 75–96.

MUTLU, CAN E. 2011. 'A de facto cooperation? The increasing role of the European Union on improved relations between Georgia and Turkey'. *Comparative European Politics* 9(4), 543–556.

NYERS, PETER. 2019. *Irregular citizenship, immigration, and deportation.* New York: Routledge.

OSIANDER, ANDREAS. 2001. 'Sovereignty, international relations, and the Westphalian myth'. *International Organization* 55(2), 251–287.

SANDSET, TONY. 2021. 'The necropolitics of COVID-19: Race, class and slow death in an ongoing pandemic'. *Global Public Health* 16(8–9), 1411–1423.

SQUIRE, VICKI. 2017. 'Governing migration through death in Europe and the US: Identification, burial and the crisis of modern humanism'. *European Journal of International Relations* 23(3), 513–532.

SQUIRE, VICKI. 2020. 'Hidden geographies of the "Mediterranean migration crisis"'. *Environment and Planning C: Politics and Space.* DOI: 10.1177/2399654420935904.

STIERL, MAURICE. 2016. 'A sea of struggle: Activist border interventions in the Mediterranean sea'. *Citizenship Studies* 20(5), 561–578.

STIERL, MAURICE. 2018. 'A fleet of Mediterranean border humanitarians'. *Antipode* 50(3), 704–724.

STIERL, MAURICE. 2019. *Migrant resistance in contemporary Europe.* London: Routledge.

TAZZIOLI, MARTINA. 2015. *Spaces of governmentality: Autonomous migration and the Arab uprisings.* Lanham, MD: Rowman & Littlefield.

VALLET, ELISABETH. Ed. 2014. *Borders, fences and walls: State of insecurity?* New York: Routledge.

VAUGHAN-WILLIAMS, NICK. 2012. *Border politics: The limits of sovereign power.* Edinburgh: Edinburgh University Press.

VIRNO, PAOLO. 2004. *A grammar of the multitude: For an analysis of contemporary forms of life.* New York: Semiotext(e).

WALIA, HARSHA. 2021. *Border and rule: Global migration, capitalism and the rise of racist nationalism.* Black Point, Nova Scotia: Fernwood Publishing.

WALKER, R. B. J. 1993. *Inside/outside: International relations as political theory.* Cambridge: Cambridge University Press.

20
Prisons and camps

Anna Schliehe

20.1	Introduction	325
20.2	Building secure states through incarceration and encampment?	328
20.3	Designing security—institutional creation of order and control	331
20.4	Living in securityscapes—enforced intimacy and the microworlds of prisons and border camps	334
20.5	Conclusion	337

READER'S GUIDE

In this chapter, prisons and camps are explored alongside their inherent security logics and security practices from the global to the intimate. By exposing the visceral realities of encampment and incarceration, from the micro-practices to the macro-issues on a global scale, we can question security for whom and at whose expense. By asking these questions, we gain better insights into how a generated need for national and international security has led to unprecedented numbers of people who are incarcerated or displaced.

20.1 Introduction

Illustrative case studies on the topics explored in this chapter are available on the online resources to help take your understanding of prisons and camps further: http://www.oup.com/he/Grayson-Guillaume1e.

Spaces of incarceration are inherently bound to security. 'Securing' certain people in dedicated spaces of imprisonment and detention camps, prisons, and a range of other closed institutions is intended to increase levels of safety. Therefore, security logics underpin how and why categories of people are incarcerated. Holding people in place and separating them from society at large is both a physical act and symbolic. Achieving security through locking up, or separating certain groups, is also inherently embodied

*To identify these hierarchies when security is mobilized, see **Sections 1.3** and **3.2***

and emotional. Confining people in locked places is often harmful to those who are imprisoned. It also affects large parts of a socio-political order: prison architects; lawyers, magistrates, and judges; staff; families, friends, and loved ones; children whose parents are in prison; parents whose children are imprisoned; and whole families who are detained upon crossing a border. Security as a political mobilization has an impact on a large number of people in society. Here, it naturalizes the exceptional situation of camps and prisons as viable solutions to various forms of insecurity.

For more on security as a political mobilization, see **Section 2.4**

Building on Lauren Martin and Matthew Mitchelson's (2009, 460) definition, we understand imprisonment/detention as an intentional practice that restricts individual movement and imposes particular regimes on detainees' time and space. Importantly, 'holding' human beings without their consent in these institutions is characterized by 'purposeful violence'and is connected to what Martin and Mitchelson (2009, 460) call 'specialized networks of public monies, private corporations, and marginalized labor'. While we refer to 'prisons' and 'camps' in this chapter, they are part of a global panoply of institutions that have many names and diverse locations. Therefore, it is important to assess them in their wider context. It can be challenging to make sense of a wide range of experiences as 'prisons' and 'camps' can describe very different institutions. They also have many similarities and are sometimes used inter-changeably.

Chapter 4 extensively explores political violence

See **Zoom-in 20.1** on the global dimensions

The emergence of carceral spaces as we know them can be traced back to the late eighteenth century which saw the birth of the first state-funded prisons. Certainly detaining people against their will and keeping some groups contained in designated areas are much older practices that can be traced at least to the Roman Empire. In the past forty years, hyper-incarceration by a 'punitive' state apparatus has become an issue in many socio-political orders as an increasing range of activities are criminalized under new legal regimes, including the 'war on drugs', zero-tolerance policing, and more (see Table 20.1 on rates of incarceration).

 ZOOM-IN 20.1 A GLOBAL PHENOMENON

The global prison population has grown in unprecedented ways in recent decades. According to World Prison Brief (2021), over 11 million people are in prison around the world, one third of whom are awaiting sentencing by a court. The United States has the highest total number of prisoners relative to its overall population. While prisoner numbers have increased globally, there has been little simultaneous increase in resources for prison systems. Thus, overcrowding and dangerous conditions are increasing.

Globally, the refugee population has also been rising with nearly 26.4 million officially registered refugees and at least 82.4 million people around the world that were forcibly displaced according to the United Nations High Commissioner for Refugees (UNHCR 2021). The UNHCR states that around half of the refugee population are children and, on average, one in every ninety-five persons on earth had to flee their home due to conflict or persecution—many of whom are forced to live in camps.

Table 20.1 World incarceration rate (Prison Policy Initiative 2021) and total number of prisoners (WPB 2021)

Country	Number of prisoners per 100,000 people	Total number of prisoners	Total population in 2020 (World Bank n.d.)
USA	664	2,068,800	329,484,120
Brazil	357	811,707	212,559,410
Russian Federation	329	472,226	144,104,080
China	121	1,710,000	1,410,929,360
India	35	478,600	1,380,004,390

Table 20.2 Largest refugee camps in 2020 (estimates) (UNHCR 2021)

Refugee camp, country	Estimated number
Kutupalong, Bangladesh	800,000
Dadaab, Kenya	200,000
Kakuma, Kenya	150,000
Za'atari, Jordan	76,000

Camps have also historically been a defining feature of a range of practices from genocide to migration control, as well as being an outcome of global security arrangements (see Table 20.2).

As carceral spaces, prisons and camps reflect specific patterns of prejudice that bring intersections of racial, colonial, social, economic, and gendered inequalities into view. They are also spaces of political violence, surveillance, and punishment that often render certain populations, their political claims, and living situations invisible. We thus need to ask critical questions about security to analyse the hierarchies underpinning incarceration as it is designed, made (in)visible, (im)mobilized, experienced, and/or resisted. To help find some answers, we will demonstrate how different dimensions of security and insecurity are embedded in the carceral, how they are created and experienced, and how they tie in with issues like legitimacy, authority and violence. We will address where carceral security is located, for whom carceral institutions might produce security, and at whose expense. Security here is both seen as a process that is ever-changing and as a prescribed goal that justifies the very existence of carceral spaces.

This chapter is organized as follows. In Section 20.2, we illustrate how the growth of prisons and camps is connected to state building and national and global dimensions of security. In Section 20.3, we consider how order and security are institutionally produced—that is, how are these intrinsically designed into spaces of incarceration (Moran et al. 2018)? In Section 20.4, we introduce the lived experience of incarceration and its relations to security. We will learn about the microworlds of prisons and camps, including how security is inherently intimate in its everyday occurrence.

See **Chapter 15** for more on surveillance

See **Section 3.3** for more on hierarchies and how they relate to security

Legitimacy and authority are discussed in **Sections 4.3–4**

The relevance of these different questions is explained in **Sections 5.3.1.2–3** and **5.3.2.3**

On security as a process, see **Section 2.3.2**

Design is covered in **Chapter 16**

This will reveal how incarcerated people describe their lived experience as emotional and embodied. In Section 20.5, we will synthesize these points and consider practices of resistance and the abolition movement.

20.2 Building secure states through incarceration and encampment?

Prisons and camps are global phenomena. Although they officially serve different functions, they affect the incarcerated in existential ways. Both are carceral spaces. They have similar institutional traits and are sometimes almost indistinguishable. Both prisons and camps exist to separate 'criminal', 'deviant', or 'migrant' others from the rest of society to make it safer and distinguish between 'us' and 'them'. As citizens, we may learn about the existence of prisons from an early age through the media; 'locking people up' becomes an intuitive paradigm for delivering security and justice. However, we need to ask ourselves if we are, in fact, enhancing security in a sociopolitical order by incarcerating people, putting them into detention camps, or indeed letting them fend for themselves in makeshift border camps.

*See **Chapter 9** on the production of threats and its relation to identity*

The increased presence of camps and, more generally, the global expansion of confinement, needs to be analysed as in terms of the security claims and mobilizations underpinning them. This includes how these have been legitimized by pointing to growing threats from social phenomena like criminality and migration (Martin and Mitchelson 2009). Thinking critically about security then means that we ask ourselves how we can contextualize the global expansion of a confinement industry, how we can draw links between historical legacies including colonialism and slavery to these contemporary dynamics, and how we can assess individual institutions such as prisons and camps as a form of state power.

*To understand what security does, see **Chapter 2***

20.2.1 Mass incarceration and the prison industrial complex

The concepts of mass incarceration and a 'prison industrial complex' have emerged from the United States largely due to its extremely high number of incarcerated people (see Table 20.1). The idea that prisons are an 'industry' refers to how Jamie Peck (2003, 226) links the rise of mass incarceration with the rise of economic models which put the profit of privatized carceral institutions—which are tied to the number of prisoners incarcerated—ahead of other central values such as human rights. Ruth Wilson Gilmore (2007, 26) identifies prisons as 'partial geographic solutions to political economic crises [e.g., de-industrialization, falling real wages, growing economic inequality] organized by the state, which itself is in crisis'. Imprisonment has become an easy response to the multi-causal social problems that are connected to poverty. As such, the 'prison industrial complex' is increasingly connected to business, military production, and public punishment as prisoners provide labour, often for free, to produce goods, military gear, or provide public services (e.g., waste removal; firefighting) (Davis 2000).

Mass incarceration, the exponential increase of people in prisons, is a paradox as it cannot be explained by an increase in criminality. Mass incarceration leads to lower criminality levels as imprisonment levels rise (see Peck 2003). So how can we explain the continuing rise in incarceration rates? Many studies point to the fact that imprisonment exacerbates poverty, destitution, separating families, and intergenerational trauma. These then become identified problems that are symbolic of social disorder that requires security mobilizations. In many cases, these mobilizations specifically target 'problem' groups (e.g., those who are homeless) by criminalizing the problem (e.g., vagrancy laws). These actions reflect classist, gendered, and racialized strategies that have been shown to maintain longer-standing hierarchies in the United States (and elsewhere). Loïc Wacquant (2009, 198) describes the well-established racial disparity in incarceration rates and argues that urban ghettoes are also prisons as

> both belong to the same genus of organisation, namely, institutions of forced confinement: the ghetto is a manner of 'social prison' while the prison functions as a 'judicial ghetto'. Both are entrusted with enclosing a stigmatised population so as to neutralise the material and/or symbolic threat that it poses for broader society from which it has been extruded.

This underlines the importance of considering wider socio-political contexts and orders, the type of hierarchies at work in a given society, and how different types of confinement and wider structures of the state are connected. Mass imprisonment stems not just from crime but also from racism, sexism, and other forms of difference and exclusion.

As Martin and Mitchelson (2009) and Peck (2003) point out, mass incarceration and the 'prison industrial complex' as an idea, institution, and infrastructure connected to interests have been exported from the US to a variety of countries in the global north and global south. Internationally, like in the United Kingdom, Australia, and France, corporate security firms manage detention centres (for migrants or minors) and prisons, creating a lucrative global industry. Incarceration is increasingly geographically dispersed and diversified 'as people are housed in ocean freighter hulls, in jails and prisons, in airports, and a variety of currently undisclosed locations' (Martin and Mitchelson 2009, 472). Given this variety in carceral spaces, how can we critically compare different sites of imprisonment to better understand how they are supposed to provide security and for whom? Crucially, what is missed if we ignore hierarchies that are reproduced via mass incarceration? Who is incarcerated on an industrial scale? Can certain groups ever feel 'secure' if they are the 'product' of the prison industrial complex? How do individual experiences and global trends intertwine? These questions are also important with regards to camps.

*On the importance of socio-political orders and hierarchies, see **Sections 1.2** and **3.2–3***

*We explore these enablers in **Section 3.3***

*The questions 'security for whom?', 'how?', and 'at whose expense?' are examined further in **Sections 5.3.1.2–6** and **5.3.2.3***

20.2.2 Looking beyond the European camp complex

The Mediterranean Island of Lampedusa in southern Italy is identified by Claudio Minca (2015, 74) as one of many points of friction in the European camp complex.

Here 'serene' holiday-makers and desperate asylum seekers come into direct contact before migrants are interned in camps by local authorities. The contrasts in worlds are stark:

> Sometimes these floating bodies reach the shore to die namelessly, other times they try to escape the police to avoid being interned, in both cases provoking a momentary disruption in the routinized slow pace of the holiday goers. (Minca 2015, 74)

Lampedusa in Italy. Calais in France. Moria in Greece. These are but some of the migrant camps that have spread across Europe. Yet, there has been no decisive action from politicians, or policy-makers to address the underlying issues that have made the emergence of these camps possible. Camps produce borders between inside and outside as well as within the camps themselves (Freedman 2018). Borders are intimately linked with questions around mass incarceration we raised in Section 20.2.1. Primarily, what are the impacts on 'those that mobilize [borders] to guarantee the "security" of their populations, and those that are trying to cross them to improve their own individual security' (Freedman 2018, 403)?

Chapter 19 investigates borders and security

What becomes immediately clear, however, is that the European camp complex goes beyond national agendas. It sits within a global network of sites and practices. 'Fortress Europe' exists alongside camps in Bangladesh for Rohingya refugees, refugee camps in Kenya for Somalis, or camps in Jordan for Syrian refugees, to name just a few (see Table 20.2). For example, the Rohingya of Myanmar form one of the largest refugee groups in the world. In Bangladesh, living in camps exposes them to high levels of stress including scarcity of food, restrictions on movement, and safety concerns (see Riley et al. 2017). Moreover, populations like the Rohingya are severely affected by multiple forms of individual and collective violence. The effects of environmental stressors associated with life in refugee camps were found to play a pivotal role in perpetuating experiences of trauma. In Jordan, various population movements from the on-going conflict in Syria have produced a high number of refugees. The Jordanian state has struggled with the realities of being a host for close to 700,000 Syrian refugees in a country of 10 million and has deployed practices that have segregated refugees from local citizens (Dalal et al. 2018).

Chapter 4 discusses different forms of political violence

While contexts, living conditions, and experiences differ across these different cases, Gil Loescher and James Milner (2005, 153) argue that 'protracted refugee situations are a critical and growing element in continuing conflict and instability'. They refer to contexts in Africa where direct security concerns, including armed refugee populations and the spread of conflict across borders, and indirect security concerns, such as tensions over the allocation of scarce resources, are issues. Looking at the prevalence of camps raises broader questions about connections between global mobility and national responses, and about whose security counts more: and at whose expense? What is the purpose of camps when the security, and rights of forced migrants and refugees to be offered sanctuary is enshrined in international law? These situations raise fundamental questions about our socio-political orders—the role and legitimacy of borders and their constitutive security practices, the rights of individuals, and the responsibilities of states. Most directly, they raise troubling questions about how (little) we value human life.

20.2.3 Camps, prisons, and the production of security

In some contexts, prisons and camps are different forms of exclusion. Camps separate migrant/refugee populations, who have not committed any crimes, from their host society. Prisons are fortified sites of control for people who have been convicted of a crime and sentenced by a court of law. However, the differences in practice are becoming less clear. Lived experiences in open prisons can be less restrictive than in many refugee camps. Migrants can find themselves locked up in detention centres that resemble many prisons with their walls, barbed wire, guards, and surveillance systems. As this section shows, prisons and camps are used to separate and produce hierarchies by restricting the freedoms of those deemed to be 'offenders' or 'foreign bodies'. Prisons and camps are thus important to national and international productions of security.

Nowhere is this more pronounced than in the opaque and nebulous global sites of incarceration connected to military interventions. Camps like Guantánamo Bay in Cuba, Abu Ghraib in Iraq, or Bagram in Afghanistan are examples of sites of incarceration that exist beyond the reach of national and international law. The oppression of Uighurs and other Muslim minorities in China is connected to the existence of 're-education' camps set by the Chinese government in Xinjiang. The exact number of Uighurs detained such camps and their living conditions remain a guarded secret (Stern 2021).

Section 4.3 discusses the question of legitimacy and security

Looking at the global scale of incarceration and encampment raises many questions. These include: is it possible to produce security through incarceration? How does incarceration produce security? For whom does it produce security and at whose expense? Can we justify making some insecure through practices of incarceration and physical exclusion to maintain 'security' for others? And if so, where should lines be drawn between just and unjust practices?

20.3 Designing security – institutional creation of order and control

Prisons and camps are the materialization of an interplay between security and space for the purposes of excluding groups from a socio-political order. They are supposed to generate security and use security to govern detainees. Thus, the design of prisons and camps is important. Yet, in spite of the growing emphasis on their role in the provision of security (Maguire and Low 2019), these institutions are bound up in various paradoxes. Can security be achieved by design? Are prisons secure? If so, for whom? Do camps increase security and, if so, for whom? Can incarceration be legitimate? In this section, we explore these spaces of security by focusing on how they produce security through their architecture and institutional practices. The examples in this

Chapter 16 examines the links between design and security

section demonstrate important spatial dimension of security practices and reveals otherwise hidden ways of actively creating 'security'.

20.3.1 Planned prisons

One of the guiding architectural design principles for prisons is to incorporate security into its features. To isolate prisoners, prisons are often located 'at a distance' from wider society. Both human-made structures—like high walls, barbed wire, and heavy doors—and natural aspects of the landscape—like cliffs, forests, or rivers—are often used to increase that distance (Goffman 1991 [1961], 15). Michel Foucault (1991 [1972]) classically noted the connections between these security features and 'discipline' which he understood as the coercive management and correction of people through different means. The task of maintaining an internal order in prison is identified as similarly important. Thinking through the aspects of security in individual carceral spaces is thus based on architecture and human organization as well as symbolic meaning.

As many studies show, prison architecture is infused with meaning (Pratt 2002). This meaning-making process derives from state and societal attitudes towards prisoners and justice more generally. Through daily operations, those who live and work in prisons also shape the security regime and atmosphere. At its most extreme, prisoners in isolation cells, or the most secure parts of a high-security estate, can spend most hours of the day confined in small barren cells with little distraction—all in the name of security. The US Supermax prison is often described as the most inhumane and extreme form of incarceration, due to extreme levels of isolation, lack of association, and lack of physical activity, as well as often very long sentences (Reiter 2012).

Designing security in a prison is thus a combination of architectural features and internal management practices to manage often large numbers of people, some of whom have few incentives to cooperate. While it is generally assumed that fewer security measures are preferable, there can also be dangers associated with prisons that remove many of them (Crewe et al. 2014). When power is under-used and staff are less visible, or even absent, the tone and quality of prison life can deteriorate. Prison staff are vital to managing everyday relationships and access to items. Designing safe prisons, then, requires focusing on the forms of interpersonal engagement between staff and prisoners, as much as on built-in security and surveillance features.

*See **Section 3.2** for more on relations of power*

In these often large-scale and densely occupied spaces, (in)security is built into their architectural, managerial, technological, and interpersonal features. This is to create opportunities to visibly maintain order and discipline. Equally important, however, and more elusive, are the features that cannot be designed, like interpersonal relationships and moral climate.

20.3.2 Camps as constructions (of power)

Camps can vary even more than prisons in how they are planned, designed, and built as well as the underlying rationales for their existence. There is a growing global spread of the use of encampments that includes 'concentration, detention, transit, identification, refugee, military, and training camps' that are located across authoritarian and democratic regimes (Minca 2015, 74). While all camps work with a mixture of custody, care, control, and forms of violence (both manifest and latent) as we may find in prisons, their aims and structures are less uniform (Minca 2015). Thus, how are security and violence produced in, and through, camps?

For example, in the case of the European border regime, many detainees are incarcerated in detention centres, or in border camps, that are not dissimilar to prisons with regards to their architectural design and forms of control. People are controlled through high walls, barbed wire, surveillance systems, the need to undergo security checks when entering and leaving the facility. Similar to prisons, forms of coercion and restricted mobility are used to manage detainees. However, one major difference with prisons lies in the connection between camps, forms of political violence, and its perceived legitimacy by those subjected to it. Bénédicte Michalon (2013, 45), for instance, details how the whole experience is seen by detainees held in camps as 'an act of unjustified violence by people who do not consider themselves criminals'.

> See **Sections 4.3–4** for a discussion of legitimacy and authority

In makeshift refugee camps, carceral dynamics are primarily enforced by state security apparatuses. Camps are generally comprised of temporary structures built by individual migrants in spaces separated from the rest of society through the imposition of internal practices of border management by state authorities that place them outside of the protections of the normal socio-political order (see Davies et al. 2017). In being separated from society, camp dwellers are left alone to manage extreme conditions. Camps generally lack basic infrastructure like running water, sanitation, or electricity. To further reinforce the symbolism of exclusion, external security forces like the police regularly intervene to destroy any makeshift infrastructure that may have been established in the camps, arrest camp dwellers, and impose 'order' and 'security' in ways that produce more insecurity in the end. Tellingly in terms of the hierarchies that are at play in this mobilization of security, camp dwellers are subject to gross forms of violence and insecurity in the name of preventing them from harming, by their sheer presence, the wider society. Thus, structural violence, oppression, and insecurity are embedded into the camp. Beyond coercive measures, the lack of supportive actions by the state (support that is required under international law) has security consequences for migrants/refugees. Inaction also leads to insecurities.

When considering the production of (in)security in spaces like prisons and camps, it is important to keep in mind who benefits from the creation of order and control, and at whose expense. How should we understand the connections between forms of political violence experienced in carceral spaces and those who manage them? Is this too reductive? What responsibility lies with the people who plan and build these structures but do not manage them? What about the people in government who make laws or the people who vote for them? What about those who write about, teach, or study carceral institutions? Prisons and camps are challenging environments that can dehumanize their occupants and generate anxiety. They are also the product of

> **Sections 2.4 and 3.3** explain how security is a political mobilization that produces hierarchies

security mobilizations that transpose ideas about what it is to be safe, who is a threat as well as who 'we are' and 'they are' into a material form. As we will now see, there are multiple sources of political violence for those living in such securityscapes.

20.4 Living in securityscapes—enforced intimacy and the microworlds of prisons and border camps

> On the notion of securityscape, see **Zoom-in 20.2**

We can refer to prisons and camps as securityscapes. These are spaces which are infused with the effects of security mobilizations. Despite the variety and complexity of securityspaces, there are common (in)securities in the lived experience of inmates, refugees, and migrants. In order to contextualize these experiences, we will focus on the camps in Calais, France and the experiences of prisoners in the United Kingdom.

For more than twenty years, the region of Calais has been an intermediate destination for migrants and refugees who hope to cross the channel to the United Kingdom (Debuyser 2021). The poor living conditions for refugees and migrants in Calais are connected to specific decisions. First, a welcome centre for migrants was closed in 2002 due to pressures from the British government. Second, since that time, France has done nothing to provide the camps with basic infrastructure. There has thus been a continuous cycle of makeshift camps being built and then being forcibly cleared.

Many more of these makeshift refugee encampments exist in Europe. There, growth is reaching unprecedented scales. For example, the so-called 'new jungle' camp in Calais was 'the largest [of] such site in northern Europe … which by the end of [2015] housed 6000 refugees, rising to 10,000 in 2016' (Davies et al. 2017, 1263). Makeshift camps are characterized by many insecurities (see below), even if camp dwellers often self-organize to provide basic daily sustenance and basic infrastructures with the help of local volunteers (Sandri 2018). While the camp in Calais, known as the 'new jungle', was dismantled by security personnel and police in 2016, other makeshift camps have been built since then. Moreover, refugees continue to come to Calais and remain subject to coercive security measures.

> **Section 3.4** explores how security can be challenged and resisted

 ZOOM-IN 20.2 SECURITYSCAPES

Securityscapes is a term that encapsulates a variety of ideas and situations (see Maguire and Low 2019). While some adopt the term to describe a distinct landscape that is contained—like an airport, a gated community, a stadium, or indeed a prison or camp—some use it to grapple with spatial and temporal aspects of security as process (see Section 2.3.2). This includes how security shapes and frames feelings and imaginary elements as well as infrastructure and our built environment. This means that we should view security not only as contingent to a particular place and time, but as a dynamic affecting wider symbolic meanings. These symbolic meanings contribute to how it is imagined and justified, mobilized and enacted, and challenged and resisted.

Prisons in England and Wales have one of the highest (total and per head of population) numbers of prisoners in Europe. There are 118 prisons that differ in their security categorization (from open to high security), mode of operation (privately or publicly run), size, and physical characteristics. These differences stem from 'their individual histories, geographic locations, management ethos, physical (or "situational") security measures and commitment to "social" methods of containment and control' (Jewkes and Johnston 2006, 8). However, there are common experiences that characterize imprisonment for most prisoners. These are connected to having to:

- live in a locked space that is not of one's choosing;
- share space and resources with a group of people with little to no control over who they are;
- adhere to a particular regime enforced by the institution which includes:
  - rigid management of one's time;
  - little to no choice over forms of occupation;
  - limited access to necessities like food or healthcare; and
  - controlled access to communication with people outside the prison walls.

Moreover, the effects of prisons as security spaces do not end with being released from prison; they continue into probation and beyond. This arises from the structural and social obstacles facing prisoners' reintegration into society.

What is already apparent is how, for both dwellers in camps and prisoners, the camp and the prison reach into the most intimate and fundamental parts of their being. These securityscapes produce deep emotional and embodied effects that connect to the feelings of (in)security they generate. To understand the forms of violence that emerge from the everyday experiences of security spaces, we will detail some of their effects. These everyday experiences and effects cover both imposed security measures set by institutions to impose control over individuals, and affective internal effects experienced by individuals related to personal safety. Some overarching questions will follow us through this section: where can we locate these intimate dimensions of security? What kinds of security are meaningful to prisoners and camp dwellers? Who benefits from impositions of security? Is security experienced as a condition of possibility, or impossibility, in these securityscapes?

Important scholarship on border camps has outlined the challenging living conditions faced by camp dwellers (Sigona 2014). During fieldwork in Calais, researchers have highlighted physically insecurities generated from makeshift tents, unsanitary conditions, scarce access to fresh water and cleaning products, the spread of dangerous pathogens, irregular access to food and drinking water; threats to bodily integrity through violence from other camp dwellers and the police, psychological harm, and other forms of injury/illness (Davies et al. 2017, 1279). Scholarship on prisons in the UK has highlighted that certain parts of the prison system also struggle with challenging living conditions including unsanitary conditions in cells (Schliehe and Crewe 2021), a lack of access to healthcare (Stoller 2003), physical violence from officers or other prisoners (McGuire 2018), and psychological issues from social isolation.

A particular aspect of prison life worth noting is the constant need to maintain a public façade due to the lack of privacy. In prison, any space can be observed, entered, and thoroughly searched by prison staff at any time. The absence of privacy limits feelings of personal autonomy, deprives prisoners of control over their immediate space, and exposes them almost perpetually to forms of sensory intrusion—for example, noise, smells, and any lack of hygiene from other occupants—that are typically found in communal living spaces. Living in a prison can involve sensory overcrowding, physical and psychological crowding, and, conversely, isolation and sensory deprivation (at the same time). Yvonne Jewkes (2018) writes that the effects can be so severe that serving a long sentence is known to accelerate the ageing process, and lead to chronic or terminal illnesses.

Prisons and camps as securityscapes expose their inhabitants to rules and regulations set by 'security personnel'. In the case of prisons, the security personnel's main roles are custodial: locking and unlocking, checking locks, maintaining discipline, and being responsible for the internal security of the prison. Their centrality in the life of prisoners goes beyond 'security'. They regulate visits, provide meals and other necessities, control and manage prisoners' movements through the prison, and can initiate disciplinary proceedings to punish bad behaviour. They also are providers of 'care': they are expected to change prisoners' behaviours and act as role models, mentors, counsellors, teachers, social workers, and so on (Crawley 2006).

In border camps, these interactions are less structured and therefore more arbitrary than in prisons. Nonetheless, 'the border at Calais has been produced as a site of "security" and control by the French and UK authorities' (Freedman 2018, 411). While the makeshift camps of Calais, unlike enclosed camps in other parts of Europe, do not prevent the movement of residents, they are regularly raided by police who try to discourage refugees from remaining in the camps, while at the same time preventing them from moving elsewhere. Widespread police brutality has been reported as well as physical attacks and violence from members of the public (Freedman 2015). Fear of this violence as well as the forced removal meant that residents of the 'new jungle' considered public urban spaces in Calais unsafe or off-limits (Davies et al. 2017).

In both cases, we can clearly see that the production of the security for some produces forms of violence and insecurity for others. It is also clear that security personnel contribute to these dynamics through their coercive, repressive, protective, and/or caring roles. Security staff, for instance, may perceive their duties as part of a state-designed coercive institution that should stand in opposition to the safety and security of individual detainees.

The forms of political violence that can be identified in both border camps and prisons extend beyond the immediacy of securityscapes. Camps dwellers and prisoners live their lives in 'limbo', unsure as to their future, and stuck in a situation where they have little control over what might happen next. Jane Freedman (2018, 412) reports that in Calais, refugees expressed dismay not only about the unsafe conditions for themselves and their families but also about 'their frustrations of being stuck in this "no man's land", unable to reach the UK'. Such experiences and projections towards the future are not homogeneously felt. They are strongly determined by gender and age, with 'women experiencing specific forms of insecurity and violence' (Freedman 2018, 412).

Prisoners also face many forms of deprivation once released from prison. For example, many women and men are homeless once released, making them prone to a persistent cycle of short-term imprisonment. As with camp dwellers, female prisoners face additional difficulties to their personal security and are noted as being at particular risk of extreme poverty, homelessness and suicide when leaving prisons (Kendall 2013). Many prisoners are fearful of what the future will bring and feel that they are 'abandoned' by the state. Some even describe prison as a lifeline compared to the extreme challenges of life on release (Crewe and Ievins 2020).

These dilemmas are made more painful by high levels of material and psychological deprivation, the intensity of the effects of short imprisonment or encampment periods, and by having primary caring responsibilities that either cannot be undertaken while incarcerated or are highly disrupted by being in camps. Securityscapes, prisons, and border camps 'stay' with people much longer than the actual time spent in their confines. Like living in a camp, imprisonment leaves marks. For some, these marks are physically 'inscribed on their bodies' (Moran 2014, 43).

For example, these inscriptions can take the form of poor dental hygiene, malnutrition, and poor health. Incarceration also 'sticks' psychologically, behaviourally, and individually—people feel they can be 'spotted' even without any physical markers. Both formal and informal stigmas present barriers to participating in civic society. Living in such insecure conditions can cause a crisis of legitimacy. Prisons (and camps) are not consensual communities, and 'as such, they are susceptible to abuses of power and to breakdowns in order' (Liebling 2004, 462).

Poor living conditions produce personal insecurity and can be understood as a form of structural violence. As Freedman (2018, 411) argues, 'the violence may be interpreted as indirect but is in no way abstract'. Importantly, the lack of legitimacy felt about how security is mobilized in these spaces and the sheer lack of personal or collective security has a profound impact on the moral standing of individual institutions but also socio-political orders at large. What do these individual experiences tell us about our stances towards the (in)security of prisoners and camp dwellers? What does it say when some people feel more secure within carceral environments than outside? How do the taken-for-granted representations of prisoners, forced migrants, refugees, and asylum seekers match their realities? What do these individual experiences tell us about our socio-political orders and at whose expense are they produced and maintained?

On the concept of structural violence, see **Section 4.2.1**

20.5 Conclusion

In this chapter, we outlined striking similarities and intriguing parallels between prisons and camps to how they are intimately connected to questions of security and political violence. We also revealed some important differences in type and scale of incarceration and the need for careful comparison. On different scales, from individual experiences to institutional practices and national, or global trends, this chapter showed the detrimental effects of prisons and camps. Nevertheless, both continue to be considered solutions to a variety of problems surrounding 'security', however defined. Asking critical questions throughout revealed politically important paradoxes that surround prisons and camps. Thus, there is a need for political reflection and engagement when contemplating locking up or restricting the freedom of people in such fundamental ways. Securityscapes make clear the importance of what it means to be human and to be treated as a person of moral worth. In contemporary discussions, this is routinely ignored in favour of an abstract sense of 'security'. Therefore, we wanted to underscore why we should be inherently critical about detaining people and why we should challenge security as a governing logic.

We should also pay attention to the agency of prisoners and camp dwellers. They continue to develop strategies to resist, challenge, survive, and even make the best of these extreme mobilizations of security. For example, despite the often-negative experiences of living in camps, these sites can be a setting for 'the creation of new forms of refugee citizenship and solidarity' (Freedman 2018, 412; see also Dalal et al. 2018; Sigona 2014). Prisons, for certain people in certain circumstances, can be positive, enabling individuals to break free of old behaviours and identities.

Some have called for the abolition of camps and prisons. Anti-carceral and abolitionist movements have a long tradition, including Women Against Prison in Australia and other anti-carceral feminist critiques (e.g., Carlton and Russell 2018). Alliances have developed and activists like Angela Davis (with Rodriguez, 2000), criminologists like Thomas Mathiesen (2016), and geographers like Ruth Gilmore (2007) have combined their scholarly work with abolitionist activism. There is also a long tradition of activists rallying to support solidarity activism for the residents of camps (e.g., Rigby and Schlembach 2013). On the whole, despite varying forms of activism and solidarity, prisons and camps increasingly feature security mobilizations globally. By exposing the visceral realities of encampment and incarceration, from the micro-practices to the macro-issues on a global scale, we can question security for whom and at whose expense.

Questions for further discussion

1. Are prisons and camps necessary for our collective sense of security in a socio-political order? If so, why, and how?
2. Whose security should be paramount when deciding to exclude individuals from wider society?
3. Do you think countries with low rates of imprisonment are less safe than those with a higher rate? If so, why might this be?
4. Borders produce individual and structural inequalities. What would a world without them look like?
5. In light of the prison industrial complex and vast numbers of incarcerated people, is abolition a viable solution?

Further reading

Weima, Yolenda. 2021. 'Ethically (un)bounding camp research: Life histories within and beyond camp boundaries'. *AREA*. https://doi.org/10.1111/area.12760.
  An important contribution highlighting research ethics in the field and the changing nature of camp boundaries. Very attentive to the importance of space and place and the voice of research participants in Burundi refugee camps.

Axster, Sabrina, Ida Danewid, Asher Goldstein, Matt Mahmoudi, Cemal Burak Tansel, and Lauren Wilcox. 2021. 'Colonial lives of the carceral archipelago: Rethinking the neoliberal security state'. *International Political Sociology* 15(3), 415–439.
  This collective discussion highlights how mass incarceration, police brutality, and border controls impact marginalized and racialized communities across the world.

Moran, Dominique and Jennifer Turner. 2022. 'Carceral and military geographies: Prisons, the military and war'. *Progress in Human Geography*. DOI: 10.1177/03091325221080247.
  An important paper highlighting the connections between different institutions of security and thus situating spaces of confinement, surveillance, and monitoring in deep histories of violence.

Dickson, Andonea J. 2021. 'The carceral wet: Hollowing out rights for migrants in maritime geographies'. *Political Geography* 90. doi.org/10.1016/j.polgeo.2021.102475.
  An interesting article exploring the sea as an important space connected to prisons and camps. It examines how the sea has been used to ignore rights and how it has allowed governments to use maritime environments and more broadly the condition of *wetness* to hold migrants beyond the juridical order and administrative bodies of the state.

Mei-Singh, Laurel. 2020. 'Accompaniment through carceral geographies: Abolitionist research partnerships with Indigenous communities'. *Antipode* 53(1), 74–94.
  A fascinating and challenging read which proposes abolitionist research practices that bring Indigenous politics and carceral geographies into critical dialogue. It highlights racism's practices of criminalization and containment while contributing new ideas to understand radical, syncretic placemaking as part of an expansive practice of liberation.

References

Carlton, Bree and Emma K. Russell. 2018. 'Women against prison: Anti-carceral feminist critiques of the prison'. In *Resisting carceral violence: Women's imprisonment and the politics of abolition*, edited by Bree Carlton and Emma K. Russell. Basingstoke: Palgrave Macmillan.

Crawley, Elaine. 2006. 'Doing prison work: The public and private lives of prison officers'. In *Prison readings: A critical introduction to prisons and imprisonment*, edited by Yvonne Jewkes and Helen Johnston. London: Routledge

Crewe, Ben and Alice Ievins. 2020. 'The prison as a reinventive institution'. *Theoretical Criminology* 24(4), 568–589.

Crewe, Ben, Alison Liebling and Susie Hulley. 2014. 'Heavy-light, absent-present: Rethinking the "weight" of imprisonment'. *The British Journal of Criminology* 65(3), 387–410.

Dalal, Ayham, Amer Darweesh, Philipp Misselwitz, and Anna Steigermann. 2018. 'Planning the ideal refugee camp? A critical interrogation of recent planning innovations in Jordan and Germany'. *Urban Planning* 3(4), 64–78.

DAVIES, THOM, ARSHAD ISAKJEE, and SURINDAR DHESI. 2017. 'Violent inaction: The necropolitical experience of refugees in Europe'. *Antipode* 49(5), 1263–1284.

DAVIS, ANGELA, with DYLAN RODRIGUEZ. 2000. 'The challenge of prison abolition: A conversation'. *Social Justice* 27(3), 212–218.

DEBUYSER, CLAIRE. 2021. 'Calais's migrants continue to face an interminable violation of their human rights'. *Equal Times*, 5 February. www.equaltimes.org/calais-s-migrants-continue-to-face?lang=en#.YN4YYG7RZB0 (last accessed 21 February 2022).

FOUCAULT, MICHEL. 1991 [1972]. *Discipline and punish: The birth of the prison*. London: Penguin.

FREEDMAN, JANE. 2015. *Gendering the international asylum and refugee debate*. Basingstoke: Palgrave Macmillan.

FREEDMAN, JANE. 2018. '"After Calais": Creating and managing (in)security for refugees in Europe'. *French Politics* 16, 400–418.

GILMORE, RUTH W. 2007. *Golden gulag: Prisons, surplus, crisis, and opposition in globalising California*. Berkeley, CA: University of California Press.

GOFFMAN, ERWIN. 1991[1961]. *Asylums: Essays on the situation of mental patients and other inmates*. London: Penguin Press.

JEWKES, YVONNE. 2018. 'Just design: Healthy prisons and the architecture of hope'. *Journal of Criminology* 51(3), 319–338.

JEWKES, YVONNE and HELEN JOHNSTON. Eds. 2006. *Prison readings: A critical introduction to prisons and imprisonment*. London: Routledge.

KENDALL, KATHLEEN. 2013. 'Post-release support for women in England and Wales: The big picture'. In *Women exiting prison: Critical essays on gender, post-release support and survival*, edited by BREE CARLTON and MARIE SEGRAVE. London: Routledge.

LIEBLING, ALISON. 2004. *Prisons and their moral performance: A study of values, quality and prison life*. Oxford: Oxford University Press.

LOESCHER, GIL and JAMES MILNER. 2005. 'The long road home: Protracted refugee situations in Africa'. *Survival: Global Politics and Strategy* 47(2), 153–174.

MAGUIRE, MARK and SETHA LOW. Eds. 2019. *Spaces of security: Ethnographies of securityscapes, surveillance, and control*. New York: New York University Press.

MARTIN, LAUREN L. and MATTHREW L. MITCHELSON. 2009. 'Geographies of detention and imprisonment'. *Geography Compass* 3(1), 459–477.

MATHIESEN, THOMAS. 2016. *The politics of abolition revisited*. London: Routledge.

MCGUIRE, JAMES. 2018. Understanding prison violence: A rapid evidence assessment. HM Prison & Probation Service. https://assets.publishing.service.gov.uk/government/uploads/system/uploads/attachment_data/file/737956/understanding-prison-violence.pdf (last accessed 21 February 2022).

MICHALON, BÉNÉDICTE. 2013. 'Mobility and power in detention: The management of internal movement and governmental mobility in Romania'. In *Carceral spaces: Mobility and agency in imprisonment and migrant detention*, edited by DOMINIQUE MORAN, NICK GILL, and DEIRDRE CONLON. Farnham: Ashgate.

MINCA, CLAUDIO. 2015. 'Geographies of the camp'. *Political Geography* 49, 74–83.

MORAN, DOMINIQUE. 2014. 'Leaving behind the "total institution"? Teeth, transcarceral spaces and (re)inscription of the formerly incarcerated body'. *Gender, Place & Culture* 21(1), 35–51.

MORAN, DOMINIQUE, JENNIFER TURNER, and ANNA K. SCHLIEHE. 2018. 'Conceptualizing the carceral in carceral geography'. *Progress in Human Geography* 42(5), 666–686.

PECK, JAMIE. 2003. 'Geography and public policy: Mapping the penal state'. *Progress in Human Geography* 27(2), 222–232.

Pratt, John. 2002. *Punishment and civilization*. London: SAGE.
Prison Policy Initiative. 2021. *States of incarceration: The global context 2021*. www.prisonpolicy.org/global/2021.html (last accessed 22 February 2022).
Reiter, Keramet A. 2012. 'Parole, snitch, or die: California's supermax prisons and prisoners, 1997–2007'. *Punishment & Society* 14(5), 530–563.
Rigby, Joe and Raphael Schlembach. 2013. 'Impossible protest: Noborders in Calais'. *Citizenship Studies* 17(2), 157–172.
Riley, Andrew, Andrea Varner, Peter Ventevogel, M. M. Talmur Hasan, and Courtney Welton-Mitchell. 2017. 'Daily stressors, trauma exposure, and mental health among stateless Rohingya refugees in Bangladesh'. *Transcultural Psychiatry* 54(3), 304–331.
Sandri, Elisa. 2018. '"Volunteer humanitarianism": Volunteers and humanitarian aid in the Jungle refugee camp of Calais'. *Journal of Ethnic and Migration Studies* 44(1), 65–80.
Schliehe, Anna K. and Ben Crewe. 2021. 'Top bunk, bottom bunk: Cellsharing in prisons'. *British Journal of Criminology* 62(2), 484–500.
Sigona, Nando. 2014. 'Campzenship: Reimagining the camp as a social and political space'. *Citizenship Studies* 19(1), 1–15.
Stern, Julia. 2021. 'Genocide in China: Uighur re-education camps and international response'. *Immigration and Human Rights Law Review* 3(1), 1–33.
Stoller, Nancy. 2003. 'Space, place and movement as aspects of health care in three women's prisons'. *Social Science and Medicine* 56(11), 2263–2275.
UNHCR. 2021. *UNHCR's refugee population statistics database*. www.unhcr.org/refugee-statistics (last accessed 21 February 2022).
Wacquant, Loïc. 2009. *Punishing the poor: The neoliberal government of social insecurity*. Durham, NC: Duke University Press.
World Bank. n.d. *Population, total*. https://data.worldbank.org/indicator/SP.POP.TOTL (last accessed 22 February 2022).
World Prison Brief. 2021. www.prisonstudies.org (last accessed 21 February 2022).

Index

#BlackLivesMatter, *see also* police and policing; social movements; resistance; United States of America, African-Americans 10, 63–64, 91, 140, 314
Afghanistan 41, 73, 79, 80, 105, 107–108, 133, 180, 193, 198, 201, 244–246, 249, 261, 266, 275, 281, 316, 331
Africa (*see* Chapter 14) 21, 44, 107, 108, 145, 146, 173, 174, 175, 206, 207, 211, 213, 216, 229, 231, 232, 234, 318, 330
Ahmed, Sara 148
algorithms (*see* Chapter 15)
Algeria 21–23, 27, 145
  Algerian War of Independence (1954–1962) 21–23, 122, 124, 129
Anarchism 21, 68, 123–124, 230, 237
Anthropocene (the), *see also* environment, environmental security (*see* Chapter 18)
Appadurai, Arjun 141, 144, 146
architecture, *see also* urban spaces and dynamics (*see* Chapter 20) 29, 42, 58, 77, 85, 259–260, 266, 297, 314
Arctic (the) 291, 297
Arendt, Hannah 183, 319
armed conflicts (*see* Chapters 7 and 8) 7, 21, 157, 161, 189, 196, 200, 297
armed forces and the military, *see also* militarisation; Security Sector Reform (*see* Chapters 7 and 8) 8, 19, 21, 25, 31–32, 41, 48, 62, 66, 67, 75, 80, 82–83, 98–99, 145, 148, 157, 166, 192, 193, 195, 196, 209, 214, 234, 241, 245, 246, 259, 262, 266–268, 274, 276, 278, 281–283, 285, 292, 294, 297, 319
  non–state armed forces/paramilitaries (*see* Chapter 8) 31, 57–58, 112, 180, 209, 266

arms control, *see also* weapons, weapons-systems 263, 281–286
Artificial Intelligence (AI), *see also* technology; weapons, weapons–systems (*see* Chapter 15) 262–263, 265, 280, 281, 285, 316
asylum seekers, *see also* camps; migration and migrants; refugees; prisons (*see* Chapters 19 and 20) 189, 198
Australia 27, 44, 73, 76, 179, 201, 215, 217, 291, 318, 320, 329, 338
authority, *see also* violence (political) xii–xiv, 19–20, 26, 30, 40, 45, 47–49, 54–55, 60–61, 64–67, 88, 92, 109–110, 122–124, 125–126, 132, 134, 139–140, 155, 165, 178, 190–192, 196, 212, 215, 247, 260, 274, 310–313, 320–321, 327, 331, 333
autonomous weapons, *see also* artificial intelligence (*see* Chapters 15 and 17)

Bangladesh 6, 327, 330
Benjamin, Walter 65, 134, 259, 319
biometrics, *see also* bodies and body politics; digital security; surveillance (*see* Chapters 15 and 19)
bodies and body politics, *see also* biometrics (*see* Chapters 9, 10, 19, and 20) 12, 13–14, 39, 57, 59, 72, 80, 83, 97, 110, 131, 182–184, 198, 214, 215, 233, 244, 245, 248, 260, 273–277, 279, 282–283,
Bolivia 232
borders (*see* Chapters 19 and 20) 38, 44, 54, 76, 80, 82, 83, 98, 100, 140, 149, 173, 175, 178, 181–182, 195, 197, 206–208, 211, 239–240, 242, 244, 281,

Bosnia 165
Bourdieu, Pierre 12, 59
Brazil 23, 58, 83, 89, 93, 95–96, 97, 111, 113, 115, 146, 164, 216, 327
  'favelas' [urban slums], *see also* urban spaces and dynamics 23, 58, 115
Burundi 239

Cambodia 194
camps, *see also* asylum seekers; migration and migrants; refugees; prisons (*see* Chapters 19 and 20) 29, 45, 80, 106–107, 109, 135
Canada 19, 44, 55–56, 73, 75, 76, 79, 82, 90, 93, 108, 148, 174, 179, 181, 201, 237, 297, 309–311
capitalism and forms of accumulation, *see also* class, economic factors (*see* Chapter 14) 12, 20, 45, 68, 78, 97, 144, 149, 180, 218, 251, 262–264, 285, 294, 298–303, 312–313, 320–321, 322, 328–329
Caribbean, the 21, 143–144, 145
challenges to security, *see* resistance
China (People's Republic of) 7, 13, 45, 76, 78, 113, 116, 178, 192, 215, 217, 263, 274, 294, 327, 331
cities, *see* urban spaces and dynamics
citizenship, *see also* identity; nationalism; othering; political belonging; xenophobia (*see* Chapter 11) xii, 13, 31, 34, 41–43, 44, 62, 64, 83–84, 113–115, 116, 127, 140, 147, 149, 150, 190, 192, 196, 210, 215, 237, 245, 259, 264, 265, 294, 296, 311, 314, 316, 322, 328, 330, 337–338

civilians 7, 53, 60, 106, 107, 115, 117, 122–124, 128, 132–133, 135, 196, 267, 284
class ix–xii, 3, 11–12, 13, 21, 26–27, 31, 38–40, 41, 43–44, 50, 55–56, 58–59, 68, 75, 79, 81, 82, 84, 89, 90, 141, 142, 146, 153, 160, 165–166, 174, 175, 176, 182, 189, 195, 216–218, 242, 259, 275, 276, 292, 294, 299–300, 310, 312–320, 328–329, 337
  definition 12
climate change, *see also* Anthropocene (the); environment, environmental security (*see* Chapter 18) 5, 10, 25, 29, 47, 54, 59, 114, 192, 218, 231, 232, 237, 265, 266, 310, 312
Cohn, Carol 10, 109–110, 157, 265
Cold War (1947–1991) 8, 79, 110, 144, 157, 173, 190, 191, 274, 278, 282–283, 285, 287, 292, 296
Colombia 54, 73, 80, 114–115, 125, 126, 128, 135, 166, 196
colonialism/coloniality, *see also* decolonial thinking (*see* Chapter 9) 7, 8, 15, 19–20, 21–24, 44, 61–63, 66, 68, 76–79, 90–91, 161, 167, 173, 174, 175, 179–180, 190–191, 195, 197–199, 215, 218, 225–236, 249–251, 275, 280–282, 284–285, 292, 294–295, 305, 328
common–sense, *see also* critique 2, 5, 9, 276–277
Congo, Democratic Republic of 132, 194, 196, 235
contingency, *see also* critique x–xi, 3, 4–5, 7–8, 10, 19–20, 25, 29–30, 32, 38–39, 40–41, 43, 61, 72–73, 75, 83, 133, 134, 142, 173, 279, 281, 305
Côte d'Ivoire 53, 182
counterinsurgency (*see* Chapter 8) 21, 23, 31, 53, 82, 97, 108, 144, 190, 193, 196, 287

counterterrorism, *see also* terrorism (clandestine political violence; *see* Chapter 8) 32, 40, 82, 181, 201, 248, 250
COVID-19, *see also* health, health security 37, 53, 192, 206, 214, 214, 215, 216–219, 313, 316
Crenshaw, Kimberlé W., *see also* intersectionality 11, 160
crime, (organized) criminality (*see* Chapters 6 and 20) 25, 26, 30, 32, 40, 56, 58, 60, 65, 66, 73, 77, 79, 80, 82, 83, 88, 115, 125, 128, 131, 159, 181, 183, 210, 247, 261, 276, 284
critique (*see* Chapters 1 and 5) ix–xi, xiii, 27, 29, 32–33, 36–38, 41, 43, 47, 49, 54, 67, 89, 97, 99, 100, 105, 124, 134, 143, 145, 148, 172, 156, 157, 160, 165, 166, 175, 176, 184, 196, 190, 194–201, 213, 224, 244, 246–249, 258, 263–268, 274, 286, 296, 298, 304, 312, 313, 319, 327, 329, 338
Cuba 331
culture ix–xii, 3, 11, 12–13, 19–21, 28, 38, 41, 43–44, 48–49, 50, 55, 59, 64, 67, 75, 88, 94, 105, 107–110, 113, 145, 148, 161, 172, 173, 176–177, 179, 182, 198, 200, 251, 257, 262, 264–265, 284, 285, 316
  definition 13
cybersecurity, *see* digital security

data, datafication, *see also* cybersecurity; surveillance (*see* Chapter 15) 32, 54, 95, 215, 310, 316–317
decolonial thinking, *see also* colonialism/coloniality; western-centrism (*see* Chapter 9) 7, 68
cosmologies/*cosmopraxis* 142, 149–152, 303
defence and security industry, *see also* security professionals 19, 81, 225–226, 262–263, 285, 328

design, security and design (*see* Chapter 16) 29, 32, 41–42, 46–47, 58, 77, 79, 80, 85, 97, 106–107, 163, 241, 248, 251, 275, 276, 281, 285, 320, 331–337
deterrence, *see also* nuclear weapons 39, 60, 259–261, 274, 278, 282–283, 287, 313, 318–321, 322
development, security-development nexus (*see* Chapter 12) 5, 8, 18, 26, 31, 32, 34, 42, 79, 80, 83, 144, 207, 211, 212, 226, 231, 232, 235–236, 292, 295, 298, 299–301, 303
digital security (*see* Chapter 15) 19, 25, 31, 58, 93, 97, 217, 261, 266, 277, 310–311, 316–317
disability ix–xii, 3, 11, 13–14, 15, 33, 38, 41, 43–44, 54, 55, 75, 81, 141, 144, 146, 160–161, 163, 165, 197, 207, 211, 242, 276, 281
  definition 13–14
discourse, *see also* meaning-making processes; security as discursive mobilisation 15, 28, 31, 32, 37, 47, 78, 123, 140–143, 148, 152, 159, 161, 172, 176–178, 179, 180, 182–183, 193–194, 197, 199, 207, 209, 215, 224, 230, 257, 278, 279, 284–285, 295, 296, 297, 298, 305, 313, 315, 320–321
domestic abuses, *see also* femicide; gender 53, 56, 58, 217
domination, *see also* injustices; oppression ix–xii, 2–3, 6–8, 11–14, 30, 36–37, 38–41, 47–49, 54–55, 57, 64, 66, 81, 82–83, 91, 97, 141, 143, 149, 160–161, 164–166, 211, 218, 240, 245, 252, 268–269, 275, 285, 292–294, 300, 301–302
  definition 3
Dominican Republic 140, 149, 153

INDEX

drones, *see also* weapons, weapon–systems 54, 80, 97, 108, 183, 189, 240, 241–242, 243, 246, 248, 249, 251, 261–262, 266, 281–282, 285, 310, 312, 314
drugs, *see* war on drugs
Du Bois, W. E. B. 150, 175, 180, 319

Ebola, *see also* health, health security 37, 206, 207–208, 211, 213, 214, 215, 216
economic factors xii–xiii, 25–26, 31–32, 54, 58, 59, 64, 77–79, 82–83, 180, 189, 191, 192, 195, 200, 217–218, 232, 294, 299–300, 302–303, 312–315, 328–329
Ecuador 232, 234, 294
Egypt 126
El Salvador 83
Elias, Norbert 91–92
emotions (politics of) 56, 148
energy resources and security (*see* Chapter 18) 46, 210, 230, 232, 292, 296–297
Enloe, Cynthia 106, 116, 160
environment, environmental security, *see also* climate change, energy security (*see* Chapter 18) 10, 29, 54, 56, 58, 82–83, 151, 174, 189, 192, 211, 231–236, 265, 279, 283, 318, 320
  environmental degradations (*see* Chapter 18) 3, 6, 25, 29, 116, 189, 206, 210, 237
  natural disasters (*see* Chapter 18) 41, 161, 200, 232, 297, 304, 310
ethnicity ix–xii, 3, 11, 12, 13, 21, 38, 39, 41, 43–44, 55, 75, 81, 82, 108, 111, 133, 141, 142, 173–178, 216, 217, 312–315
  definition 12
euro-centrism, *see* western-centrism
European Union (EU) 44, 174, 179, 193, 196, 201, 292, 318, 329–330
everyday (the) (*see* Chapter 10) i, xiii, 6, 10–11, 12, 26, 30–31, 41–43, 48–49, 76, 87–88, 107, 141, 153, 177, 181, 213, 215, 216–218, 239, 242, 257, 259, 260, 264, 269, 281, 292, 328–329, 331–337
exception (the), *see also* law; legitimacy; rule of law 27, 31, 34, 63, 91, 125–126, 131, 217, 246–247, 316, 326, 331–337
extraction, *see* natural resources

failed state (idea of), *see also* state (the) 180, 191, 192–194, 198, 210
Fanon, Frantz 68, 145
femicide, *see also* gender; sexual violences; sexuality (*see* Chapter 10) x, 53, 55–56, 64
feminisms, *see also* gender (*see* Chapter 10) 7, 148, 248, 338
food (security) 6, 19, 112, 162, 189, 212, 214, 218, 227, 230–231, 265, 277, 292, 294, 297, 299, 330, 335
Foucault, Michel 127, 319, 332
framing, *see* security as framing
France 21, 23, 45, 47, 53, 78, 88, 91, 92, 93, 95, 99, 140, 145, 147, 162, 174, 175, 180, 182, 183, 191, 250, 258–259, 274, 329, 330, 334, 335, 336
freedoms (individual), *see also* balance (security-liberty); exception (the); law; liberalism; rule of law 18, 19, 21, 27, 30, 31–32, 44, 112, 150, 162, 190, 211, 246, 269, 331, 338

Galtung, Johan 55, 56, 57, 274, 277
gender, *see also* Lesbian, Gay, Bisexual, Trans, Queer + (LGBTQ+); sexuality (*see* Chapter 10) ix–xii, 3, 11, 12, 15, 28, 32, 38, 41, 43, 44, 50, 53, 55–56, 57, 64, 66, 68, 75, 76, 79, 81, 82, 83, 84, 85, 97, 109, 110–111, 116, 133, 141, 142, 144, 146, 153, 174, 180, 189, 193, 194, 197–198, 200, 212, 213, 215, 216, 217, 233, 242, 244, 248, 275, 281, 303–304, 312, 313, 314, 316, 317, 320, 327, 329, 337, 338
  definition 12
genocide, *see also* Holocaust (the) 21, 53, 54, 56, 68, 108–109, 131, 144, 146, 153, 195, 276, 327
geopolitics 108, 175, 191, 199–200, 234, 246, 257–258, 263, 270
Germany 21, 68, 75, 93, 95, 173, 175, 179, 260,
Gramsci, Antonio 39–40
Guatemala 53, 77, 144, 153
Guinea 207, 216

Hague Convention (1899) 108, 280
Haiti 23, 140, 149, 310
health, health security (*see* Chapter 13) 5, 8, 18, 19, 21, 25, 27, 28, 29, 30, 31, 32, 37, 40, 44, 47, 53, 56, 59, 72, 76, 79, 80, 82, 83, 92, 111, 113, 127, 129, 146, 159, 163, 164, 189, 192, 195, 259, 260, 262, 265, 292, 299, 312, 319, 335, 337
heteronormativity, *see* gender
hierarchies, *see also* power (relations of); order (socio–political); class; culture; disability; ethnicity; gender; ideology; political belonging; race and racialisation; religion; and sexuality (*see* Chapters 1, 2, 3, 4, and 5) x–xii, 92, 93, 94, 96, 107, 115, 132, 133, 144, 151, 156–158, 162, 164, 165, 172, 175, 177, 180–182, 189, 194, 195, 196, 206, 208, 211, 214, 215, 216, 218, 224–225, 227, 233, 240–241, 247, 250, 257, 258, 259, 260, 268, 276, 279, 280–281, 292, 295, 299–301, 304, 309, 312, 314, 316–317, 328–330, 331, 333
  definition 43
historicity, *see also* critique, 5, 8, 20–24, 25, 29, 32, 38–39, 40–41, 43, 48–49, 61–64, 72–73, 75, 78, 82–83, 134, 141, 207, 225–236, 240, 249, 280–281

HIV/AIDS, *see also* health, health security 37, 82, 206, 211, 212, 213, 214,
Holocaust (the), *see also* genocide; race and racialisation 68, 107, 133, 108–109, 117, 144
homelessness, *see* unhoused people
human rights ix–x, 19, 27, 30, 45, 167, 192, 193, 207, 215, 218, 246, 318–320, 328, 331–337
human security, *see also* security, as condition of possibility 5, 19, 26–27, 34, 45, 180, 192, 193, 196, 197, 198, 199, 206, 207, 208, 211–213, 214, 283, 292–293, 298–300, 303
humanitarian intervention, *see* human security
humanitarianism (*see* Chapter 12) 45, 80, 191, 192, 197, 198, 283, 284, 287, 318, 321

ideas xi–xii, 3, 33, 37, 41, 42–49, 49, 54, 74, 111, 115, 165, 176, 190–192, 217, 298–299
  definition 45
identity[/–ies], *see also* citizenship; nationalism; othering; political belonging; xenophobia (*see* Chapters 9, 10, and 11) ix–xii, 32–33, 37, 40–41, 42–49, 54, 74, 76, 79, 84, 95, 294–295, 310–315, 320–321, 331–337
  definition 44
  predatory identities 141, 143–149
ideology xi–xii, 11, 12–13, 21, 31, 38, 41, 43–45, 55, 61–64, 75, 113, 140, 146, 173–176, 178, 191–192, 260, 300, 303
  definition 12–13
India 31, 66, 78, 85, 91, 164, 178, 231, 274, 327
Indigenous peoples 15, 21, 43–44, 53, 55–56, 60, 61, 82–83, 106, 144–146, 150–151, 153, 165, 166, 180, 219, 229, 230–231, 232, 234–235, 236, 293, 294–296, 303, 312–314, 317, 320, 322, 339

Indonesia 113, 193, 216, 231
inequalities, *see also* domination; hierarchies; oppression; power (relations of) 10, 12–14, 39, 64, 72, 82–83, 178
infrastructure (*see* Chapters 15, 17, and 20) xi–xii, 5, 7, 33, 37, 41–42, 42–49, 54, 55, 58, 59, 74, 76, 85, 92, 106–107, 109, 113, 126, 131, 146, 176, 184, 189, 191, 195, 208, 209, 257, 260, 294–295, 314
  definition 46
institutions, *see also* security as institutional mobilisation (*see* Chapter 20) xi–xii, 3, 8, 14, 29–30, 32, 38, 40, 42–49, 54, 59, 74, 88, 90–91, 92–93, 95–97, 107, 108, 109, 112, 226, 292, 297–298, 310
  definition 46
international institutions, *see also* United Nations, United Natins Development Programme, World Bank, World Health Organization 7–8, 43, 109, 208, 212–213, 218, 292, 297
interest 4, 5, 6–7, 20, 30, 33, 37, 41, 42–49, 54, 74, 90–91, 109, 113, 115
  definition 45
  national interest 8, 45
international (humanitarian) law, *see also* exception (the); law; legitimacy 58, 62, 64, 108, 109, 280, 284
International Monetary Fund (IMF), *see also* institutions, international institutions 191
international system 45, 274, 283, 299, 302
intersectionality xi–xii, 3, 11, 14, 25, 43, 75, 81, 141, 142, 148, 158, 160–162, 164, 165, 166, 174, 175, 189, 217
  definition 11
intervention (military), *see also* human security, Responsibility to Protect (R2P) 54, 62, 63, 73, 80, 191, 192, 197
Iran 66
Iraq 23, 66, 91, 122, 129, 140, 266, 275, 276, 316, 331
Ireland (Republic of, and Northern Ireland) 57, 91, 93, 127, 131, 167, 176

Israel 60, 85, 132, 135, 147, 148, 267–268, 274

Japan 19, 75, 93, 113, 124, 161, 200
Jordan 327, 330

Kenya 327, 330
knowledge production 2, 8, 10–11, 12, 14, 26, 30, 31–32, 41, 43–44, 48, 150–151, 156, 193, 195, 285

land, land rights and conflicts (*see* Chapter 14), *see also* natural resources; property, property rights 144, 294, 298–299, 302–303
landmines, *see also* weapons and weapon–systems 7, 189, 280, 283
law, *see also* exception (the); freedoms (individual); international law; legitimacy; rule of law 19–20, 27, 31–32, 38, 40, 43–44, 47, 63, 64–65, 72–73, 79, 80, 134, 140, 161, 228, 231, 240, 284
Lebanon 113, 124
legitimacy, *see also* violence (political) ix, xii, 26, 28, 30, 38, 40, 45, 49, 55, 61–64, 66, 90–92, 95–97, 109–110, 122, 125–126, 215–216, 232, 274–275, 279, 285–286, 310, 320–321, 328, 330–331, 337–338
  use of force 60, 61–67, 73, 88, 90–91, 96–97, 108, 127–129, 195–196, 421–422, 274, 281–282, 285
Lesbian, Gay, Bisexual, Trans, Queer + (LGBTQ+), *see also* gender; sexuality; citizenship; identity; political belonging (*see* Chapter 10) xi, 34, 81, 317
liberalism, *see also* democracy (liberal) 26–27, 41, 44, 45, 229, 262
Liberia 207, 216, 237
Libya 126
Lukes, Steven 39–40

Marx, Karl 6, 78, 230
masculinities, *see* gender
Mauritania 173
Mbembe, Achille 232, 319

meaning–making processes, *see also* discourse; security as discursive mobilisation; productive processes 10, 19, 21, 28–29, 32, 40, 55, 56, 59, 65, 73–74, 76, 79, 82, 84, 172, 214
media, social media 13, 32, 37, 75, 265, 277
methodology, *see also* security questions ix–xii
Mexico 73, 83, 115, 140, 146, 149, 153, 159, 164, 215, 314–315, 319, 321
migration and migrants, *see also* asylum seekers; camps; refugees (*see* Chapter 19) xi, 21, 44–45, 76, 82–83, 140, 142, 146, 149, 176, 181, 198, 294–295, 297, 327, 329–331, 332–337
militarisation (*see* Chapter 7) 32, 234–236, 284–285, 292–293, 328
military, *see* armed forces and the military (*see* Chapters 7, 8, 16, and 17)
mines and mining industry, *see* natural resources (*see* Chapter 14)
mobility and travel, *see also* migration and migrants (*see* Chapter 19) 80, 178–179, 183
Myanmar 47, 216, 330

Namibia 113
national interest, *see* interest
national security 19, 41, 115–116, 206, 209–211, 216–217, 278, 296–298
nationalism, *see also* citizenship; identity; othering; political belonging; xenophobia (*see* Chapter 11) 21, 112, 144, 148
natural resources, *see also* environment, environmental security (*see* Chapters 14 and 18) 6, 19, 54, 56, 218
necropolitics, *see also* Mbembe, Achille 318–320
Netherlands (the) 75, 191, 231
New Zealand (Aotearoa) 44, 60, 76, 179, 250
Nigeria 167, 207
non-humans and non-human world, *see* environment and environmental security; technology (*see* Chapters 15 and 18) 56, 58, 59, 66, 149, 151, 318
non-violence, *see also* violence (political) 19, 47–49, 66, 105, 129, 268, 285
North Atlantic Treaty Organisation (NATO) 41, 80, 193, 201, 292
North Korea, People's Republic of 79, 110, 274
Norway 19, 130
novelty, claims to, *see also* historicity 5
nuclear weapons, *see also* weapons and weapon–systems 19, 46, 53, 60, 83, 110–111, 124, 157, 174, 261, 265, 274, 277, 278, 281, 283, 284, 287, 293
nuclear deterrence 60, 83, 278, 283

oppression, *see also* domination 3, 8, 12–14, 25, 31, 37–41, 47–49, 66, 81, 82–83, 141–142, 158–160, 165–166, 217–218, 246–247, 334–338
definition 3
orders (socio-political), *see also* domination; hierarchies, power (relations of) (*see* Chapter 3) xi–xiv, 2–3, 5–8, 11–14, 20, 30–33, 37–41, 56, 60–61, 63, 64–67, 72, 73–76, 81–84, 87–88, 89–92, 95–97, 100, 105, 122, 125–126, 129–132, 141, 144–146, 158–159, 171–172, 175–176, 180, 195–198, 216–218, 224–225, 231, 260, 262, 285–286, 303–304, 325–328, 331–335, 337–338
definition 38
Orientalism, *see also* colonialism/coloniality 147
othering, *see also* citizenship; identity; nationalism; political belonging; xenophobia (*see* Chapters 9 and 11) 32, 39, 44, 76, 79, 83, 163–164, 171–172, 182, 198, 211, 310, 314–315, 334–335

Pacific-island states 284, 292, 300
Pakistan 54, 111, 113, 274
Palestine 60, 85, 124, 132, 135, 237, 267–268
pathologization, *see also* authority; health, health security; medicalisation of security; security as discursive mobilisation 65
patriarchy, *see also* domination; gender; order (socio-political) (*see* Chapter 10) xii, 3, 141, 303
peacebuilding, peacebuilding operations 108, 193, 194, 196, 197, 199, 201
Peru 232, 234
Philippines, the 79, 84, 91
police and policing (*see* Chapters 6 and 20) 6, 10, 21, 30, 32, 44, 53, 54, 57–58, 60, 62, 65, 72–73, 75, 79, 80, 82–84, 108, 113, 115, 125–126, 134, 180–181, 195, 224, 228, 260, 281, 314
defunding movement, police reforms 30, 96–97, 313
militarization of, *see also* militarization (*see* Chapters 6 and 7) 6, 21–22, 80, 88, 98–100, 292
political belonging, *see also* citizenship; identity; nationalism; othering; xenophobia (*see* Chapter 11) 5, 3, 11, 13, 38, 41, 43–44, 55, 75
definition 13
political violence, *see* violence (political)
politics (as struggle and context), *see also* historicity 13, 19, 37–38, 42–43, 46, 47–48
definition 42–43
popular culture, *see also* culture 13, 48–49, 59, 80, 99, 105, 113, 116, 117, 179, 240, 262, 285, 314
power (relations of), *see also* hierarchies; orders (socio-politiocal) (*see* Chapter 3) xi–xiv, 10, 26–27, 32–33, 38–41, 45, 49, 55–56, 59, 61, 64–67, 72, 73–75, 81, 82, 134, 165–166, 174–177, 192–193, 196, 199–200, 227, 233–234, 241, 264, 273–274, 334–337

definition 38
as co-constitution 38–41, 87–88, 142–143, 151–152, 165
as framing, *see* security, as framing
to coerce 3, 39–40
to deter 39–40
prisons, *see also* camps (*see* Chapter 20) 21, 40, 44, 54, 58, 60, 66, 67, 73, 84, 131, 132, 159, 277
privatisation and private actors 23, 31–32, 37, 46–47, 54, 61, 65, 88, 89, 106, 192, 212, 215, 217–218, 224, 226, 232, 233–236, 239, 240, 241, 243, 248, 251, 252, 262–263, 285, 310, 317, 320, 326, 328–329, 335
productive processes, *see also* meaning-making processes 3, 10, 14, 19–20, 21, 23, 27, 28–29, 47–49
property, property rights (*see* Chapter 14) 24, 27, 54, 58, 89, 106, 125, 131, 144, 196, 302

queer (theory and identity), *see also* gender; sexuality (*see* Chapter 10) 7, 34, 110, 148, 150, 156–158, 312, 317

race and racialisation (*see* Chapters 9, 10, and 11) ix, xi–xii, 3, 6, 11, 12, 20–21, 32, 38, 41, 43–44, 55–56, 58–59, 60, 63, 65, 73, 75, 76, 79, 80, 82–83, 95–97, 109, 110–111, 113–115, 140–142, 144–149, 160–162, 194–195, 197–198, 217–218, 229–236, 242, 249–251, 275, 281, 312–315, 316–320, 329–330
definition 12
radicalization (*see* Chapter 8) 181, 215
refugees, *see also* asylum seekers; camps; migration and migrants (*see* Chapters 19 and 20) 21, 45, 80, 161, 178, 185, 198, 210, 243, 300
reification, *see also* domination; othering; oppression; sociology (*see* Chapters 9, 10, 11, and 19) 6–7, 12, 28, 38–40, 144
definition 6
religion ix, xi–xii, 3, 11, 13, 21, 31, 38, 41, 43–44, 55, 58, 66, 75, 79, 81, 82–83, 147, 162, 174, 178, 181, 183, 275
definition 13
resistance, *see also* everyday (the); non-violence; social movements (*see* Chapter 3) 10–11, 28, 32–33, 37–40, 47–49, 66, 75, 82, 108, 124, 134, 183, 199–200, 225, 302–303, 313, 338
as direct and formal 47–48, 99–100, 140, 334–337
as informal and indirect 48–49
resource extraction (*see* Chapters 14 and 18) 54, 218
Responsibility to Protect (R2P), *see also* human rights; human security; humanitarianism; intervention (military) 45, 62, 63, 192
risk(s) 10, 19, 25–26, 29, 37, 79, 80, 81–82, 88, 126, 129, 144, 172, 181, 183, 207, 208, 215, 216–218, 240, 241, 242, 252, 263, 265, 268, 284, 292, 302, 310, 315, 316–317, 320–321
rule of law, *see also* freedom(s); international law; law; legitimacy; and exception (the) 61–64, 88, 91, 94, 97, 98–99, 134, 178, 191, 199, 224, 233
Russia (and Union of Soviet Socialist Republics (1922–1991)) 7, 60, 68, 113, 191, 261, 274, 297, 327
Rwanda 144, 195, 276

Said, Edward, *see also* Orientalism 50, 147
Second World War (1939–1945) 106, 107, 122, 124, 145, 190, 240, 257, 266
security, *see also* meaning-making processes; private actors and dynamics in security; productive processes; security questions; security professionals; violence (political) ix–xiv
balance, security-liberty 19–20, 27, 132, 246–247
debates in security studies x, 8, 24–25, 45, 193, 296–303
as condition of impossibility 7, 30–31, 54–55, 128–134, 164
as condition of possiblity 7, 30–31, 54–55, 131
as discursive mobilisation 9–10, 14, 19, 21, 28, 32, 37–38, 43, 45, 80, 81, 140–142, 214–215, 225, 296, 298–299
as framing x, 2–3, 10–11, 14, 19–20, 25–26, 28–32, 37–41, 45, 48–49, 61, 63, 64–67, 73–74, 79, 80, 82, 84, 133, 141–143, 178, 181–183, 193–194, 207–208, 209, 215, 218, 231, 292, 298
as insecurities (*see* Chapter 10) 19, 31, 40, 61, 82, 84, 126, 132–133, 144, 158–160, 162–164, 175–177, 236, 241–242, 303–304, 318–320, 334–337
as institutional mobilisation xii, 5, 21, 32, 43–44, 46, 224–225
as material mobilisation xii, 31, 43–44, 214–215, 224–225, 317, 329–330
as mobilisation ix–xiv, 9–10, 14, 19–20, 26, 29–33, 37–41, 42–49, 54–56, 61, 64–67, 71–72, 73–84, 88, 100, 126, 129–132, 141–143, 173–174, 178, 193–194, 195–196, 206, 209, 214, 217–218, 224–225, 246, 274, 285–286, 292, 320–321, 328, 334–335, 337–338
objective understanding of 25–27, 29
as political choice ix, 3, 9–11, 14, 19–20, 28–29, 32–33, 37, 44, 46, 47–49, 268–269
as political claim ix, xii, 9–11, 14, 19–20, 26–33, 37–38, 44, 46–47, 54, 75, 130–131, 165, 195, 240–241, 259, 275–276, 281–284
as political struggle 3, 10, 19, 26–33, 37–38, 47–49, 54, 55, 72–73, 81–82, 84, 105, 195–196

as material mobilisation 31, 43–44, 46–47
as political mobilisation x–xii, 20, 29–33, 54, 214–215
as symbolic mobilisation xii, 27, 44–45, 54–56
subjective understanding of 3, 9–11, 13, 25–27, 29, 39–40, 45
security questions (methodology)
who (can) 'speak' security? xi, 26, 28, 37, 38, 60, 75–76, 124, 140, 195
security for whom? xi, xiii, 19, 38, 60, 76, 79, 81, 85, 88, 91, 93, 95, 123, 125, 158, 178, 181, 183, 190, 194–198, 208, 212, 247, 249, 252, 263, 274, 280, 294, 310, 327, 329, 331, 338
security where? xi, 38, 43, 59, 60, 75, 76–78, 81, 85, 88, 92, 93, 105–109, 113, 115, 133, 158, 161, 162–164, 166, 189, 190, 194, 198–201, 214, 231, 233–234, 241, 246, 249, 252, 258, 268, 269, 281–282, 293, 294, 312, 315, 316–318, 319, 327, 330, 331–337
security when? xi, xii, 19, 20, 21, 24, 25, 29, 38, 39, 44, 49, 54–55, 56, 60, 62, 63, 65, 66, 78–79, 82, 90, 91, 106, 107, 110, 112, 122, 123, 126, 133, 140, 141, 149, 151, 158, 162–164, 190, 198–201, 207, 208, 213, 215, 216, 228, 241, 243, 246–248, 261, 266, 275, 279, 282, 284, 286, 292, 294, 296, 304, 310, 316, 318–320, 330, 332, 333, 337–338
security from what? (passim) xi, 25, 38, 60, 79, 81, 85, 95, 122, 125, 140, 141, 190, 194–198, 207, 208, 209, 212, 252, 274, 295, 296, 317
security how? (see esp. Chapters 15, 16, and 17) xi, 26, 60, 80–81, 85, 88, 93, 212
security why? (passim) xi, 60, 81–82, 143, 206, 208, 212, 266

security for what purpose? (passim) xi, 38, 60, 81, 82–83, 112–115, 125, 141, 172, 206, 208, 212–216, 224, 233, 236, 248, 252, 258, 263, 269, 316
security at whose expense? (passim) xi, 38, 76, 81, 83–84, 85, 91, 95, 140, 141, 156, 158, 160, 162, 166, 172, 174, 190, 194, 224, 233, 235, 236, 246, 248, 249, 252, 266, 274, 280, 318, 327, 330, 333, 337, 338
security professionals, see also experts/expertise; knowledge production 10, 19, 20, 26, 30–31, 40, 44, 67, 81–82, 88, 92–97, 110–111, 144, 224, 259, 263–268, 285, 293, 318–320, 334–337
Security Sector Reform (SSR) 191–192, 196
September 11th, 2001 attacks 5, 27, 32, 126, 192, 315, 316
Sexuality [/ies], see also gender; queer; LGBTQ+ (see Chapter 10) ix–xii, 3, 11, 12, 21, 38, 41, 42–44, 55, 75, 81, 166, 189, 200, 313–315, 317
definition 12
sexual violences, see also femicide; gender; sexuality; violence (political) (see Chapter 10) 111, 146
Sierra Leone 54, 207, 216, 226–228, 230–232, 235
slavery 21, 24, 225, 229–236, 305, 328
small arms, see also weapons-systems 29, 261, 274, 276–277
social movements, see also resistance 9–10, 19, 21, 30, 45, 63, 106, 124, 126, 140, 233–236, 285, 292, 302–303, 318–319, 338
sociology, see also under critique 3, 5–6, 19–20, 25–26, 29–33, 38–41, 43–44, 72–73, 75, 83, 134
Somalia 108, 132
South Africa, Republic of 89, 91, 106–107, 116, 124, 134, 147–148, 177

South Korea, Republic of 85, 110–111, 200, 215
sovereignty, see also Right to Protect (R2P); state (the) (see Chapter 19) 45, 63, 77, 78, 123, 175, 178–179, 190, 191–192, 196, 197, 207, 232, 274, 282
Spain 48, 93, 99, 173, 176
Sri Lanka 113
state (the) 3, 8, 12–14, 19, 21, 27, 31, 37–39, 42–43, 44, 48, 61–65, 78, 83, 123, 129–132, 173–174, 180–181, 191–195, 207–208, 209–211, 216–218, 241, 283, 295–297, 298–299, 301–304, 310–311, 314–315, 317–320, 328–329
European state-building and policing (see Chapters 2 and 6)
state-building 185, 191–192, 193, 196–197, 199, 201
surveillance (see Chapter 15) 5, 21, 50, 54, 80, 89, 90, 91, 93, 97, 127, 128, 129, 163, 182–183, 210, 215, 225, 260, 264, 282, 316–318, 320, 321, 327, 328–329, 331–337
Syria 79, 122, 126, 132, 178, 297, 330

targeted killing, see drones
technology, see also cybersecurity; data, datafication; infrastructure (see Chapters 15, 16, and 17) xii–xiii, 6, 31–32, 45, 53, 54, 60, 77, 80, 106, 123, 163, 210, 217, 316–317
territory, see also state (the); sovereignty (see Chapters 14 and 19) 38, 39, 44, 59, 62, 78, 80, 82–83, 106, 122, 125, 126, 127, 132–133, 135, 142, 190, 195–196, 259, 297, 300
terrorism (clandestine political violence); see also counterterrorism (see Chapter 8) 25, 27, 28, 32, 40, 47, 85, 98, 147, 159, 163, 180, 181, 183, 184, 192, 199, 200, 209, 210, 211, 240, 250, 264, 285,
definition 123–124

threats, *see also* security (*see esp.* Chapters 8, 9, 13, and 18) ix, xii, 3, 9–10, 13, 14, 20, 21, 24, 25–26, 28, 29–30, 34, 37–38, 39, 40, 42, 43–44, 45, 49, 54, 58, 59, 62, 63, 65, 71, 73, 74, 76, 77, 79, 81, 82, 83, 84, 113, 114, 116, 157, 162, 163, 174, 176, 181, 188–189, 195–196, 198, 200, 228, 234, 240–243, 249, 250, 258, 260, 264, 266, 274, 275, 283, 286, 310, 311, 313, 316, 317, 321, 328, 329, 334, 335
torture 21, 23, 27, 67, 108, 124, 129, 131, 149, 165
transformation, *see also* critique xi–xiv, 3–4, 6–8, 14, 21–22, 26, 30–31, 38–39, 47–49, 54–55, 59, 61, 65, 66, 72–73, 78, 100, 134, 164–166, 241, 251–252, 300–304
  definition 6–8
Troubles, the (1968–1998), *see also* Ireland 57–58, 131
Turkey 110, 113, 318, 319

Ukraine 60
unhoused people 30, 42, 114, 159, 259, 260, 329, 337
Union of Soviet Socialist Republics (1922–1991), *see* Russia
United Kingdom of Great Britain and Northern Ireland 53, 54, 57–58, 65, 66, 78, 91, 96, 106, 107, 111, 113, 114, 153, 164, 174, 179, 191, 201, 215, 262–263, 274, 284, 292, 329, 334, 335, 336
United Nations (UN) 15, 19, 43, 62, 63, 73, 189, 193, 205, 297, 326
United Nations Development Programme (UNDP) (*see* Chapter 12), *see also* institutions, international institutions 8, 26, 299
United States of America, *see also* #BlackLivesMatter 7, 10, 41, 44, 45, 58–59, 66–67, 73, 75, 76, 78–79, 80, 82–83, 88, 93, 96–97, 113–114, 122, 140, 144, 147, 150, 158–159, 163, 175–176, 179, 180, 183, 191, 192, 201, 217–218, 233–234, 244–246, 274, 275, 278, 285, 292, 294, 309–311, 314–315, 316–317, 327, 329, 331, 332
  African–Americans 64, 139–140, 175
urban spaces and dynamics 23, 29, 42, 46–47, 58–59, 77, 90, 258–260, 267, 281
use of force, *see* legitimacy; authority

Vietnam 21, 68,
violence (political), *see also* legitimacy; authority; non-violence (*see* Chapter 4) xii–xiv, 2–3, 8–11, 12–14, 31–32, 40, 42, 47–49, 71–74, 80–84, 92, 105, 107, 108–109, 112, 122, 123–126, 132–133, 141, 143–149, 158–166, 171–172, 176–178, 180–181, 189, 193–196, 200–201, 207–208, 212, 214, 216–218, 224–225, 226–236, 241–242, 266–267, 274–282, 284–285, 292–294, 298–304, 313–315, 318–321, 326, 331–337
  as constitutive 56, 90, 124, 125–126, 143–151
  definition, *see* 54, 56
  discrete/structural violence 55–56, 58, 60, 64, 65, 79, 82–83, 93, 95–96, 99, 100, 159, 162, 200, 227–228, 230, 233–236, 245, 251, 277, 283, 294–295, 298, 299, 300–304, 333, 337
  intentional/unintentional violence 55–56, 59, 60, 276, 318–320, 334–337
  manifest/latent violence 25–26, 56, 57, 58, 60, 93, 181, 224, 228, 230, 233, 234, 235, 236, 333
  material violence 14, 56, 57, 58, 59, 76, 78, 159, 163–164, 226, 228, 235, 294–295, 297–298, 300–304, 337
  physical violence 3, 25–26, 76, 78, 82–83, 88, 90–91, 95–96, 124, 125, 146, 158–159, 163–164, 212, 228, 243, 275–276, 280, 283–284, 286, 294, 302–304, 325–326, 334–337
  psychological violence 58, 76, 78, 146, 163–164, 302–304, 334–337
  symbolic violence 5, 49, 55, 57, 59, 60, 68, 76, 79, 82–83, 146, 159, 226, 228, 236, 245, 282, 285, 294, 295, 302–304, 325

walls, *see also* design, security and design (*see* Chapter 20) 54, 140, 267, 312–314, 320, 322
war, war and society (*see* Chapters 7 and 8) 58, 62–63, 71–73, 74, 76–79, 80, 82–84, 123, 124, 125, 128–129, 133, 206, 258, 261–269, 278
war on drugs (*see* Chapter 5) 10, 40, 316, 326
  drugs/narcotics/opioids 40, 72–73, 74, 76, 78–82
Weber, Max 62, 125
weapons and weapons–systems (*see* Chapters 16 and 17) 29, 31, 79, 209, 211, 247
  non-lethal weapons 275–276, 281
weapons of mass destruction, *see also* nuclear weapons 282–284
western–centrism (eurocentrism), *see also* colonialism/coloniality 61–63, 76, 88–89, 107, 161–162, 191, 197, 199, 211, 228–232
World Bank 180, 231
World Health Organization (WHO) (*see* Chapter 13) 37, 164

xenophobia, *see also* citizenship; identity; othering; nationalism; political belonging (*see* Chapters 9 and 11)

Yemen 132, 183, 284

Zedner, Lucia 20
Zimbabwe 73, 113, 148